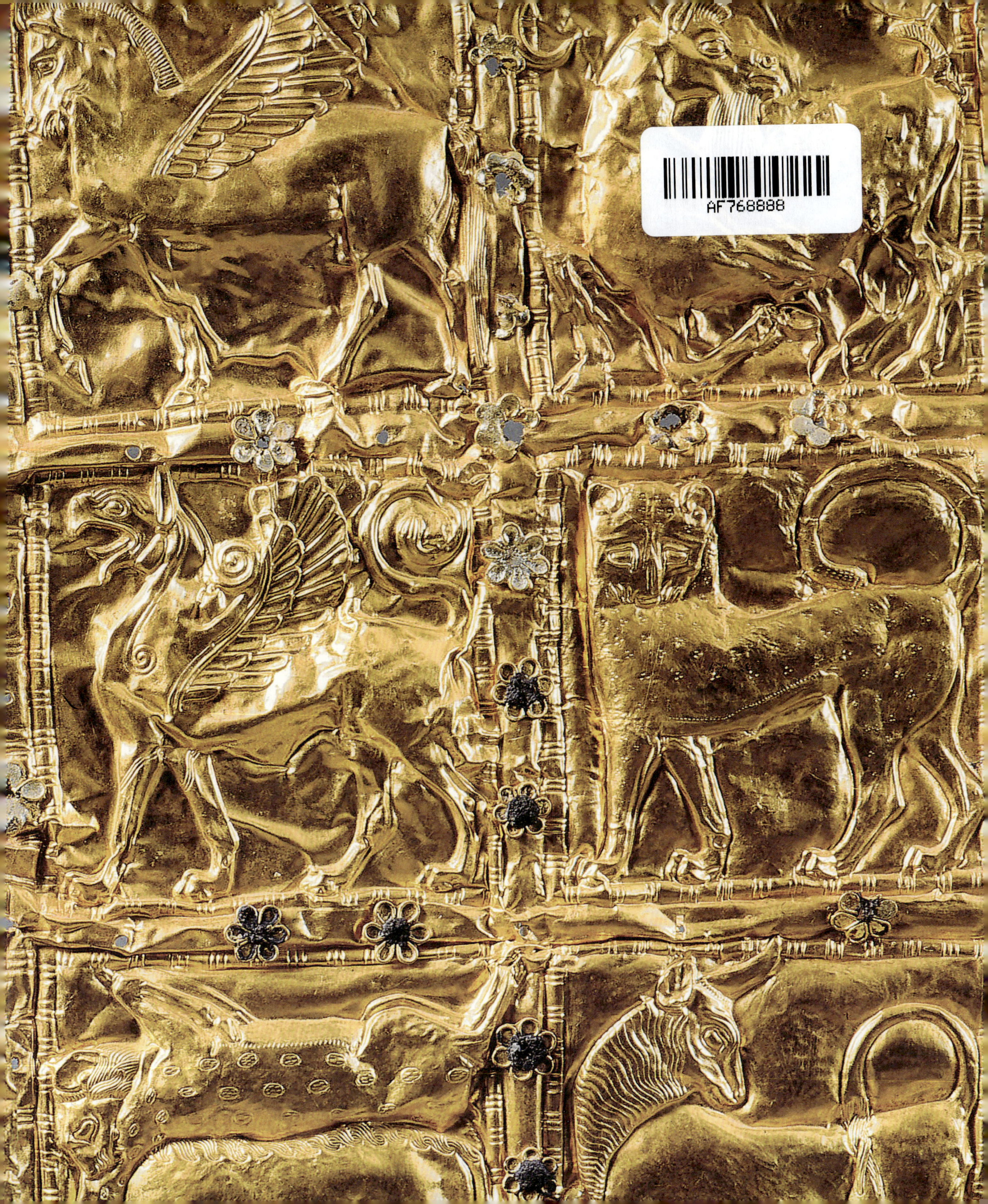

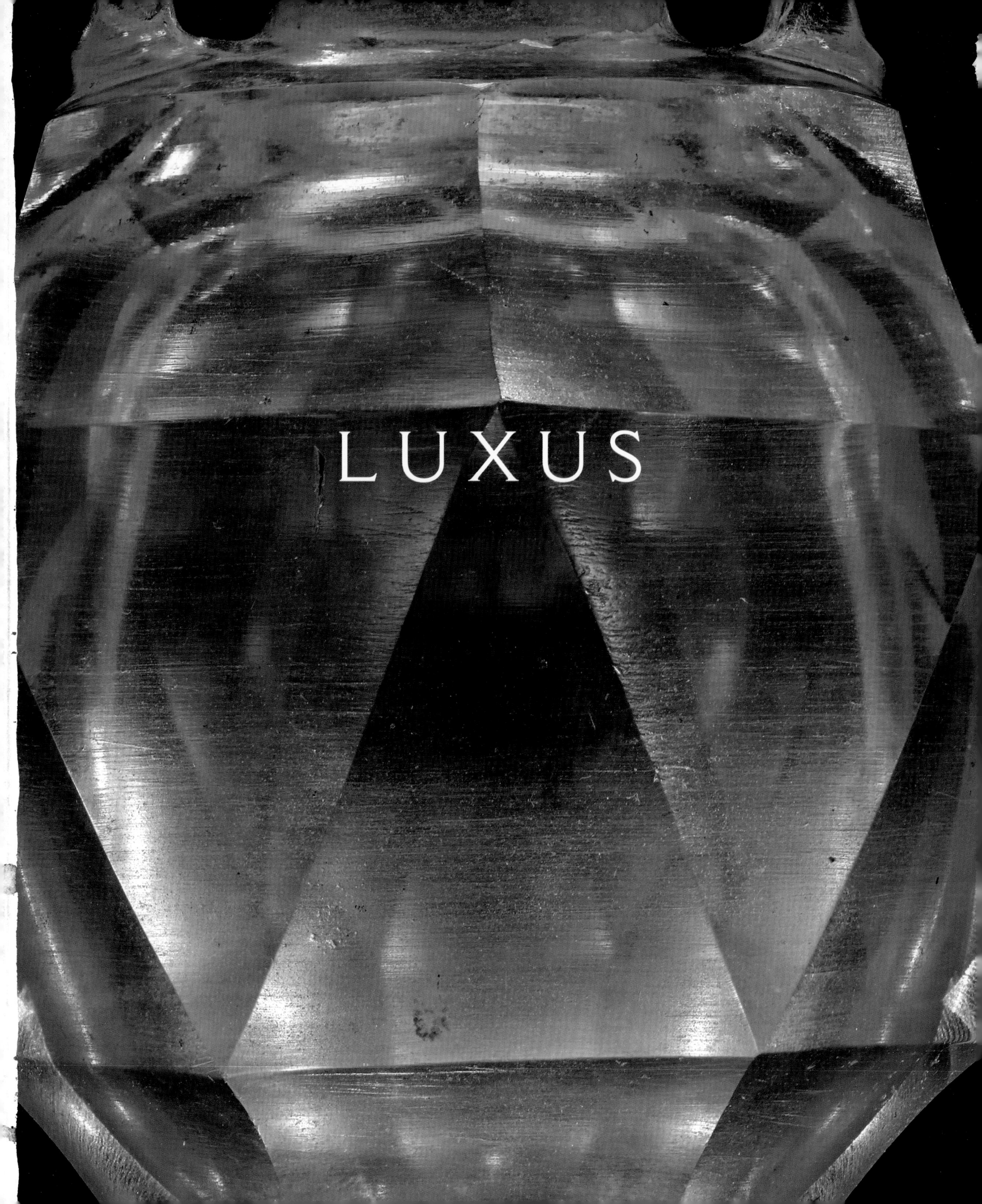
LUXUS

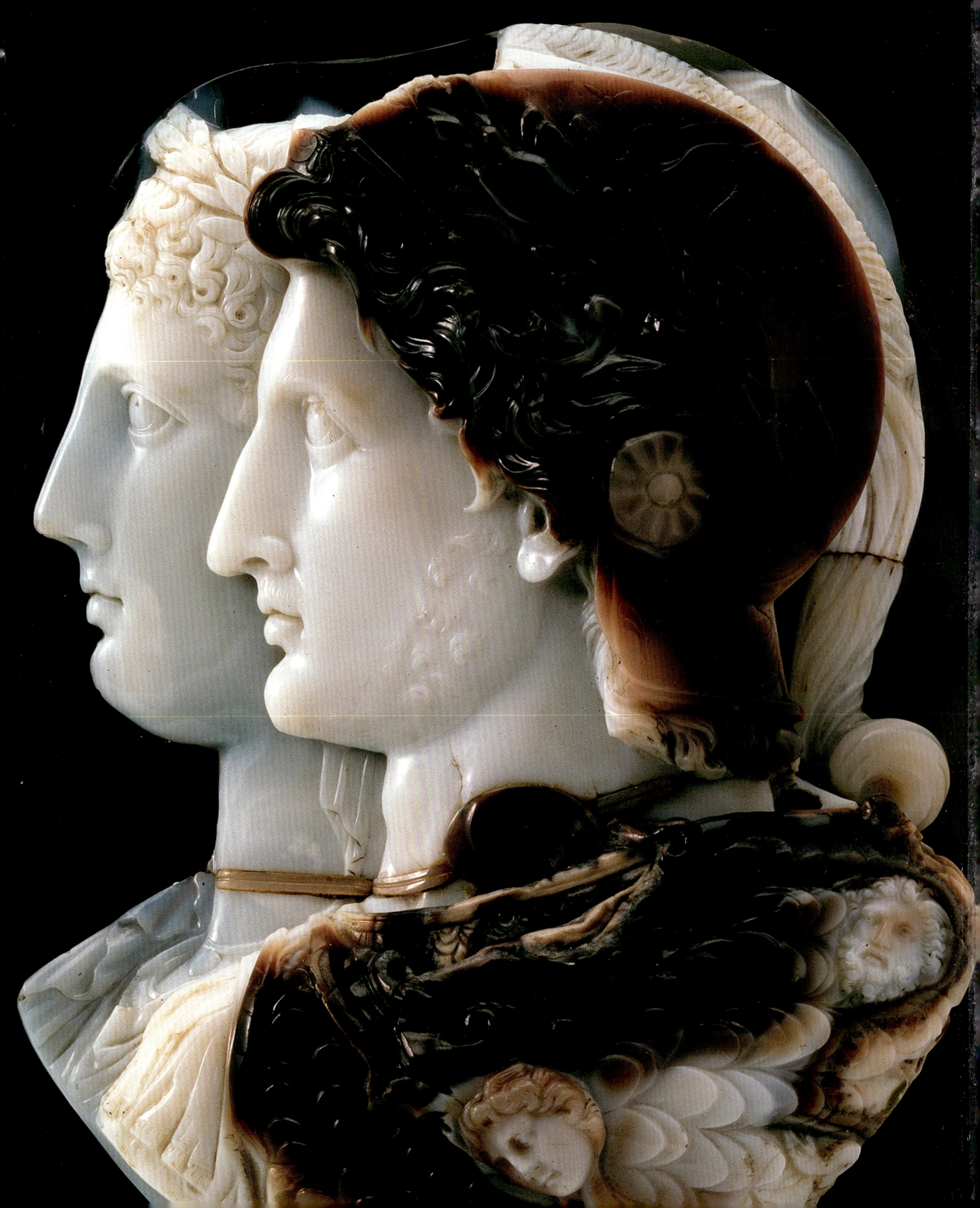

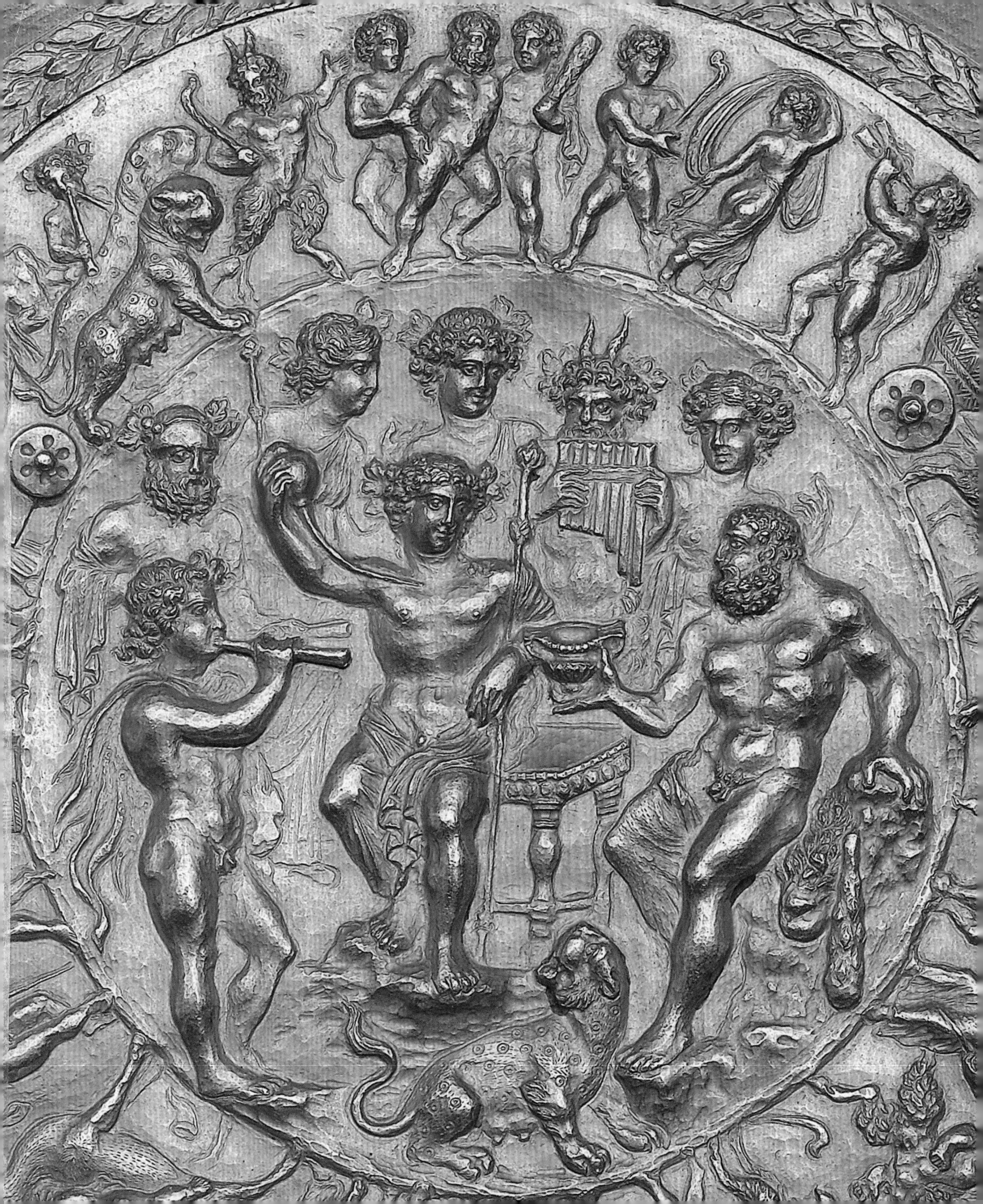

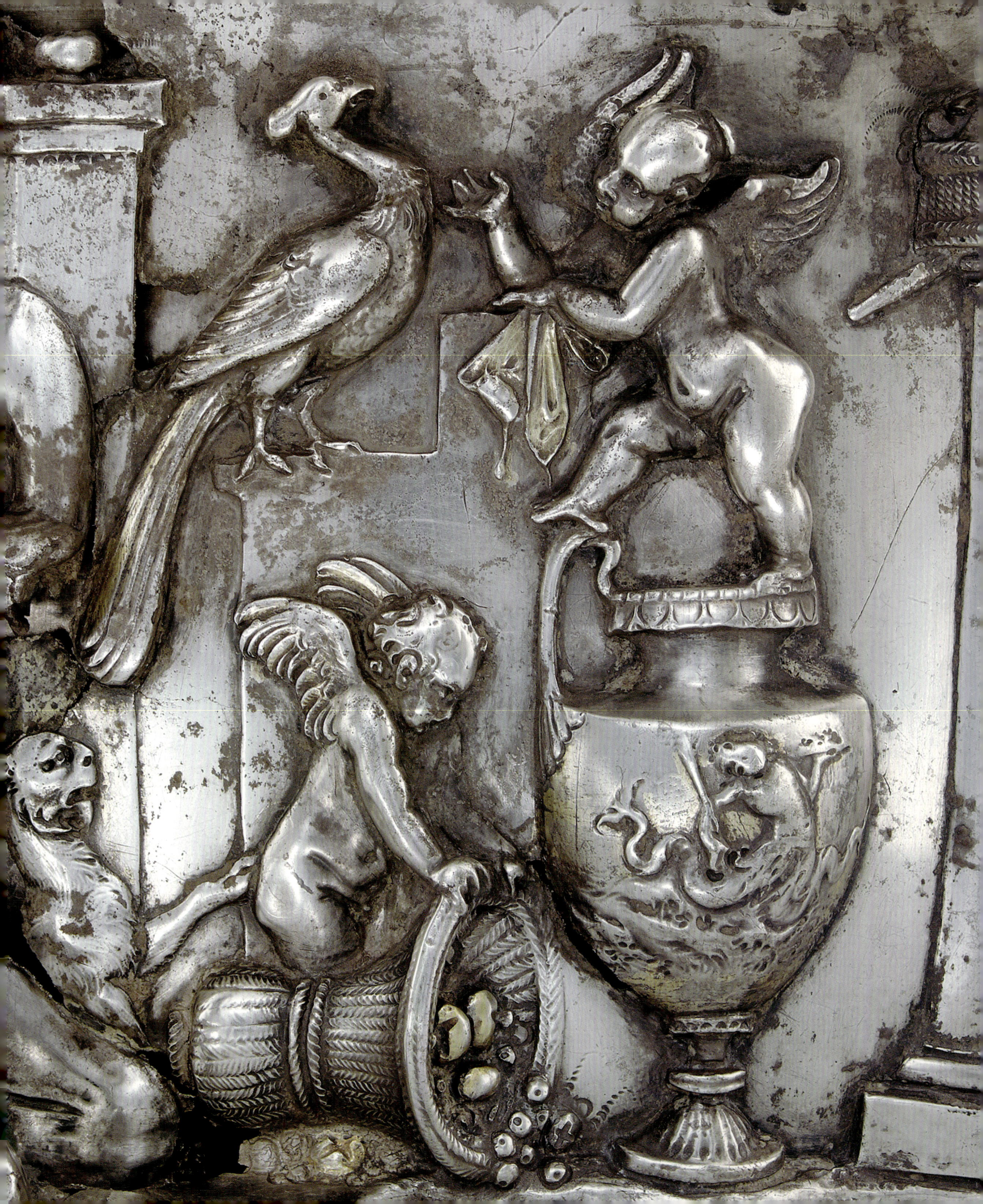

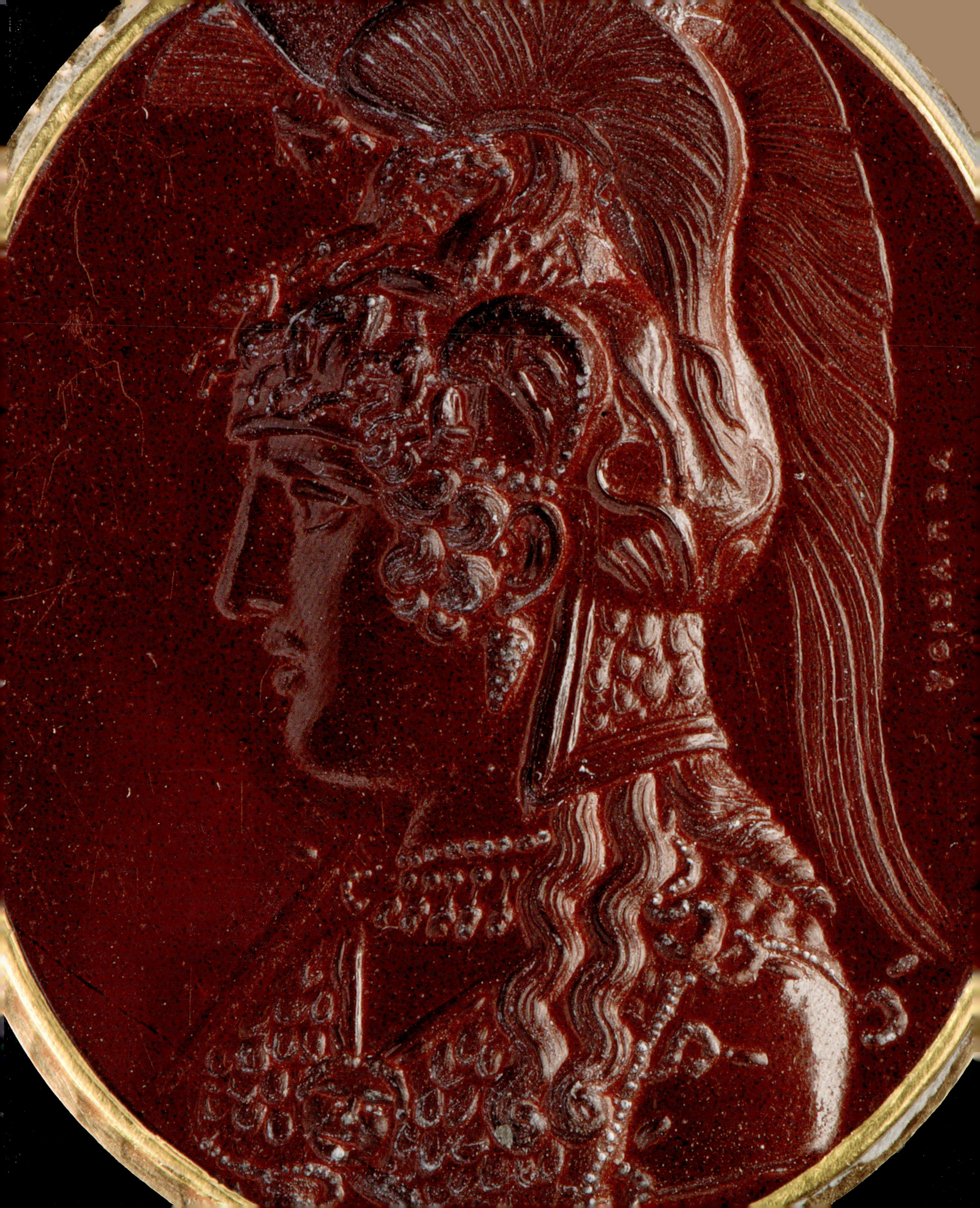

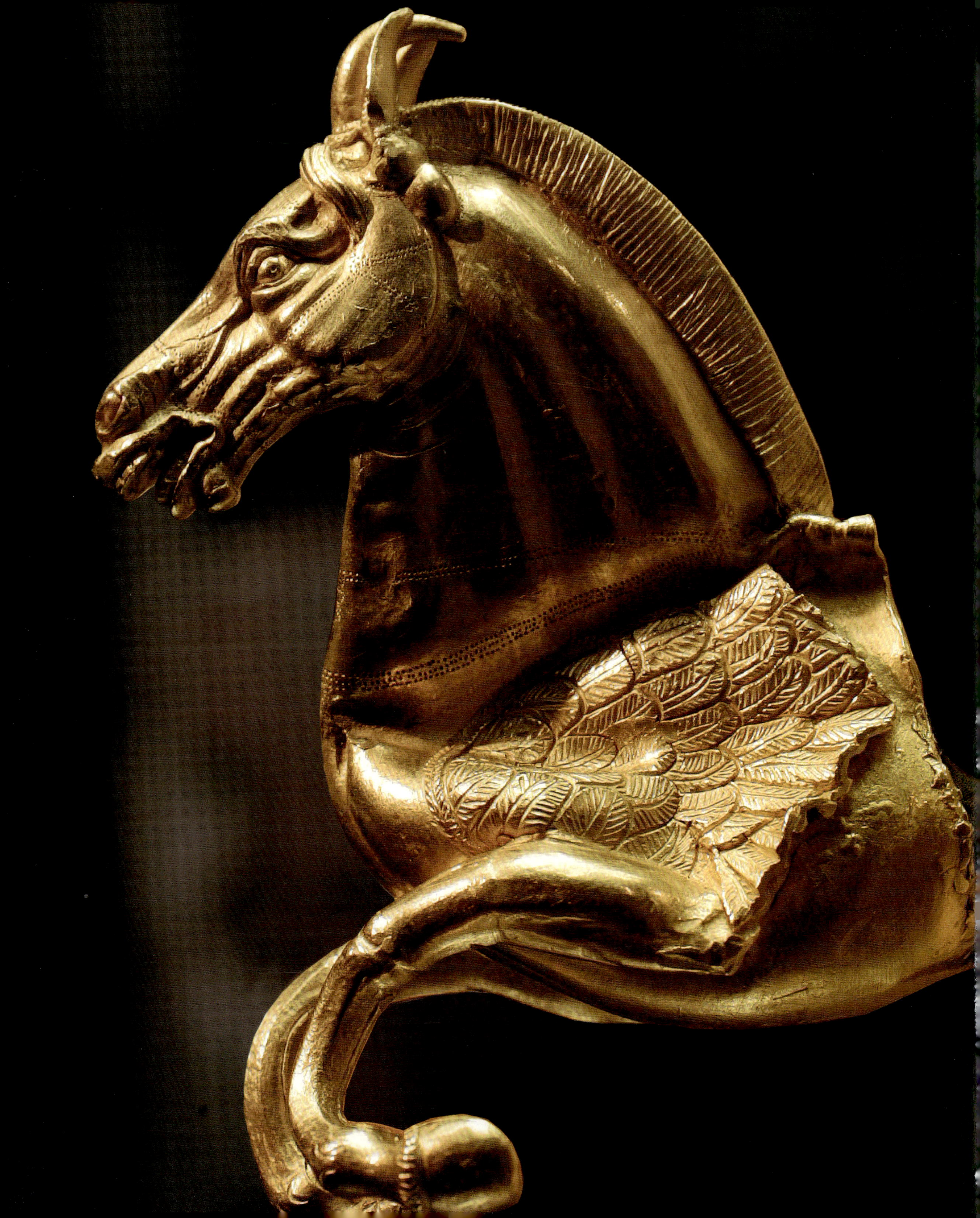

LUXUS

The Sumptuous Arts of Greece and Rome

Kenneth Lapatin

The J. Paul Getty Museum
Los Angeles

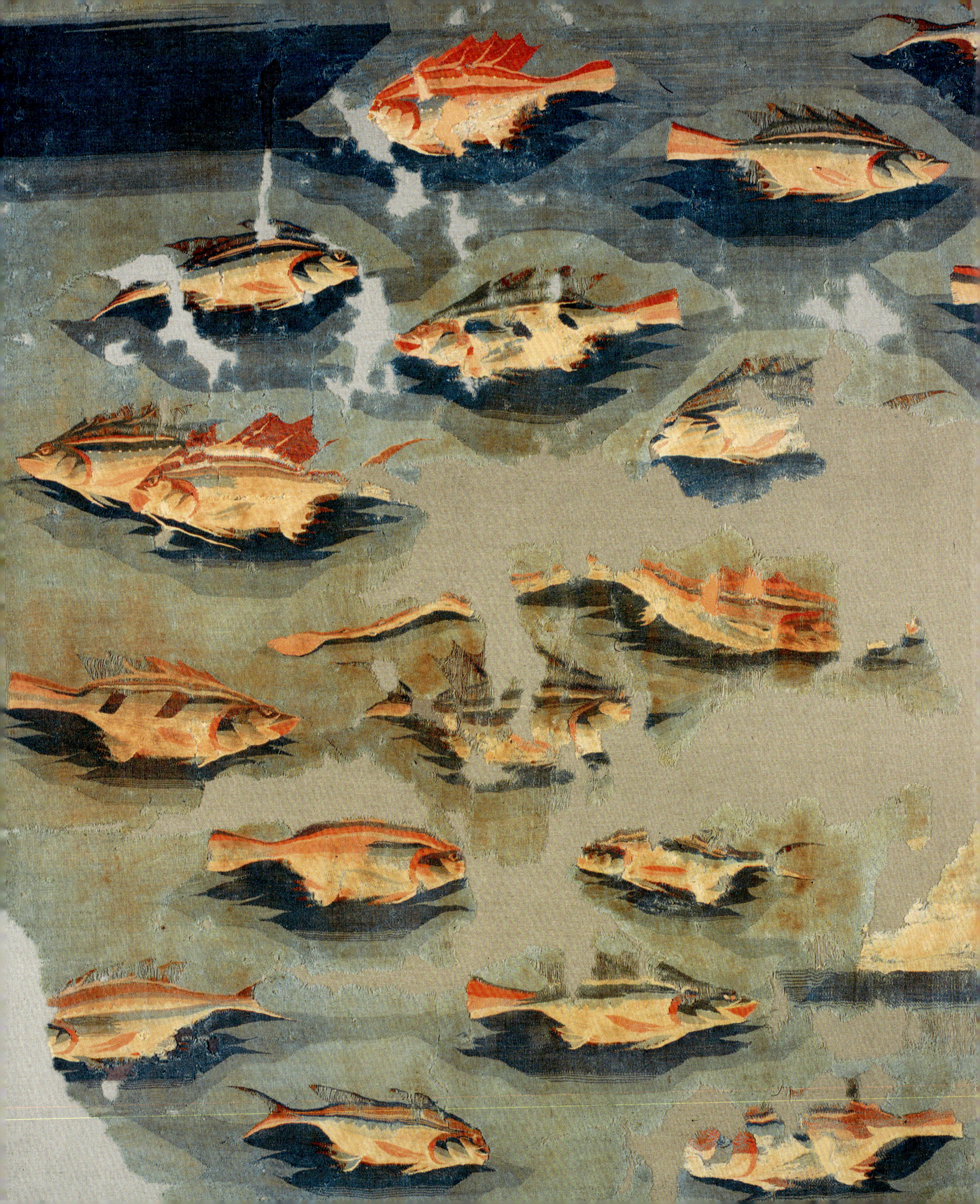

CONTENTS

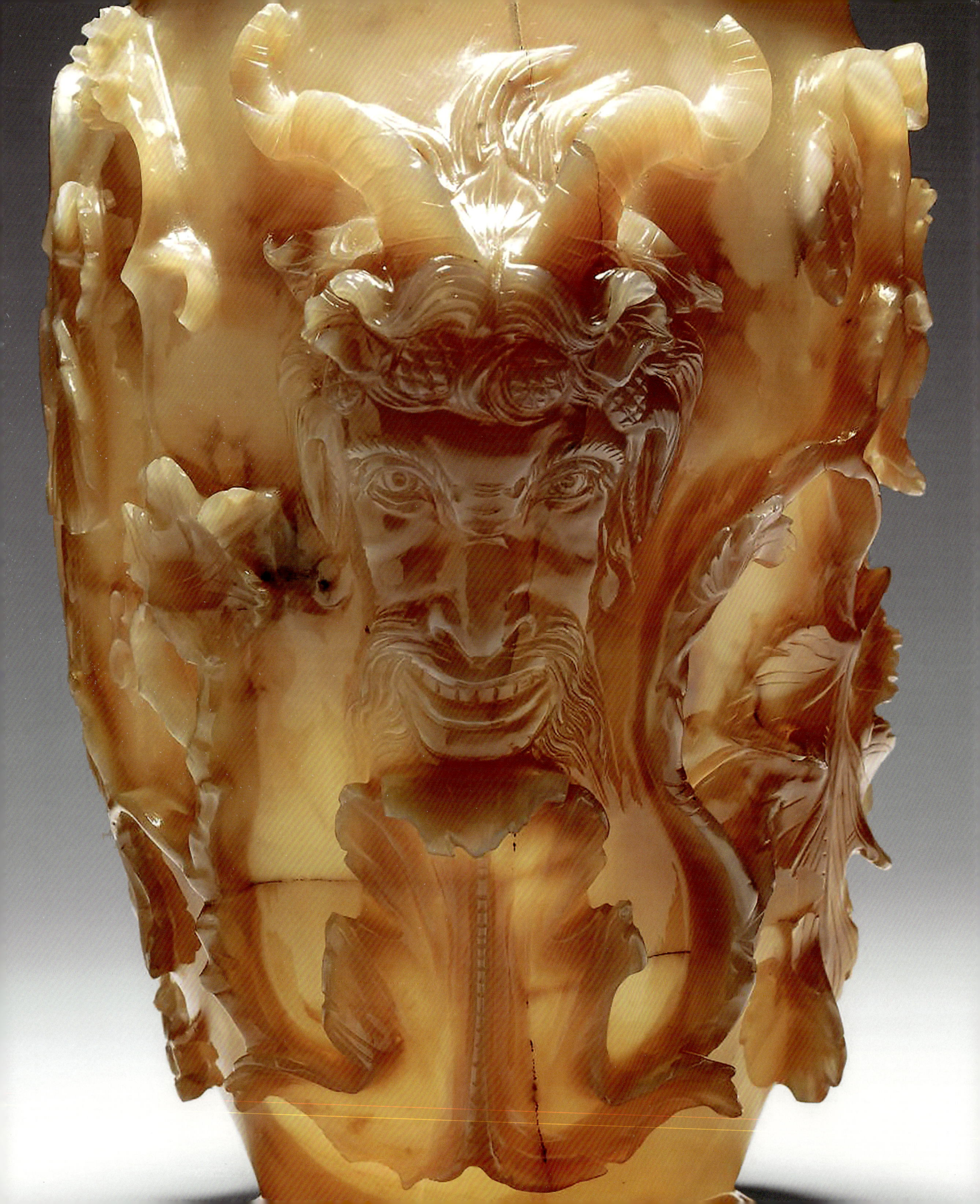

FOREWORD

The arts of the ancient civilizations of Greece and Rome played a significant role in the culture not only of those societies but also of the Middle Ages, Renaissance, and Enlightenment, and indeed still draw us in today. Yet the objects that have pride of place in our museums and books devoted to antiquity—as beautiful, finely crafted, and illuminating as they may be—are not necessarily those that were most highly valued by the ancients themselves. The familiar statues of marble and bronze, along with painted ceramics, wall frescoes, and other architectural features, are not the masterpieces lauded by Greek and Latin authors. Rather, they are the accidental survivals of time and fortune, privileged by durability rather than status or value.

The works of art most highly prized by the ancients were those crafted from the most luxurious and splendid materials: gold and silver, precious and semiprecious stones, ivory, pearls, coral, amber, and fine woods. To be sure, most ancient gold and silver objects have been melted down, and those made of ivory and other organic materials have disintegrated. But exquisite artifacts fashioned from these and other sumptuous substances survive in far greater number than is usually acknowledged, and the quality of these objects, both technical and aesthetic, leaves no doubt as to the consummate skill of their creators. This book focuses on a selection of the finest such objects, thirty-four of which are in the collection of the J. Paul Getty Museum, and all of which are accompanied here by splendid photographs and detailed commentaries.

As with any culture—but especially those remote from us in time and place—it is critical to a proper understanding of classical art that it be seen in its broader cultural, historical, and archaeological context. This is achieved here admirably by Kenneth Lapatin, a curator in the department of Antiquities at the J. Paul Getty Museum. His introduction addresses the diverse contexts of Greek and Roman luxury arts and their varying ancient and modern receptions, tracing how the supreme creations of ancient artists have sometimes been relegated to the "minor arts"—an anachronistic and totally inappropriate categorization. The three chapters that follow present an in-depth examination of the materials, techniques, myths, functions, and ideologies surrounding precious metals (gold and silver), hard stones (intaglios, cameos, vessels, and statuettes), and organic materials (ivory, fine wood, amber, pearl, coral, and textiles). The qualities and associations that made these materials so desirable to the ancients were many and varied, from their exotic origins, luminosity, malleability, and durability to their perceived magical or mystical powers.

Ancient texts frequently mention these luxury objects as products of master craftsmen, the possessions of elites, and dedications to the gods. They were prized and envied, lauded and —by those of more puritan inclination—denigrated. Some were recovered from archaeological contexts that reveal something of their function as grave goods or votive offerings; others seem never to have gone underground and were apparently transferred from ancient treasuries to ecclesiastical or princely collections and eventually to modern museums. All are admirable and, although often small in scale, richly reward close inspection.

This study offers a valuable counterpoint to the standard textbook accounts of the arts and culture of the classical world. It shows how artifacts fashioned in precious materials played a crucial role in defining and articulating the beliefs and aesthetics, the crafts and technologies, and the political and economic networks of antiquity. Scholars of ancient civilizations, admirers of *virtù*, and the curious general reader alike will discover a wealth of new insights and visual pleasures in this exquisite material.

Timothy Potts
Director, The J. Paul Getty Museum

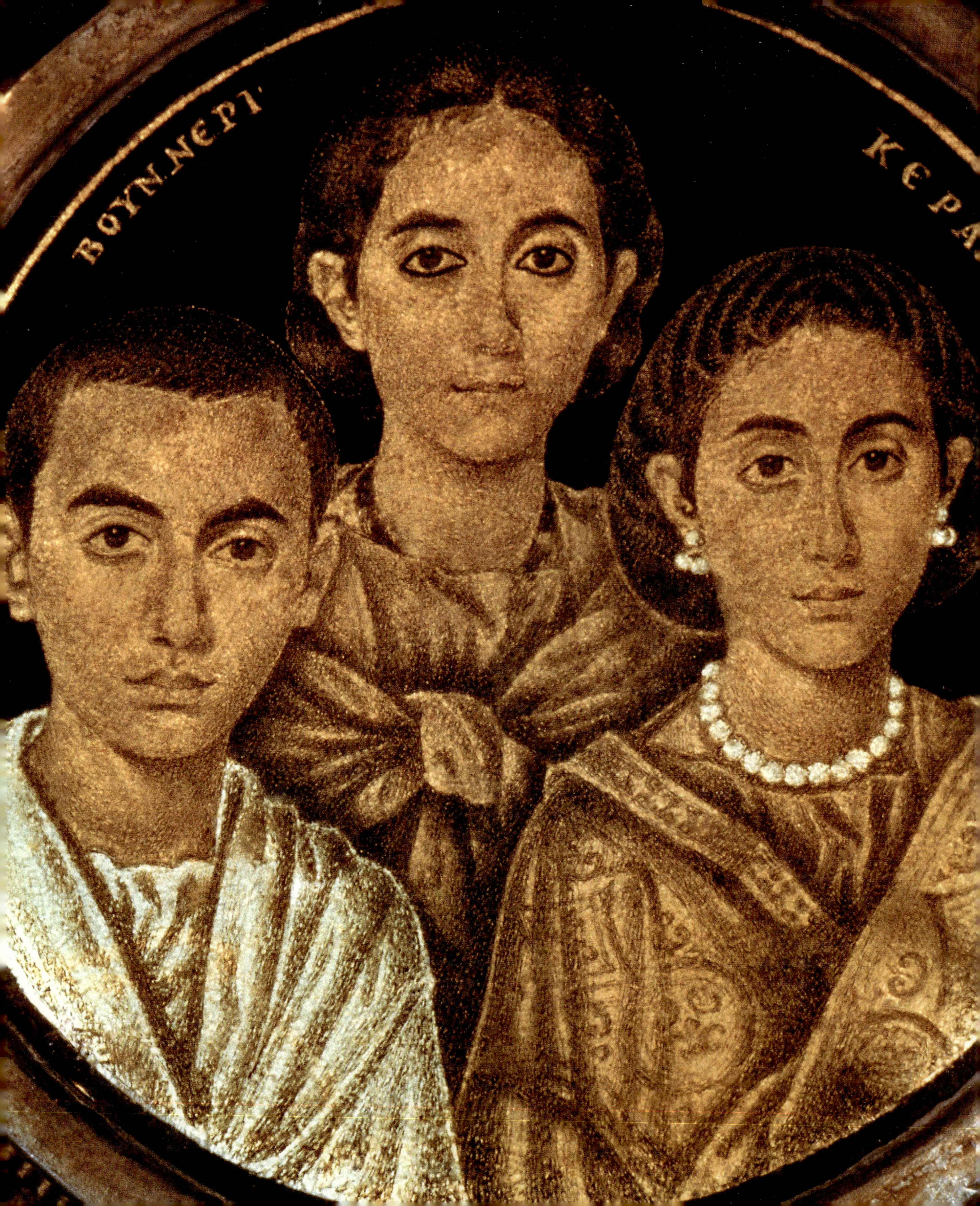
BOYN.NEPI
KEPA

INTRODUCTION

HISTORIES AND CONTEXTS

The Latin noun *luxus* is derived from the verb *luctor*, to dislocate or to sprain (rather than from *lux*, light). *Luxus* denotes something overextended, something in excess, and thus indulgence, extravagance, opulence, and soft living. Its derivatives, the noun *luxuria* and the verb *luxurio*, cognate with the English *luxury*, carry these connotations and more. They indicate immoderate growth, swelling, even the rankness of plants; and when used in reference to persons or animals, willful or unruly behavior, disregard for moral restraints, and licentiousness. No wonder, then, that luxury, in Roman antiquity, was not widely praised. In Latin poetry and prose *luxus* was frequently invoked pejoratively. In the earliest surviving instance of the word, about 160 BC, the playwright Terence writes of "a youth destroyed by *luxus*."[1] A century later, the historian Sallust described the Late Republic as "a state corrupted by *luxus* and sloth." Further such references abound.[2]

What defines luxury varies greatly with time and circumstance. Among the definitions offered by the *Oxford English Dictionary* is a "thing desirable but not indispensible"; Coco Chanel, in contrast, observed that luxury is a necessity that begins where necessity ends. Certainly luxuries are not frivolities, but the values ascribed to things are not constant. Jade was rated more highly than gold in ancient China and Mesoamerica. In early modern Europe, coffee and chocolate were prized—and certain varieties are still considered luxuries today.[3] In the ancient world, luxury was about experience as much as, if not more than, objects: banquets with fine wines, sumptuous dishes, and lavish entertainment; the experience of delightful music, perfumes, and aromatics; hot baths and other sensual pleasures; and even extravagant funerals.[4] In ancient Greece attitudes toward luxury were more ambivalent than in Rome. Archaic Greek aristocrats consciously adopted the refined lifestyle of the regions to the east, especially that of Lydia, as a form of differentiation and self-definition. The delicate, fine garments of expensive materials (often colored with premium dyes), fragrances, gold jewelry, and sensuality connoted by the word *habrosune* were praised by such poets as Sappho, Alkaios, and Alkman. Others, such as Xenophanes and Simonides, disparaged luxury, for sumptuous living had sociopolitical as well as moral implications, and the sumptuary laws that sought to curb it were usually, at root, about much more than morals.[5] Luxury, in short, has always been contentious.

In Classical Greece, the word *tryphe* (softness or delicacy) had largely negative associations. The verb *tryphao* (to live luxuriously or sumptuously) was applied to children, women, or effeminate men, and like its Latin counterparts, connoted extravagant, licentious, or wanton behavior. Luxury goods, derived from the east, became unfashionable around the time of the Persian Wars in the early fifth century BC, but they never disappeared. They were, of course, especially suspect in democratic Athens, where they were recast negatively and stigmatized decisively as feminine and tyrannical in origin. But fine imports nevertheless remained desirable, and expensive, well-crafted goods of precious materials, wherever produced, continued to convey elitist connotations of wealth, education, refined taste, and cosmopolitanism.[6] The mid-fourth-century inventories of the sanctuary of Artemis at Brauron, for example, indicate that women regularly dedicated luxurious garments (*tryphemata*) to the goddess.[7] And in Aristophanes's *Wasps*, produced in 422 BC, as elsewhere, one character describes archly how to succeed at a drinking party: "Praise some metal vessel, inspect the ceiling, admire the woven hangings of the hall."[8] The possession and appreciation of extravagant accoutrements not only demonstrated wealth and refinement but also were associated in the popular imagination with the excesses of kingship and tyranny. The fourth-century orator Isokrates considered the Persians, whose wealth was legendary, "ruined by *tryphe*," and later historians wrote repeatedly of the slippery slope from *ploutos* (wealth) to *tryphe*, to hubris, to *apoleia* (destruction).[9]

Yet *tryphe* was not an entirely negative concept. Although the word does not appear earlier than the fifth century BC, it soon came to embody Homeric *arēte* (aristocratic excellence). To be sure, in the wake of the Persian Wars luxury goods were frequently attacked as foreign and effeminate, yet Herakleides of Pontos, in his treatise *Peri hedones (On Pleasure)*, praised Persians and Medes as magnanimous and magnificent because they enjoyed the greatest luxury without sacrificing their manly courage.[10] Thucydides, in the *History of the Peloponnesian Wars*, reports that the Athenian Alkibiades argued that his sumptuous displays, rooted in the Homeric concept of *kleos* (glory), brought honor and greater power not only to himself but also to his city.[11] In Plato's *Gorgias*, Kallikles positively links *tryphe* with both *hedone* (pleasure) and *eleutheria* (freedom), for a free man should not enslave his appetites: it is those without power who are unable to satisfy their desires.[12] Luxury, thus, could be viewed as a mark of autonomy. Aristotle (who reportedly was fond of wearing multiple finger rings) similarly connects *tryphe* with freedom and aristocratic rank in the *Nicomachean Ethics*.[13]

In the Hellenistic period, as vast riches and exotic substances flooded the Greek world in the wake of Alexander's conquests, rulers not only delighted in extreme wealth but also consciously employed *tryphe* as a matter of state policy. Luxurious displays and extravagant banquets embodied their refinement, wealth, and power. The prosperity of the kings was a manifestation of the favor of the gods, and royal prestige relied upon exhibiting it. The Ptolemies who ruled Egypt employed displays of magnificence, beneficence, and delicacy as a major component of a calculated political strategy. And because it was often linked to the wine god Dionysos, theirs might even be called a philosophy of excess.[14] In the

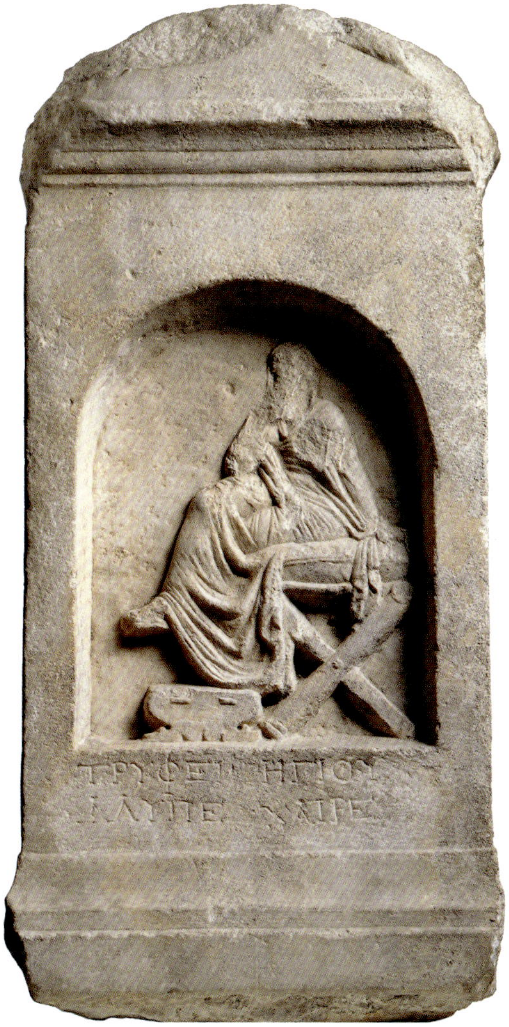

Figure 1

Gravestone of Tryphe, ca. 150–100 BC. Marble, H: 60.5 cm; W: 29.3 cm; D: 17.6 cm. Princeton University, The Art Museum, y1992-48, Gift of the Committee for the Excavation of Antioch to Princeton University. This gravestone from Seleucia Pieria (the port of Antioch) is inscribed ΤΡΥΦΕΙ ΗΓΙΟΥ ΑΛΥΠΕ ΧΑΙΡΕ (To Tryphe, [wife, or daughter] of Egias / Farewell, you [who are now] without pain). The deceased sits cross-legged, head resting on her hand, in the pose of the famous statue of the patron goddess of the city, the Tyche of Antioch, commissioned from the sculptor Eutychides shortly after the founding of Antioch in 300 BC.

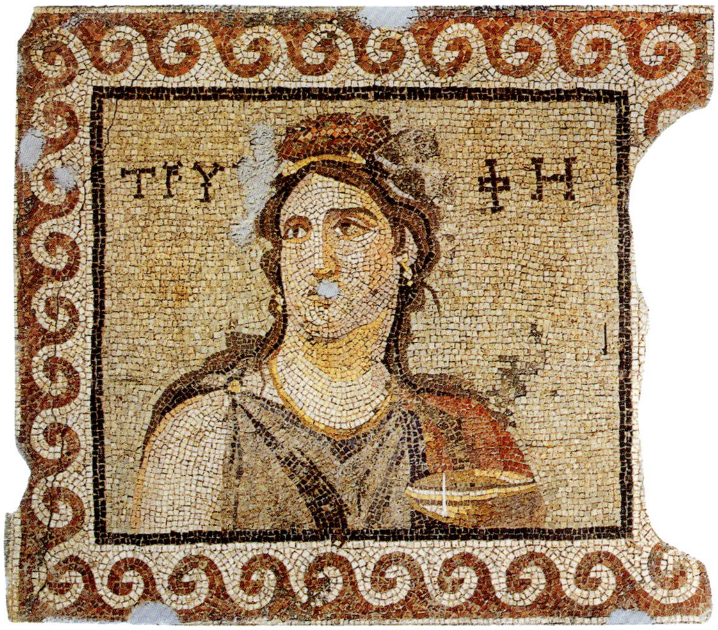

Figure 2

Tryphe holding a golden bowl, ca.250–275 BC. Mosaic, H: 95 cm. Antakya, Hatay Museum, 1015. From Room 3 of the House of Menander, Daphne. The personification of the good life wears a gold necklace, earrings, and hair ornament, as well as red and purple garments.

grand procession and sumptuous banquet hall of Ptolemy II Philadelphos (r. 283–246 BC), both described at length by Kallixeinos of Rhodes, Ptolemaic luxury reached the height of extravagance and ostentation as precious objects were exhibited on an unprecedented scale.[15] Later Ptolemies, such as Ptolemy III and IV, were actually dubbed Tryphon, and by the second century BC the epithet had become one of the ruler's official titles: Cleopatra V Tryphaina was the mother of the famous Cleopatra VII. Such positive ideologies of luxury naturally trickled down, and Tryphon also appears as the personal name of a poet, a gem engraver (plate 107), and other individuals in the Hellenistic and Roman periods. A second-century BC tombstone depicts a woman named Tryphe in the guise of a goddess (fig. 1).[16] Centuries later, *tryphe* continued to be depicted positively as the personification of living well in mosaics from the Roman East (fig. 2), while a young girl aptly named Crepereia Tryphaenea was buried in central Rome in a tomb richly appointed with gold jewelry inset with beryls, pearls, and engraved gems, a silver mirror, an amber wand, two amber combs, and an articulated doll of ivory.[17]

Yet from Archaic Greek poets and rulers to Roman moralists, ancient thinkers considered the desire to possess and enjoy more than nature required—a desire that was easily inflamed—to be potentially disruptive. Luxury, it was feared, led not only to softness and effeminacy but also to corruption. Roman historians such as Livy idealized the past and attributed the social and political chaos of the Late Republic to the influx of luxury: "No republic was ever greater, none more virtuous or richer in good example, none into which luxury [*luxuria*] and avarice entered so late, or where poverty and frugality were so honored. For it is true that the less wealth there was, the less desire there was. More recently, riches have imported avarice and excessive pleasures with a craving for luxury [*luxum*] and wantonness to the ruination of ourselves and everything else."[18]

Centuries earlier, soon after the beginning of Rome's territorial expansion and increased importation of foreign goods and customs, Cato the Elder, according to Plutarch, not only personally lived "in a contracted way in order to correct and moderate the extravagance of others," he also ran for the office of censor in order to "cut and sear to some purpose the hydra-like luxury [*tryphe*] and effeminacy of the time."[19] When he won, he raised taxes on sumptuous living. Sumptuary laws had been imposed by early Roman kings, as well as Archaic Greek tyrants. While ostensibly designed to protect public morals, such legislation also aimed to constrain competition among the wealthy and especially encroachment by the nouveau riche on the prerogatives of the established upper classes. These laws were rarely successful, for if their goal was to limit ostentation, prosecution merely brought to the perpetrator the attention he or she sought.[20] A sacred law from the sanctuary of Despoina at Lykosoura in Arcadia, for example, forbade participants in religious processions from wearing fine robes or gold jewelry. The penalty for infractions was to dedicate the offending object in the sanctuary.[21] Likewise Harpokration reports that if a maiden who served Athena on the Acropolis at Athens wore gold ornaments, those became sacred, that is to say, the property of the goddess.[22] What better way to draw attention to oneself and one's means?

Most ancient sumptuary laws, however, were not intended to restrict the possession of luxury objects but rather to limit expenditure on luxurious practices, such as extravagant funerals and large banquets. At such occasions ambitious individuals could build social connections and advance on the path to power. Luxury goods were customarily displayed at these events, and possession of them has always been significant.[23] Beautifully crafted objects, made of fine materials, often imported from afar, brought status as well as pleasure. Thus, for all the negative views, luxurious living was highly attractive, and asceticism and desire were constantly in conflict. Even Roman philosophers, such as Cicero and Seneca, who railed against luxury, lived extremely well. Cicero spent millions on his villas and, according to the historian Dio Cassius, Seneca had a collection of five hundred expensive tables, with ivory legs and citrus-wood tops. In his treatise, *On the Good Life*, the philosopher questioned his own conscience: "Why don't you live according to your principles? Why do you have such elegant furniture?"[24]

Elaborate furniture made of expensive imported materials, gold and silver plate, hard stone vessels, gems, jewelry, and other luxury goods are not the standard subjects of modern art histories of the ancient world. Although they were prized by the Greeks and Romans, praised or denigrated by ancient authors, dedicated to the gods in temples and deposited with the dead in tombs, such objects, which survive in large numbers and in a better state of preservation than one might think, have in more recent times been erroneously designated *minor arts*. There was no such category in the ancient world, although well-crafted objects were recognized and valued, and there were, as early as the fifth century BC, celebrity craftsmen whose creations were highly prized. The importance of these objects was in part monetary, but they were also conduits of diverse values—emotional, spiritual, intellectual, aesthetic, and perceptual—which contributed to their exchange value. Indeed, the cost of things, in antiquity as today, was an important gauge of their significance.[25] The materials used were not only exotic but were also characterized by their radiance; that these shiny, gleaming,

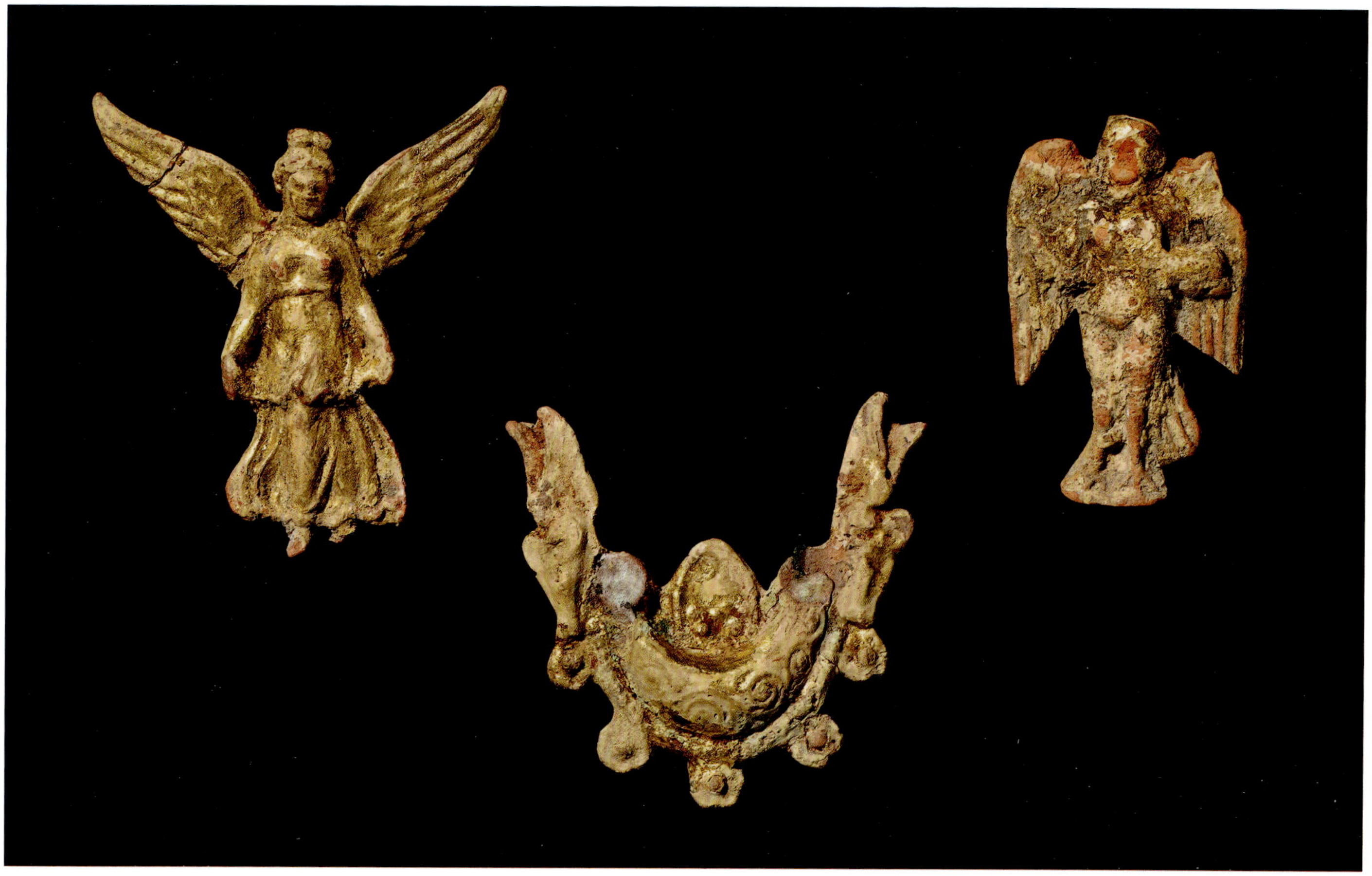

Figure 3
Imitations of gold earrings, ca. 300–100 BC. Gilt-terracotta, H: 3.9 cm (Nike), 3.3 cm ("boat"), 3.0 cm (Siren). London, British Museum, 1856,1001.104; 1856,1112.11; 1898,0223.6. The Nike and "boat" earrings are both from Cyrenaica; the Siren is from Crete. Compare plates 27, 29, 31.

reflective, or translucent objects seemed to produce light contributed greatly to their appeal. Their luminosity made them seem alive, even divine; they were experienced with pleasure by those who saw and handled them; they produced positive sensations and evoked wonder and awe. Many, moreover, were designed to be held in the hands, used in intimate settings, inspected closely and admired.[26]

The materials could also be copied, emulated, imitated, and forged. Ancient glass frequently resembles hard stone, either clear rock crystal or banded agate (see fig. 23); fake gold jewelry and luxury furniture attachments intended to be deposited in tombs, rather than used in life, were often fashioned from gilt terracotta and stucco (fig. 3); and various gemstones and even pearls were forged.[27] The physical qualities of the genuine materials were frequently—but not always—enhanced by the quality of workmanship. Although precious materials were sometimes entrusted to craftsmen of lesser skill, in the hands of masters they were transformed into truly affecting works of art.

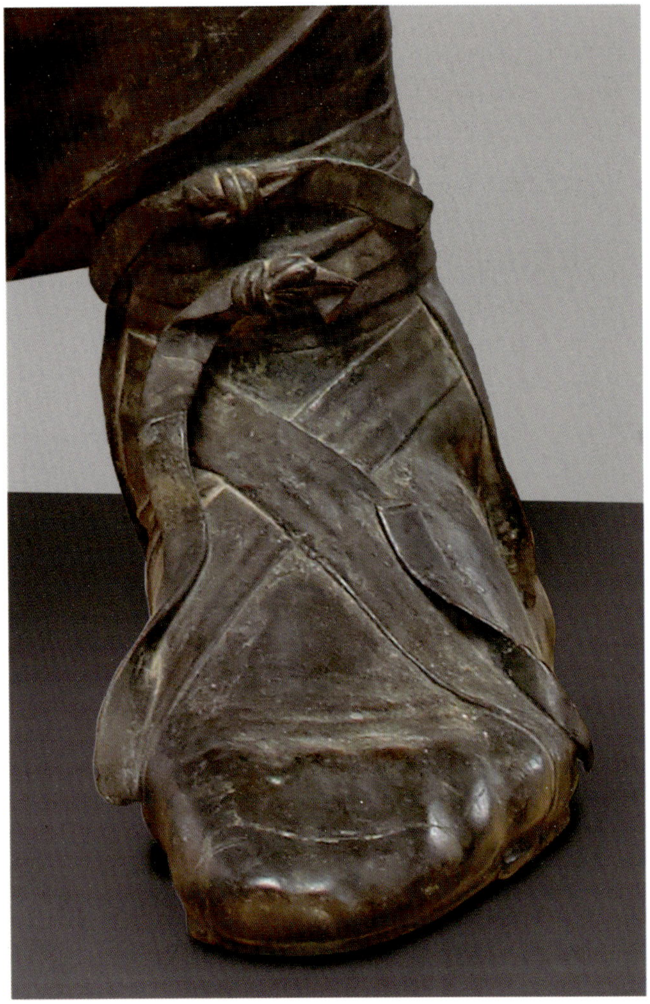

Figure 4
Foot of a monumental statue of Tiberius, from Herculaneum, AD 37. Bronze, H (of statue): 2.46 m. Naples, Museo Archeologico Nazionale, 5615. Despite its detail, the quality of this bronze portrait of a Roman emperor does not approach that of work in other, more precious media. Compare feet of statues carved of ivory, plates 152, 165.

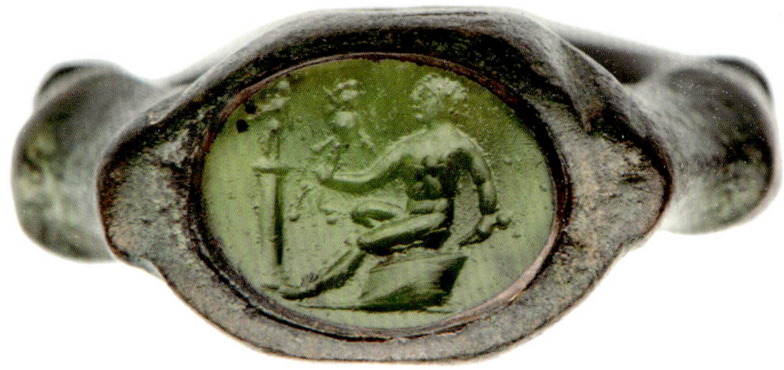

Figure 5
Diomedes and the Palladion, ca. AD 200–300. Green plasma intaglio set in a bronze ring, H: 8 mm, W: 10 mm. Boston, Museum of Fine Arts, 27.782. Diomedes sits on an altar, sword in one hand, the ancient statue of Pallas Athena in the other. Before him stands a statue of Poseidon on a column. Compare the much finer renditions of the same scene, plates 94, 96.

Today art historians have frequently shied away from making qualitative judgments about ancient artifacts, and there is, to be sure, a lot to be learned from objects of all sorts. But differences in quality are readily visible and should be acknowledged and appreciated, not only across but also within media. The modeling and execution of a bronze statue of the emperor Tiberius dedicated at Herculaneum in AD 37, for example, is certainly admirable, as seen in a detail of his footwear (fig. 4), but it pales in comparison to the ivory foot of a composite statue carved a century later (plate 165; compare also plate 153). The theft of the Palladion (the legendary statue of Pallas Athena sacred to the Trojans) was a popular subject in ancient art and was represented by some of the ancient world's most skilled gem engravers, including Felix and Dioskourides, the carver of the signet ring of the emperor Augustus (plates 94, 96). The quality of their work becomes clear when compared to a representation of the same scene by a less accomplished carver (fig. 5).

While gold, silver, gems, and other luxury products of ancient Egypt and the Near East, of the Bronze Age Aegean, and of the European Middle Ages stand at the center of modern studies of their material culture, those of Greece and Rome, although investigated in considerable depth by some specialists, have largely been overlooked. Beginning in the sixteenth century with the second edition of Giorgio Vasari's *Lives of the Most Excellent Painters, Sculptors, and Architects* (1568), which aimed, among other things, to valorize the author's own practice, architecture, sculpture, and painting have been enshrined as the principal subjects of modern art history, while other crafts have been sidelined. Thus architecture in stone, sculpture in marble (and bronze to the degree that it survives), and painting on ceramics and plaster are the principal foci of Greek and Roman art history. Yet painted pots were of little interest to ancient writers on art. The ancients were keenly interested in other objects, especially those fashioned from sumptuous materials, which, as in other periods and cultures, were often more consequential than those privileged today. Along with the sculptors Polykleitos, Praxiteles, and Lysippos, and the painters Apelles, Parrhasios, and Zeuxis, workers in precious metals, gemstones, and fine textiles, such as Akragas, Boëthos, Mentor, Mys, Mnesarchos, Pyrgoteles, Dioskourides, Tryphon, Theodoros, Akesas, and Helikon, were praised by classical writers.[28] Pheidias, the most celebrated of all ancient artists, was famous *not* for the marbles of the Parthenon, which today are often attributed to his genius, but for his monumental gold and ivory (chryselephantine) statues. These were widely acclaimed—and frequently represented in other media—less for their stylistic innovations than because they so vividly conveyed the otherworldly power of their divine subjects. The splendor of their materials—semiprecious stones, fine woods, rock crystal, glass, and amber, as well as gold and ivory—contributed to their mimetic success by presenting convincing simulacra of Olympian radiance.[29] In the *Iliad*, *Odyssey*, and other ancient texts, the gods are described as bright, shining, and luminous. Although they might disguise themselves and appear on earth in some other form, their resplendence, more often than not, reveals their true nature. Heroes recognize the gods by their blazing eyes, luminous flesh, and elaborate drapery. In the *Homeric Hymn to Aphrodite*, the goddess appears before the mortal Anchises "wearing a robe more brilliant than gleaming fire," "her cheeks radiant with divine beauty."[30] Something of these qualities can be seen in preserved works of ancient goldsmiths, their shining gold not only modulated by skillful modeling but also enhanced by the addition of colored enamels (plates 19, 27, 30, 33, 35) and precious stones (plates 35–39, 41, 43).[31]

Gold, ivory, gemstones, and other sumptuous materials frequently had spiritual qualities ascribed to them. Incorruptible, gold was "the child of Zeus... the most excellent of possessions," according to the Greek poet Pindar,[32] and numerous ancient texts indicate that gold and silver vessels played crucial roles in ancient religious festivals, not to mention symposia and other events with significant sociopolitical implications. Surviving inventories make it abundantly clear that temples were built to house gold and silver dedications, along with gemstones, ivory, fine woods, and luxurious textiles.[33] The great expense and exotic origins of these materials added to their appeal, manifesting the wealth and power, as well as the piety, of their donors. Pausanias, writing in the middle of the second century AD, considered Greeks of earlier times "to have been especially lavish in honoring the gods, and not at all miserly of resources, in that they imported ivory from India and Ethiopia to make statues"; Pliny the Elder observed that "tusks fetch a vast price and supply a very elegant material for images of the gods."[34] Indeed, when visiting Rhodes in the first century, the philosopher Apollonios of Tyana reputedly said he would much prefer to see a gold and ivory statue in a small sanctuary than a cheap clay image in a large one.[35] It was not just the scale of Pheidias's statues that made them famous, but their splendid materials and skilled craftsmanship, which mutually reinforced one another. This was recognized by Maximus of Tyre, who, in the second century, wrote that "the Greek manner of honoring the gods uses what is most beautiful on earth, in purity of raw materials, in human shape, and in artistic precision."[36]

Yet Greek and Roman works in hard stones, gold, and ivory, not to mention silver, fine woods, amber, textiles, and other sumptuous materials, have come to be neglected in modern histories of art, although they rank among the outstanding and best-preserved products of classical civilization and were arguably the most important to the ancients themselves. The focus of modern histories of ancient art on marble and bronze statuary, Greek pottery, and Roman frescoes and the almost wholesale exclusion of works in other media has skewed our views of past artistic production and taste, as well as of religious practices and social, economic, and political relations. To give but one example: in the middle of the sixth century BC, the inhabitants of Phokaia, an Ionian Greek city on the western coast of Anatolia, decided to abandon their city rather than submit to the Medes. Herodotos reports: "They loaded onto their ships their children, women, and household property, and above all the images of the gods from sanctuaries and other dedications, everything, in fact, *except bronzes, stonework, and paintings*, and they sailed to Chios" [emphasis added].[37] The Phokaians abandoned the very objects that lie at the heart of modern art histories. In specialized textbooks, just as in more general surveys of art history, virtually all illustrations devoted to Greek art depict objects made of either ceramic or stone. The exceptions are inevitably bronze statues or plaster models, and occasionally coins, with few if any objects in other, more valuable materials. To be sure, items superbly fashioned of sumptuous substances are not always so well preserved as pots or marbles, but they *do* survive in far greater quantities than the standard treatments of ancient art would lead one to believe.

Why are exquisitely wrought and ideologically potent luxury arts habitually overlooked in modern accounts of Greek and Roman art? Their counterparts, after all, are regularly included in histories of ancient Near Eastern, Egyptian, Aegean Bronze Age, Etruscan, Late Antique, and medieval art. Survival, although certainly a factor, is not the answer. Ancient Greek and Roman gemstones of every period, for example, far outnumber preserved bronzes. And yet Greek bronze "originals"—whether they actually survive or are merely identified in Roman marble "copies"—dominate modern studies of ancient art. They are prominent in the first half of Book 34 of Pliny's *Natural History*, but Pliny also devoted Book 33 to gold and silver and Book 37, the culmination of the *Natural History*, to precious stones.[38] He and other ancient authors leave no doubt about the importance of these materials, even if Pliny himself was deeply concerned with their potentially corrupting influence.[39]

As Pliny and others make clear, gems performed vital functions as personal insignia, tokens of political affiliation, and dedications in sanctuaries. Imported from abroad and worked with great skill, they were deemed to have mythical and magical, as well as aesthetic and economic, characteristics. As magical charms, they could inspire love, guarantee faithfulness, cure the sick, and avert the evil eye. Certain stones might make one lecherous or more convincing in court; they might predict storms or prevent scorpion bites. But such beliefs hardly accord well with the vision of the rational ancients *we* have constructed. Could the Greeks and Romans, revered as the inventors of democracy, philosophy, and theater, the establishers of law, builders of roads, aqueducts, and so much more that we hold dear, have been so irrational?[40] This is just one of the reasons that gemstones, a mainstay of classical studies through the eighteenth century, now dwell largely in specialist publications, where they tend to be demystified through "scientific" modes of analysis and categorization by shape, style, and date. Their great value to early modern collectors unfortunately created an active market for forgeries, which still bedevil the field, providing yet another reason for their exclusion from the art historical canon.

The demotion of ancient Greek and Roman sumptuous arts into the category of minor arts (now inadequately rehabilitated as decorative arts), and their relegation to the margins of art history, can be traced along a variety of trajectories. These trends overlap, interact, and mutually reinforce one another. Anachronistic notions of what constitutes "art" have proved detrimental to the study of objects created from sumptuous materials. In the ancient world all art objects had a function. The temples, statues, and painted pots that fill modern text- and coffee-table books on Greek and Roman art were created to serve religious, social, political, and other purposes. The same holds true for sumptuous objects, such as the ivory figure that originally formed part of a lyre dedicated to Hera at Samos (plate 149) or the silver *hydria* and gold wreath deposited in a Macedonian tomb at Vergina (plate 67). These objects operated in the same contexts as more modest artifacts, but because they were fashioned from valuable and exotic or even mythical and magical substances, they could better fulfill their functions as votives, funerary offerings, and status-enhancing commodities. The inherent properties of these luxurious materials, moreover, permitted greater technical elaboration and caused them to be entrusted to superior craftsmen, who fashioned products of higher quality. Precious votives, such as the lyre originally inlaid with amber, or the now-fragmentary life-size gilt-silver bull offered to Apollo at Delphi (plate 60), could garner greater divine favor than bronzes or marbles, for in antiquity humility was not a virtue. Artists might revel in some aesthetic breakthrough, but patrons made offerings to the gods in the hope of receiving "something pleasing in return."[41] At the beginning of the *Iliad*, the priest Chryses, spurned by Agamemnon, prays to Apollo: "Hear me, Apollo! God of the silver bow... If I ever roofed a shrine to please your heart, ever burned the long rich bones of bulls and goats on your holy altar, now bring my prayer to pass."[42] As Pausanias recognized, the gods should be honored lavishly.

A similar aesthetic operated in the cemetery, as evidenced by ancient sumptuary legislation seeking to restrict displays of wealth that might upset the status quo.[43] In private homes, gold and silver vessels (some inlaid with semiprecious stones)—produced in the same shapes as ceramics, decorated in the same styles, and with many of the same scenes (plates 25, 48–50, 62–64, 70, 76, 78)—would have impressed visitors far more than clay pots, however finely decorated. Thus, according to Thucydides, the Athenians were duped into launching the disastrous Sicilian expedition of 415 BC by the inhabitants of Egesta, who entertained the Athenian ambassadors and ships' crews "in their private houses, collecting together all the cups of gold and silver in Egesta itself, borrowing others from the neighboring cities, Phoenician and Hellenic, and then letting each host produce them at banquets as though they were his own property. All used pretty much the same articles and everywhere there was a great abundance of them, so that the Athenians were astonished and when they got back to Athens told everyone of the vast quantities of valuable objects they had seen."[44]

Sumptuous objects were embedded in life, and the strict categorization of artifacts by media—essentially an academic enterprise—is not attested before the sixteenth century, when academies of art, concerned not only with the practice but also with theories of art, began to enshrine the triad of architecture, sculpture, and painting. In the first edition of Vasari's massively influential *Lives of the Most Excellent Architects, Painters, and Sculptors*, which he conceived amid the splendor of Farnesine Rome and published in 1550, he lauded the creative and formative role of gold work and gem engraving. In the 1568 revision of this fundamental text, however, he demoted the sumptuous arts and elevated painting within what was to become the canonical triad, even promoting it to first place in his title. Vasari's aim was to promote a concept of *disegno* (creative design) and to advance his own status in contrast to his rivals, among them the goldsmith Benvenuto Cellini.[45]

The impact of Vasari's efforts, however, was not immediate. Connoisseurs continued to read ancient authors and to covet gems as well as marbles. In the seventeenth century, Franciscus Junius wrote of Akesas the weaver as well as Apelles the painter; and in the eighteenth century, J. J. Winckelmann, also immersed in ancient texts, made his reputation producing a major catalogue of Philipp von Stosch's collection of engraved gems (1760) and privileged this medium on the title page of his monumental *History of Ancient Art* (1764). In fact, having seen little original Greek sculpture or painting, Winckelmann, like many others, believed that the history of Greek art could be written just as well from glyptic as from any other evidence.[46] Thus gems continued to inform the practice and study of painting, sculpture, and architecture long after Vasari, as is evident from the engravings adorning the late eighteenth-century publication of the collection of the duc d'Orleans, which depict gem cutting as a beacon to those practicing other crafts (fig. 6).[47]

Over the years, art historical ideologies have contributed to the displacement and demotion of items fashioned from semiprecious stones and other sumptuous materials from the lofty position they held in ancient art and culture (as well as in the Middle Ages and the Renaissance). When Greek art is placed on the procrustean bed of the triad of architecture, sculpture, and painting, the sumptuous arts suffer: ruined temples, after all, are but empty shells, past repositories of precious offerings; marbles stand in for the bronze and chryselephantine images admired by ancient authors; and painted pots fill the gap

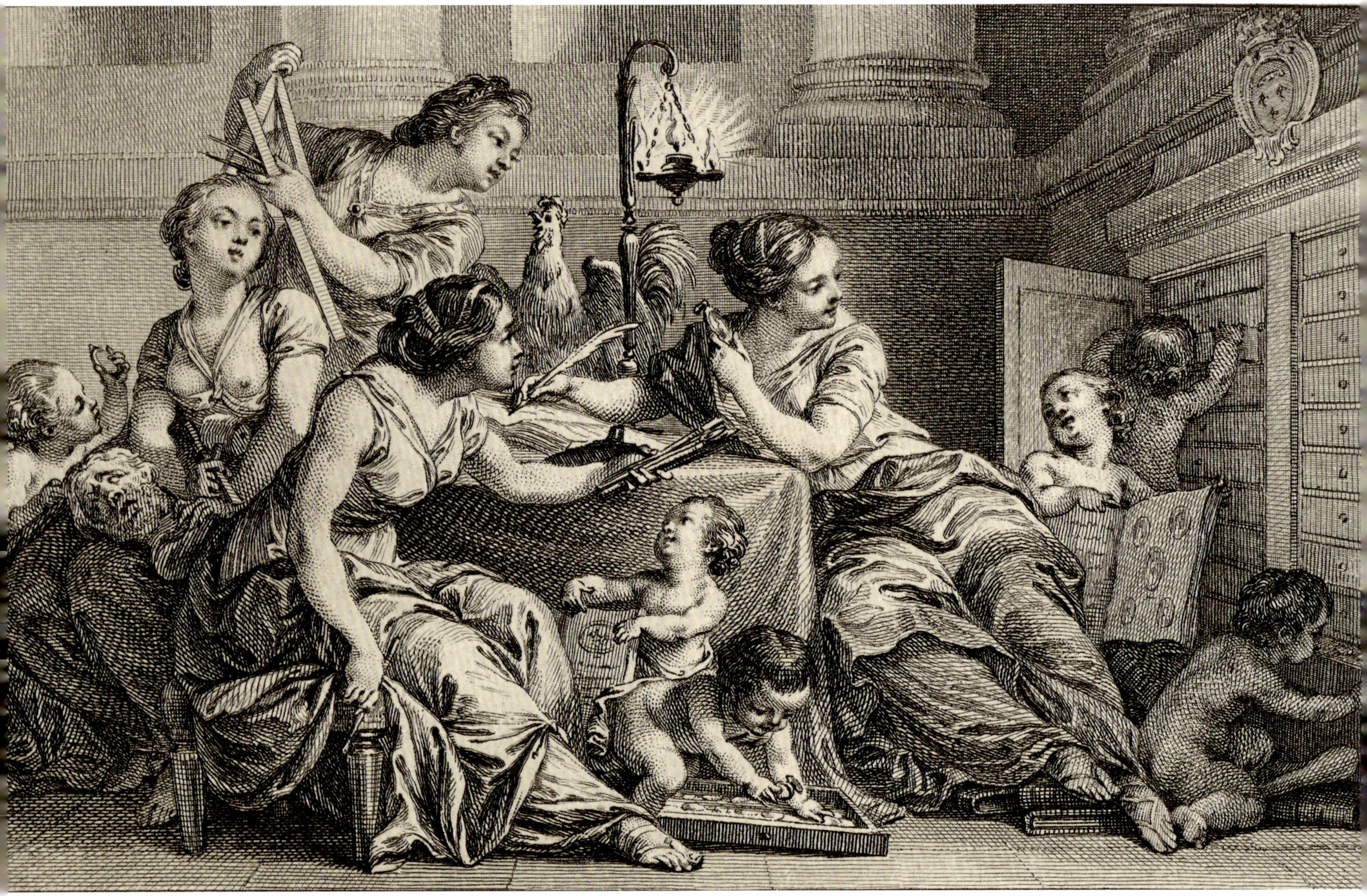

Figure 6

The personification of Glyptic (center right) illuminates Architecture, Sculpture, and Painting. Vignette on page 1 of the first volume of G. de La Chau and G. M. Le Blond, *Description des principales pierres gravées du cabinet de S. A. S. Monseigneur le Duc d'Orleans, premier prince du sang* (Paris, 1780); vignette designed by Charles Nicolas Cochin and engraved by Augustin de St. Aubin in 1779.

created by the loss of celebrated panel paintings. Indeed, owing to the exaltation of painting, ceramics have become a major subfield of ancient art history, with the names of Exekias and Euthymides on the lips of successful students in undergraduate art history survey courses.[48]

That decorated pots have acquired an aesthetic significance inordinately greater than they had in antiquity leads us to another trajectory along which the sumptuous arts have suffered—that of "good taste." As Winckelmann declared at the beginning of his *Reflections on the Imitation of Greek Works in Painting and Sculpture* (1755), "der gute Geschmack" is often considered to have "had its origins under the skies of Greece."[49] Winckelmann's idea of good taste, which he optimistically thought was "becoming more prevalent throughout the world," was naturally no closer to that of the ancient Greeks than is our own today. Such notions, closely allied to postantique hierarchies of media, have undermined the study of the sumptuous arts. The pervasive ideological construct of Greek taste as "pure" and "simple," which served Winckelmann in his campaign against the Rococo, went on to play a significant role not only in the elevation of ceramics[50] but also in the debate over polychromy in the early and mid-nineteenth century.[51] Romantic notions of "art for art's sake," the English art critic John Ruskin's crusade against ornament, and, more recently, the modernist aesthetic of "less is more" have all figured in the intellectual and moral shifts that have contributed to the devaluation of opulent artifacts prized by the ancients.

Modern preferences for white-stone sculpture and less costly, and thus putatively more democratic, ceramics—preferences that have been projected onto the Greeks, despite the explicit and copious testimony of ancient texts to the contrary—also mask political, moral, and racial agendas. In their role as proto–Anglo-Europeans, the Greeks have been repeatedly praised for having created "perfect" forms from common materials. Painted pots are, paradoxically, both considered to have been within the reach of Everyman and simultaneously extolled as high art. Indeed, antimaterialist sentiment was so pervasive in the nineteenth century that the simplicity of a red-figured vase or an Athenian marble was seen as the height of perfection.[52] How, in contrast, was it possible for finely crafted sumptuous objects, long the possessions of elites, to serve as embodiments of the art of a people we consider to have been free, democratic, and rational?

Ancient texts reveal that gold wreaths were awarded to foreign potentates by a sycophantic Athenian demos.[53] Yet, because most surviving examples of ancient sumptuous arts have emerged from tombs outside modern Greece, such objects have all too often been perceived as the products of barbarian—that is, non–Western European—aesthetics. The scene on the technically and materially splendid gilt-silver bowl excavated in 1929 from a Thracian tomb near Duvanli in central Bulgaria (plate 63), for example, compares favorably to Athenian red-figured pots, yet it and similar objects were characterized by a prominent art historian as aesthetically "second-rate"[54]—despite the sophisticated characterization of the charioteers, the poses of the warriors on the coursing chariots, and the various positions of their shields, each emblazoned with a distinct device. Although the style of this *phiale* is clearly related to that of late fifth-century BC Athenian pots and marbles, it has been suggested that this and other such objects were commissioned from itinerant Greek craftsmen by rich, gaudy barbarians. The insinuation—contradicted by the incontrovertible record of temple inventories and ancient literature—is that no right-thinking Greek would be attracted by such an item, that such ornate and opulent objects are somehow not *truly* Greek. The Duvanli *phiale*, however, is certainly Athenian. Although found in Thrace, it was excavated with red-figured pottery, which no one has ever suggested is anything other than imported Athenian ware; it weighs 428 grams (approximately the weight, 431 grams, of an Attic mina); and its iconography—*apobatai* (warriors mounting and dismounting from racing chariots)—is manifestly Athenian. Such warriors appear on Panathenaic prize amphorae as well as on the Parthenon frieze.

Prevalent interpretations of Greek art, perhaps derived from Platonic notions of ideal form, allow little tolerance for vibrant color or rich surface effects, although these are as evident in Late Archaic marbles and Late Classical ceramics as in other, less copiously preserved media. We have ascribed restrained and rational principles of organization to Greeks across the board. Precious objects recovered abroad or composed of imported—literally exotic—materials have been perceived and denigrated as the products of aberrant, foreign, even "Oriental" sensibilities, with all the essentialist baggage of such terms, despite the fact that the Greeks and Romans looked to other ancient civilizations, not just for materials and markets but also for cultural models.[55] The forms of the vast majority of pre-Hellenistic Greek gems, for example, are modeled on Egyptian scarabs, but their backs, or rather tops, are seldom illustrated, and some of their beetles have actually been cut away.[56]

Copious ancient evidence makes it clear that the ancients produced and enjoyed such objects and admired complex polychromatic compositions, which are increasingly being sought—and found—on ancient marbles. Such polychromy is still discernible in the surviving painted decoration of the *korai* on the Acropolis and on an elaborate painted and gilded marble throne from the Tomb of Eurydike at Vergina, as well as in fanciful objects like the Shield of Achilles (described at length in *Iliad* 18).[57] That many surviving examples of Greek luxury art were not only recovered abroad but also date to the Hellenistic period—a period long considered "decadent" or "degenerate"—may be another reason for their having been dismissed as evidence of genuine Greek sensibilities.[58]

Although postantique classifications of media and anachronistic notions of good taste have contributed to the marginalization of ancient Greek sumptuous arts, some of the major monuments treated in our traditional art histories focus explicitly upon them. The Parthenon frieze, whatever it represents, depicts men and women carrying musical instruments, metal vessels, ritual implements, and fine furniture, and it culminates in the folding of a (presumably elaborately woven) textile, all of which are mentioned in the inscribed inventories of the temple. The famous grave stele of Hegeso (fig. 7) depicts a scene repeated on numerous funeral monuments: a well-dressed young woman, seated on a finely wrought chair with a footstool, inspects an item of jewelry brought to her by an attendant.[59] Terracotta votive plaques from Lokri, which have lost most of their polychromatic decoration, illustrate the importance of textiles and metal plate as well as the sophistication of ancient furniture (fig. 8).[60] While metal vessels dominate one composition, the other features a woman who stands before an ornate chair and places a folded cloth in an elaborate chest adorned with inset figural panels depicting Athena striking down Pallas (or Enkelados) and a youth grasping the wrist of a maiden. Such scenes, which seem to have served as exempla for women, are actually preserved in furniture appliqués, for example, the so-called Morgan Ivory in New York (plate 147). Like the lost Chest of Kypselos at Olympia, described at length by Pausanias,[61] such objects, and those represented on thousands of other artifacts, populated the ancient city of images no less than black- and red-figured pots, and they served to convey social, religious, and political messages through their materials as well as their decoration. This iconography of the precious communicated wealth, power, and prestige in the home and in the city, in the cemetery and in the sanctuary.

Another reason for the absence of Greek sumptuous arts from our histories of art seems to be their presumed inadequacy to the task of tracing the evolution in the naturalistic depiction of the human figure, the interpretative framework that continues to dominate the study of Greek art, although it is not employed in the analysis of the art of many other cultures. Greek stylistic development toward greater naturalism, a topic of interest to ancient writers (as well as to early moderns like Vasari and Winckelmann), is today easily delineated through hundreds of preserved marbles (Roman interleaved with Greek) and thousands of painted pots. The potential of pottery, hardly mentioned by ancient literary sources, to "indicat[e] the successful progress of Painting and design" was recognized in the eighteenth century by the self-styled Baron d'Hancarville, who sought to increase the value of Sir William Hamilton's collection of ceramics.[62] The canonical styles of Greek art, however, similarly evolved and can be traced across

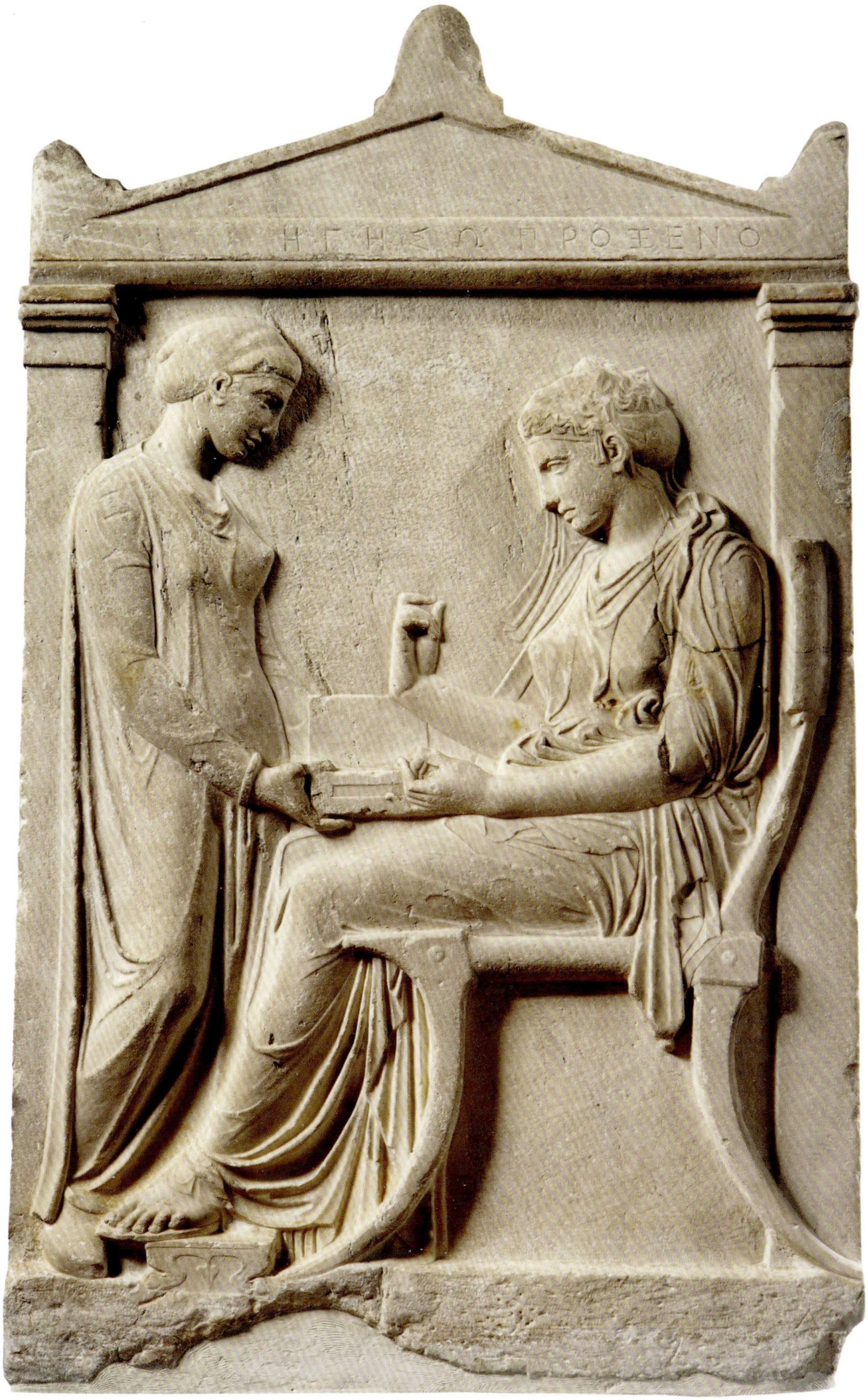

Figure 7
Grave stele, from the Kerameikos cemetery, Athens, ca. 400 BC. Marble, H: 1.58 m. Athens, National Archaeological Museum, 3624. Hegeso, the daughter of Proxenos, examines a necklace, originally painted, taken from a jewelry box brought to her by a slave girl.

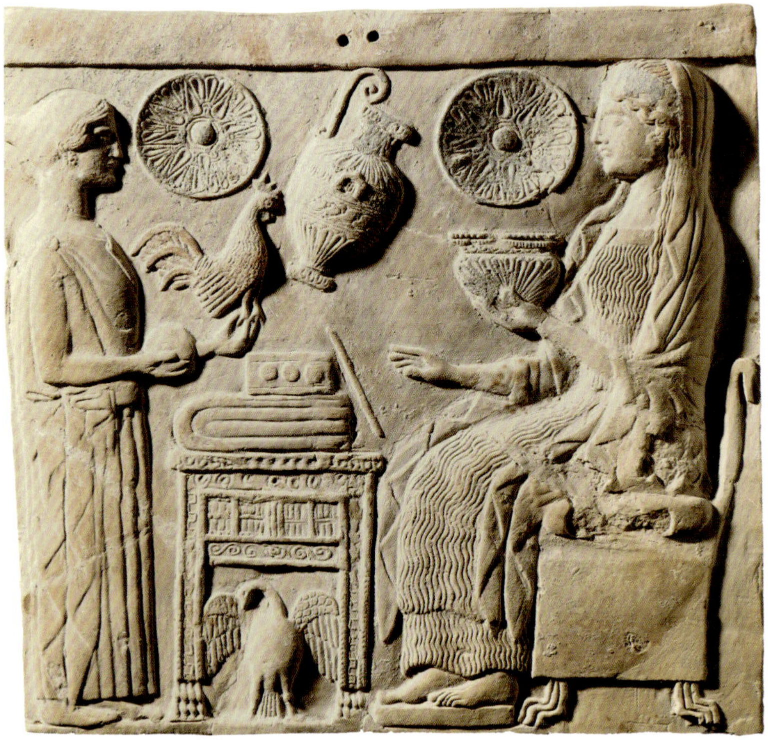

a

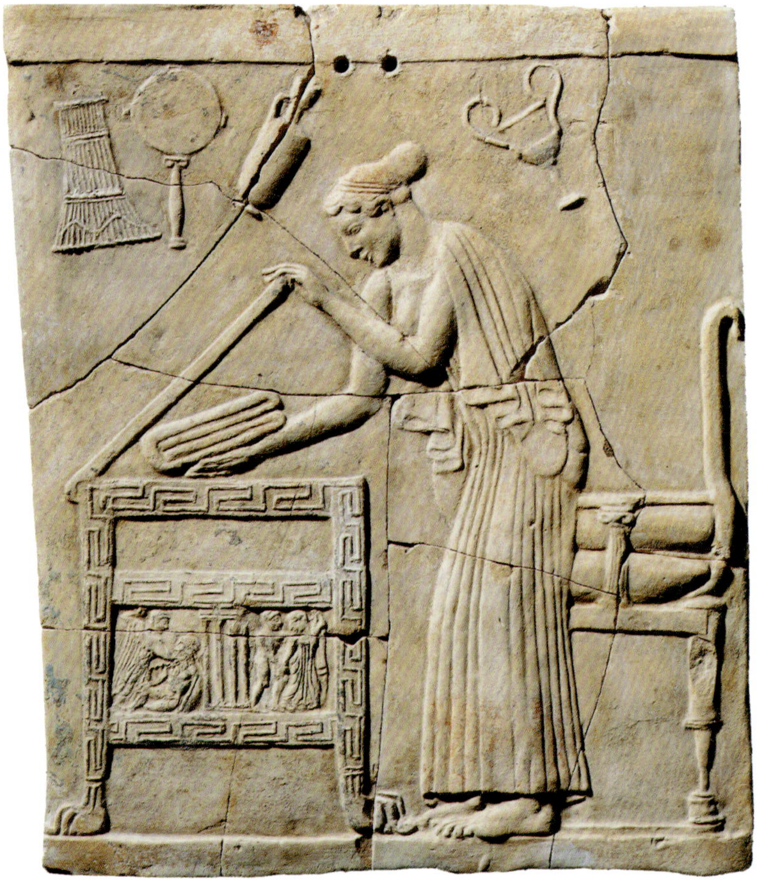

b

Figure 8a, b
Two votive plaques to Persephone, from Lokri (southern Italy), ca. 470–450 BC. Terracotta, (a) H: 28 cm, W: 28 cm; (b) H: 26 cm, W: 21.5 cm. Reggio Calabria, Museo Nazionale. In these plaques, metal vessels, luxury furniture, and precious textiles are all depicted among objects offered to the goddess.

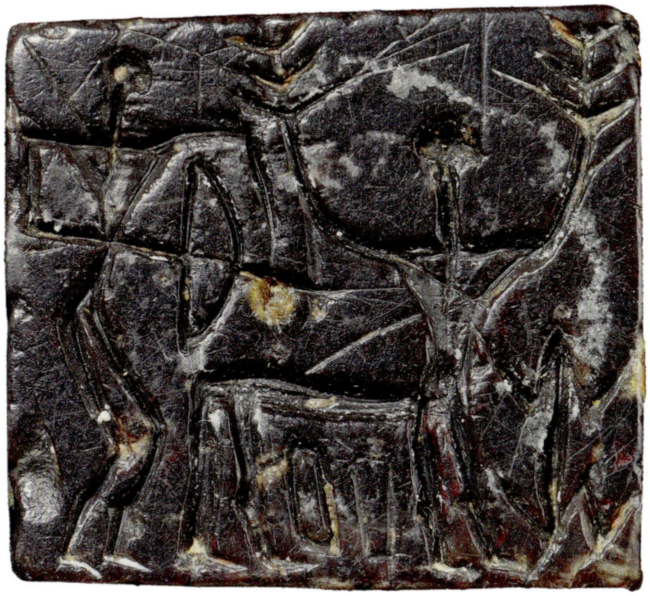

Figure 9
Archer and a Centaur, ca. 700 BC.
Black serpentine tabloid intaglio,
H: 22 mm; W: 20 mm; D: 10 mm
Paris, Bibliothèque nationale de
France, Cabinet des médailles, M 5837.

media. An engraved tabloid, perhaps depicting Herakles and Nessos, said to be from Crete but arguably Peloponnesian (fig. 9), and repoussé gold diadems recovered from tombs in Athens's Kerameikos cemetery (plates 3, 4) are no less Geometric in style than Dipylon amphorae; Rhodian gold plaques depicting the *Potnia Theron* (Mistress of the Animals) (plate 5) are as orientalizing as the "Lady of Auxerre"; a fourth-century BC chalcedony intaglio depicting a Nike assembling a trophy (plate 86) demonstrates well the much-vaunted advances in mimesis made by artists in the Classical period; and the evolution of the differing styles of Hellenistic and Roman art are likewise to be discerned in precious materials.

The ancients did not live in an exclusively red, black, or white world. Not only were their architecture and sculpture brightly painted, gilded, and even inlaid, but sanctuaries as well as the homes of the elites (who set the standards for other members of society) contained vessels and jewelry made of precious metals alongside polychromed ivories, opulent furniture, rich textiles, and so on. These objects were not merely decorative, but politically, socially, and religiously potent. Excavations have recovered many such objects (and others never went underground). The sumptuous arts, however, have paradoxically been accorded less, rather than more, attention since the advent of scientific archaeology. The art histories of Junius and Winckelmann, although they followed the Vasarian tradition of privileging painting, sculpture, and architecture, were still attuned to what we might call the visual culture of the Greeks, for they relied heavily on the diversity of objects mentioned in ancient texts. Today, however, the Vasarian, academic model has taken firm hold. Style has come to dominate. Primed to believe that painting, sculpture, and architecture are the only true arts, and concerned with what we understand to have been daily life in a democratic society, we have been misled by the disproportionately high survival rate of ceramics and stone, try as we may to remind ourselves otherwise. The products of ancient marble carvers and pot painters, fine as they are, are not fully representative of ancient art and are certainly not characteristic of what the Greeks and Romans themselves valued most in their material culture. We might not be able to recover the most remarkable products of classical civilization, but to ignore the physical and literary evidence for the appearance, technique, and functions of the luxury arts in antiquity is, quite simply, to impoverish the past.

The chapters that follow attempt to move beyond anachronistic and reductive art histories and to return the sumptuous arts of ancient Greece and Rome to their rightful place. Three kinds of evidence are adduced: archaeological, literary, and art historical. These rarely overlap but are often complementary. Primacy is given to the archaeological evidence, that is, to the objects themselves, even though not all the artifacts presented in the following pages were scientifically excavated by professional archaeologists. Indeed, some of them never went into the ground. Literary evidence for the existence, production, and uses of luxury objects, as well as ancient attitudes toward them, is abundant and is presented at some length in the chapters that follow. Ancient literary texts in a wide variety of genres provide vivid testimony to the diverse roles played by items similar to those presented in the plates (for the specific objects actually described by the ancients rarely survive). The third category of evidence, the art historical, is no less important and also quite abundant. It includes depictions of luxury objects in other media, such as Roman frescoes and reliefs bearing images of finely wrought silver (see figs. 20, 21) or a linen mummy wrapping with a painted representation of a woman wearing numerous rings set with gems (see fig. 25). These clearly illustrate how ubiquitous the luxury arts were in the visual culture of the ancient world and, along with the literary evidence, help to contextualize the surviving artifacts.

In the end, the diverse evidence is best combined, and in this way techniques of production, contexts of use, and the real and symbolic values of ancient objects fashioned from precious materials can be reconstructed. Even creations that no longer survive can, to some extent, be recovered if we bring together the evidence left to us with a healthy dose of imaginative thought. Standing some 12.5 meters (forty feet) tall, the gold and ivory statue of Athena that Pheidias fashioned as the centerpiece of the Parthenon on the Acropolis was a repository for the wealth of Athens at the height of her empire. The value of the figure's gold alone was equal to the city's annual military budget, and the materials and scale of the statue demonstrated the power of the *polis*, just as its iconography asserted the divine favor the *demos* enjoyed. Not a scrap of the statue itself survives, only a few blocks ascribed to its base and cuttings in the floor of the temple. But the descriptions of numerous ancient authors and representations of the statue in a wide variety of media—from stone reliefs and red-figured vases to coins, lamps, gems, and jewelry (plates 19, 92), and even buttons for clothes—provide a good impression of the appearance of the figure, even if not the experience of viewing it. For that we must bring to bear surviving objects made of the same materials: ivory hands, faces, and feet; gold reliefs; inlays of precious stones, such as those presented on the following pages.

Pheidias's statue of Zeus at Olympia was just as large as the Athena, but because the god was depicted sitting, rather than standing, he appeared larger. One ancient author complained that Pheidias miscalculated his proportions: if the god stood, he would unroof the temple.[63] But such incongruity must have been deliberate: both statues were too large to be contained by the interiors of their temples. They represented the Olympian gods' epiphanies on earth and captured the imaginations of ancient viewers. Located at a Panhellenic shrine, Pheidias's Zeus was more than the patron of a single polis and thus seems to have had an even wider appeal. The statue's technique also seems to have been more complex than that of the Athena. Pheidias combined techniques of shipbuilding, furniture making, and metalworking to fashion the inner core, ivory veneers, and gold sheeting of the Athena. But for the Zeus, both physical evidence gained from the excavation of Pheidias's workshop at Olympia and the detailed descriptions of ancient authors suggest that the sculptor went even further, employing gold-backed glass to create the illusion of shimmering, transparent embroidered drapery (plates 55–59). Both statues likely had precious stones for their eyes, and pigments added to their ivory flesh evoked naturalistically the ethereal complexion of the gods. These statues, sadly, do not survive. But through the combination of archaeological, literary, and art historical evidence we can envision what the Greeks and Romans themselves indisputably considered to be the most outstanding works of art.

NOTES

1 Terence, *Adelphi* 760: *Adulescens luxu perditus.*

2 Sallust, *Bellum Catilinae* 53.5. See also Dubois-Pelerin 2008; Lapatin 2008; and below.

3 On concepts of luxury in general, see, e.g., Sekora 1977; Berry 1994. See also Clark 1986. On the relativity of values, see Appadurai 1986 and, most recently, Papadopoulos and Urton 2012. For hierarchies of materials and individuals in Archaic and Classical Greece specifically, see Kurke 1999; M. Miller 1997. For brief surveys of Greek and Roman luxury objects, see Henig 1983; Henig 2006, 217–23; La Rocca 1986; Reeder 1988; Kloft 1996; Sparkes 2006, 213–16; Boardman and Wagner 2012; Lapatin 2008, 2014, 2015.

4 Bernhardt 2003; Weeber 2003, 2006; Aßkamp 2007; Dubois-Pelerin 2008; Lapatin 2008; Fontanella 2009; Zanda 2011.

5 Kurke 1992. On ancient sumptuary legislation, see, most recently, Bernhardt 2003; Di Pasquale and Bruun in Fontanella 2009, 40–51; Zanda 2011; Brøns 2014, 184–217.

6 Harward 1982, 57–79; Miller 1989, 1997. See also Davidson 1998.

7 Cleland 2005; Brøns 2014.

8 Aristophanes, *Wasps* 1214–15.

9 Isokrates 5.124. See especially R. Gorman and V. Gorman 2007, who place the prevalence of this thought in Roman, rather than Hellenistic, historiography.

10 Herakleides, fragment 55: Athenaios, *Deipnosophistai* 12.512a–d.

11 Thucydides 6.16.

12 Plato, *Gorgias* 491e–92c. Of course, this position is not necessarily Plato's and may have been intended as a critique.

13 Aristotle, *Nicomachean Ethics* 1122a.18–1123a.23, 1125a.11–12. Aelian, *Varia Historia* 3.19.

14 Passerini 1934; Tondriau 1948; Cozzoli 1980; Heinen 1983; Briant 2002; Ager 2006.

15 Kallixeinos *apud* Athenaios, *Deipnosophistai* 196a–203b; see Rice 1983; Calandra 2011; Erskine 2013.

16 Grave stele of Tryphe, Princeton, y1992-48: Ridgway 1994, 34–37, no. 10 (with previous bibliography); Kondoleon 2000, 139; Lapatin 2003, 82–83. See also an early second-century inscription from Aphrodisias recording honors awarded to Tryphe, the daughter of Menodotos (Reynolds, Roueché, and Bodard 2007, no. 12.707). Surviving Aphrodisian inscriptions also attest to six men called Tryphon.

17 Mosaic from Daphne 1977: Balty, "Tryphe," *LIMC* 7:96–97, no. 1 (with previous bibliography); Cimok 2000, 182; Kondoleon 2000, 74, fig. 9. Other mosaics depict Tryphe lounging comfortably together with Bios (the male personification of life) either bejeweled on a banquet couch or stretched out on the ground; e.g., Antakya, Hatay Archaeological Museum, 862 (Cimok 2000, 54–55); Toronto, Royal Ontario Museum; Mura Sommella 1983.

18 Livy, *History* 1, preface 11–12.

19 Plutarch, *Cato* 5, 16, 18, translation by B. Perrin, 1914.

20 In addition to the sources cited in note 5 above, see also Berry 1994; Wyetzner 2002; Dubois-Pelerin 2008; Dari-Mattiacci and Plisecka (2010) 2012. See also below.

21 *IG* 5.2.514; Dittenberger 1920, 131–32, no. 999: "It is not permitted to enter the temple of the Lady goddess with any object of gold on one's person, unless it is intended for an offering; or to wear a purple or brightly-colored or black garment, or shoes, or a finger-ring. But if one enters wearing any forbidden object, it must be dedicated to the temple." See also Brøns 2014, 184–217.

22 Harpokration 1.59 (ed. Dindorf), s.v. *arrhephorein*.

23 See, e.g., Clark 1986.

24 Dio Cassius 61.10.3; Seneca, *De vita beata* 17.2.

25 Hardiman 2012, 268–69; Pollitt 1974, 63–66.

26 For the operation of such aesthetics in Mesopotamia and Byzantium, see Winter 1994; Kalavrezou 2012. See also Cutler 1994 (with a more sociological perspective). For the sensual experience of material objects as well as poetry—*aisthesis* (sensation), the root of aesthetics—especially in the Hellenistic period, see Porter 2012, 49. For the properties of, and responses to, specific materials, as well as their size, see the individual chapters that follow.

27 De Juliis 1984, 88–95; Vickers 1994, 1999b; Williams 2003.

28 See, e.g., Junius 1694 (ed. 1991); Overbeck 1868.

29 Lapatin 2001, 2005.

30 *Homeric Hymn to Aphrodite* 5.85.

31 See also Ogden 1993a.

32 Pindar, frag. 209 Bowra, 222 Snell-Maehler; compare Pindar, *Olympian* 1.1–2.

33 For precious objects in temple inventories, see, e.g., Linders 1972, 1975, 1987, 1997; Lewis 1985; Aleshire 1989; Vickers and Gill 1994, esp. 33–76; Harris 1995; Hamilton 2000; Vickers 1999a; Lapatin 2005; Brøns 2014. See also Rouse 1902.

34 Pausanias 5.12.3; *NH* 8.31.

35 Philostratos, *Vita Apollonii* 23.

36 Maximus of Tyre, *Oration* 2.3.

37 Herodotos 1.164.

38 Apart from a single chapter (8), Pliny's Book 37 is omitted entirely by Jex-Blake and Sellers 1896, as are most of Books 33 and 36. For the coherence of Pliny's design and ideology, see Isager 1991; Carey 2000. More recently than Jex-Blake and Sellers, J. J. Pollitt has devoted six chapters (totaling over a hundred pages) of his sourcebook, *The Art of Ancient Greece* (1990) to sculpture, three to painting (over fifty pages), and one to architecture (twenty-five pages). The decorative arts, in contrast, are treated in a single chapter of 15 pages, one third of which are given over to Pausanias's description of the Chest of Kypselos.

39 See note 36 above and Wallace-Hadrill 1990; Lapatin 2012.

40 See, e.g., Dodds 1951; Gordon 2011; Mastrocinque 2011; Nagy 2011; Rubel 2014.

41 See, e.g., Athens, National Museum, 39. This stele from Orchomenos is inscribed "Alxenor of Naxos made this: just look": Boardman 1978, fig. 244. The quote is from the dedication of Mantiklos to Apollo: Museum of Fine Arts, Boston, 03.997: Boardman 1978, fig. 10.

42 *Iliad* 1.43–48; translation by R. Fagles, 1998.

43 See, e.g., Ampolo 1984, 71–102; Garland 1989; Toher 1991; Morris 1992/93; Seaford 1994, 74–87; Hunt 1996, esp. 18–19; and note 5 above.

44 Thucydides 6.46.

45 Collareta 1995; see also Rubin 1995; Belozerskaya 2005. Vasari altered his title from *Le Vite de più eccellenti Architetti, Pittori, et Scultori* in 1550 to *Le Vite de più eccellenti Pittori, Scultori, e Architettori* in 1568.

46 Junius 1694 (ed. 1991); Winckelmann 1760, 1764; see also Leppmann 1970, 193.

47 La Chau and Le Blond 1780; see also P. Zazoff and H. Zazoff 1983, esp. 145–46.

48 Although known to collectors much earlier, ancient ceramics became symbols of status only in the mid-eighteenth century, when Greek wares were recognized in Italy (by Winckelmann, among others); see, e.g., Cook 1997, esp. 276–80. This shift is evident in Pompeo Battoni's 1767 portrait of the "Grand Tourist," Prince Karl Wilhelm Ferdinand, later Duke of Braunschweig and Lüneburg, who, apparently under the direction of Winckelmann, posed with pots as props, rather than with the more customary Roman architecture or sculpture; see Wilton and Bignamini 1996, 81–82, no. 39; Jenkins and Sloan 1996.

49 Winckelmann 1755 (1987 ed.), 2–3: "Der gute Geschmack, welcher sich mehr und mehr durch die Welt ausbreitet, hat sich angefangen zuerst unter dem griechischen Himmel zu bilden."

50 Vickers and Gill 1994, 1–32.

51 Bluhm et al. 1996; Van Zanten 1977.

52 See, e.g., Jenkyns 1980, 298–330.

53 Lawton 1995, 30–34; see also Harris 1995, 104–5, 230–32, 238 (for dedications of wreaths sent to Athena from members of the second Athenian confederacy [378–338 BC]).

54 Williams 1996, 236.

55 See, e.g., M. Miller 1997; Gruen 2011.

56 See, e.g., Boardman 1968a, esp. 55 and pl. XL.

57 See, e.g., Ginouvès 1994, 154–61, figs. 135–37; Reuterswärd 1960; Richter 1968a, esp. 14–15; Manzelli 1994; Panzanelli, Schmidt and Lapatin 2008; Brinkmann, Primavesi, and Hollein 2010; Grand-Clément 2011.

58 See, e.g., Winckelmann 1764; also the commentary of Donohue 1995, esp. 331–32, 335; and the apologia of R. Richardson 1911, 247.

59 See, e.g., Athens, National Archaeological Museum, 3624 (Stewart 1990, pl. 477).

60 Quagliati 1908, 196–200 (esp. fig. 47), 215–16 (fig. 63); Richter 1966, figs. 604, 386; Pruckner 1968; Brøns 2014, 29–32.

61 Pausanias 5.17.5–19.10.

62 d'Hancarville 1766–67, 1:168. See also Haskell 1984; Vickers and Gill 1994; Jenkins and Sloan 1996, 40–64. Of course, it was not until the twentieth century that the enormous corpus of Athenian ceramics was heroically classified by John Beazley, who also provided numerous anonymous craftsmen with names and thus, significantly, expanded the potential for biography in the Vasarian mode. Although best known for his work on pots, Beazley also wrote a catalogue of gems (Beazley 1920 [2002 ed.]). See also Kurtz 1985; Robertson 1991; Whitley 1997; Beard 2003.

63 Strabo, *Geographika* 8.3.30 (353–54).

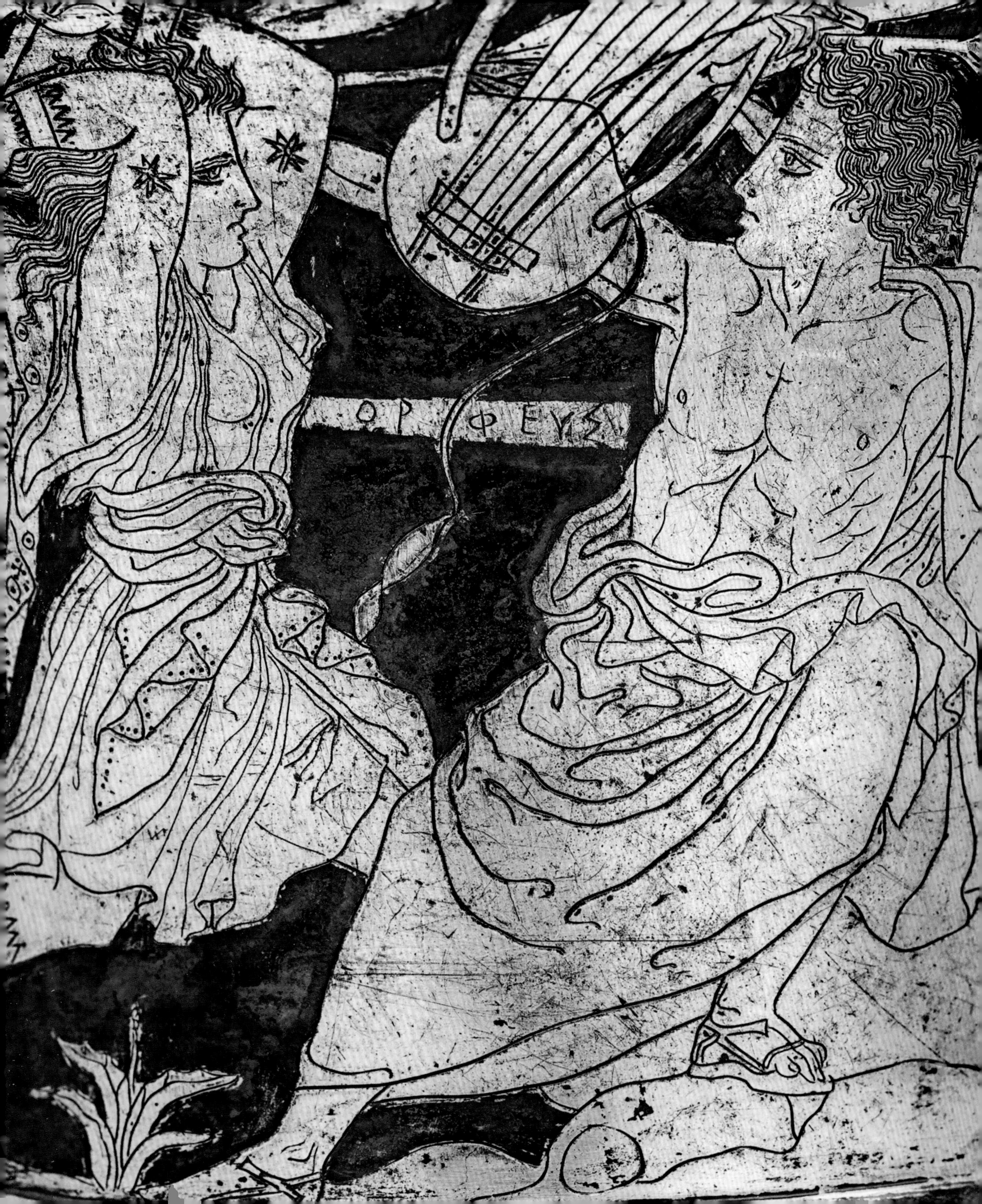
ΟΡΦΕΥΣ

CHAPTER ONE

METALS

Water is best, but gold shines like fire,
blazing in the night, supreme of lordly wealth.

—Pindar, *First Olympian Ode,* ca. 470 BC

GOLD

Water is the universal source of life, especially prized in the arid lands surrounding the Mediterranean, but, from the earliest days, humans have also cherished gold. Its bright shine draws attention, and its warm luster has long been associated with the sun. Unlike other metals, it is incorruptible. Thus gold seems to share something with the divine. Its rarity, too, makes it precious, bringing prestige to those who possess it. Although imperishable, gold is also extremely malleable and versatile in the hands of skilled craftsmen. It is easily worked and readily melted down and reused—hence the relative scarcity of survivals from the distant past. Most of what has come down to us from Greece and Rome was buried in antiquity, usually in tombs or hoards, but gold objects have also been found in destruction levels at a variety of sites and occasionally in shipwrecks.

Sophisticated gold vessels, jewelry, and ceremonial weapons were produced in the great preclassical civilizations of the Aegean Bronze Age, as well as in those of Egypt, the ancient Near East, and others further afield. The skills of Bronze Age goldsmiths are reflected in the Linear B tablets written by Mycenaean scribes and remembered in the poetry of Homer, where the houses of Alkinoos and Menelaos are said to have been decorated impressively with the metal. The Shield of Achilles and the Cup of Nestor, described in considerable detail in the *Iliad*, and the brooch given to Odysseus by his wife Penelope in the *Odyssey*, which depicted a hound capturing a fawn, are all presented as masterpieces of precious metalwork. Golden vessels and weapons were among the prizes awarded to the heroic victors of legendary athletic contests. The preeminence of gold in the Greek imagination is, perhaps, best reflected in the Ages of Man, as expounded by the seventh-century BC poet Hesiod, who describes the degeneration from eras of gold to silver to bronze to iron, a concept readily taken up by later writers and persisting to this day.[1]

Contradictory mythical traditions about gold (*chrysos* in ancient Greek; *aurum* in Latin) abound. Pliny the Elder writes that the Phoenician prince Kadmos discovered it at Pangaion in Thrace while searching for his sister Europa, who had been carried off by Zeus. Pliny, however, also mentions other accounts that credit Thoas, king of Taurian Chersonesos on the northern shore of the Black Sea; or Aiakos, son of Zeus; or Sol, son of Okeanos, who first found the metal at Panchaia, a rich island in the Red Sea.[2] The Roman fabulist Gaius Julius Hyginus, a freedman of the emperor Augustus and superintendent of the imperial library on Rome's Palatine Hill, in contrast, attributes to Kadmos the production of bronze, saying that it was Aiakos who discovered gold at Panchaia.[3] The Late Antique *Chronicum Alexandrium*, meanwhile, not unreasonably credits the god Mercury (Hermes to the Greeks), patron of commerce as well as thieves, with discovery of the metal. The early fifth-century BC poet Pindar, for his part, simply calls gold "the child of Zeus."[4]

In addition to its exotic mythical origins and aesthetic and ideological qualities, gold was thought to possess medicinal, magical, mystical, and moral properties. Thus the ring of the Lydian king Gyges, or alternatively that of the Phrygian Midas, both of whom ruled over the rich lands of western Asia Minor, was said to make its wearer invisible. The rationalist Pliny dismisses that tradition, but he does report that the metal could protect against poison; relieve ulcers; cure fistulas, warts, and hemorrhoids; and, if boiled in honey and cumin and applied as a liniment to the navel, act as a gentle laxative.[5] Sixth- and fifth-century BC Greek poets, for their part, invoke images of weighing, refining, and testing precious metals as stable metaphors for the essential personal qualities of aristocrats, such as nobility, authenticity, and consistency. Theognis, Simonides, Pindar, and Bacchylides employ precious metals as key terms in a discourse of self-constitution and moral testing; such terms constituted the ethically charged conceptual frame in which the noble self and its proper relations with peers was articulated, in contrast to falsehood, baser behaviors, base metals, and counterfeits.[6]

In nature, gold exists in two forms: primary or *reef* gold, which occurs as small particles in veins or lodes embedded in quartz and must be mined; and secondary or *placer* gold, which appears where such rocks have been eroded by water or wind and the metal has been released from its matrix, naturally reconcentrated, and deposited in sand or gravel beds—usually associated with former or existing streams—as flakes, grains, or nuggets. Mining reef gold is a laborious procedure that requires hammering the rock, grinding it to powder, then washing the powder to separate the gold from the mineral debris. Alluvial deposits of placer gold are recovered much more readily by panning or sieving, and this gold can be easily worked in its natural state. Small particles can be joined by hammering and do not have to be smelted.[7] Precious gold flakes can also be filtered from auriferous water through thick woolen fleeces: hence the myth of the Golden Fleece, set in Colchis on the eastern shores of the Black Sea, another area rich in gold. In fact, the ancient geographer Strabo wrote in the first century that there "the mountain torrents are said to bring down gold, and the barbarians catch it in sluices perforated with holes and in fleecy skins."[8]

Ancient authors associated gold with exotic animals, such as large Indian ants that supposedly dug for the metal and fantastic griffins that guarded gold fields in remote lands (figs. 10,

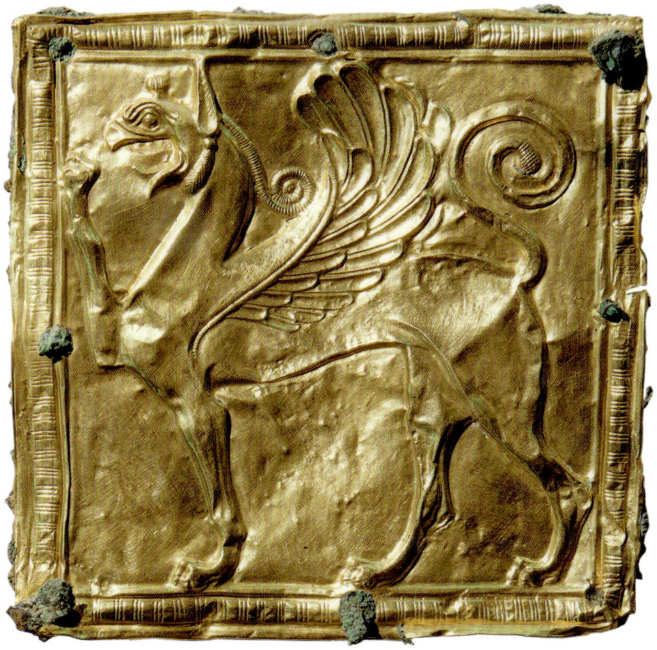

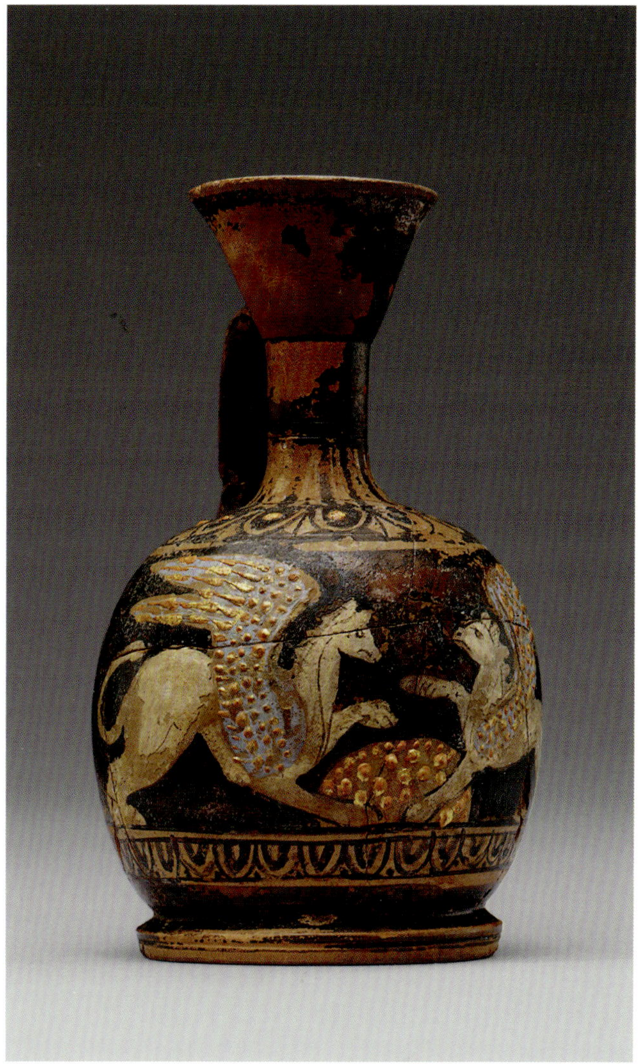

11). The first story might reasonably derive from the sighting of ants fortuitously removing some gold-laden sand from the earth while digging their burrows, although Herodotos writes of huge ants—"larger than a fox, but smaller than a dog"—so fleet of foot that men could escape them only when riding swift camels. Some have suggested that these were, in fact, pangolins (scaly anteaters) or marmots.[9] The legend of the griffins, meanwhile, seems to be rooted in the fact that skeletons of small, four-legged, beaked dinosaurs—along with fossilized nests containing their eggs—were revealed by the same erosive process that brought gold to the surface on the eastern steppe. Hence the composite lion-eagle beast linked to far-off sources of gold is not some wild fancy of Greek writers but rather a reasonable explanation of strange, but observed, natural phenomena.[10]

Gold occurs rarely in central Greece and Italy, but sources in Thrace, Asia Minor, Egypt, and Spain were all exploited in antiquity, as were those on the Adriatic, in Pannonia, the Alps, and farther afield in Africa, India, and beyond. Herodotos mentions Hyperborean sources, in the far north, which might indicate deposits in the Urals; he also writes of gold obtained

Figure 10
Plaque with griffin, ca. 600–550 BC. Gold, H: 10 cm. Delphi, Archaeological Museum, 9756. Griffins, composite beasts with a lion's body and an eagle's head and wings, were believed to guard the gold fields at the remote edges of the ancient Greek world. This hammered plaque, originally attached to a sheet of bronze, was worked from both front and back employing the repoussé technique. The form was raised by hammering from the rear. Then surface details of the animal's tail, wing, knob, and comb and the border were enhanced from the front. This is one of several linked panels depicting animals, both real and fantastic, which originally formed part of the gold garments of a life-size chryselephantine (gold and ivory) figure that was damaged in antiquity and buried beneath the Sacred Way in the Sanctuary of Apollo at Delphi (see plate 10).

Figure 11
Two griffins guarding a large gold nugget on an Athenian red-figured squat *lekythos*, ca. 380 BC. Terracotta, H: 8 cm. London, British Museum, 1894,1204.2.

by the Carthaginians who sailed beyond the Pillars of Herakles (Strait of Gibraltar) to the Atlantic coast of Africa.[11] Most famous in ancient literature is the gold of Asia Minor, where the mythical king Midas of Phrygia and the historical and legendarily rich king Croesus of Lydia became synonymous with vast wealth—and poor judgment. The story of Midas's improvident desire to transform everything he touched into gold is best told by the Roman poet Ovid in the *Metamorphoses:* Taking pity on the thoughtless monarch, the god Dionysos generously allowed Midas to wash away the deadly gift at the source of the Paktolos River, which thereafter flowed abundantly with gold dust.[12] This river ran through Sardis, capital city of the Lydians, and Herodotos describes in detail the wealth that accrued to Croesus, including the magnificent offerings the king dedicated to Apollo at Delphi, hoping to win the god's favor:

> He slaughtered three thousand of every kind of appropriate animal and burnt in a huge pile a number of precious objects—couches overlaid with gold or silver, golden cups, and other richly colored garments—in the hope of binding the god more closely to his interest.... He melted down an enormous quantity of gold into one hundred and seventeen ingots about eighteen inches long, nine inches wide, and three inches thick; four of the ingots were of refined gold weighing approximately a hundred and forty-two pounds each: the rest were alloyed and weighed about a hundred and fourteen pounds. He also caused the image of a lion to be made of refined gold: it weighed ten talents. This statue, when the temple at Delphi burned down [in 546 BC], fell from the gold bricks that formed its base and lies now in the Treasury of the Corinthians. It lost about three and half talents in the fire, and now weighs six and a half. This was by no means all that Croesus sent to Delphi; there were also two huge mixing bowls, one of gold, which was placed on the right-hand side of the entrance to the temple, the other of silver, on the left. These were also moved at the time of the fire, and the golden one, which weighs nearly a quarter of a ton, now stands in the Treasury of the Klazomenians.... I must not forget to mention the figure of a woman, in gold, four and half feet high, said by the Delphians to represent the woman who baked Croesus's bread.[13]

Ancient authors and modern scholars offer various explanations for why Croesus might have dedicated a large gold statue of his baker, or mistakenly was thought to have done so.[14] The lion was the symbol of Lydia, and in it can be recognized a self-representation of Croesus at the most important Greek oracular shrine, Delphi (the statue's fall also paralleled his own, which was predicted by the oracle). Croesus also dedicated a huge gold shield at Delphi and made similar offerings, equal in weight, to Apollo's oracle at Branchidai (Didyma) near Miletos, closer to his home, and smaller gold offerings elsewhere. His predecessor, Gyges, whom the seventh-century BC Greek poet Archilochos called *polychrysos* (rich in gold), is said to have dedicated to Apollo at Delphi six golden mixing bowls together weighing 30 talents as well as other gold and silver items of considerable weight.[15]

Nothing that can be linked with absolute certainty to these rich Lydian dedications has been found at Delphi, although it is possible that some of the precious items excavated in 1939 in a cache buried in antiquity underneath the Sacred Way (plates 10, 60, 151, 152) might come from one of the treasuries mentioned by Herodotos.[16] At the Lydian capital of Sardis, however, copious evidence for ancient gold refining has been recovered from the very period of Croesus's reign (561–547 BC). Although recent research indicates that the placer gold of the Paktolos River was pure, the Lydians also employed the naturally occurring alloy of gold and silver. Pliny called gold with more than 20 percent silver *electrum;* Herodotos called it *leukos* (white) gold.[17] To guarantee the value of coinage, which was invented in Lydia in the first half of the sixth century BC, slightly before the time of Croesus, these two precious metals and the small amounts of copper that were also naturally present needed to be refined. First, these elements were separated by *cupellation*, which consisted of melting the electrum with lead in small hearths and furnaces and then blasting the mixture with high heat (ca. 1,100°C) that oxidized the lead and other base metals, leaving the gold and silver unaffected. The two noble metals were then further divided by a second process called *cementation*: the alloyed metal was hammered into thin sheets and placed into coarse ceramic containers with acidic salts and heated for several hours or even days to a temperature high enough for salt vapors to penetrate the metal and draw the silver out and into the walls of the inert vessel, leaving pure gold. Similar processes were described by Agatharchides as having been used in Ptolemaic Egypt. Additional refinement processes, such as amalgamation using mercury, were developed later. Excavations of a refinery at Sardis have recovered gold globules and scraps of foil, coarse pottery embedded with gold particles, lead, slag, hearths, furnaces, and nozzles from bellows and blowpipes, as well as charcoal and burnt brick. It is estimated that the excavated refinery, probably one of several, was capable of producing several hundred kilograms of pure gold annually.[18]

Ancient authors suggest that the Lydians derived their wealth not only from the gold-bearing waters of the Paktolos but also from mines in the mountains near Sardis. Writing in the first century, Strabo reports that mining operations had taken place at other sites in Asia Minor and Thrace:

> **The wealth of Tantalos and the Pelopidai arose from the mines around Phrygia and Sipylos; that of Kadmos from those round Thrace and Mt. Pangaion; that of Priam [king of Troy] from the gold mines at Astyra near Abydos, of which there are still small remains—here the amount of earth thrown out is considerable, and the excavations are signs of mining in olden times; and that of Midas from those round Mount Bermios; and that of Gyges and Alyattes and Croesus from those in Lydia and from the region between Atarneos and Pergamon, were there is still a small deserted town, whose lands have been exhausted of ore.**[19]

In Greece itself, Herodotos saw gold mines on the north Aegean island of Thasos. The mines lay on the southeast coast of the island, facing Samothrace. Herodotos and other authors report that richer mines existed on the mainland, eight kilometers to the north, at Skapte Hyle (the place name means diggable matter). In the fifth century BC these mines alone yielded the islanders 80 talents of gold annually. Half a millennium later Pliny reported that Thasos also produced amethyst and opal.[20]

The Cycladic island of Siphnos, too, was renowned for its mines, both gold and silver. Silver mines have been recorded at Agios Sostis on the island's northeast coast, where labyrinthine chambers are cut into the rock, and an abundance of slag is present nearby, both on land and underwater. Gold deposits have also been traced at Agios Ioannis, Apokofto, and Aspros Pyrgos in the southeast. These were first exploited in the early Bronze Age, but it was in the late sixth century BC that the inhabitants of the island set aside a tithe of the wealth derived from their mines to erect the most lavish of the treasury buildings at Apollo's sanctuary at Delphi. Today the surviving architectural blocks and fine marble friezes of the Siphnian Treasury (see fig. 29) are prime attractions of the museum there. Less well preserved is the temple the Siphnians dedicated to the same god at home. Herodotos reports that the Siphnians' prosperity declined after they were attacked by pirates from Samos. Pausanias, however, records a tradition that Apollo punished the islanders, who, having sent him tribute annually, became greedy and reneged on their vow, so the god flooded their mines. Most of the mines that have been explored by modern archaeologists are inland and well above sea level, but what appear to be gold deposits have also been sighted underwater around old workings on the seabed near Agrimbela on the east coast of the island.[21]

Gold was not the basis of currency or the principal medium of monetary exchange in ancient Greece.[22] It was, however, more conspicuous and thus fitting for occasions where displays of opulence were appropriate—or necessary. Mythical examples include gold crowns, belts, and sandals, swords, spears, bows and arrows, helmets, shields, and breastplates, flutes, lyres, thrones, couches, tables, horse-trappings, and chariots of gods and heroes—and a golden apple was the prize in the Judgment of Paris.[23] At religious festivals the horns of sacrificial animals were gilded, and victorious athletes, soldiers, and other dignitaries were awarded golden crowns, which, more often than not, they were expected to dedicate in turn to the gods. Indeed, numerous ancient images in marble and bronze of victors "crowning themselves" more likely depict them removing the crowns, prior to offering them in thanks. Ancient inventories recording the treasures stored in temples on the Athenian Acropolis, at Delos, and elsewhere list not only numerous gold crowns, offering bowls, and other vessels but also gold necklaces, bracelets, belts, finger rings, pins, stalks of wheat, and such stray objects as nails and other architectural and decorative components, as well as unwrought gold, not to mention numerous items of gilt silver. These were dedicated by a wide range of individuals, either in fulfillment of a vow or in hope of some future benefice.[24] Inscriptions from the Acropolis at Athens record gold vessels dedicated by Rhoxane, the wife of Alexander the Great, and others from the sanctuary of Apollo at Didyma indicate that among gold crowns, jewelry, and vessels dedicated to the god and his twin sister, Artemis, were offerings made by King Seleukos I of Syria and his son Antiochos.[25] The so-called Lindian Chronicle, an inscription from the sanctuary of Athena Lindia at Rhodes, dating to 99 BC, records, in chronological order, gifts offered to the sanctuary. It begins with dedications of legendary figures—the Telchines, early metalworkers; Kadmos; Minos; Herakles; heroes of the Trojan War, including Helen, who dedicated her gold bracelets—and includes such historical figures as the pharaoh Amasis (570–526 BC), who reputedly offered two gold statues and ten offering bowls.[26] None of these objects survives, and we have only very few items of plate from the Archaic period, when gold vessels seem to have been used more for religious and state offerings than for personal use, although Pindar describes a solid gold bowl as "the peak of possessions."[27] A magnificent inscribed gold bowl said to be from Olympia is a notable survival (plate 9).

Although frequently offered to the gods, gold was by no means removed from economic considerations. The narrator of the *Iliad* opines that the Lykian warrior Glaukos had his wits taken away by Zeus when he traded a golden panoply worth one hundred oxen for bronze armor worth only nine. Other Homeric heroes present gold and other precious materials as gifts to friends or ransom to enemies with an eye toward their economic as well as symbolic value.[28] Precise rates of exchange, of course, fluctuated over time. In the late fifth century BC, gold was worth eleven to sixteen times more than silver.[29] Economic value and aesthetics were, in any case, not mutually exclusive; rather, they reinforced one another. From large vessels to small earrings, gold items were fashioned with great skill—and their weights frequently coincide with standard monetary measurements; indeed, sometimes their weight is inscribed upon them (see plates 23, 24, 48, 49).[30] Pliny remarked that skilled craftsmanship made worked gold (and silver) more valuable, and a late fifth-century BC inscription records that a Carian slave who was a goldsmith sold for twice the normal price.[31] Historical associations might also, on occasion, have increased the esteem in which objects were held. Ultimately, however, weight and purity, rather than fine workmanship, determined the value of most objects and led, over time, to the vast majority of ancient gold and silver being melted down. Xenophon, for example, reports that the Persian king Cyrus the Younger was willing to dismantle his gold and silver throne in order to pay the Spartan general Lysander, and there are many other recorded instances of conversion of private, civic, and religious plate in order to overcome financial difficulties.[32]

While few large-scale gold objects survive from antiquity, there is copious evidence for gold (as well as gilt) statues erected by both the Greeks and the Romans.[33] Kypselos, who ruled Corinth in the seventh century BC, is said to have dedicated a gold statue to Zeus at Olympia, although some authors attribute it to his son, Periander.[34] In the Temple of Apollo at Delphi, besides Croesus's "baker," there was a gold statue of Apollo, which was seen by Pausanias in the second century.[35] And when the Spartans likewise sought to offer a gold statue to Apollo, they sent messengers to Sardis to buy the material from Croesus, who, ever generous, gave it to them as a gift.[36] The source of the metal fashioned into the statue of solid gold (at least according to Pliny) that the late fifth-century BC Sicilian Sophist Gorgias of Leontini later dedicated at Delphi remains unknown. Its subject, however, is recorded: Gorgias offered the god a portrait of himself! Earlier, the Macedonian king Alexander I (r. 494–452 BC) had erected gilded portraits of himself at both Delphi and Olympia. In the fourth century, another golden statue was erected at Delphi: a portrait of the courtesan Phryne by Praxiteles. Athenaios, citing the second book of Alketas's treatise *On the Offerings at Delphi*, reports that the image, offered by the citizens of Thespiae, was of solid gold and stood prominently on a marble pillar between portraits of the Spartan king Archidamos and Philip II of Macedon. It was inscribed "Phryne of Thespiae, the daughter of Epikles." Whether or not the statue was really *solid* gold, it outraged the Cynic philosopher Krates, who declared it "a votive offering of the profligacy of Greece."[37]

The statues of Alexander, Gorgias, and Phryne were made after the Persian Wars, when wealth poured into Greece. Herodotos reports that among the Persian troops that set out for Greece from Sardis in 480 BC were two thousand soldiers with golden pomegranates on the butt-ends of their spears, one thousand with golden apples, and nine thousand with silver pomegranates. The ten thousand elite Persian troops called "Immortals" were also adorned with vast quantities of gold,[38] and the precious metals worn by the Persian general Mardonios, along with the furniture and plate captured in the Persian camp immediately after the battle of Plataia, amazed the Spartan king Pausanias, who found therein

> **many tents richly adorned with furniture of gold and silver, many couches covered with plates of the same, and many golden bowls, goblets, and other drinking-vessels. On the carriages were bags containing silver and golden kettles; and the bodies of the slain furnished bracelets and chains, and scimitars with golden ornaments—not to mention embroidered apparel, of which no one made any account.... When all the booty had been brought together, a tenth of the whole was set apart for the Delphian god; and hence was made the golden tripod which stands on the bronze serpent with the three heads, quite close to the altar. Portions were also set apart for the gods of Olympia, and of the Isthmus.... It is said that the following circumstance happened likewise at this time. Xerxes, when he fled away out of Greece, left his war-tent with Mardonios: when Pausanias, therefore, saw the tent with its adornments of gold and silver, and its hangings of divers colors, he gave commandment to the bakers and the cooks to make him ready a banquet in such fashion as was their wont for Mardonios. Then they made ready as they were bidden; and Pausanias, beholding the couches of gold and silver daintily decked out with their rich covertures, and the tables of gold and silver laid, and the feast itself prepared with all magnificence, was astonished at the good things which were set before him.... During many years afterwards, the Plataians used often to find upon the field of battle concealed treasures of gold, and silver, and other valuables.**[39]

The wealth of the Persians was legendary, and their display of riches later served as both a positive and a negative example. As Athens' power increased in the course of the fifth century BC, most of the tribute paid by her subject allies was silver, but some took the form of gold coin or bullion.[40] In the 460s BC, the Athenians struggled to gain control of the gold mines on Thasos and the mainland opposite, eventually founding a colony at Amphipolis. Gold from Skapte Hyle is mentioned in fragmentary late fifth-century inscriptions listing the treasure stored on the Athenian Acropolis, and it seems that some of the nearby mines eventually came into the possession of the Athenian general and historian Thucydides, perhaps through the dowry of his wife. His family, like hers, apparently had connections in the area, and he spent his exile there, just as the Athenian tyrant Peisistratos had a century earlier.[41]

According to inventory lists inscribed on marble slabs in the late fifth and early fourth centuries BC, the temples on the Athenian Acropolis, like others elsewhere, served as repositories for numerous golden vessels: *kraters*, *kylikes*, and especially *phialai* (ritual offering bowls). Gold jewelry, too, was dedicated to the gods, as was weaponry (including the gold sword of Mardonios, which is said to have weighed 300 darics—about five-and-a-half pounds).[42] Gilt furniture, musical instruments, and baskets are also listed in the inscriptions.[43]

In the aftermath of the Persian Wars, gold and silver plate appears to have been more frequently possessed, displayed, and utilized by wealthy individuals. Plutarch writes of the Athenian Anytos, the son of Anthemion, who was particularly fond of the profligate Alkibiades, and invited him to a dinner party. Alkibiades initially refused the invitation, but, having drunk to excess at his own house, he went, and seeing the tables covered with gold and silver cups, he ordered his servants to take away half of them. Anytos's other guests were indignant at this rude and insulting conduct, but Anytos said that, on the contrary, Alkibiades had shown great consideration and tenderness in taking only a part when he might have taken all.[44] We don't know how Anytos's plate was displayed, but silver and gold (or less likely bronze) vessels and platters are arrayed on, above, and below a stepped *kylikeion* (sideboard) in a frieze depicting a nocturnal banquet painted on the facade of a richly decorated Macedonian tomb of the late fourth century BC (fig. 12).[45] Plutarch reports elsewhere that Alkibiades was said to have "made daily use at his table of many gold and silver vessels, which belonged to the commonwealth, as if they had been his own."[46] This seems to be a reference to the story, told most fully by the orator Andokides, that following his victory in the chariot race at Olympia in 416 BC Alkibiades "asked the leaders of the Athenian deputation to lend him the processional vessels, alleging that he intended to use them for a celebration of his victory on the day before the sacrifice; he then abused the trust placed in him and refused to return them, as he wanted to use the golden basins and censers before Athens did so. Naturally, when those strangers who did not know that they belonged to us saw the state-procession taking place after that of Alcibiades, they imagined that we were using his vessels."[47]

In addition to the reserves of the state, which might be melted down at any time as needed, there was enough gold and silver plate in private hands in Athens that the year after Alkibiades's victory at Olympia, when the Athenians set out on the expedition to conquer Sicily, officers and soldiers on the deck of every ship "poured libations from vessels of gold and silver," according to Thucydides.[48] Such wealth, however, was far from mere show. Thucydides reports that desire for the precious metal was a crucial factor in the Athenian decision to invade the island.

Athens' fortunes plummeted in the fourth century BC after the loss of its maritime empire, but gold plate was still being recorded in the inventories of the Acropolis temples and was often mentioned in the speeches of orators. Demosthenes speaks of "gold vessels, weighing a mina [100 drachmai, or 431 grams] each," and it was the norm for plate to be made up in round figures corresponding to the weight of coinage.[49]

The circulation of precious metals in the Greek world seems to have increased dramatically as a result of the plundering of Apollo's sanctuary at Delphi in the 350s BC. It has been estimated that 4,000 talents of gold (103,440 kilograms) and 10,000 of silver were taken by the Phokaians and paid out to mercenaries. Dedications were melted down, minted into coin, and distributed widely. Subsequently, the coins could be refashioned into new precious objects.[50] Further north, Philip II of Macedon (r. 382–336) gained control of the rich mines around Mount Pangaion in Thrace in 358 BC and exploited them fully. He reportedly extracted 1,000 talents (25,860 kilograms) of metal annually; Pliny preserves a tradition that the king slept with a golden goblet under his pillow.[51] Philip's son, Alexander the Great, established his principal mint at nearby Amphipolis. Alexander's conquest of the Persian Empire, including Egypt, which had been ruled by the Persians since 525 BC, brought a flood of gold to the Mediterranean. At

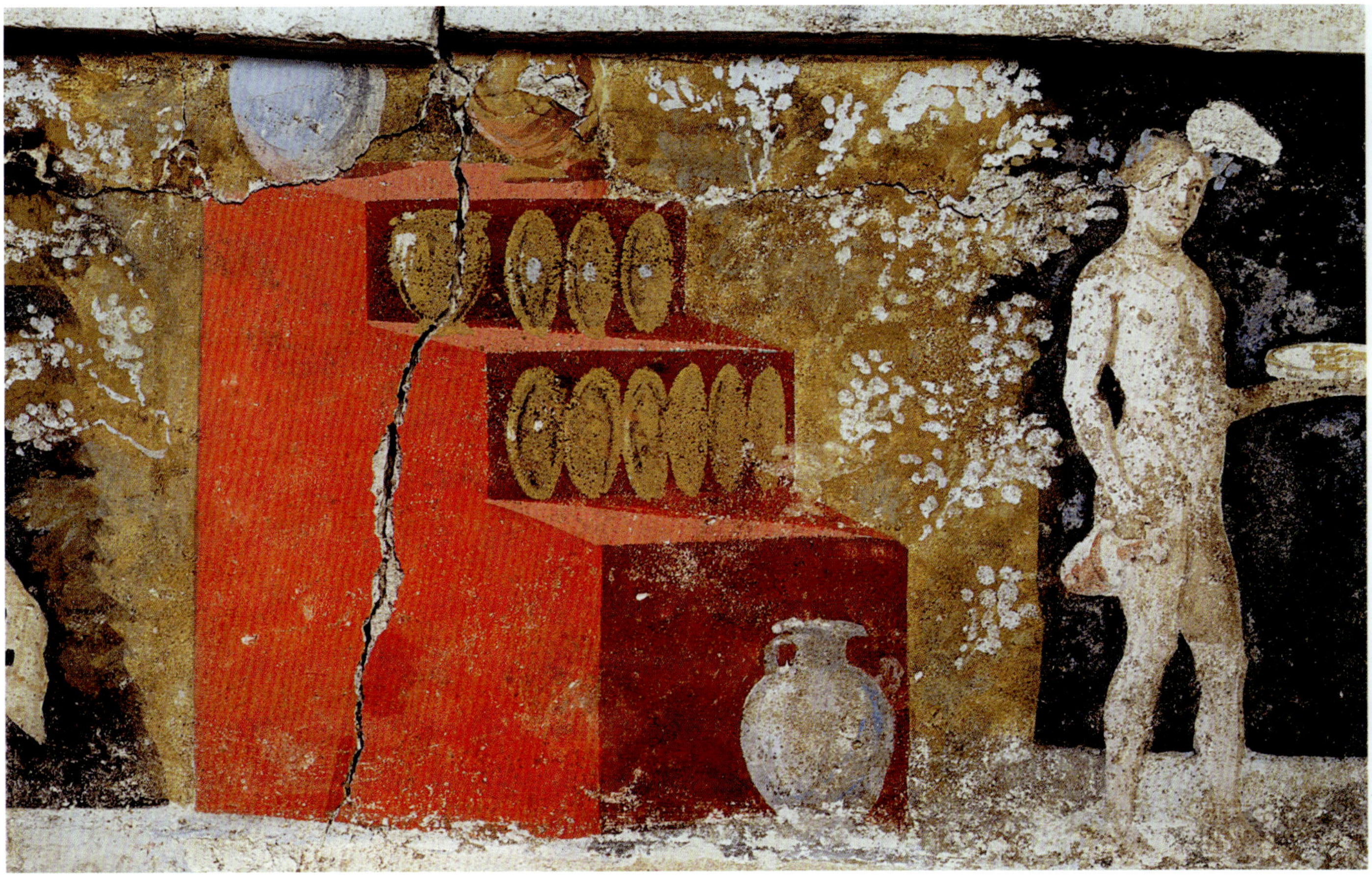

Figure 12
Painted facade (detail) of a Macedonian tomb at Ayios Athanasios, near Thessalonike, late fourth century BC. H (of frieze): 35 cm. A large red *kylikeion* (sideboard) laden with gold and silver vessels demonstrates how ancient plate might have been displayed at a *symposion*. A young male servant carries a pitcher and bowl toward banqueters reclining on couches and entertained by a flute girl.

Susa he captured some 40,000 talents of gold and silver and another 9,000 of minted gold coins; from Persepolis he is said to have obtained a treasure of 120,000 talents of gold and silver (more than 3,000,000 kg). He and his successors issued far more gold coinage than Greece had ever seen, and gold jewelry became more common—and more elaborate (plates 35–41).[52] One of his generals, Hagnon of Teos, is said to have had the soles of his sandals attached with golden nails.[53] Gold was also fashioned into thin threads and woven into textiles. Although said to have been invented by King Attalos of Pergamon, and thus called "Attalid cloth," such items are mentioned in the Homeric poems, Greek temple inventories, and have been recovered archaeologically from fifth- and fourth-century BC contexts in Attica and Macedonia (plates 174, 176), as well as in southern Italy and the Roman cities on the Bay of Naples buried by the eruption of Mount Vesuvius in AD 79.[54]

Greeks of the Classical period seem to have been reluctant to deposit gold vessels and jewelry in tombs. Most such objects that have survived to this day have been recovered from rich burials in southern Italy and on the shores of the Black Sea. In those areas the taste for gold, rendered beautiful by immigrant Greeks and local goldsmiths, was indulged in by both chieftains grown rich from trading grain, timber, and other natural resources and Greek merchants and settlers, who may have adopted local customs. While some of their treasures are clearly the work of local craftsman, others are highly refined works in unadulterated Greek style, suggesting that they were either imports or the products of Greek craftsmen who settled abroad in order to profit from serving wealthy foreign clients (plates 18–23, 25–28).[55]

In Hellenistic Egypt, the Ptolemies, ruling in the wake of Alexander's conquests, prospected extensively for gold and other precious materials in Upper Egypt and Nubia (present-day Sudan), sources previously exploited by the pharaohs, and perhaps in Arabia as well. The eastern desert, between the Nile and the Red Sea, was the main gold-producing area. It also yielded gems and semiprecious stones, such as agate, amethyst, emerald, chalcedony, cornelian, and turquoise. The Ptolemies organized expeditions and founded cities to reap the benefits of their explorations, which included herds of elephants that could be utilized for war as well as for ivory.[56] The great wealth that flowed into the Ptolemaic capital of Alexandria is best illustrated by the lengthy description of the Grand Procession of Ptolemy II that opened the Ptolemaia festival of circa 275 BC written by Kallixeinos of Rhodes and preserved in Athenaios's compilation *Deipnosophistai* (*The Learned Banqueters*). For page after page Kallixeinos describes thousands of people—men, women, and children—almost all wearing sumptuous garments and gold crowns, carrying gold vessels, torches, and other implements, some dressed as satyrs, Silenoi, and Nikai, others as personifications of Greek cities and distant lands. Accompanying them were musicians with golden instruments and carts bearing golden statues of gods and personifications, vast amounts of gold and silver plate and luxury furniture, jewelry, golden weapons, gilt palm trees, enormous gem-encrusted wreaths, a golden cornucopia 45 feet long, and an enormous golden phallus, 180 feet long, sacred to Dionysos.[57]

This vast assemblage of wealth is lost, and so are other impressive works noted by ancient literary sources and inscriptions carved in stone, such as the golden statue, adorned with diamonds, of the deceased and deified princess Berenike mentioned in the Canopic decree of 238 BC. The Seleucid king Antiochos I Soter was honored by the inhabitants of Ilion with a gold equestrian statue erected inside the Temple of Athena there, and the Pergamene king Attalos I received a golden statue inside the Temple of Apollo. The Ionians voted his successor, Eumenes II, a golden crown and a statue to be set up wherever he desired, and in 183/182 BC, Eumenes and his brothers were honored by the Aitolians with golden statues in the sanctuary at Thermos "because of their virtue and their goodwill towards the gods." At Pergamon itself a less exalted personality, Diodoros, a wealthy *gymnasiarch*, was celebrated: he was voted a shrine and various statues, including two of gold. Meanwhile, back in Alexandria, Ptolemy VIII and his wife erected a gold statue in honor of Hieron, their children's tutor, on account of his virtue and goodwill.[58]

Just how many other such commissions were made, or how involved individual rulers were in them, we do not know. The Macedonian king of Syria Antiochos IV Epiphanes (215–164 BC) seems to have been exceptional in his particular interest in precious metalworking; he is said to have regularly visited the shops of gold- and silversmiths to "discuss the latest fashions and taste."[59] Such wealth was not available to all, of course, but it modeled behavior. The lovesick reaper Bukaios in Theokritos's tenth *Idyll* says that he would erect golden statues of himself and his beloved as votives to Aphrodite, if only he were as rich as Croesus.[60]

It was this Hellenistic world of Alexander the Great's successors, rather than the idealized "Golden Age" of the fifth century BC, that the Romans encountered when they conquered the rich Greek cities of southern Italy and Sicily in the late third century BC, then Greece itself in the second century, and Ptolemaic Egypt in the first.[61] Prior to the resulting flood into

Rome of gold and other riches, the Romans exhibited no great appetite for the metal, or so they liked to think. Roman ideology held that strong native peasant values were corrupted by foreign luxury. Pliny takes great pains to argue that gold rings were not worn in early Rome and that it was the Etruscan king Tarquinius Priscus (r. 616–579 BC) who first presented a gold *bulla* to his son, for having killed an enemy in battle. Pliny also reports that when Rome was sacked by the Gauls in 390 BC, no more than 1,000 pounds of gold could be found for ransom, but by 156 BC the treasury held some 17,410 pounds. By 49 BC Julius Caesar could withdraw 15,000 gold ingots (plus considerably more in silver and in coin) to cover his expenses.[62]

The Etruscans, Rome's neighbors, sometime rulers, and eventual subjects, were rich in metals. They obtained gold from sources in the Pennine Alps, along the Po River (in the region the Romans later called Cisalpine Gaul) as well as from abroad.[63] Early Romans, however, seem to have been ambivalent about the metal. In order to curb ostentation the so-called Twelve Tables, a law code dating to the fifth century BC, limited the amount of gold that could be buried with the deceased: jewelry was banned, but dental prostheses were allowed. This attempt to limit luxury parallels those of early Greek lawgivers, such as Solon at Athens, Zaleukos at Lokri, and Charondas at Catania, who in the seventh century BC promulgated laws prohibiting private displays in personal adornment as well as ceremonies.[64] In 396 BC, when the Roman general Marcus Furius Camillus refused to fulfill his vow and send a tithe of the booty from the long and difficult conquest of the Etruscan city of Veii to Apollo at Delphi, the women of Rome collected their jewelry to melt down in order to fashion a gift for the god, gathering enough for only a single gold *krater*.[65]

In the early years of the Roman Republic, gold seems to have been destined for temples and the public treasury and for modest personal adornment, but Roman conquests abroad eventually brought much booty. According to Florus's second-century *Epitome* of Roman history, "richly adorned statues of gold" were paraded in the triumphal procession following the victory of Pyrrhus in 275 BC,[66] and Livy reports that in 216 BC the Syracusans presented to the Roman senate a golden statue of Victory weighing 220 pounds.[67] After the disastrous defeat of the Roman army by Hannibal at Cannae that same year, the Oppian Law limited possession of gold to a half ounce per person, and in 210 BC the consul Levinus urged members of the senate to donate to the state treasury all gold, silver, and bronze except that to be used for personal rings, a *bulla* for the eldest child, and an ounce of gold for the adornment of women. By 209 BC, the year Rome conquered Tarentum, the gold reserves of the treasury amounted to 4,000 pounds, but far more wealth flowed into the city, for Livy reports that 30,000 slaves were taken, as well as a huge amount of silver, both wrought and coined, and 83,000 pounds of gold.[68]

After the defeat of Hannibal by Scipio Africanus at Zama in 202 BC, the Oppian Law was eventually repealed, though only after a long and spirited debate as to whether women's desire to adorn themselves in gold would lead to ever more corrupting extravagance and dissipation.[69] Following the conquest of Macedon in 168 BC, Lucius Aemilius Paullus displayed, in a triumphal procession famous for its opulence, the gold and silver plate that had belonged to the Macedonian king Perseus, including a sacred bowl set with jewels weighing ten talents.[70]

Pliny claimed that "it was conquered Asia that first sent luxury to Italy, since Lucius Scipio brought over 1,400 pounds of engraved silverware and gold vases weighing 1,500 pounds for his triumphal procession" in 189 BC. But it was Attalos III's bequest of the kingdom of Pergamon to Rome in 133 BC that brought with it the riches of Asia Minor. Hence, according to Pliny, Rome "learnt not merely to admire but also to covet foreign opulence."[71]

Roman rapacity soon alienated the subject populations of Asia Minor, and various ancient sources report the brutal death, half a century later, of the Roman ambassador Manius Aquilius, son of a notoriously corrupt governor. To rebuke the Romans for their thirst for gold, the Pontic king Mithradates VI Eupator ordered the unfortunate Roman to be brought into the theater at Pergamon, where molten gold was poured down his throat. A generation after Aquilius's death, the general Marcus Licinius Crassus, the richest man in Rome, who profited greatly from his eastern campaigns and was credited with introducing luxury to Rome, is said to have perished by being similarly forced to "drink" molten gold by the Parthians at the end of his ill-fated expedition against them.[72]

Despite such setbacks, the Romans conquered the shores of the Mediterranean and beyond, and mineral wealth from the provinces flowed into the capital. Baetica (southwestern Spain and southeastern Portugal) came into their possession in 197 BC and other Spanish provinces soon thereafter. The Tagus River became a byword for wealth in Latin literature: its gold-bearing sands are mentioned by Catullus, Ovid, Juvenal, and Martial, among others.[73] Pliny wrote that no gold was more perfect than that obtained from the Tagus in Spain, the Po in Italy, the Maritza in Thrace, the Sarabat in Asia Minor, and the Ganges in India.[74] The same author describes in detail large-scale hydraulic mining operations that took place at Las Médulas in northwestern Spain, where rivers were diverted and extensive aqueduct systems were constructed to provide water to wash the earth and separate the metal. This process undermined the hills and ravaged the landscape, creating the "ruins of mountains" (*ruina montium*) visible to this day. He further states that Galicia and Lusitania yielded 20,000 pounds of the metal annually.[75]

In the first century BC Roman power spread to Gaul, where, according to Diodoros, "there is gold in great quantities.... It is not mined so there is no hardship.... Gold is collected from the surface by men who grind or crush lumps after washing out the earthy material with water. A large amount was amassed chiefly for the ornaments worn by men and women in the form of bracelets and heavy necklaces of solid gold. Much gold was placed in temples as a dedication to the gods."[76] Julius Caesar invaded Britain in 55 BC, and by the first century AD the Romans were exploiting gold mines at Dolaucothi in Wales, employing open pits, underground tunnels, and extensive waterworks to extract the metal, as they had in Spain.[77] Gold was also mined in Dalmatia and Illyria, on the Adriatic coast, and at Pannonia farther east.[78] In the early second century, Trajan's advance into Dacia (modern Romania) brought further rich sources of gold into Roman hands.[79]

Little Roman gold survives, apart from coinage and jewelry, but inscribed ingots of the purified metal (fig. 13) indicate something of the highly controlled nature of its production, at least by the late third century. Ancient literary sources mention many golden images and much plate being displayed in triumphal processions. While no large-scale gold statues survive, some idea of the appearance of these images might be gained from hollow gold busts that probably served as military standards (plates 51, 52).

Few gold vessels are preserved from Roman antiquity (plates 48, 49), but Pliny reports that natural electrum was sometimes favored for goblets as it was thought to change appearance in the presence of poison.[80] Other sources suggest that despite increasing wealth and the wide use of silver by the wealthy throughout the empire, the use of gold vessels was restricted to the imperial household between the reigns of Tiberius and Aurelian.[81] Earlier, however, the lack of any such restrictions led to reports, by the orator Messala according to Pliny, "that the triumvir Antony used vessels of gold in satisfying all the indecent necessities, an enormity that even Cleopatra would have been ashamed of.... Antony alone cheapened gold by this contumely of nature. How he deserved to be proscribed—but proscribed by Spartacus," who forbade anyone in his camp from possessing gold or silver.[82]

Techniques

Whether carefully refined from ore or gathered from streambeds in flakes and nuggets, gold can be worked with tools as simple as a hammer and punch. Separately fashioned pieces of gold can be joined by percussion, and the metal can easily be hammered to various thicknesses, from sheet, to foil, to leaf.[83] Pliny famously remarked that a single ounce of gold can yield 450 sheets of leaf, four inches square, and modern stamping

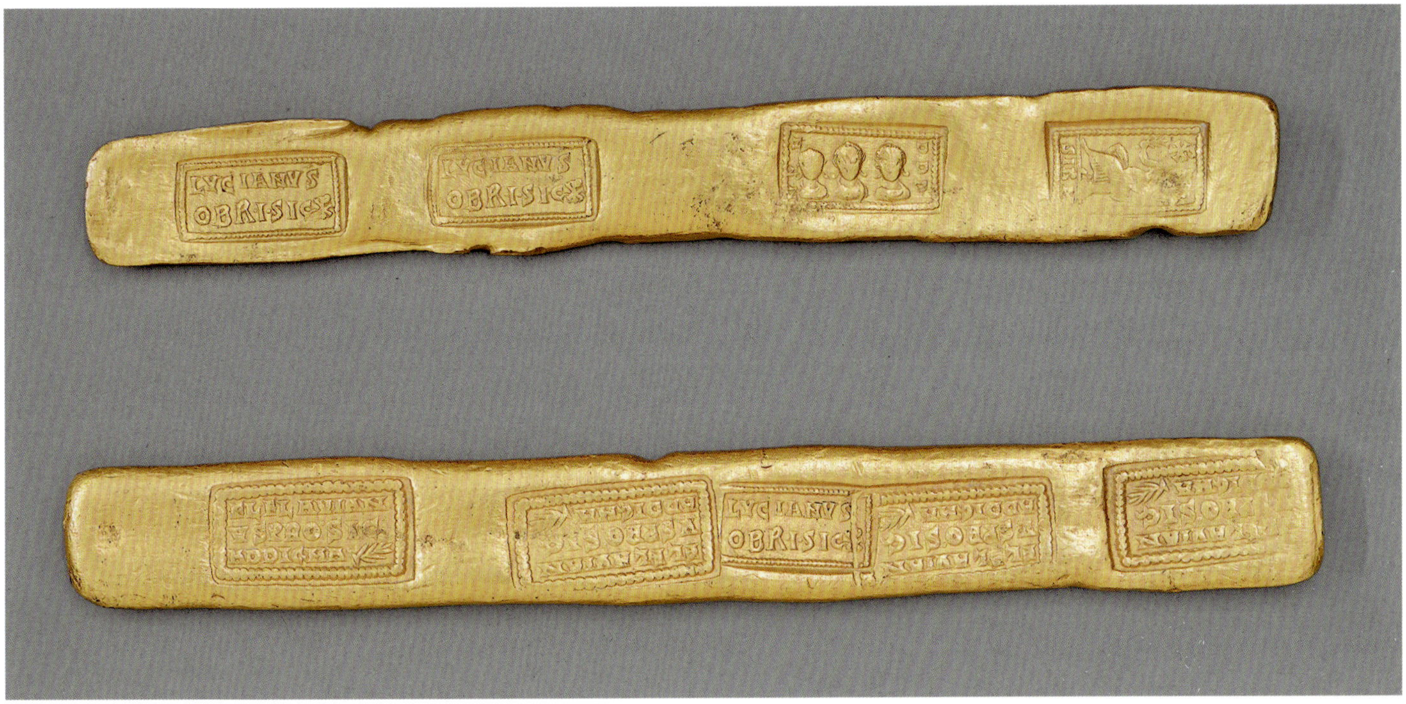

Figure 13
Inscribed ingots from Krazna, Translyvania, ca. AD 367–80. Gold, L: 17 and 19.3 cm; Wt: 372 and 472 grams. Paris, Bibliothèque nationale de France, Cabinet des médialles 56.342-43. Cast gold ingots were stamped by Roman imperial officials to guarantee their purity. In the third and fourth centuries, if not before, gold coins were melted into ingots, which were tested before being reminted into coin or employed for some other purpose. These ingots have been stamped by officials from mints at Sirmium (in Romania): LVCIANVS OBR I SIG (Lucianus stamped this *obryzium* [pure gold] of the first quality) and FL FLAVIANVS PRO SIG AD DIGMA (Flavius Flavianus, assayer, stamped this according to the sample).

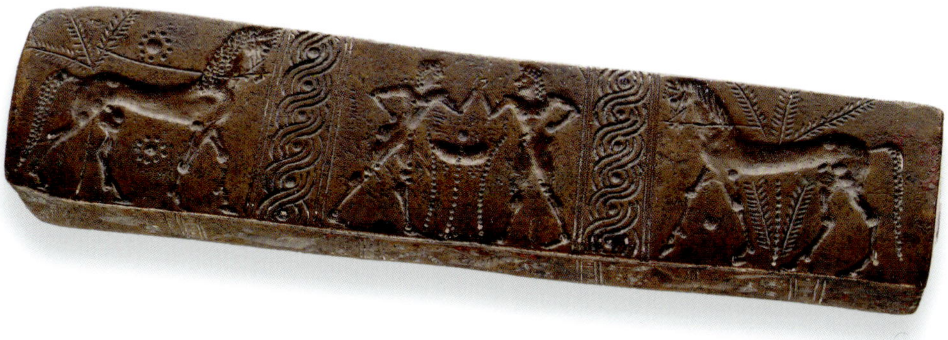

Figure 14
Four-sided matrix, from Corfu, ca. 700–650 BC. Bronze, L: 12.5 cm; H: 2.5–2.9 cm; Thickness: 0.95–1.1 cm. Oxford, Ashmolean Museum, G. 437. This matrix, intended for use in hammering gold or silver sheet, depicts on its wider side two men competing over a tripod cauldron flanked by guilloches and horses, and on the thinner side, upside down, the suicide of Ajax, a triton, dolphin, and an owl. The other wide side, not seen here, has a bull, lion, two swans, boar, griffin, stag, and a cock and hen; and the other thin side a dog chasing four hares through the brush.

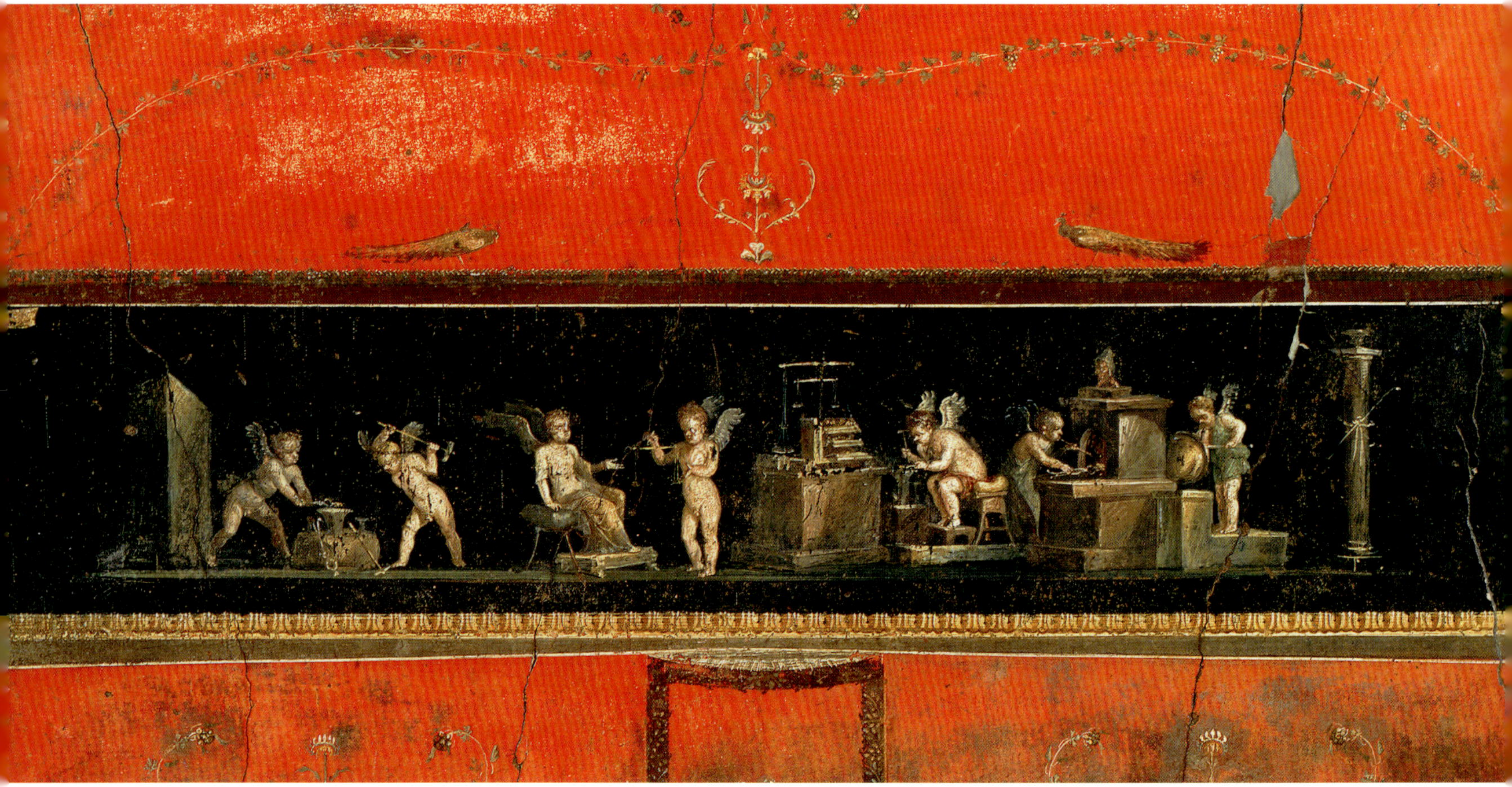

Figure 15
Fresco of cupids and psychai playing at goldsmithing, from the east wall of a dining room in the House of the Vettii (VI.15.1) at Pompeii, ca. AD 62–79. Fresco. At left two cupids work gold on an anvil: one holds the material with tongs; the other raises a large hammer for a heavy strike, perhaps preparing gold sheets. In the center, a customer sits comfortably before a cupid who is weighing merchandise in a pair of scales. Behind him are other scales of various sizes and a display cabinet with three open drawers. Next a cupid crouches over an anvil, working with a small hammer and tongs. Behind him a psyche heats a flaming furnace with a blowpipe while moving tongs into it. On the other side of the furnace, perhaps taking advantage of its radiant heat, another psyche shapes a large gold vessel with a hammer.

machines can produce even more.[84] Such thin leaf is suitable for gilding, and gold was regularly applied to silver, bronze, wood, marble, pottery, glass, and other materials. Burnishing, hammering, or the use of binders such as egg, honey, resin, animal or vegetal glue, or bole (sticky clay) would guarantee adherence. Thicker foil could also be applied to underlying materials, and sheets, thicker still, could be fashioned into objects—hollow or solid—entirely of gold. The only tools necessary were a hammer and anvil, though punches, stamps, matrices (fig. 14), and gravers of different kinds were regularly used to render decorative motifs. These were generally hammered from behind with the gold placed over a soft material (leather, pitch, or lead); or the gold might be pressed into a mold or matrix (of wood, stone, or metal) to take a predetermined form. Likewise a more or less elaborate stamp might be used to fashion a repeated pattern. When the metal is moved, but not removed, the technique is called *embossing*; when this is done from the front it is *chasing*, from behind *repoussé* (fig. 16). Usually these techniques are used in combination, with preliminary work done from behind, to raise the relief, and fine work chased afterward. Different tools, of course, would render different effects: thin and thick lines, curved or V-shaped in section (the profile of the cut), circles, triangles, or squares. Occasionally, engraving was employed. This entailed removal of the metal by cutting sharp lines with a chisel or graver, which was the usual technique for cutting gold seal rings.

Embossing, through both repoussé and chasing, appears in Geometric Greek gold work on gold diadems interred with the deceased (plates 3, 4). These bear the same motifs seen in Geometric pottery: complex meanders, stars, and human figures whose bodies are composed of lozenges, triangles, and circles. Some molds, with similar motifs, also survive.

Gold was also cast, which was a useful technique for making multiple identical elements for a larger ensemble. Goldsmiths employed the lost-wax process, making a model of the desired object in wax, investing it in a clay mold, firing the mold and melting out the wax; then pouring molten gold into the resulting cavity to create a gold version of the original lost-wax object. However, because casting requires a relatively large amount of gold, not to mention costly fuel (gold melts at 1,064°C = 1,948°F) and other infrastructure, it was not often used for small-scale production. Cast gold, moreover, often suffers from imperfect surface effects, such as porosity, roughness, or cracking, and objects frequently require extensive cold working after casting.

Granulation • Granulation is the method of affixing small gold spheres (which can be just a fraction of a millimeter in diameter) to a gold sheet (e.g., plates 1, 2, 5–8). While pure gold melts at 1,064°C, gold alloyed with silver melts at slightly lower temperatures, so such alloys could be used as a solder

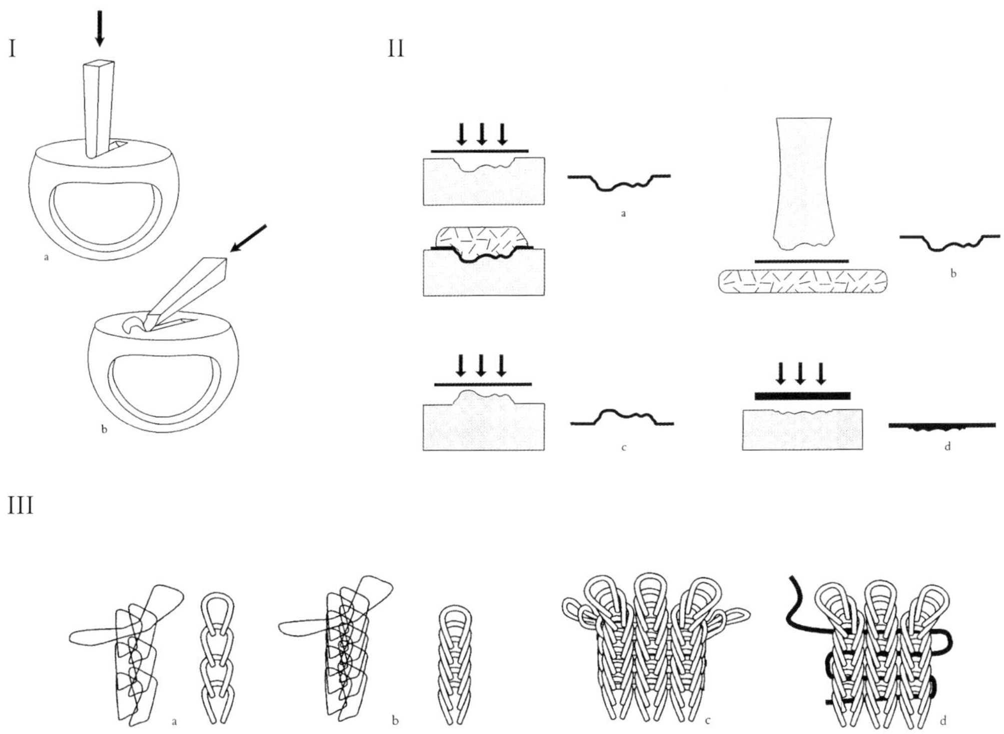

Figure 16
Gold-working techniques: embossing (Ia) consists of pushing the soft metal to create a new shape; engraving (Ib) is cutting and removing the metal, leaving a sharper edge. Sheet metal can be driven into a preformed die or matrix using a hard, but flexible material like pitch (IIa), stamped with a punch (IIb), pressed over a form in relief (IIc), or an inset matrix (IId). Complex, flexible chains of gold wire can be created by a combination of simple loop-in-loop strands either woven or sewn together (III). After Williams and Ogden 1994, figs. 10, 12, 24.

for pure gold, although their paler color contrasts with pure yellow gold. Copper lowers the melting point of gold further still and lacks the disadvantage of lightening the color. The Leyden Papyrus of circa AD 325 recommends that goldsmiths melt down Ptolemaic gold coins for certain uses, "for they contain copper."[85] Another recipe recommends a 2:1 gold to copper ratio for such solders.

Granulation was first practiced in ancient Mesopotamia, spreading west from there to Egypt, Phoenicia, Greece, and Etruria. Small spheres of gold could be formed by heating gold clippings on a block of charcoal and allowing surface tension to create spheres as the clippings melted. Another method was to drip molten gold into water. Once cooled, the spheres could be soldered with a gold/silver alloy or be coated with a mixture of a copper salt and animal glue (to hold them temporarily in place), and then heated, melting the copper but not the pure gold elements. This process is called colloidal hard soldering or diffusion bonding.[86]

Filigree • Filigree is similar to granulation, only strips of wire rather than spheres of gold are attached to a backing. Wires can be straight or curved, plain, beaded, or twisted. Since the Middle Ages, goldsmiths have fashioned wire by pulling it through successively smaller holes in a draw plate, leaving microscopic traces of long parallel lines. Ancient goldsmiths, however, fashioned wire by cutting long, flat strips from gold sheet and first twisting, then rolling them. As the sheets are rolled, the seams close, but often a spiral gap remains visible, especially under magnification (see plate 1). Once formed, wire can be beaded, woven, or shaped into still more complex forms. It can then be attached to a larger ensemble, as filigree, woven into chain, or used to connect other elements. Wire can also be utilized to form the borders of *cloisons*, into which colored stones or enamel (a glass paste fused to the underlying metal surface by firing) might be placed.

Gold Glass • Thin gold sheets, hammered with figural images by means of the repoussé technique, were, from at least the fourth century BC, placed behind rock crystal and glass and inset into jewelry and plaques destined for luxury furniture. Pliny mentions stones from Epirus and Egypt that were backed with gold foil (*quae brattea aurea sublinuntur*), and fourth-century BC Athenian temple inventories record the existence of crystal or glass seals set in gold. Two unidentified objects, of crystal or glass interworked with gold (*hyalina diachrusa*), are mentioned among the sumptuous objects carried in the Grand Procession of Ptolemy II Philadelphos at Alexandria in the early third century BC. There is good reason to believe that a similar technique was used to enliven the drapery worn by Pheidias's monumental statue of Zeus at Olympia, or at least that of the Nike held in his hand.[87] In the Hellenistic period thinner gold foils, cut with decorative vegetal and figural patterns, were sandwiched between nesting glass bowls, creating splendid visual effects (plate 55). Later, artists developed sophisticated techniques of pricking or stippling the glass with the point of a needle, as well as adding pigment, to render striking coloristic and chiaroscuro effects (plates 56–59).

SILVER

Silver, like gold, has mythical origins, but they are not quite so glorious. Pliny reports that the metal was discovered either by the legendary Athenian king Erichthonios or by Aiakos, king of the nearby island of Aigina, while Hyginus says that it was first found by the Scythian king Indus, who introduced it to Erichthonios.[88] On account of its bright, light color, the metal was particularly associated with the moon goddess Selene. Ancient poets dubbed Aphrodite, Artemis, and the sea nymph Thetis "silver-footed," a reference to their radiant white skin. *Argyros* in Greek, *argentum* in Latin, silver was the material of numerous divine attributes and accoutrements, such as thrones and couches, but perhaps most famously the bow of Apollo, who, at the beginning of Homer's *Iliad* and elsewhere, is called *argyrotoxos* (silver-bowed). Breastplates and shields, too, were occasionally made of or adorned with silver, and elite corps in the armies of Alexander the Great and his successors were known as *argyraspides* (those with silver shields).[89] Excavations at the sanctuary of Zeus Olympia have yielded numerous bronze helmets offered as dedications to the god, several with silver decoration. One particularly fine example is of the Illyrian type (fig. 17).[90] There is also both linguistic and physical evidence for silver horse-trappings, statues and statuettes, inlays and appliqués, sword hilts, and even shoe buckles, not to mention tableware. Of course, when untarnished and polished, silver is highly reflective, and thus it was also used for mirrors (although cheaper bronze was more common and tin was sometimes used). Most silver in the Greek and Roman world, however, seems to have been minted into coins, and in ancient texts the word for the metal frequently denotes money.[91]

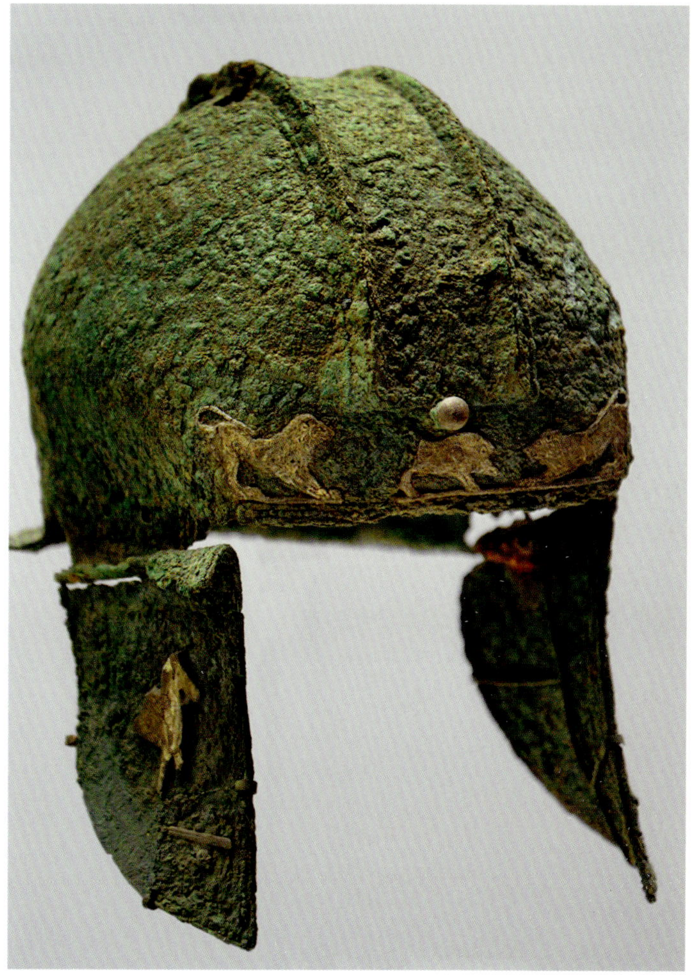

Figure 17
Helmet, from Olympia, ca. 530 BC. Bronze with silver appliqués, H: 26.5 cm. Olympia, Archaeological Museum, B 5316. Horsemen on the cheek pieces and two lions confronting a boar over the brow adorn this Illyrian-type helmet.

Silver was obtained from many of the same places as gold. In the Homeric poems several silver objects, especially vessels, have Phoenician associations. Both literary and archaeological evidence indicate that silver was mined on Mount Pangaion in Thrace, at Lydia in western Anatolia, and at Colchis on the eastern shore of the Black Sea, as well as on the Aegean islands of Siphnos and Lesbos. Thorikos and especially Laurion in eastern Attica brought great wealth to Athens at its height in the fifth century BC, although some of these mines seem to have been exploited earlier. The Attic mines were owned by the state, overseen by ten magistrates (*poletai*) elected annually, but worked by private contractors, who purchased leases, usually for terms of three years.[92] They paid the state a fixed price, usually a talent, and one twenty-fourth of their income, which was gained by the exploitation of large slave populations that toiled under harsh conditions. Herodotos tells of the discovery of a particularly rich vein at Laurion in 483 BC, which Themistokles convinced the Athenians not to distribute to the people but rather to use to finance the construction of ships (100 talents for 200 triremes), thus enabling the Athenian victory over the Persians at Salamis a few years later and the subsequent growth and maintenance of their maritime empire.[93] According to Xenophon, Nikias, son of Nikeratos, owned 1,000 slaves who worked in the mines; he rented them to the Thracian Sosias for one *obol* each a day; Hipponikos rented out 600; and Philomedes 300.[94] There must have been several such operations. When, in 413 BC, the Spartans occupied Dekeleia in northern Attica, 20,000 slaves are said to have run away.

Estimates of the total number of mines in Attica and their yield vary, but in the fifth century BC the state is thought to have received up to 1,000 talents annually from hundreds, if not thousands, of mines. Despite lower prices for silver as the wealth of Asia flowed into Greece in the wake of Alexander's conquests, mining continued in Attica, on and off, until 103 BC, when the mines were closed following a slave revolt. Among the archaeological features for processing silver ore preserved at Thorikos and Laurion are washing tables, cisterns, grinderies, smelters, work rooms, and slave quarters.[95]

In the west, Spain was the richest source of silver exploited by the Romans, having previously been developed by the Carthaginians. Pliny reports that Hannibal extracted 300 pounds a day from mines at Baebelone, and Strabo mentions several other rich sources on the Iberian peninsula, which the Romans took over from their predecessors, including a mountain not far from Castlon, in the Sierra Cazorla, that is called "silver mountain."[96] The silver mines of Gaul were worked by locals before the Roman conquest. Julius Caesar praised the subterranean engineering of local tribesmen.[97] Ancient mines have been identified in Provence, Savoy, Oisans, L'Argenière, Aquitania, and Hérault. Britain, conquered by the emperor Claudius in AD 43, also supplied Romans with the metal, as did Dalmatia and Dacia.[98]

Tons of silver coin, bullion, and finished goods flowed back to Rome from various conquests. The great wealth displayed in triumphs during the later Republic was catalogued by Livy and Pliny, among other ancient authors. Livy's account of the booty Scipio displayed in his triumph of 189 BC, after the defeat of the Seleucid king Antiochos III at the Battle of Magnesia the previous year, is highly specific: "224 military standards, 134 images of towns, 1,231 ivory tusks, 234 gold crowns, 137,420 pounds of silver, 224,000 Attic tetradrachmas [3,862 kilograms of silver], 321,070 *cistophoroi* [4,094 kilograms of silver], 140 gold coins, 1,423 pounds of silver vases—all with engraved surfaces—and 1,023 pounds of gold."[99] Just a few years earlier, in 197 BC, Titus Quinctius Flamininus defeated the Macedonian king Philip V at Kynokephalai, and, according to Livy, on the second day of his triumphal celebration at Rome "gold and silver, worked, unworked, and coined was carried in procession. The unwrought silver came to 43,270 pounds, while wrought silver included vessels of every sort, most embossed, some works of outstanding craftsmanship; there were also many made of bronze and ten silver shields as well. Of the silver coinage there were 84,000 Attic tetradrachmas."[100] And in 196 BC Lucius Stertinus returned from his proconsulship in Spain bringing 50,000 pounds of silver to the Roman treasury, which, according to Livy, financed the construction of two arches topped by golden statues.[101]

Silver, unlike gold, is rarely found in a native state. It must be separated from ore by crushing, grinding, and washing, and from baser metals, usually lead, through cupellation. The ancients perfected these techniques and regularly achieved extremely high degrees of purity. Slightly harder than gold (2.7 vs. 2.5 on the Mohs scale),[102] and more brittle, silver is worked by many of the same techniques. It can be shaped by freely hammering a sheet or pressing it into matrices, by casting it in molds, or turning it on a lathe. Individually fashioned components can be joined mechanically by rivets or metallurgically by solder. Vessels as well as sheet can be decorated in high or low relief through the techniques of repoussé, stamping, chasing, or engraving.[103] Separately made reliefs (*emblemata*) were often set into cups or bowls. Cicero reports that Verres, the corrupt Roman governor of Sicily, employed a team of silversmiths to reset ancient *emblemata* from bowls he had appropriated into new, more fashionable vessels,[104] and numerous ancient authors praise the decorative work of ancient silversmiths.

Additional adornment of silver vessels and other items with decorative reliefs of gold was not uncommon, and gilding could be achieved by fusion (i.e., burnishing) or by the application of thin leaf combined with an organic binder (animal or vegetable glues such as fish glue, egg white, resin, or gum arabic), and, from at least the first century BC, with mercury.[105] Niello, a black silver, copper, or lead sulfide, was sometimes applied as an inlay, creating another attractive color contrast. Although perhaps known in the Bronze Age, niello (*nigellum* in Latin) was employed in Roman works in silver, statuary as well as plate, as early as the first century AD, when it is mentioned by Pliny; it seems to have been especially popular from the third century on.[106]

Silver rings, earrings, bracelets, and necklaces are known,[107] but gold seems to have been preferred for jewelry. For plate, however, silver was much more common than its more precious cousin, and it survives in considerably greater numbers.[108] The shapes of silver cups, bowls, pitchers, and other vessels often parallel those of ceramics, and there has been much debate in recent years as to the precedence of one medium over the other.[109] In the Archaic and Classical periods we find wide-bowled *kylikes* and high-handled *kantharoi,* as well as flat-shouldered *kalpides* (plates 62, 64). Some of these have gilded and incised figural decoration that recalls the finest red-figured pottery (plates 63, 64). The Hellenistic period has yielded elegant cups and bowls (plates 68, 69). And from the Roman period we have a wealth of shapes, notably in hoards of entire sets of silver intended for both eating and drinking (*argentum escarium* and *argentum potorium*). Perfume vessels, pails, and other implements for the bath constituted a third category of luxury vessels (*argentum balneare*).[110] Wide, shallow ritual bowls for pouring libations (*phialai* in Greek; *paterae* in Latin), often with fluting or other decoration, were derived from ancient Near Eastern prototypes and had a long life. Inventories of Greek temples inscribed in stone record the dedication of hundreds of such objects, which were often fashioned according to fixed weights or monetary values, such as one or two minai (1 mina = 100 drachmai), and surviving vessels are often of standard weights, or are inscribed with such measurements, effectively demonstrating their dual function—as attractive products of decorative art and as easily convertible high-value "banknotes." Interestingly enough, several of the objects recorded in the inventories of the Parthenon, although recorded in Attic drachmai, seem to have been made in round numbers of Persian darics or sigloi.[111]

The great hoards of Roman silver that have been recovered from the houses and villas on the Bay of Naples, which were buried and thus preserved by the eruption of Mount Vesuvius in AD 79, and from numerous individual deposits throughout the empire, but especially in present-day France, Germany, Switzerland, and Britain, appear mostly to be personal or family treasures, hidden in times of uncertainty and never recovered.[112] A few, however, such as that discovered by a farmer near Berthouville in Normandy in 1830 (plates 77, 78), are temple deposits, as indicated by their votive inscriptions (to Mercury Canetonensis in the case of the Berthouville cache), dedicated by a variety of individuals whose names are recorded on them.[113]

Decorated silver plate was highly valued, by both individuals and institutions, as indicated in the accounts of Roman triumphal processions and temple inventories cited above—and not just for its monetary value. Highly wrought figural imagery, often scenes from myth, ritual, or idealized/normative daily life, adorned cups, pitchers, and other vessels. Dionysiac (or Bacchic) imagery was particularly popular, understandably, as was skillfully rendered exuberant vegetal ornament. Cicero's speeches against Verres (70 BC) catalogue the corrupt Roman governor of Sicily's obsession with obtaining figured plate of every kind, in addition to other valuable items. Pliny mentions several Greek silversmiths by name, and the works of these "old masters" fetched astronomical prices: Lucius Licinius Crassus (191–140 BC) paid 100,000 sesterces for a pair of chased goblets by the artist Mentor, who reputedly made only four pairs of cups, the others of which were lost in fires that destroyed the Temples of Artemis in Ephesos (in 356 BC) and on the Capitol.[114] After Mentor, Pliny reports, the silversmiths "most admired were Akragas, Boëthos, and Mys. Works by all of these exist on the island of Rhodes—one by Boëthos in the temple of Athena at Lindos, some goblets engraved with Centaurs and Bacchants by

Akragas in the temple of Father Liber or Dionysos in Rhodes itself, goblets with Silenoi and cupids by Mys in the same temple." As for other silversmiths, Pliny continues:

> **Hunting scenes by Akragas on goblets also had a great reputation. After these in celebrity are Kalamis and Diodoros.... Next praise is awarded to Stratonikos of Kyzikos, Tauriskos, and Ariston and Eunikos of Mitylene and Hekataios, and around the period of Pompey the Great Pasiteles, Poseidonios of Ephesos, Hedys, Thrakides, who engraved battle scenes and men in armor, and Zopyros who engraved the Athenian Council of the Areopagos and the Trial of Orestes on two goblets valued at 12,000 sesterces. There was also Pytheas, one of whose works sold at the price of 10,000 denarii for two ounces: it consisted of an embossed base of a bowl representing Odysseus and Diomedes in the act of stealing the Palladion. The same artist also fashioned some very small drinking cups in the shape of cooks known as "The Chefs in Miniature," which it was not allowed even to reproduce by casts, so liable to damage was the fineness of the work.[115]**

Even if we dismiss Pliny's complaint that in his own day (the first century AD) "this art so declined that it is now only valued in old specimens, and authority attaches to engravings worn with use even if the very design is invisible," the passages quoted above contain much valuable information. Of course, nothing survives from the hands of the masters named therein, but the scenes Pliny describes—centaurs, maenads, Silenoi, and cupids—are common on extant Roman silver vessels, as are hunting and battle scenes. Although not the work of Zopyrus, two surviving silver cups depicting the Trial of Orestes may be ancient copies or imitations of half of the famous pair.[116] Slight variations exist between the two, and one of them so closely resembles a cup depicting Odysseus in the Underworld in size, technique, details of moldings, etc., as to suggest that they might have been a pair—or at least part of a larger set manufactured by the same workshop. In any case, Pliny mentions that silver cups might be made, or reproduced, based on plaster models or casts, and multiple ancient plasters of metal vessels survive (fig. 18). These could have been used to make not only copies of vessels in precious metal but also replicas in glass and terracotta. Indeed, some terracotta "Arretine" bowls closely resemble preserved silver vessels.[117] Famous scenes could also be adapted to other uses: Pytheas's expensive *emblema* depicting Odysseus and Diomedes stealing the Palladion might well stand behind the depiction of the same scene on the neck of a silver pitcher from Berthouville (compare plate 77), the body of which depicts other scenes from the Trojan War that recall the work of Thrakides, "who engraved battle scenes and men in armor." Publius Curtilius Agatus, a silversmith who apparently earned his freedom through his skills, is represented on his grave monument making a cup with a dancing satyr (fig. 19), a figure type known in many other media, including engraved gems.[118]

All these silver objects, called *crustae, emblemata*, or *scyphi homerici* by other Roman authors, such as Cicero, Vergil, Petronius, Martial, and Suetonius, were not only employed at elite banquets but were also themselves objects of desire and the subjects of learned discourse. In antiquity, as today, it was bad form to drink on one's own, and we know not only from the prevalence of paired vessels among survivals but also from Cicero's comment about Verres stealing "many pairs of cups" (*scyphorum paria complura*) that silver vessels were often produced as sets.[119] Indeed, we can imagine a participant in a Greek *symposion*—or a Roman *convivium*—first inspecting his own cup and then comparing it to that of a companion, and this becoming a launching point for discussion, for the examination of the imagery on drinking cups is a recurring motif in Hellenistic and Roman literature. A poem by the epigrammatist Antipater of Thessalonike, for example, accompanied the gift to Lucius Calpurnius Piso of two silver cups adorned with maps of the heavens:

> **Theogenes sends to Piso these skillfully wrought bowls,**
> **And both of us together contain the heavens.**

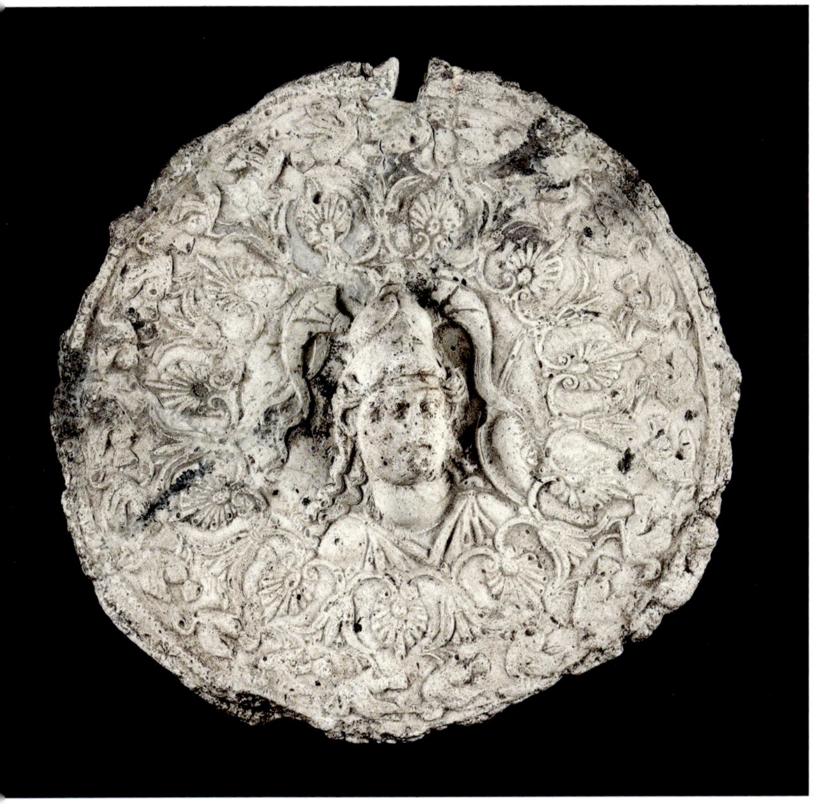

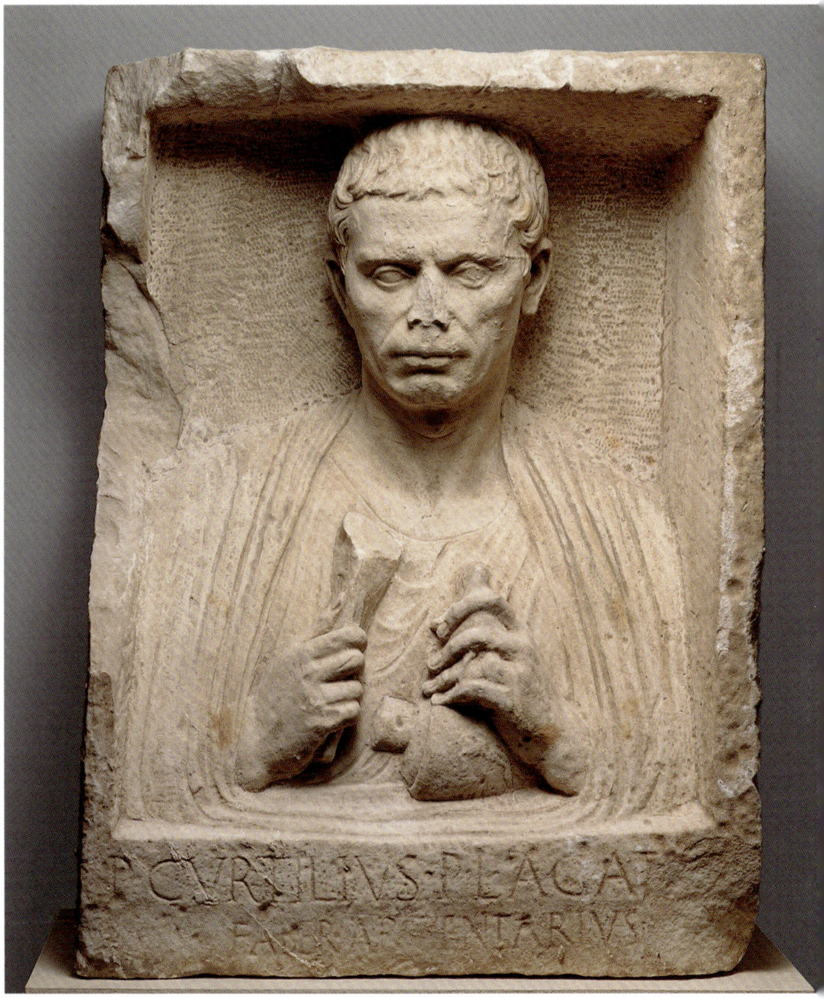

Figure 18
Cast of a metal medallion, from Memphis in Egypt, ca. 340–330 BC. Plaster, Diam. (max): 15 cm. Hildesheim, Pelizaeus-Museum, 1109. The central bust of Athena is surrounded by two concentric friezes of lotuses and palmettes and birds. The goddess herself wears a *peplos* pinned at her shoulders and a triple-crested helmet. Her spear and a diminutive shield are above her left shoulder (compare plate 19).

Figure 19
Grave relief of a silversmith, ca. AD 1–25. Marble, H: 79.9 cm; W: 58.5 cm; D: 31.7 cm. Malibu, JPGM, 96.AA.40. Inscribed: P CVRTILIVS P L AGAT . . / FABER ARGENTARIVS (Publius Curtilius Agatus, freedman of Publius, silversmith). Although depicted at work, this prosperous ex-slave wears his "Sunday best," a loosely draped toga and ring on his left hand, both marking his status. The hammer in his right hand is broken, and he holds a punch in his left as he refines the embossed decoration on a cup before him. He has already fashioned the figure of a dancing satyr on the cup, into which he has temporarily placed a wooden plug to prevent any damage from the force exerted from the exterior.

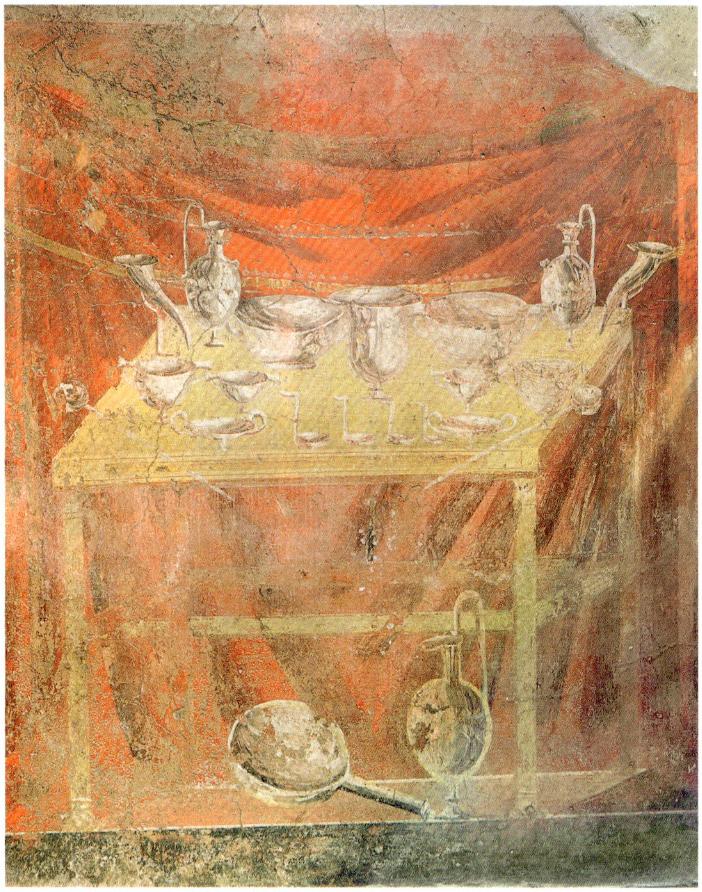

Figure 20
Fresco of a silver service from the Tomb of Gaius Vestorius Priscus at Pompeii, ca. AD 75. Priscus died at age twenty-two, after being elected *aedile* (junior magistrate), and was honored by the town council, which allocated funds for the construction of his tomb. On this wall a table is laden with paired vessels comprising a set of *argentum potorium* (silver for drinking). Various pieces of silver appear elsewhere in the tomb, along with other images crucial to the construction and projection of Priscus's social and political identity, including depictions of the magistrate seated on a *curule* chair, a gladiatorial combat, exotic animal hunt, luscious gardens with fountains and peacocks, Nilotic scenes, a banquet, couches, writing implements, and bags of money.

Figure 21
Frieze of metal vessels and sacred implements (detail), from the Temple of Divine Vespasian and Titus, ca. AD 87. Marble, H: 1.02 m. Rome, Musei Capitolini (Tabularium). The handle of the *urceus* (pitcher) takes the form of a Silenos wearing a goatskin. The vessel has a winged Victory on the neck; on the body a hunter with a spear confronts a lioness and panther, and below a rhinoceros attacks a bull. This decoration seems to refer to the hunts (*venationes*) and animal combats sponsored by the Flavians, who were responsible for the construction of the Colosseum. The poet Martial describes in detail how a rhinoceros, an animal rarely seen in Rome previously, tossed two steers in games in the Colosseum, and the animal was widely disseminated on coinage of the emperor Domitian. The *patera* (libation bowl) to the right features the head of Zeus Ammon surrounded by a series of overlapping leaves.

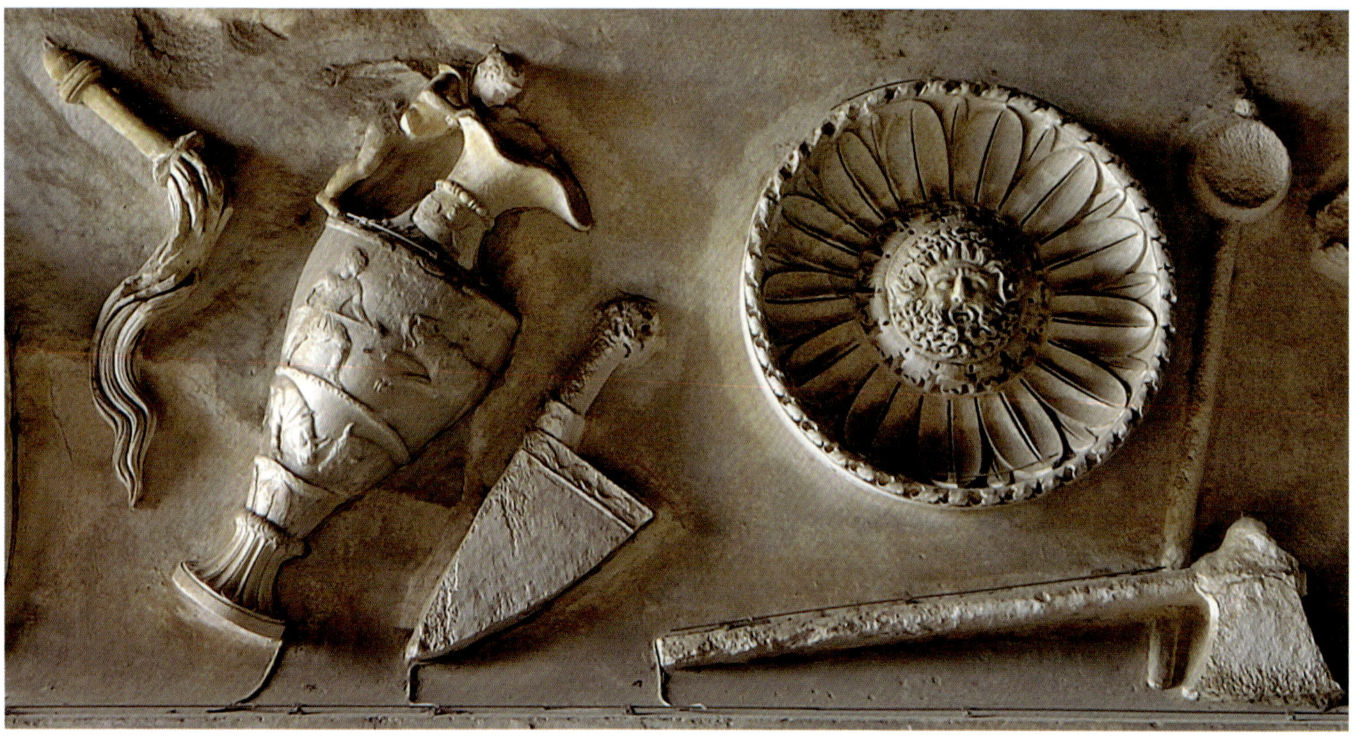

> **We two are cut from a sphere, and one of us**
> **Contains the southern constellations, the other the northern.**
> **No longer consult Aratos, for if you empty us both**
> **You will see all the phenomena.**[120]

That highly decorated cups were intended to be read in pairs, sometimes even as puzzles, is also clear in a scene in Vergil's third *Eclogue*, where the shepherd Menalcas challenges Damoetas to name the astronomer depicted on a cup, the "work of the divine Alcimedon." These cups, in the rustic setting of Vergil's poem, are carved of beech wood, but both the motifs—grapevines and ivy clusters, acanthus and Orpheus, as well as astronomers—and the technical vocabulary—*caelatum* (engraved), *torno* (burin)—are more appropriate to silver.

In the *Satyricon*, Petronius demonstrates how one might read the imagery on ancient silver cups to flaunt one's erudition and high culture, albeit with a large dose of social criticism. The boorish, but exceedingly rich ex-slave Trimalchio, who enters the narrative relieving himself into a silver piss-pot, tries to impress his dinner guests, but he blithely misinterprets the scenes on his own silver vessels, garbling mythological references to the delight of the reader, learned Roman and modern scholar alike:

> **When it comes to silver, I'm a connoisseur; I have goblets as big as wine-jars, a hundred of 'em more or less, with engraving that shows how Cassandra killed her sons, and the dead boys are laying so naturally that you'd think 'em alive. I own a thousand bowls which Mummius left to my patron, where Daedalus is shown shutting Niobe up in the Trojan horse, and I also have cups engraved with the gladiatorial contests of Hermeros and Petraites: they're all heavy, too. I wouldn't sell my taste in these matters for any money!**[121]

The famous gladiators Hermeros and Petraites may seem unlikely subjects for Roman silver, but gladiators named Petraites (as well as Tetraites and Hermes among others) appear on ancient glass vessels roughly contemporary with the *Satyricon*.[122] More commonly depicted on Roman silver are scenes closely related to the wine god Dionysos, which is understandable given the sympotic context of most of these objects. Narrative scenes from mythology, such as those mentioned above, as well as imagery relating to philosophy and to the theater (which, by definition, is Dionysian) also contributed to the self-fashioning of users as cultured literati. A few vessels bear explicit political imagery.[123]

Like gold, silver was imitated in other materials and represented in other media. Precious vessels frequently appear as accessories in Roman wall paintings, but in the tomb of Gaius Vestorius Priscus, located just outside the so-called Porta del Vesuvio north of Pompeii, an entire service (*ministerium*) of drinking silver is represented on the north wall, for such an assemblage was a significant element in the construction of the aspiring young man's social and political identity (fig. 20).[124] Silver was also an important component of temple treasuries with ritual as well as economic functions. Thus, *paterae* (libation bowls) and *urcei* (pitchers) are included among the religious paraphernalia carved in high relief on the marble frieze of the Temple of Divine Vespasian and Titus in the Roman Forum (fig. 21).[125] A decade earlier, Pliny reported that

> **fashions in silver plate undergo marvelous variations owing to the vagaries of human taste, no kind of workmanship remaining long in favor. At one time Furnian plate is in demand, at another Clodian, at another Gratian . . . at another time the demand is for embossed plate and rough surfaces, where the metal has been cut out along the painted lines of the designs . . . and other pieces of plate we decorate with filigree, so that the file may have wasted as much silver as possible. The orator Calvus complainingly cries that cooking pots are made of silver but it is we who invented decorating carriages with chased silver.**

Pliny goes on to complain of silver bedsteads and large platters owned by imperial slaves and freedmen that weighed 100, 250, even 500 pounds.[126]

Silver statues, too, are recorded, both archaeologically and in literary sources.[127] Many statuettes survive, but the remains of a remarkable life-size silver bull, with gilded horns and dewlap, were excavated under the Sacred Way in the sanctuary of Apollo at Delphi (plate 60). Assembled on a copper armature in the sixth century BC, it was damaged by fire and deliberately buried along with other precious offerings to the god a century later.[128] Pliny remarks that "the opinion that the use of silver was first transferred to sculpture for making statues of the divine Augustus, as a result of the flattery characteristic of those times, is false. For in the triumphal procession of Pompey the Great [in 61 BC] we find that a silver statue of Pharnakes I, king of Pontus [ca. 185–169 BC], was carried and likewise one of Mithradates Eupator."[129] Pliny records that silver statuary was popular already in late second-century BC Rome: "Not only are men mad for silver in great quantity, but they are perhaps even mad for it in the form of works of art, and this has been true for so long a time now that we today pardon ourselves. Gaius Sempronius Gracchus [153–121 BC] had some figures of dolphins he bought for the price of 5,000 sesterces per pound."[130]

It was, however, in the early reign of Augustus that things got out of hand. According to the historian Dio Cassius, "when the Senate and the people once again contributed silver for statues of him, he set up a statue not of himself, but of *Salus Publica, Concordia,* and *Pax*."[131] Suetonius reports that Augustus "even melted down silver statues that had already been set up in his honor, and with the total proceeds from these he dedicated gold cauldrons to Apollo on the Palatine."[132] Dio also reports that the emperor Claudius modestly accepted but one silver portrait along with bronzes and marbles that had been voted to him.[133] Nero preferred golden images, but Domitian "permitted no statues to be set up in his honor unless they were of gold and silver and were of certifiable weight."[134] Nerva allegedly refused to be portrayed in precious metal, and this seems to have set the tone for his successors, but in AD 176, after the death of Faustina the Younger, the senate voted to erect silver statues of Marcus Aurelius and his late wife in the Temple of Venus and Rome.[135]

Of course, silver statues depicting the gods and other offerings continued to be produced. The *Acts of the Apostles* record that in AD 54, the Ephesian silversmith Demetrios organized opposition to Christian evangelists sent by the apostle Paul in order to protect his trade; and according to a fragmentary Ephesian inscription, in AD 104 a certain C. Vivius Salurarius dedicated to Artemis twenty-nine silver statues, some gilded, to be carried regularly in processions through the city. Stored in the *pronaos* of the goddess's temple, the statues ranged in weight from three to seven pounds. Nine of them represented the goddess herself, while others depicted Trajan and Plotina, the reigning emperor and his wife, personifications of the Roman senate, the equestrian order, and the Roman people as well as of the city of Ephesos, the demos, various city councils, and historical and mythological founders of the city.[136]

Silver statuettes of divinities survive from various sites throughout the Roman Empire, as do images of emperors (plate 80),[137] but the quantity of precious metal objects that has been melted down and recycled is incalculable. The many objects mentioned above provide but an inkling of the riches of the ancient world and the diversity of contexts in which they served. The surviving artifacts illustrated on the following pages, more numerous than generally assumed, offer an explanation for the praise accorded such items by ancient authors and their great cultural significance.

NOTES

Pindar, *First Olympian Ode*, translated by Diane Arnson Svarlien.

1 On Greek gold in general, see Strong 1966; Higgins 1980; Mylonas 1983; Musti et al. 1992; Tolstikov and Treister 1996. See also Homer, *Iliad* 11.632, 18.478–608; *Odyssey* 19.228–31; Hesiod, *Works and Days*; Plato, *Kratylos*. On the ideological valences of gold, see Laum 1924 and esp. Kurke 1995, 1999. See also Daumas 1956.

2 *NH* 7.56.

3 Hyginus, *Fabulae* 274.

4 Pindar, frag. 209 Bowra, 222 Snell-Maehler. For Zeus turning himself into gold to seduce Danae, see Gantz 1993, 299–304.

5 *NH* 33.4, 25.

6 Kurke 1995, 1999.

7 *NH* 33.19.

8 Strabo, *Geographika* 11.2.19; see also *NH* 33.15; Chkonia and Lordkipanidze 2007; Kacharava et al. 2008.

9 Herodotos 3.102, 116; compare *NH* 33.21. For pangolins, see G. Jennison cited by Graham 1957, 118n43.

10 Mayor 2000.

11 Herodotos 4.196.

12 Ovid, *Metamorphoses* 9.85–193.

13 Herodotos 1.49–52; slightly adapted from the translation by A. de Sélincourt, first published 1954.

14 Plutarch, who was a priest at Delphi, explains that Croesus's stepmother attempted to poison him, but his life was saved by his baker (*Moralia* 403e–f; *De Pythiae oraculis* C. 16 and 92); see also Xenophon, *Hellenica* 7.126; *Cyropaedia* 5.539. For the suggestion that "baker" was a euphemism for courtesan, see Garrett and Kurke 1994, 82–83.

15 Herodotos 1.92 and 1.14; Archilochos, frag. 19 = Plutarch, *De tranquillitate animi* 10.470b–c. Two standards of weight were employed regularly in ancient Greece. In each one, 100 dramchai = 1 mina; and 60 mina = 1 talent. In the Attic-Euboic system, 1 drachma = 4.31 grams; 1 mina =431 grams; and 1 talent = 25.86 kg. In the Aeginetic standard (which was similar to that of the Persians), 1 drachma = 6.3 grams; 1 mina = 630 grams; and 1 talent = 37.80 kg. If Croesus dedications followed the Aeginitic standard, they would weigh 1,134 kg. If Herodotos or his source translated them into the Attic system, they would weigh 775.8 kg.

16 Amandry 1939, 1977, 1991; Petrakos 1977; Lapatin 2001.

17 On *electrum*, see *NH* 33.80. The term *electros* appears earlier, in Sophokles, *Antigone* 1037; on *leukos*, see Herodotos 1.50. The Greek *elektros*, or *elektron*, also refers to amber.

18 On gold from the Paktolos and the Sardis refineries, see Ramage and Craddock 2000; Bruce 2014.

19 Strabo, *Geographika* 13.1.23; slightly adapted from the translation by H. L. Jones, 1929.

20 Herodotos 6.47; *NH* 37.121 and 130. For the mines of Thasos, see Wagner and Weisgerber 1988; R. Shepherd 1993, 128–35; Domergue 2008, passim.

21 On Siphnos, see Herodotos 3.57; Pausanias 10.11.2; Bent 1885; Wagner, Weisgerber, and Kroker 1985; Shepherd 1993, 116–27; Domergue 2008, passim.

22 See, e.g., Kurke 1999.

23 LSJ, 2009–12; Hesiod, *Works and Days* 109–26; see also Ovid, *Metamorphoses* 1.89–112. Also the virgin hunter Atalanta was undone by golden apples, given to her suitor Hippomenes by Aphrodite; see, e.g., Ovid, *Metamorphoses* 10.560–707.

24 On horns and on gold crowns to soldiers, see *NH* 33.11; on gold offerings in sanctuaries, see Linders 1972, 1975, 1987, 1997; Lewis 1985; Aleshire 1989; Vickers and Gill 1994, esp. 33–76; Harris 1995; Vickers 1999a, 1999b; Hamilton 2000; Lapatin 2005. On dress pins specifically, see Brøns 2014, 40–45, and appendix 4. For textiles in general, see Brøns 2014, passim. See also Rouse 1902.

25 See Harris 1995, 105, 229, 234–35; Kosmetatou 2004b.

26 Higbie 2003.

27 Pindar, *Olympian* 7.1–4.

28 *Iliad* 6.212–36, 24.232–37; *Odyssey* 8.430–32, 438–40.

29 Harris 1995, 269–71; see also Vickers 1989a, 1989b; Treister 1996, 251–52, 344.

30 See, e.g., Vickers and Gill 1994; Gill 2008; see also Künzl 1978; Baratte 1985, 1992; Lorber 2008.

31 *NH* 33.2: *aurum argentumque caelando carius fecimus*. Panagopoulou 2007, 326.

32 Xenophon, *Hellenika* 1.5. Panagopoulou 2007, 352.

33 While it is often difficult to determine from a literary description, or mere mention, of a statue whether it was gold or gilt, a difference in vocabulary sometimes make this clear: *chryseos* (golden) can be ambiguous; clearer are *chyusendetos* (inlaid with gold), *chryselatos* (of beaten gold), *chrysodetos* (set in gold), *chrysoeides* (goldlike), *chrysostrophos* (made of twisted gold), *chrysotos* (gilded), *epichrysos* (gold-plated), *perichrysos* (ringed with gold), *holochrysos* (of solid gold); see LSJ and Harris 1995. For the statues in general, see Pekàry 1968; Vermeule 1974; Lahusen 1978; Krumeich 2007, 167–68.

34 Pausanias 5.2.3; Strabo, *Geographika* 8.353, 378; Diogenes Laertius 1.7.96; compare Plato, *Phaedrus* 236B.

35 Pausanias 10.24.5; see Frazer 1913, ad loc.

36 Herodotos 1.69.

37 Athenaios, *Deipnosophistai* 13.59 (591B): Keesling 2006; Krumeich 2007, 167.

38 Herodotos 7.41 and 83.

39 Herodotos 9.80–83; slightly adapted from the translation by Rawlinson, 1858.

40 Harris 1995, nos. II.20, V.54, 57, 59, 61, 63, 65.

41 *IG* I^{3}, 396.105, 118; Aristotle, *Constitution of the Athenians* 15.2; Thucydides 4.105; Herodotos 1.64, 9.75; Casson 1926, 68–70.

42 Demosthenes 24.129; the weight of the sword is not given in inventories inscribed on stone.

43 See note 24 above.

44 Plutarch, *Alkibiades* 16.1.

45 Tsimbidou-Avloniti 2005.

46 Plutarch, *Alkibiades* 13.

47 Andokides, *Against Alkibiades* 4.29.

48 Thucydides 6.32; see also Vickers and Gill 1994, 41, 45.

49 Demosthenes 24.184; Lewis 1985; Vickers and Gill 1994, 40; Lorber 2008.

50 Diodoros 16.56.3–6. Miles 2015; Davies 2007; Chankowski 2011,

51 *NH* 33.14.

52 On Philip, see Diodoros 16.8; Greek Geological Institute report: *Archaiologikon Deltion* 37.326 and 38.322; on Hellenistic jewelry, see Higgins 1980; Reeder 1988; Despini 1996; on Alexander, see Diodoros 17.65–66, 70–71; Callataÿ 1989; Miles 2015.

53 *NH* 33.14.

54 *NH* 33.19; Homer, *Odyssey* 5.232, 10.543; cf. Vergil, *Aeneid* 3.483, 4.264, 8.167, 11.75; Cleland 2005; Brøns 2014, esp. 71–74. On survivals from Athens: London, Victoria and Albert Museum, T220–1953 (Beckwith 1954; Barber 1991, 206); from Vergina: Andronicos 1984, 191–95, figs. 156, 157; from Taranto: Taranto, Museo Nazionale Archeologico, 1.238, 50.625bis, 108.256, 6.484 (De Juliis 1984, 339–40, nos. 277–80); from the Vesuvian cities: Naples, Museo Archeologico Nazionale, 110834; Soprintendenza Archeologica di Pompei, 78548. See also British Museum, GR 1772,0314.191 (Gem 4048), a rock crystal vessel containing a fragment of gold cloth, formerly in the collection of Sir William Hamilton (Vickers 1997b, 265).

55 Strong 1966; Musti et al. 1992; Williams and Ogden 1994; Vickers and Gill 1994; Marazov et al. 1998; Reeder 1999; Kalashnik 2004; Nikolov 2007; Trofimova 2007; Marazov 2011.

56 On Ptolemaic prospecting and mining in Egypt, see Belozerskaya 2006, 2–47; R. Klemm and D. Klemm 2013, esp. 12–15.

57 Kallixeinos *apud* Athenaios, *Deipnosophistai* 5.197C–203B; see Rice 1983; Pollitt 1986, 280–81; Erskine 2013; Miles 2015.

58 Polybios 18.16; Scott 1931, 101–4; see also Krumeich 2007, 168.

59 Athenaios, *Deipnosophistai* 5.193D; Polybios 26.1.

60 Theokritos, *Idyll* 10.32–35.

61 The Romans conquered and looted Syracuse in 211 BC, Capua in 210, Tarentum in 209, Eretria in 198, Macedon in 194 and 164, Aetolia and Ambracia in 187, Asia Minor in 186, Corinth in 146, and Athens, Olympia, and Epidauros in 87–85.

62 *NH* 33.14–16, 55–56; Gaius Marius the Younger in 82 BC removed 14,000 pounds of gold from Praeneste and the Capitoline temples.
63 Livy 31.45; *NH* 33.21; O. Davies 1935, 63–64 (see pp. 71 and 74 for fourth- and sixth-century literary evidence for possible gold working in Sardinia and Bruttium); R. Shepherd 1993, 141–42; Domergue 2008.
64 See Introduction, esp. notes 5, 20, and 43.
65 Plutarch, *Camillus*; Diodoros 14.93.2–4; Vickers and Gill 1994, 63.
66 *Epitome* 1.13.27.
67 Livy 22.37.2–5.
68 Livy 23.16.7ff. Such numbers render paltry the 112 pounds of gold crowns displayed by Marcus Fulvius Nobilior in celebration of his triumph over the Aetolian Greeks and capture of Ambracia twenty years later (Livy 39.5.13–16).
69 Livy 34.1–8.
70 Plutarch, *Aemilius Paullus* 32–33; Beard 2007.
71 *NH* 33.148–49. See also Gruen 1992.
72 Appian, *Mithradatic Wars* 3.21; *Roman History* 12.16; Dio Cassius 40.27; NH 33.44; Mayor 2010.
73 On Tagus, see Catullus 29.19; Ovid, *Amores* 1.15.34; Juvenal 3.55; Martial 1.49.15, 686.5, 7.88.7, 8.78.6, 10.17.4, 10.96.3, 12.2.3.
74 R. Shepherd 1993, 9.
75 *NH* 33.4.66, 78; O. Davies 1935, 100–103, 110–12; R. Shepherd 1993; Orejas and Sánchez-Palencia 2002; Domergue 2008.
76 Diodoros 5.26.1–27.1 and passim. For other ancient sources on Gallic gold, see O. Davies 1935, 76–77, 79, 82; Shepherd 1993, 170–81; Domergue 2008.
77 R. Shepherd 1993, 397–404.
78 O. Davies 1935, 186–89; Polybios 34.10.
79 R. Shepherd 1993, 153–69; O. Davies 1935, 198–206.
80 *NH* 33.23.
81 Tacitus, *Annals* 2.33; Scriptores Historiae Augustae, *Aurelian* 16.
82 *NH* 33.49–50.
83 More detailed discussions of techniques are found in Becatti 1955; Hoffmann and Davidson 1965; Higgins 1980; Ogden 1982; Nicolini 1990; Odgen 1992a; Williams and Ogden 1994; Despini 1996; Williams 1998; Ramage and Craddock 2000; Treister 2001; Sas and Vilvorder in Sas and Thoen 2002, 27–34; Baldini and Guaitoli 2009.
84 *NH* 33.19. See Hackens and Winkes 1983; Ogden 1991, 1993a.
85 Caley 2008, 23.
86 See, e.g., Ogden 1992a, 1992b, 1993b; and note 83 above.
87 *NH* 37.106; Harris 1995, nos. II.37, V.164. See also Lapatin 2001, 82–83, esp. n. 212.
88 *NH* 7.57; *Fabulae* 274.
89 LSJ, 236–37; *OLD*, 166–67.
90 Olympia Museum, B 5316 (Mallwitz and Herrmann 1980, 92–93, no. 52, pl. 52; A. Yalouris and N. Yalouris 1987, 64–65; Frielinghaus 2011, 252–53, no. C50).
91 See note 22 above.
92 Aristophanes, *Wasps* 659; Aristotle, *Constitution of the Athenians* 47.
93 Herodotos 7.144; compare Plutarch, *Themistokles* 4; Thucydides 6.91.7.
94 Xenophon, *On Revenues* 4; compare Plutarch, *Nikias* 4.2.
95 See, e.g., Conophagos 1980 (for Laurion). For other sources, see O. Davies 1935; R. Shepherd 1993; Panagopoulou 2007; Domergue 2008.
96 *NH* 33.96–97; Strabo, *Geographika* 3.2.11.
97 Caesar, *Gallic Wars* 7.22.
98 O. Davies 1935; R. Shepherd 1993; Domergue 2008.
99 Livy 37.59.3–5.
100 Livy 34.52.4–5.
101 Livy 32.27.3–4.
102 See chapter 2, note 2.
103 Simon 1966; Strong 1966; Stefanelli 1991; Sherlock 1996.
104 Cicero, *In Verrem* 2.4.24.
105 Oddy 1981; Drayman-Weisser 2000.
106 *NH* 33.46; Oddy, Bimson, and La Niece 1983.
107 Higgins 1980; Despini 1996.
108 Strong 1966 remains the standard overview. See also Kent and Painter 1977; Oliver 1977; Stefanelli 1991.
109 See Vickers and Gill 1994; Vickers 1999b.
110 Stefanelli 1991; Guzzo 2006a; for a brief survey, see Oliver 2004.
111 Lewis 1985; Aleshire 1989; Vickers 1989b, 1990a; Vickers and Gill 1994; Harris 1995; Hamilton 2000.
112 See, e.g., Maiuri 1933; Gehrig 1980; Cahn and Kaufmann-Heinimann 1984; Baratte 1986, 1988; U. Pappalardo 1986, 2003; Baratte and Painter 1989; Boetzkes and Stein 1997; Painter 2001; Guzzo 2006a, 2006b; Johns 2010.
113 Babelon 1916; Lapatin 2014. See also Griffiths 1943; Springer 1949; Baratte 1992.
114 *NH* 33.147, 154–55.
115 *NH* 33.156–57.
116 Oliver 2004, 20–21 (with further references).
117 *NH* 35.156. Reinsberg 1980; Reeder Williams 1976; Strong 1966, 138–39.
118 See, e.g., British Museum, 1867,0507.160 (Gem 3513).
119 Cicero, *In Verrem* 2.2.47.
120 Translation adapted from W. R. Patton, *The Greek Anthology*, vol. 3 (London and New York, 1917), no. 541.
121 Petronius, *Satyricon* 52.
122 For Petraites, see Corning Museum of Glass, 57.1.4: Whitehouse 2001, 62–64, no. 534; for Tetraites and Hermes, see Metropolitan Museum of Art, 81.10.245: Picón et al. 2007, 379, 492–93, no. 445. Petraites is also mentioned in an inscription at Pompeii (*CIL* 4.538). For a detailed analysis of Trimalchio's silver, see Castiglione 2006.
123 Vermeule 1963; Baratte 1991; Kuttner 1995.
124 For the tomb of Gaius Vestorius Priscus, see Spano 1943; Dentzer 1962; L. Richardson 1988, 362–63; A. Cooley and M. Cooley 2004, 128, no. F88; Tamm 2005; Cormack 2007, 597.
125 De Angeli 1992; Rodríguez-Almeida 1994, 200–203; Buttrey 2007. See also Martial, *Liber Spectaculorum* 22.
126 *NH* 33.139–40; see also 33.144–46; adapted from the translation by H. Rackham, 1952. Also Martial, *Liber Spectaculorum* 4.39.
127 Vermeule 1974.
128 Amandry 1977; Amandry 1991, 202–50.
129 *NH* 33.151.
130 *NH* 33.147.
131 Dio Cassius 54.35.2.
132 Suetonius, *Augustus* 52.
133 Dio Cassius 60.5.4–5.
134 Suetonius, *Domitian* 13.2.
135 Dio Cassius 71.31.1.
136 *Acts* 19:24ff.; Rogers 1991, 80–126.
137 Bendinelli 1937; Baratte 1998b; Sena Chiesa 1998, 2008; Riccardi 2002.

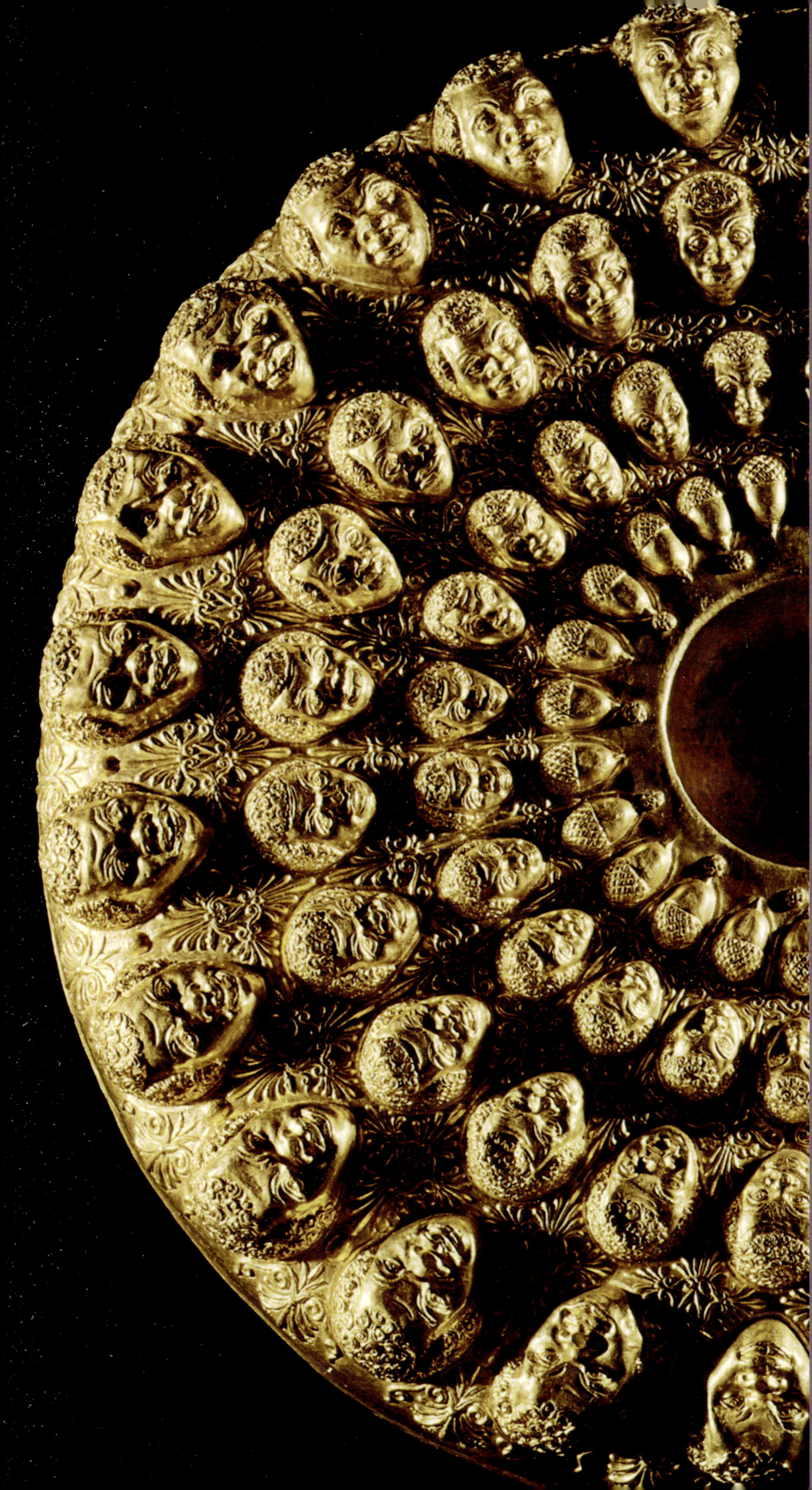

CHAPTER ONE

METALS

PLATES 1–80

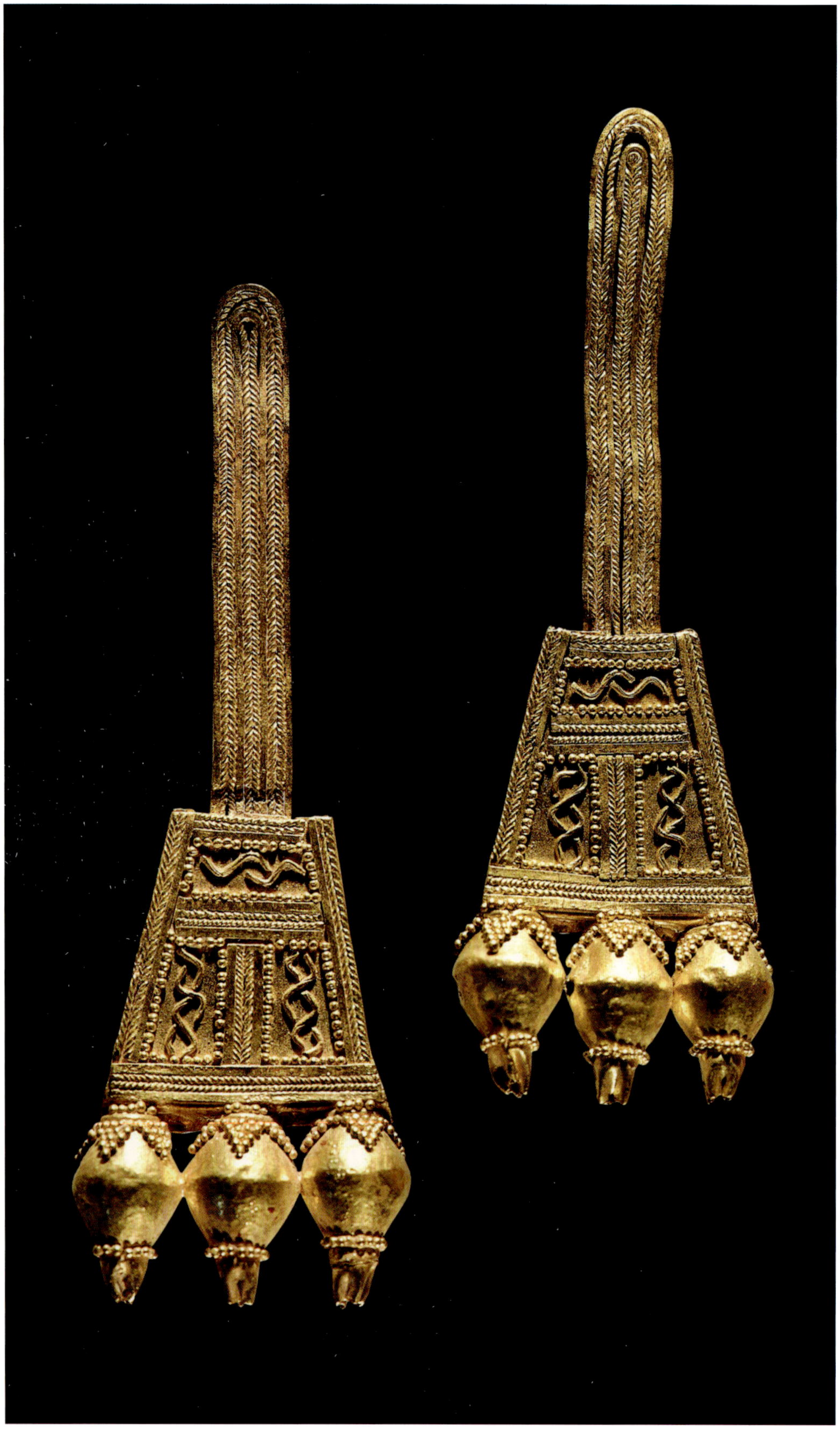

Plate 1
Pair of earrings with geometric decoration, ca. 850 BC. Gold, H: 6.4 and 6.5 cm; W: 2.5 and 2.1 cm; Wt. 5.9 and 6.2 grams

Plate 2 (opposite)
Pair of earrings with geometric decoration, ca. 750–700 BC. Gold, Diam (disks): 2.8 cm; Wt: 18.3 and 18.7 grams

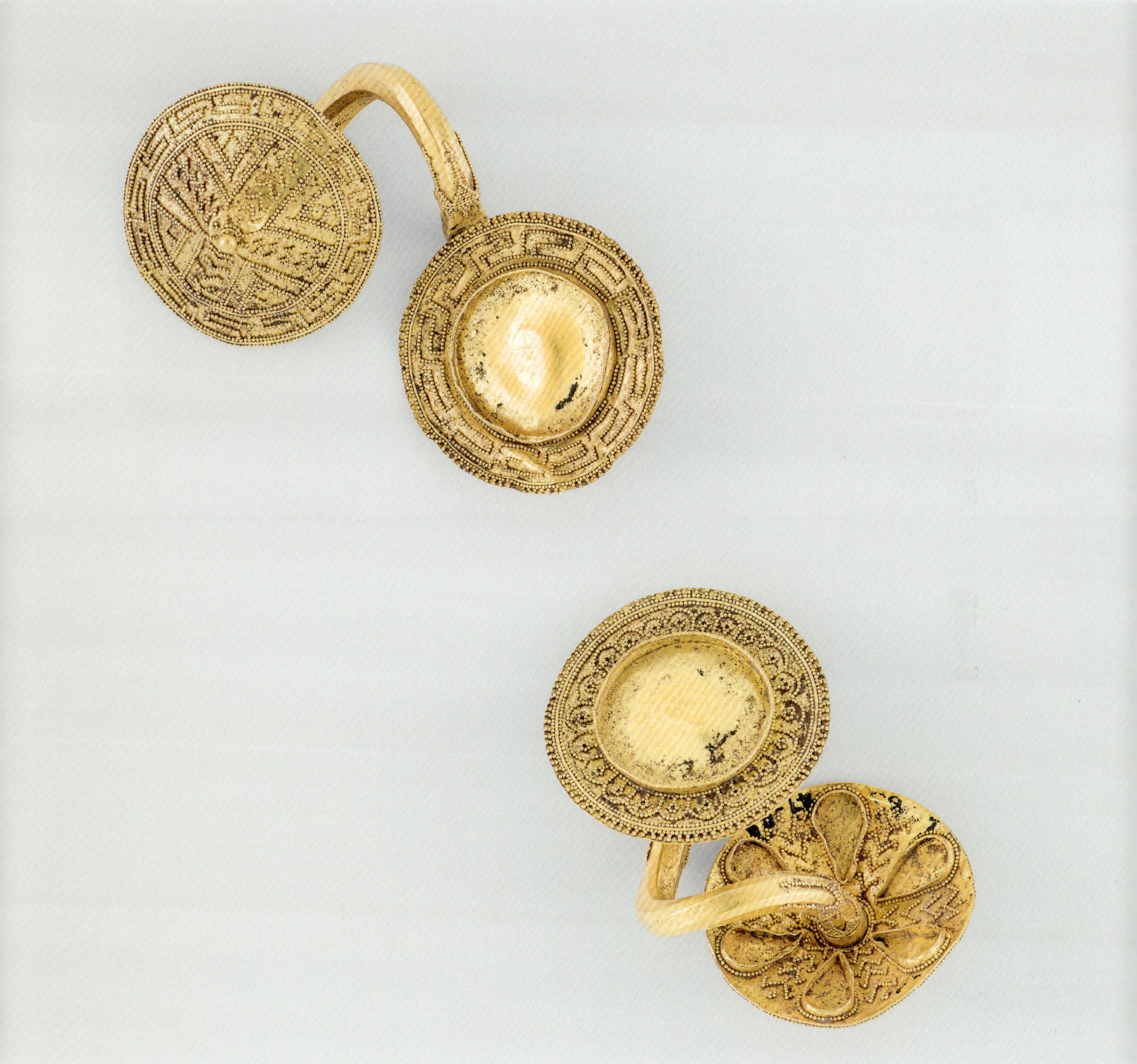

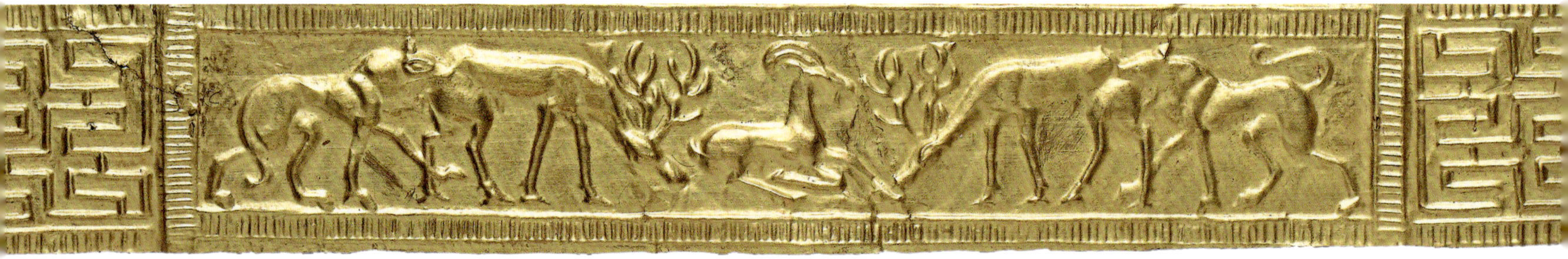

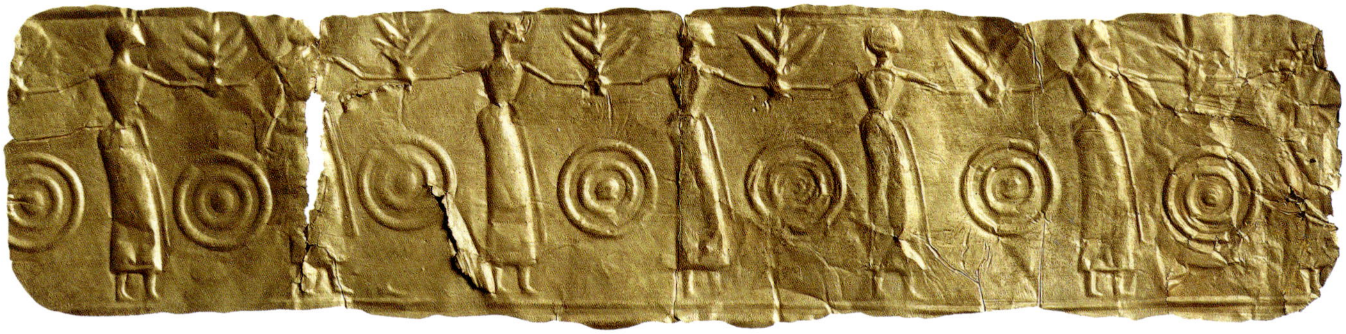

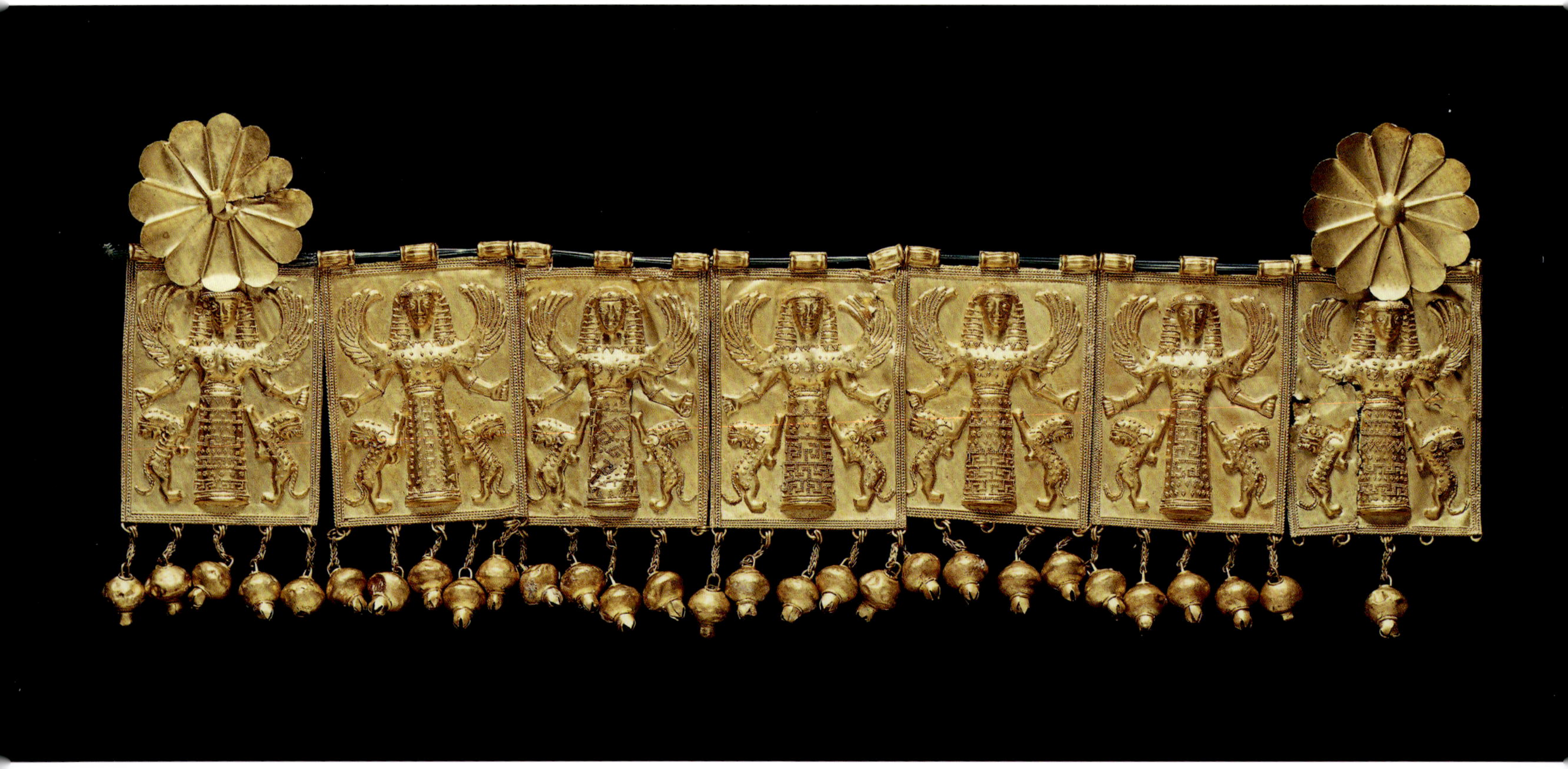

Plate 3 (opposite, top)
Diadem with animals, ca. 760–720 BC. Gold, L: 38.5 cm; H: 3.4 cm; Wt: 20.7 grams

Plate 4 (opposite, middle)
Diadem with dancing women, ca. 700 BC. Gold, L: 15.5 cm; H: 3.5 cm; Wt: 15 grams

Plate 5 (opposite, bottom)
Necklace or pectoral with Artemis as Mistress of the Animals, ca. 660–620 BC. Gold, H (plaques): 4.2 cm; L: 22.2 cm; Wt. 52.8 grams

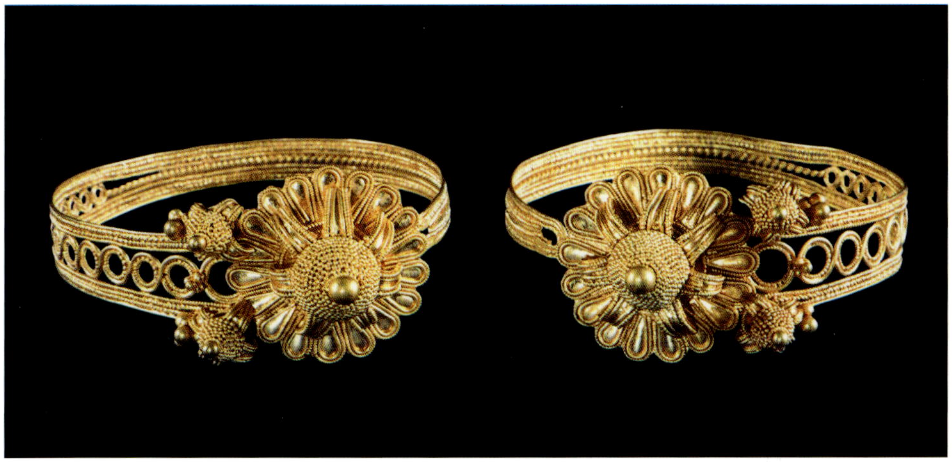

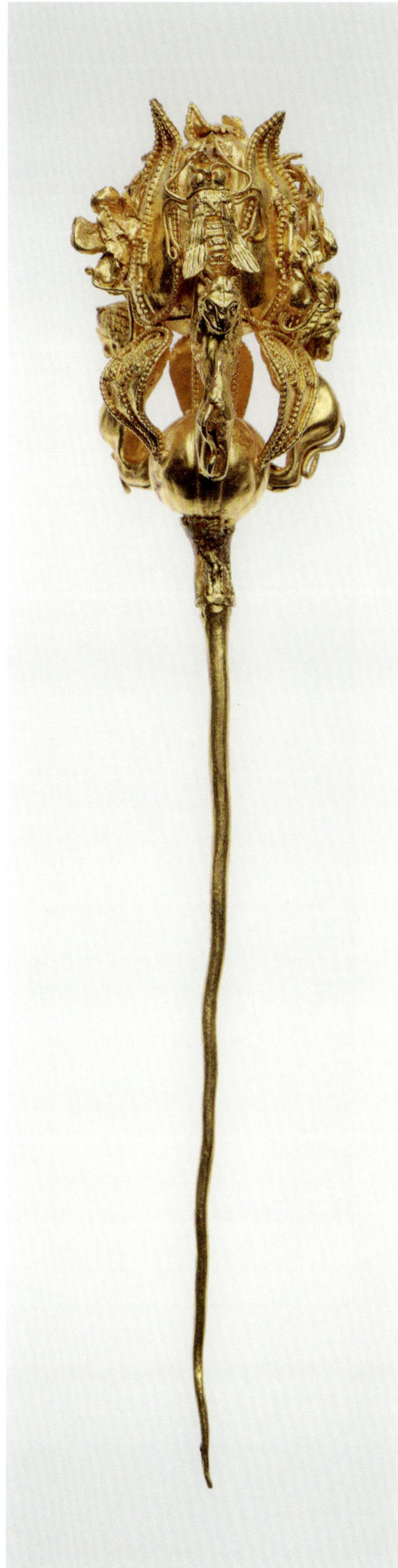

Plate 6
Pair of earrings with rosettes, ca. 510 BC. Gold, Diam: 5.5 and 5.7 cm

Plate 7
Dress pin with animals, ca. 475–450 BC. Gold, L (pin): 11.8 cm; L: (head) 4.2 cm; Wt. 14.2 grams

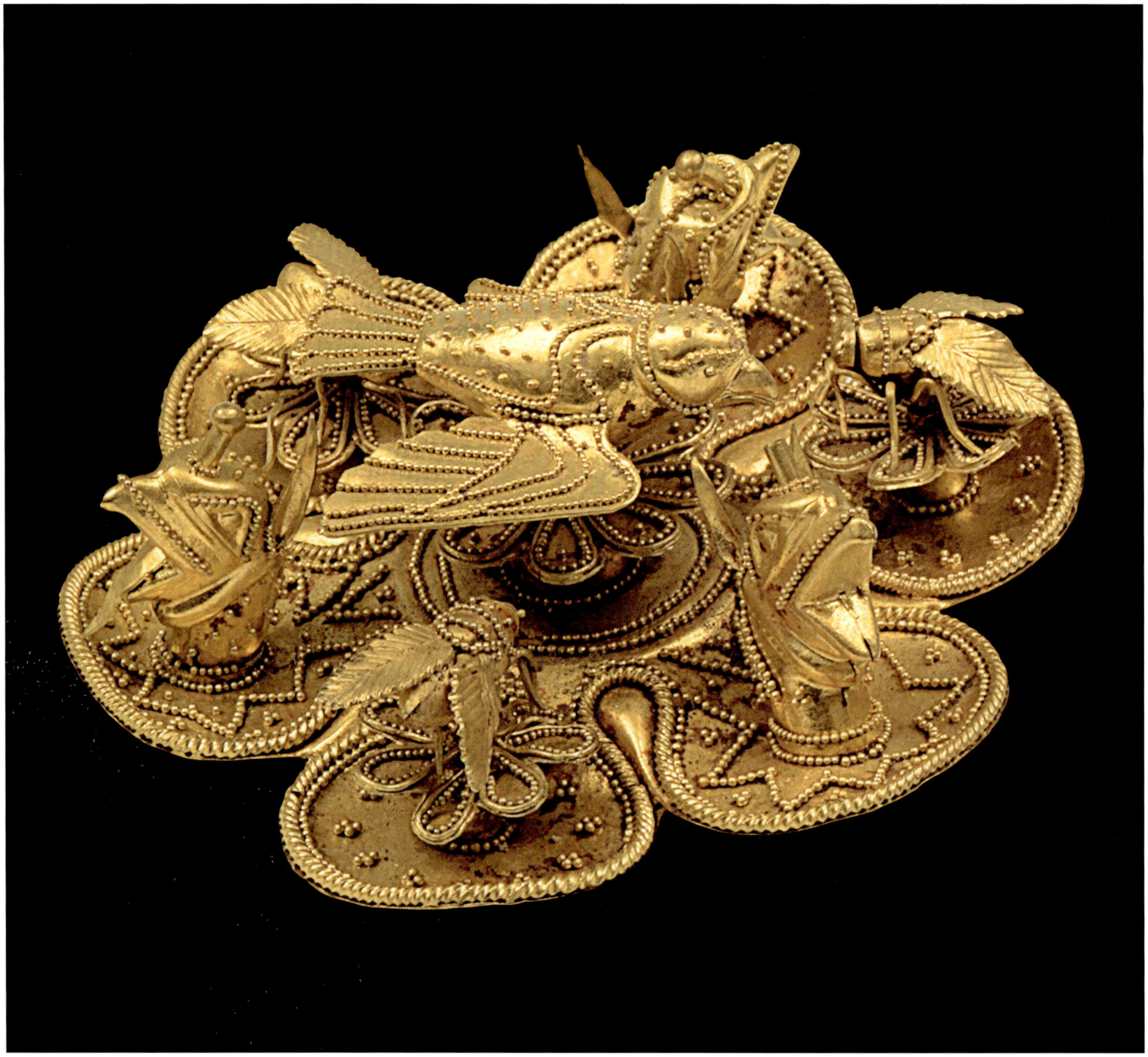

Plate 8

Rosette with winged animals, ca. 650 BC. Gold, Diam: 4.6 cm

Plate 9 (opposite)

Phiale (libation bowl), dedicated by the sons of Kypselos, ca. 625 BC. Gold, H: 15 cm; Diam: 16.8 cm; Wt: 835.5 grams

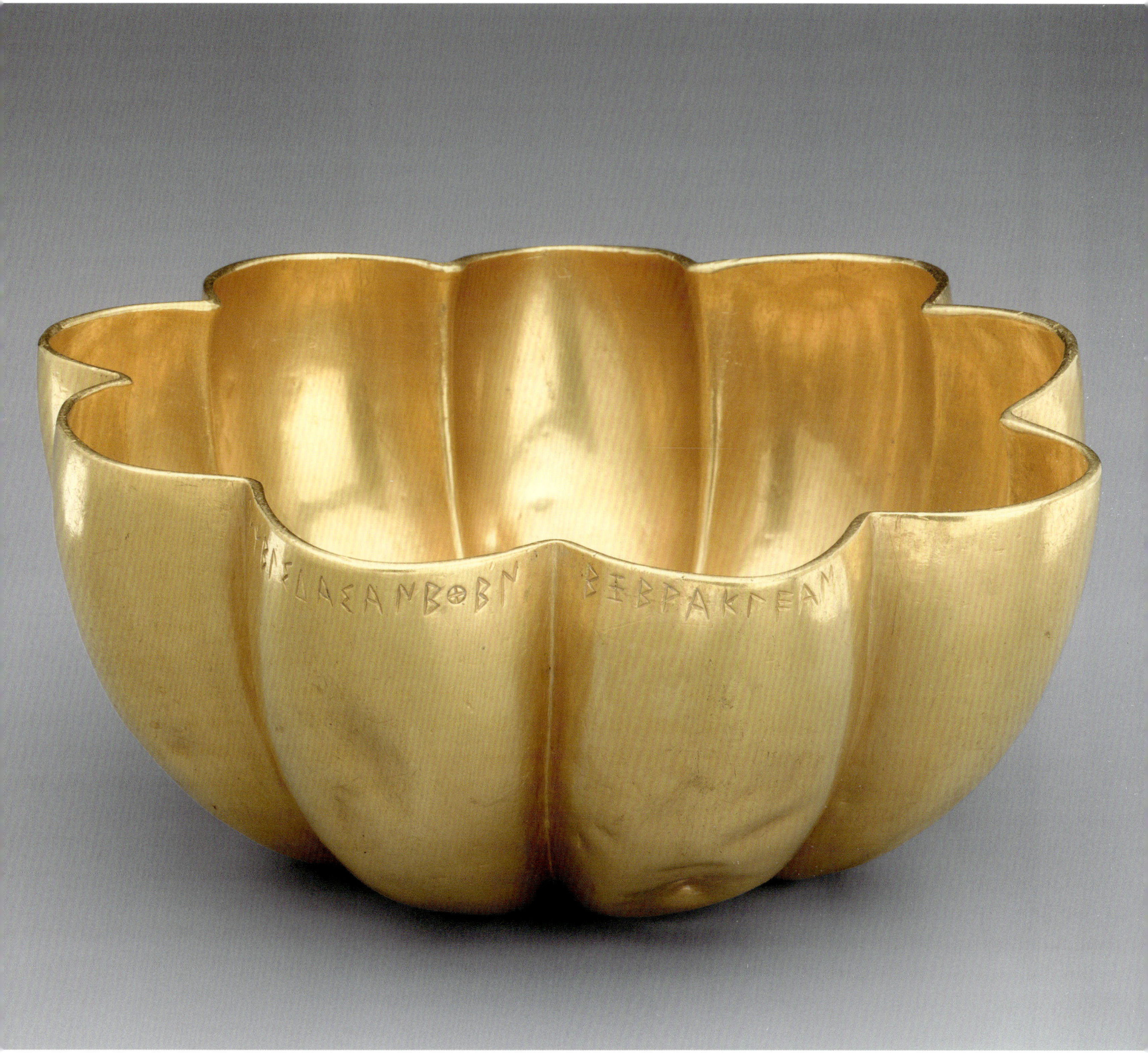

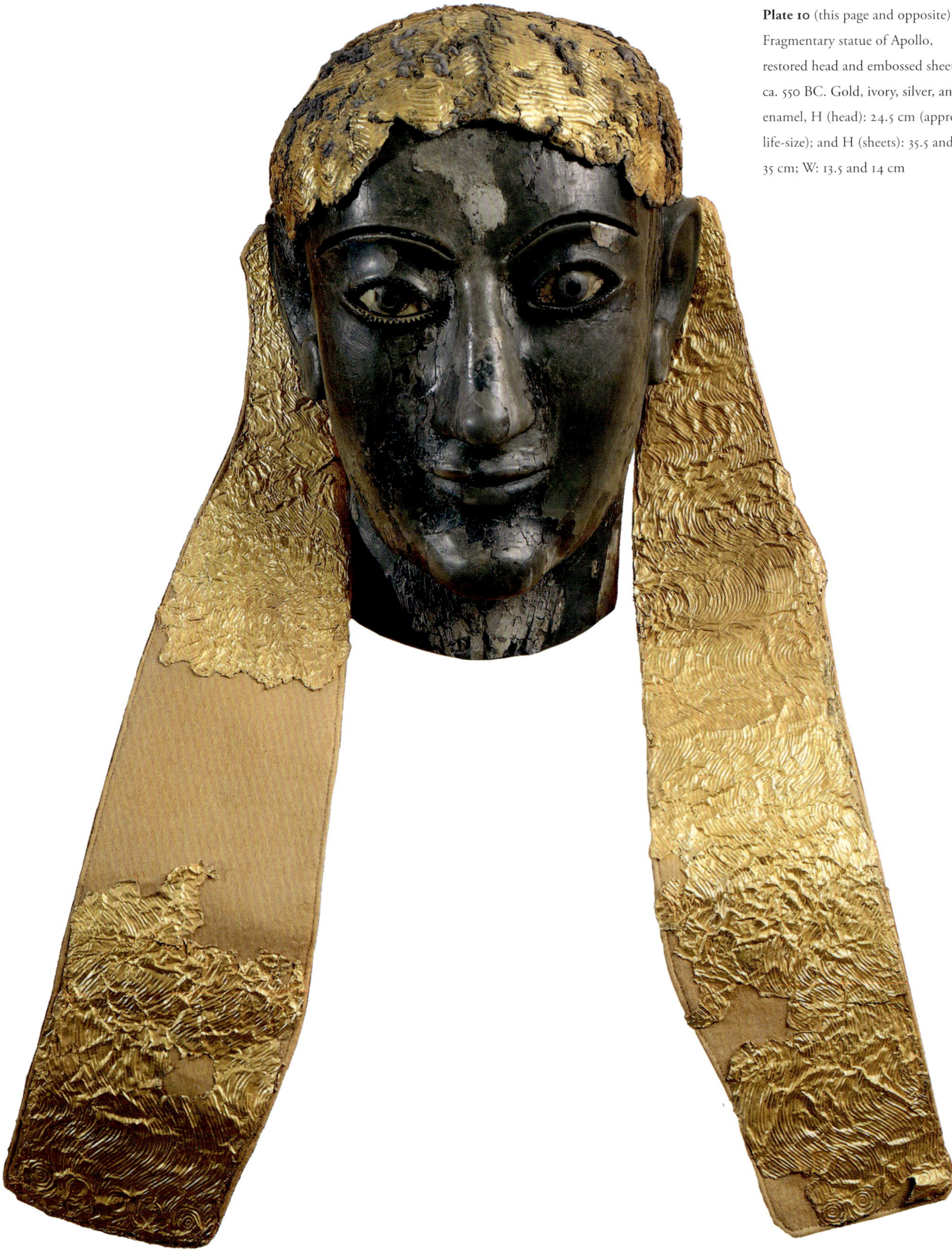

Plate 10 (this page and opposite) Fragmentary statue of Apollo, restored head and embossed sheets, ca. 550 BC. Gold, ivory, silver, and enamel, H (head): 24.5 cm (approx. life-size); and H (sheets): 35.5 and 35 cm; W: 13.5 and 14 cm

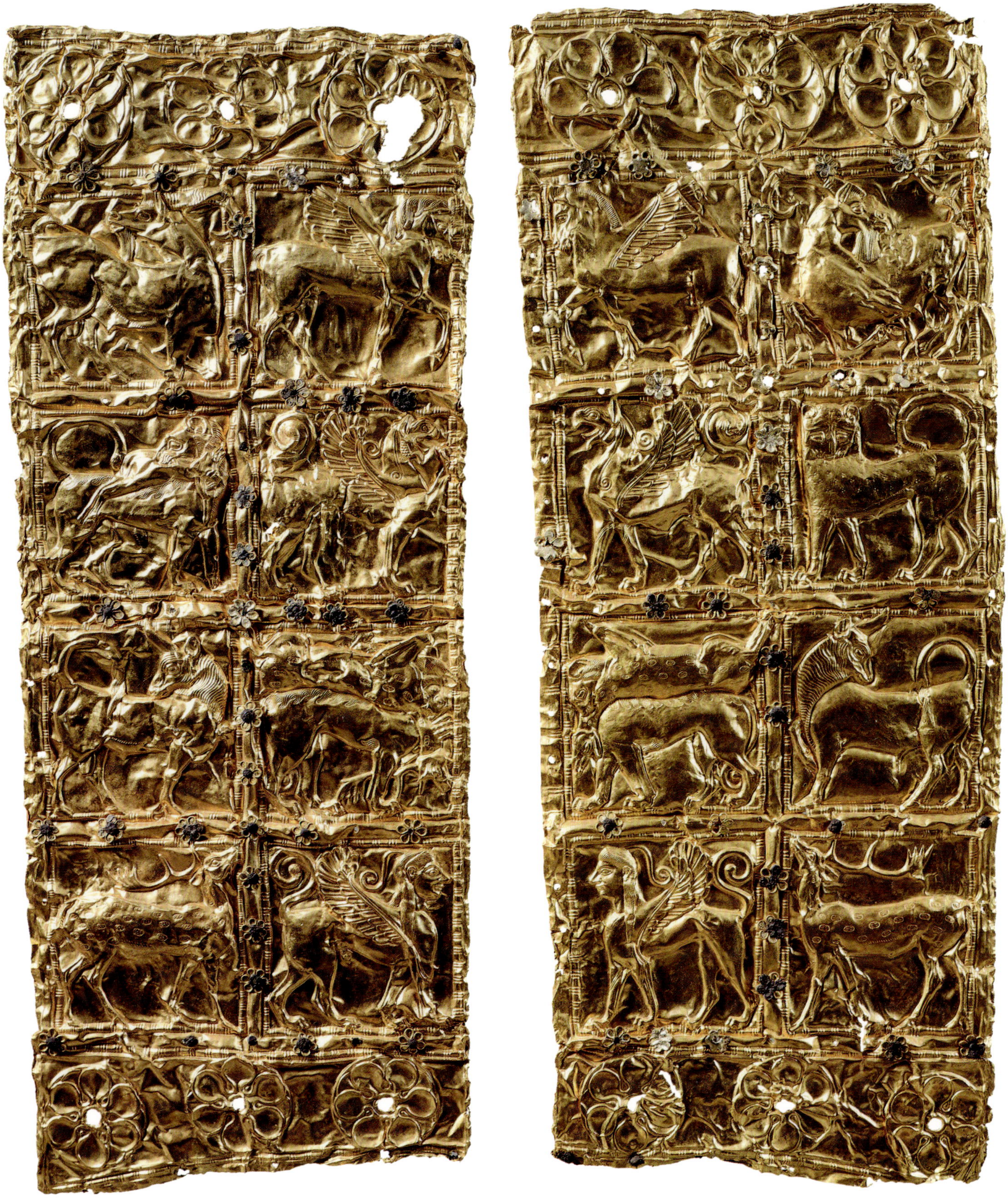

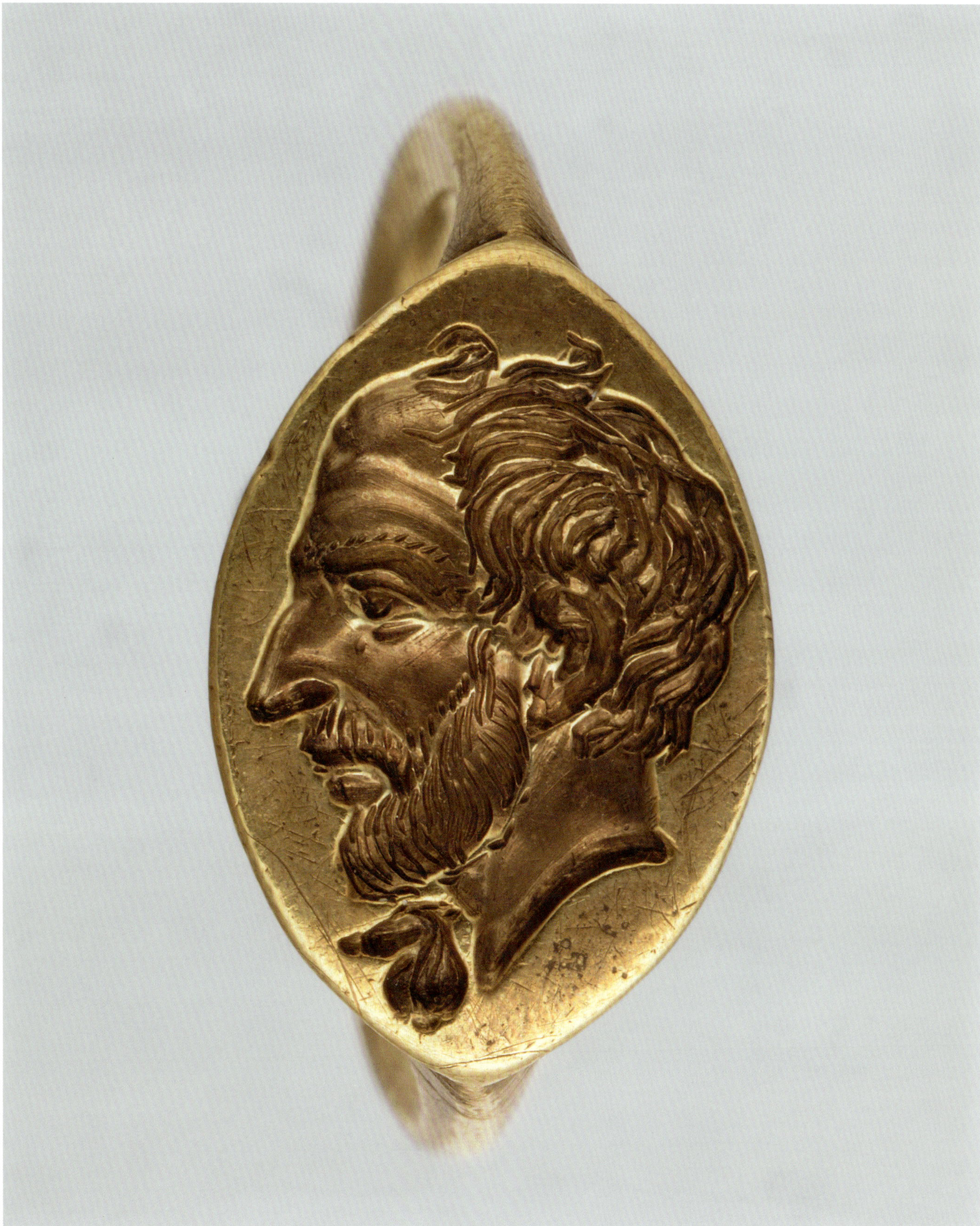

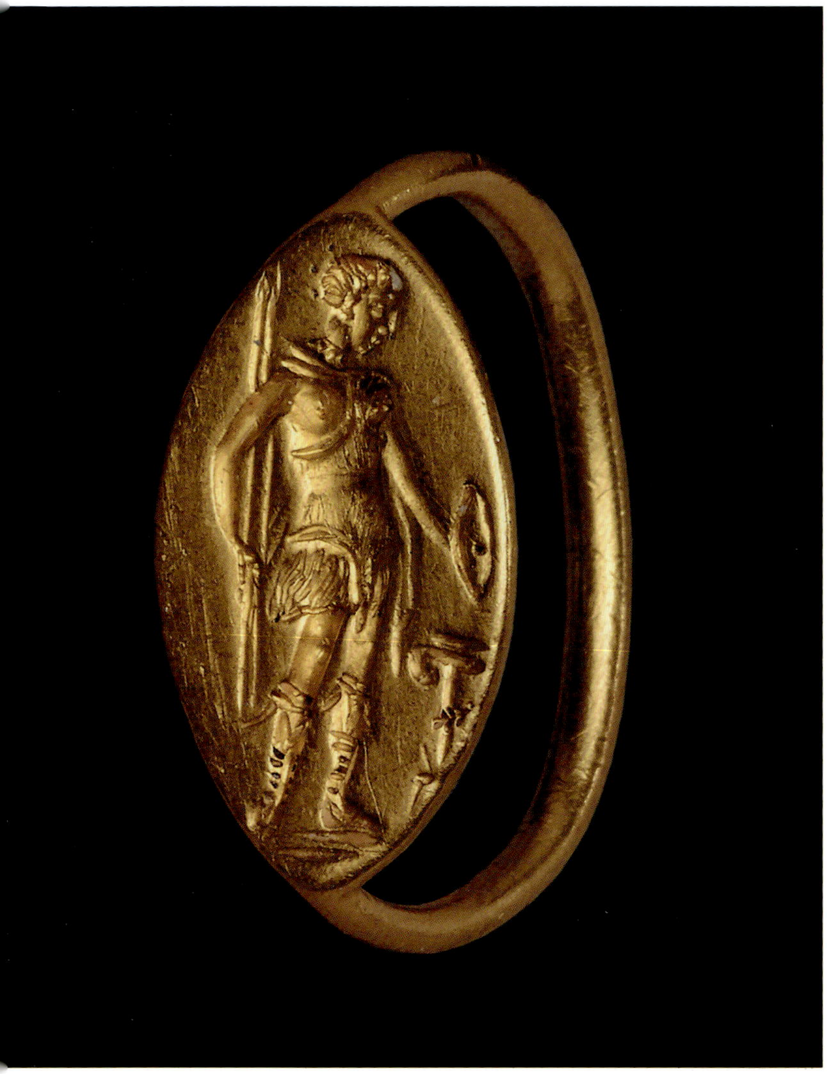

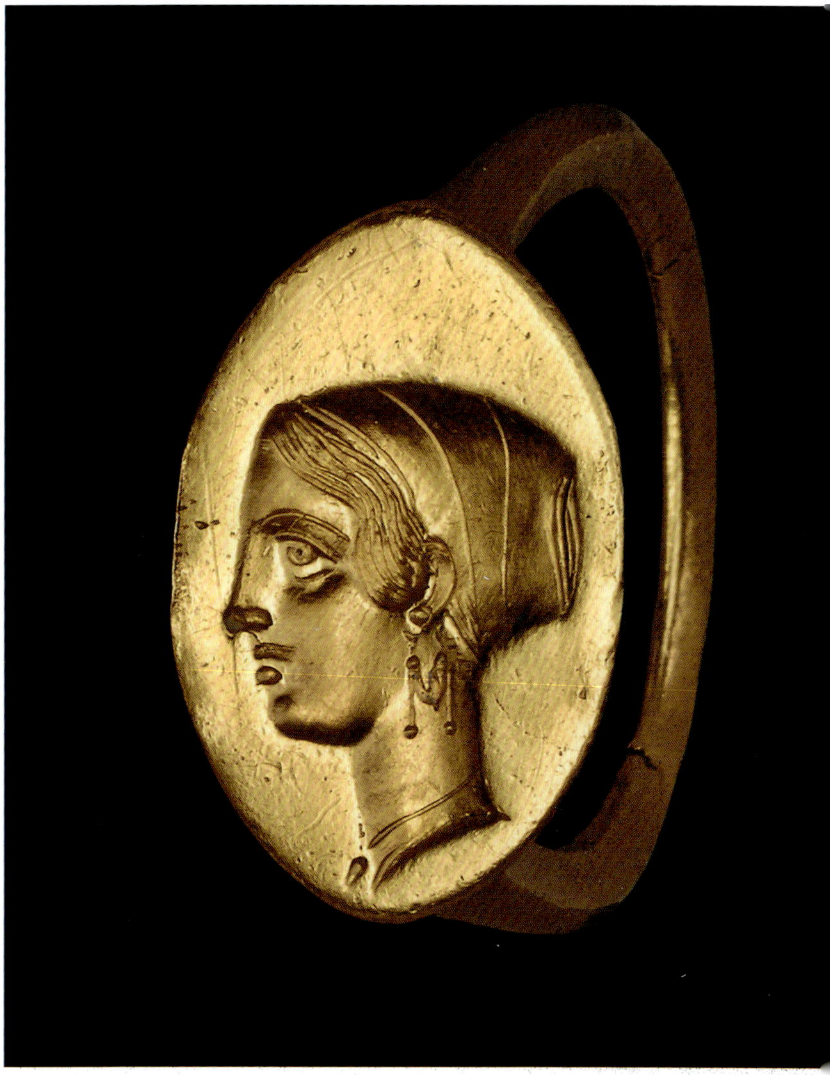

Plate 11 (opposite)
Ring with bearded man and phallos,
ca. 440–430 BC. Electrum,
H (bezel): 1.7 cm; Wt: 5.9 grams

Plate 12
Ring with Artemis pouring a libation,
ca. 450–425 BC. Gold, H: 1.8 cm;
Wt: 4 grams

Plate 13
Ring with head of a woman,
ca. 400–350 BC. Gold, H (bezel):
1.9 cm; Wt: 8.9 grams

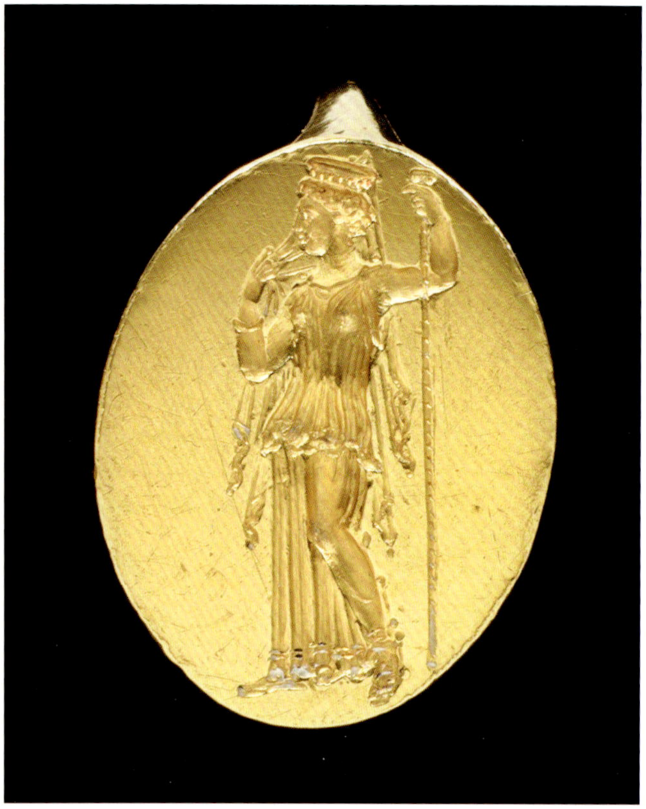

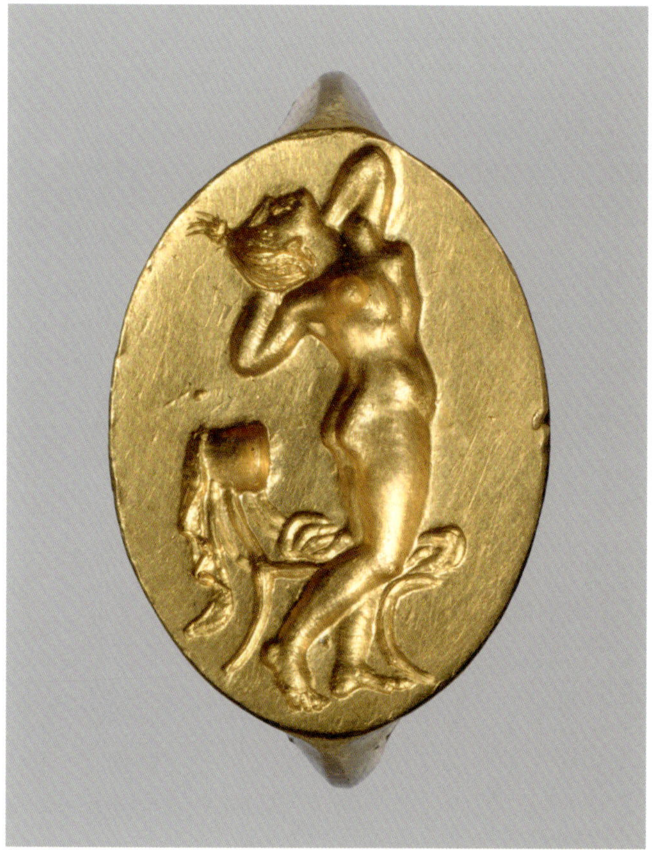

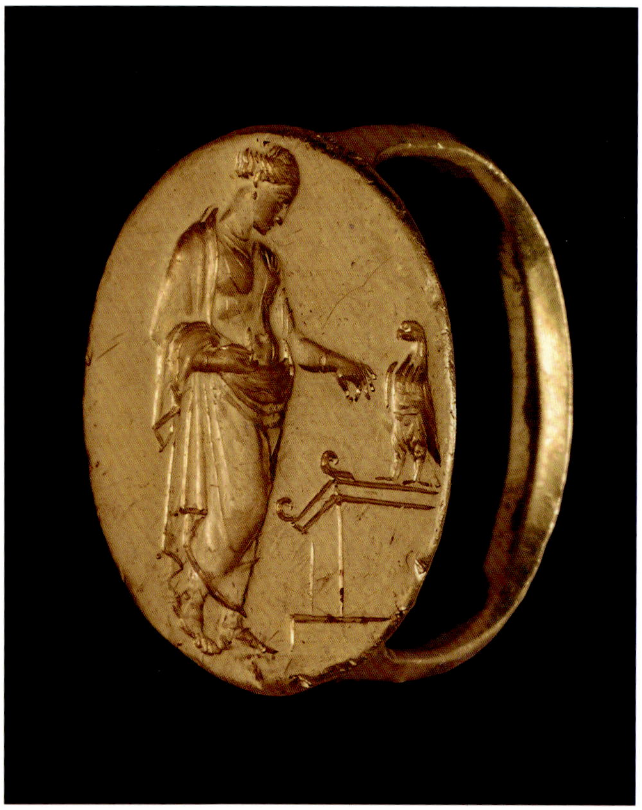

Plate 14 (top, left)
Ring with a goddess, ca. 400–300 BC. Gold, H: 2.2 cm: Wt: 15 grams

Plate 15 (left)
Ring with woman and eagle on altar, ca. 350 BC. Gold, L (bezel): 2 cm; Wt: 11.3 grams

Plate 16 (above right)
Ring with nude woman, ca. 400–380 BC. Gold, H (bezel): 2 cm; Wt: 15.8 grams

Plate 17 (opposite)
Ring with the *Erotostasia*, ca. 350 BC. Gold, H (bezel): 2.2 cm; W (bezel): 1.7 cm; Wt: 12 grams

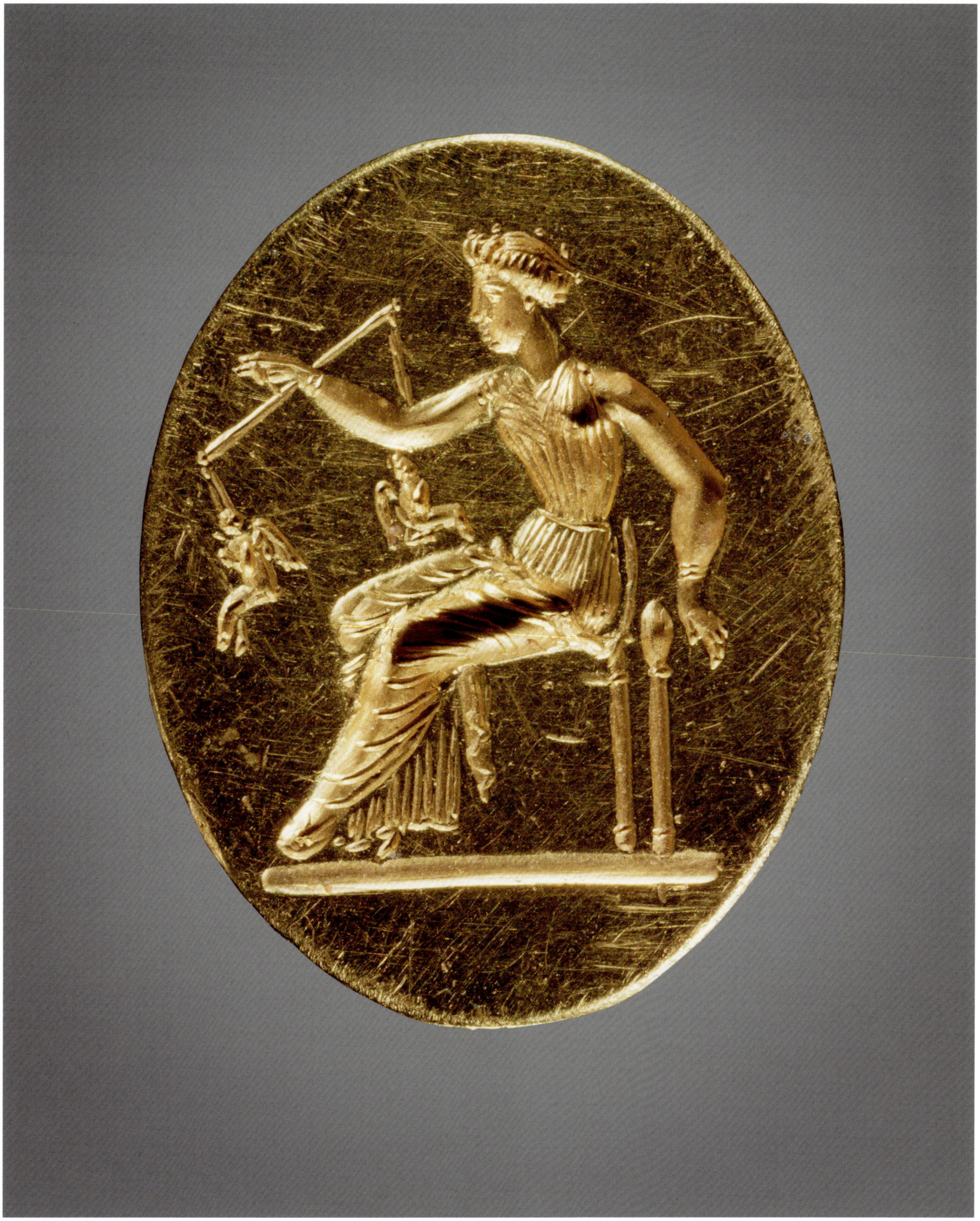

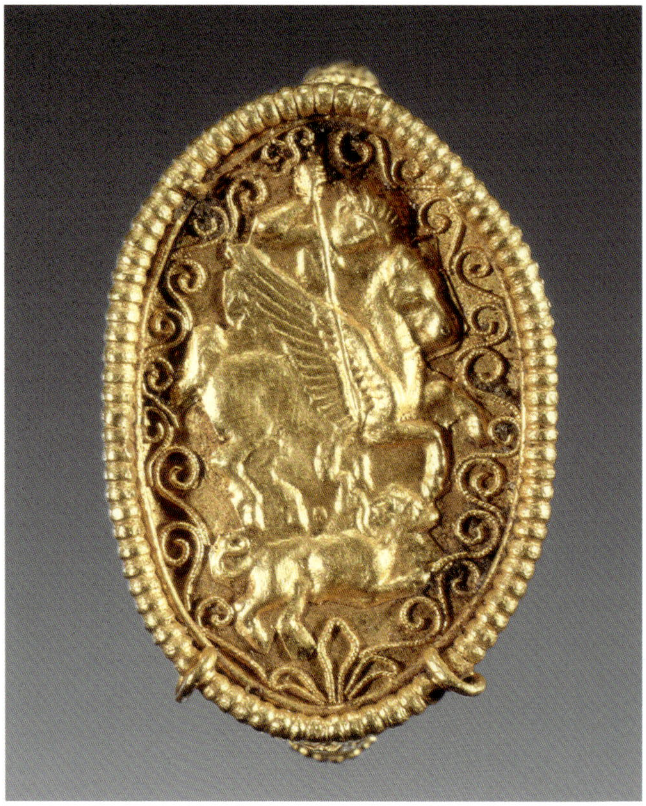

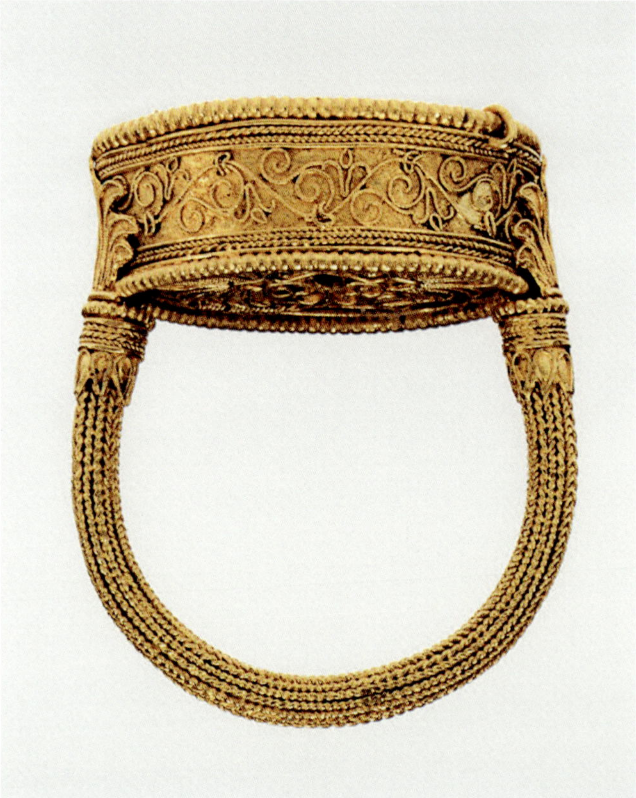

Plate 18 (two views)
Ring with Bellerophon, Pegasos, and the Chimaira, ca. 350–300 BC. Gold, H (bezel): 2 cm; W (bezel): 1.4 cm; D (box): 0.8 cm; Wt: 8 grams

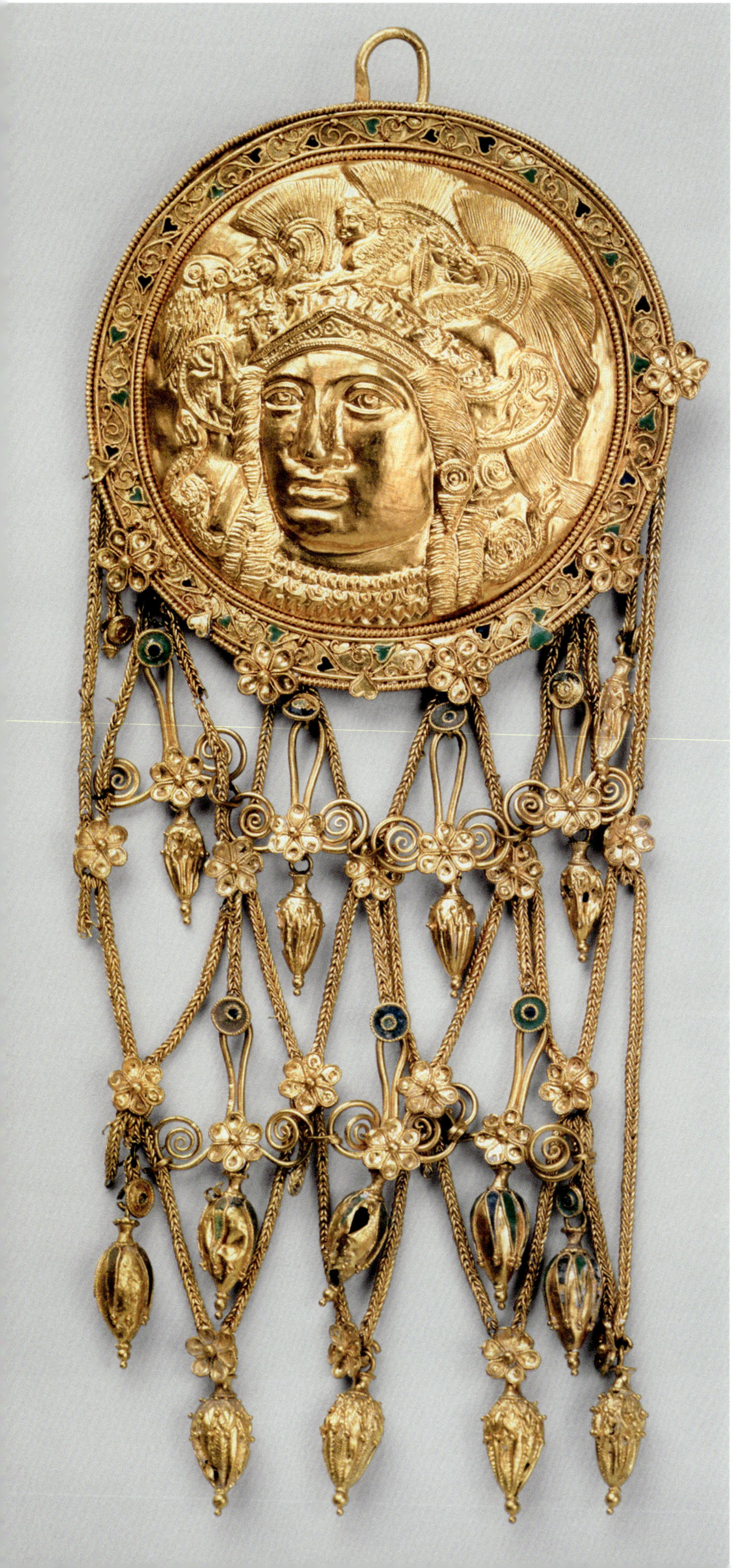

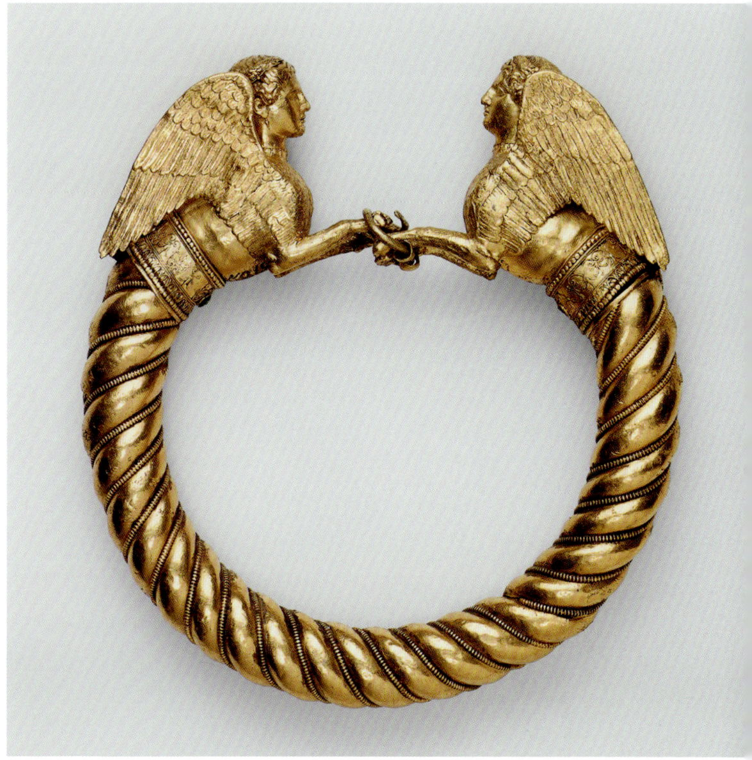

Plate 19

Pendant disk with head of *Athena Parthenos*, ca. 400–350 BC. Gold and enamel, H: 18.5 cm; Diam: 7.2 cm; Wt: 85.3 grams

Plate 20

Bracelet with sphinxes, ca. 400–350 BC. Gold and enamel, H: 11.5 cm; W: 10 cm; Wt: 176.2 grams

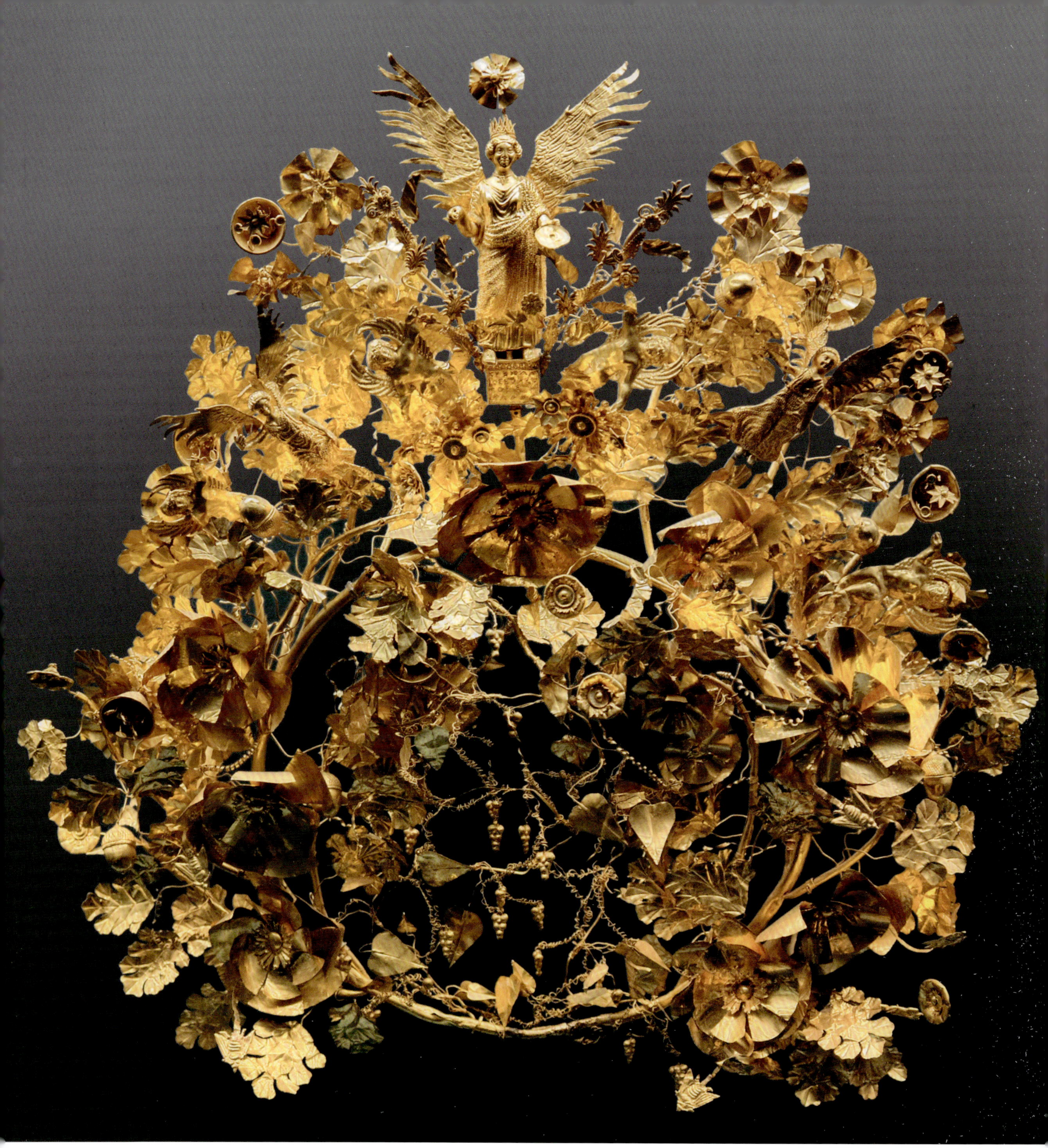

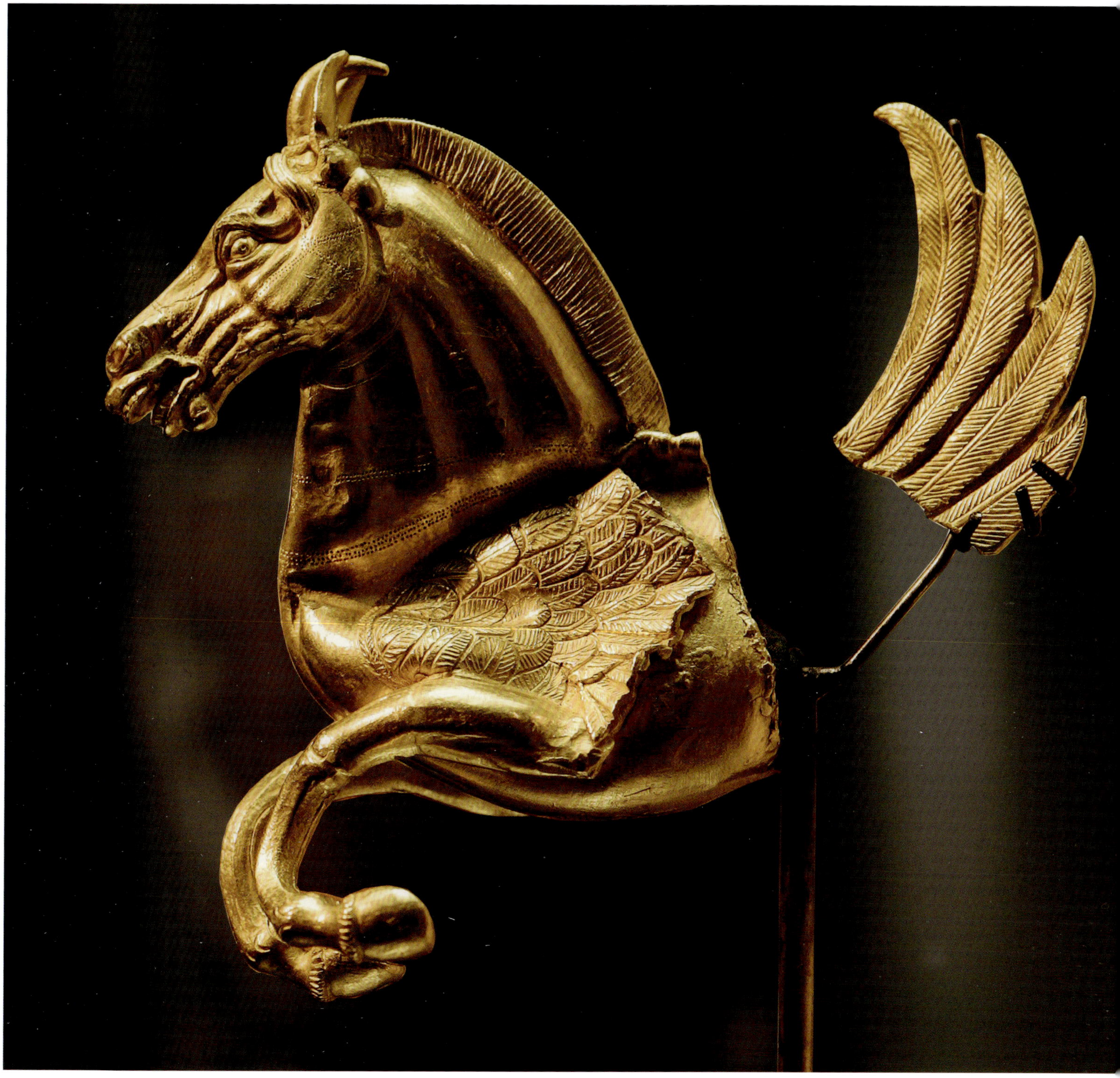

Plate 21 (opposite)
Wreath with Nikai and Erotes, dedicated by Kreithonios, ca. 350–300 BC. Gold, H: 37 cm; Diam: 19 cm

Plate 22
Pegasos protome, ca. 350 BC. Gold, H: 14.8 cm; Wt: 475.5 grams

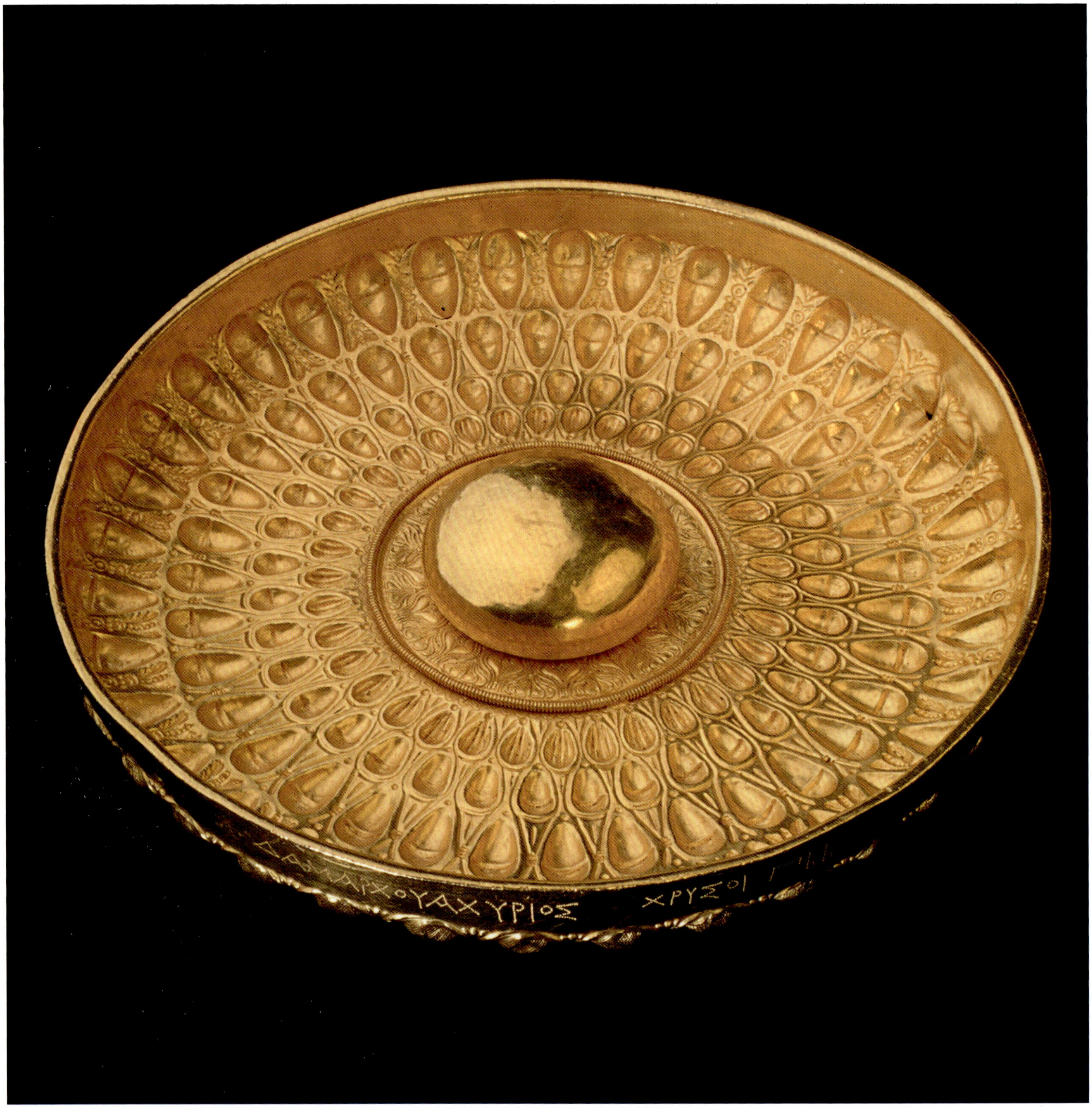

Plate 23

Phiale (libation bowl) with acorns, beechnuts, and bees, dedicated by Demarchos, son of Achyris, ca. 325–275 BC. Gold, H: 3.7 cm; Diam: 22.8 cm; Wt: 982.4 grams

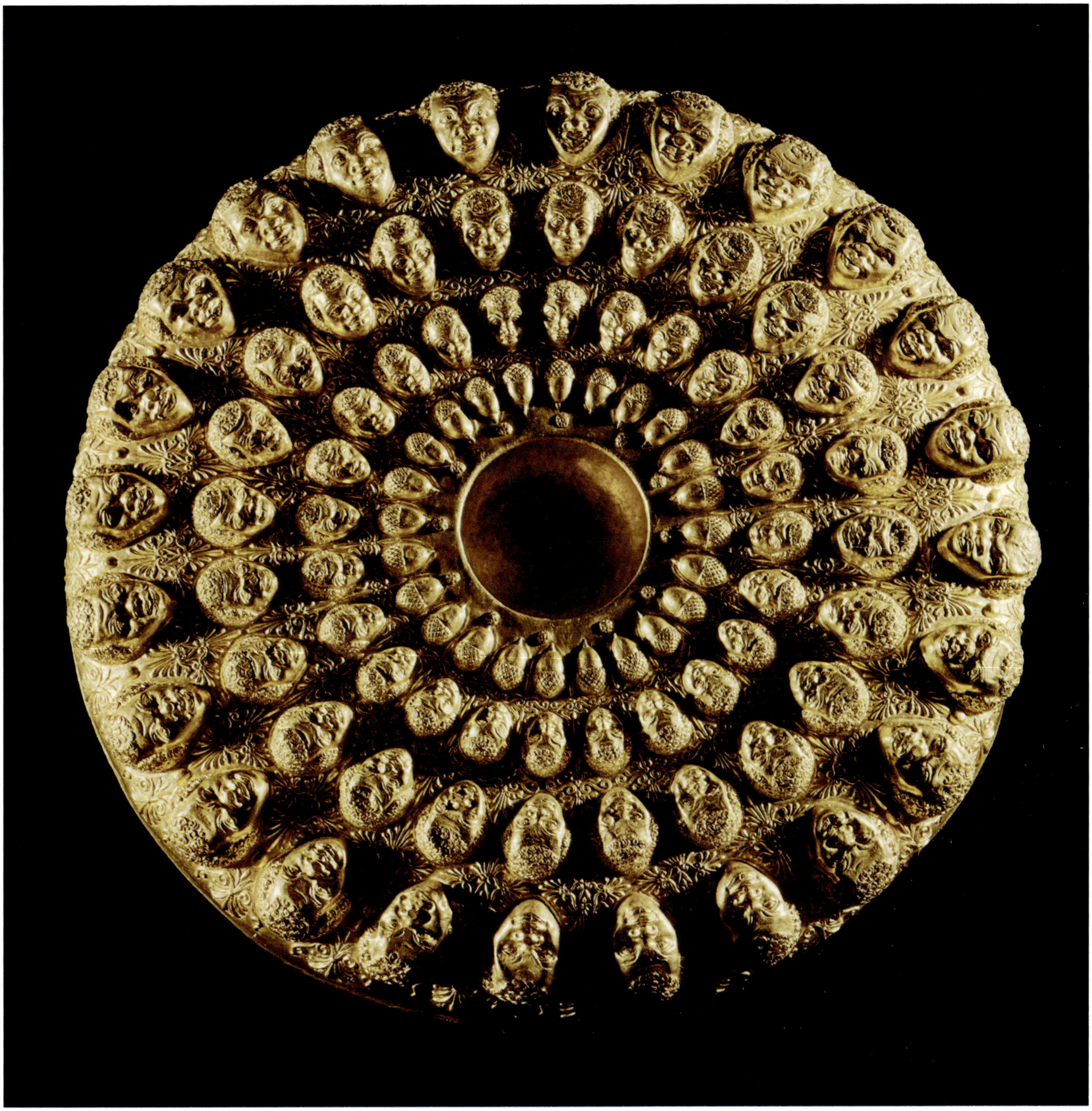

Plate 24

Phiale (libation bowl) with Ethiopians and acorns, ca. 325–275 BC. Gold, H: 3.5 cm; Diam: 25 cm; Wt: 845.7 grams

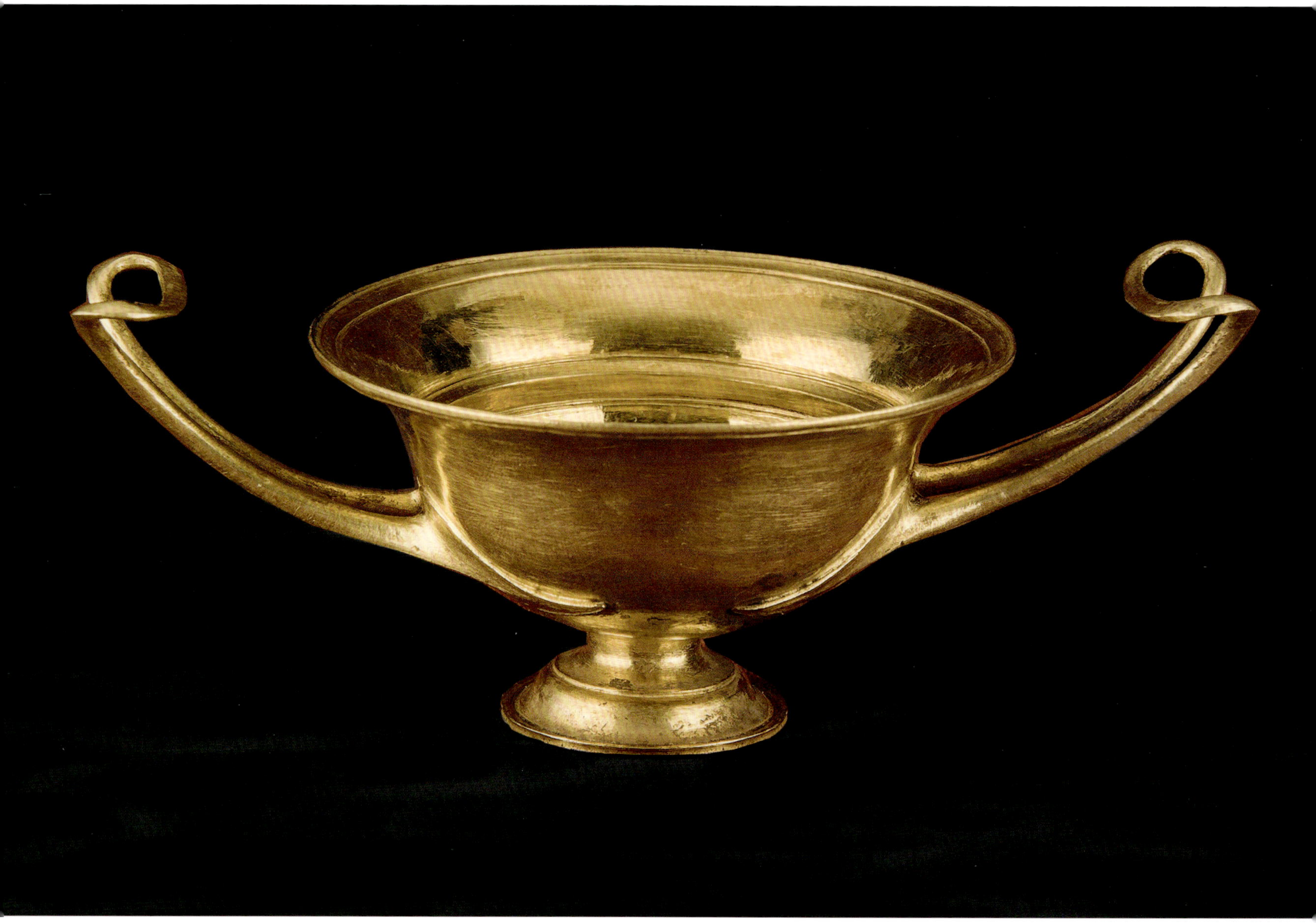

Plate 25
Kylix, ca. 350–300 BC. Gold, H: 5.9 cm; Diam: 9.5 cm; Wt: 228 grams

Plate 26 (opposite)
Necklace, ca. 330–300 BC. Gold and enamel, L: 37.8 cm; H: 6 cm; Wt: 241.7 grams

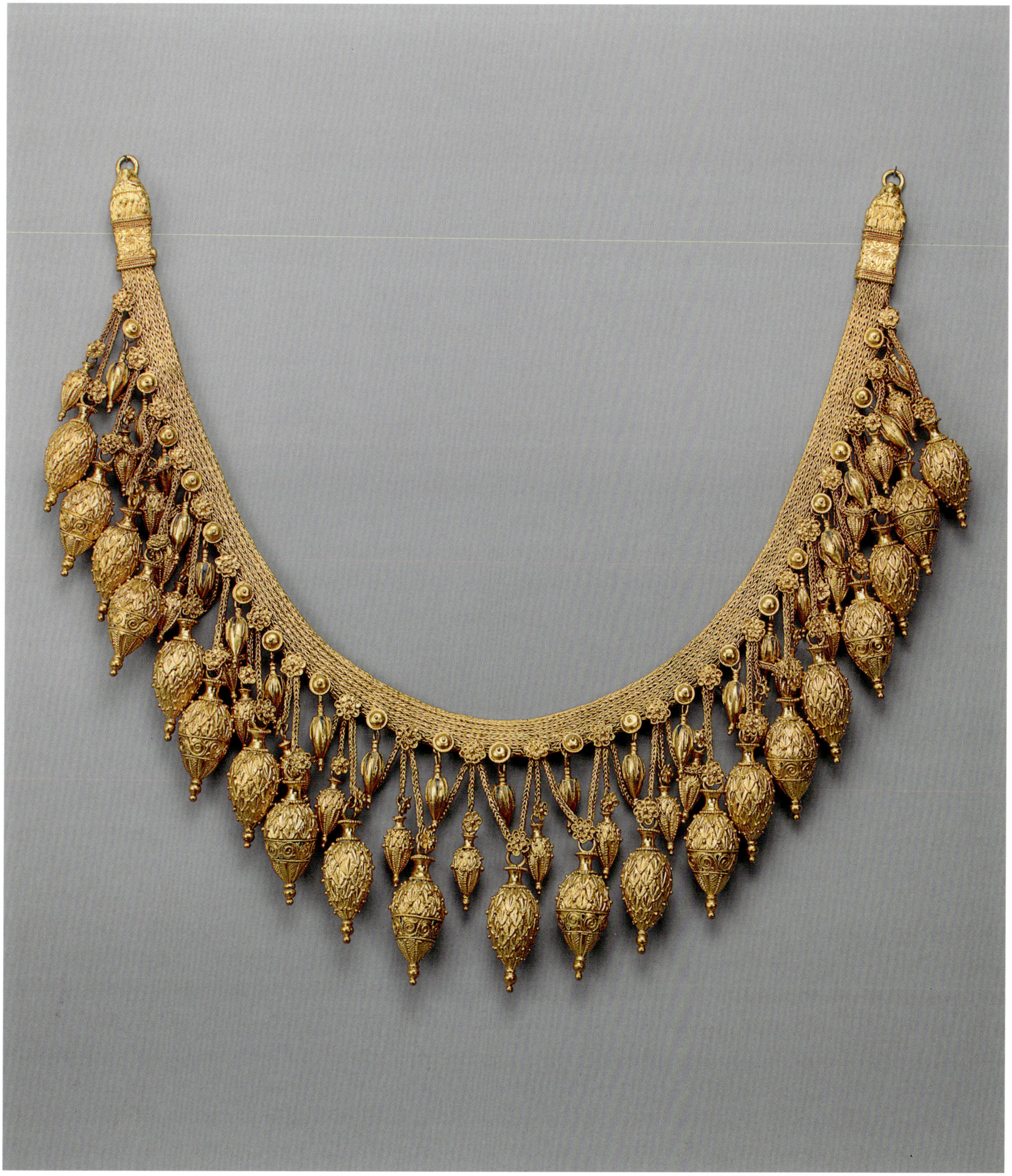

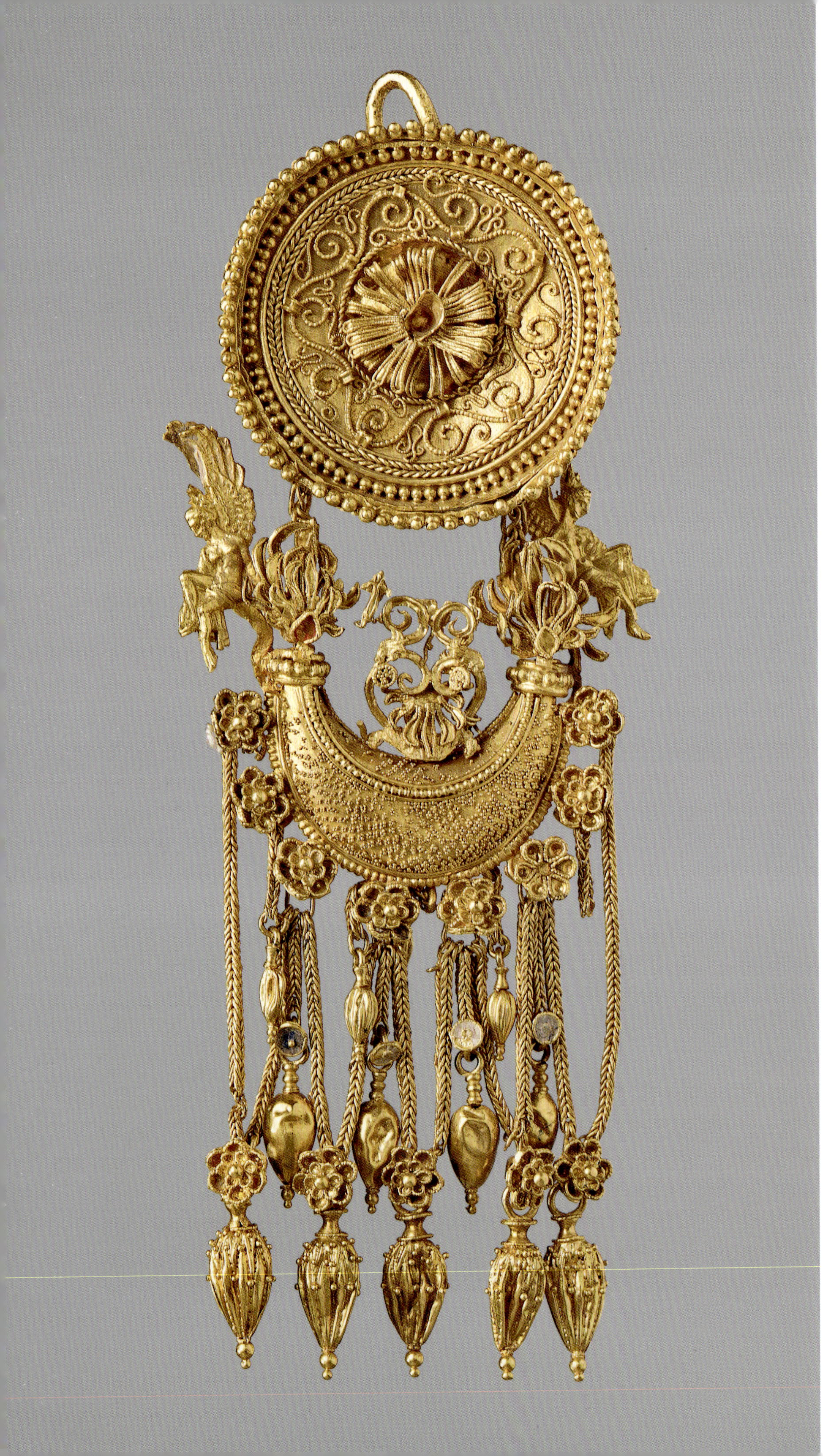

Plate 27
Earring with Nikai, ca. 350 BC. Gold, cinnabar, and enamel, H: 9 cm; Diam (disk): 2.8 cm; Wt: 23.4 grams

Plate 28 (opposite top)
Pair of earrings with Artemis, ca. 375–300 BC. Gold, H: 4.4 and 4.6 cm; W (each): 2.5 cm; Wt (each): 8.6 grams

Plate 29 (opposite bottom)
Pair of earrings with Ganymede and the Eagle of Zeus, ca. 330–300 BC. Gold, H (each) : 6 cm; Wt: 15.1 and 16.5 grams

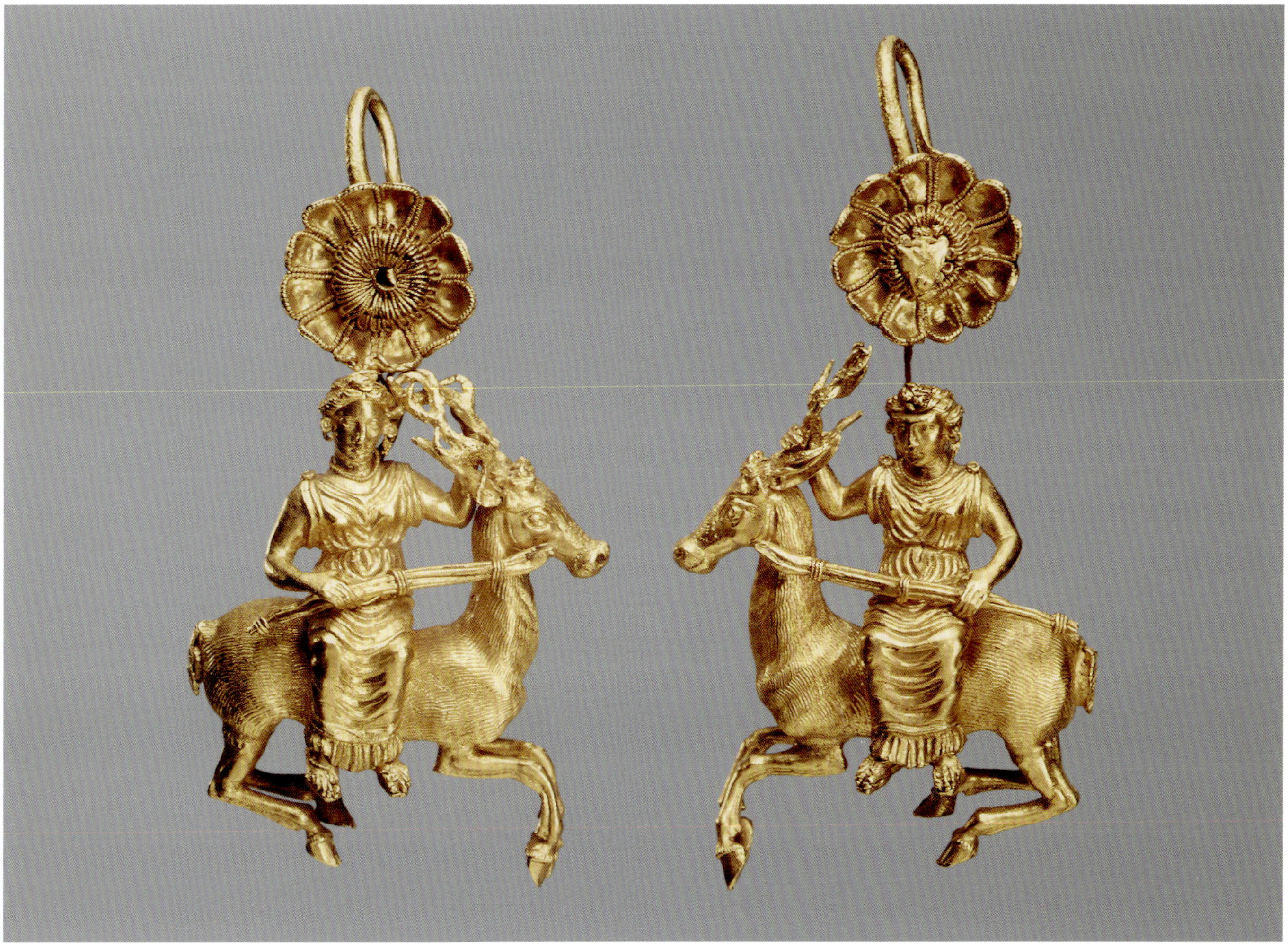

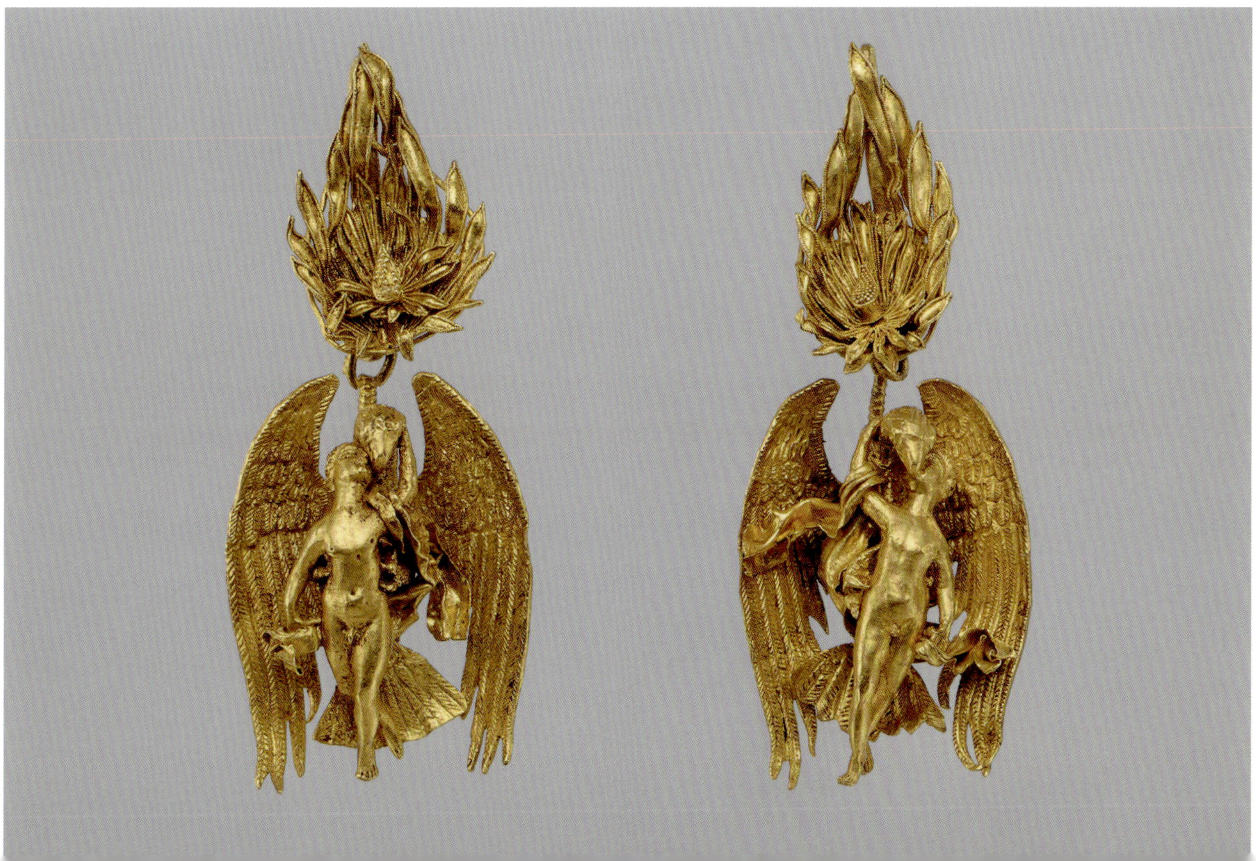

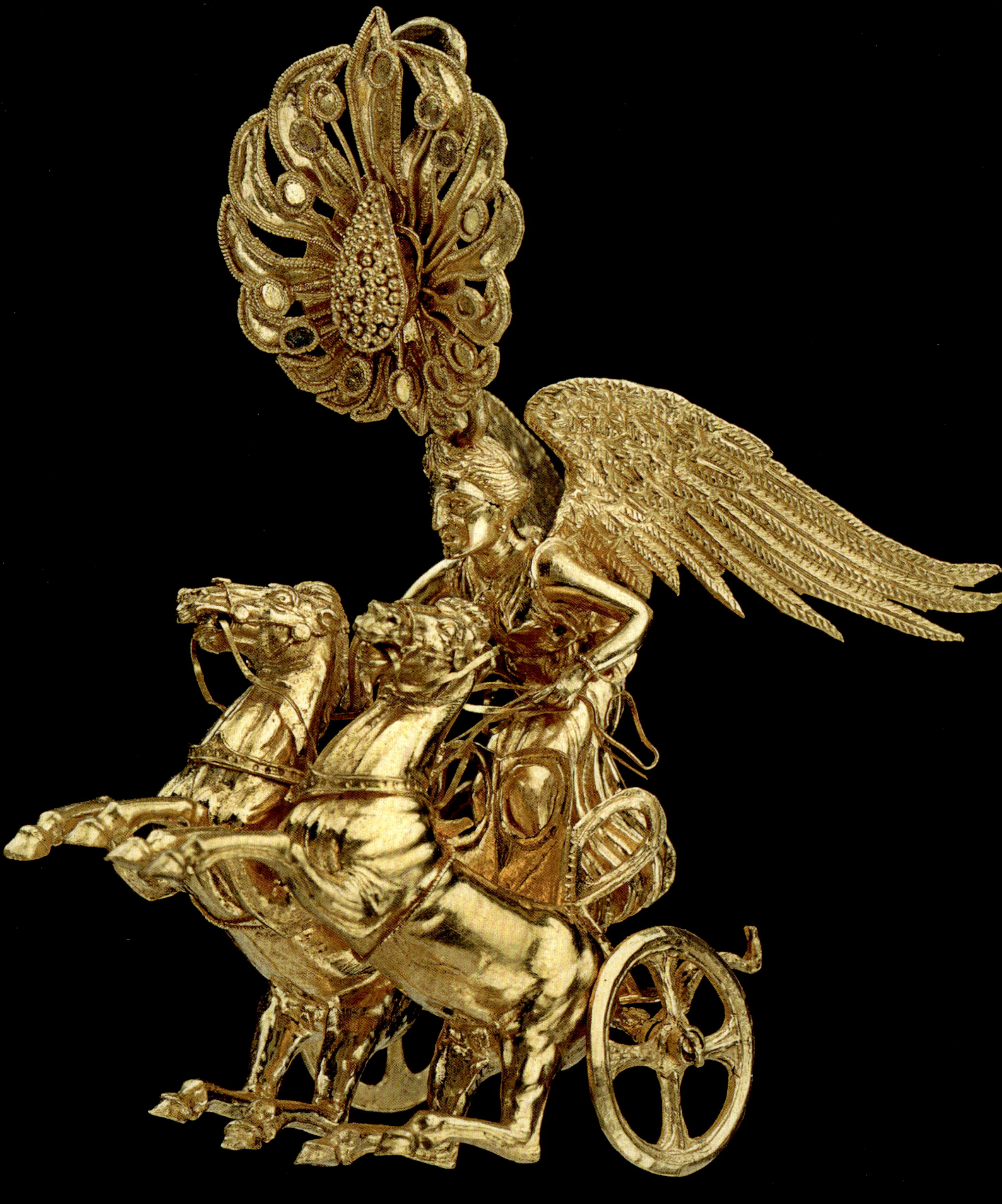

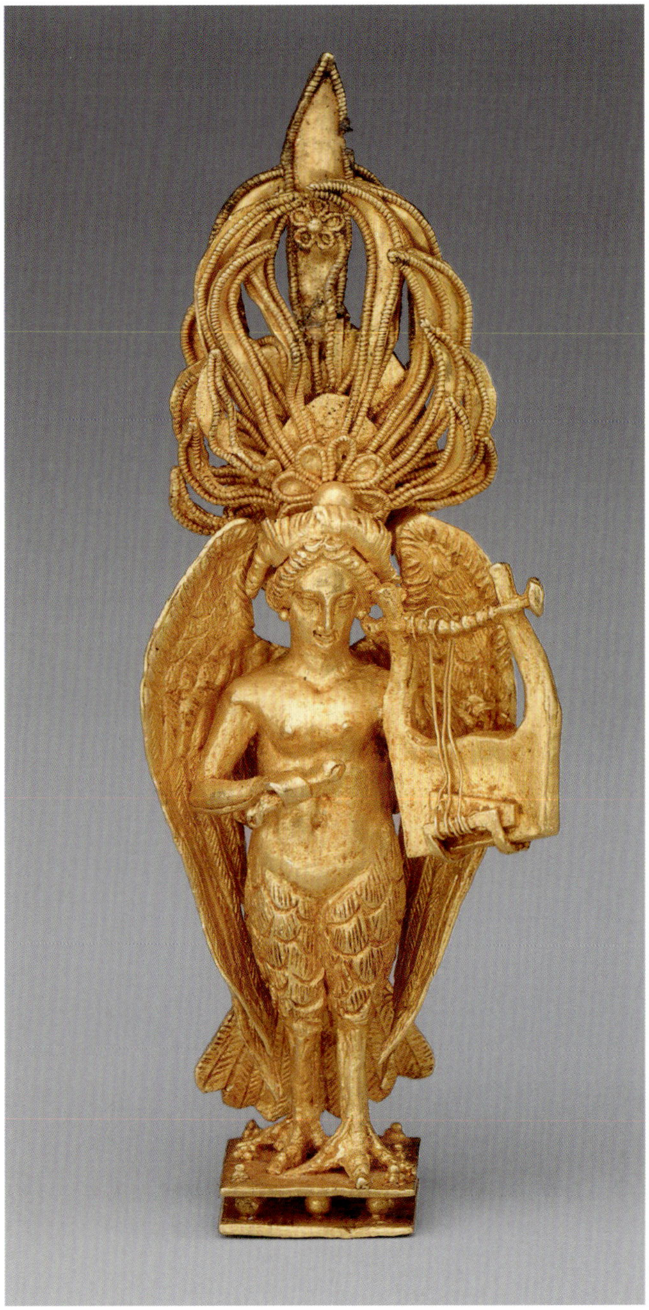

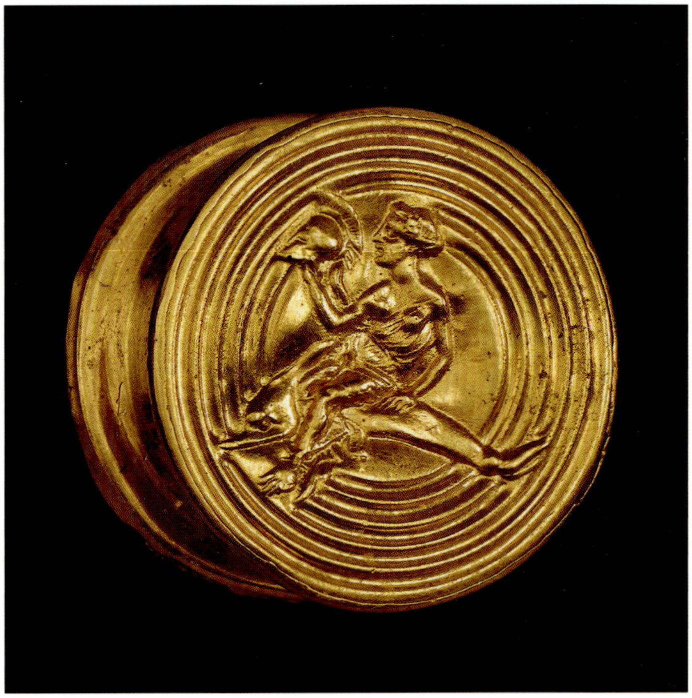

a

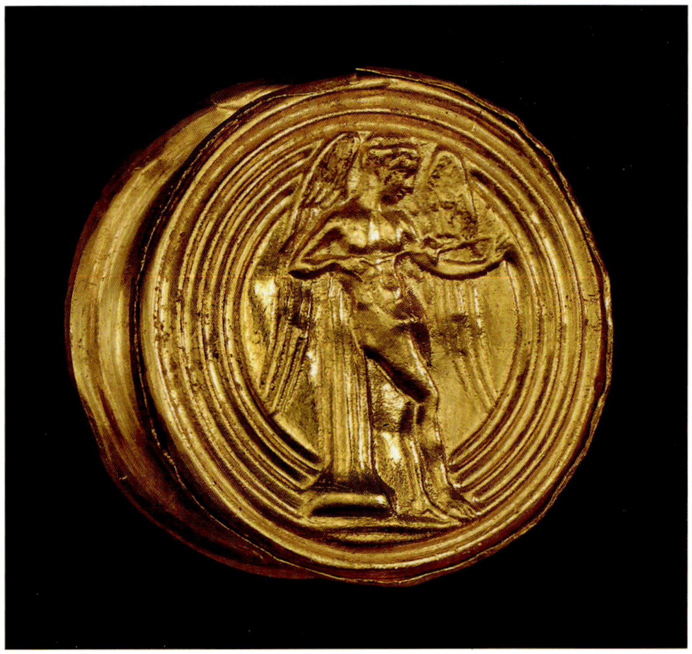

b

Plate 30 (opposite)
Earring with Nike driving a chariot, ca. 350–325 BC. Gold and enamel, H: 5 cm; Wt: 15.8 grams

Plate 31 (above)
Earring with Siren, ca. 330–300 BC. Gold, H: 4.4 cm; Wt: 7.3 grams

Plate 32 (two views)
Ear reel with Nereid and Eros, ca. 350–330 BC. Gold, Diam: 2.3 cm; D: 1.1 cm; Wt: 4.1 grams

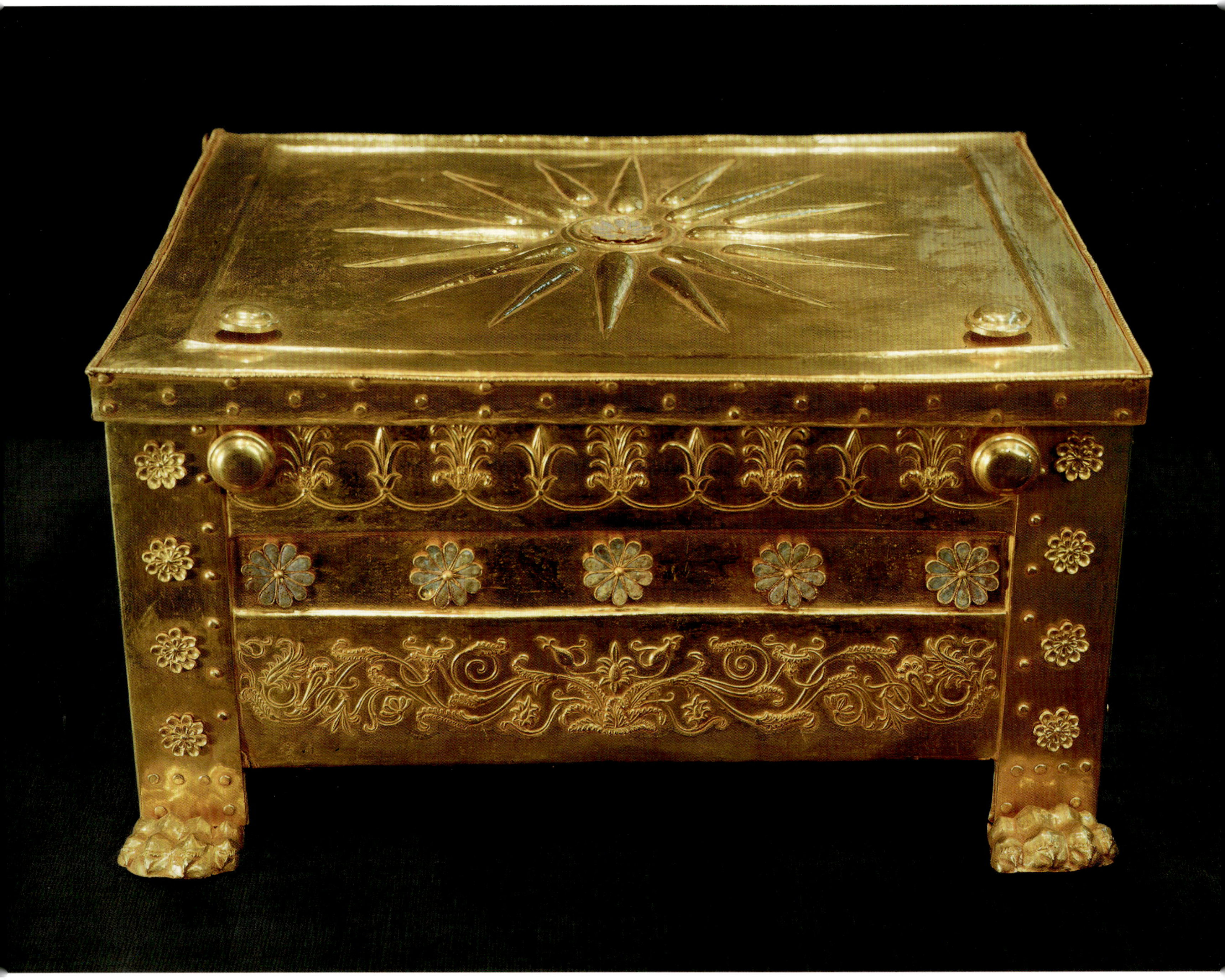

Plate 33
Larnax, ca. 336–316 BC. Gold and enamel, H: 20.7 cm; W: 41 cm; D: 34 cm; Wt: 7.790 kg

Plate 34 (opposite)
Gorgon appliqué, ca. 336–316 BC. Gold, H: 3.6 cm; W: 3.5 cm

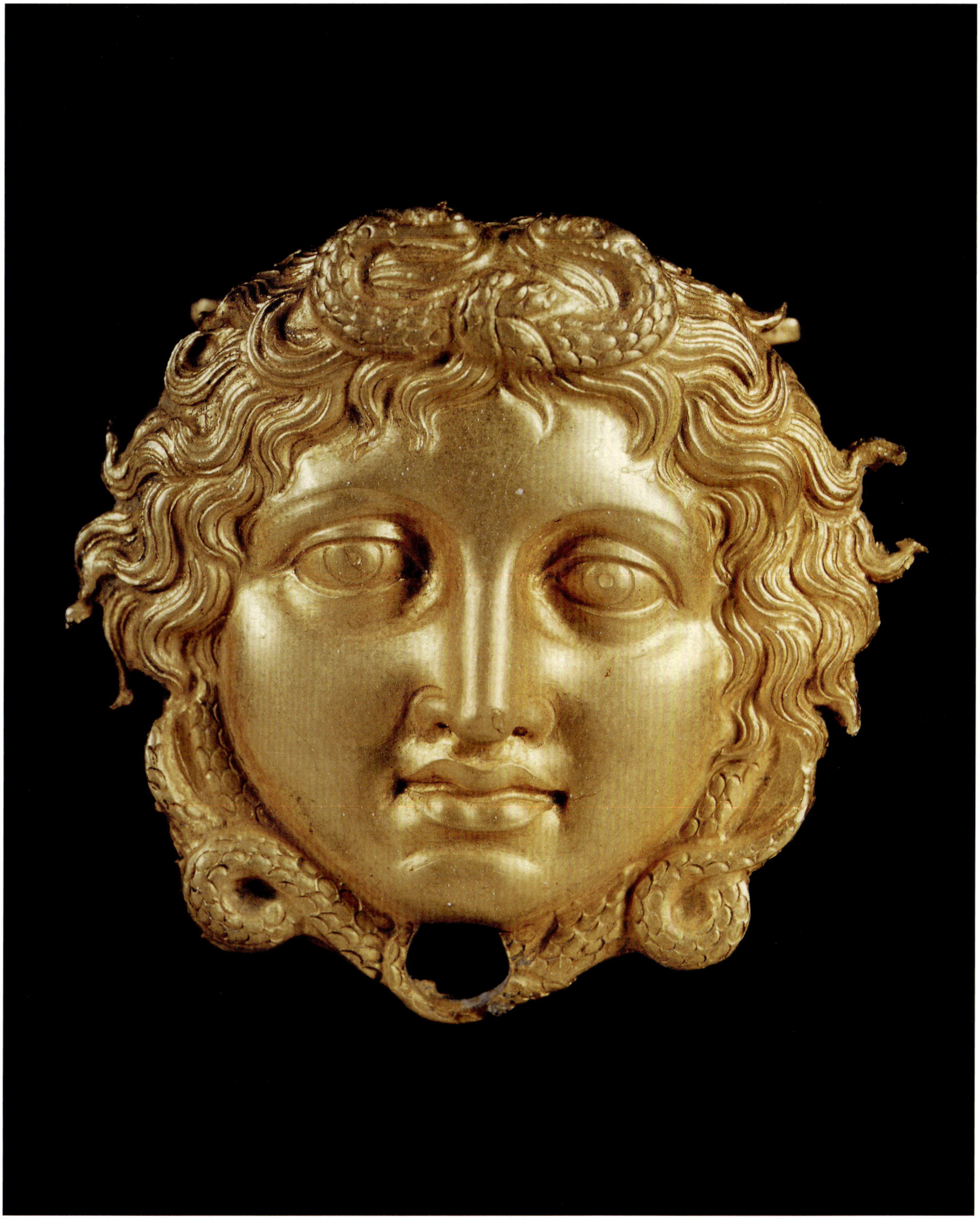

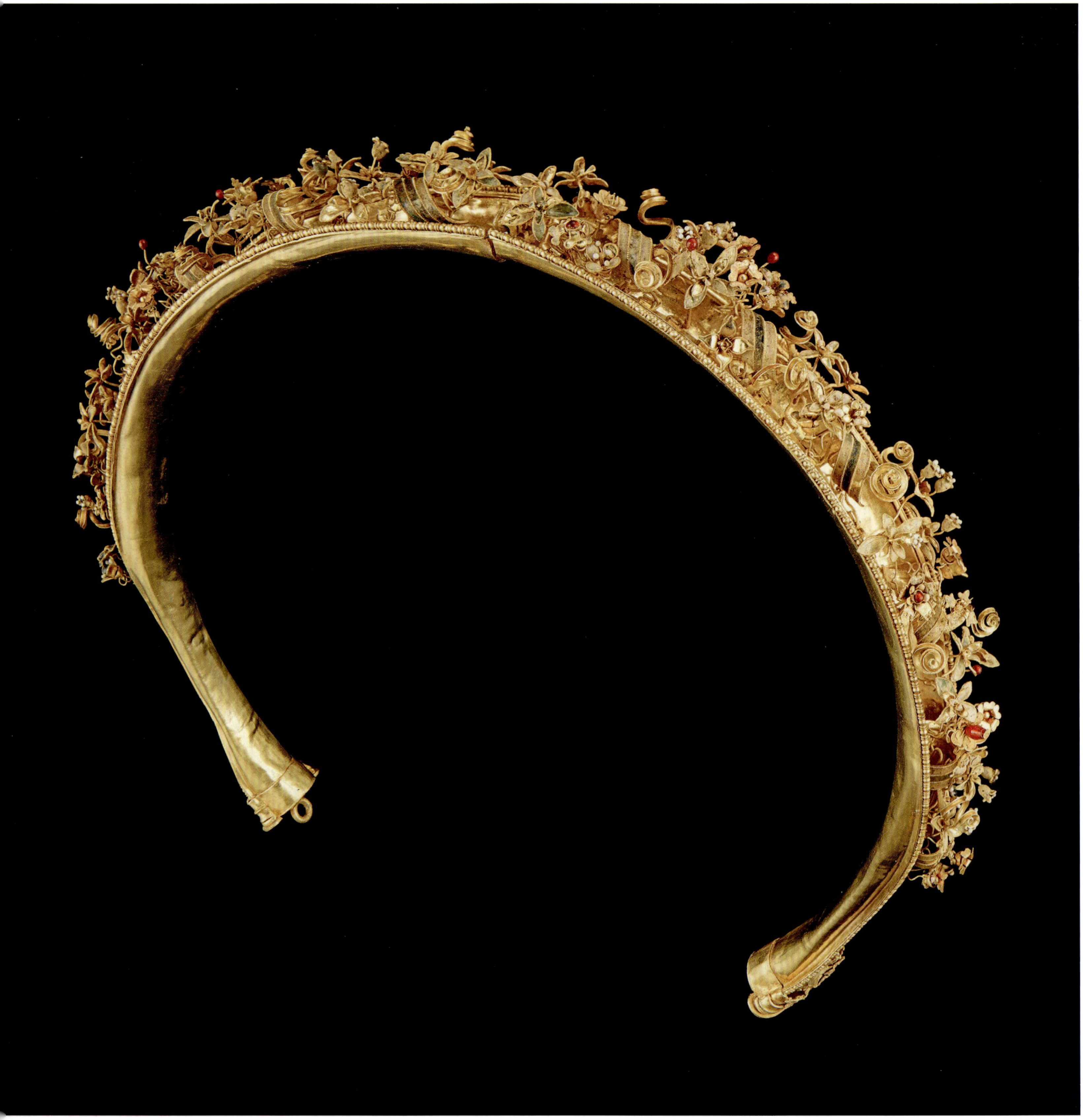

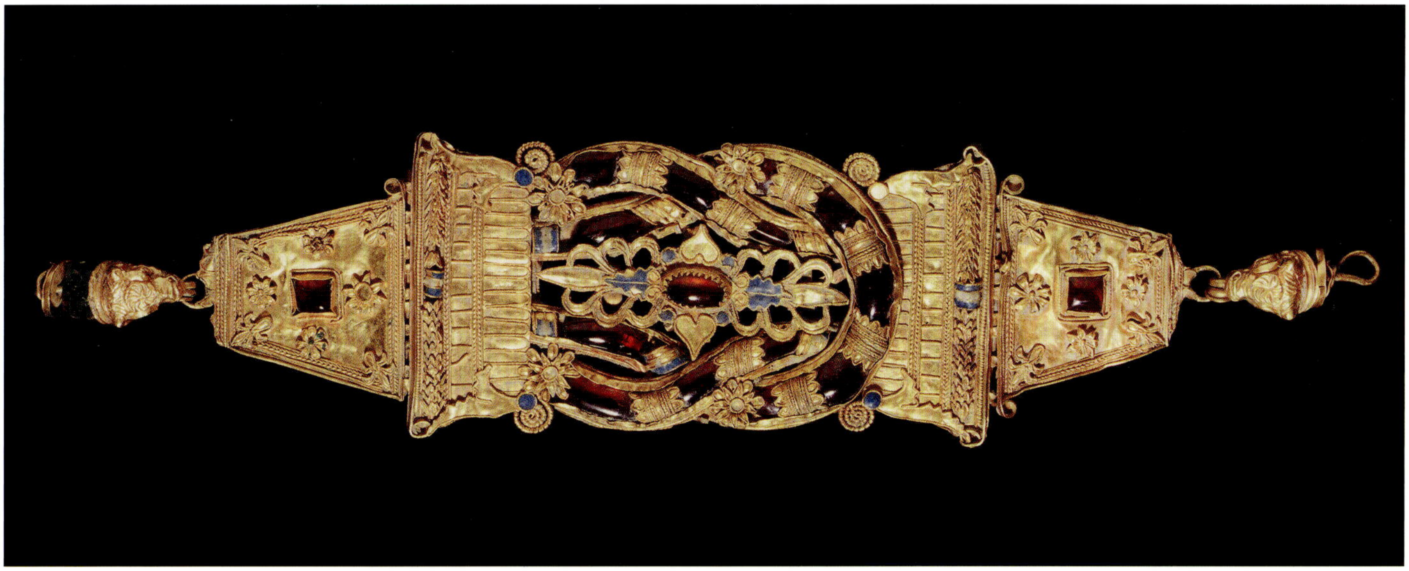

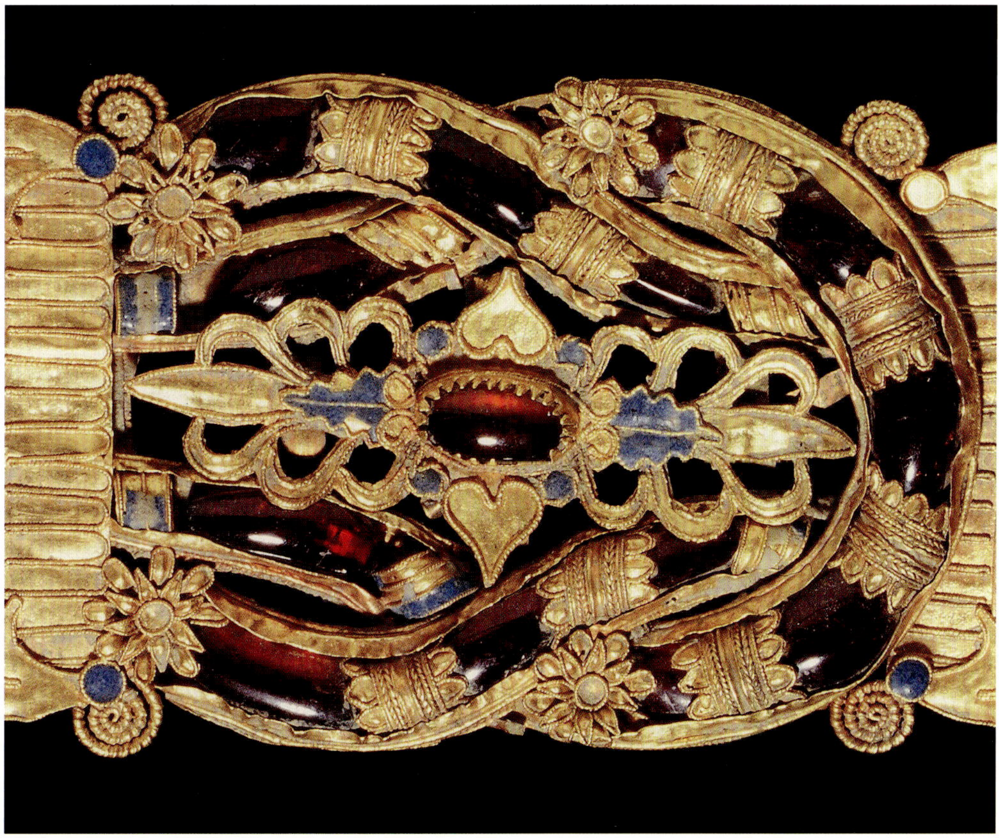

Plate 35 (opposite)
Diadem, ca. 200 BC. Gold, enamel, cornelian, and garnet, L: 47.2 cm; Wt: 145 grams

Plate 36
Diadem in the form of a Herakles knot, ca. 200 BC. Gold with garnet, agate, glass paste, and enamel, L: 52.5 cm; H: 4.5 cm

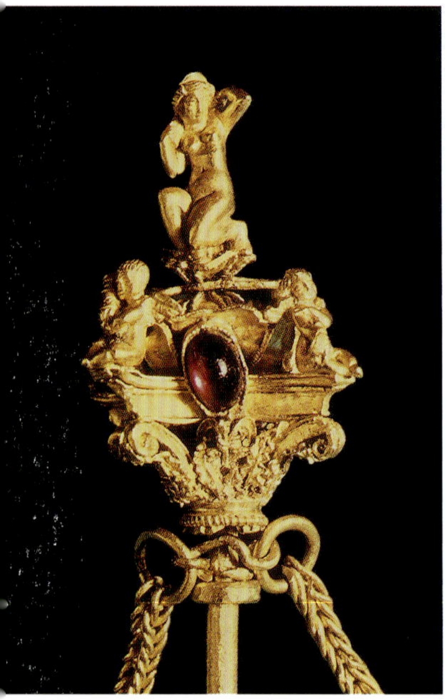

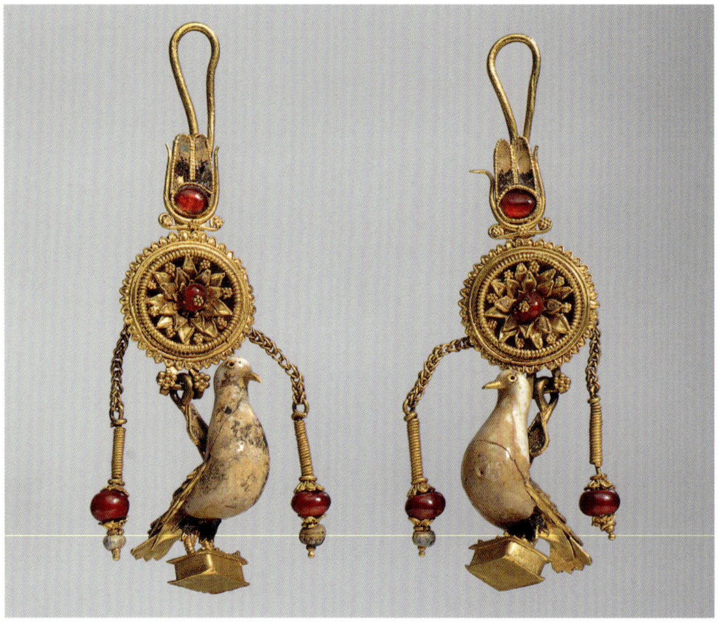

Plate 37 (far left)
Dress pin with crouching Aphrodite (detail), ca. 300–200 BC. Gold and garnet, H (figure): 1.8 cm

Plate 38 (near left)
Pair of earrings with doves, ca. 150–100 BC. Gold, enamel, garnet, and cornelian, H: 6.5 cm

Plate 39 (below)
Pair of armbands with Tritons and Erotes, ca. 200 BC. Gold, H: 25 and 26.5 cm; Wt (each): 186.5 grams

Plate 40 (opposite)
Assemblage of jewelry, ca. 220–100 BC. Gold, garnet, cornelian, pearl, and glass

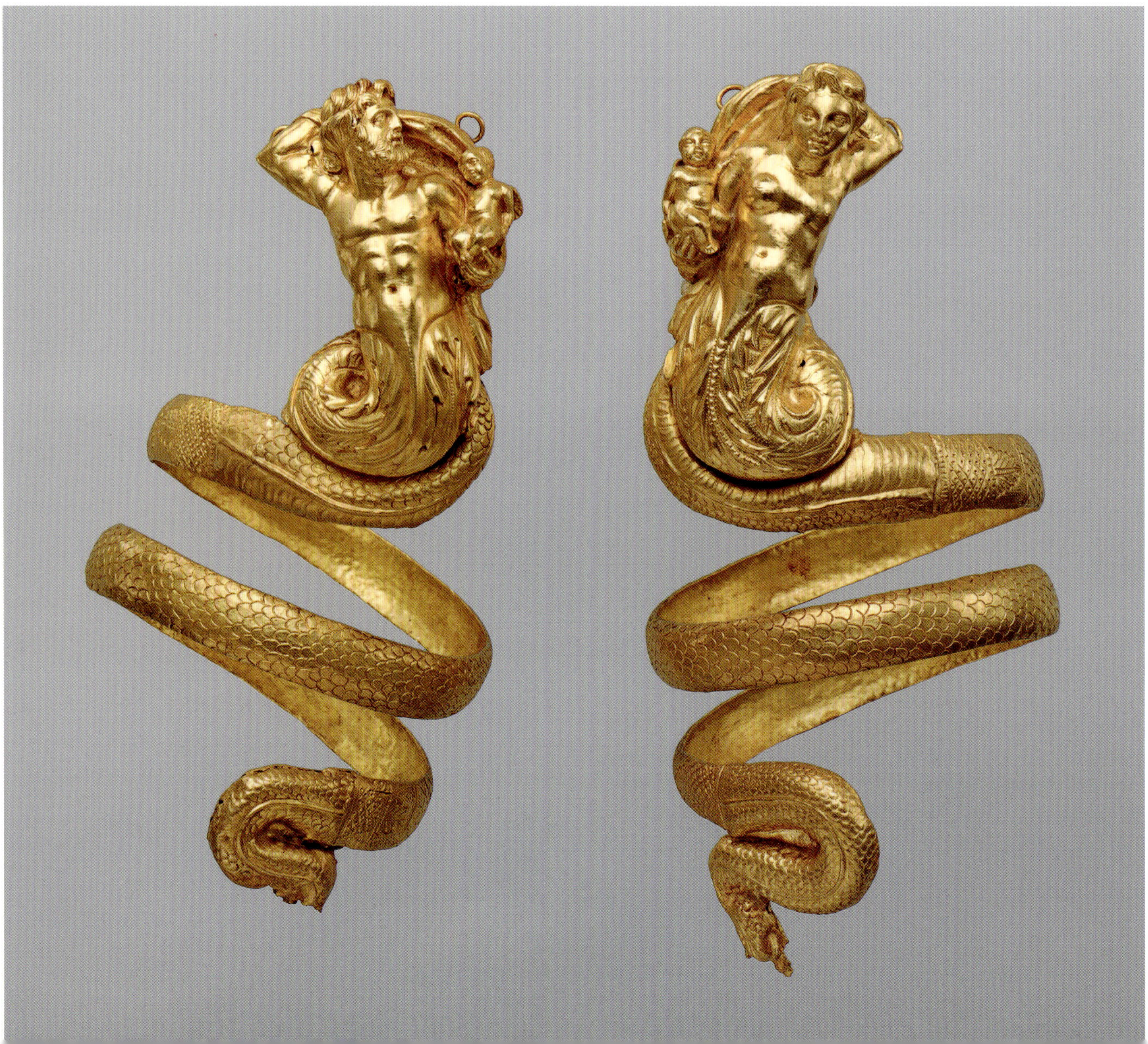

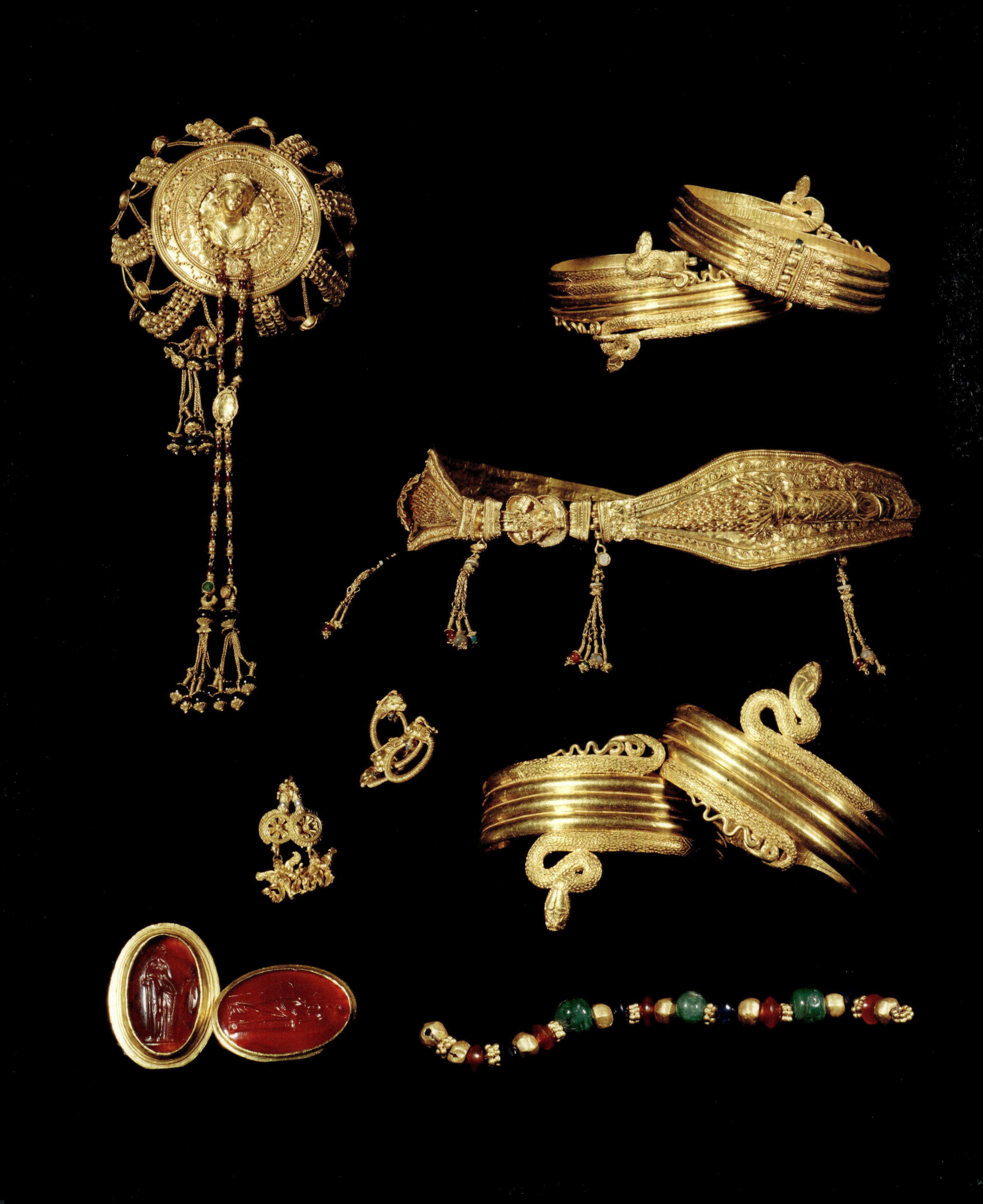

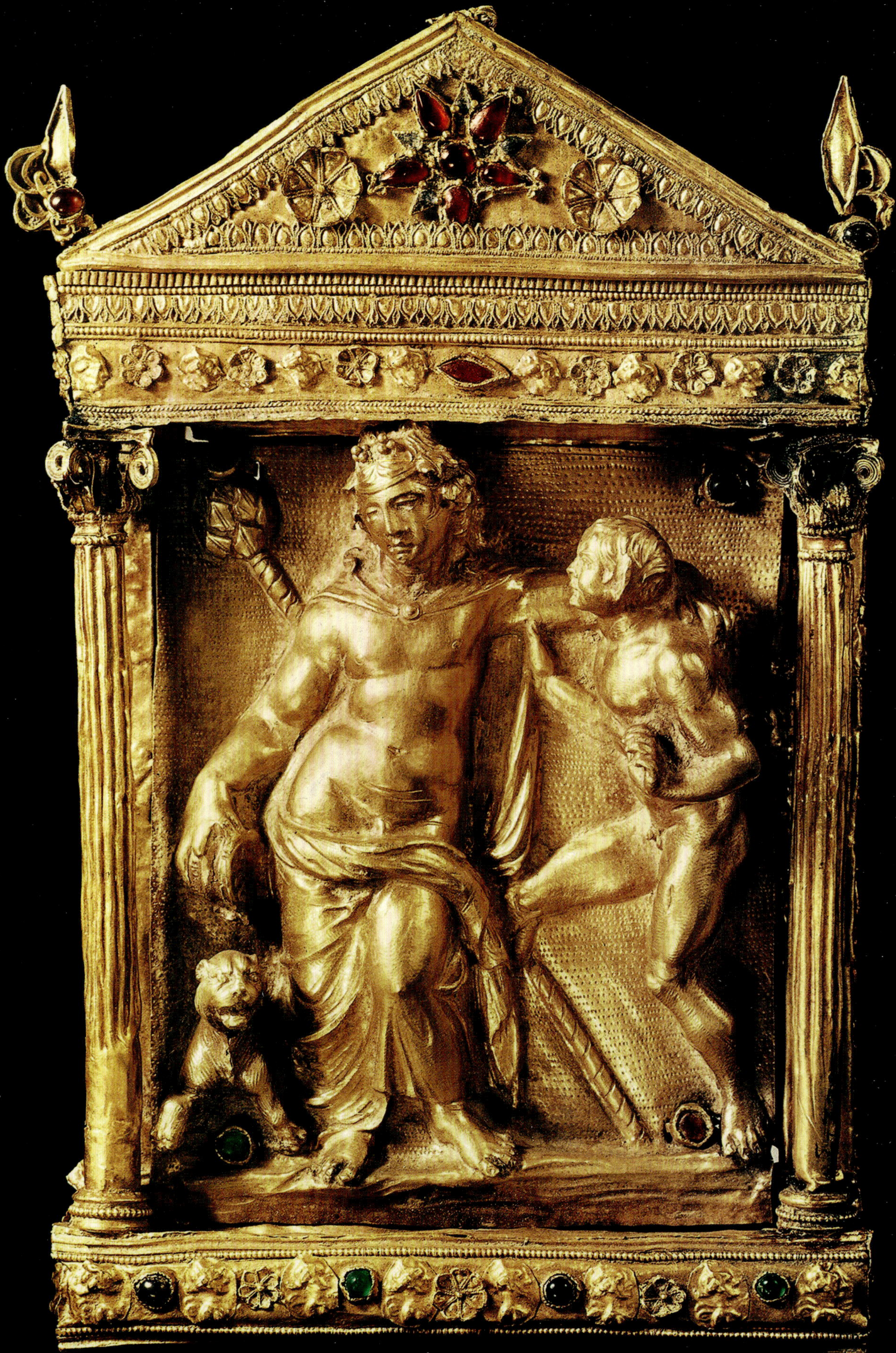

Plate 41 (opposite)
Miniature shrine with Dionysos, ca. 200–100 BC. Gold, cornelian, and glass, H: 14.5 cm; W: 9 cm

Plate 42
Head of a satyr, ca. 200–100 BC. Gold, H: 4.1 cm

Plate 43
Pair of earrings with Ethiopians, ca. 200 BC. Gold and garnet, H: 1.8 cm

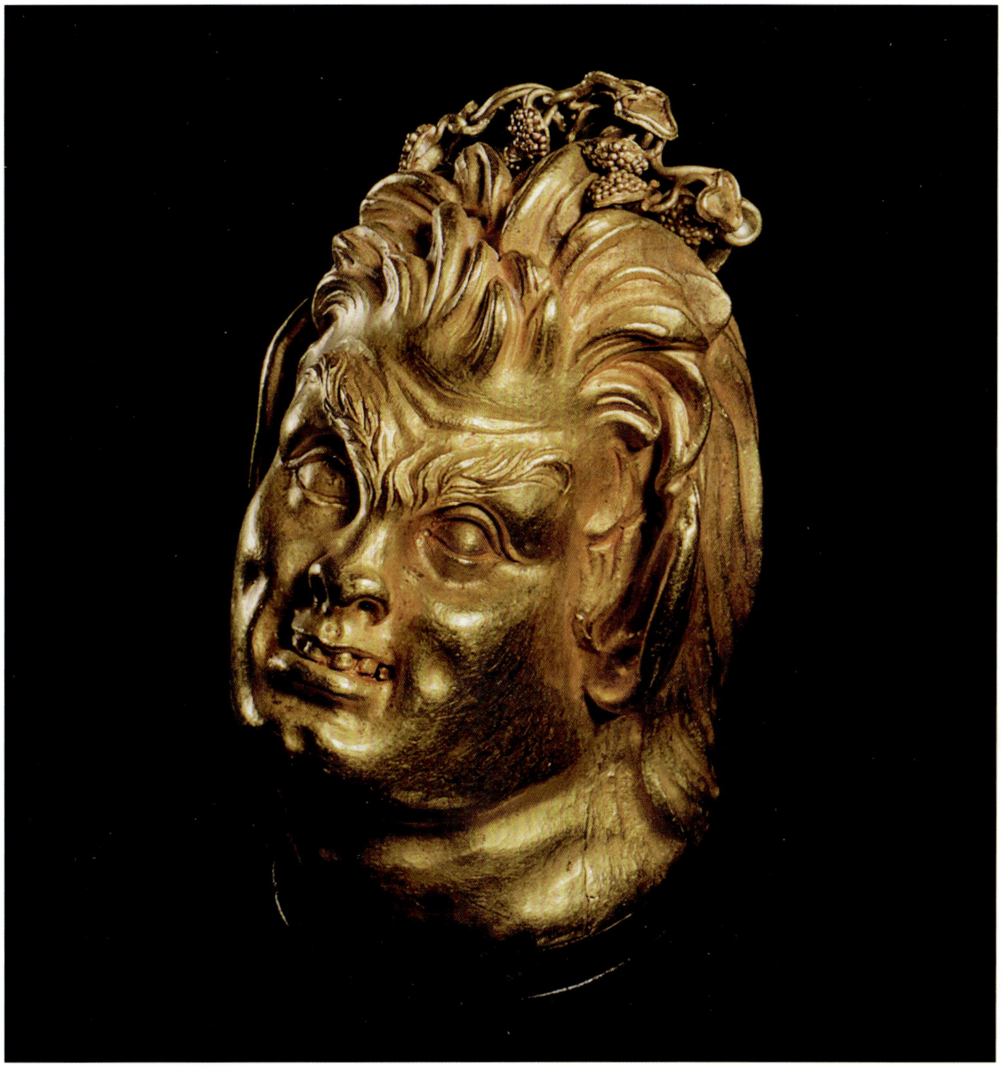

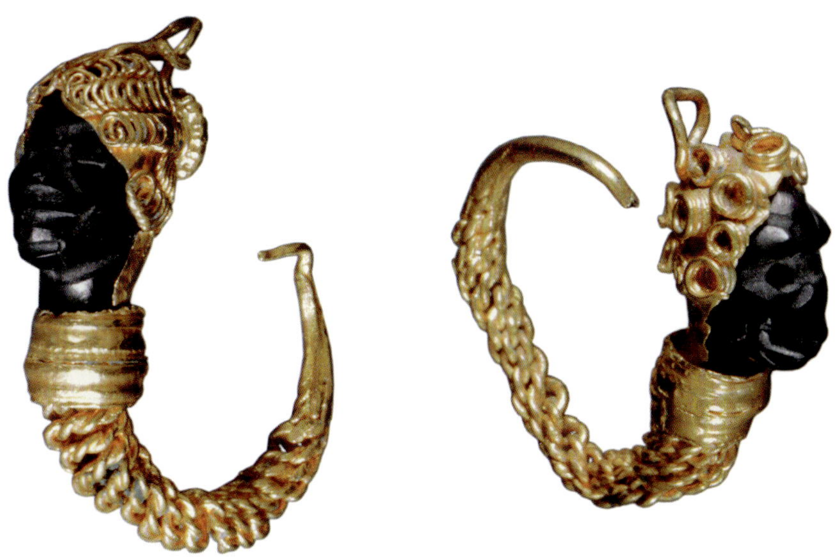

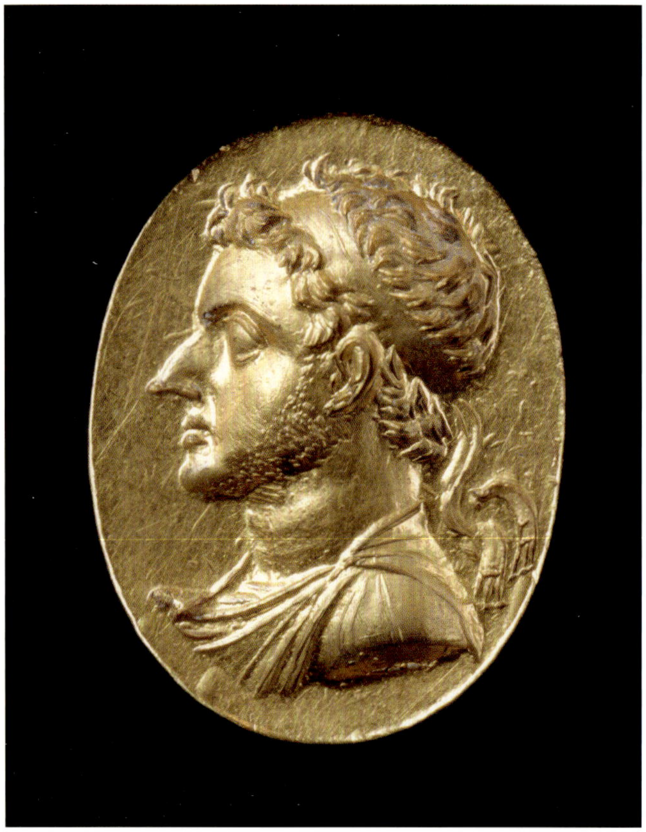

a

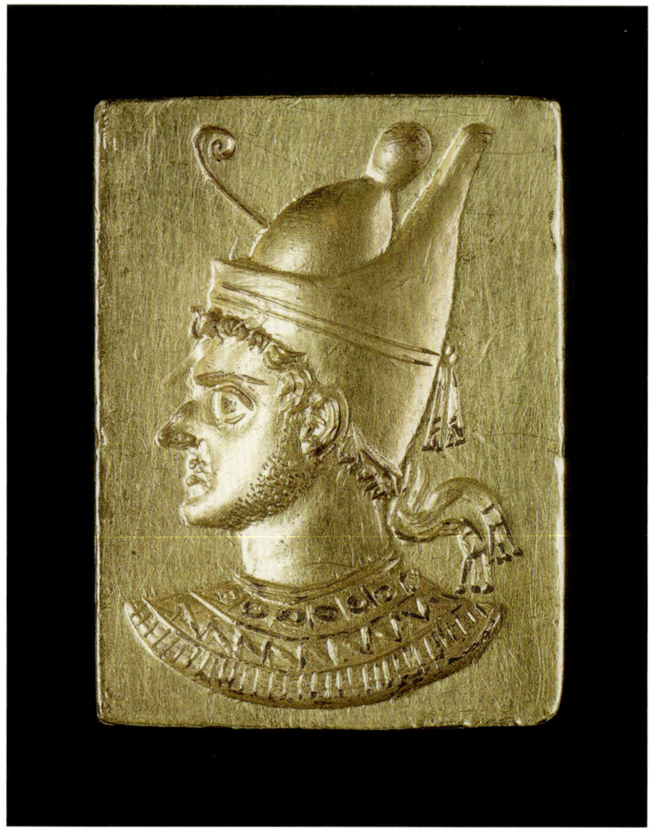

b

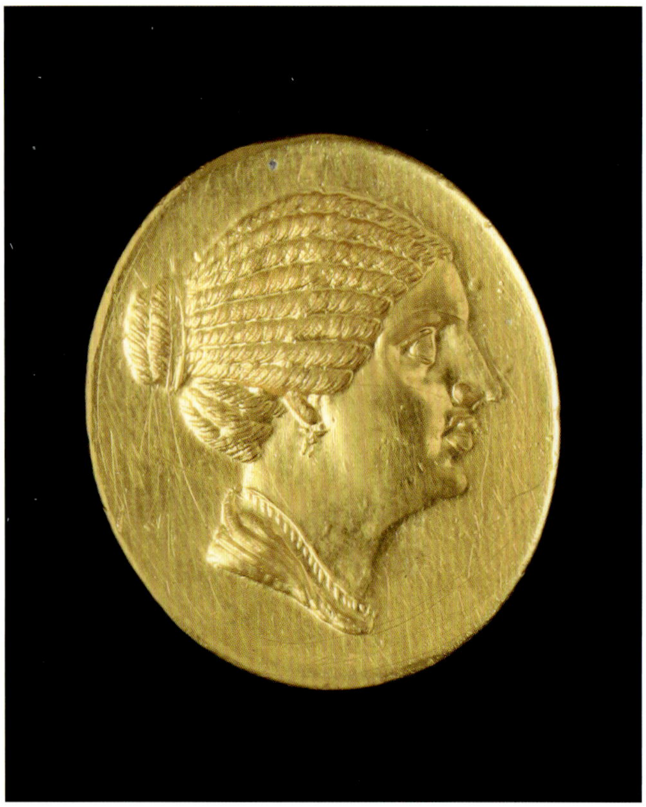

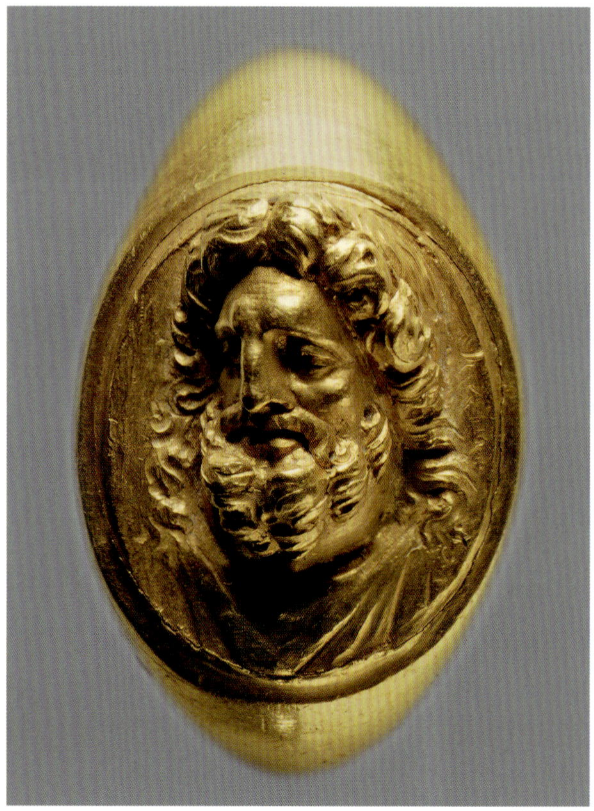

Plate 44a, b (opposite, top row)
Pair of engraved rings depicting a Ptolemy, ca. 186–145 BC. Gold, H: 3.4 and 2.6 cm; W: 2.5 and 1.9 cm

Plate 45 (opposite, bottom left)
Ring with head of a woman, ca. 300–200 BC. Gold, H: 2.9 cm; W: 2.4 cm

Plate 46 (opposite, bottom right)
Ring inset with cast bust of Jupiter, ca. 50 BC–AD 20. Gold, H (bezel): 1.5 cm; W (bezel): 1.2 cm; Wt: 14 grams

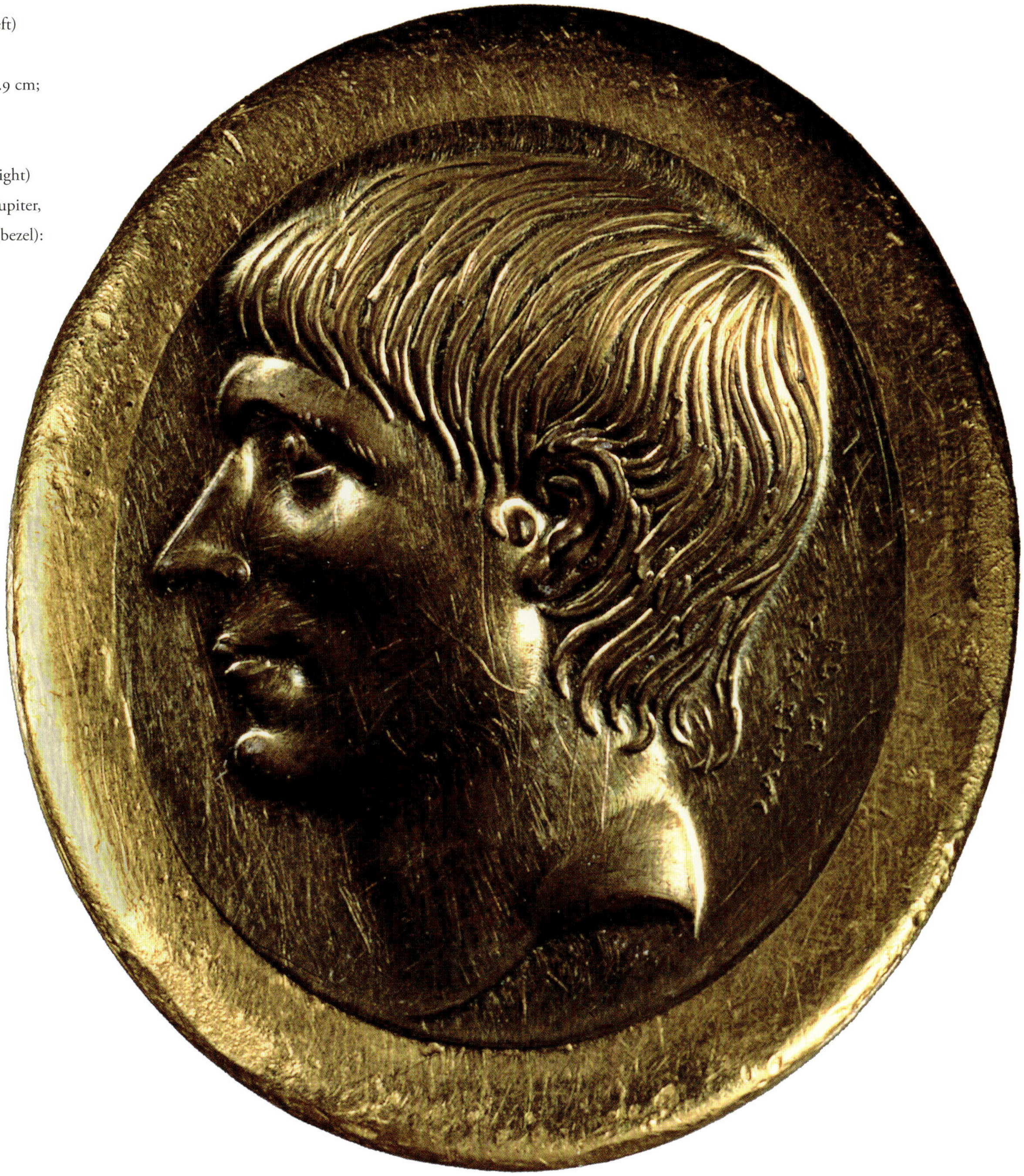

Plate 47
Ring signed by Herakleidas, ca. 300–100 BC. Gold, H: 3.3 cm; W: 2.9 cm; Wt: 93.2 grams

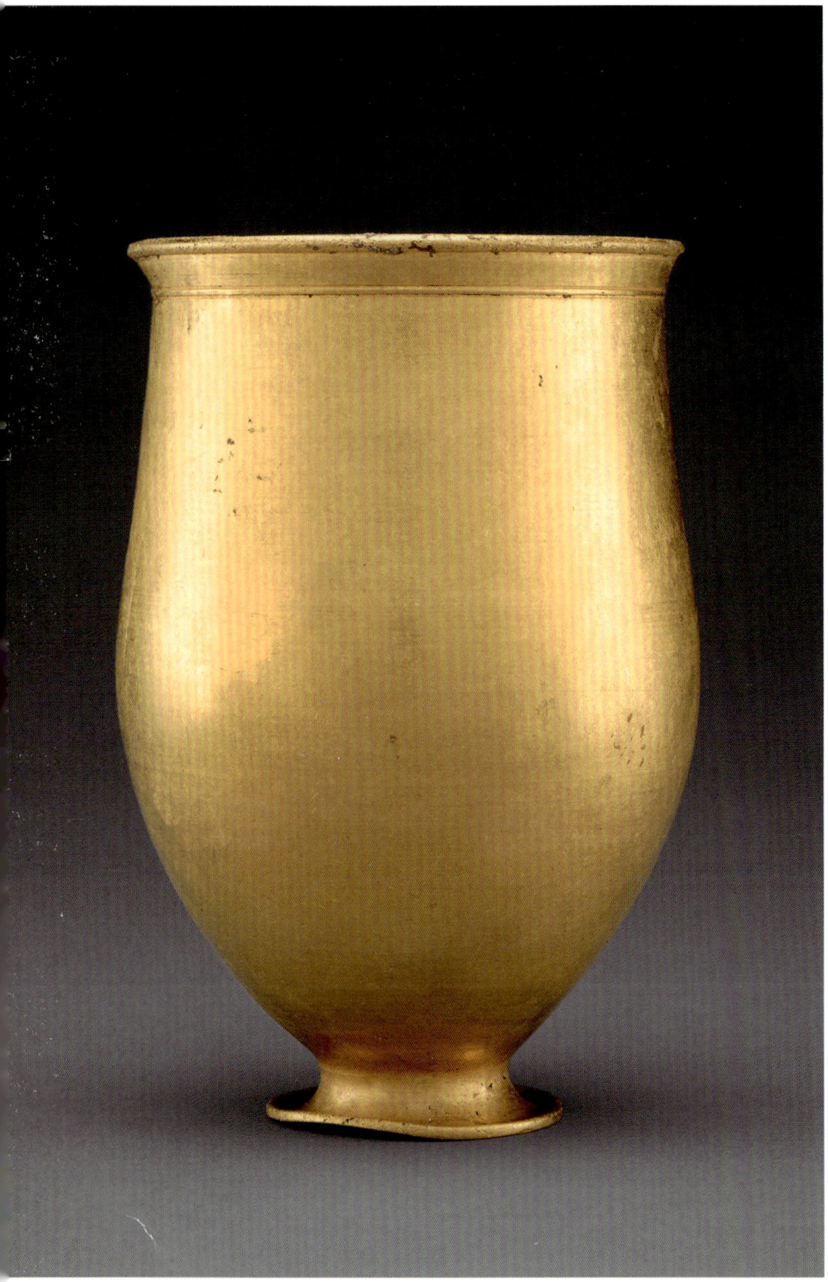

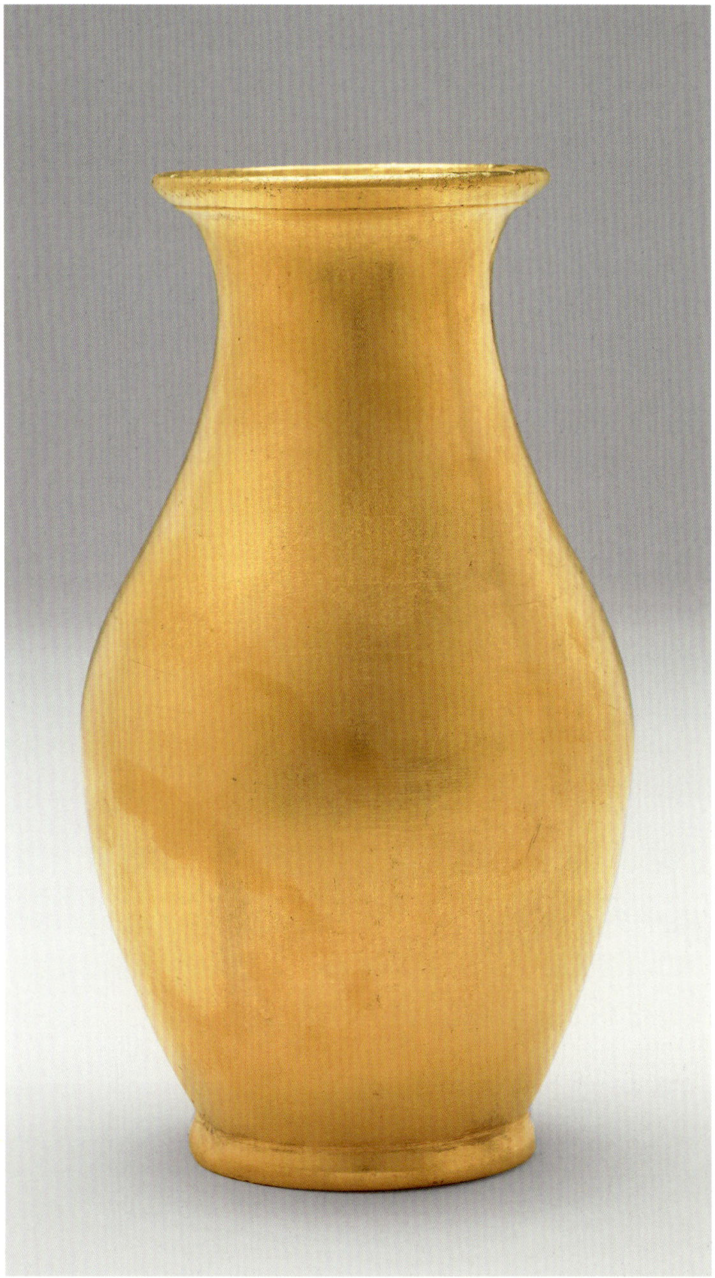

Plate 48
Beaker, ca. 25 BC–AD 50. Gold, H: 13.7 cm; Wt: 656.2 grams

Plate 49
Pitcher, ca. 25 BC–AD 50. Gold, H: 19 cm; Wt: 673 grams

Plate 50 (opposite)
Double-spouted lamp, ca. AD 50–79. Gold, H: 15.1 cm; L: 32.2 cm; Wt: 801 grams

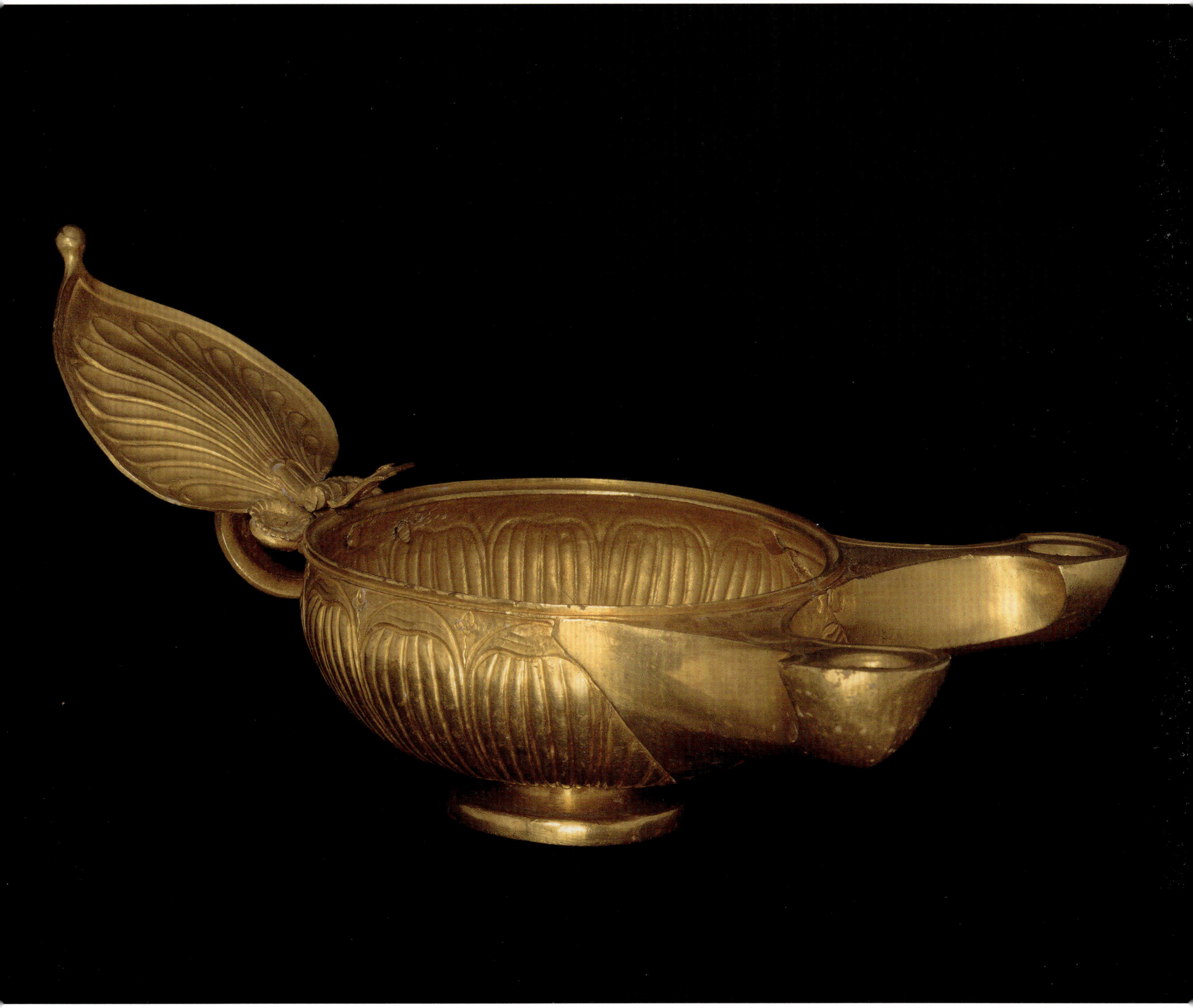

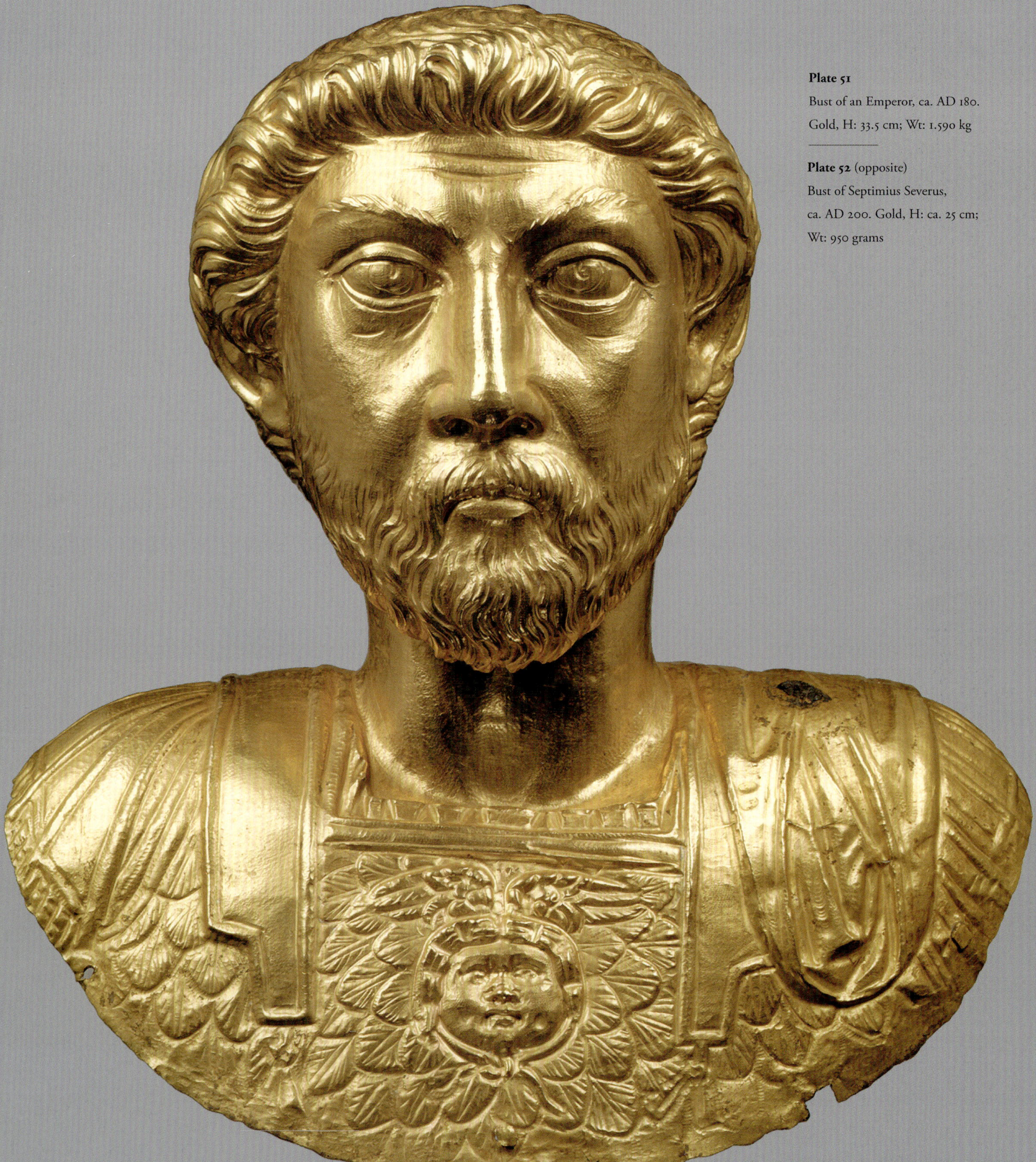

Plate 51
Bust of an Emperor, ca. AD 180.
Gold, H: 33.5 cm; Wt: 1.590 kg

Plate 52 (opposite)
Bust of Septimius Severus,
ca. AD 200. Gold, H: ca. 25 cm;
Wt: 950 grams

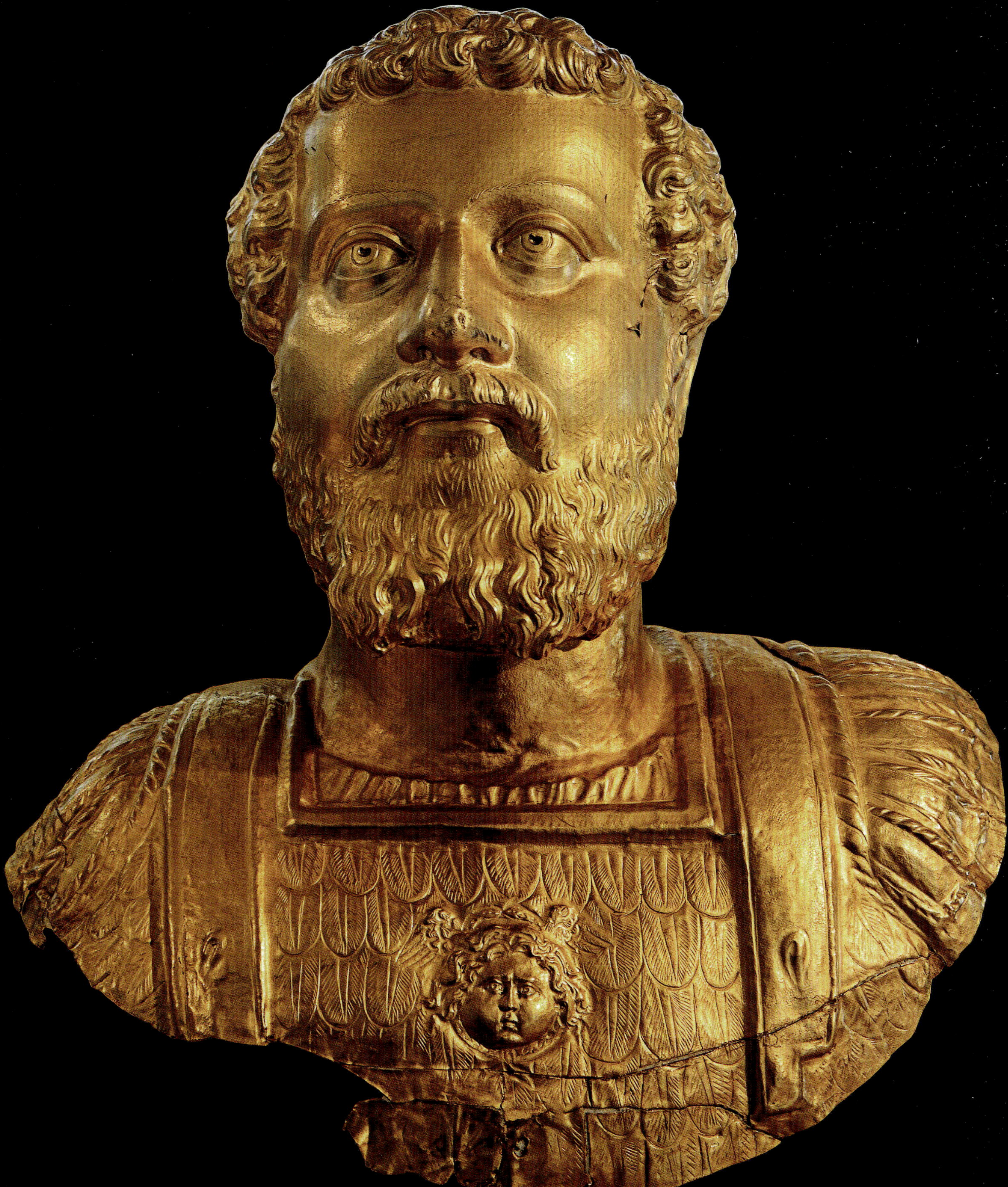

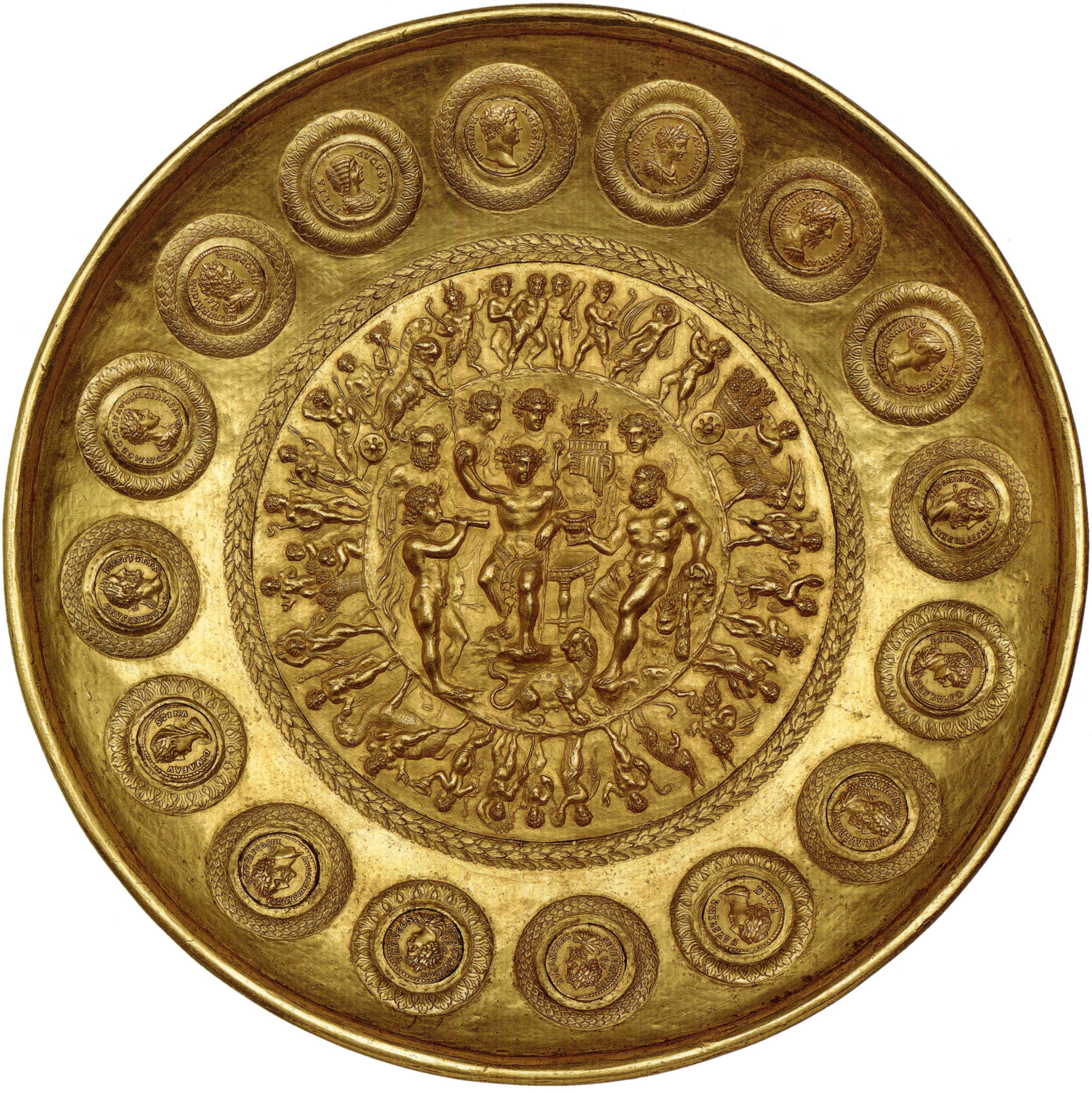

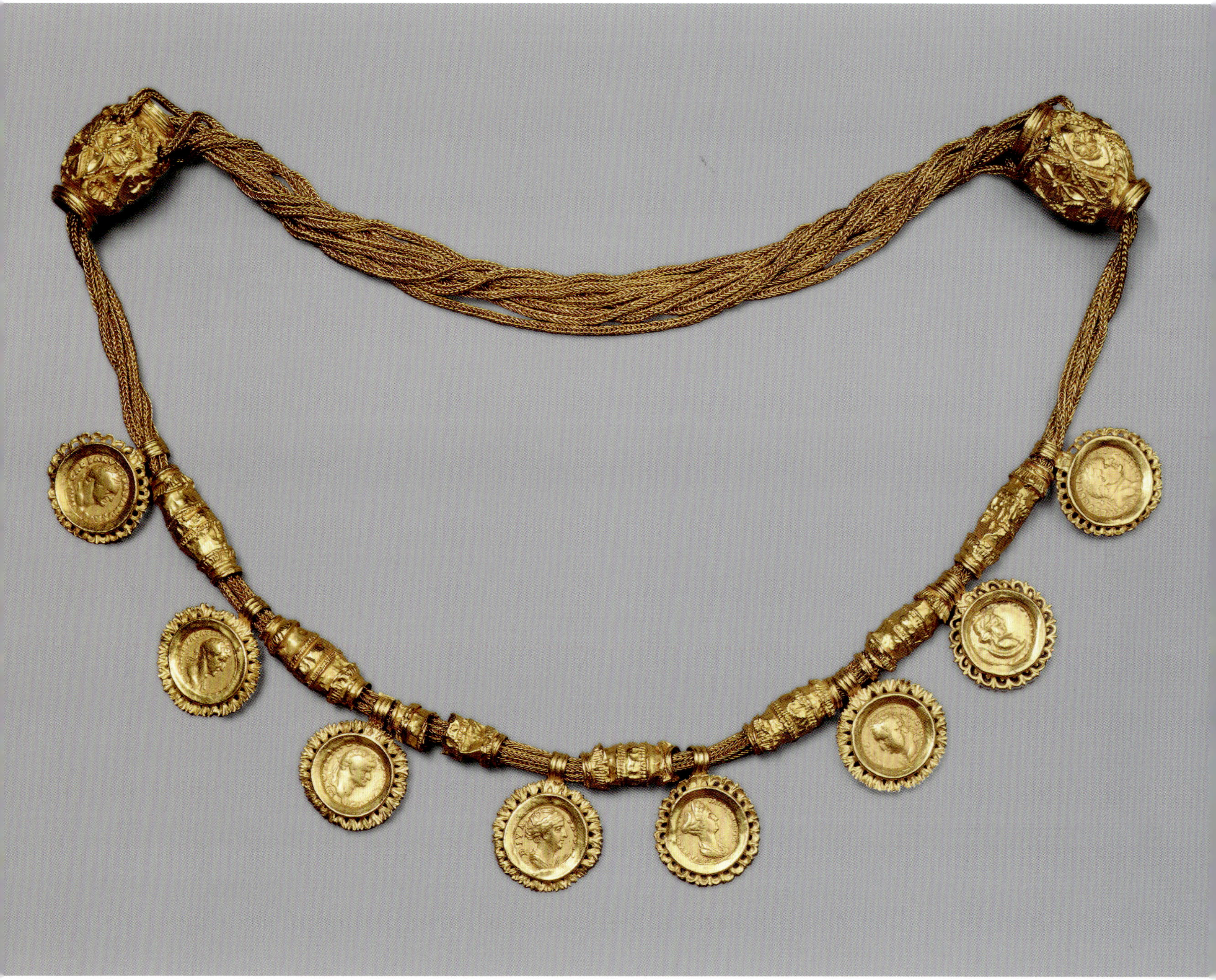

Plate 53 (opposite)
Patera from Rennes, ca. AD 210.
Diam: 25 cm; Wt: 1.35 kg

Plate 54
Necklace, ca. AD 200–300. Gold,
L (extended): 91.4 cm; Diam
(medallions): 2.7 cm

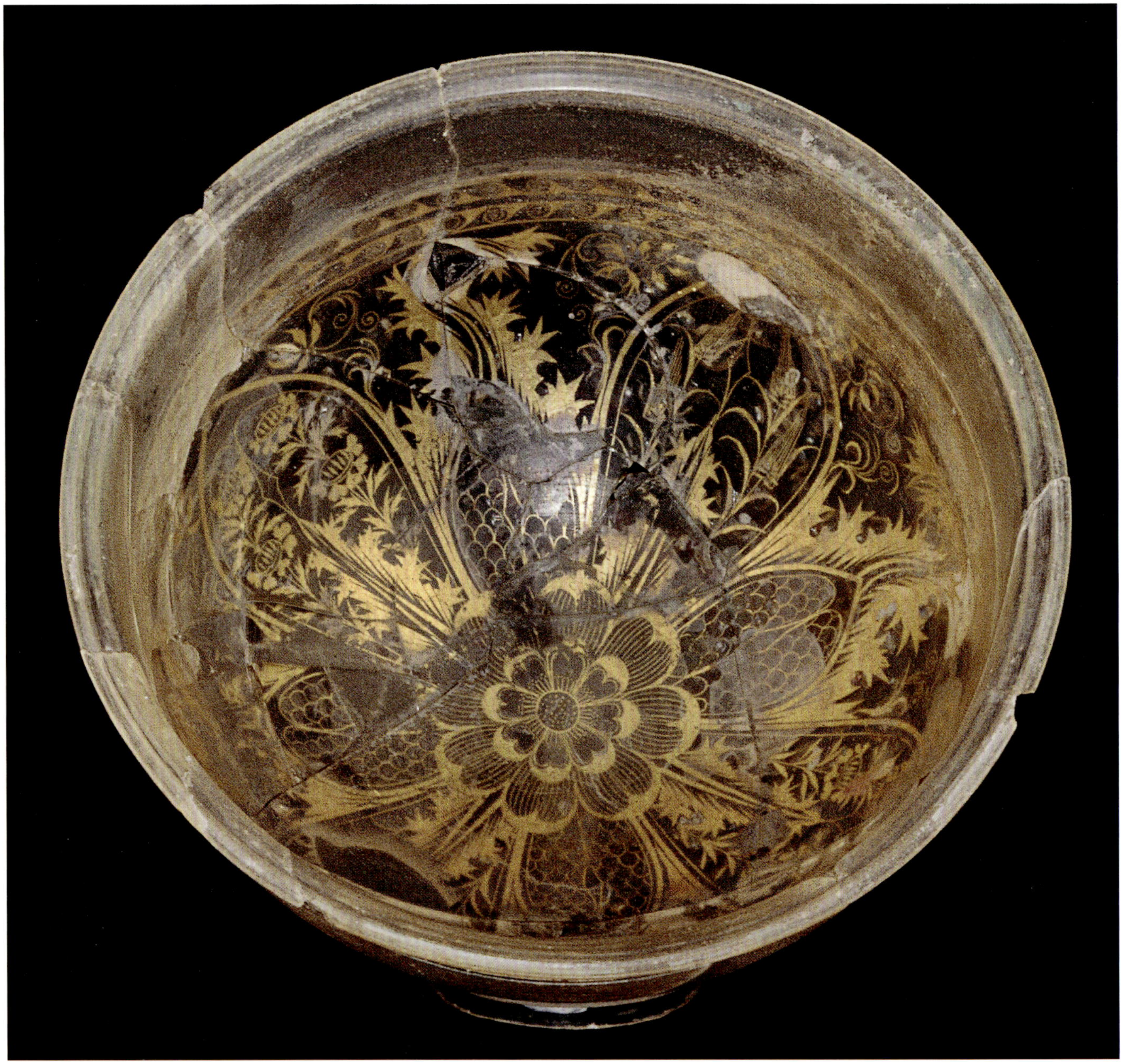

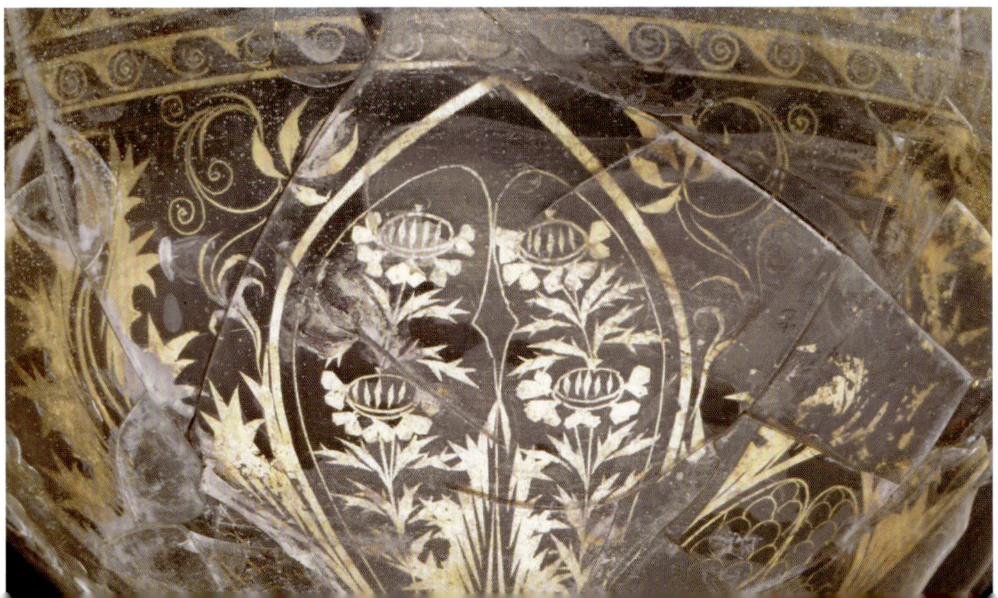

Plate 55 (above)
Bowl with floral decoration,
ca. 250 BC. Gold glass, H: 11.4 cm;
Diam: 20.3 cm

detail, plate 55

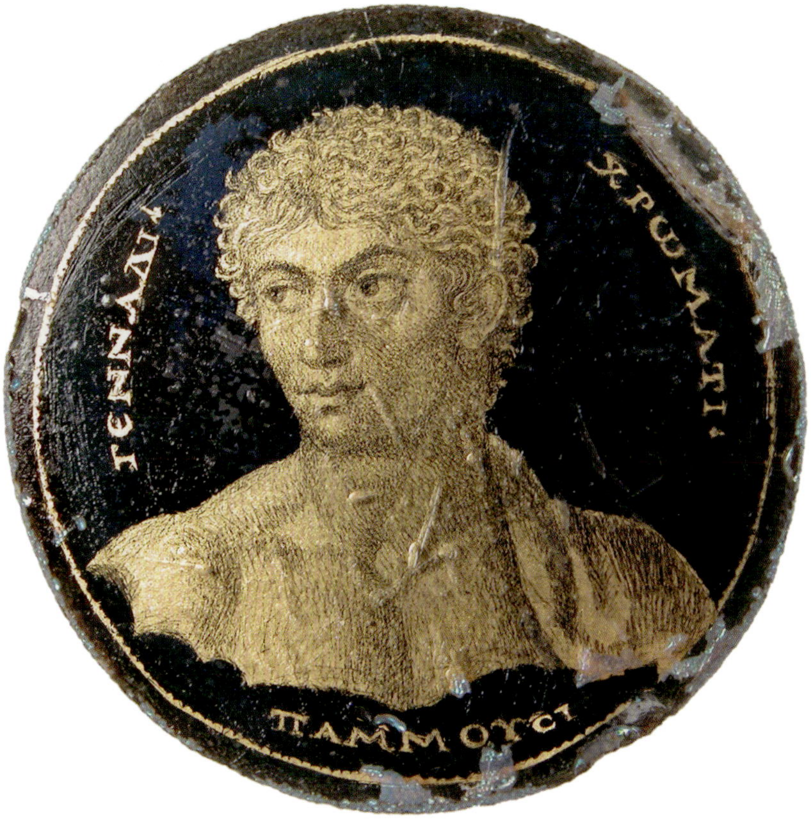

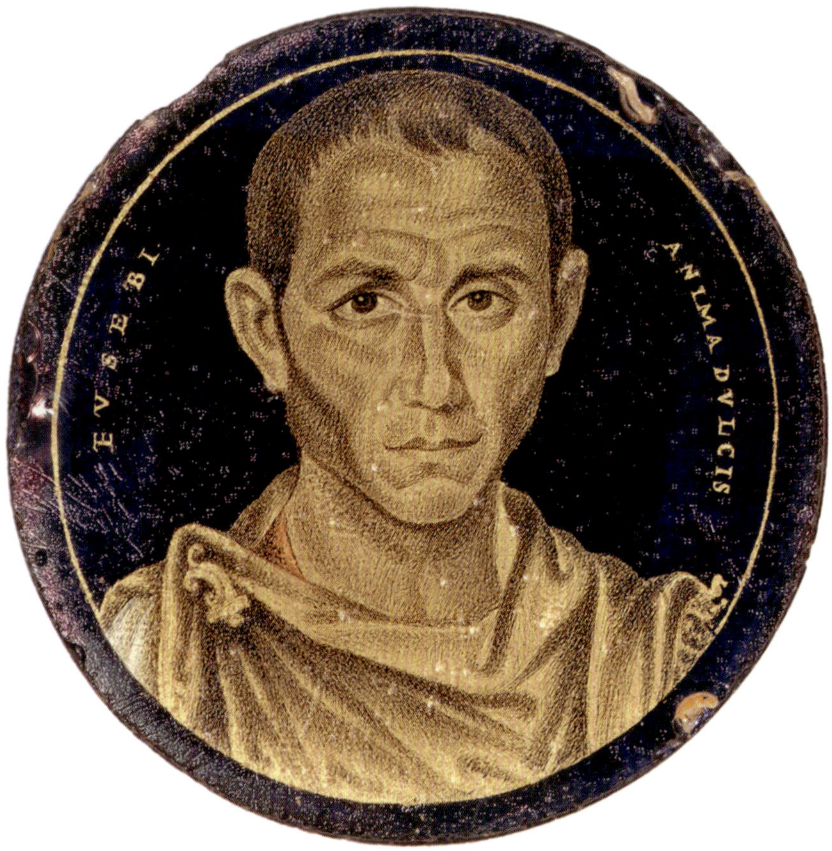

Plate 56

Portrait of Gennadios, ca. AD 250–300. Gold glass, Diam: 4.1 cm

Plate 57

Portrait of Eusebius, ca. AD 225–50. Gold glass, silver, and pigment, Diam: 4.8 cm

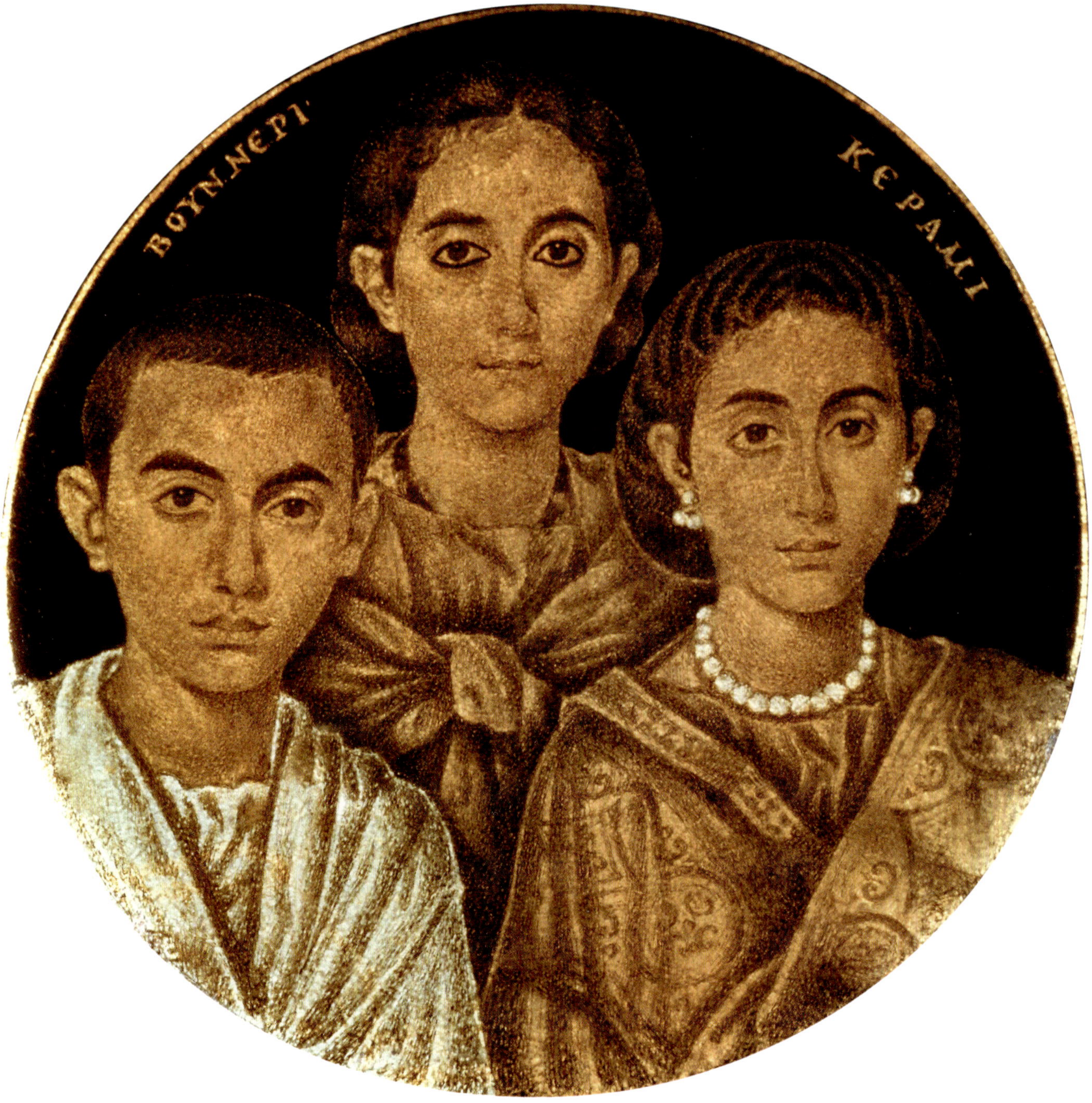

Plate 58
Portrait of two women and a youth, ca. AD 250. Gold glass and silver, Diam: 6.1 cm

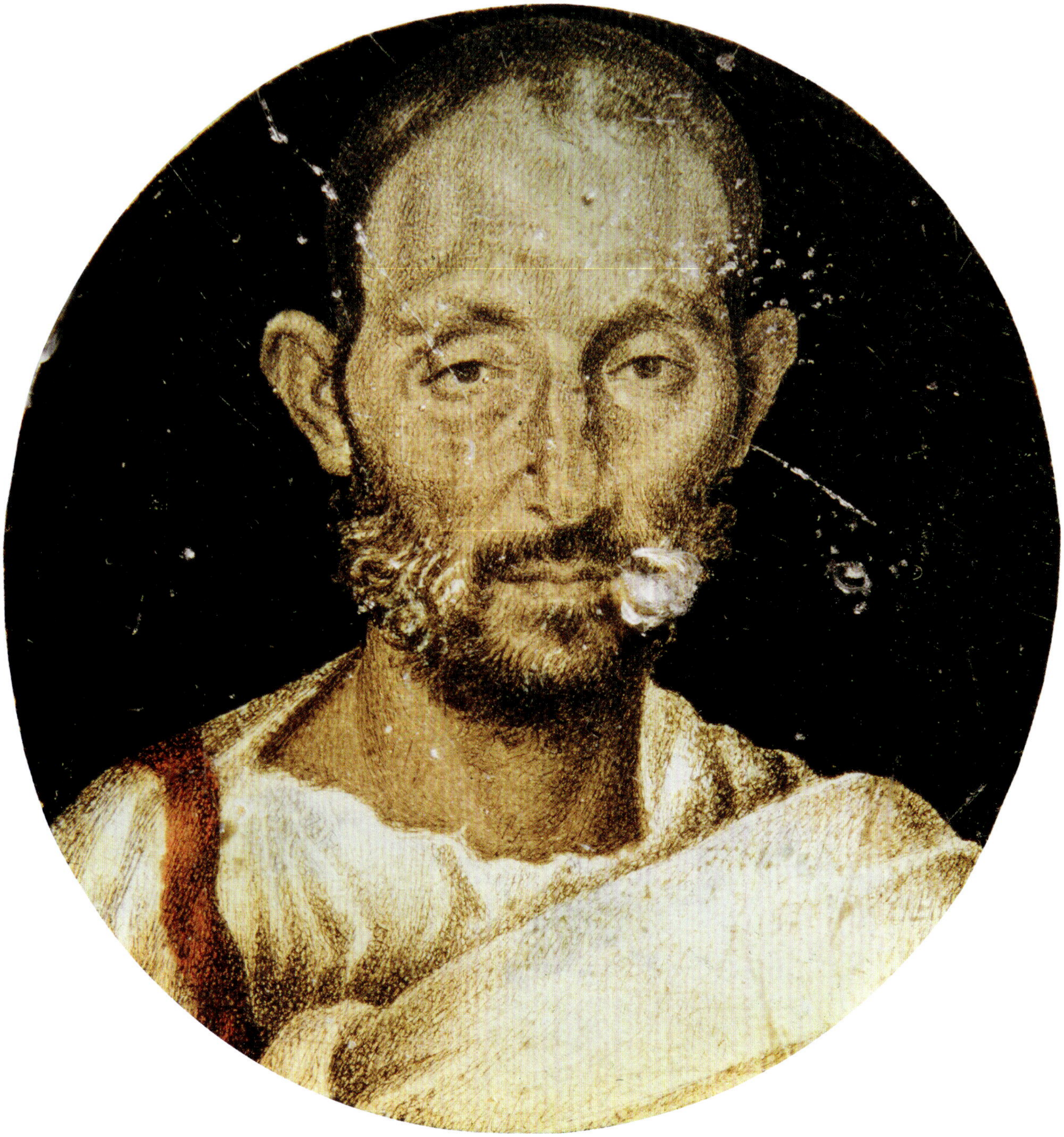

Plate 59
Portrait of a bearded man, ca. AD 200–250. Gold glass and pigment, Diam: 4.4 cm

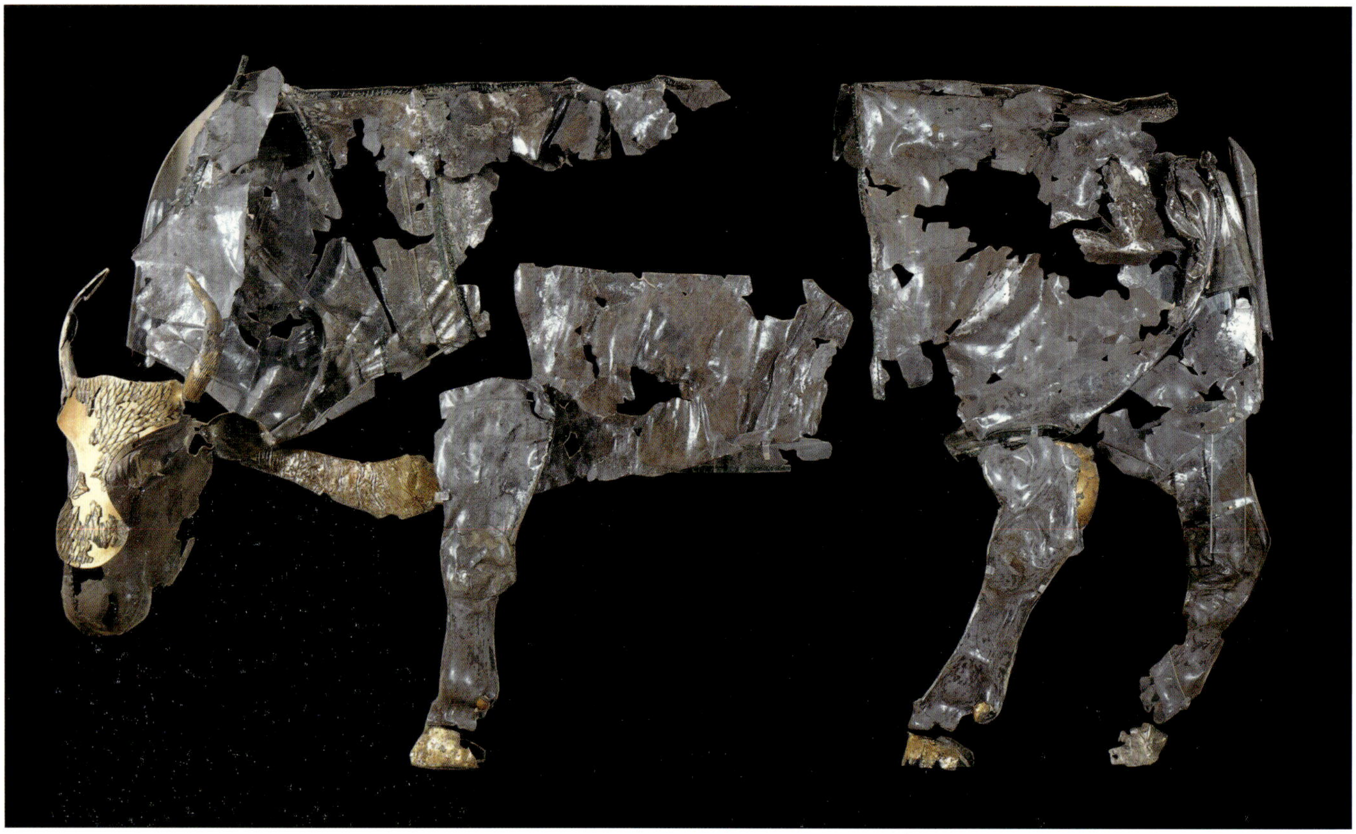

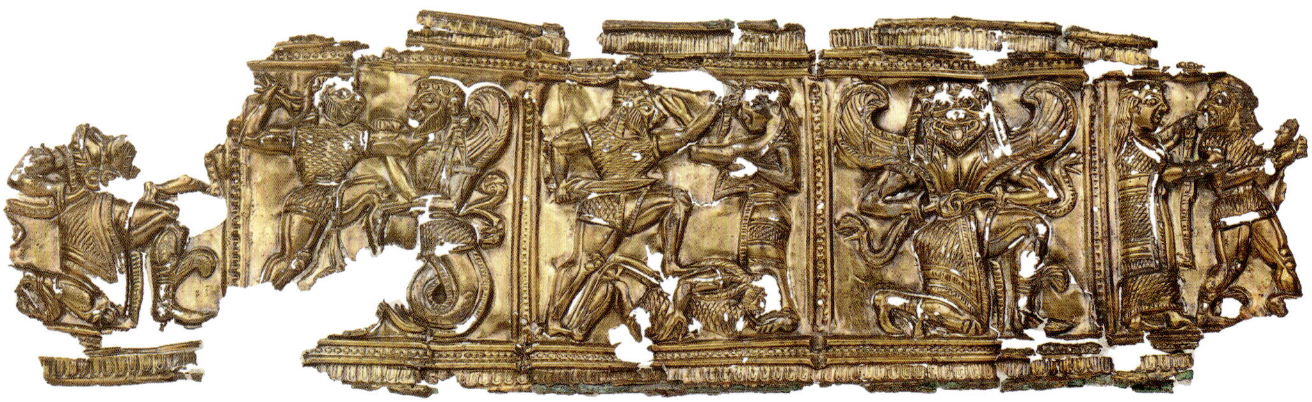

Plate 60

Bull, ca. 600–550 BC. Silver, gold, and copper, original H: ca. 1.25 m; L: ca. 2.30 m

Plate 61

Fragmentary strip with mythological scenes, ca. 540–530 BC. Silver and gold, H: 9 cm; L: 27.5 cm

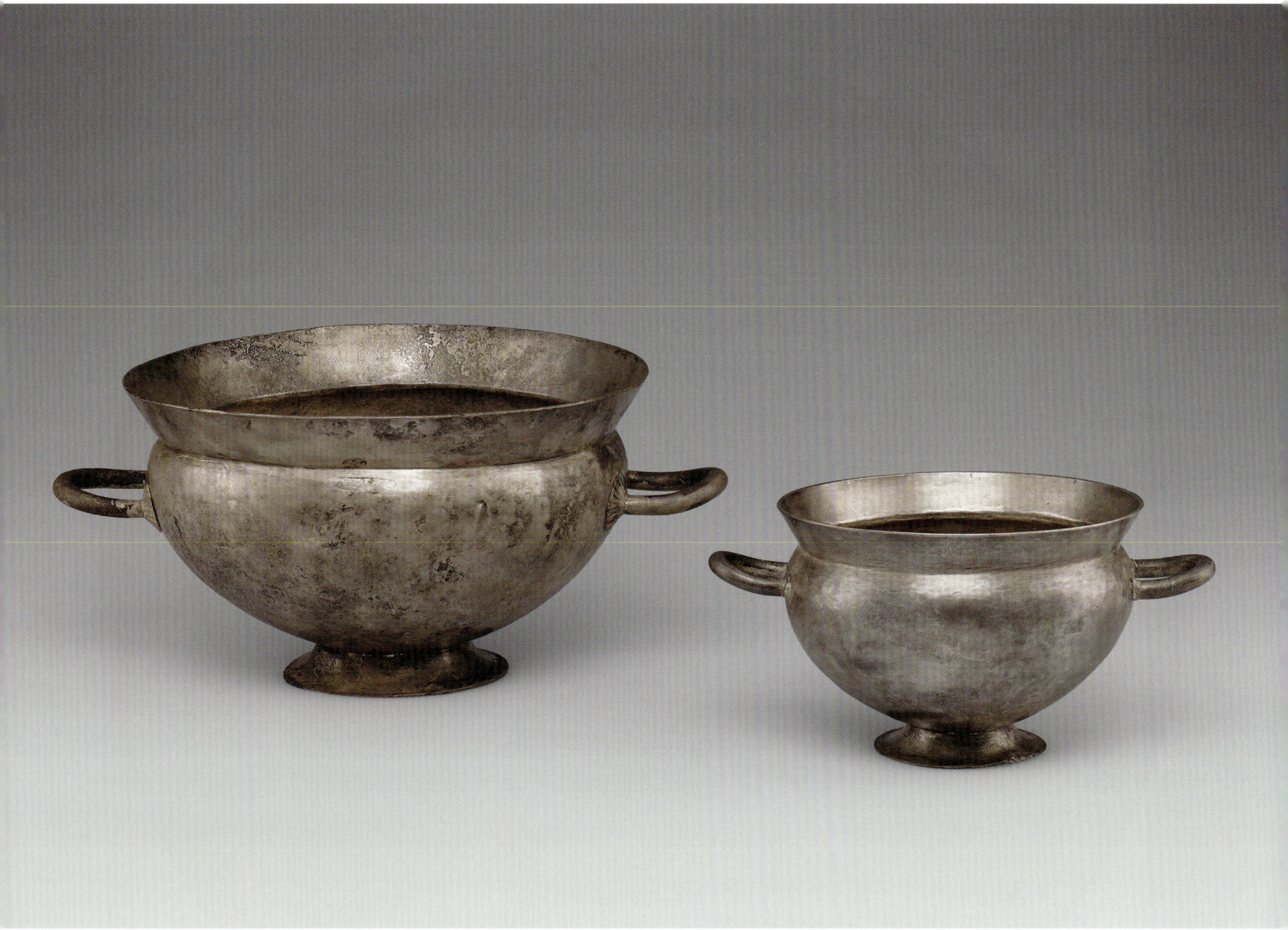

Plate 62
Two *kylikes,* ca. 625–575 BC. Silver, H: 10.2 and 7.4 cm; W: 22 and 14.7 cm; Diam: 16.5 and 10.7 cm; Wt: 362.7 and 192.1 grams

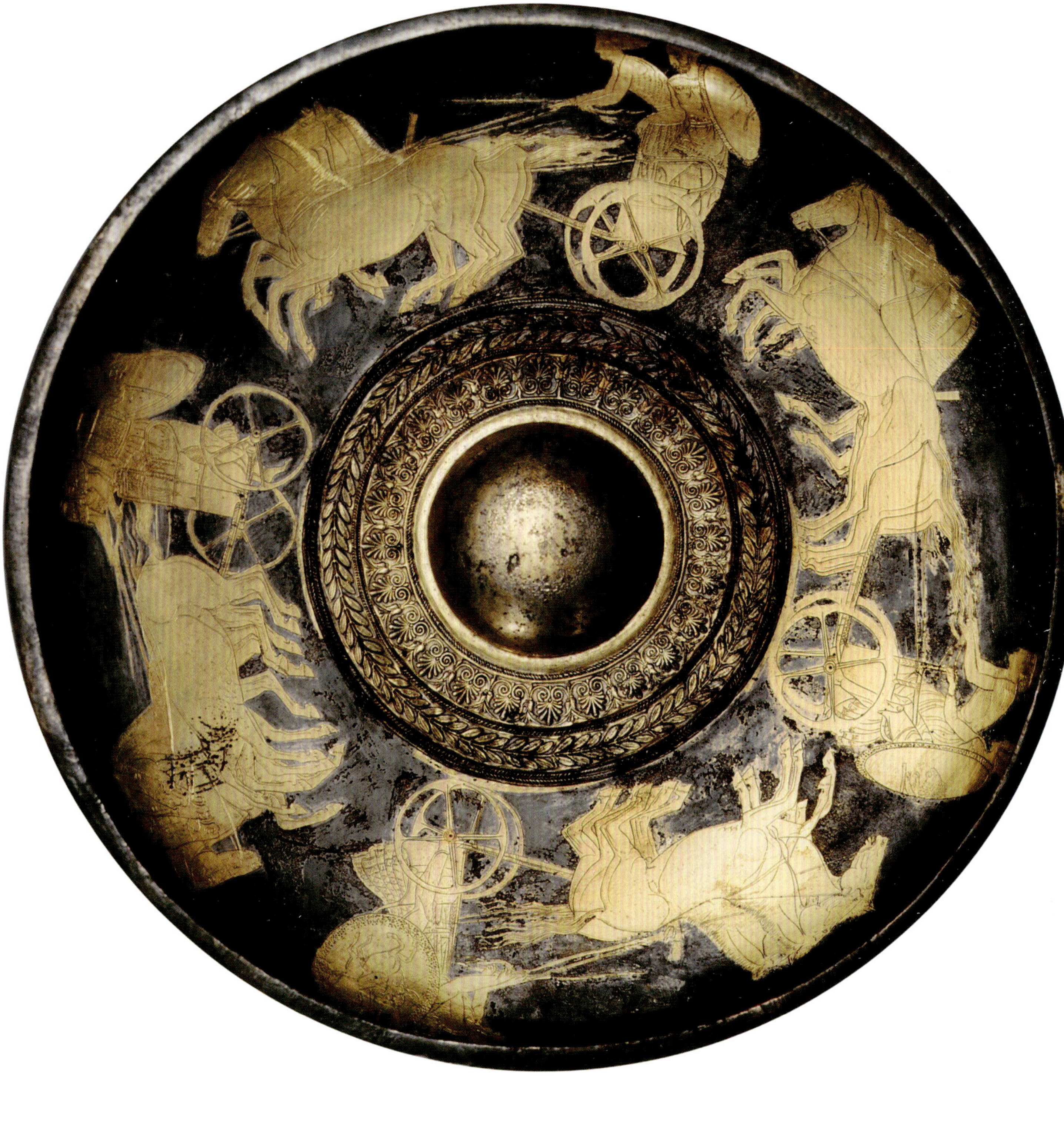

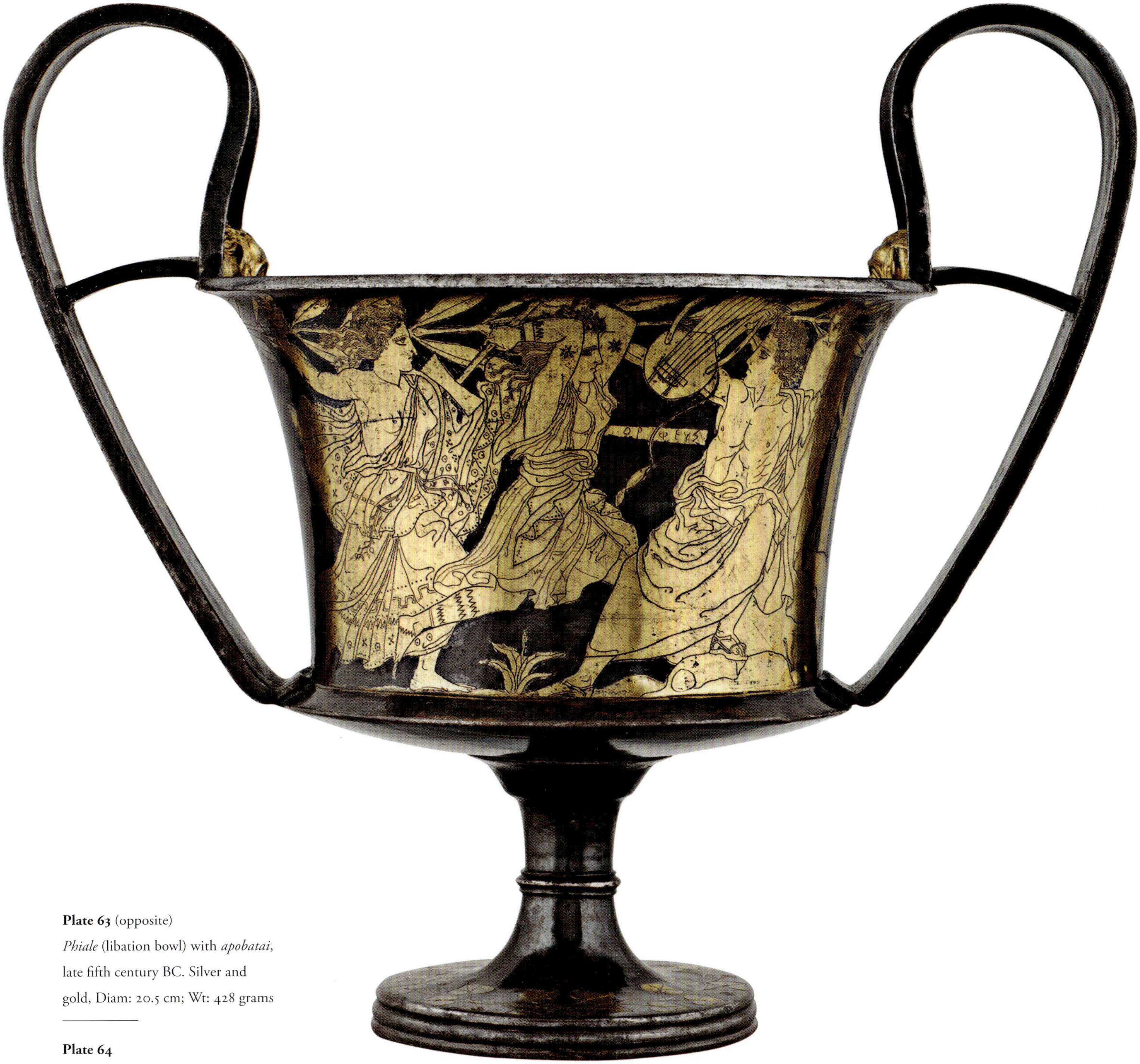

Plate 63 (opposite)
Phiale (libation bowl) with *apobatai*, late fifth century BC. Silver and gold, Diam: 20.5 cm; Wt: 428 grams

Plate 64
Kantharos with the death of Orpheus, late fifth century BC. Silver and gold, H: 16.4 cm; Diam: 11.8 cm; Wt: 408.9 grams

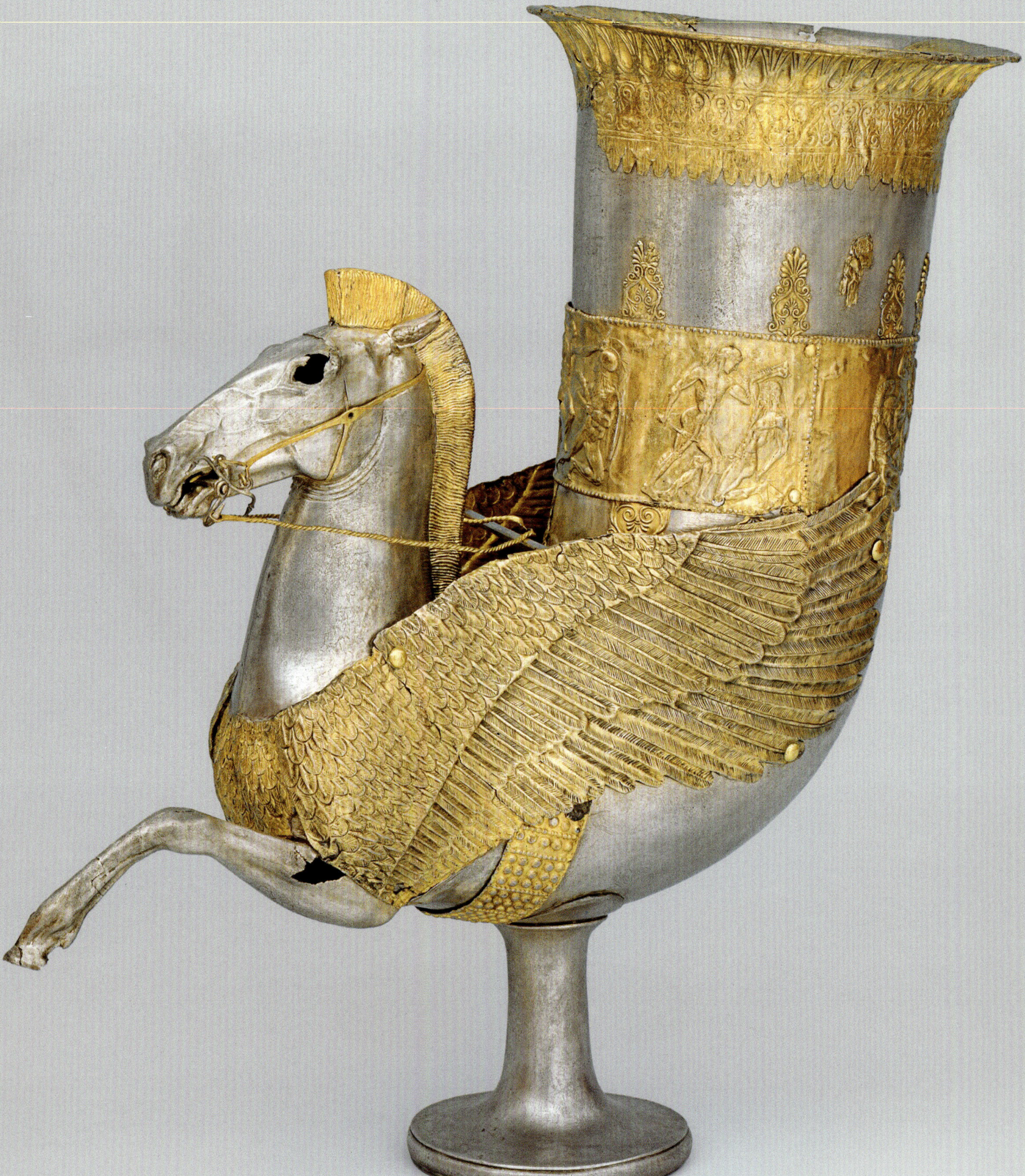

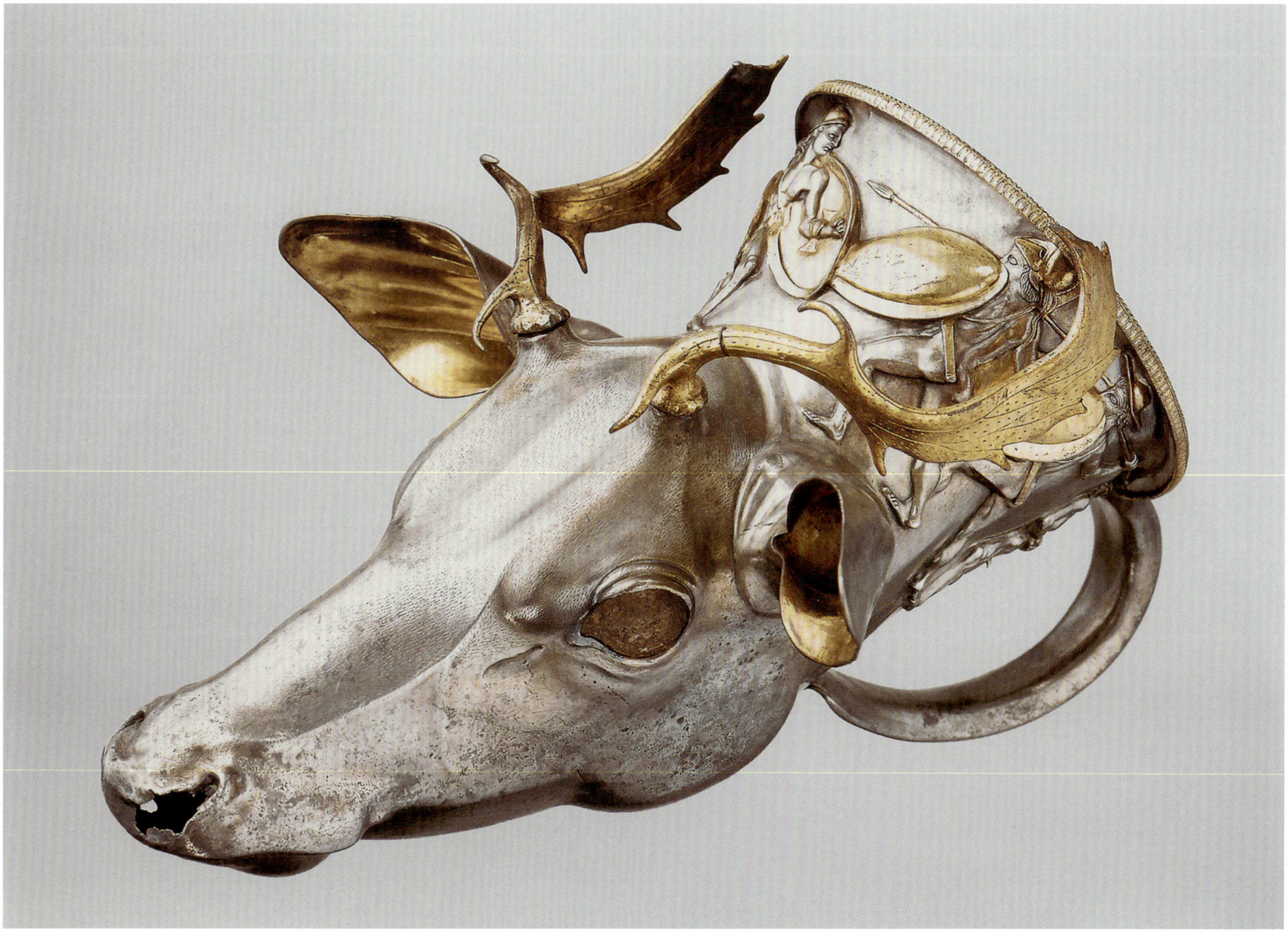

Plate 65 (opposite)
Rhyton in the form of Pegasos, ca. 400 BC. Silver and gold, H: 37.3 cm; Wt: ca. 1.43 kg

Plate 66
Stag's head rhyton with warriors, ca. 400 BC. Silver and gold, L: 29 cm; Diam: 12.8 cm; Wt: 829.2 grams

Plate 67
Hydria and wreath, ca. 310 BC. Silver and gold, H (hydria): 54 cm; Wt (hydria): 2.3 kg

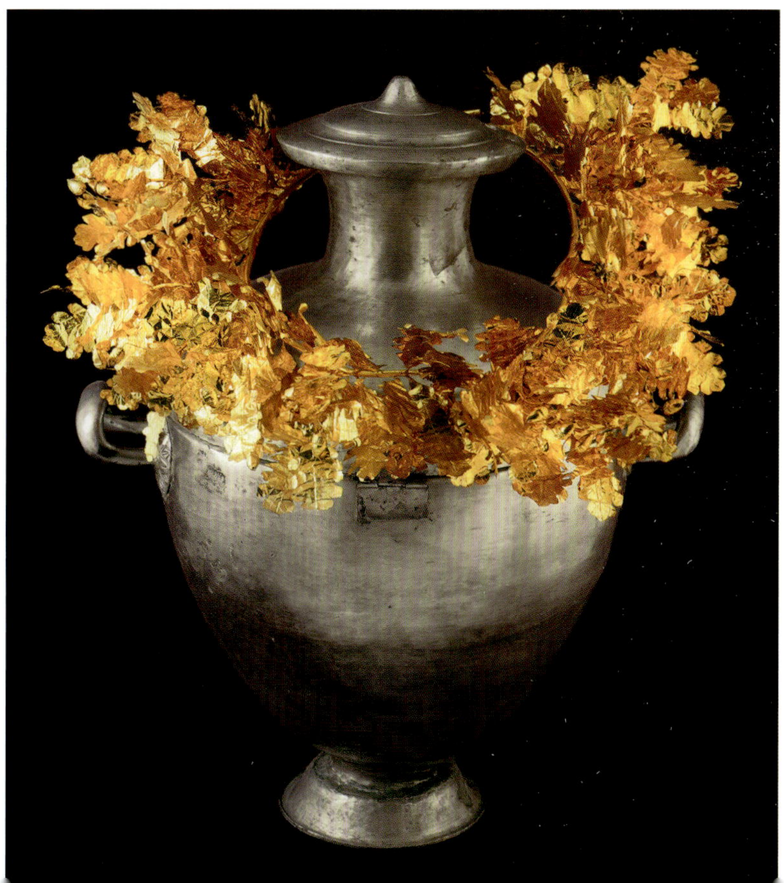

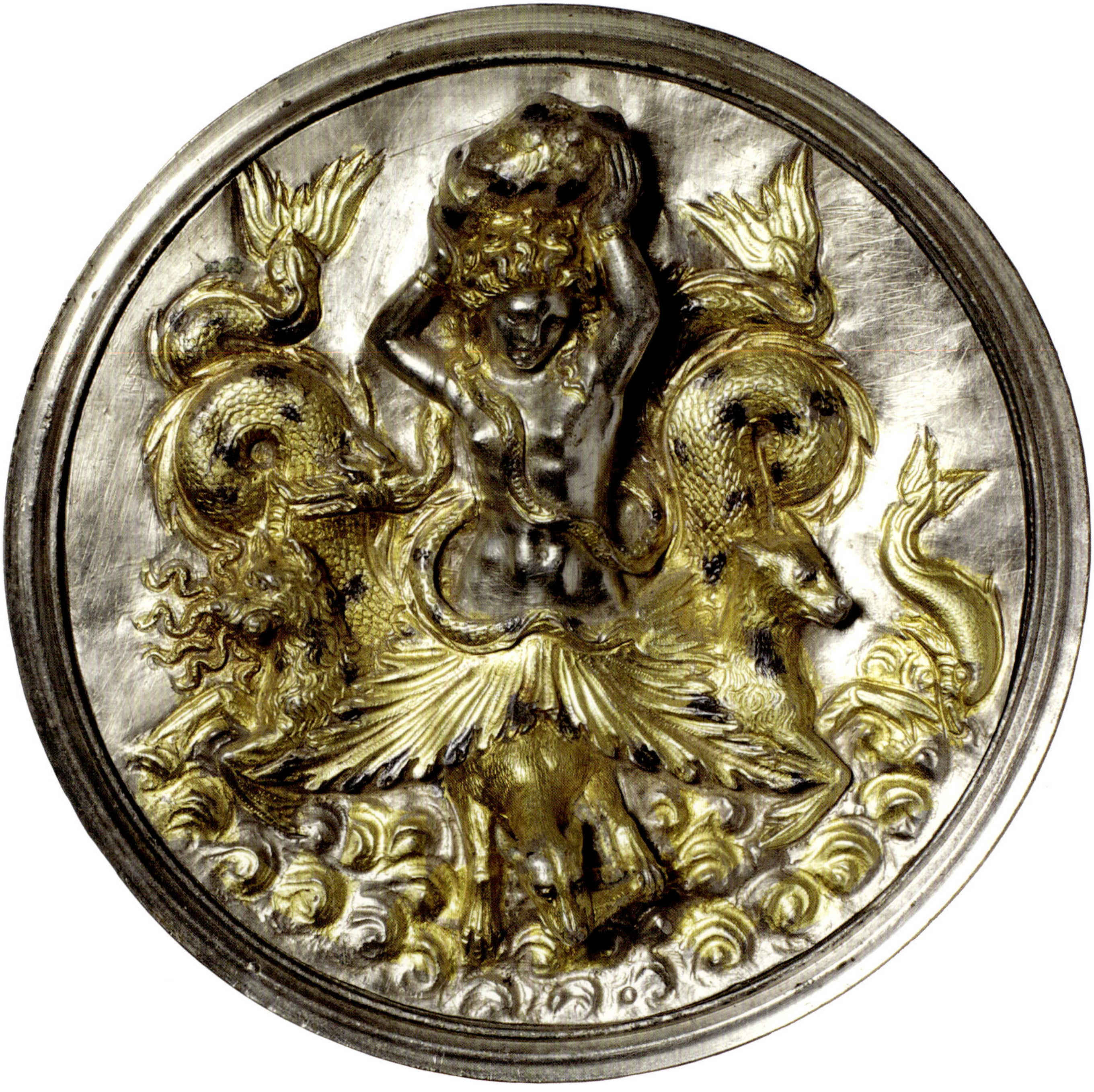

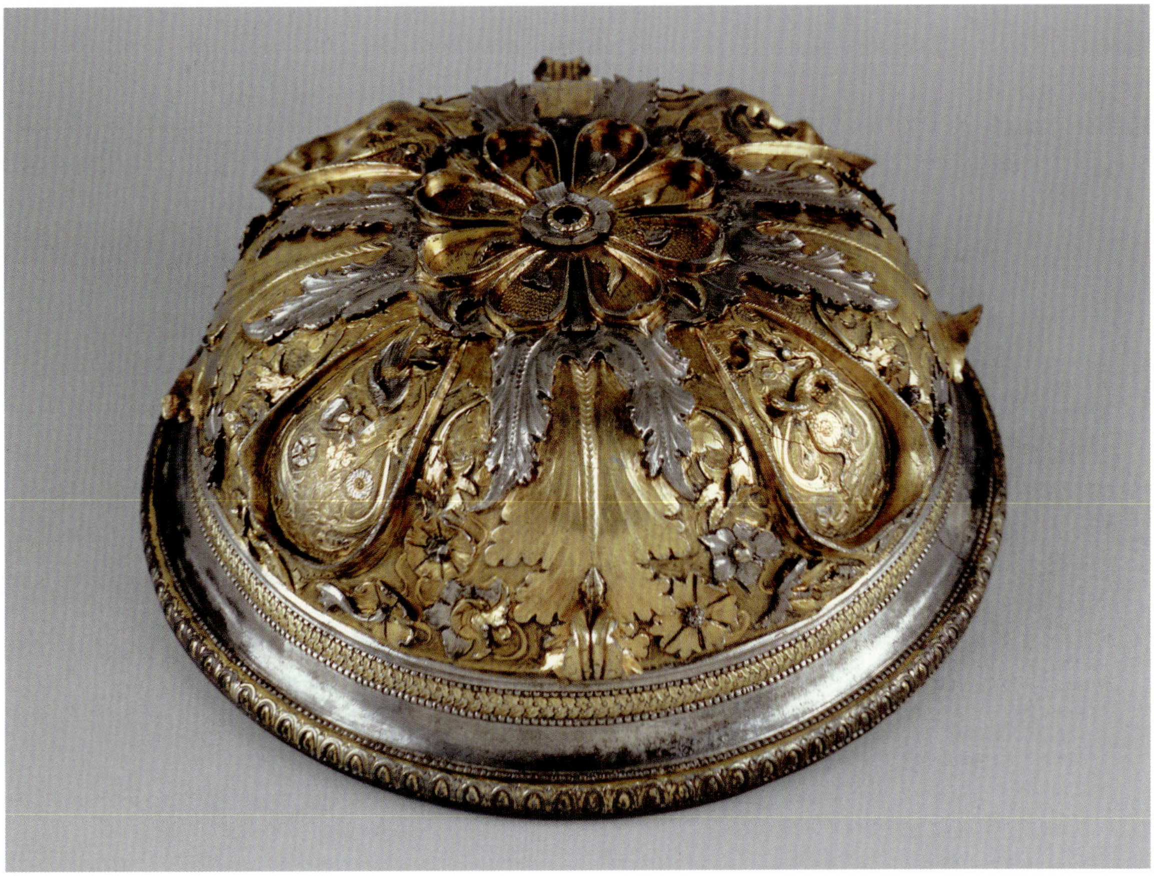

Plate 68 (opposite)
Emblema with Skylla, ca. 300–212 BC. Silver and gold, Diam: 10.5 cm; Thickness: 2 cm; Wt: 81 grams

Plate 69
Hemispherical bowl with floral decoration and small animals, ca. 200–100 BC. Silver, gold, and garnet, Diam: 18.3 cm; Wt: 1.280 kg

Plate 70
Net-patterned bowl, ca. 100–1 BC. Silver, gold, and garnets, H: 5.1 cm; Diam: 20 cm; Wt: 433.8 g

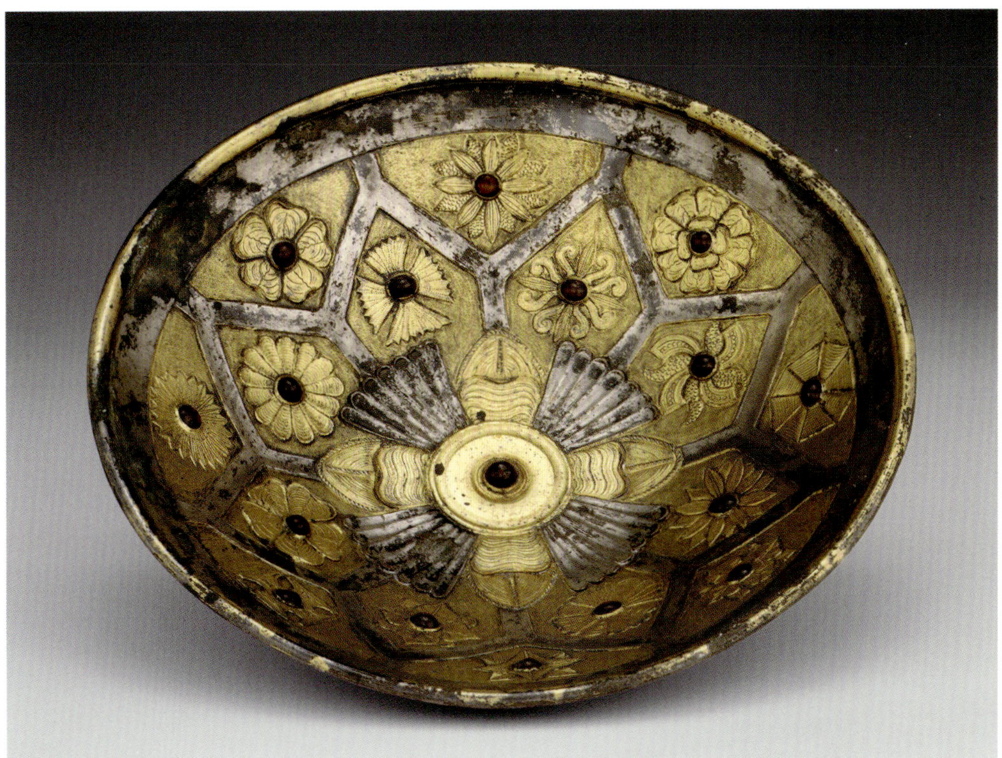

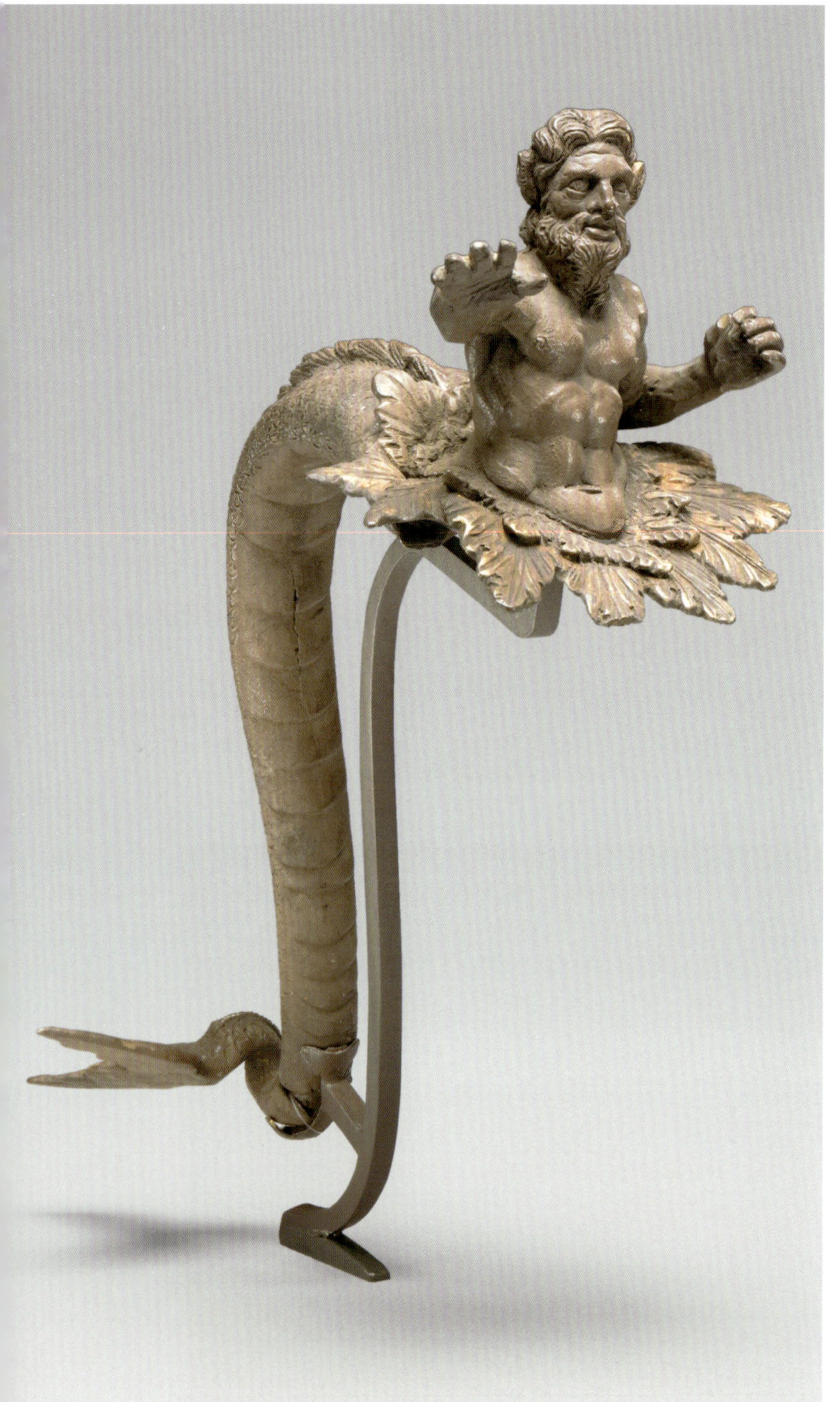

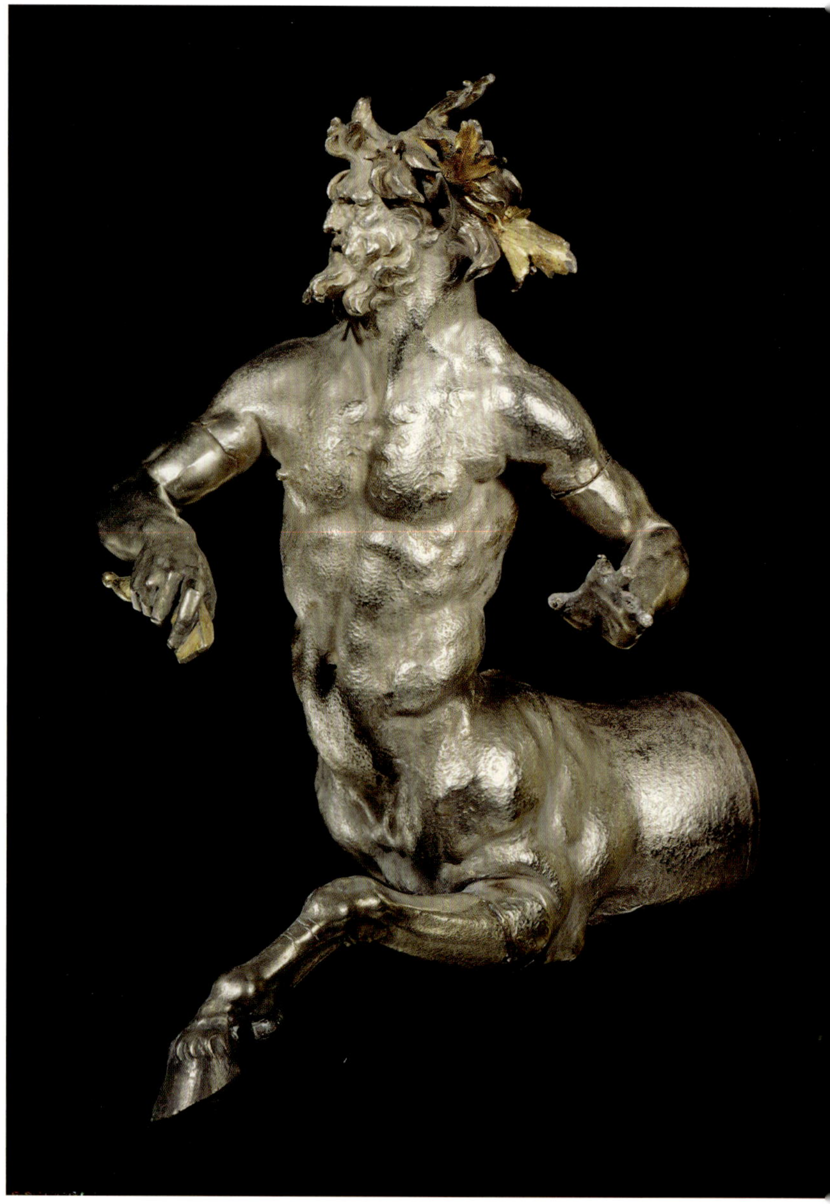

Plate 71
Handle in the form of a Triton,
ca. 100–50 BC. Silver and gold,
H: 27 cm; W: 9.5 cm; Wt: 455.3 grams

Plate 72
Centaur protome from a rhyton,
ca. 160 BC. Silver and gold,
H: 22 cm; Wt: 689 grams

Plate 73 (opposite)
Stag rhyton, ca. 50 BC–AD 50.
Silver, gold, garnet, and glass,
H: 27.4 cm; L: 46 cm; Diam:
12.6 cm; Wt: 899.6 grams

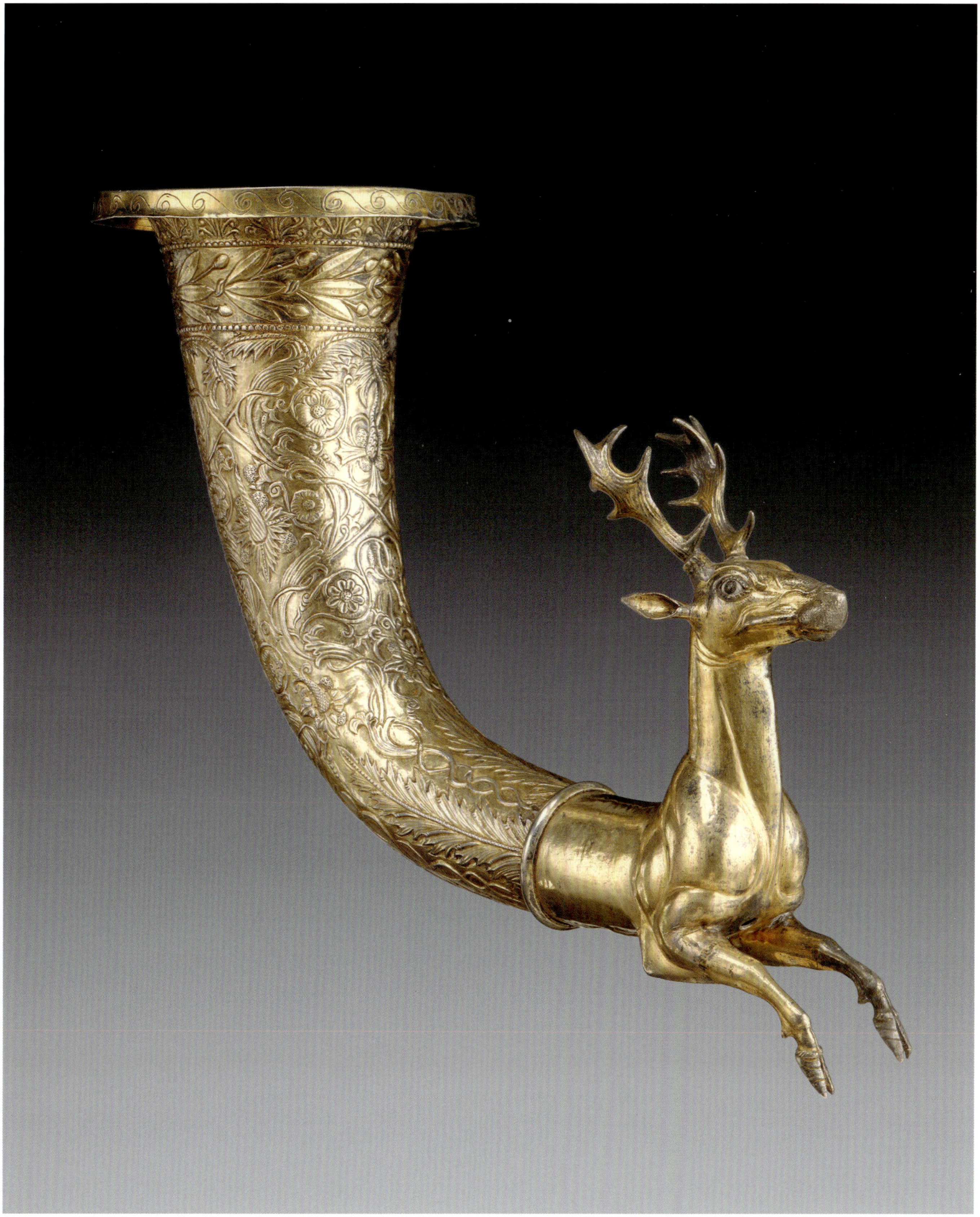

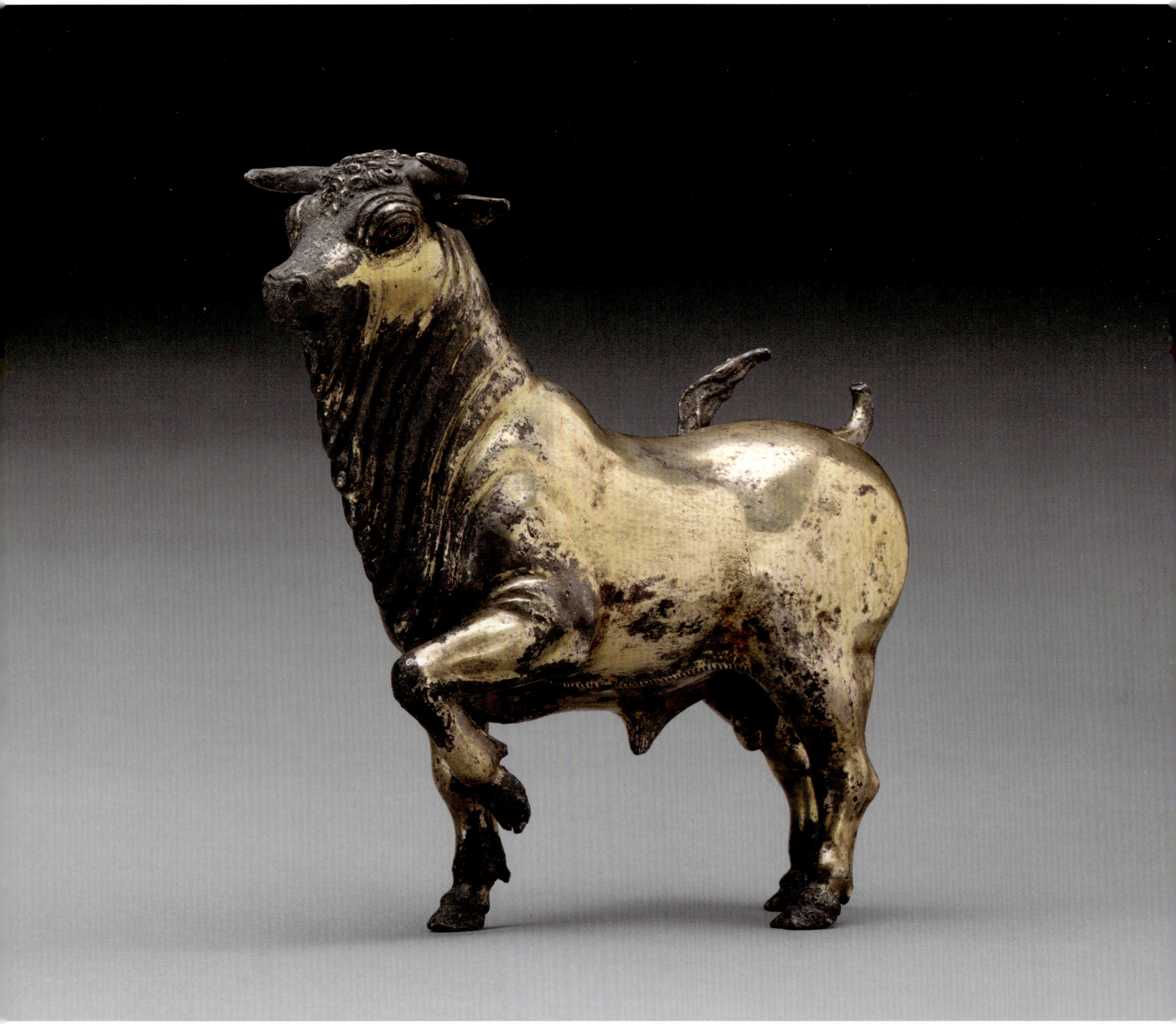

Plate 74

Statuette of a bull, ca. 100 BC–AD 79. Silver and gold, H: 14 cm; Wt: 475 grams

Plate 75

Cup in the form of a bull's head, ca. 100 BC–AD 100. Silver and gold, H: 12.1 cm; Diam: 9.5 cm; Wt: 274 grams

Plate 76

Skyphos with Priam before Achilles, signed by Cheirisophos (Hoby Cup), ca. AD 1–25. Silver and gold, H: 10.9 cm; W (including handles): 21.7 cm; Wt: 975.5 grams

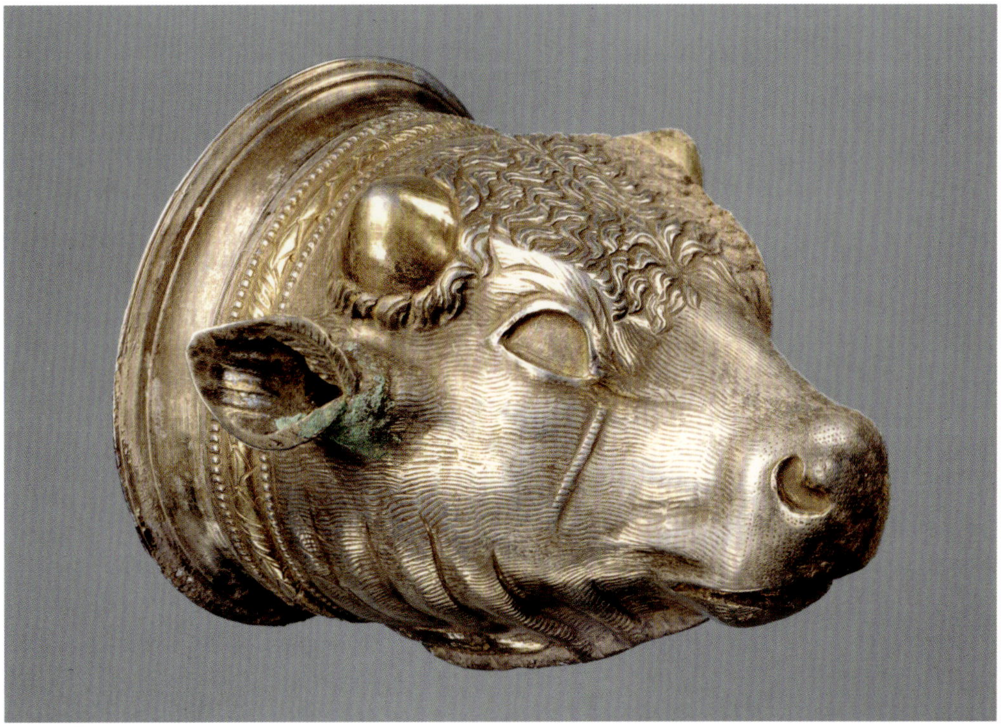

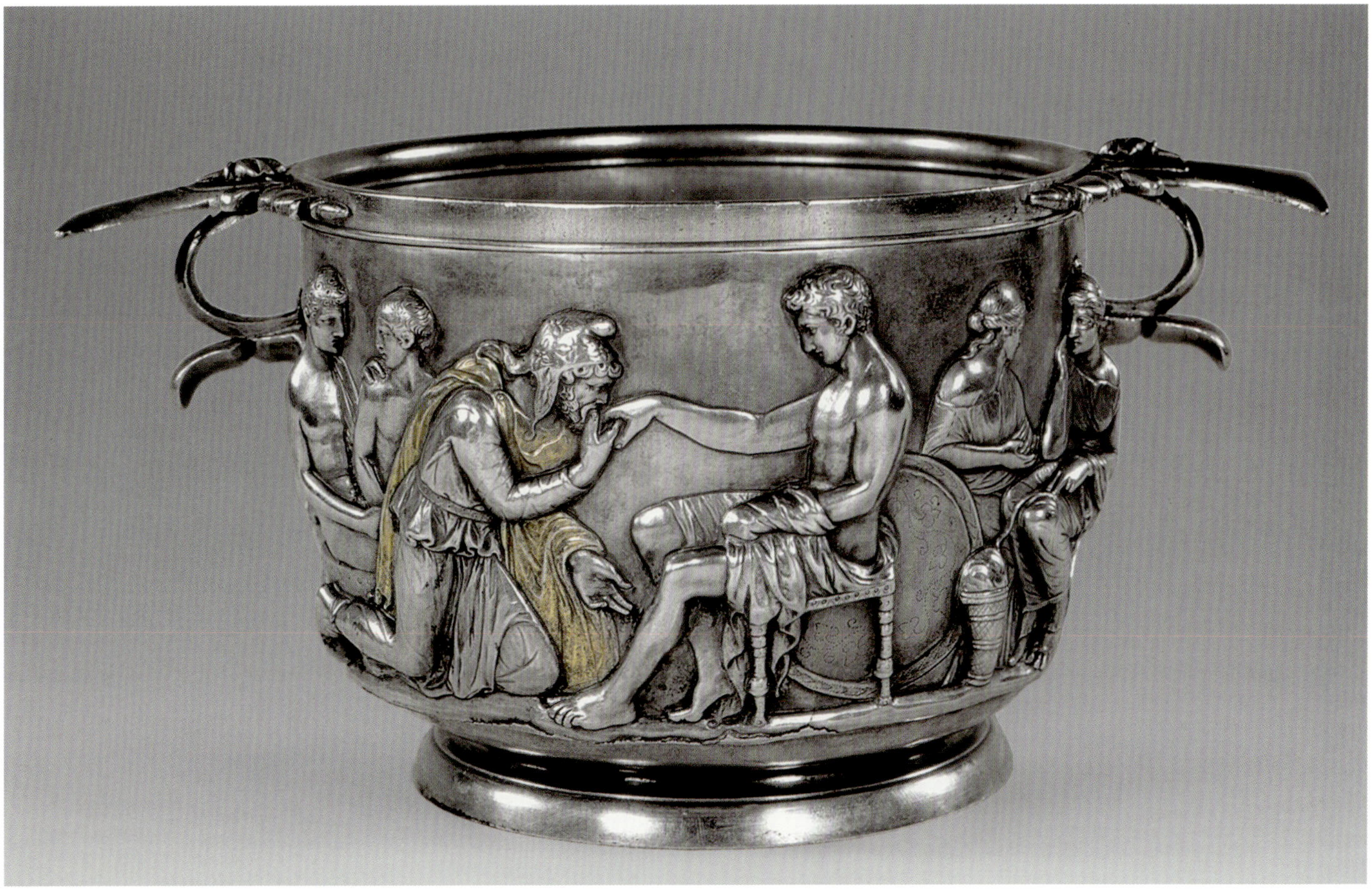

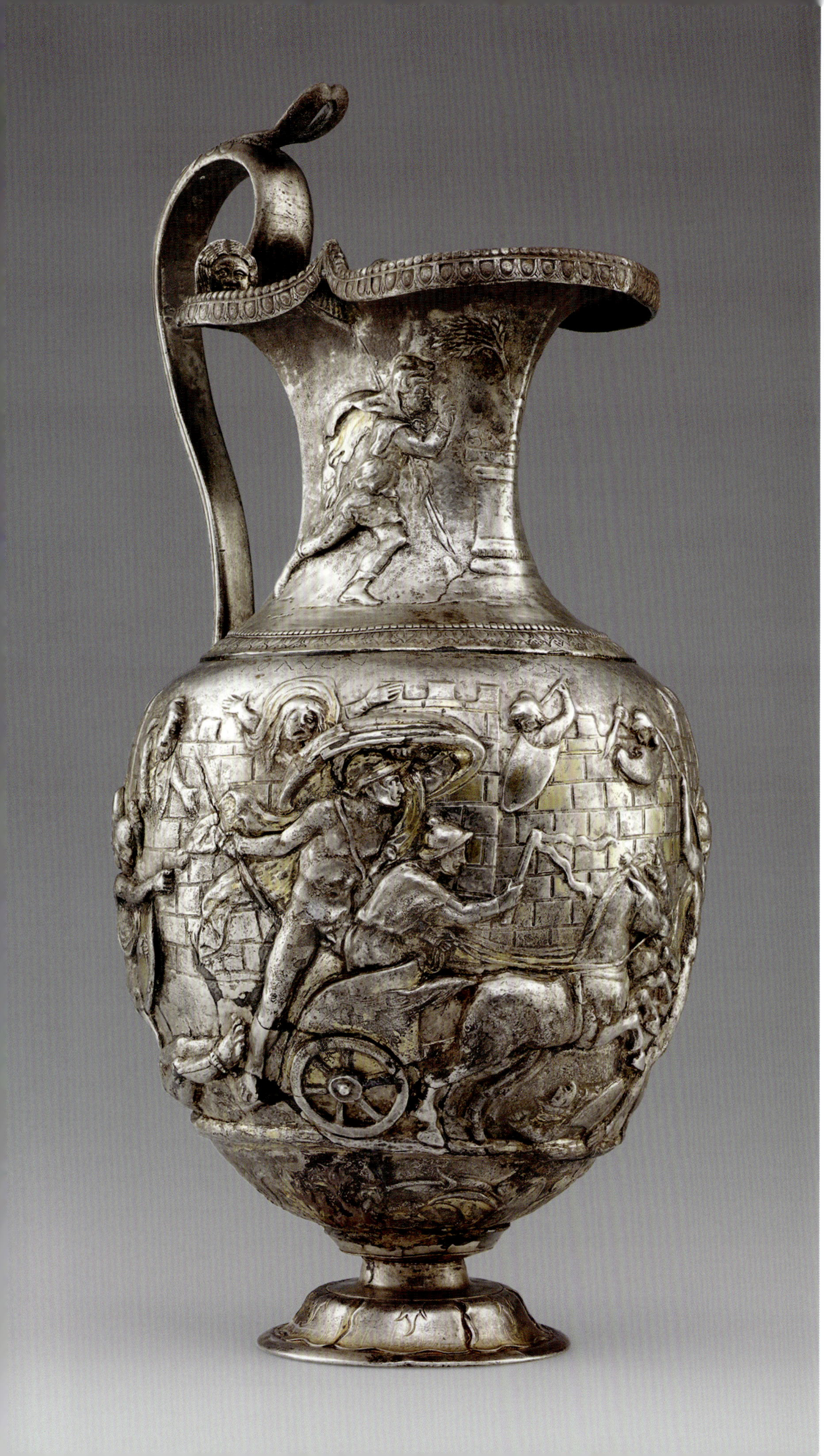

Plate 77
Pitcher with Achilles, AD 1–100.
Silver and gold, H: 31.5 cm;
Wt: 1.159 kg

Plate 78 (opposite, top)
Cup with Centaurs, ca. AD 1–100.
Silver and gold, H: 11.6 cm;
W (including handles): 21.6 cm;
Diam: 15 cm; Wt: 1.653 kg

detail, plate 78 (opposite, bottom)

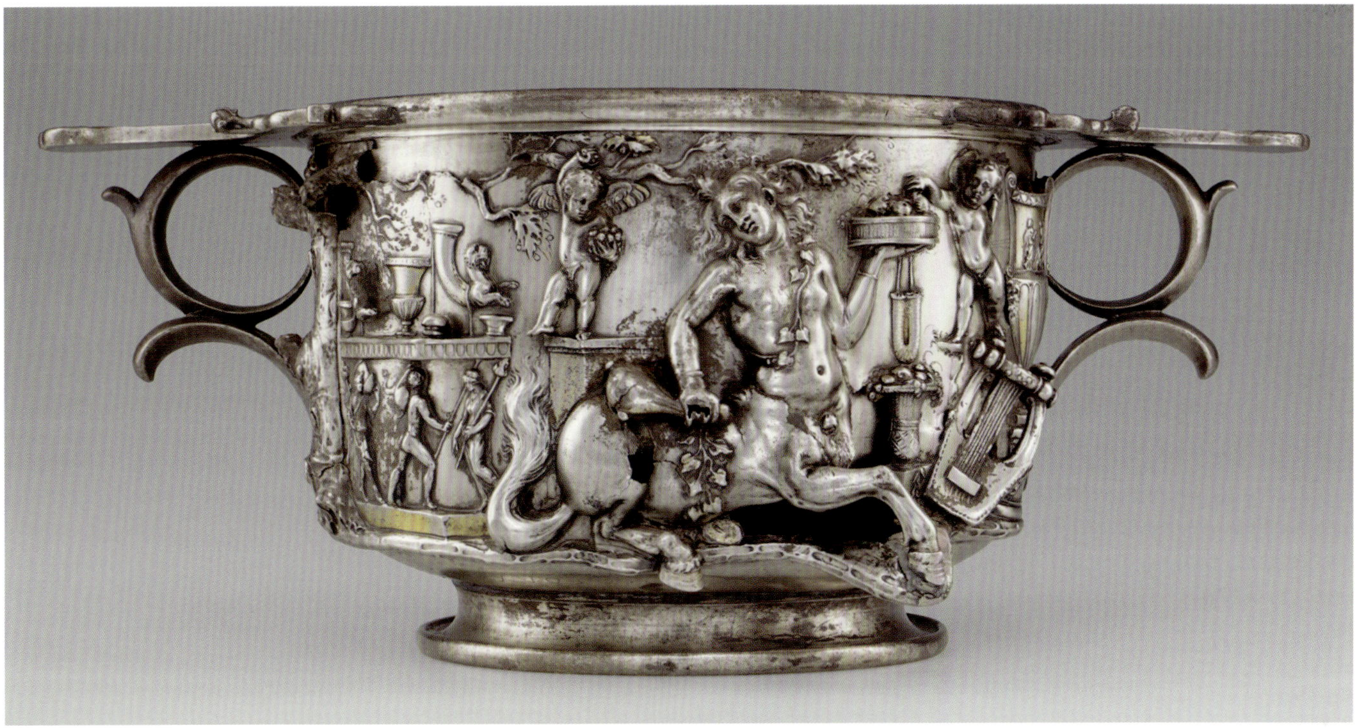

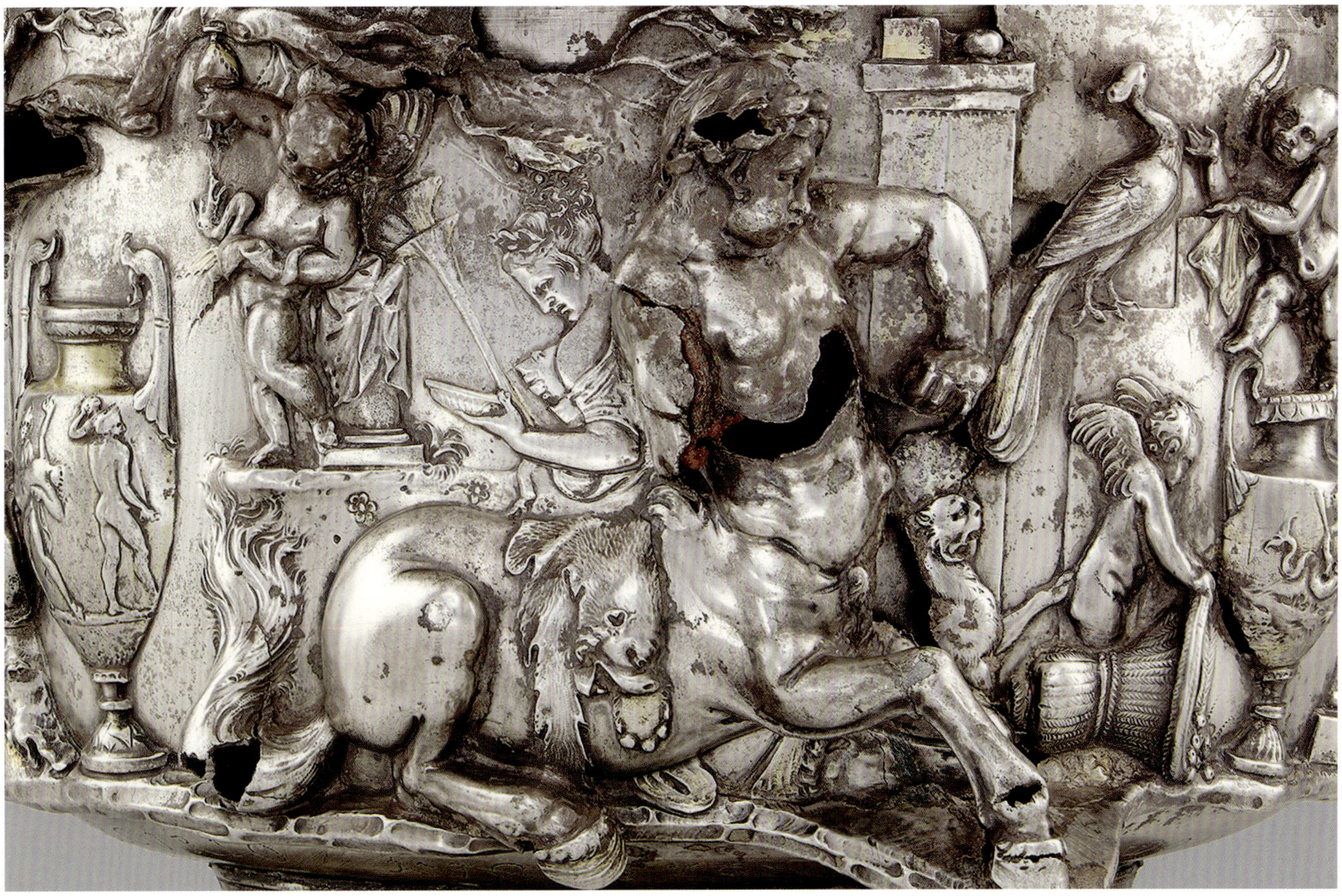

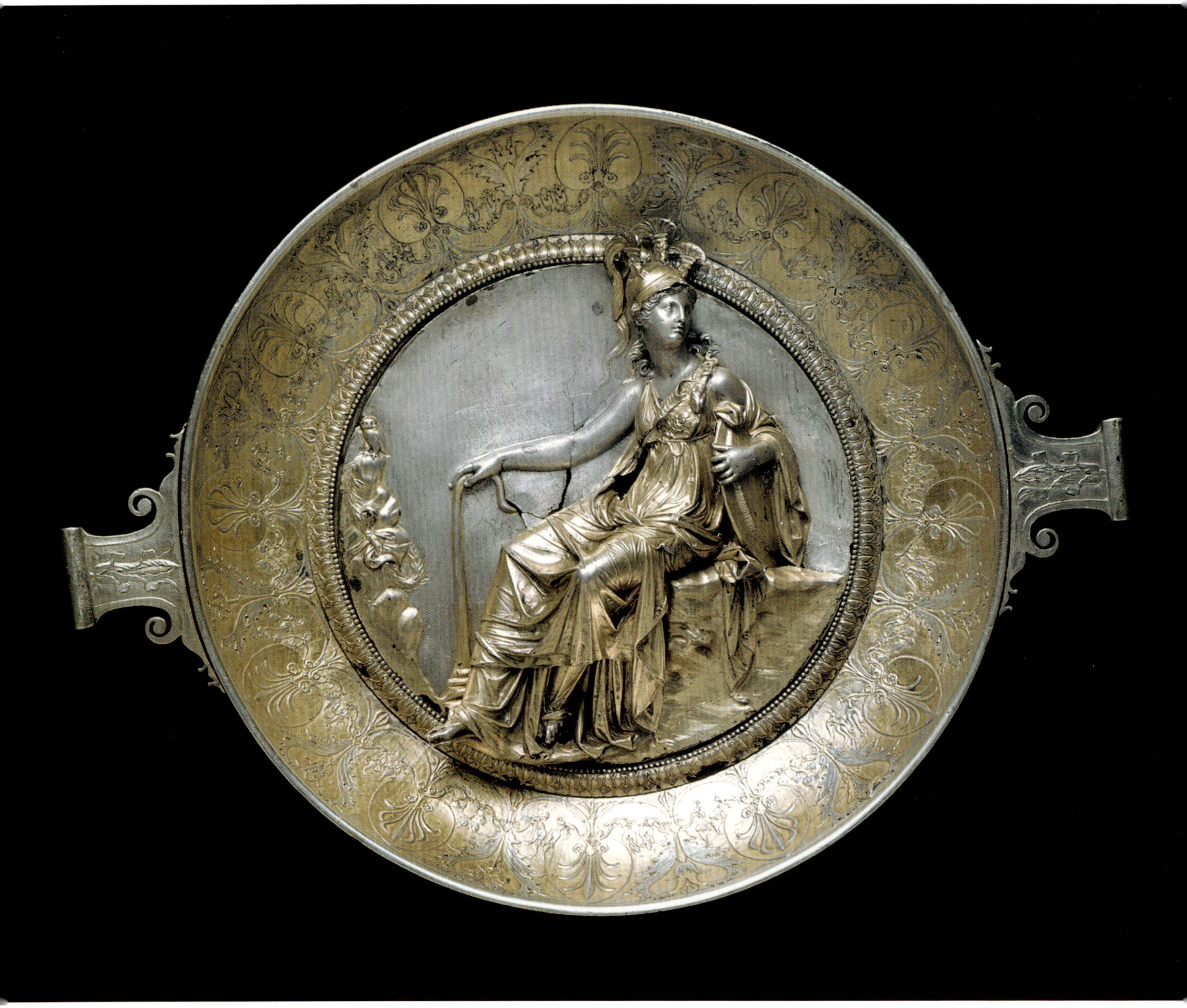

Plate 79
Cup with a medallion of Athena, ca. 75–50 BC. Silver and gold, Diam: 32.5 cm (cup); 16 cm (emblem); Wt: 1.984 kg

Plate 80 (opposite)
Bust of Lucius Verus, AD 161–69. Silver, H: 55 cm; W: 51 cm; Wt: 2.850 kg

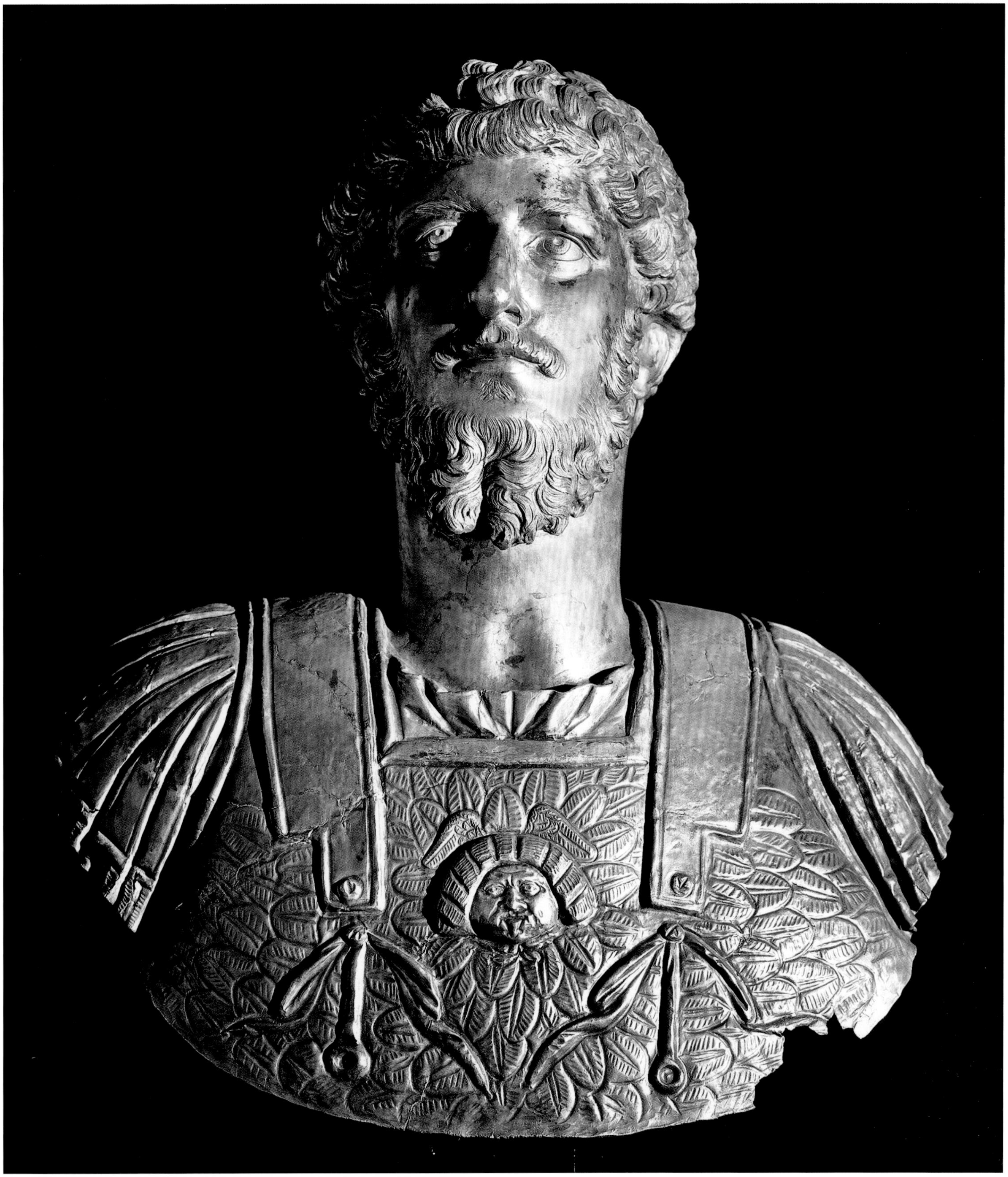

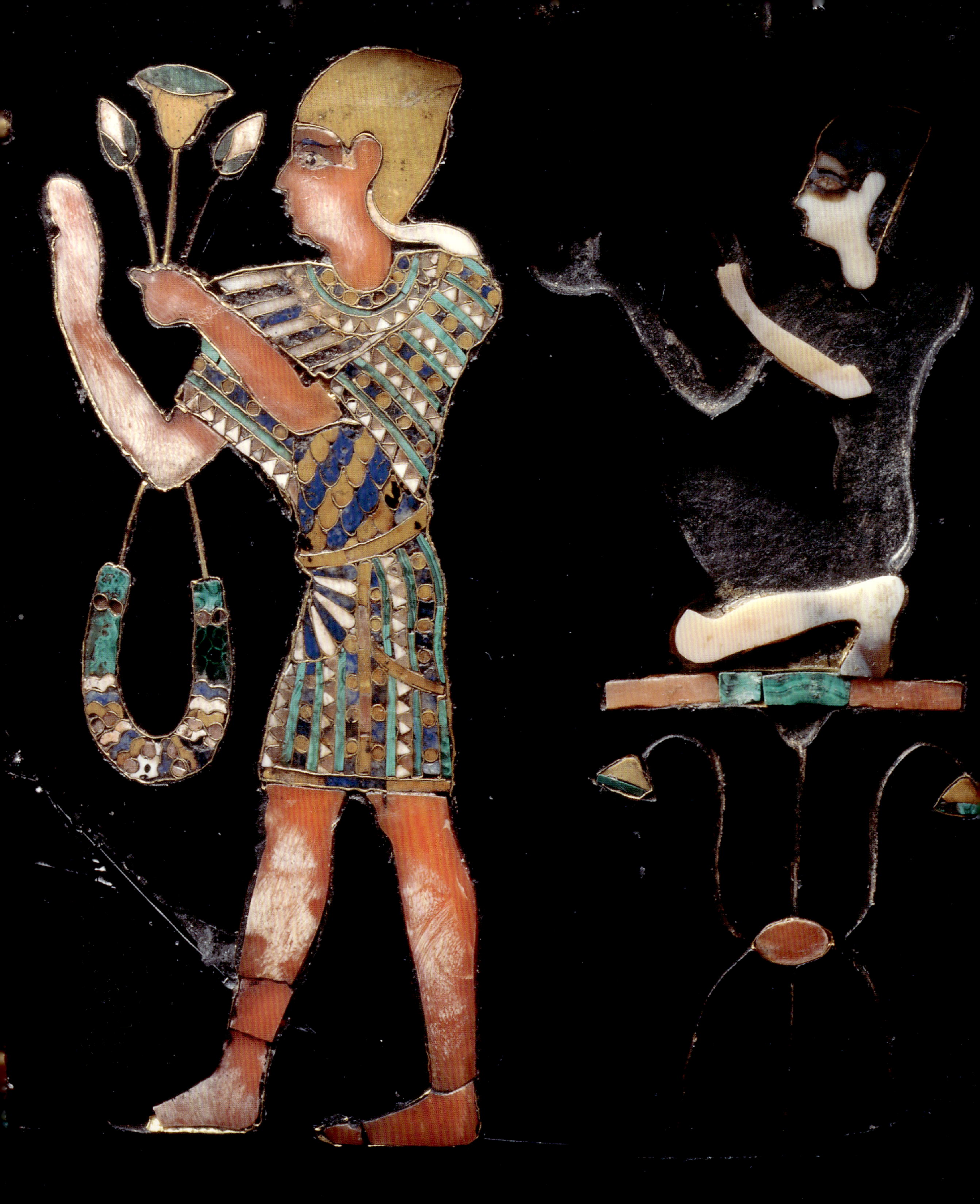

CHAPTER TWO

HARD STONES

Brightly colored minerals, like precious metals, have long fascinated humans. Gemstones such as agate, amethyst, cornelian, jasper, rock crystal, and sardonyx are today considered only semiprecious, but they were prized by Greeks and Romans, as by their Minoan and Mycenaean predecessors and their neighbors in Egypt and the ancient Near East. Found in the beds of streams and rivers, later quarried from the depths of the earth and imported from afar, they were first carved into seals and amulets in Mesopotamia and the Indus Valley as early as the seventh millennium BC. They continued to serve these functions on the shores of the Mediterranean, where, in the first millennium BC, Archaic, Classical, and Hellenistic Greek engravers fashioned them, and other minerals, into works of lasting beauty, as did their successors under the rule of Rome.[1]

Glyptic, a word derived from the ancient Greek verb *glyphein*, meaning to carve or engrave, designates the art of working hard stones. Soft stones, such as serpentine and marble (2 and 3 on the Mohs scale),[2] can readily be cut with metal drills, chisels, and other tools, but the colorful gemstones more often used for intaglios, cameos, vessels, and statuary are considerably harder. These are predominantly quartzes and chalcedonies (microcrystalline quartzes), which rate 6.5–7.5 Mohs, and cannot be cut by metal tools alone (copper is 3 Mohs, iron is 5). Materials as soft as reeds, however, can be used to cut hard stones when they are charged with powdered abrasive mixed with olive oil, as the abrasive, not the tool, actually does the cutting. Abundantly

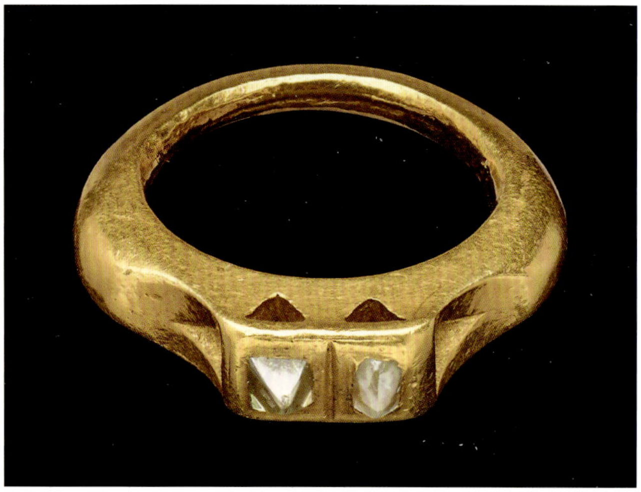

Figure 22
Ring set with two natural octahedral (double, pyramid-shaped) diamonds, third century AD. Gold and diamonds, Diam: 2.2 cm. London, British Museum, 1917,0501.790.

available sand, which is mostly quartz, is effective on many softer stones, but emery, a form of corundum (9 Mohs), readily available on the island of Naxos, was the abrasive commonly used by ancient gem engravers.[3]

Diamonds (10 Mohs) were also known in antiquity, and the Romans occasionally set them uncut into rings (fig. 22). The hardest known natural substance, diamonds can easily be crushed and reduced to powder and used as an abrasive. Pliny mentions several varieties of *adamas* (literally, unconquerable), which he reports were used to cut other gems. Pliny asserts that *adamas* is magnetic, and other references in Latin and Greek texts sometimes seem to concern different materials, perhaps iron or some other metal. Thus the precise meaning of the term in ancient texts remains uncertain.[4]

Indeed, despite frequent similarities in terminology, the seemingly recognizable names of many gemstones mentioned in ancient texts do not necessarily denote the cognate minerals familiar to us. The word *sappheiros*, for example, was used to describe a brilliant blue stone, but one with flecks of gold therein, thus lapis lazuli, not sapphire. The word *jaspis* appears to refer to translucent stones of diverse colors, including chalcedony, not the various opaque stones that we call jaspers. *Topazios* was the ancient word for translucent green peridot, not what we call topaz. In this case confusion arises because the stone was found on a small island in the Red Sea off the coast of southern Egypt that was called Topazios in antiquity (today known as Zabargad, or St. John's Island). Writing in the second century BC, Agatharchides reported that the Ptolemaic governor Philo brought the stone from "Serpent Island" to the Ptolemaic Queen Berenike I, a story repeated by Pliny, who cites the Mauritanian king Juba II as his authority. Pliny further relates that the stone "is a greenish variety of its own, and when first discovered, was preferred to any other . . . and in general its color tends to resemble the tints of the leek."[5] *Smaragdus,* often translated as emerald, seems to have been applied to a variety of dark green stones, most of which might have once been called plasmas or prases, but which modern gemologists would likely identify as quartzes or chalcedonies.

Cornelian, a translucent chalcedony, was the most common material for engraved gems. Reddened by iron oxides, it ranges in color from light orange to dark brown. It takes its name from the cornel fruit, *cornus mas*, which it was thought to resemble. The variant *carnelian* is the result of a false etymology that associated the stone with the color of flesh, *carnis*. Pliny states that the term *sard* (Greek *sardion*), which continues to be used to describe some darker cornelians, is derived from the city of Sardis in Asia Minor. Onyx, from the Greek word for fingernail on account of its thin white layer over another darker color, is actually another form of chalcedonic microcrystalline quartz. So is sardonyx, which has red, yellow, and brown layers and might just as well be called banded agate, although sardonyx is conventionally used to describe stones having more regular, parallel layers. The variant usages of terms today within the disciplines of archaeology and art history, not to mention geology, compound such confusions.

Pliny describes the exotic origins and specific characteristics of more than two hundred different gemstones in the culminating book of his encyclopedic *Natural History*. Indeed, he opens Book 37 by emphasizing the great importance of these materials:

> **Precious stones: a subject in which the majestic might of Nature presents itself to us, contracted within a very limited space, though, in the opinion of many, nowhere displayed in a more admirable form. So great is the value that men attach to the many varieties of these gems, their numerous colours, their constituent parts, and their singular beauty, that, in the case of some of them, it is looked upon as no less than sacrilege to engrave them, for signets even, the very purpose for which, in reality, they were made. Others, again, are regarded as beyond all price, and could not be valued at any known amount of human wealth; so much so that, in the case of many, it is quite sufficient to have some single gem or other before the eyes, there to behold the supreme and absolute perfection of Nature's work.**[6]

Of the forty works by ancient authors Pliny names at various points in his *Natural History* as sources for his research into gems (including books by King Juba of Mauritania and by the emperor Augustus's right-hand man Maecenas), only the *Peri lithon* (*On Stones*) of the polymath Theophrastos, pupil and successor of Aristotle, survives. Pliny translated verbatim several passages from Theophrastos's Greek. Theophrastos was particularly interested in the sources, formation, and other properties of stones that make them exceptional. He enumerates their color, density, hardness, and texture; ascribes many of their particularities to their derivation from fire or water; and describes their diverse reactions to these elements. Of course, many of the characteristics of these stones were not well understood. Darker and lighter sards, for example, were thought to be male and female, respectively, and similar gender distinctions were ascribed to other gems.[7] Following Theophrastos's ideas about the watery origins of some stones, Pliny writes that rock crystal is a petrified form of ice—and thus a suitable material from which to fashion cups for cold drinks.[8] Other stones, such as sardonyx, were ascribed exotic origins, such as Arabia and India, although recent research has revealed they were also found much nearer to hand, for example in Thrace.[9] Such misinformation was perhaps promulgated by merchants and/or carvers seeking to increase the value of their products or to protect their sources. But even if a good deal of what ancient authors convey about gemstones is not factually correct, such writings are nonetheless valuable because they provide information about ancient beliefs, values, and motivations.[10]

The Greeks and Romans, like other peoples before and since, frequently ascribed magical properties to gemstones, the names of which in ancient languages were sometimes associated with their origins or perceived powers: as mentioned above *adamas* was seen as "unconquerable"; *lingourion* was believed to be petrified lynx urine, although Pliny dismissed this story as legend.[11] The word *amethyst* was thought to derive from the Greek *a-methe,* "without drunkenness." Believed to guard against inebriation, it was particularly appropriate for representations of Dionysos and his circle: two poems preserved in the *Palatine Anthology* describe amethysts carved with images of the wine god and Methe, the female personification of drunkenness.[12] Conversely, it might serve for an image of the more sober Apollo (plate 97).

The hue, brightness, and luster of many stones elicited wonder, especially as these characteristics changed with the intensity of light and the angle of view. Color was particularly important, and some stones were thought, through sympathetic magic, to increase fertility, ease childbirth, and to protect against or help to heal disease, scorpion bites, stomach ailments, and eye and other afflictions. Written sources list a host of powers attributed to various stones: protection against the evil eye; the guarantee of safe travel; proficiency in speaking; victory in the courts, in athletic events, or in love; even, under the right combination of circumstances, the power to make one invisible.[13] Thus, the allure of even the finest of engraved gemstones lay in their material as well as their skillfully crafted imagery—as was also the case for uncut and poorly carved gems.

The expansion of the Hellenistic world in the wake of the conquests of Alexander the Great facilitated the export of exotic stones from India and elsewhere to the Mediterranean.[14]

True emeralds, once rare, became more readily available, as did garnets—both are recorded in Hellenistic temple inventories on Delos, as well as in archaeological finds (plates 36–38, 68, 69, 90, 91, 137)—and, eventually, true sapphires (which were imported from India and Sri Lanka and, depending on color, might be called *hyacinthos*, *asterias*, or *crateris*).[15] Such exotic stones feature prominently in the *Lithika* of the early Hellenistic epigrammatist Poseidippos of Pella, recently recovered on a papyrus scroll reused in antiquity to wrap a mummy. The wide geographic distribution of the stones' origins was clearly intended to signal the taste, wealth, and power of Poseidippos's Ptolemaic patrons, who not only mined emeralds in Egypt's southern desert but also imported precious stones from the islands of the Red Sea and beyond.[16] And, as many literary critics have observed, the small scale and exquisite craftsmanship of the gem-engraver provided a fitting analogy for the refined art of the poet.[17]

Being harder than quartzes, emeralds and garnets were less frequently engraved. Polykrates, the sixth-century BC tyrant of Samos, reportedly considered a gold ring set with a *smaragdus* his most valuable possession. It was said to be the work of Theodoros, a master of both monumental and miniature sculpture.[18] When Polykrates's friend Amasis, the pharaoh of Egypt, advised him to give up what he most treasured lest the gods punish him for being too fortunate, the Samian threw the ring into the sea, but it was returned in the belly of a fish presented to him by a local fisherman, leading Amasis to abandon Polykrates before he was, in due course, destroyed by the gods. Pausanias and other ancient authors report that Polykrates's ringstone was green, but Pliny saw a sardonyx, said to be Polykrates's seal, that had been dedicated by the empress Livia in the Temple of Concord at Rome, where it was set in a golden cornucopia—he thought it much less impressive than other gems there.[19] According to some ancient authors, Polykrates's gem was uncut, but Strabo mentions its engraving,[20] and Clement of Alexandria describes its device: a lyre.[21] Poseidippos, for his part, self-referentially adds to his description of this gem a poet who plays the lyre.[22] Other engraved emeralds are recorded: in 86 BC, according to Plutarch, Ptolemy XI offered Lucius Licinius Lucullus a gold ring with a green stone (*smaragdos*) bearing the king's portrait, a gift the Roman patrician was reluctant to accept.[23] The ancients also valued green stones, which were thought to confer benefits on the eyes.[24] Pliny describes several varieties of *smaragdus*, of which he writes:

> **There is no stone, the colour of which is more delightful to the eye; for whereas the sight fixes itself with avidity upon the green grass and the foliage of the trees, we have all the more pleasure in looking upon the *smaragdus*, there being no green in existence of a more intense colour than this. And then, besides, of all the precious stones, this is the only one that feeds the sight without satiating it. Even when the vision has been fatigued with intently viewing other objects, it is refreshed by being turned upon this stone; and lapidaries know of nothing that is more gratefully soothing to the eyes, its soft green tints being wonderfully adapted for assuaging lassitude, when felt in those organs. . . . When the surface of the *smaragdus* is flat, it reflects the image of objects in the same manner as a mirror. The Emperor Nero used to view the combats of the gladiators upon a *smaragdus*.**[25]

The colors of some stones could be—and certainly were—enhanced by dyeing and heating, as well as by immersion in honey; Pliny recommends Corsican honey particularly. This is not as far-fetched as it might sound, for honey can penetrate the microstructure of the mineral and, when heated, it caramelizes or carbonizes, turning the stone, or parts of it, orange, brown, or black. Various other recipes for changing the color of stones survive from ancient Mesopotamia and later Greek papyri. The yellow, orange, and brown bands of agates, especially, were often produced artificially, and some stones were forged outright (e.g., by dyeing rock crystal to look like amethyst, beryl, or emerald). Pliny knew "no other trickery practiced against society with greater profit."[26] Glass became cheap and widespread after the first century BC and

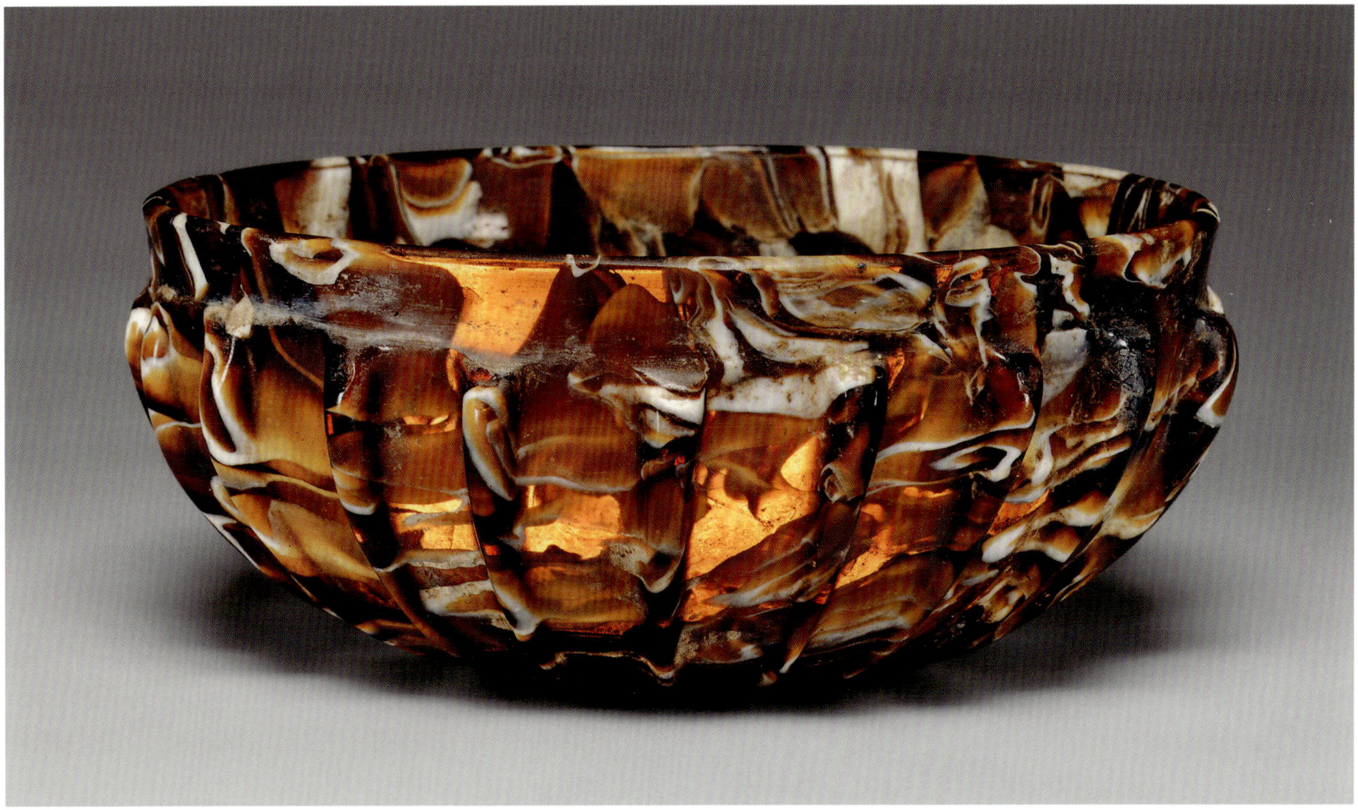

Figure 23
Ribbed bowl imitating irregularly banded agate, first century BC–first century AD. Glass, H: 7.5 cm; Diam: 18 cm. Malibu, JPGM, 72.AF.37 (compare plates 119–128).

was frequently produced in different colors (or none) so as to imitate more precious hard stones. It could be made dark green like emerald or malachite, blue like lapis lazuli, variegated like banded agate (fig. 23) or murrhine (plates 133, 134), or clear like rock crystal, as Pliny noted. Indeed, he also remarked, "glass gems are for the masses."[27]

The magnifying effects of rock crystal were recognized in antiquity, but there is no evidence that lenses made out of that stone—or any other material—were used by ancient gem engravers.[28] It has, however, been suggested that the craft, passed from father to son, might have profited from the hereditary nature of myopia. In any case, gems were carved using a slurry of abrasive powder suspended in oil, which darkened as it combined with the detritus of stone and tool worn away in the process of engraving, so that much of the carving was effectively done "blind." Neither Theophrastos nor Pliny provides much information about the techniques used by ancient engravers, but the process appears to have changed little over the millennia, apart from the advent of power tools and more readily available diamond powder today, in contrast to less

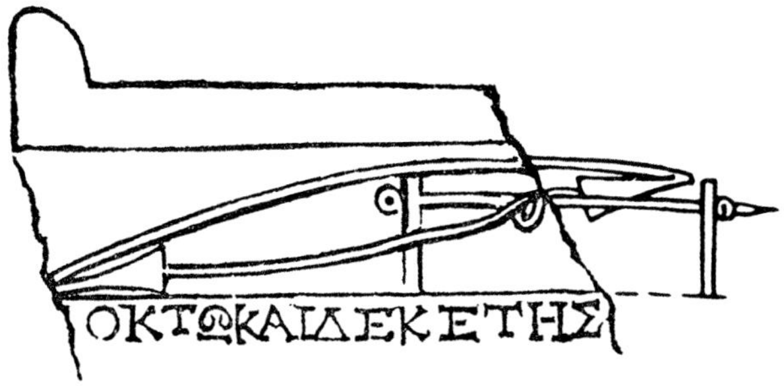

Figure 24
Drawing of the fragmentary gravestone of Doros, an eighteen-year-old *daktylou-koiloglyphos* (engraver of gems for rings), who lived in Asia Minor in the second century AD, depicting a horizontal lathe powered by a bow.

durable corundum (emery). (Although corundum, 9 on the Mohs scale, is just below diamond at 10 Mohs, in absolute terms diamond is estimated to be more than one hundred times harder than corundum and a thousand times harder than quartz, which rates 7 Mohs.)

The fragmentary gravestone of an eighteen-year-old gem engraver preserves an image of a horizontal lathe powered by a bow, which seems to have been the principal instrument of ancient gem cutters (fig. 24).[29] Bits of different shapes—wheels, cones, balls, for the most part, rather than drills—similar to modern dental instruments, were slotted into the lathe, charged with an abrasive slurry, and the carver applied the stone to the spinning tool. Although it seems likely that some jewelers' lathes might have been powered by heavier wheels or foot pedals, high speeds were not necessary and can be detrimental to the fine work of gem engraving, occasioning the loss of abrasive through excessive centrifugal force or—worse—loss of control.

Ancient engravers, like modern ones, probably fashioned their own tools: differently shaped bits designed to create different cuts. It also appears that carvers began by using bigger tools to remove larger areas of stone and then proceeded to smaller, finer tools—and finer-grade abrasives—for details. This is also suggested by the evidence of unfinished gems where tool marks have not been polished away. Final polishing was achieved using files as well as wooden tools, leather, felt, and cloth, dipped in increasingly fine slurry.[30]

INTAGLIOS

Intaglios, from the modern Italian word *intagliare* (to cut into), were carved into the stone, creating a negative space, so that when the gem was pressed into wax, clay, or some other soft material it created a relief impression that was the reverse of the image in the stone itself. Thus inscriptions that were intended to be read in impression were cut in reverse. Some inscriptions, including occasional carvers' signatures, were engraved so they could be read on the stone itself, suggesting that these gems were also intended to be admired in their settings, for which there is ample literary testimony, especially in Hellenistic and Roman epigrams. Nonetheless, depending on the color or veining of the stone, the image carved into it might be difficult to see in the gem itself. Indeed, there must have been something magical about seeing, say, a portrait emerge from the impression of a hard-to-read multicolored intaglio (plates 85, 87). Poseidippos, in fact, writes of such phenomena, contrasting both the appearance of the same stone when wet and dry, and of an intaglio and its impression:

> This is a cunning stone. When oiled,
> a lustre, a miracle of mirage, follows its entire mass.
> Yet when dry, an engraved Persian lion
> shines brilliantly, stretching against the lovely sun.[31]

> No river rolled this stone onto its banks, but at one time
> the well-bearded head of a snake held it,
> streaked with white. The chariot engraved upon it,
> resembling a white mark on a fingernail, was carved
> by the eyes of Lynkeios. For after an imprint is taken
> the chariot is seen, but on the surface you do not see any
> projections.
> In which fact resides a great marvel of labor,
> how the craftsman while straining did not damage his eyes.[32]

Ancient writers praised not only the carvers of elaborate scenes, sometimes by name, but also stones that appeared to have images formed spontaneously therein. Pliny describes an agate that belonged to King Pyrrhos of Epiros "upon which were to be seen the Nine Muses and Apollo holding a lyre; not a work of art, but the spontaneous produce of Nature, the veins in it being so arranged that each of the Muses had her own peculiar attribute." Wonder at the complex imagery that could be depicted in such a small space was, and remains, a key element of the appeal of engraved gemstones, which reward close examination. Indeed, the same vocabulary of praise for subtle, refined, detailed work was applied by ancient critics to both poetry and works of art.[33]

Intaglios used as seals, called *sphragides* in Greek (singular: *sphragis*) and *sigilla* in Latin (singular: *sigillum*), were often closely associated with their owners; the ensuing image was known in Greek as a *charakter*. In Sophokles's *Elektra* the protagonist accepts that her brother Orestes has returned only when he shows her the seal of their father, Agamemnon.[34] Similarly, in the *Trachiniai* Deianeira gives Lichas an impression of her ring to show to her husband, Herakles, "as a token that he will surely recognize."[35] Pressed into wax or clay, intaglios could seal letters, chests, or storerooms. In Aischylos's *Agamemnon*, when the king returns from Troy, his wife, Klytemnestra, sends him a message stating that he will find his treasures intact, with no seal broken.[36] In Aristophanes's comedy *Thesmophoriazousai*, the chorus of Athenian women complains that their husbands' seals make it difficult for them to steal wine and oil from the household stores.[37]

States and other corporate entities had official seals. Those of Athens are mentioned in the speeches of fourth-century BC orators; and impressions of the public seals of local magistrates and the official seals of neighboring and more distant states have been found among the sealings recovered from the excavations of ancient archives at a variety of sites, although the documents they accompanied are almost always lost. At Delos, for example, impressions of the official seals of Naxos, Mykonos, Ephesos, Kolophon, and Tralles, as well as of officials serving the Seleucid kings, have all been found; likewise at Seleukia on the Tigris.[38]

According to Diogenes Laertius, the Athenian lawgiver Solon decreed in the early sixth century BC that gem engravers should not keep copies of the seals they carved so as to protect their clients against identity theft.[39] Nonetheless, more than half a millennium later, Lucian described a method of casting duplicate seals from impressions and thus gaining surreptitious access to letters and other secured items.[40] The archaeological record, however, provides ample evidence for the wide repetition of devices on engraved gems, whether representations of gods in various guises, personifications, mythological and genre scenes, animals, or even objects, such as anchors, vessels, and lyres. Distinctive and finely carved portraits are exceptional (and the selection of images presented here privileges such skillfully produced items). The fact of the matter is that engraved gemstones, though valuable, were not so precious that small, cursorily carved examples with repetitive subjects, produced serially by a number of modest workshops, were not widely available to what we might consider the ancient equivalent of the middle class.[41]

Well-to-do individuals might commission from master craftsmen their own portraits or other meaningful images on their seals. The Roman dictator Sulla apparently chose an image of the surrender of the Numidian king Jugurtha, whom he brought to Rome in chains. Pompey's signet featured a lion holding a sword; Julius Caesar's seal depicted his ancestor, Venus Victrix—the armed Venus.[42] Augustus is reported to have employed different seals during the course of his life. He first used a pair of identical sphinx intaglios found among his mother's effects and took advantage of the fact that he could entrust one to his lieutenants to seal letters in his absence. When gibes about the inscrutability of the mythical beast became too much, he adopted a seal of Alexander the Great, the connotations of which were abundantly clear. Eventually he commissioned his own portrait from Dioskourides, a skilled engraver originally from Aigai in Asia Minor, some of whose gems survive to this day, as do several produced by his three sons, who followed him in the craft (plates 95, 96, 109, 114).[43]

Although ancient literature does provide a few examples to the contrary, most devices engraved on gemstones must have pleased their owners. Kallikrates, who lived in Alexandria during the rule of Ptolemy III in the later third century BC, wore an image of Odysseus on his seal ring: he also named his children Telegonos and Antikleia after characters related to the hero of the *Odyssey*, a new edition of which the king had commissioned from his scholars in the Mouseion.[44] Commodus is said to have had an Amazon on his ring because of the pleasure he took in seeing his mistress Marcia so attired—and she evidently lived up to the masquerade by taking part in his assassination![45] Seal devices might serve as omens: Plutarch tells of the fourth-century BC general Timoleon's lieutenants vying to lead a charge against the enemy, each being unwilling to follow another: "wishing, therefore, to decide their order by lot, Timoleon took a seal-ring from each of the leaders, and after casting all the rings into his own cloak and mixing them up, he showed the first that came out, and it had by chance as the device of its seal a trophy of victory [compare plate 86]. When the young men saw it, they cried aloud for joy and would no longer wait for the others, but all dashed through the river as fast as they could and closed with the enemy."[46] Centuries later, on New Year's day in AD 68, Nero's *puer delicatus* Sporus gave the emperor a ring set with a gemstone inscribed with the Rape of Persephone, which was later considered to be a harbinger of his death.[47]

Seal devices may also have punningly referred to their owners' names. It is easy to imagine a lion intaglio belonging to someone with one of the *Leo*-stemmed names common in Greece, for women as well as men. *Leaena*, the lover of the tyrannicide Aristogeiton, was allegedly honored for her bravery by the Athenians with a bronze statue of a lioness.[48] *Leontia* and *Leontodama* are other feminine names attested by epigraphic sources; and there are many male ones: *Leon, Leontas, Leonides, Nikoleon,* and so forth. A Greek called Nikias or a Roman named Victor might well use a winged victory as a device. In the *Birds* Aristophanes wrote of many Athenians with avian nicknames, images of which could conceivably have been represented on their seals.[49]

As early as the fifth century BC there is evidence of seal rings being given as tokens of friendship. In his description of Polygnotos's painting of the Underworld, Pausanias mentions a certain Isaios who gave his friend Phokos a gold ring with an inscribed stone.[50] Plutarch reports that the Spartan general Klearchos gave the doctor/historian Ktesias a ring depicting dancing *karyatides*, "which he might show to his kindred and friends in Sparta."[51] Centuries later, Ovid referred to his friends wearing rings bearing his portrait, while Chariton, Martial, and other authors wrote of portraits on rings being given as mementos to friends and lovers, both real and fictional.[52]

Some gem devices indicated philosophical or political leanings. Intaglios of Sokrates seem to have been especially popular, and Cicero has his friend Atticus joke about the many Epicureans who wore rings with images of the founder of their school.[53] A fine Late Republican intaglio depicting Demosthenes and signed by the carver Apelles (plate 99), however, might indicate more than admiration for the ancient Athenian statesman or desire for oratorical success. Cicero titled his speeches against Mark Antony the *Philippics*, recalling Demosthenes's diatribes of the same name against Philip of Macedon; the owner of Apelles's gem might well have harbored Republican sympathies. Wearing a glyptic image of a ruler openly signaled one's allegiance. Lucullus rejected Ptolemy XI's gift of an emerald engraved with his portrait. The philosopher Athenion is reported to have returned from Asia to Athens in 88 BC wearing a gold ring engraved with the portrait of the Pontic king Mithradates.[54] Centuries later, Saint Ambrose recalled having read that certain persons who wore rings bearing portraits of Brutus and Cassius, the assassins of Caesar, were condemned to capital punishment.[55] Late in the reign of Tiberius it could even be considered a capital crime to carry a ring or a coin stamped with Augustus's image into a privy or a brothel.[56] Pliny mentions that the emperor Claudius marked the particular status of those who had free access to him by the gift of gold rings engraved with his image.[57] Josephus, meanwhile, reports that following the death of Caligula, his co-consul Gnaeus Sentius Saturninus passionately urged the senate to regain the liberties it had been robbed of, forgetting that throughout his speech he still wore a ring with a portrait of the detested tyrant. This, however, was noticed by Trebellius Maximus, who removed Saturninus's ring and smashed the image.[58] Upon the death of their owners, seal rings were buried or consigned to the pyre, though they could be passed on to heirs.[59] Pompey's ring was delivered to Julius Caesar, and the premature removal of Tiberius's ring (bearing Dioskourides's portrait of Augustus) from his finger was considered a harbinger, if not a cause, of his death.[60]

CAMEOS

In contrast to intaglios, which were cut into the stone and intended to replicate their imagery, in reverse, when used as seals pressed in softer materials, cameos were carved in relief and functioned, for the most part, as decorative objects. (A few of the numerous ancient clay impressions recovered from a Hellenistic archive on Delos, however, demonstrate that cameos could occasionally be used as seals.)[61] Although miniature sculpture in hard stone, notably amulets, had long been produced in ancient Egypt and the Near East, and the beetles of scarabs, which were popular in Archaic Greece, might in a sense be considered cameos, reliefs that exploited the layered multicolored structure of banded agate to create polychrome compositions with striking effect appear to have been invented in the Hellenistic period, perhaps as early as the third century BC. The origins of the modern term *cameo* remain uncertain, but Pliny mentions several multicolored gemstones suitable for the carving of reliefs, using the Greek term for relief *ektypon*: *gemmae quae ad ectypas scalpturas aptantur*; Seneca similarly describes a cameo of the emperor Tiberius: *imago Tiberii Caesaris ectypa et eminente gemma.*[62]

Cameos were produced with the same basic tools and techniques as intaglios, albeit inverted, that is to say by cutting away excess stone around the image to create a raised relief, rather than cutting the image into the stone. Although this technical reversal can be compared to, say, the earlier shift from black- to red-figure in Athenian vase painting, like that change it was not as simple as it might appear. First, to be most effective visually, cameos could not be carved from any stone but required multilayered banded agates, usually sardonyxes, the colors of which, as mentioned above, were often artificially enhanced. This allowed a light figure to stand out from a dark background, or vice versa, or in exceptional cases allowed for multilayered compositions (plates 102–118).

The time and effort needed to carve a cameo is considerably greater than that required to produce an intaglio, not just because more stone must be cut away but also because in fashioning a cameo in relief there is considerably less surface contact between the rotating circular tool and the convex surface of the gem. This is in contrast to an intaglio, where the circular tool has greater contact with the concave image it creates. Even more time is needed to produce cameos of high quality, for during the modeling of rounded, raised forms the tool often has just the slightest, tangential contact with the stone. Thus many less accomplished cameos are quite flat, while truly exceptional ones achieve a remarkable modeling of sculptural forms—the result of painstaking work. Some of these cameos even have undercut features (plates 109, 115), making them unsuitable for use as seals, a reminder that cameos were typically meant to be seen and admired in their own right.

Carving through differently hued layers of stone allows the engraver to distinguish not only foreground from background but also details, such as flesh from hair or drapery, and to create such colorful effects as blushing cheeks or mottled animal skins. Similarly, a master carver might cut an overlying band of stone so thinly as to suggest the transparency of drapery (plate 105) or to create the illusion of the play of light and shadow and thus illusionistically model a figure's body (plate 116). The peculiarities of any given stone can both create challenges for the carver and be exploited by him, for the layers of banded agates are not always straight or regular, and their thickness and direction cannot necessarily be predicted from surface features visible before carving. The master carver therefore must be adept not only at following the undulating layers of the stone but also at adapting the design to avoid or exploit some unexpected feature that might arise in the course of carving. For example, the layers of the so-called Gonzaga Cameo (plate 103), widely believed to be one of the earliest surviving cameos and to depict Ptolemy II Philadelphos and his sister/wife Arsinoe II (although other sitters and dates have been proposed), might appear to be regular when the object is seen straight on, with a thick white layer sandwiched between two dark brown ones. Oblique views, however, reveal irregular waves of white that undulate and drop back on the right side, above, and forward at the shoulder. At the bottom, moreover, the layers are intermingled, and white rises up through the brown. How much of this was evident to the carver before he began carving we cannot know. It seems that while he must have planned to place the Medusa's head on the aegis in the white layer, he may have been surprised by more white rising up further to the right and adapted his composition during the course of carving, masterfully adding another head—that of a bearded, wild-haired male identified as Phobos (the personification of terror).

CONTEXTS

Small intaglios and cameos were set into rings, and larger ones might be worn as pendants or otherwise used as decoration, as were uncut stones, which were employed in a variety of contexts. According to Pausanias, the throne of Pheidias's statue of Zeus at Olympia was "adorned with gold and precious stones," and the excavation of Pheidias's workshop there has turned up numerous fragments of rock crystal, as well as glass, amber, shell, and other materials. Plato reports that the eyes of Pheidias's statue of Athena in the Parthenon were precious stones, perhaps chalcedonies; and Pliny writes of a marble statue of a lion on the tomb of a Cypriot king, the eyes of which were set with bright green stones.[63]

In antiquity, as today, some individuals wore jewelry ostentatiously, to flaunt their wealth, to make a fashion statement, or both. Aristophanes scoffed at the youth of his day loading their fingers with onyxes; Plato was said to have criticized Aristotle's luxurious clothing and multiple rings; and Martial disparaged a certain Carinus who "wears six rings on each finger and does not take them off at night, or even when he bathes." The poet was kinder toward his friends. Statius, for his part, writes of a father who "set afire with vivid jewels" the fingers of his eleven-year-old son; and Seneca complains about people who wore gem-studded rings on every joint (*in omno articulo gemma disponintur*). Quintilian warns aspiring orators not to "overload their hands with rings, which should under no circumstance encroach upon the middle joint of the finger," presumably so as not to distract the audience.[64] Surviving statues and other representations demonstrate that wearing rings higher on the finger was popular in antiquity, as it was in the Renaissance, and a fragmentary mummy shroud from Roman Egypt (fig. 25) illustrates how several rings might be worn simultaneously.

In antiquity, as today, such ostentation seems to have been particularly prevalent among successful entertainers. According to Pliny, the famous fourth-century BC Theban musician Ismenias, a man "in the habit of displaying great numbers of glittering stones, a piece of vanity, on his part," learned that a *smaragdus* engraved with the figure of Amymone, the "blameless" daughter of Danaos and consort of Poseidon, was being sold on Cyprus. Ismenias, who also seems to have written about gems, sent a trusted slave with instructions to acquire the gem. When the man returned and reported that the sellers, having learned the identity of the celebrity buyer, discounted the price by a third, Ismenias was furious and declared, "By Herakles! I've been wronged, for the stone has been robbed of much of its value."[65] Pliny relates this anecdote in Latin, but it is worthwhile to note that in ancient Greek the words for price and honor were the same: *timē*.

Ancient literature also preserves references to gem-studded weapons, chariots, and, of course, vessels, which appear to have been increasingly fashionable in the wake of Alexander's eastern conquests. In fact, one of Theophrastos's *Characters* falsely boasts about the "gem-studded cups" (*lithokolleta poteria*) he brought back from his participation in Alexander's campaigns, and similar items (see plates 69, 70) are recorded in the inventories of the temples on the Athenian Acropolis as having been dedicated to Athena Polias by Alexander's wife Rhoxane.[66] According to Kallixeinos of Rhodes, a huge gold crown adorned with multicolored gems was displayed amid other precious objects in the Grand Procession of Ptolemy II Philadelphos in the early third century BC. The same author reports that a conspicuous feature at that king's great banquet was a large couch piled high with "goblets, cups, and utensils—all of gold and studded with jewels—of wondrous workmanship." Centuries later, Cleopatra held a royal symposium for Mark Antony, at which the furnishings were all of gold inlaid with gems. She also sent him love letters written on tablets of rock crystal.[67]

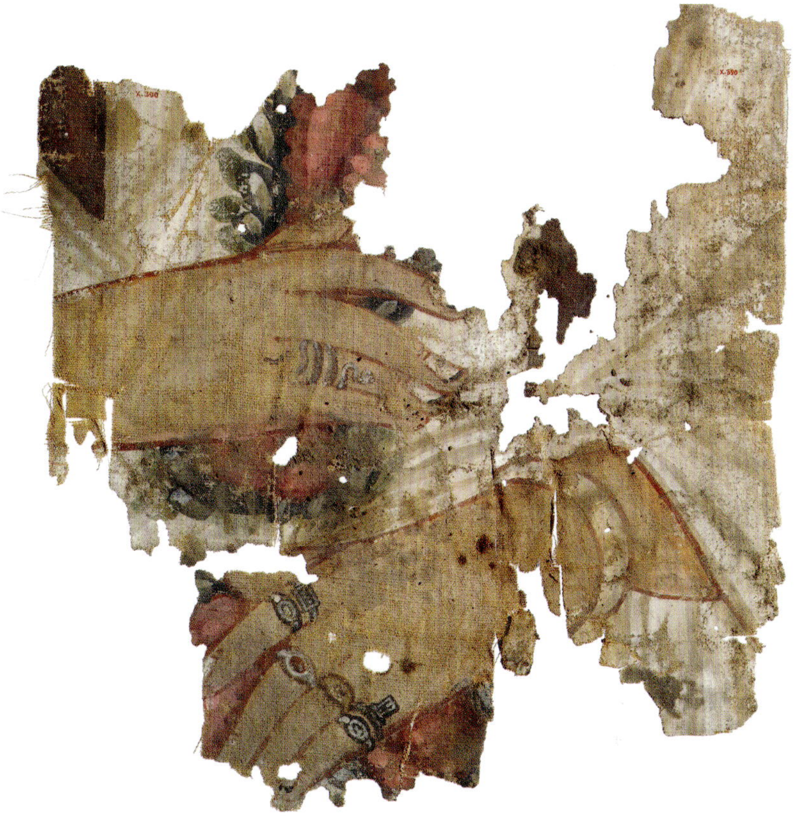

Figure 25
Fragmentary mummy shroud, from Roman Egypt, second–third century AD. Linen, H: 28.5 cm. New York, Metropolitan Museum of Art, X.390. While a single snake ring adorns the right hand, the left bears six rings, of both gold and silver, most apparently set with oval and rectangular gemstones.

The taste for gem-encrusted objects was not restricted to Hellenistic Egypt. It seems to have arisen in ancient Mesopotamia and to have spread via the Persian court, especially in the wake of Alexander's conquests. There are numerous references to precious stones in ancient Near Eastern texts, as early as the epic of *Gilgamesh*, in which a gem-studded vine with cornelian grapes, leaves of lapis lazuli, and other stones is described.[68] Similarly, the bedroom of the Persian king Darius was said to have been adorned by "a golden vine . . . with clusters of green crystals and rubies from India and other gems of every description" made by none other than Theodoros of Samos, the carver of Polykrates's ring.[69] Darius's chariot, captured by Alexander the Great at the Battle of Issos, was encrusted with gems, and the Macedonian conqueror is said to have attached a gem-encrusted neckpiece to his helmet.[70] Alexander's own funeral carriage, richly decorated with gold, was also laden with gems—and the sixty-four mules that drew it had gem-studded harnesses.[71] According to Cicero the Seleucid prince Antiochos came to Rome in the early first century BC bringing with him a jewel-encrusted cup and ladle carved from a single piece of stone (compare plate 127), as well as a lamp stand fashioned of precious stones.[72] Pompey the Great, who imitated Alexander in so many things, rode in a gem-encrusted chariot in a procession celebrating his triumph over Rome's great enemy, the Pontic king Mithradates VI Eupator, himself a passionate collector of gems and precious stone vessels.[73] Pompey dedicated Mithradates's gems to Jupiter Optimus Maximus, and they were installed in the god's temple on the Capitoline Hill. But this collection, according to Pliny, was inferior to the first brought to Rome by Pompey's sometime brother-in-law Marcus Aemelius Scaurus.[74] Scaurus's parents were both from noble old families, and he was the stepson of the dictator Sulla. He gained great wealth—and perhaps his taste for hard stones—in campaigns in Judaea and Nabataea, where he allegedly demanded enormous bribes.

Gem collecting was clearly a competitive sport. Not only did the Seleucids vie with the Ptolemies, but Julius Caesar, not to be outdone by Scaurus or Pompey, dedicated six *dactyliothecae* (literally, ring cabinets) to Venus Genetrix in the temple he built to her in his forum. The sources of this collection are unfortunately unknown, but Suetonius says he "was always a most enthusiastic collector of gems, carvings, statues, and pictures by early artists."[75] Likewise we have no information about the origin of the collection dedicated in the temple to Apollo on the Palatine by Marcellus the nephew, adopted son, and sometime heir of the emperor Augustus.[76]

More modest items, of course, were offered in Greek and Roman sanctuaries by individuals both well known and anonymous. The inventories of the Parthenon and Erechtheion on the Athenian Acropolis, as well as the Asklepieion on its south slope, and the temples of Apollo and Artemis on Delos all record gemstones offered to the gods. Often just the type of stone and its gold or silver mount are mentioned. The fourth-century BC inventories of the dedications stored in the Parthenon, for example, list a painted box dedicated by Kleito, wife of Aristokrates, the son of Oulios, who was the son of Perikles's rival Kimon. It contained a seal stone (*sphragis*) set in gold dedicated by Dexilla, as well as gold jewelry, two colored glass seals (*sphragide ualina poikila*) with gold chains, an onyx set in a gold ring, a "jasper" seal set in a gold ring, and so on. Some inscriptions describe the device engraved on the gem, such as "a large onyx depicting a priapic goat-stag weighing 32 drachmai" (approximately 138 grams). Considerably larger was an onyx that weighed 276 drachmai and half an obol, well over a kilogram![77] Perhaps this was a vessel of some sort: the famous Hellenistic cameo-cut bowl known as the Tazza Farnese (plate 124) weighs 1,418 grams (including its modern silver mount).

An early third-century BC inventory of the Athenian Asklepieion lists various rings and seals, including "chalcedony seal stones [*iaspides*] on which are represented a cavalryman and hoplite and Minos opposite the Minotaur," as well as several seals on the hand of the statue of the god in the temple, including one depicting an eagle. A seal engraved with chariot is recorded in a slightly later Asklepieion inventory inscribed in 244/43 BC.[78]

In Italy, a first-century AD inscription from the sanctuary of Diana at Lake Nemi records among the various sumptuous garments dedicated there a diadem (*basileum*) adorned with gems, a necklace of beryls (aquamarines), another with seven unspecified precious stones, two bracelets and ten earrings with gems, and a crown set with twenty-four "topazes" and eighty-four garnets.[79] Bejeweled diadems rarely survive, but they are often represented in portraits in marble and other materials (plates 118, 139).

Gem-encrusted vessels are not often preserved, though they are frequently mentioned in ancient literature. In 1955, however, a farmer in Serbia chanced upon a hoard of precious objects, dating to the early fourth century AD, including a gilt-iron parade helmet encrusted with over fifty multicolored glass gems—circular, oval, rhomboid, rectangular, and octagonal—imitating emerald, banded agate, chalcedony, and nicolo (a stone with a light blue layer atop a darker one) (fig. 26). Inscribed in Greek with the names of both its owner, *Dizzon*, and its maker, *Ayeitos* (*Avitus*?), it gives some idea of the impressive appearance of such luxury objects.[80] "Shields and greaves shining with gold and gems" are mentioned by Ovid as accoutrements fit for a Julio-Claudian prince.[81] Caligula is said to have decked his ship with precious stones, and Heliogabalus reputedly adorned his shoes with engraved gems.[82]

That real gemstones, rather than glass imitations, would be employed as decorations in the highest echelons of Roman society is made clear by finds recovered from nineteenth-century excavations of the Villa Palombara on the Esquiline Hill in Rome, which brought to light precious stones employed in an architectural context. The site has been convincingly identified as the Horti Lamiani, the gardens established by Lucius Aelius Lamia, consul in AD 3 and prefect of the city of Rome in AD 33, which were apparently bequeathed to the emperor Tiberius, embellished by Caligula, and enjoyed by subsequent emperors.[83] The architectural ornaments, now in

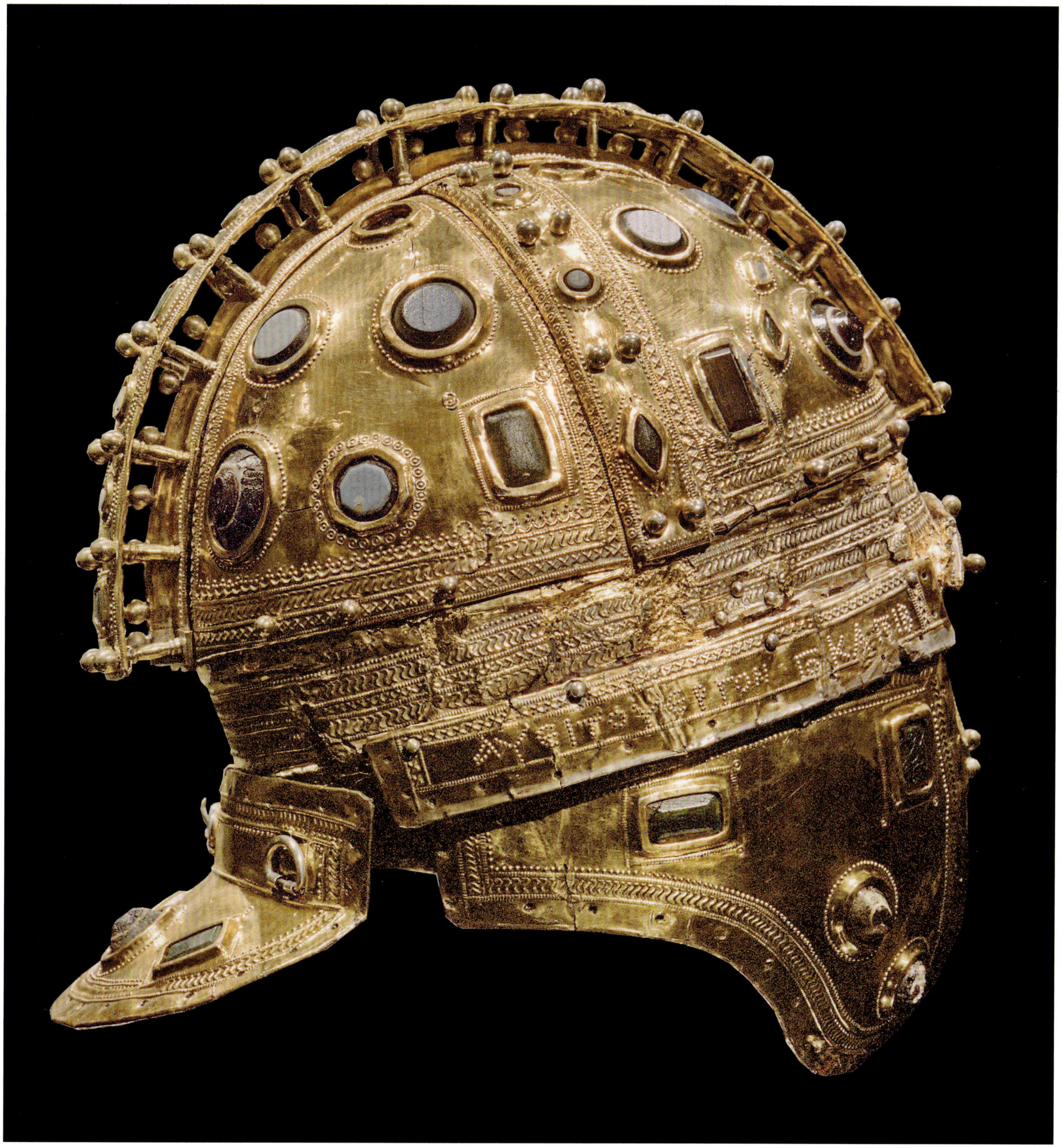

Figure 26
Gem-encrusted helmet from the Berkasovo Treasure, ca. 300–320 AD. Iron, gilt-silver leaf, and glass gems, H: 28 cm. Novi Sad, Serbia, Museum Vojvodine, AA 153.

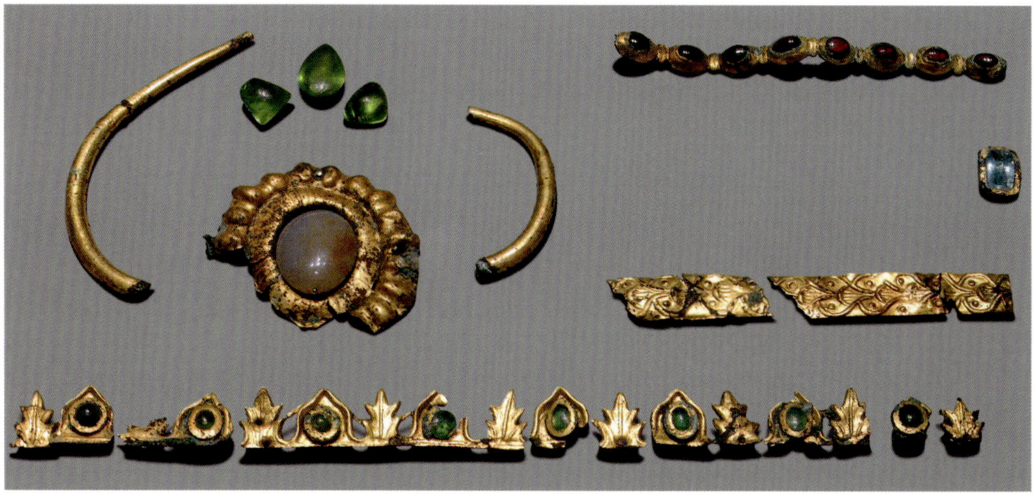

Figure 27
Fragments of decorative moldings, from the Horti Lamiani in Rome, first century AD. Gilt-bronze inset with chalcedony, peridot, garnet, and sapphire. L (lowermost fragment): ca. 28.5 cm. Rome, Capitoline Museum. Additional fragments include agates, amethysts, beryls, aquamarines, citrines, cornelians, lapis lazuli, and glass paste.

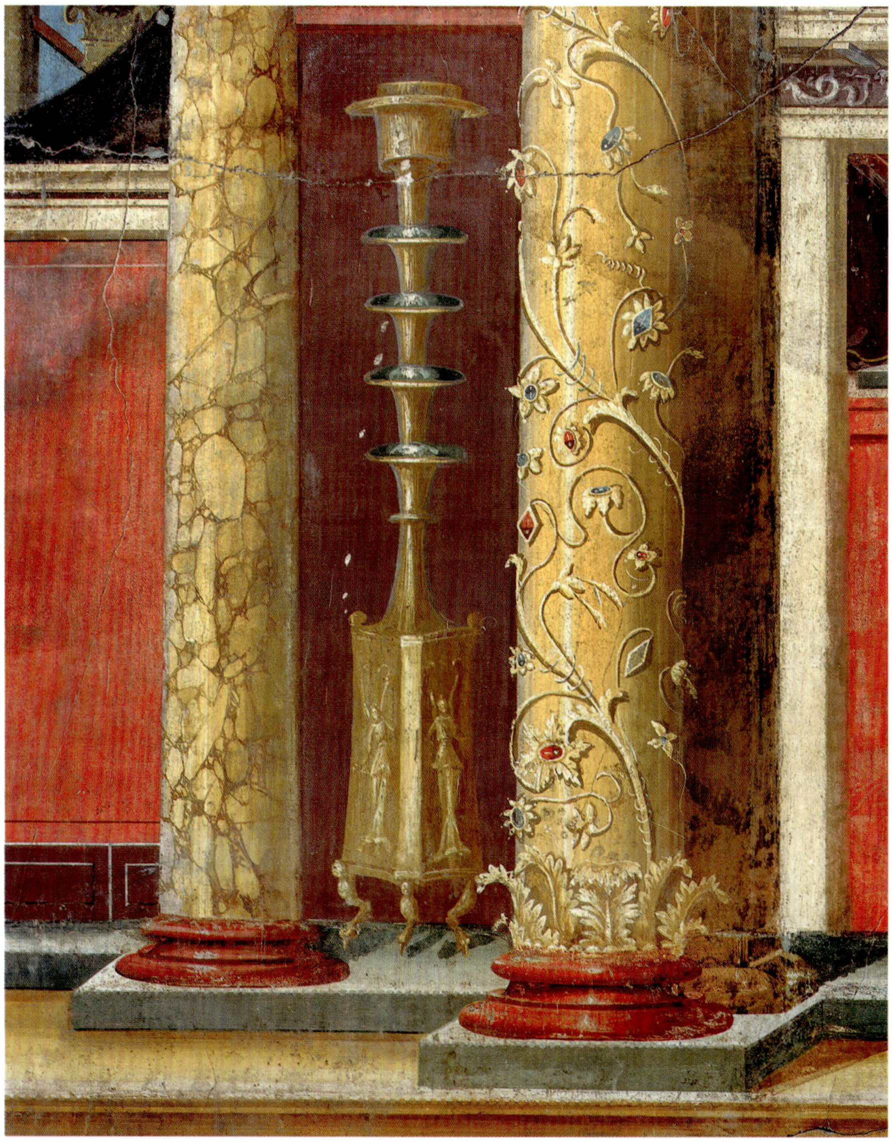

Figure 28
Fresco (detail) depicting columns adorned with gold and gem-studded tendrils from the west wall of the triclinium (Room 14) of Villa A at Oplontis, first century BC.

the Capitoline Museum, include a portion of a sumptuous *opus sectile* pavement composed of slabs of imported banded alabasters that was originally flanked by columns of yellow Numidian marble (*giallo antico*) with gilded stucco capitals and bases, and *opus sectile* pilaster capitals composed of imported colored marbles. The find includes hundreds of fragments of wood and gilt-bronze moldings set with gems, over four hundred of which were recovered: agates, amethysts, chalcedonies, cornelians, garnets, lapis lazuli, peridots, and rock crystals, as well as two sapphires, two citrines, one aquamarine, and one beryl (fig. 27). Nearly three hundred strips of banded agate veneer and a few large engraved cornelians, one depicting Europa and the bull, as well as engraved rock crystal plaques, were also excavated. Perhaps some of these elements were meant to adorn sumptuous furniture, such as the bejeweled couches, but the elaborate gem-encrusted gilt-bronze floral and architectural moldings appear to have been designed for the decoration of columns and other architectural elements. Such lavish embellishments are described in detail by Lucan in his account of Cleopatra's palace,[84] and so-called *columnae caelatae* (elaborately wrought columns) are depicted in the wall paintings of luxury villas on the Bay of Naples, such as those in the second-style triclinium of Villa A at Oplontis (Torre Annunziata) (fig. 28), a building associated with the family of Poppaea Sabina, the second wife of the emperor Nero, as well as in the House of Augustus on the Palatine.[85] Like so much else in Rome, this kind of extravagance had precedents in the Hellenistic world: the pavilion of Alexander at Susa, according to Athenaios, had columns nine meters tall decorated with gold, silver, and gems of all kinds, even Indian rubies.[86] Closer in time and place to the Esquiline finds was Nero's expansive Roman palace, the Golden House, which, among other extravagances, had rooms "entirely covered with gold adorned with gems and mother-of-pearl."[87] Luxuries of this sort were found outside the capital, too. The sites of Begram and Aï Khanoum in Afghanistan have produced fragments of vases of alabaster and rock crystal (plate 131) and plaques of rock crystal and agate, apparently furniture inlays.[88]

The Carvers

The names of more than seventy Greek and Roman gem engravers are known from their signatures on ancient stones and other inscriptions, but only eight are mentioned in ancient literary sources—all of them Greek.[89] Theodoros of Samos was credited with fashioning the seal of Polykrates; he was also a master sculptor, who, in a lost statue described by Pliny, depicted himself holding a file in one hand and miniature chariot (perhaps engraved on a scarab) in the other.[90] His countryman Mnesarchos was mentioned by Diogenes Laertius, as well as Apuleius, according to whom he "was a skillful jeweler, who excelled in the carving of gems, although he sought fame rather than wealth in exercising his art." [91] In this, however, he seems to have failed, for he is far better known today as the father of a more famous son, the mathematician and philosopher Pythagoras. More famous than both was Pyrgoteles, one of three craftsmen whom Alexander the Great is said to have allowed to fashion his image.[92] Pliny praises Apollonides and Kronios, whose work is also mentioned in Hellenistic epigrams, along with Timanthes and Tryphon.[93] Pliny and Suetonius mention Dioskourides, the gem carver of Augustus, and Dio Cassius reports that Augustus's seal continued to be used by subsequent emperors.[94] Modern gem cutters have forged the works of all of these carvers, but a handful of genuine ancient gems signed by Dioskourides and one by Tryphon survive (plates 96, 107, 109).[95] Other intaglios and cameos signed by Dioskourides's three sons, Hyllos (plate 114), Herophilos, and Eutyches, indicate that they followed their father in the trade. Several outstanding unsigned gems have been attributed to their hands and to those of other carvers, such as Epimenes, whose names are known only from inscriptions. Only one gem signed by Epimenes has come down to us, but similarities of material, pose, anatomical rendering, and other details allow other unsigned gems to be attributed to him (plates 81–83).

Likewise Dexamenos of Chios, one of the great artists of the fifth century BC; several of his gems have been found in tombs on the northern shores of the Black Sea, and the fact that he inscribed the name of his home, rather than that of his father, along with his own, suggests that he may have been working abroad. He carved several images of cranes in different positions, but the most exquisite shows the bird in majestic flight across the surface of a pale blue chalcedony (plate 84). He thus preceded by several centuries the conceit—toyed with by Poseidippos in an epigram describing a chalcedony depicting the winged horse Pegasos—of the pale blue stone representing the sky. Dexamenos's engraving bears his signature with letters neatly aligned, as in contemporary *stoichedon* inscriptions. His portrait of a bearded man on a mottled jasper, also signed, is one of the great works of early portraiture (plate 85). Dexamenos signed his gems to be read directly from the stone, rather than in reverse, on impressions, suggesting that the gem itself may have been more important than its function as a seal. Clearly, owning an engraved gem signed by a master brought its owner status and prestige.[96]

The value placed on Greek craftsmanship was such that Roman carvers often signed not only in Greek letters but also with the Greek verb *epoie* (meaning "made this"): Felix, Gaios, Gnaios, Quintos, Rufus, and Saturninus all did so.[97] Additional names are known from funerary inscriptions, which indicate that in the Roman period gem carvers might be slaves, freedmen, or free born, and in some cases reveal more about their family connections. The Latin *gemmarius* seems to refer to a gem merchant or seller of precious stones; an engraver was called *sculptor, cavator, caelator, signarius*, or *insignitor*, sometimes with the defining noun *gemmarum* added.[98]

VESSELS

Greeks and Romans, like their Bronze Age predecessors and Near Eastern neighbors, prized vessels fashioned from hard stones.[99] There is plentiful evidence for such items from ancient Mesopotamia, Egypt, and Anatolia, along with some finds from Minoan Crete and Mycenaean Greece, but information for most such classical Greek and Roman objects remains problematic.[100] It is conceivable that the "onyx" on the Athenian Acropolis recorded as weighing more than 276 drachmai (mentioned above) was a vessel of some sort,[101] but it is only in an inscription from the sanctuary of Apollo on Delos dated circa 200 BC that an onyx cup (*poterion onyxinon*), dedicated by a certain Rhomaios, is explicitly mentioned.[102] The Late Hellenistic polymath Poseidonios of Apameia (ca. 135–151 BC), for his part, mentions large Panathenaic *onyxinoi skyphoi*.[103]

Hard stone vessels seem to have been more prevalent in the ancient Near East, but physical fragments of only a few agate and rock crystal vases were recovered among the remains of more than six hundred vessels of various stones excavated at Persepolis, which was destroyed by Alexander's soldiers in 330 BC.[104] Persepolis, of course, was only one of several Persian treasuries, and Appian reports that from the mountain stronghold of Talaura, where the Pontic king Mithradates VI Eupator stored items he "inherited from Darius the Great of Persia and other mighty rulers," the Romans recovered "two thousand drinking cups made of onyx bound with gold, and many cups, wine coolers, and drinking horns, bridles for horses, etc., . . . all ornamented in like manner with gold and precious stones. The quantity of this store was so great that the inventory of it occupied thirty days."[105] Pompey displayed these objects in his Roman triumph and then dedicated them to Jupiter Optimus Maximus on the Capitoline Hill.

Murrhine Ware

It was from his conquests over Mithradates VI Eupator, according to Pliny, that Pompey first brought to Rome a taste for vessels carved from *murra*, a softer, richly colored stone.[106] The encyclopediast described the material at some length, and it is also mentioned by other ancient authors, such as Propertius, Seneca, Martial, Strabo, and Pausanias, as being of high value and a sign of great luxury. At the culmination of the *Natural History*, Pliny classes it along with *adamas*, *smaragdus*, rock crystal, and other gems as the most costly products of the earth's interior.[107] Earlier in his compendium he writes that it was mined in the east, particularly in Carmania, in Parthia, and on the coast of the Red Sea. He describes the mineral as being formed from liquid solidified underground by heat. Thus cups carved from *murra* were suitable for both hot and cold drinks. He continues:

> They shine, but without intensity; indeed, it would be truer to say that they glisten rather than shine. Their value lies in their varied colors: the veins, as they revolve, repeatedly vary from purple to white or a mixture of the two, the purple becoming fiery or the milk-white become red as though the new color were passing through the vein. Some people particularly appreciate the edges of a piece, where colors may be reflected such as we observe in the inner part of a rainbow. Others prefer thick veins and also specks and spots (any trace of transparency or fading is always a fault). The smell of the substance is also a merit.[108]

The poet Martial notes that the stone added a pleasing flavor to wine drunk from cups fashioned from it,[109] and Pliny tells of a former consul who was so fond of a murrhine cup, for which he had paid 70,000 sesterces despite its small size, that he gnawed at its rim. Apparently only small pieces of the mineral could be obtained, and these were fragile, making it all the more valuable. In fact, when the ex-consul's collection of murrhine vases was confiscated from his heirs by Nero and put on display, even fragments of a single broken cup were included in the exhibition. Titus Petronius is reported to have smashed a murrhine ladle (*trulla*) worth 300,000 sesterces so that it would not fall into Nero's hands, and the emperor himself purchased a murrhine bowl for the extraordinary price of 1,000,000 sesterces, enough to buy a thousand slaves or twenty-five thousand amphorae of the finest wine.[110] Even Emperor Augustus, who cultivated a reputation for modesty, could not refuse the allure of the material: Suetonius reports that after the defeat of Mark Antony and Cleopatra he removed for his personal use only one item from the treasury of the Ptolemies at Alexandria: a murrhine bowl.[111] Latin poets cite the material repeatedly as an example of extravagance, but no one, apparently, outdid Heliogabalus, who urinated in murrhine and onyx vessels, far surpassing the fictional Trimalchio, who relieved himself in one of mere silver. Emperor Marcus Aurelius, meanwhile, is reported to have sold his murrhine vessels and other luxuries to raise funds for the war against the Germans.[112]

Despite much past scholarly debate about the identity of the stone, the consensus today is that murrhine is fluorite, a soft, richly colored crystalline stone with many of the properties mentioned by Pliny. It has the same colors, as well as a loose crystalline structure, making it highly friable and especially susceptible to cracking during carving. Modern craftsmen working the material often immerse it in resin for reinforcement, and the ancients may have done the same, imparting to it a pleasing odor and flavor. As it is 4 on the Mohs scale, it might even be nibbled, for tooth enamel is 5.[113] Only a few ancient fluorite vessels survive (plates 133, 134).

Emerald and Garnet

Pliny also mentions small cups fashioned from other colored stones: deep green *smaragdus*, light green chrysoprase, fiery red *lychnis*, perhaps a variety of garnet, and a less valuable, brittle orange stone "full of veins and resembling a dying ember," found in Egypt near Thebes, called *Carchedonia* (Carthaginian) because it was once exported there.[114] No surviving examples of these have been identified.

Obsidian

An exceptionally hard, naturally occurring volcanic glass, obsidian was occasionally employed in antiquity for gems (plate 83), vessels, statues, and other objects. Pliny reports that it takes its name from a stone found by a certain Obsius in Ethiopia, and he repeats Xenokrates of Ephesos's statement that it was also found in India, Italy, and Spain.[115] Obsidian disks were set into the walls of Pompeian houses, apparently as mirrors, and the material was employed to produce components of furniture.[116] Two large *skyphoi* excavated in the Villa San Marco at Stabiae, south of Pompeii, each formed from one large obsidian block, are the most spectacular surviving examples of ancient obsidian vessels (plate 135). Made for a

Roman market, both are inlaid with Egyptianizing scenes rendered in a sophisticated inlay technique. Cavities cut into the body of the vessels were lined with thin gold sheet that held minute inlays of variously colored precious material: pink and white coral, cornelian, yellow jasper, lapis lazuli, and malachite. Although the imagery depicted seems to reinforce a link to Egypt (Alexandria if not Ethiopia) suggested by the exotic material itself, there were, as Pliny noted, obsidian sources much closer, particularly on the islands of Sardinia and Lipari. Analysis of these cups, however, suggests that their obsidian originated in Africa.

Rock Crystal

The best rock crystal, according to Pliny, came from India, but he also mentions sources in Asia Minor, Cyprus, an island in the Red Sea, Portugal, and especially in the Alps. The last source no doubt contributed to the belief that it was super-frozen ice: in Greek *krystallos* also means ice. The stone was fashioned into vessels in Bronze Age Greece as well as in Cyprus, Asia Minor, Egypt, and Mesopotamia. In Classical and Hellenistic Greece, however, it was used only occasionally for intaglios, and rock crystal vessels seem to have come back into fashion only in the Hellenistic period and the early years of the Roman Empire, when elegant small perfume vessels of various shapes (plate 132) were produced.[117] It is to this period that several larger drinking cups (plates 130, 131), whose forms parallel those fashioned in silver, glass, and other materials, were made.

Frequently paired with murrhine ware in Latin literature, rock crystal was highly valued. According to Pliny, Augustus's wife Livia dedicated a block weighing 150 pounds on the Capitol, and sometime later a wealthy Roman matron paid 150,000 sesterces for a single dipper. Xenokrates reputedly saw a vessel that could hold the equivalent of six gallons, and Pliny says that Nero "on receiving the message that all was lost, broke two crystal cups in a final outburst of rage by dashing them to the ground." Suetonius, however, reports that the breakage occurred when the emperor tipped over a table, and that the cups were his favorites, cut with scenes from the Homeric poems.[118] Dio Cassius, for his part, tells the story of a crystal cup accidentally broken by a slave in the presence of Emperor Augustus:

> Once, when Vedius Pollio was entertaining Augustus, his cup-bearer broke a crystal goblet, and without regard for his guest, Pollio ordered the fellow to be thrown to his lampreys. Hereupon the slave fell on his knees before Augustus and supplicated him, and Augustus at first tried to persuade Pollio not to commit so monstrous a deed. Then, when Pollio paid no heed to him, the emperor said, "Bring all the rest of the drinking vessels which are of like sort or any others of value that you possess, in order that I may use them," and when they were brought, he ordered them to be broken. When Pollio saw this, he was vexed, of course; but since he was no longer angry over the one goblet, considering the great number of the others that were ruined, and, on the other hand, could not punish his servant for what Augustus also had done, he held his peace, though much against his will.[119]

While many surviving crystal vessels are unprovenanced, excavations at various sites in Italy (including Taranto, Pompeii, Herculaneum, Capua, Rome, Aquileia, and elsewhere), at Pergamon and Kayseri in Asia Minor, Piraeus in Greece, Carthage, and elsewhere have yielded small crystal perfume containers and other objects, while larger cups have been preserved in ecclesiastical treasuries and recovered from tombs. One, discovered at Begram in Afghanistan, preserves traces of gold in its engraved decoration (plate 131).[120]

Fragments of rock crystal plaques engraved with panthers and rosettes have been excavated along with numerous decorative disks in the Horti Lamiani at Rome.[121] Two large bowls, each surviving only in a single fragment, must have been even more spectacular. Both are cameo-cut in high relief. One fragment now in Berlin is adorned with a Nereid riding a sea monster. Its style suggests a date in the late second to early first century BC. The other, now in London, is dated first–second century AD and is decorated with Bacchic figures, including an ecstatic maenad and satyr.[122]

Agate

Banded agate is formed as a geode, rather than a crystal (although it often has crystalline inclusions, which must be avoided by carvers). Such geodes can be quite large, and thus allow for the carving of large cameos, as well as vessels of various shapes. While scholars formerly ascribed surviving ancient vessels to particular locations based on their appearance, such distinctions seem to be unreliable, especially as the colors of stones were often enhanced or altered.[123]

Equally problematic is Pliny's reference to Demostratos's assertion that "the first Roman to adopt sardonyx was the elder Africanus [Publius Cornelius Scipio Africanus (236–183 BC)], and hence arose the esteem which this gemstone enjoys at Rome."[124] Scipio was famous for his victories over Carthage, but with his brother Lucius Cornelius Scipio Asiaticus he also defeated the Seleucid king Antiochos III at Magnesia in 190 BC. He may therefore have acquired his taste for the stone from the east as well as the west, but given the presence of fragments of the material in the ruins at Persepolis and its attestations in various Hellenistic courts, it seems likely that fine agate vessels reached Rome earlier.

Scholars continue to debate the date and origins of the spectacular two-sided, cameo-cut *phiale* (offering bowl) known as the Tazza Farnese (plate 124). A gorgoneion (Medusa head) carved in low relief occupies the exterior, while the interior features a complex scene of Egyptian gods and personifications. The bowl's shape, imagery, and style suggest that it was probably produced in Ptolemaic Alexandria in the late second or early first century BC. Although it is likely to have passed from Alexandria to Rome and thence Constantinople, it is first securely recorded in an early fifteenth-century drawing by Mohammed al Khayyam, a Persian artist working at the court of Timur the Great either in Samarkand or Herat. The *phiale* returned west in the fifteenth century, when it passed through the hands of Alfonso I, king of Naples; the Venetian cardinal Trevisan; and Pietro Barbo (Pope Paul II), before being acquired by Lorenzo de' Medici, upon whose death it was valued at 10,000 florins, approximately one hundred times more than Lorenzo's paintings by Fra Angelico and other Florentine masters.[125] The Tazza, which influenced the work of Botticelli, Raphael, Piero di Cosimo, Poussin, and other artists, was one of the few ancient items of hard stone Lorenzo possessed that he did not have inscribed with his own initials, whether intaglios, cameos, or vessels. The Medici holdings of ancient hard stone vessels included cups, bowls, and a tall beaker with delicately curling handles (plate 128). The shape is known from several examples, though most have been broken and recut. Another exquisitely carved agate object from the Medici collection, acquired after Lorenzo's death, is a *simpulum* (ladle) (plate 127). Archival research suggests that it is one of the thirty-nine vessels of rock crystal and eight of agate discovered in the tomb of the Roman empress Maria (d. 423) in Rome on February 4, 1544. This wealth of material was described and sketched at the time, but was dispersed soon thereafter, and other objects, many of which must have been heirlooms when buried, have unfortunately not been identified.

There is greater consensus about the date of the so-called Cup of the Ptolemies (plate 125), which entered the collection of the French royal abbey at Saint-Denis in the late ninth century and was wrongly associated with the Ptolemies by Jean Tristan de Saint-Amant in 1644, who thought it was made for Ptolemy II Philadelphos in the early third century BC.[126] The shape, Dionysiac iconography, and style of this deeply cut, high-relief agate *kantharos*, however, is more closely paralleled in Roman silver and glass vessels of the first century.

Porphyry

Quarried in the Egyptian desert, red porphyry was unsuitable for the carving of intaglios and cameos on account of its large grain, but it was used for vessels and statuary, especially in the later Roman empire, when its color was increasingly related to imperial rank and prestige. The Greek *porphyra* means "purple," and the stone likely gained value on account of its resemblance to precious purple dyes as well as its hardness and exotic origins. Ancient Egyptians appear not to have exploited porphyry, but there is some evidence that the Ptolemies did. According to

Pliny, Vistrasius Pollio, an agent of Emperor Claudius, brought porphyry statues from Egypt to Rome, but the "innovation did not meet with much approval."[127] There is, in fact, scant evidence for widespread use of the stone before the second century, in contrast to purple textiles, which were a symbol of prestige throughout the Mediterranean far earlier. A few surviving porphyry vessels, including plates, amphorae, beakers, a *pyxis*, and a *situla* now in New York (plate 136), mirror shapes that appear in other media and thus can be dated earlier than the height of the material's popularity in late antiquity, when the production of statues, basins, sarcophagi, and, of course, columns were produced in significant numbers. The closed shapes were probably manufactured as funerary vessels to hold the cremated remains of the well-to-do. Dio Cassius reports that Septimius Severus, campaigning in Britain, sensed his health waning and sent for a porphyry urn. Receiving it he remarked "Thou shalt hold a man that the world could not hold."[128]

SCULPTURE

From at least the Hellenistic period, Greeks and Romans also employed many of the hard stones discussed above to fashion statues and attachments to other objects.[129] Portraits of rulers and images of gods and heroes were the most common subjects. They might be carved from single blocks of stone or assembled from multiple components. Some were complete figures, others just busts. Some of the latter might be attached to scepters, crowns, military standards, or other objects. Such images were used in private worship, as well as in public cult celebrations, and may well have been carried in processions. Some portraits clearly follow prototypes in other materials, whether official portrait types or famous statues (plate 141). Others seem less dependent on previous creations. Female heads often have pierced ears, suggesting the original presence of earrings, presumably of gold.

Surviving components are significantly smaller than life size, but Pliny (and his sources) record larger statues: Apion Plistonices wrote of a large statue of Serapis, nine cubits (13½ feet) tall, made of *smaragdus* at Herakleiopolis in Egypt, as well as a four-cubit (6-foot) peridot statue of Arsinoe II, the sister/wife of Ptolemy II Philadelphos, that was displayed in the Arsinoeion, her shrine at Alexandria. More credible is a sixteen-inch-tall statue of Nero wearing a cuirass fashioned from smoky chalcedony that Pliny says he actually saw. He mentions obsidian statues representing the divine Augustus, four elephants (dedicated by Augustus himself), and Menelaos, ruler of Sparta, which Tiberius returned to Egypt. Pliny does not give measurements for any of these statues, but they must have been sizeable, for he explicitly states that "the substance can yield pieces bulky enough for this purpose."[130]

Considerably smaller is a minute Hellenistic garnet portrait, thought to represent Arsinoe's successor, Berenike II, perhaps intended to be set into a ring or other piece of jewelry (plate 137). A fine, creamy white chalcedony head of Antonia Minor, Augustus's favorite niece, grandmother of the emperor Caligula, and mother of the emperor Claudius, is cut at the neck for insertion into a statuette or bust (plate 139). The same seems true for the green chalcedony head of a later Julio-Claudian princess (plate 140), which given its size would have resulted in a statue approximately twenty inches tall. A considerably larger head of Augustus was recut from a portrait of Domitian (plate 143). A jasper *togatus* (plate 144), cut to allow for the addition of head, arms, and feet fashioned in another material, illustrates how such composite figures were assembled; and it is tempting to associate a stunning chalcedony left hand (plate 145) with such a figure. The chalcedony bust of a man tentatively identified as Vespasian (plate 142), in contrast, seems to have been intended for insertion into a roundel, a so-called *imago clipeata*. It has been suggested that the chalcedony bust of an Antonine woman, perhaps Empress Faustina, might originally have graced the top of a scepter.[131]

Whether used as seals or intended as a form of adornment, cut into vessels or sculpted in the round, hard stones—shining, luminous, and exotic—were fashioned by skilled craftsmen into the finest and most valuable objects of the classical world.

NOTES

1 For surveys of gems in diverse ancient cultures, see Tallon 1995; Collon 1997; André-Salvini 1999; Caubet 1999; Krzyszkowska 2005. For Greek and Roman gems, see Richter 1968b, 1971; Boardman 1970 (2001 ed.); Plantzos 1999a; Zwierlein-Diehl 2007 (with comprehensive bibliography).

2 Developed in 1812 by the German mineralogist Frederich Mohs, the Mohs scale of relative hardness rates stones that can scratch one another: 1-talc, 2-gypsum, 3-calcite, 4-fluorite, 5-apatite, 6-feldspar, 7-quartz, 8-topaz, 9-corundum, 10-diamond.

3 *NH* 37.109.

4 On *adamas*, see *NH* 37.55–61, 200, 204; Ball 1950, 242–56.

5 *NH* 37.105–9; translation by D. E. Eichholz, 1962. See also Ball 1950.

6 *NH* 37.1.

7 *NH* 37.106.

8 *NH* 37.23–32.

9 Ball 1950; G. Schmidt 2008, 10–12; Giuliani and Schmidt 2010, 90–96.

10 See, e.g., Caley and Richards 1956; Eichholtz 1962, 1965; Macrì 2009; Lapatin 2012.

11 *NH* 37.53; Theophrastos, *Peri lithon* 28.

12 *Palatine Anthology* 9.748 and 9.752: Gutzwiller 1995 (see 384n6 for references to similar epigrams in Latin).

13 *NH* 37 passim; Halleux and Schamp 1985; Macrì 2009. For so-called magical gems, see, e.g., Michel 2004; essays by Faraone, Gordon, and Nagy in Entwistle and Adams 2011.

14 Ball 1950; Boardman and Vollenweider 1978, 66–75; Reeder 1988. For garnets, which can be identified as almandine or pyrope, see Adams 2011; Thoresen and Schmetzer 2013.

15 Hamilton 2000 (Artemision Treasure B, no. 79; Apollo Treasure D, no. 139); see also *NH* 6.24; Ball 1950.

16 Bing 2005; see also *NH* 37.32; Grubessi Aurisicchio, and Castiglione 1990; Nenna 1998; Shaw, Bunbury, and Jameson 1999; Nicholson and Shaw 2000, 5–77, esp. 10–15.

17 E.g., Hutchinson 2002; Hunter 2004; Schur 2004; M. Smith 2004; Bing 2005; Kuttner 2005; Fuqua 2007, 2008; Porter 2011. See also Gutzwiller 1995.

18 Herodotos 3.40–41. For Theodoros's dates, see Vickers 1985, 13–15; for the scale of his work, see Squire 2011, esp. 284–91.

19 Pausanias 8.14.8; *NH* 37.8.

20 Strabo, *Geographika* 14.1.16.

21 Clement of Alexandria, *Paidagogos* 3.11.

22 Poseidippos, *Lithika* 9.

23 Plutarch, *Lucullus* 3.1.

24 Plantzos 1997; Faraone 2001, 2011, 2015.

25 *NH* 37.62–75; translation by J. Bostock and H. T. Riley 1855.

26 *NH* 37.195, 198. Laure Marest-Caffey kindly informs me that 90 percent of gemstones today are treated by heat or radiation to enhance their color; the majority of yellow citrine, for example, is made from heated amethyst, oxidizing its iron and changing its hue. Pliny's extreme reaction against such practices is rooted in the belief that color (rather than chemical content) is an essential quality of the stones. For color alteration in antiquity, see Nassau 1994, 6–13; Roux 1995, 39, 44, fig. 3; Tallon 1995, 84–86; Moorey in Caubet 1999, 175–88; Rosenfeld, Dvorachek, and Amorai-Stark 2003; Tressaud and Vickers 2007; Zwierlein-Diehl 2007, 312–14; Caley 2008; G. Schmidt 2008, 9–10; Giuliani and Schmidt 2010, 89–90.

27 *NH* 36.198; 35.48.

28 Plantzos 1997.

29 Doros's gravestone is often illustrated in books on ancient gems; see also Zwierlein-Diehl 2008, 14–25, esp. 16–17; Giuliani and Schmidt 2010, 81–85 (with a brief historical account of the horizontal lathe).

30 See, e.g., Mariette 1750; Natter 1754; Devoto 2003; M. Maaskant-Kleibrink in Sas and Thoen 2002, 35–39; Zwierlein-Diehl 2007, 315–25; Zwierlein-Diehl 2008, 14–25.

31 *Lithika* 13; adapted from the translation by B. Acosta-Hughes and E. Kosmetatou, 2002.

32 *Lithika* 15; adapted from the translation by M. Smith, 2004. "Snakestone" (*drakonites*) is mentioned by Pliny (*NH* 37.158), quoting an earlier source, Sotakos, who describes the hunting of snakes on chariots and killing them while they slept so that their brains would be turned to stone. Lynkeios was one of the Argonauts, renowned for his keen vision: according to Hyginus, *Fabulae* 14, he was even able see things hidden within the earth, such as gold mines. See M. Smith 2004, 112–17; Gutzwiller 1995, 388n17, notes further complex allusions in this epigram, including the derivation of *drákon* (serpent) from *drakón* (having seen). See also Macrì 2009.

33 *NH* 37.5, translation by J. Bostock and H. T. Riley, 1855. For a late Roman cameo depicting the nine muses with their attributes, see Sena Chiesa 2003. Platt 2006, 237, rightly observes that the minute dimensions of gems "demand intimacy, a prolonged and careful viewing whereby the tiny image which forms the matrix or impression expands by force of the multitude of signs it carries until it occupies huge dimensions within the mind." See also Squire 2011, esp. 259–83; and Porter 2011, 272 (on the consuming monumentality of finely wrought small objects).

34 Sophokles, *Elektra* 1222–24.

35 Sophokles, *Trachiniai* 615.

36 Aischylos, *Agamemnon* 609ff.

37 Aristophanes, *Thesmophoriazousai* 414.

38 E.g., Isokrates 17.33.34; Lewis 1955; Boussac 1992. For sealings at Seleukia on the Tigris and other sites, see also Plantzos 1999a and esp. Invernizzi et al. 2004.

39 Diogenes Laertius 1.57.

40 Lucian, *Alexander* 21–22.

41 See, e.g., Boussac 1992; Stampolides 1992; Plantzos 1999a, 73 ("Gems for the Masses"). See also the published catalogues of various provincial sites, such as Aquileia and Xanten: Sena Chiesa 1996; Platz-Horster 1987–94.

42 *NH* 37.9; Plutarch, *Pompey* 80.5; Dio Cassius 43.43.

43 *NH* 37.10. For Dioskourides and his sons, see Vollenweider 1966; Zwierlein-Diehl 2007, 117–21.

44 Euphantos *apud* Athenaios, *Deipnosophistai* 6.251d.

45 Aelius Lampridius, *Commodus* 11.

46 Plutarch, *Timoleon* 31.3–4.

47 Suetonius, *Nero* 46.

48 *NH* 34.72; Plutarch *Moralia* 505 E (*De garrulitate* [*On Talkativeness*] 8); Athenaios, *Deipnosophistai* 13.70 (596f); Polyainos, *Stratagems* 8.45; Pausanias 1.23.1–2; see also Frazer 1913, ad loc.

49 Aristophanes, *Birds* 1291.

50 Pausanias 10.30.4.

51 Plutarch, *Artaxerxes* 18.1.

52 Ovid, *Tristia* 1.7.5–8; for further references, see Zwierlein-Diehl 2007, 16–17.

53 Cicero, *De finibus* 5.3; see also Lang 2012.

54 Poseidonios *apud* Athenaios, *Deipnosophistai* 5.212.

55 Cited by Longus 1709, 40.

56 Suetonius, *Tiberius* 58.

57 *NH* 33.41.

58 Josephos, *Jewish History* 19.2.1–3.

59 Scriptores Historiae Augustae, *Aurelian*; Propertius 4.7.

60 Plutarch, *Pompey* 80.5; Suetonius, *Tiberius* 72.

61 Boussac 1988, 326.

62 Plantzos 1996a, 115–16; *NH* 37.173; Seneca, *De beneficiis* 3.26.1.

63 Pausanias 5.11; Schiering 1991; Lapatin 2001. Plato, *Hippias major* 290b–c; *NH* 37.66.

64 Aristophanes, *Clouds* 331–32; Aelian, *Varia historia* 3.19; Martial 5.61, 11.59 (compare 5.11–12); Statius, *Silvae* 2.1.134; Seneca, *Quaestiones naturales* 7.31.2; Quintilian, *Institutio oratoria* 11.3.142.

65 *NH* 37.6. The original price was six gold coins discounted to four. The denomination of the transaction in the fourth century BC is not recorded, but Pliny uses the word *aurei*, and in his day one aureus was the equivalent of twenty-five silver denari, the monthly pay of a legionary soldier. Slightly earlier, under Nero, an aureus weighed approximately 7.3 grams.

66 Harris 1995, 105, 229, 234–35; Kosmetatou 2004b.

67 Theophrastos, *Characters* 23.1–3; Kallixenos *apud* Athenaios, *Deipnosophistai* 5.202 D and 5.197 A–C; Athenaios, *Deipnosophistai* 4.147 F; Strabo, *Geographika* 15.1.69; Plutarch, *Life of Anthony*

58.11. For the procession, see Rice 1983.

68 Tallon 1995, esp. 76–78; André-Salvini 1999.

69 Athenaios, *Deipnosophistai* 12.539d, 514ff.; attributed to Theodoros by Himerios, *Eclogues* 31.8.

70 Quintus Curtius Rufus, *Historiae Alexandri Magni* 3.3.16; Plutarch, *Alexander* 32.

71 Diodoros 18.26.3–28.4

72 Cicero, *In Verrem,* 2.4.27, 62–65.

73 Appian 117.

74 *NH* 37.11.

75 Suetonius, *Divus Julius* 47.

76 *NH* 37.11.

77 Harris 1995, 51–52, no. II.37; 140, nos. V.142, 145.

78 Aleshire 1989, 203–4, nos. IV.122–26; 279, no. V.34.

79 *CIL* 14.2215; see also Rigato 2011.

80 E.g., in Sena Chiesa 2012, 235; Manojlović-Marijanski 1973. See also Gagetti 2004–5.

81 Ovid, *Ex Ponto* 3.4.103.

82 Suetonius, *Gaius* 37; see also *NH* 9.26. For bejeweled sandals, see Scriptores Historiae Augustae, *Heliogabalus* 23.4.

83 Cima and La Rocca 1986, esp. 61–65, 105–50; Cima and Talamo 2008, 82–93.

84 Lucan, *Bello civile* 10.111–26.

85 U. Pappalardo 2008, 78; Cima and La Rocca 1986, 127.

86 Chares *apud* Athenaios, *Deipnosophistai* 12.538c–d; Phylarchos and Agatharchides *apud* Athenaios, *Deipnosophistai* 539d–e.

87 Suetonius, *Nero* 31.2.

88 Rapin 1987, 1992.

89 See Zwierlein-Diehl 2005, 2007; for epitaphs, see Marvin 2008, 186–89. Satyreios, a third-century BC Alexandrian cited as a source by Pliny, should perhaps also be added. He produced a portrait of Arsinoe II on or in rock crystal, subject of an epigram by Diodoros in the *Greek Anthology* 9.776.

90 *NH* 34.83.

91 Diogenes Laertius 8.1; Apuleius, *Florida* 2.15.13.

92 *NH* 37.8. See also Stewart 1993.

93 *NH* 37.8; Poseidippos, *Lithika* 2, 5, 6, 7, 15; *Anthologia Palatina* 9.544 (ascribed to Addaios).

94 *NH* 33.154, 37.8; Suetonius, *Augustus* 50; Dio Cassius, *Roman History* 51.3.

95 On Dioskourides, see, e.g., Vollenweider 1966; Zwierlein-Diehl 1990, 2007. For a fragment signed by Apollonides, see Zwierlein-Diehl 1986, no.142.

96 For Dexamenos in general see plates 84, 85. For Poseidippos's epigram see AB 14; see, e.g., Gutzwiller 1995. A new intaglio depicting Eros and Aphrodite, signed by the master, with a *stoichedon* inscription similar to that in plate 84, has recently come to light.

97 Zwierlein-Diehl 2005, 2007.

98 Calabi Limentani 1960; Marvin 2008, 180–94, esp. 186–89.

99 See, e.g., Bühler 1973; Oliver 1975; Gasparri 1975, 1979, 2003; Alcouffe 2003; Slavazzi 2003.

100 Difficulties in understanding the surviving material, as noted by Slavazzi (2003, 437–38) among others, include its dispersal in museums and cathedral treasuries, where it is often inaccessible; its fragility, which increases its inaccessibility, often leading to lack of recorded measurements, weights, profile drawings, etc., that would aid in establishing typologies; the conservatism of technique and forms, in part attributed to the materials themselves, which leads to the replication of similar forms over long periods, as well as occasionally to unique objects; and the lack of objects scientifically excavated in well-defined archaeological contexts. Given that such objects were extremely valuable, widely traded, and retained as heirlooms, those that were buried—although many seem never to have gone underground but have for centuries been transferred from one treasury to another—may well have been deposited far from their place and time of origin.

101 Harris 1995, 140, no. V.142; see also Kosmetatou 2003, 40–41, and 2004a, who suggests this onyx was a large cameo, but her best comparandum (2003, 41n31) is actually a small cameo in the Content family collection, which is 16.8 mm in height, not 31.7 cm as listed in Sas and Theoen 2002, which, apparently, is the length of the chain to which it was attached; see Henig 1990, 40–41, no. 67.

102 Homolle 1882, 32, lines 33–34.

103 Poseidonios *apud* Athenaios, *Deipnosophistai* 11.495a.

104 E. Schmidt 1957, 91.

105 Appian, *Mithradatic Wars* 115–17.

106 *NH* 37.18.

107 *NH* 37.204.

108 *NH* 37.21–22.

109 Martial 14.113.

110 *NH* 37.18–21.

111 Suetonius, *Augustus* 71.

112 Scriptores Historiae Augustae, *Heliogabalus* 32.2; *Marcus Aurelius* 17.4; and compare *Lucius Verus* 5.3.

113 Loewental and Harden 1949; Bromehead 1952; Harden 1954; Williams 2004; Tressaud and Vickers 2007; Williams 2009, 300.

114 *NH* 37.2, 37.113, 37.104.

115 *NH* 36.196–97.

116 Haevernick 1963; Powers 2011.

117 Oliver 1975.

118 *NH* 37.23–29; Suetonius, *Nero* 47.

119 Dio Cassius 54.23.1–4; compare Seneca, *De ira* 3.40.

120 Bühler 1973; Oliver 1975; 1980, 166; Gasparri 1975, 1979, 2003. For evidence of gold added to engraved gems, see Rosenfeld, Dvorachek, and Amorai-Stark 2003.

121 Cima and La Rocca 1986, 141–44.

122 Berlin, Antikensammlung, 30219,713: Platz-Horster 2012, no. 84: London, British Museum, 1923,0401.1189 (Gem 4016): Walters 1926, no. 4016; Bühler 1973, no. 19.

123 G. Schmidt 2008.

124 *NH* 37.85.

125 See Belozerskaya 2012.

126 D. Gaborit-Chopin in Alcouffe et al. 1991, 38–40, no. 11.

127 *NH* 36.57.

128 Dio Cassius 77.15. In general, see Del Bufalo 2012; for purple, see Reinhold 1970 (both with copious references).

129 Padgett 1995; Gagetti 2006.

130 *NH* 37.75, 108, 118, 196–97.

131 Borromeo 1993, 121, notes that Faustina the Younger "was the first empress to be named *mater castrorum*; it is possible that her portrait could have adorned scepters." See also Gagetti 2006, 587–88, pls. 84–87, tables 5–6; and Gagetti 2014 for sculpture in rock crystal.

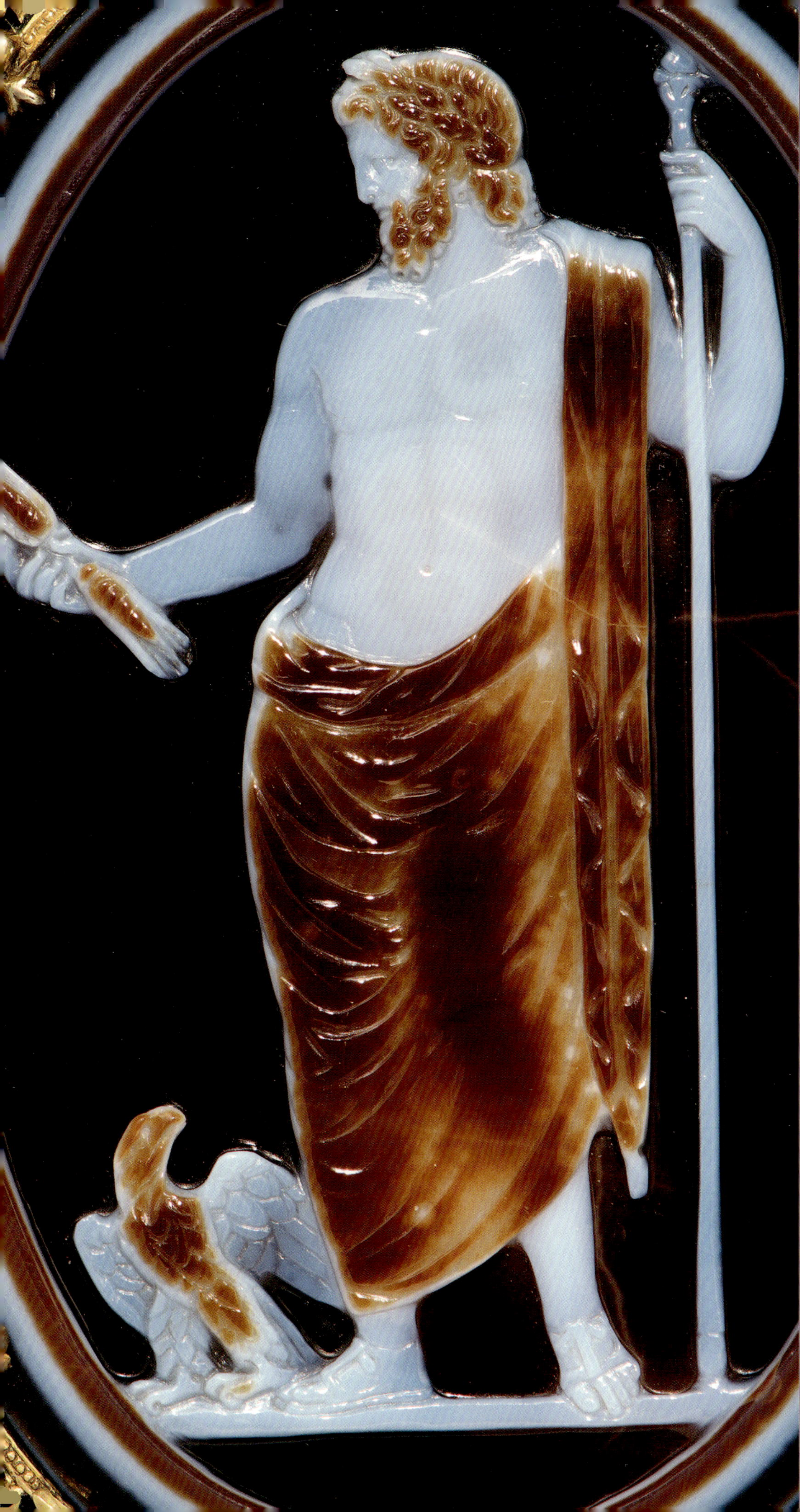

CHAPTER TWO

HARD STONES

PLATES 81–145

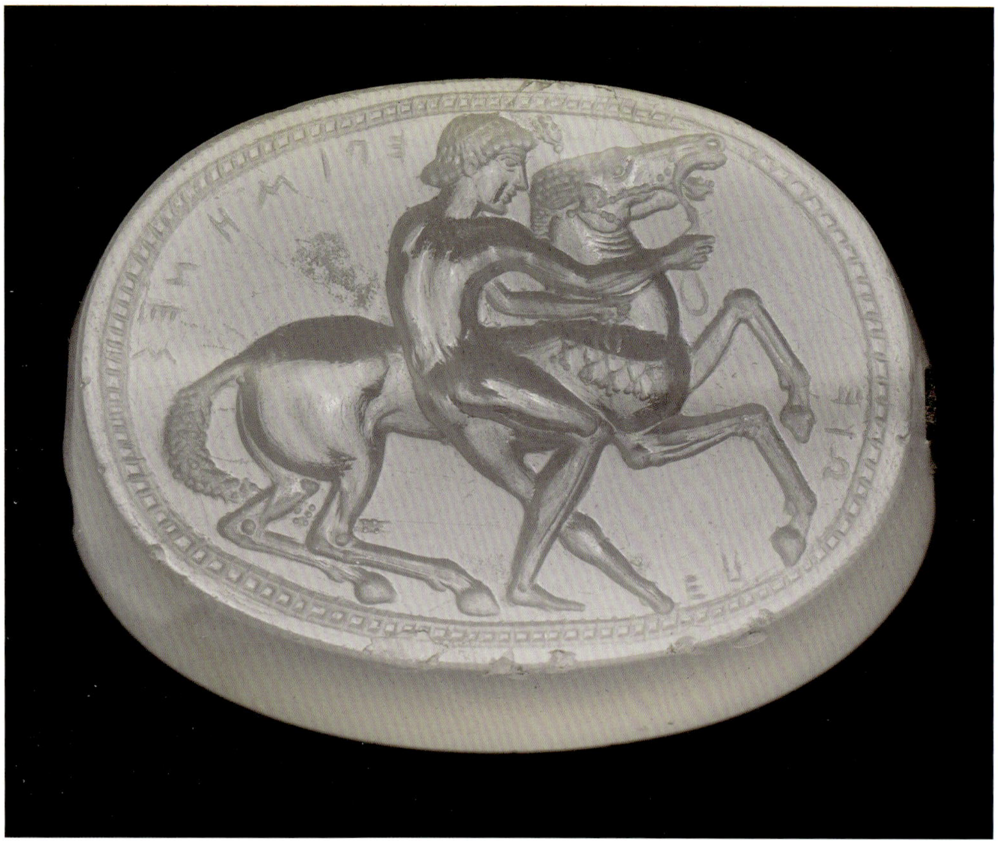

Plate 81
Scaraboid intaglio of a youth restraining a horse, signed by Epimenes, ca. 500 BC. Chalcedony, H: 17 mm; W: 19 mm; D: 9 mm

Plate 82
Scaraboid intaglio of an archer testing his arrow, attributed to Epimenes, ca. 500 BC. Chalcedony, H: 17 mm; W: 15 mm; D: 13 mm

Plate 83
Scaraboid intaglio of a youth scraping his leg with a strigil, attributed to Epimenes, ca. 500 BC. Obsidian, H (gem): 16.2 mm; W: 12.9 mm; D: 6 mm

Plate 84 (opposite)
Scaraboid intaglio of a heron, signed by Dexamenos of Chios, ca. 450–430 BC. Chalcedony, H: 17 mm; W: 22 mm

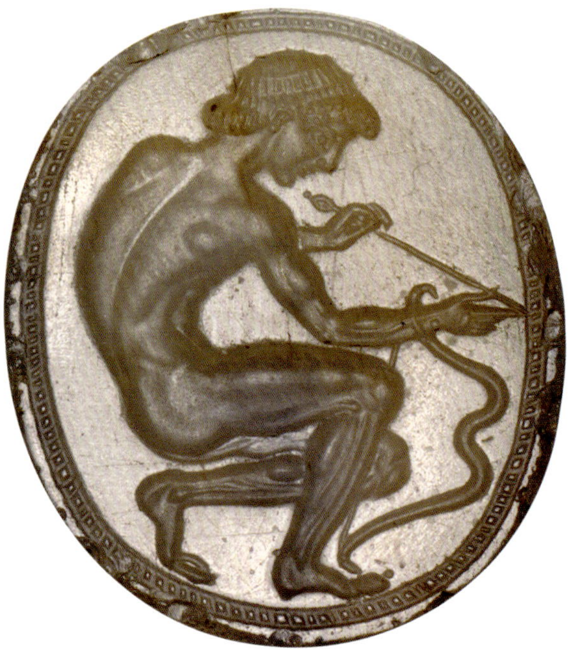

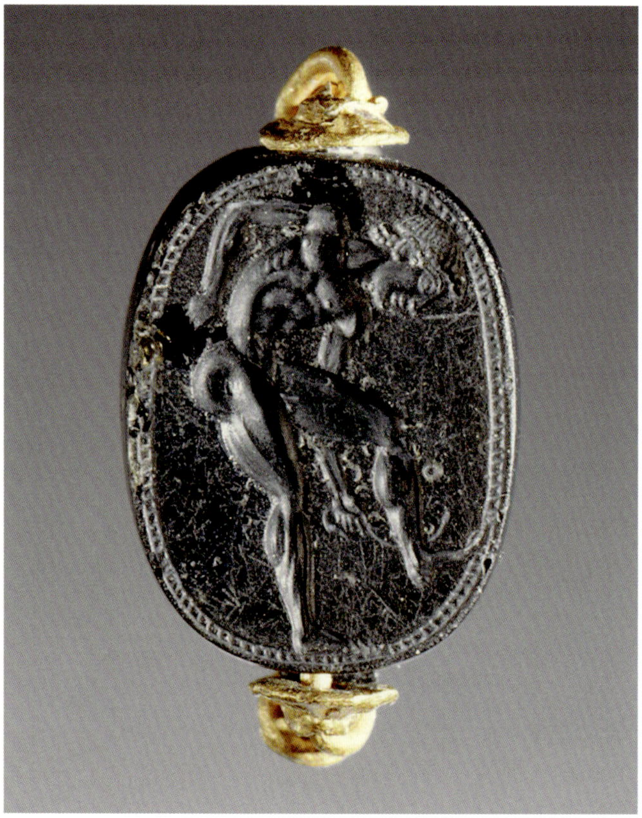

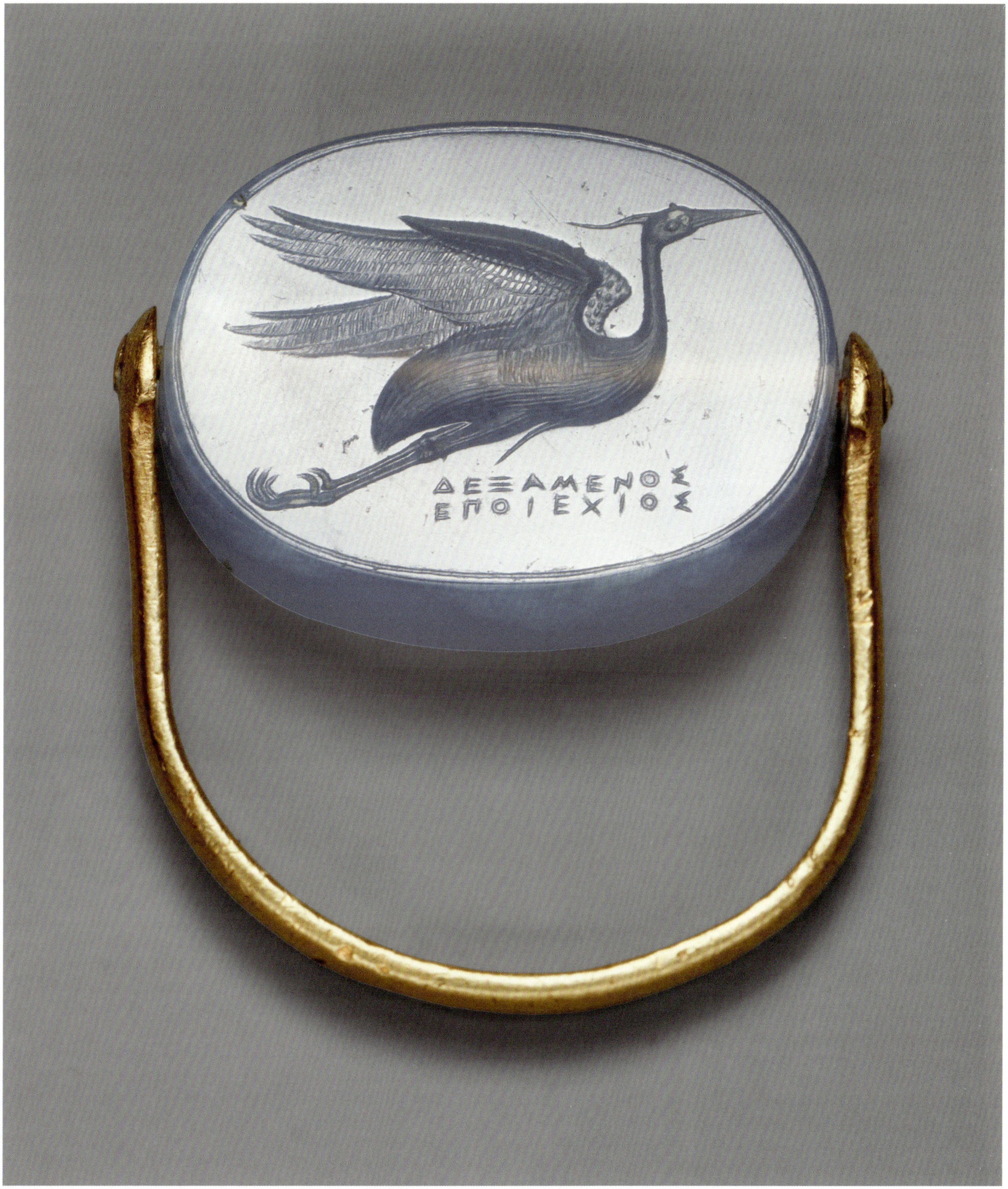
ΔΕΞΑΜΕΝΟΣ
ΕΠΟΙΕΧΙΟΣ

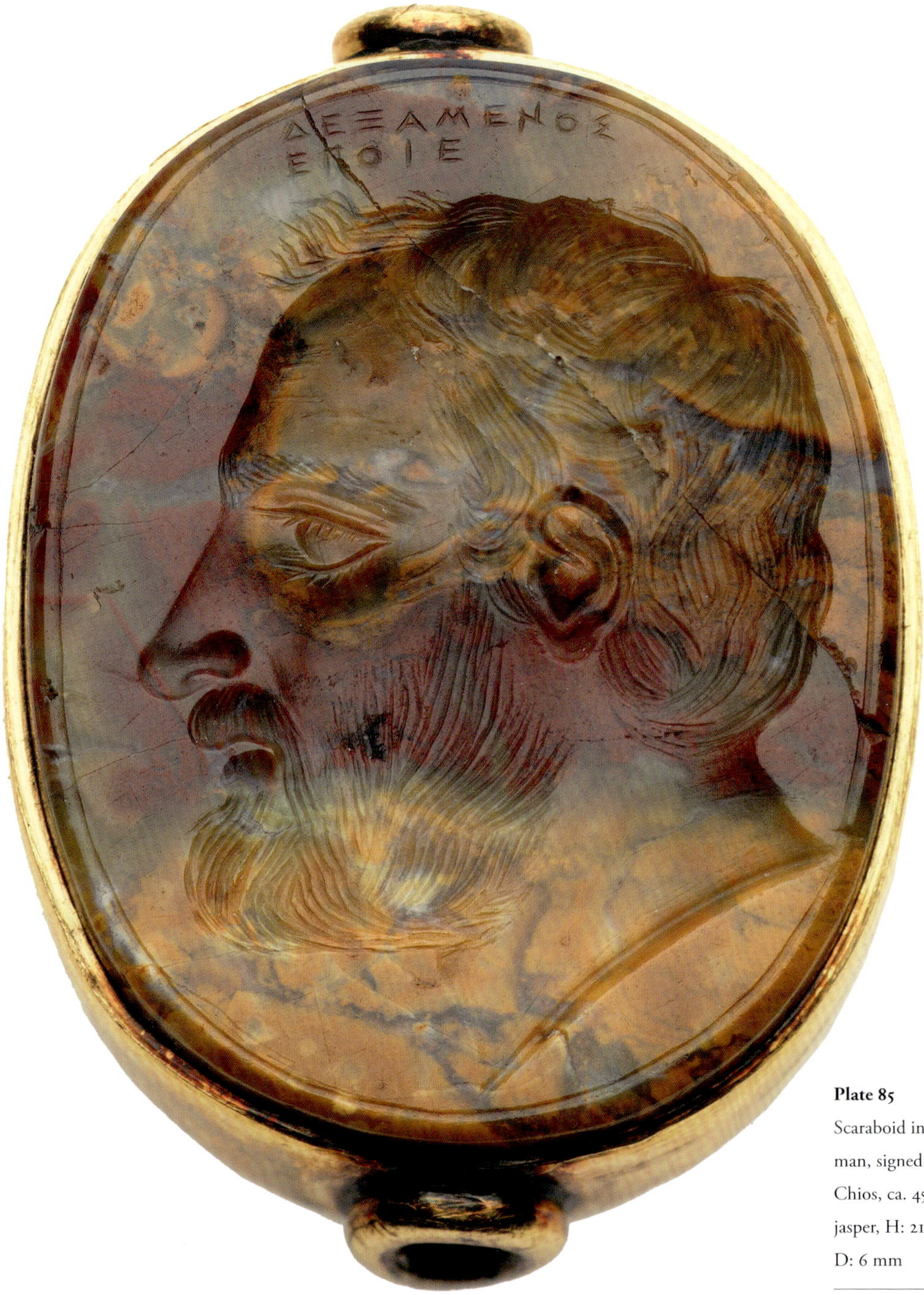

Plate 85
Scaraboid intaglio of a bearded man, signed by Dexamenos of Chios, ca. 450–430 BC. Mottled jasper, H: 21 mm, W: 17 mm, D: 6 mm

Plate 86 (opposite)
Scaraboid intaglio of Nike, signed by Onatas(?), ca. 370–350 BC. Chalcedony, H: 31 mm; W: 24 mm; D: 11 mm

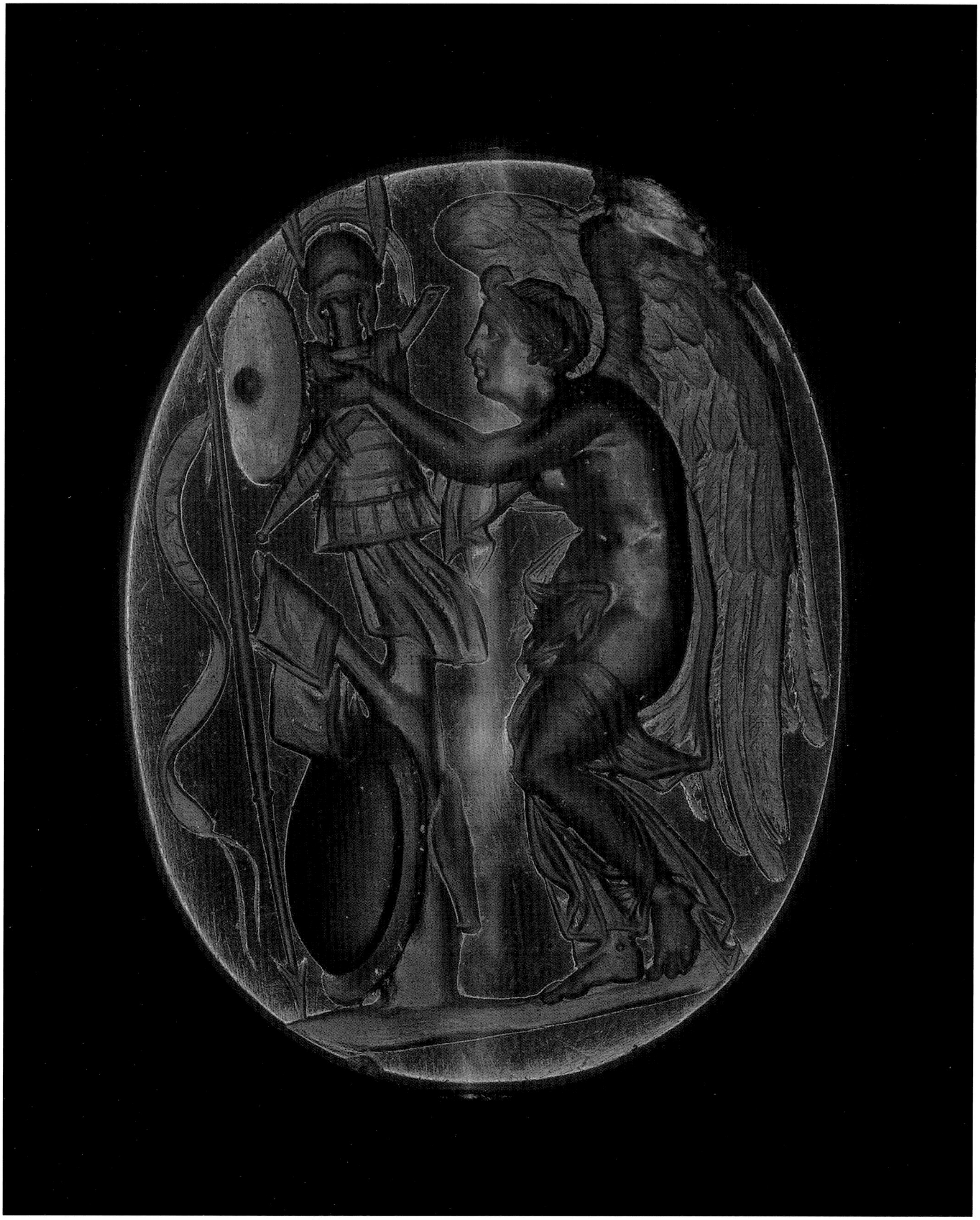

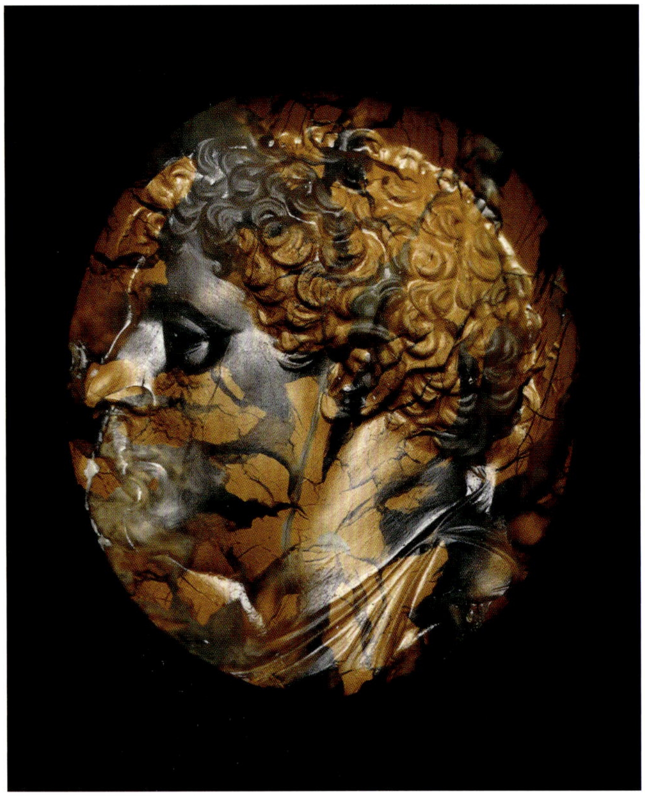

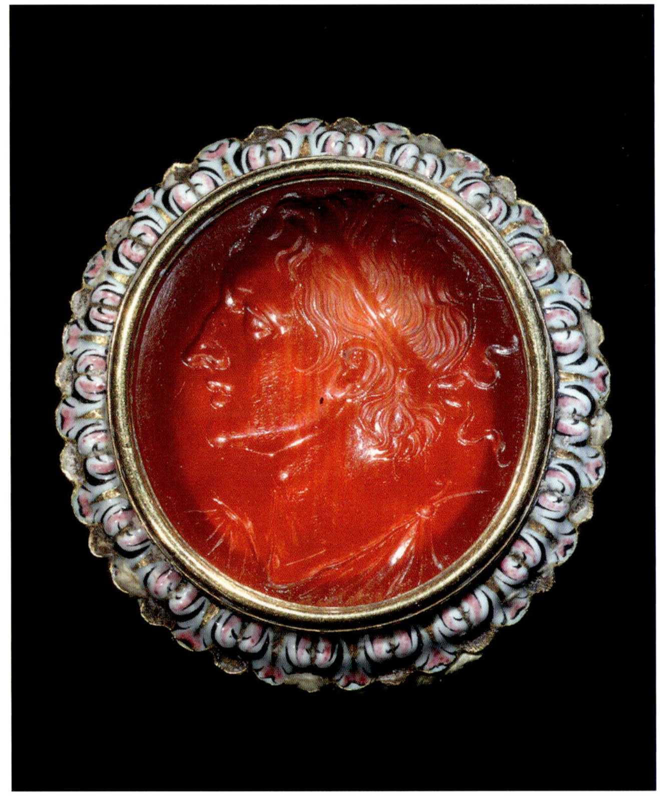

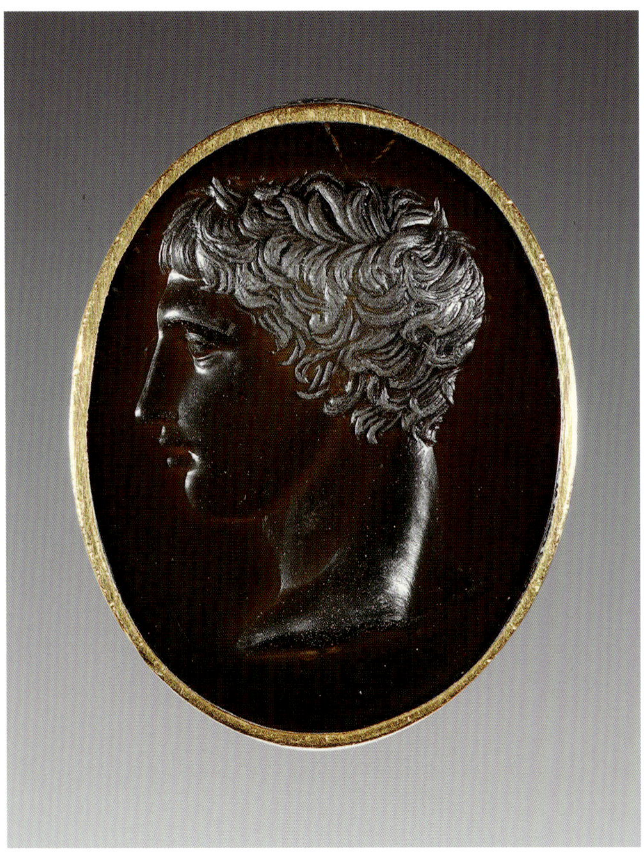

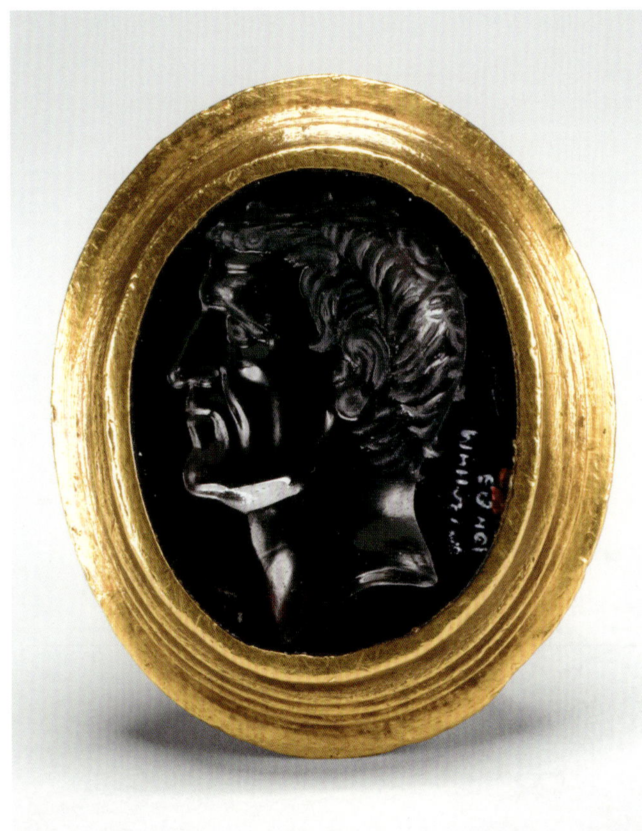

Opposite, left to right:

Plate 87
Intaglio of Philetairos of Pergamon, ca. 275–175 BC. Mottled chalcedony and jasper, H: 28 mm; W: 23 mm

Plate 88
Intaglio of a Ptolemaic king, second–first century BC. Cornelian set in a modern gold and enamel mount, H: 20 mm; W: 17 mm; D: ca. 4 mm

Plate 89
Intaglio of the *Doryphoros* of Polykleitos, ca. 50–40 BC. Dark green chalcedony, H (gem): 22.4 mm; W: 17.3 mm

Plate 90
Intaglio of a man, signed by Menophilos, ca. 150 BC. Garnet, H (gem): 23.5 mm; W: 18.5 mm; D: 7 mm; H (ring): 34.4 mm; W: 29.1 mm

Plate 91
Intaglio of Sirius the Dog Star, signed by Gaius, ca. 100 BC. Garnet, H: 21.5 mm; W: 15 mm; Thickness: 7 mm

Plate 92
Intaglio of the *Athena Parthenos* of Pheidias, signed by Aspasios, ca. 50–25 BC. Red jasper, H: 35 mm; W: 28 mm

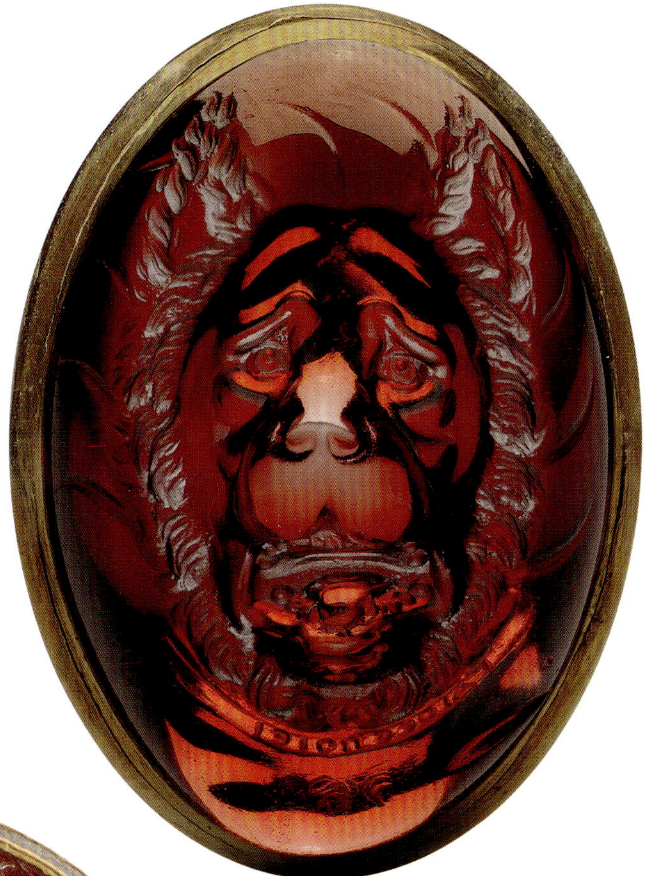

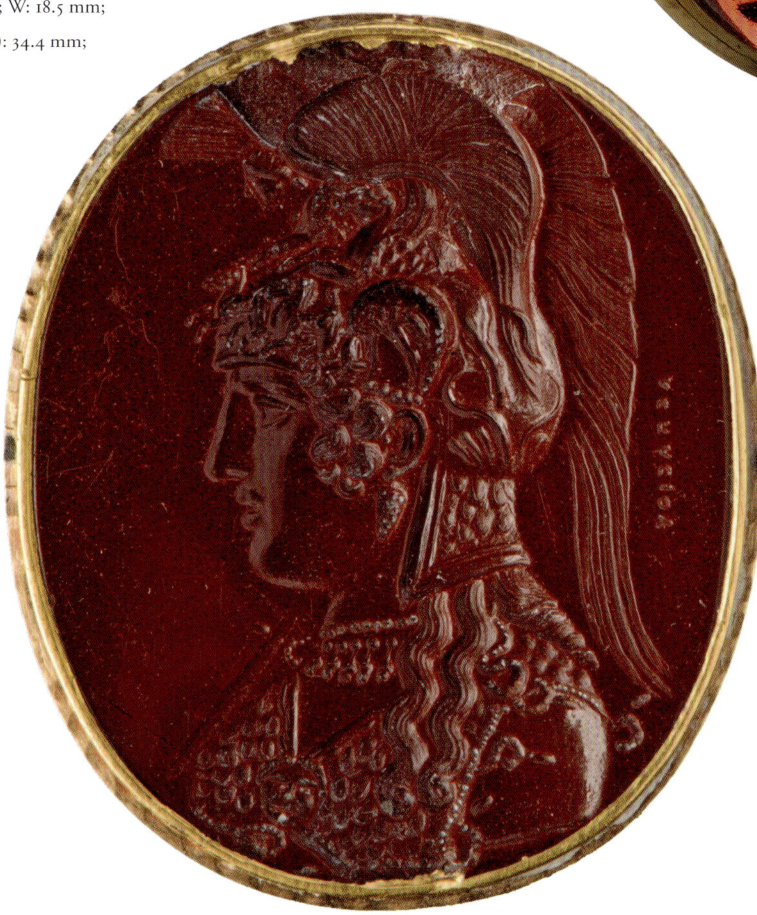

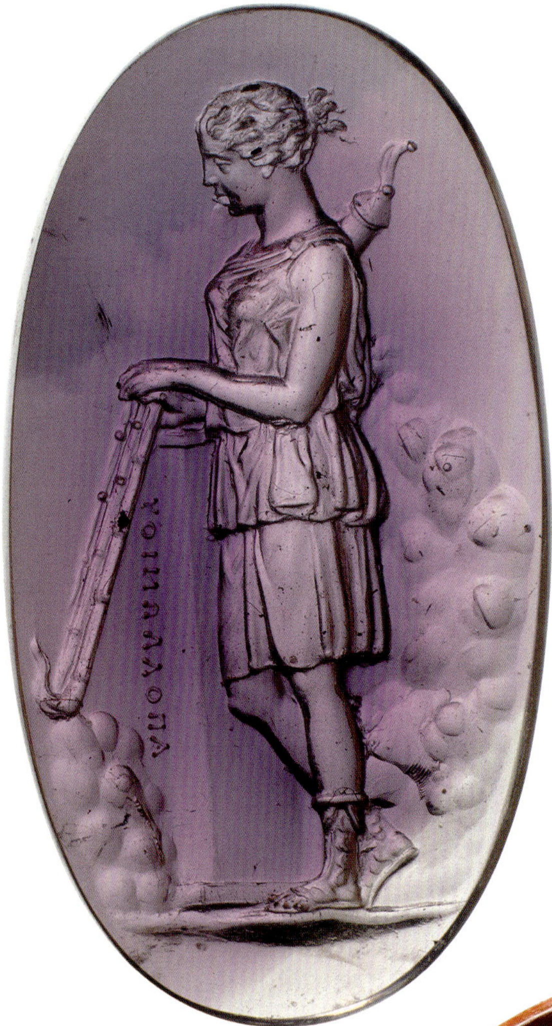

Plate 93
Intaglio of Artemis, signed by Apollonios, ca. 50–25 BC.
Amethyst, H: 25.7 mm; W: 13.8 mm

Plate 94
Intaglio of Odysseus, Diomedes, and the Palladion, signed by Felix (the Felix Gem), ca. 25 BC–AD 25.
Agate, H: 26 mm; W: 35 mm; D: 3 mm

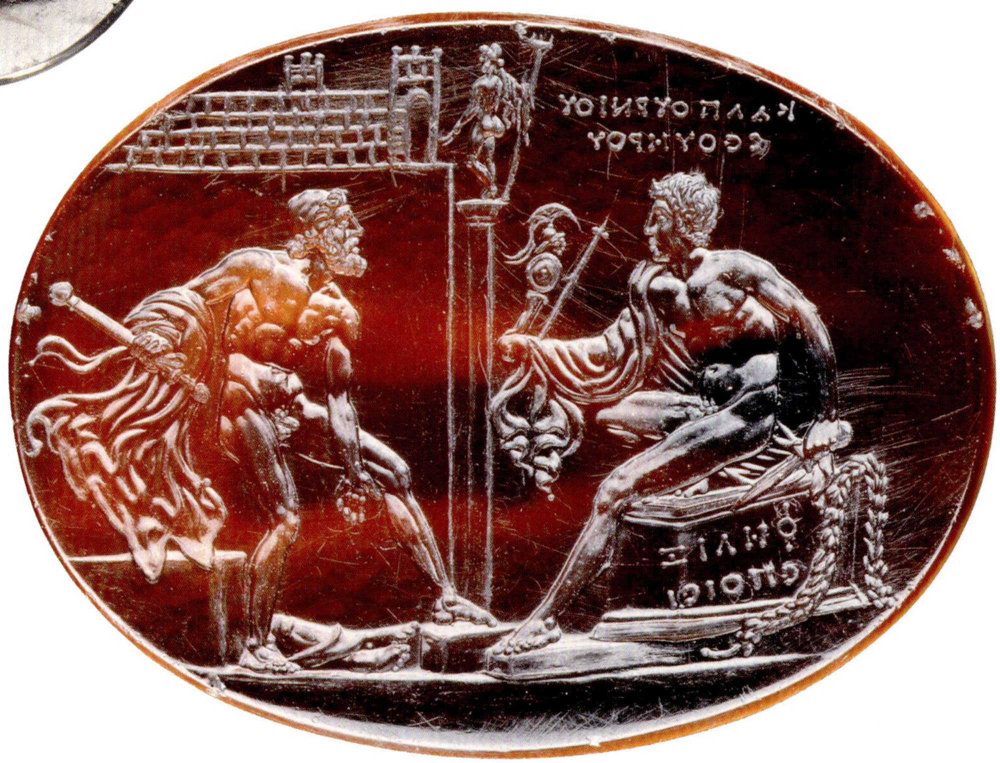

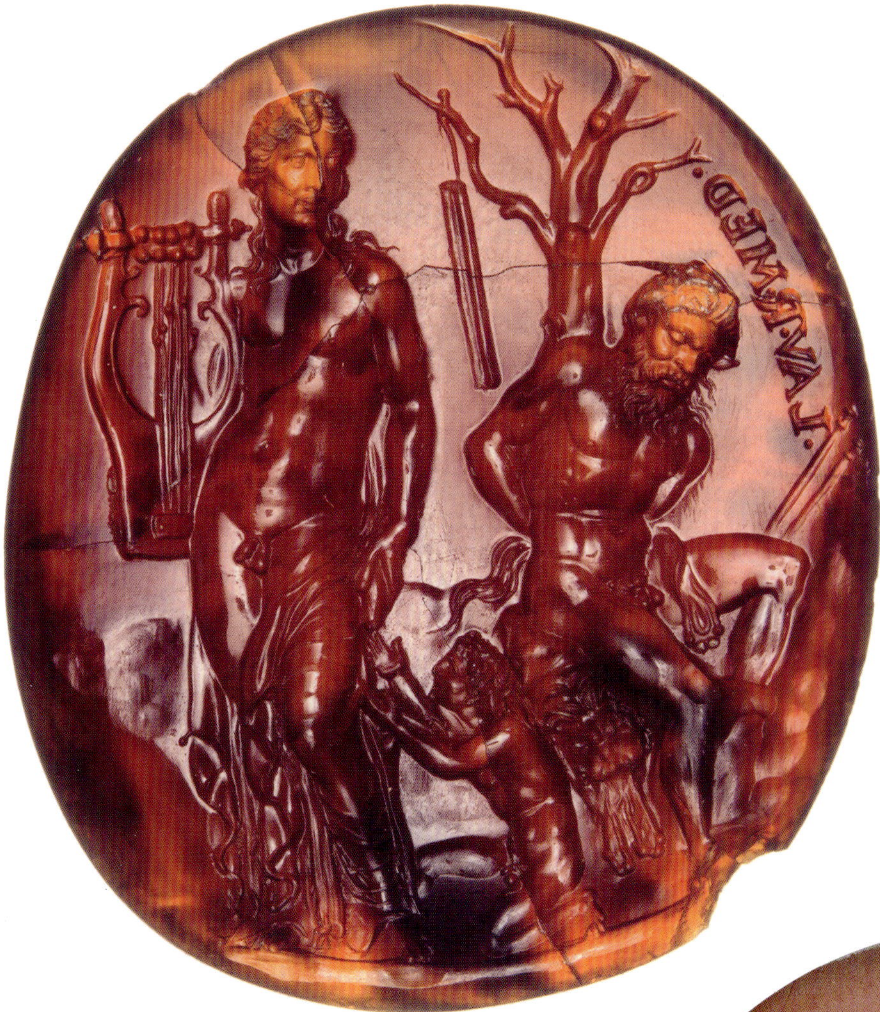

Plate 95
Intaglio of Apollo, Marsyas, and Olympos (the Seal of Nero), attributed to Dioskourides ca. 30 BC. Cornelian, H: 40.2 mm; W: 34 mm

Plate 96
Intaglio of Diomedes and the Palladion, signed by Dioskourides, ca. 40–30 BC. Cornelian, H: 17.5 mm; W: 19 mm

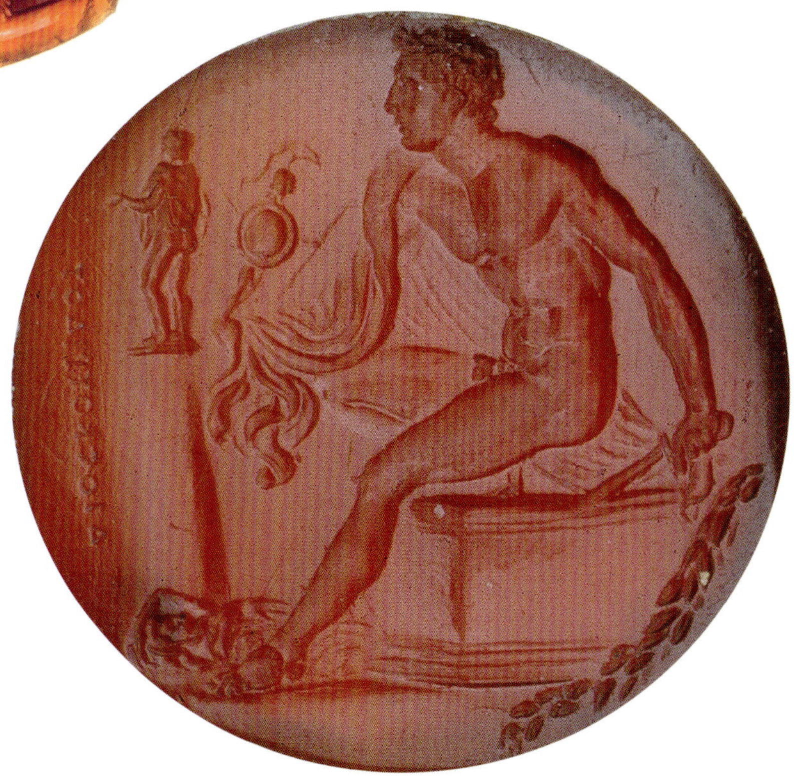

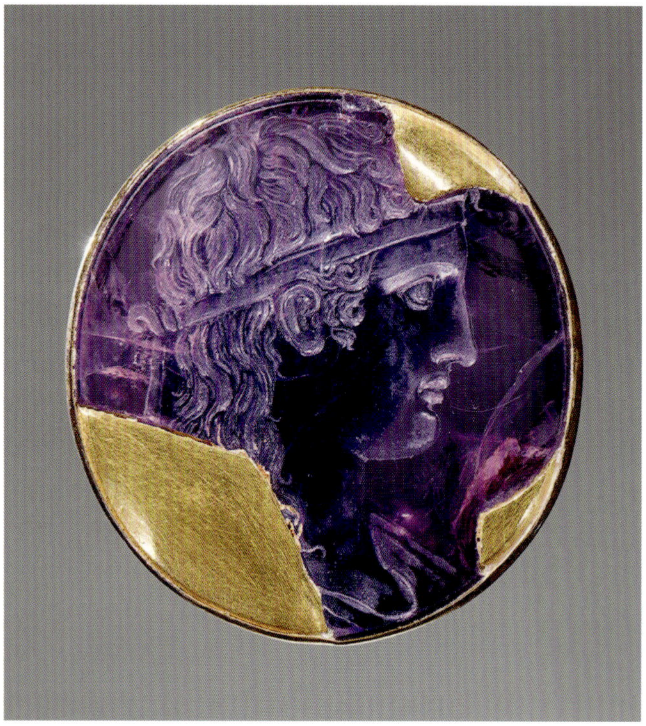

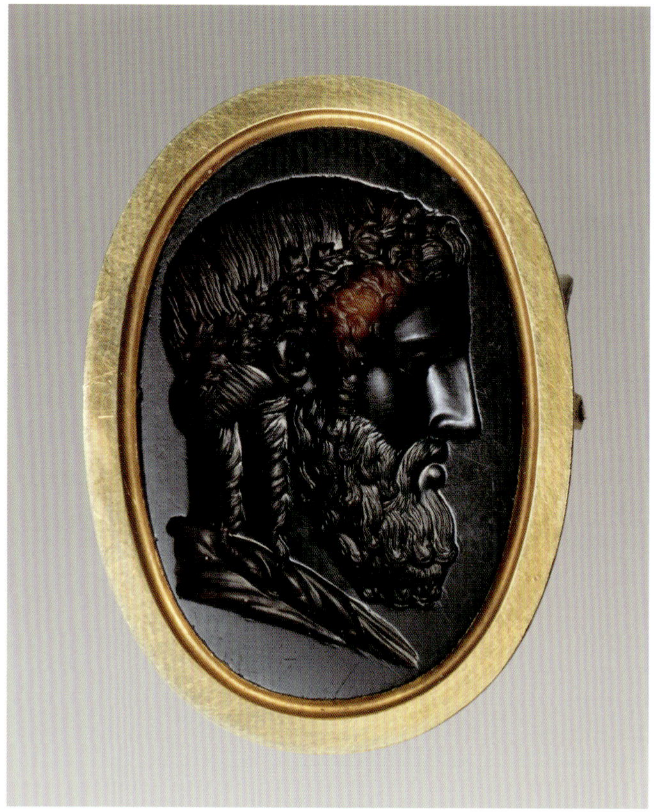

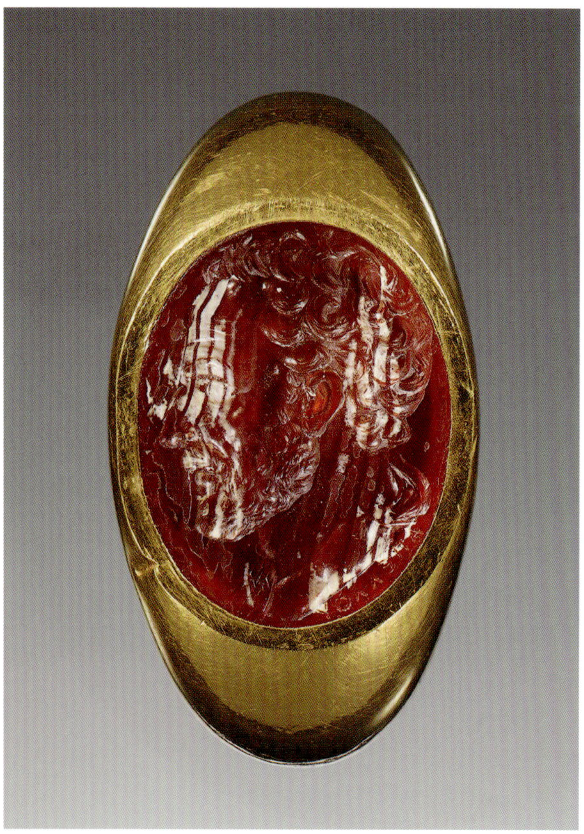

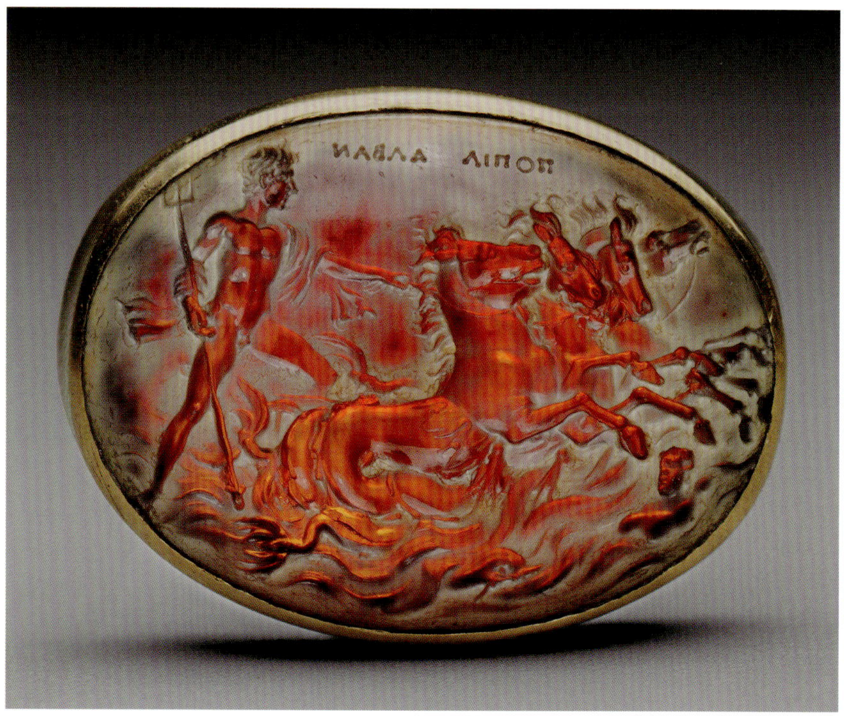

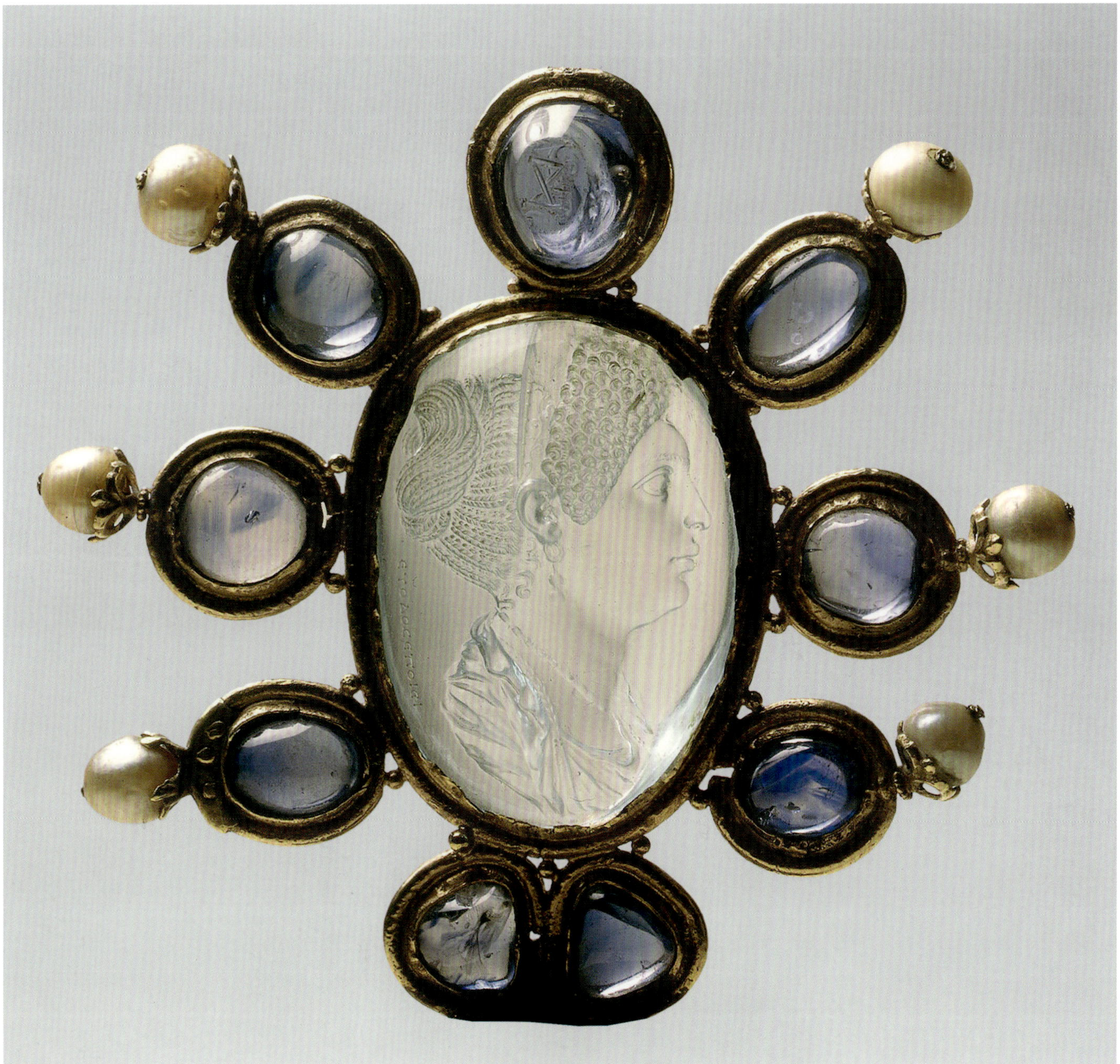

Opposite, left:

Plate 97
Fragmentary intaglio of Apollo, ca. 30–20 BC. Amethyst, H: 33 mm; W: 30 mm

Plate 99
Intaglio of Demosthenes, signed by Apelles, ca. 25–1 BC. Cornelian, H (gem): 19 mm; W: 15 mm

Opposite, right:

Plate 98
Intaglio of Zeus, late first century BC–early first century AD. Cornelian, H: 37 mm; W: 26 mm

Plate 100
Intaglio of Octavian as Neptune, ca. 31–27 BC. Cornelian, H: 17 mm; W: 21 mm

Plate 101
Intaglio of Julia, daughter of Titus, signed by Euodos, ca. 80–91. Beryl (aquamarine), in a Carolingian mount of gold, pearls, and sapphires, H (gem): 50 mm; W: 37 mm

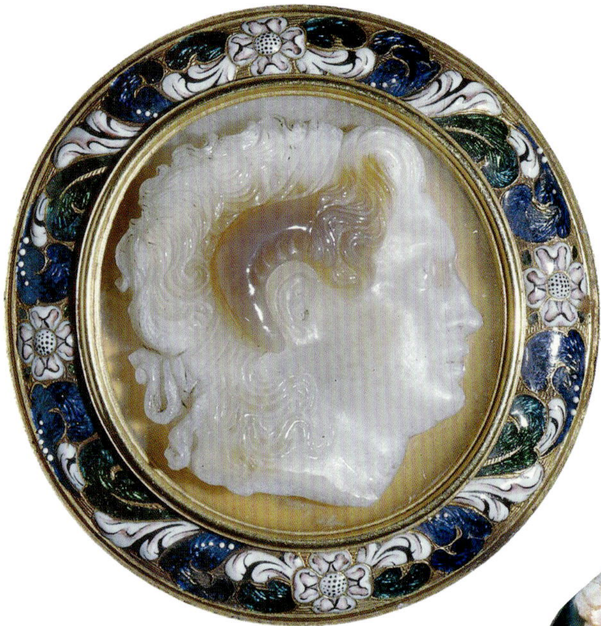

Plate 102
Cameo of Alexander the Great with the horn of Zeus Ammon in a modern gold and enamel mount, ca. 320–200 BC(?). Sardonyx, H (gem): 32 mm; W: 30 mm

Plate 103
Double portrait of male and female rulers (the Gonzaga Cameo), third century BC or later(?). Sardonyx, H: 157 mm; W: 118 mm

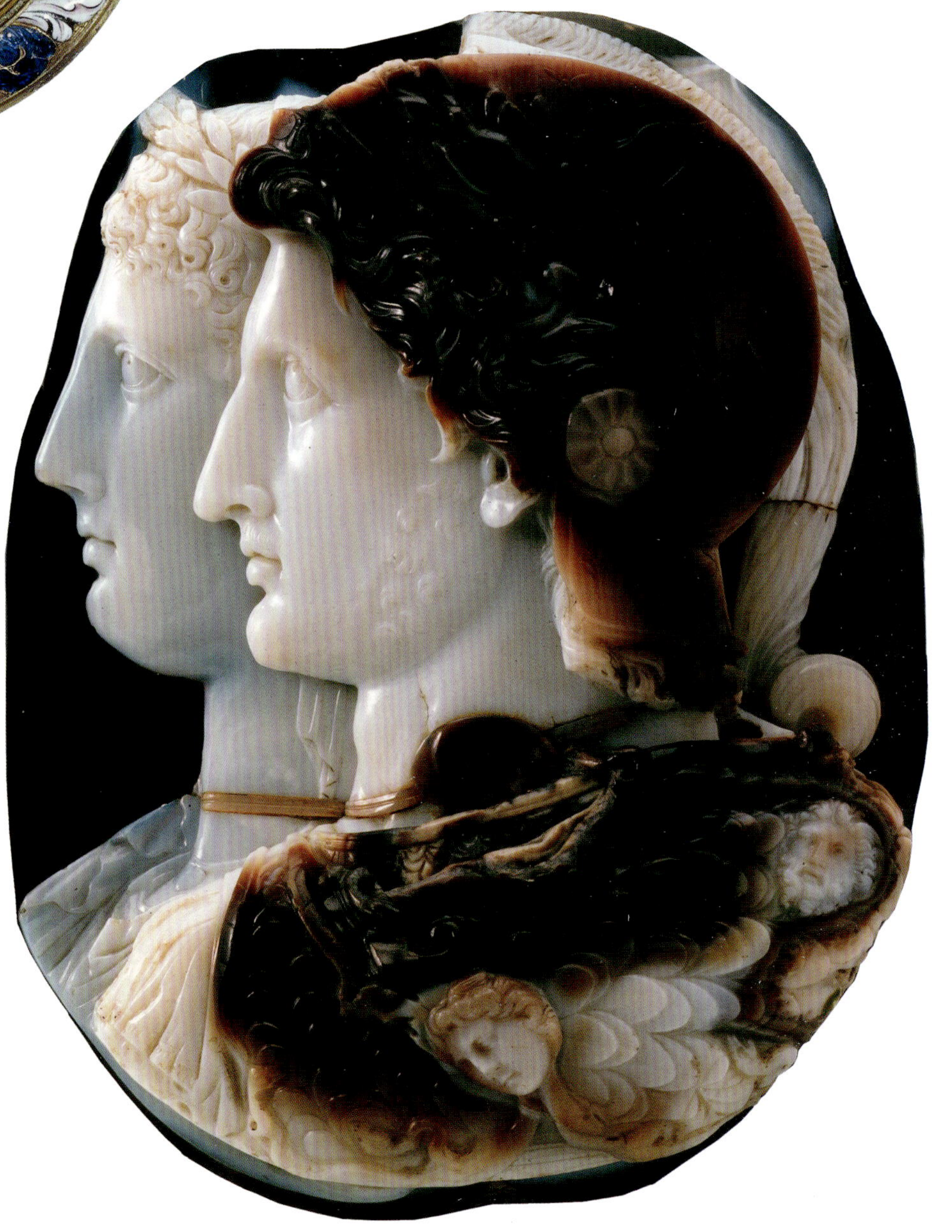

Plate 104

Cameo of Zeus fighting the giants,
signed by Athenion, ca. 150 BC.
Sardonyx, H: 29 mm; W: 35 mm

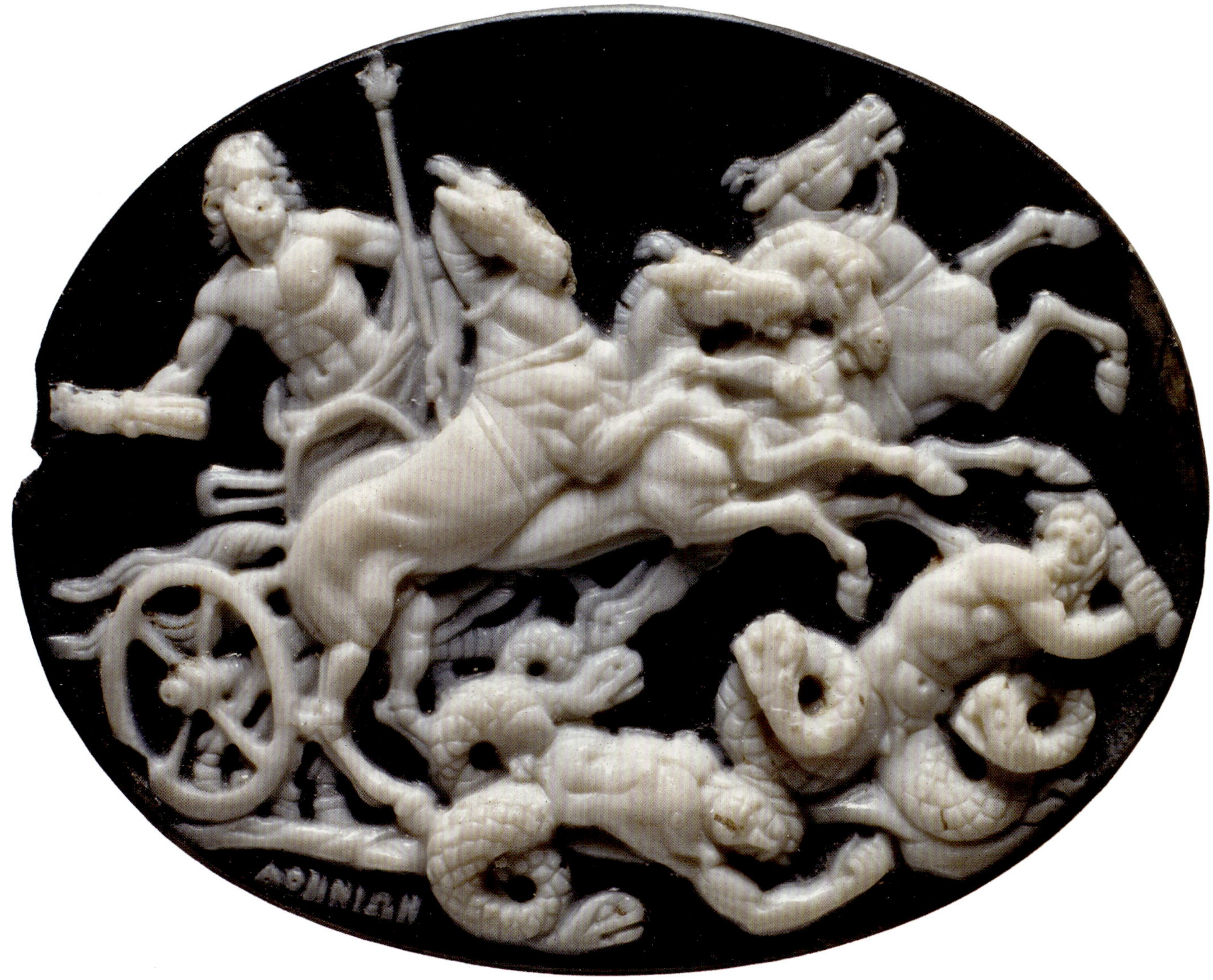

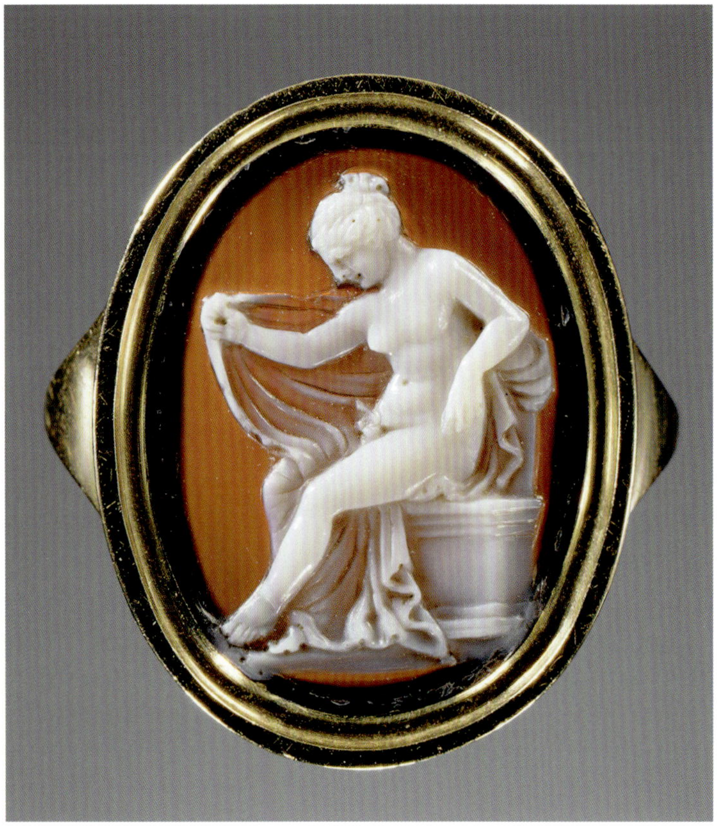

Plate 105
Cameo of Hermaphroditus revealing him/herself, attributed to Protarchos, ca. 150–100 BC. Sardonyx, H: 18 mm; W: 14 mm; D: 2 mm

Plate 106
Cameo of Dionysos and a satyr on a chariot drawn by Psychai and Erotes, ca. 50–30 BC. Sardonyx, H: 33.9 mm; W: 42.6 mm

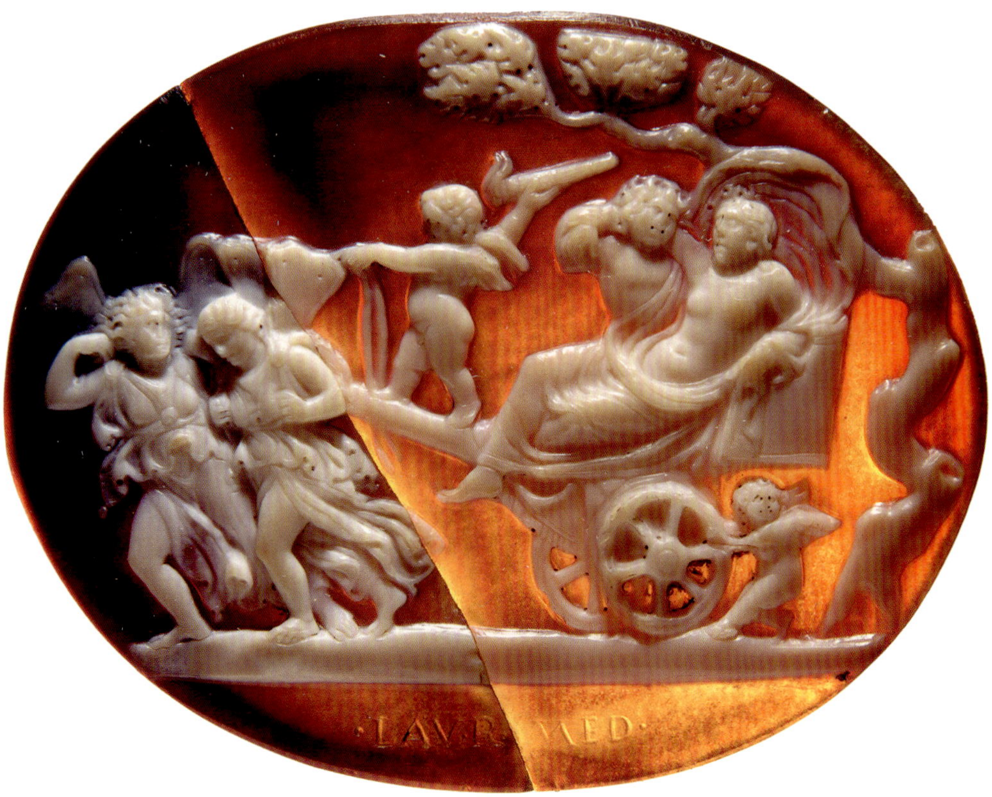

Plate 107
Cameo of the Marriage of Cupid and Psyche (?) (the Marlborough Cameo) signed by Tryphon, ca. 50–25 BC. Sardonyx, H: 37 mm; W: 45 mm; D: 2.5 mm

Plate 108
Cameo of the young Herakles, ca. 30–20 BC. Sardonyx, H: 29.9 mm; W: 23 mm

Plate 109
Cameo of Herakles leashing Kerberos, signed by Dioskourides, ca. 40–30 BC. Sardonyx, H: 25.3 mm; W: 21.3 mm

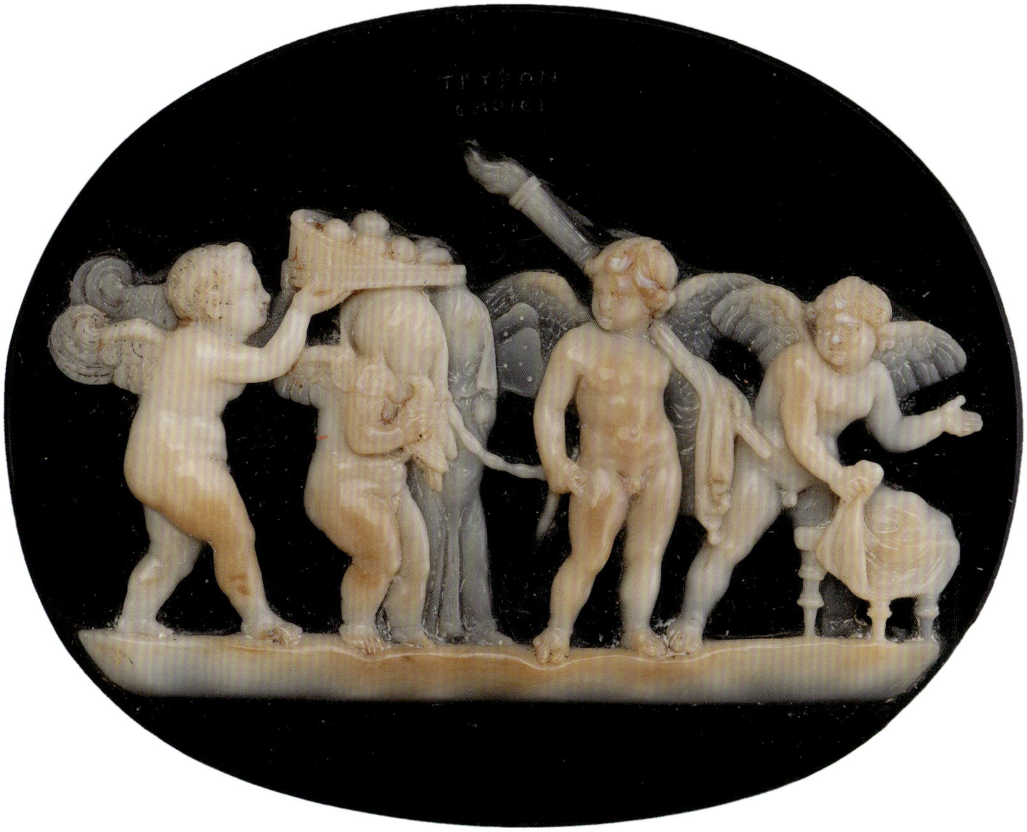

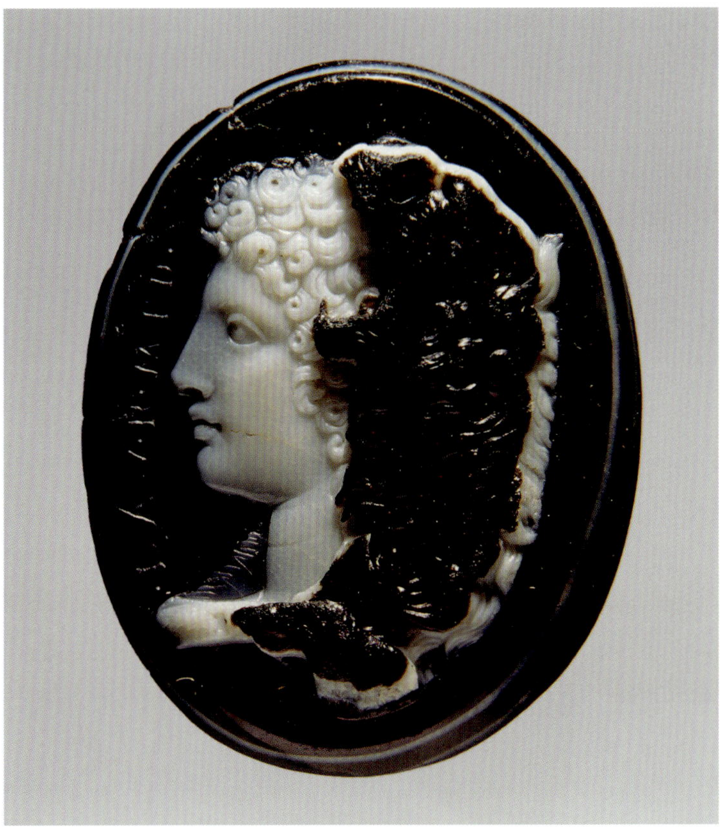

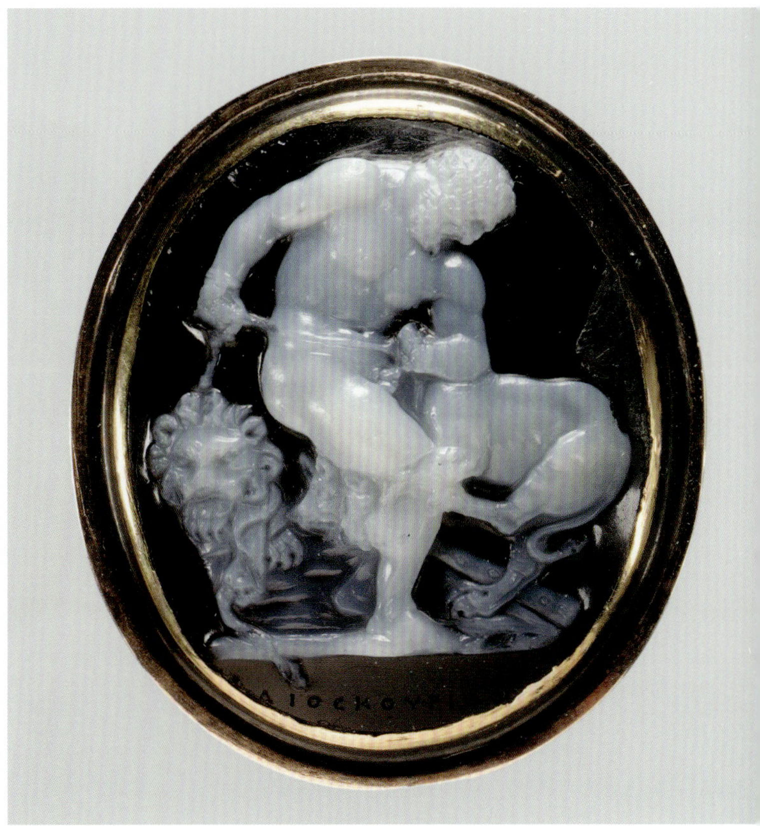

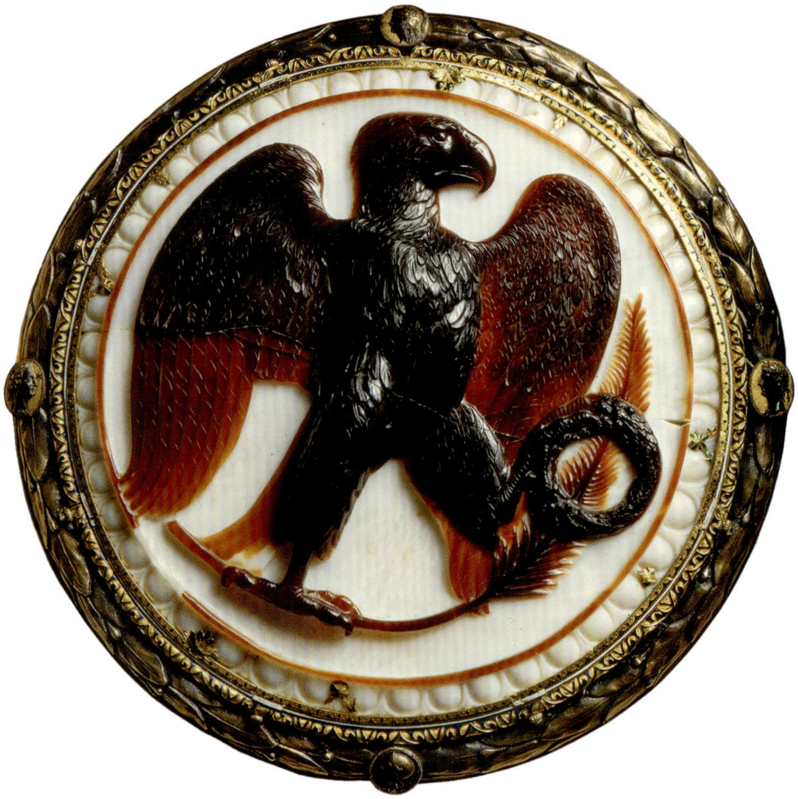

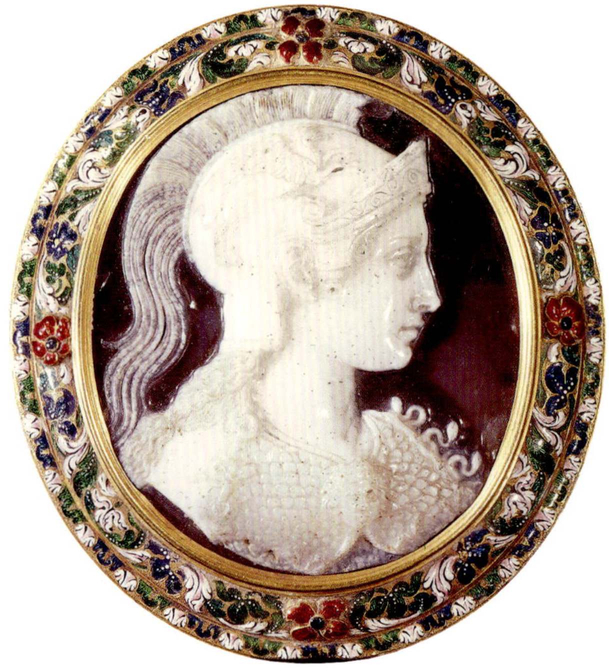

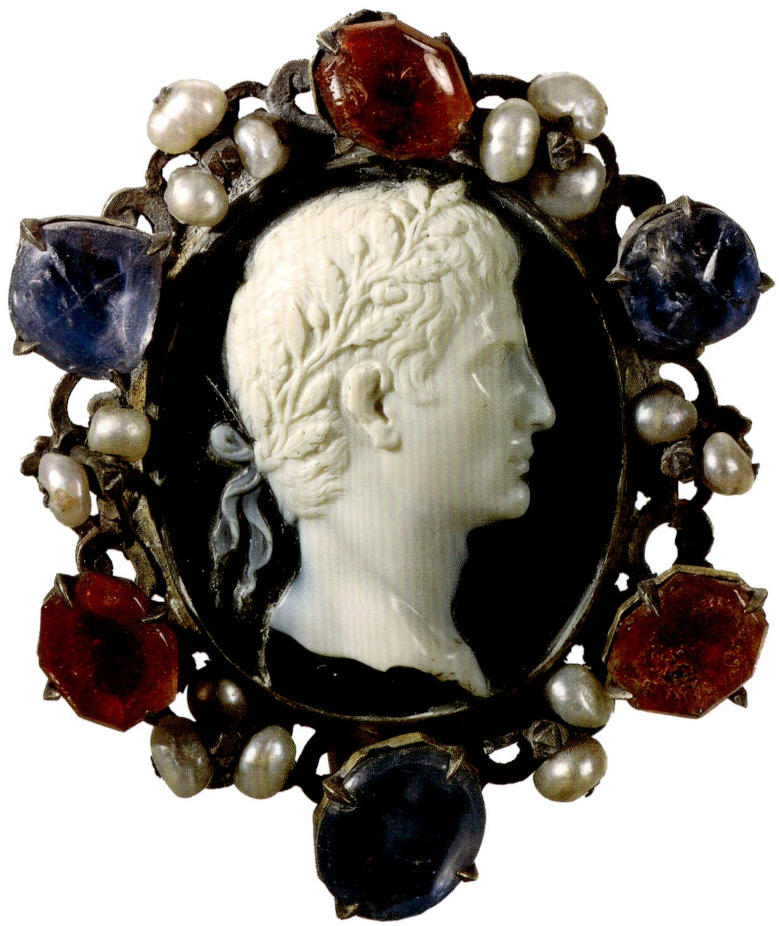

Plate 110
Cameo of an eagle, ca. 27 BC(?). Sardonyx, Diam: 220 mm

Plate 111
Cameo of Athena/Minerva, ca. 25–1 BC. Sardonyx, H: 68 mm; W: 60 mm; D: 11 mm

Plate 112
Cameo of Augustus, ca. 25–20 BC. Sardonyx, H: 49 mm; W: 40 mm

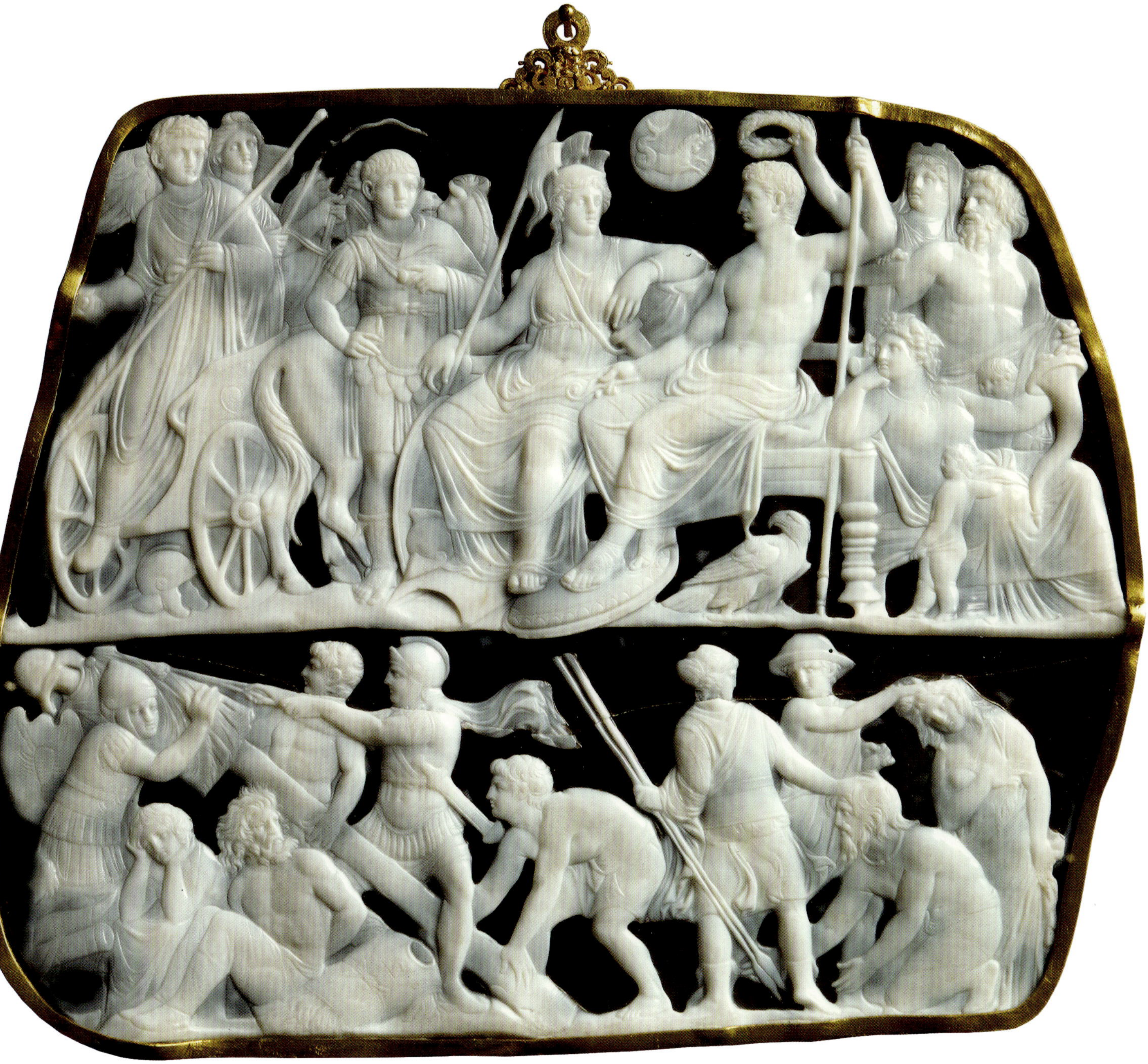

Plate 113

The Gemma Augustea, ca. 12 BC–
AD 14. Sardonyx, H: 187 mm;
W: 223 mm; D: 3.5–14 mm

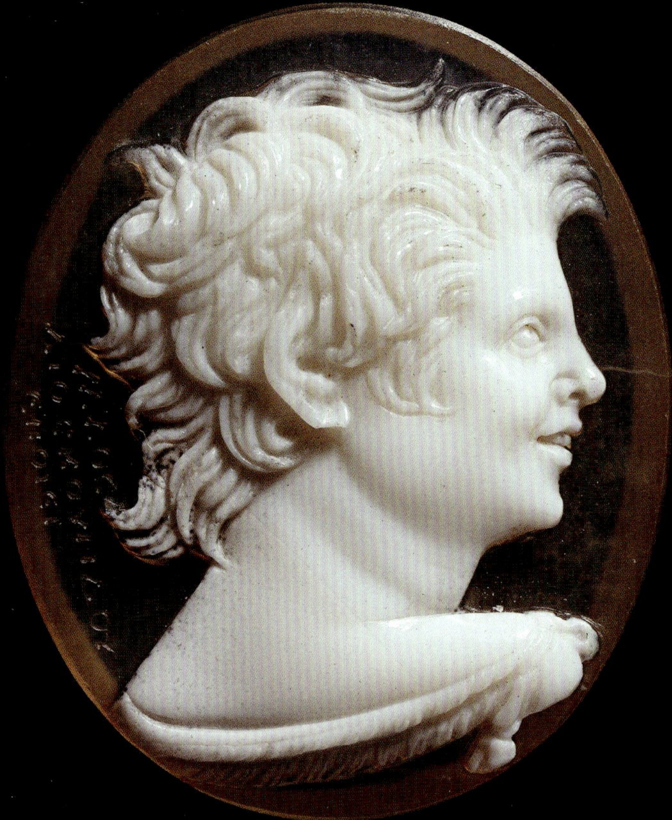

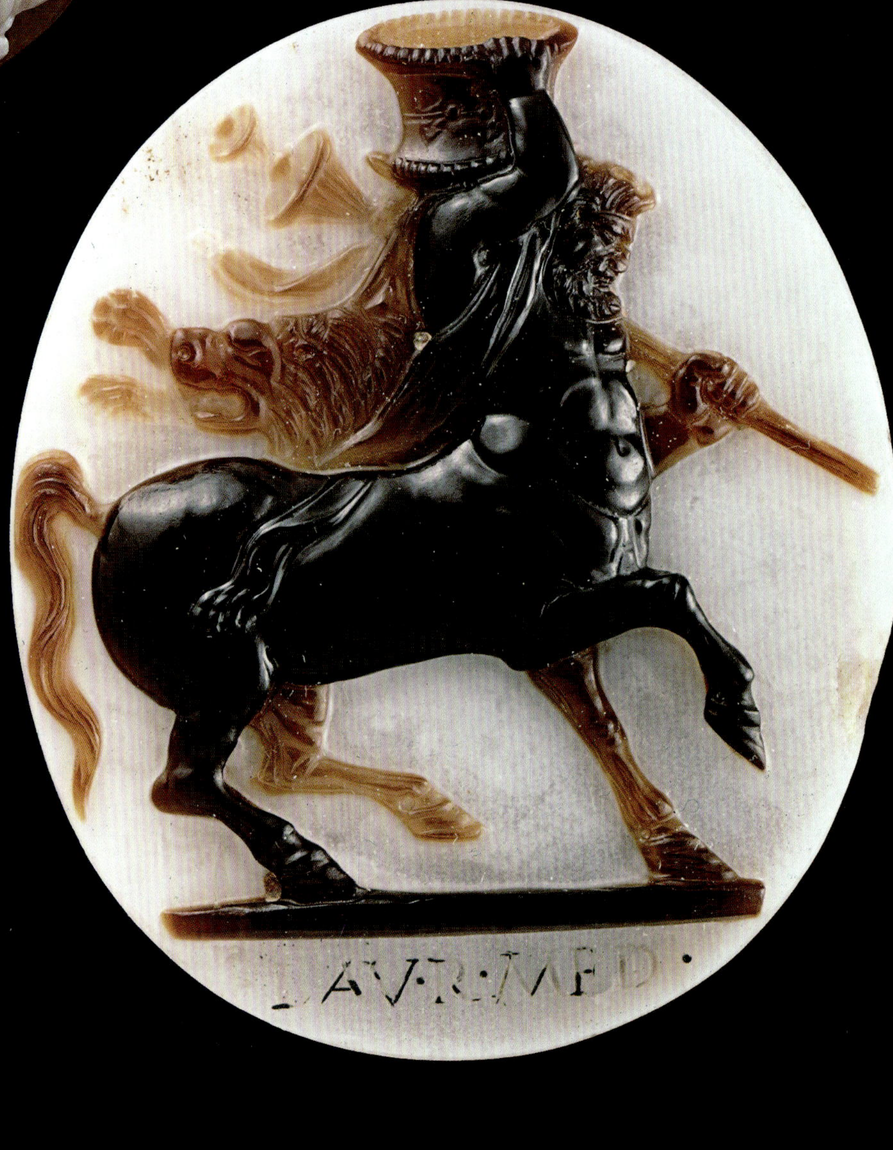
LAV·R·MED·

Plate 114 (opposite, top)
Cameo of a laughing satyr, signed by Hyllos, son of Dioskourides, ca. AD 10. Sardonyx, H: 17.6 mm; W: 14.4 mm

Plate 115 (opposite, bottom)
Cameo of a centaur, ca. AD 50–150. Sardonyx, H: 51 mm; W: 42.5 mm

Plate 116 (right)
Cameo of Jupiter, ca. AD 14–37. Sardonyx in a medieval gold and enamel mount, H: 94 mm; W: 63.5 mm; D: ca. 8 mm

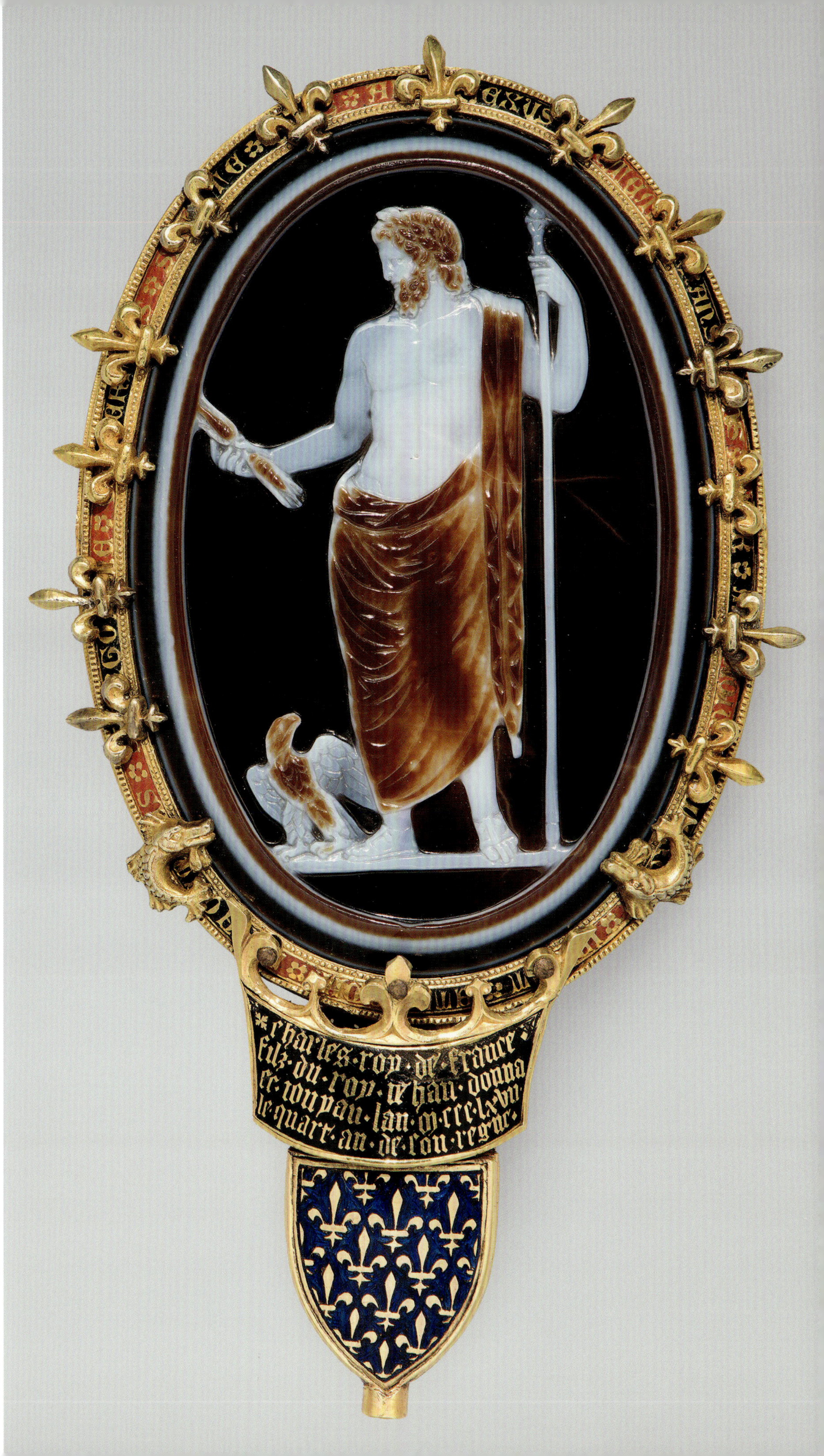

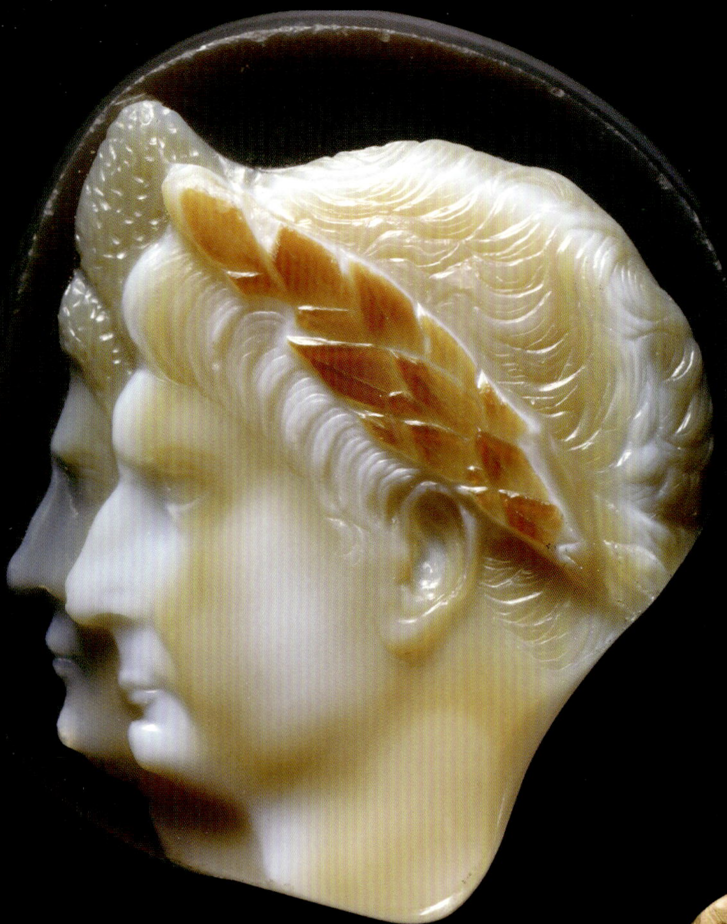

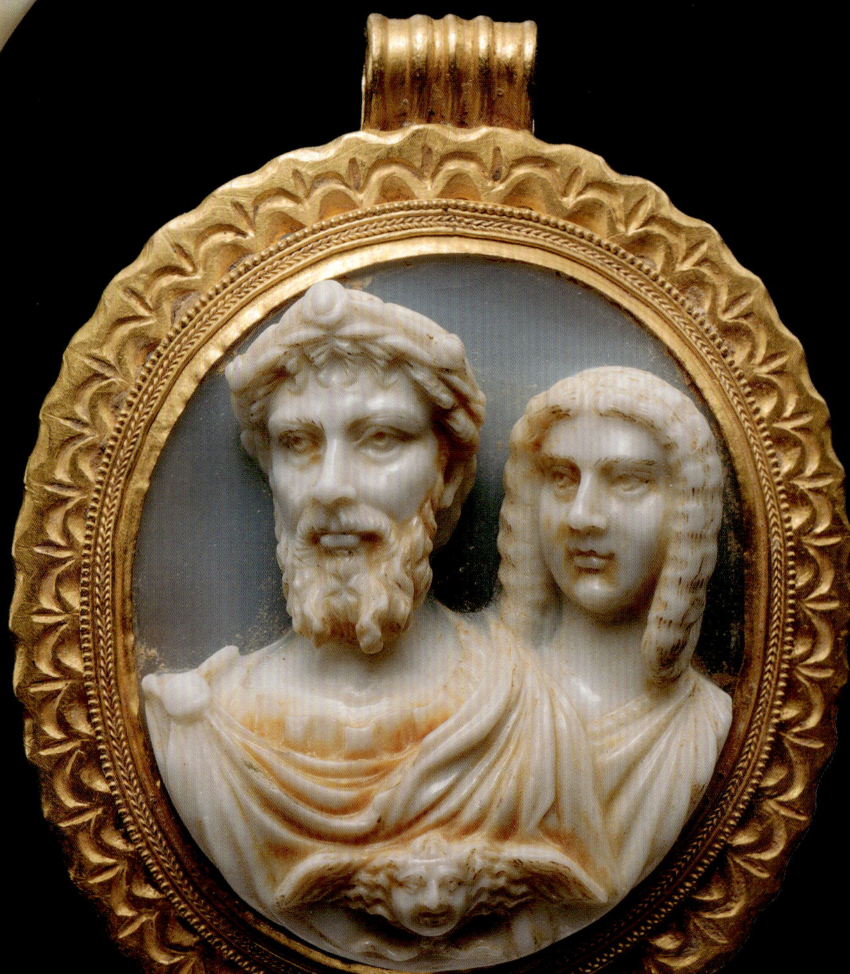

Plate 117 (opposite, top)
Cameo with double portrait of Trajan and Plotina, ca. AD 105–115. Sardonyx, H: 50 mm; W: 43 mm; D: 12 mm

Plate 118 (opposite, bottom)
Cameo with double portrait of Septimius Severus and Julia Domna, ca. 207–211. Sardonyx, H (gem): 50 mm; W: 42 mm; H (with setting): 75 mm; W: 60 mm

Plate 119
Askos, ca. 200–100 BC. Banded agate, with gold lid and foot, H: 65 mm; L: 84 mm

Plate 120
Rhyton in the form of a gazelle, ca. 300–100 BC(?). Banded agate, with gold muzzle, H: 65 mm; L: 156 mm; Diam: 59 mm; Thickness: 2 mm

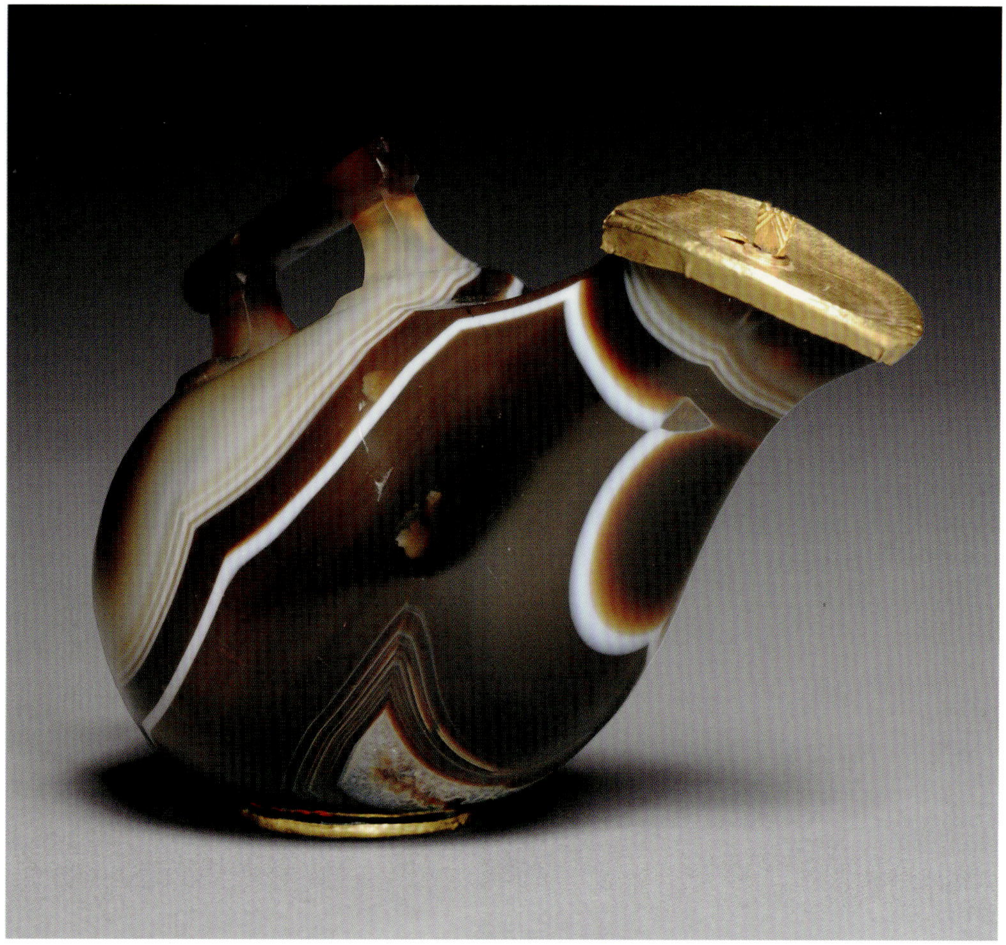

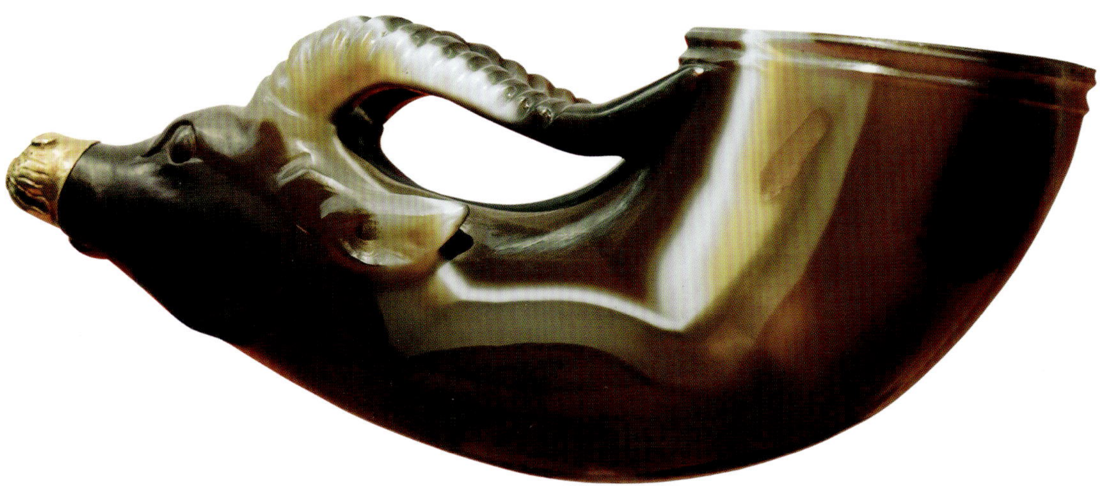

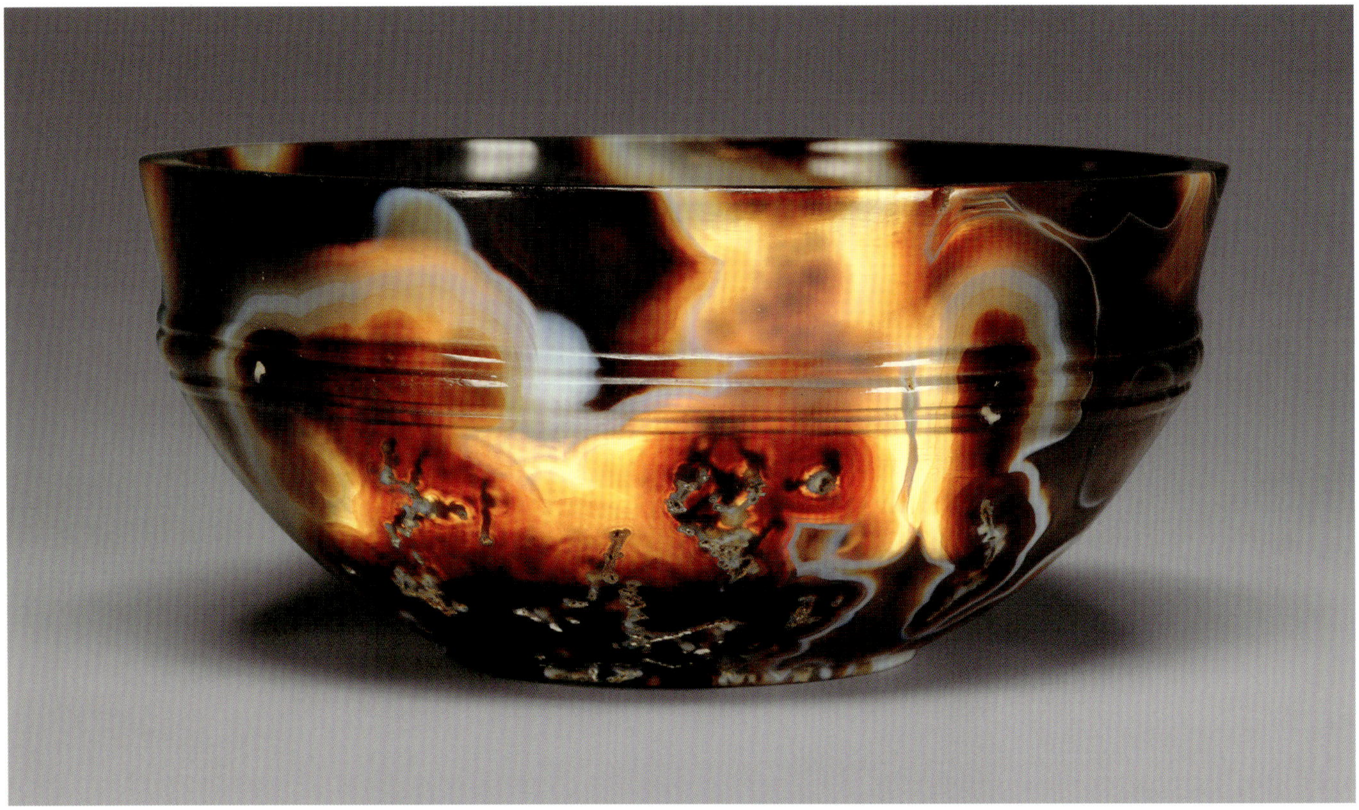

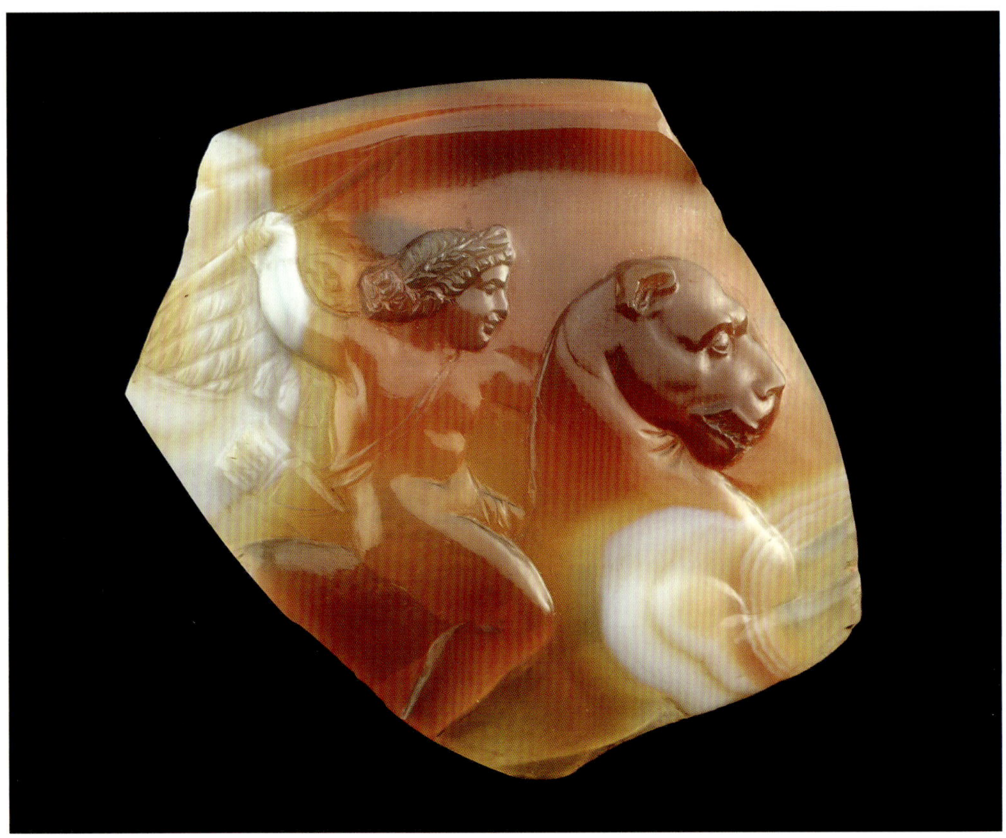

Plate 121
Bowl, ca. 300–100 BC. Banded agate, H: 42 mm; Diam: 98 mm

Plate 122
Cup fragment with Eros, ca. 100 BC–AD 100. Banded agate, H: 47.9 mm; W: 47.2 mm; Thickness: 4.2 mm

Plate 123 (opposite)
Ribbed cup (Chalice of Abbot Suger), ca. 200–1 BC. Banded agate, H (including postantique mounts): 184 mm

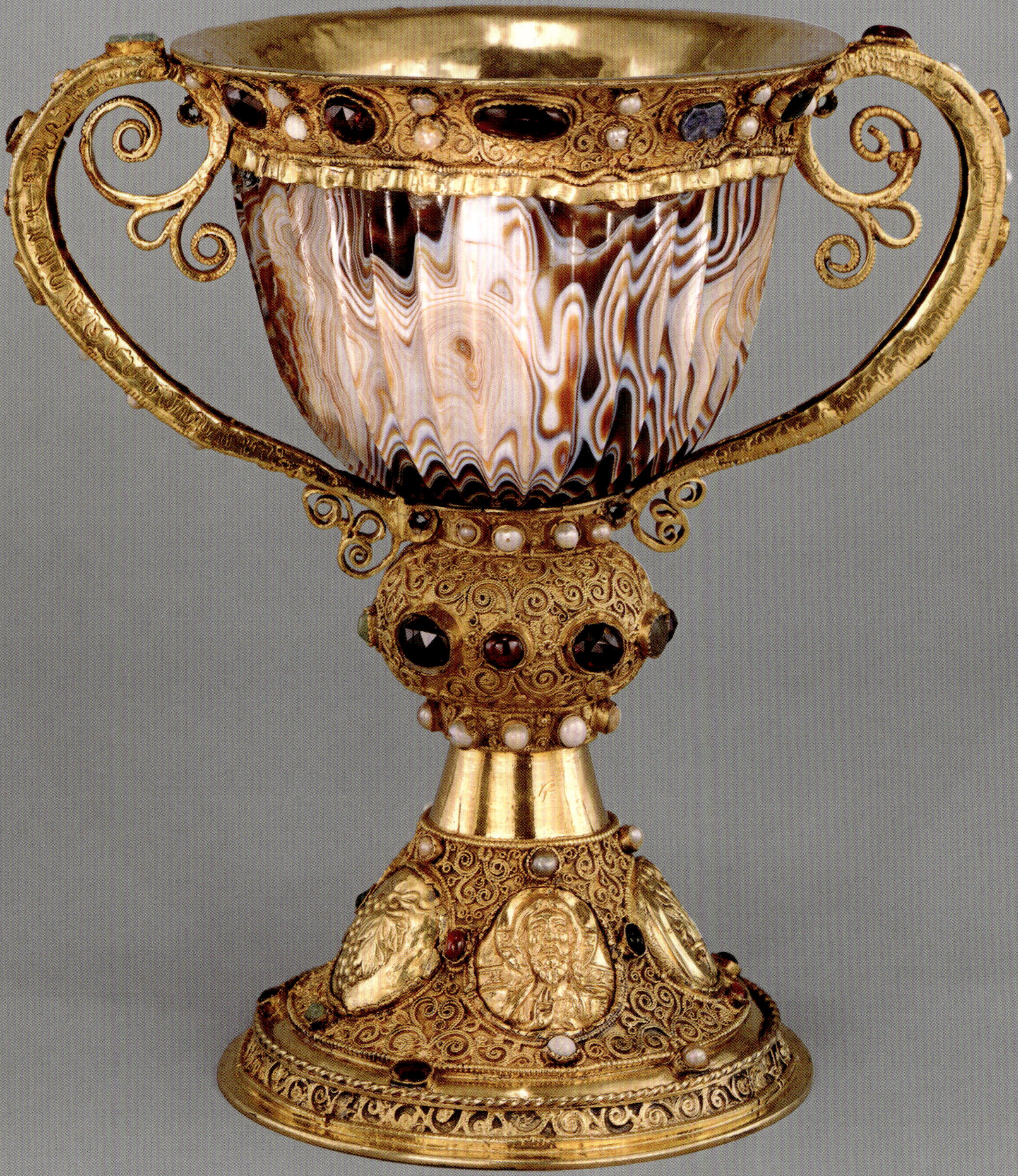

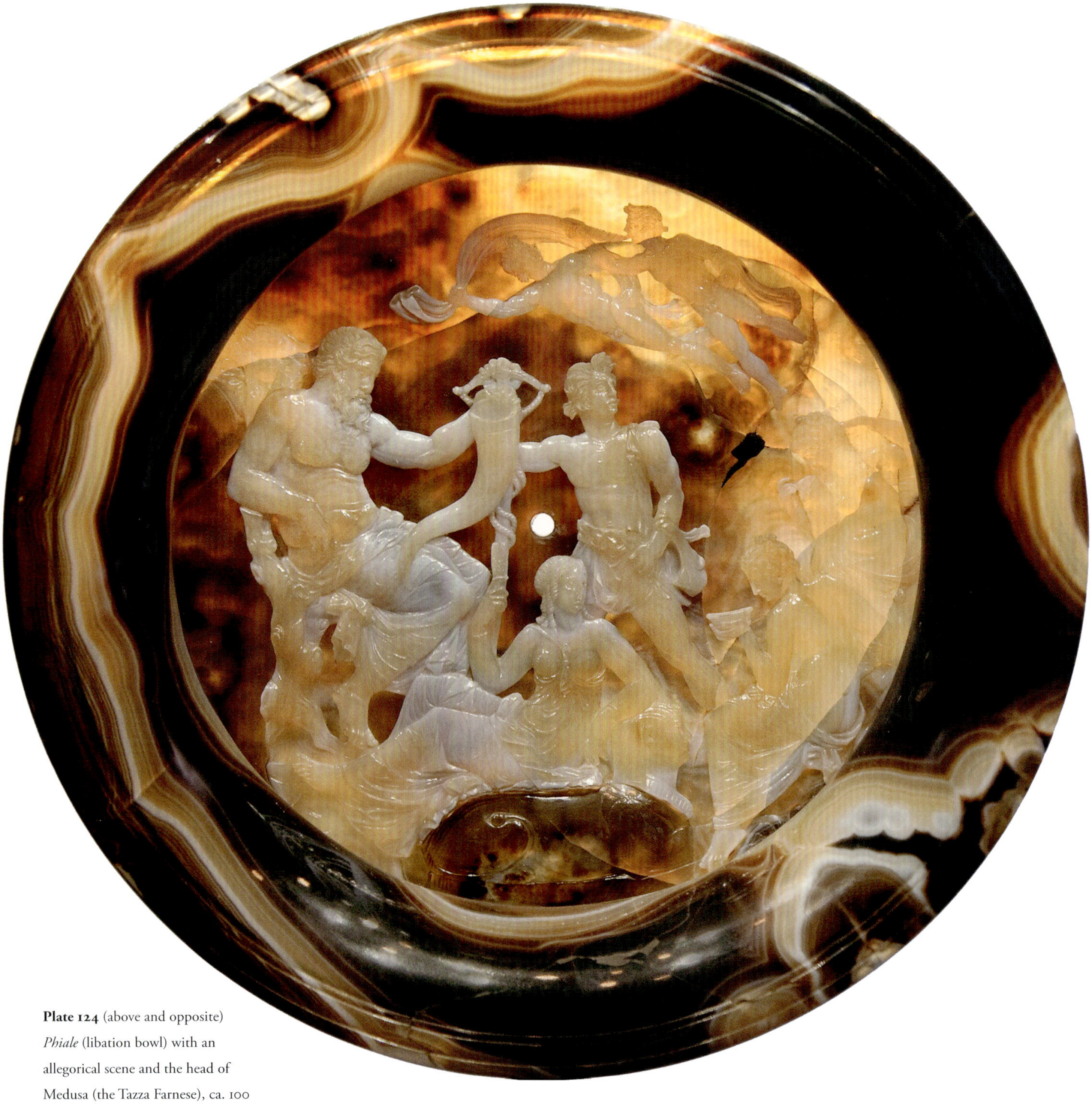

Plate 124 (above and opposite)
Phiale (libation bowl) with an allegorical scene and the head of Medusa (the Tazza Farnese), ca. 100 BC(?). Double-sided, cameo-cut, banded agate, H: 40 mm; Diam: 217 mm; Wt (including modern mount): 1.42 kg

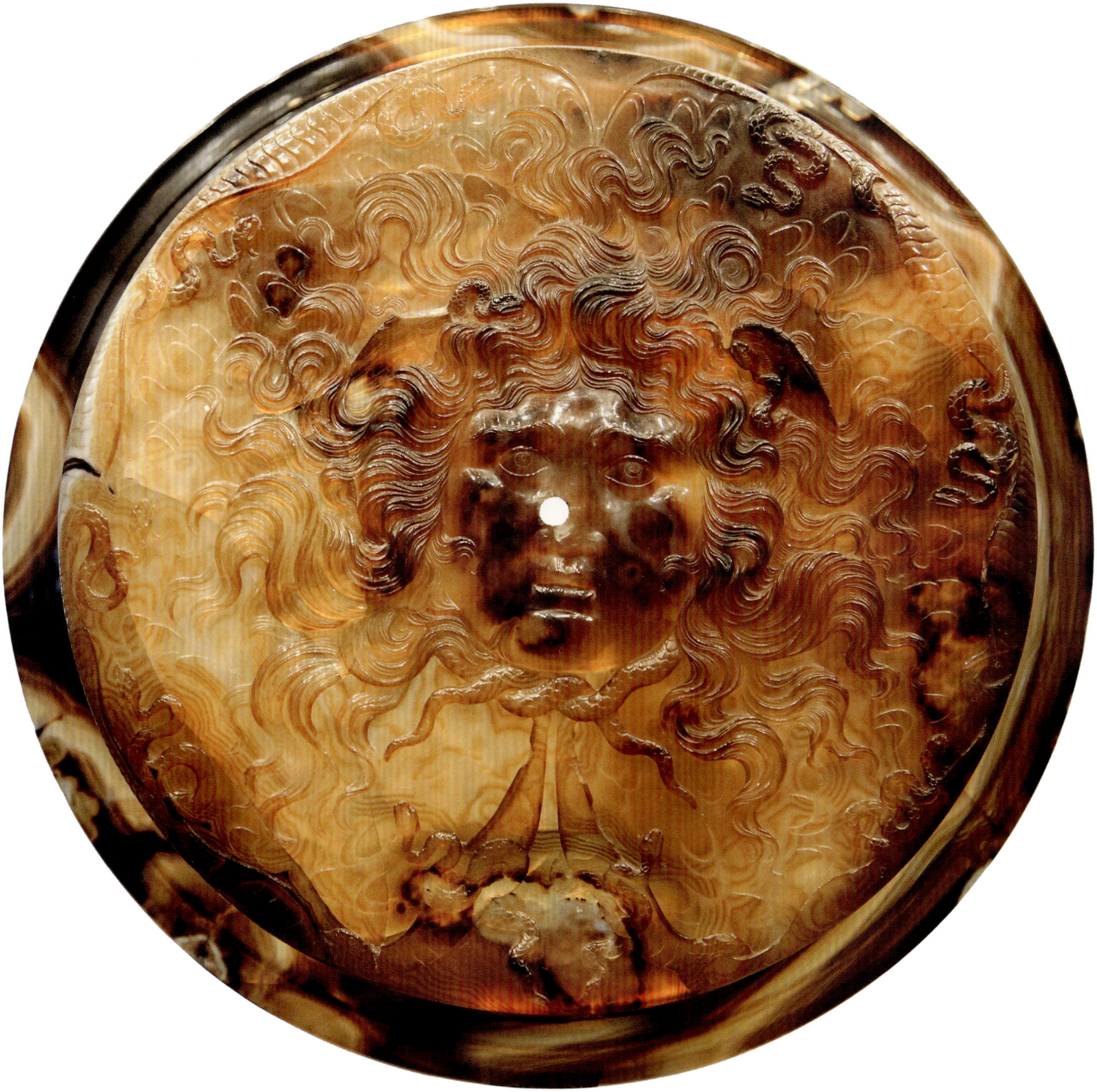

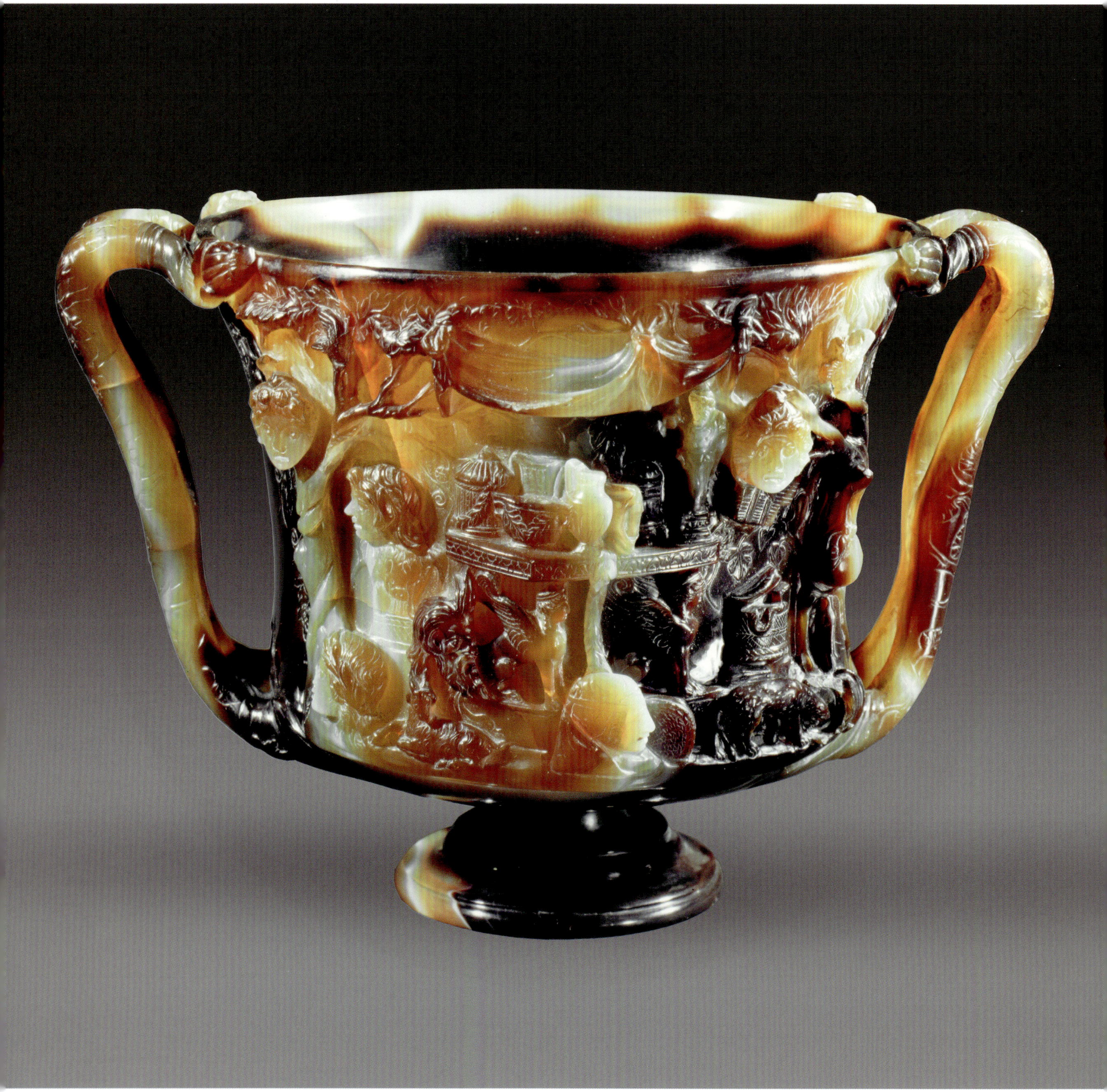

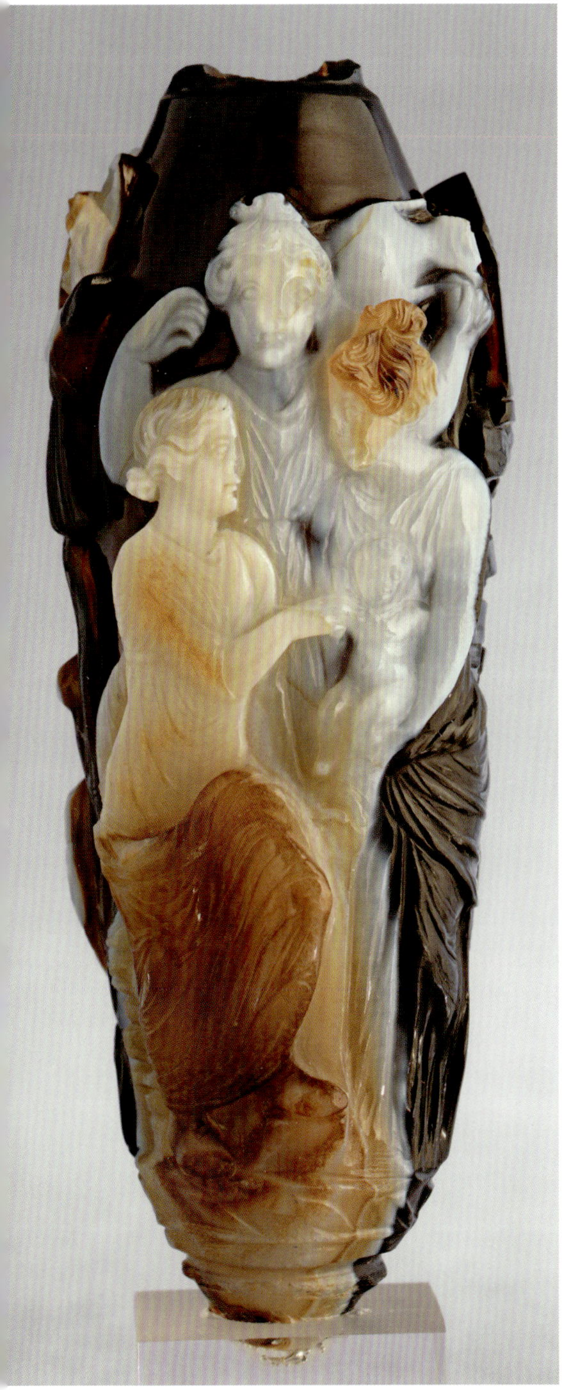

a

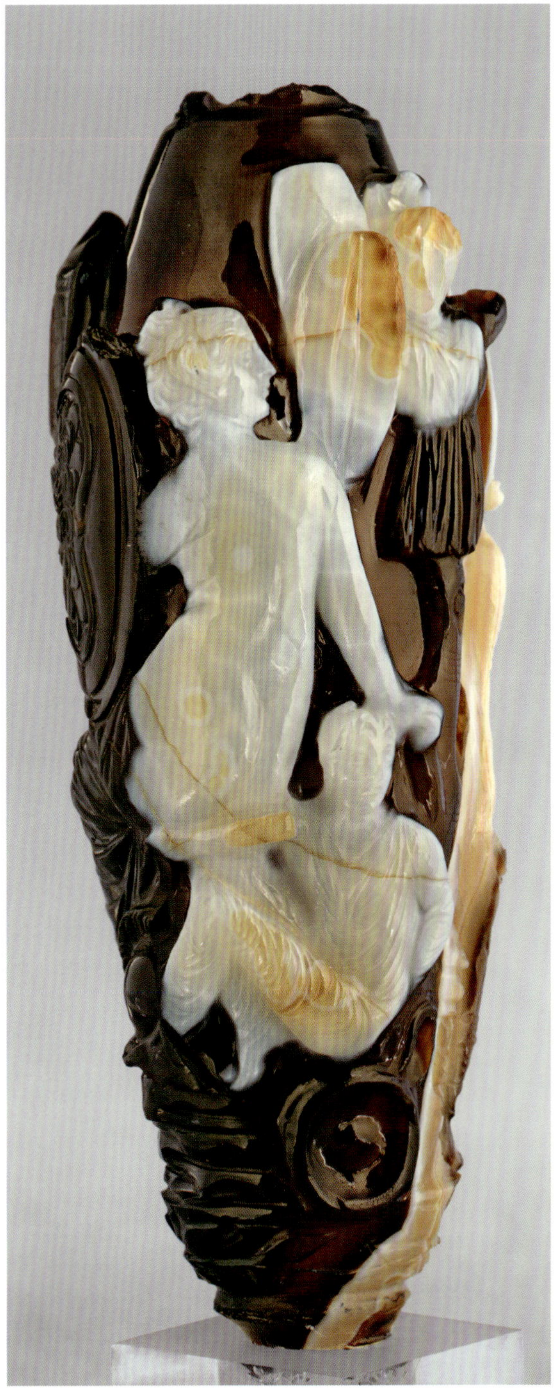

b

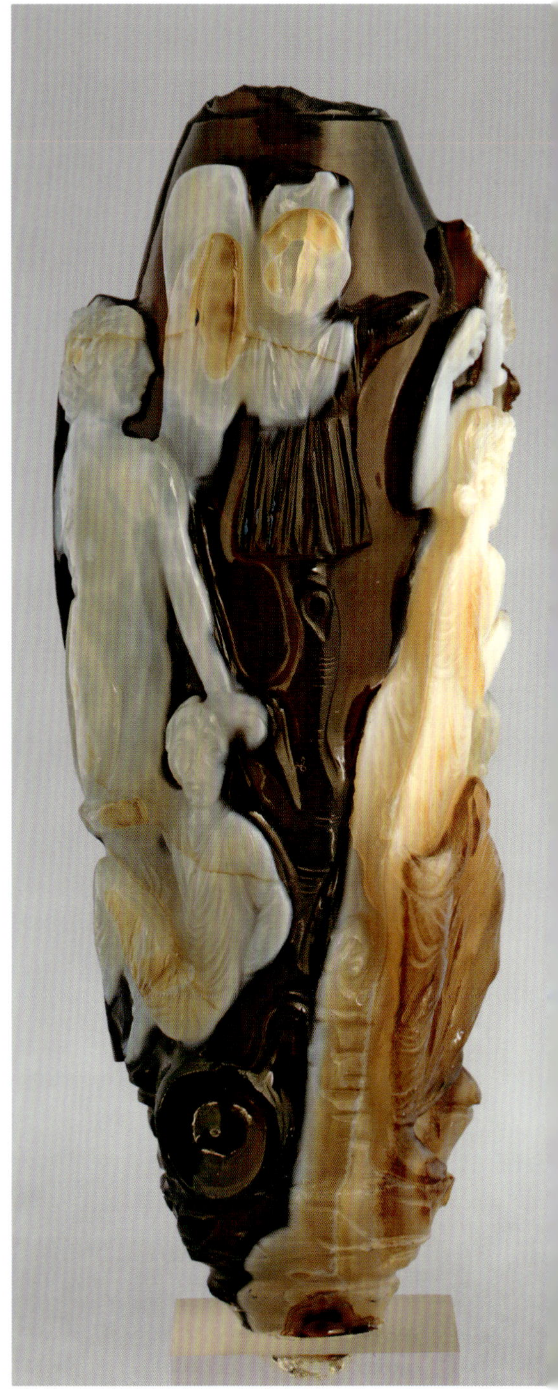

c

Plate 125 (opposite)
Kantharos with Bacchic paraphernalia (the Cup of the Ptolemies), ca. 50 BC–AD 50. Banded agate, H: 84 mm; W: 184 mm; Diam: 125 mm

Plate 126a–c
Alabastron (perfume vase), ca. 40–10 BC. Banded agate, H: 88.3 mm; Diam (max): 33.2 mm

Plate 127 (below)
Simpulum (ladle), ca. AD 1–200.
Banded agate, H: 127 mm;
Diam: 50 mm; Thickness: 2 mm

Plate 128 (right)
Cup, first century BC–fourth
century AD. Banded agate,
H: 311 mm; Diam: 117 mm;
Thickness: 3.0–3.5 mm

Plate 129 (opposite)
The Rubens Vase, ca. AD 400.
Cameo-cut agate with modern
gold lip, H: 186 mm; W: 185 mm;
D: 120 mm

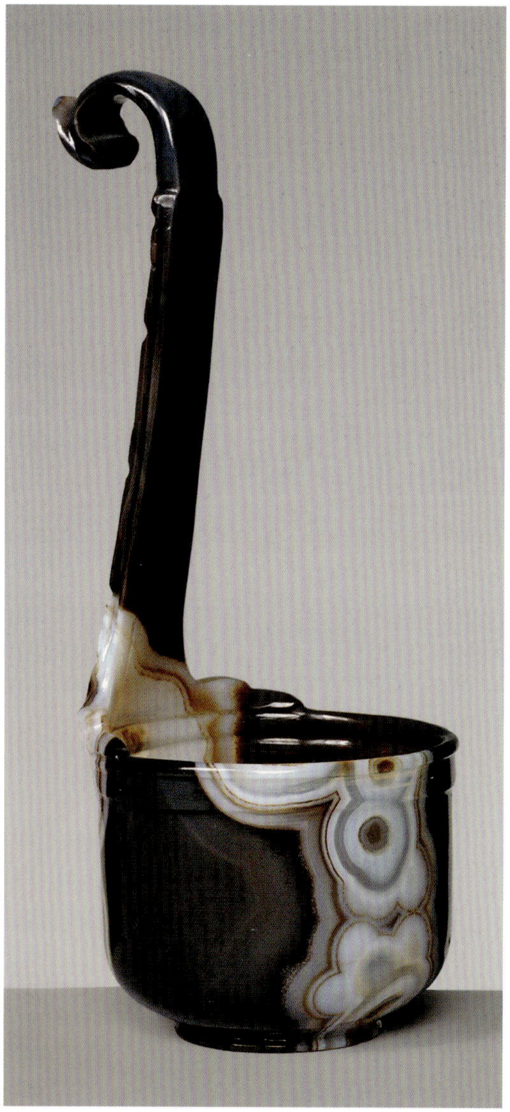

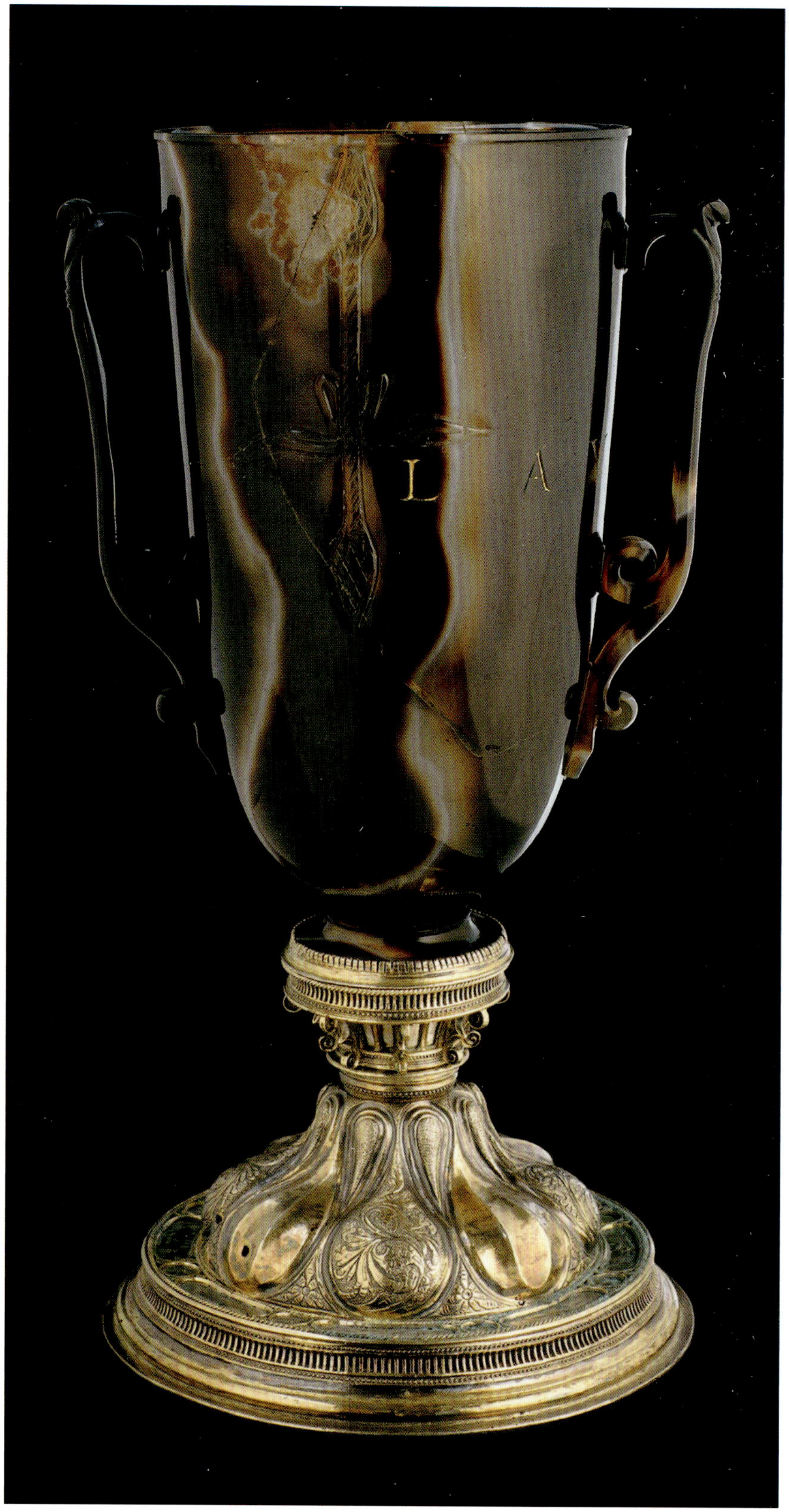

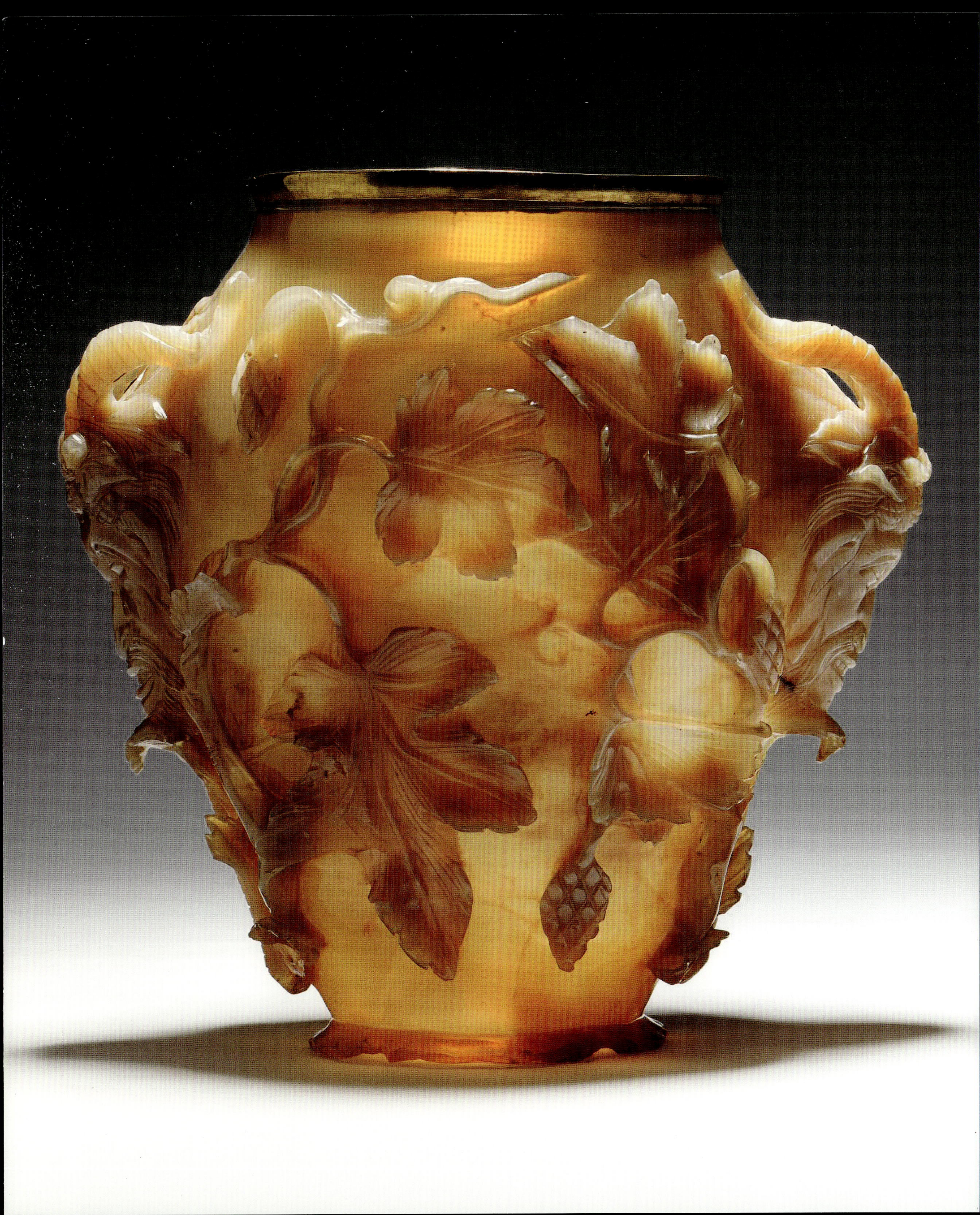

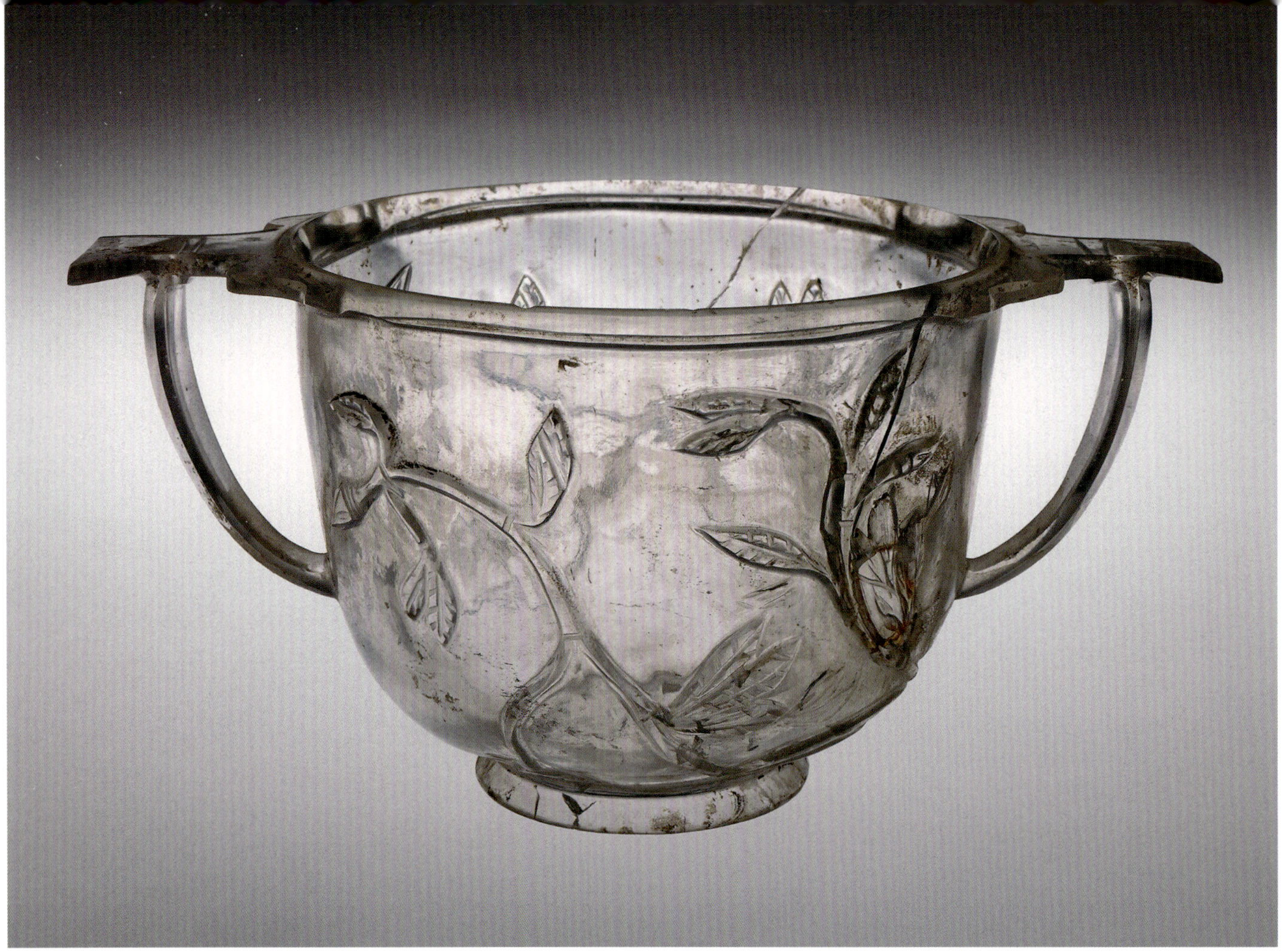

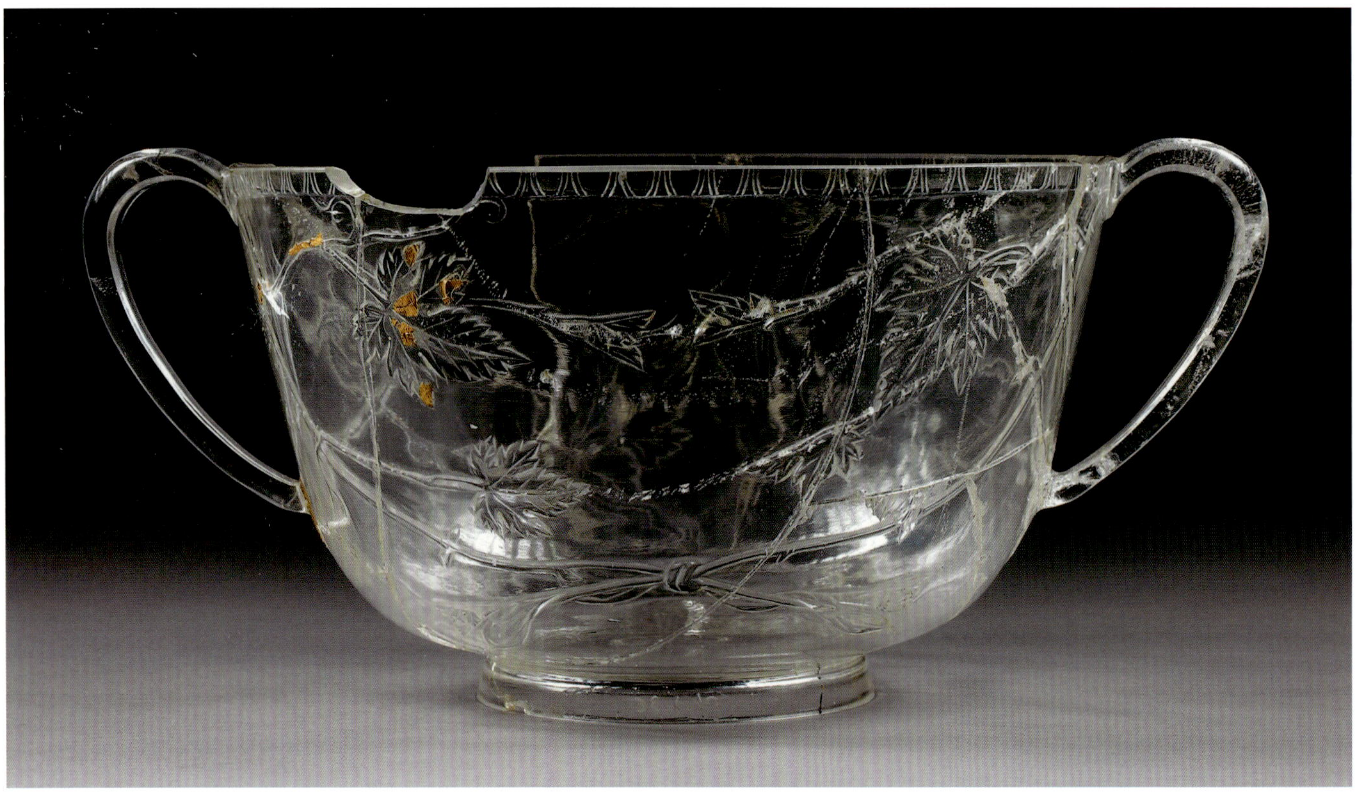

Plate 130 (opposite, top)
Skyphos, ca. 25 BC–AD 15. Rock crystal, H: 120 mm, W: 150 mm

Plate 131 (opposite, bottom)
Skyphos/Kantharos, ca. AD 1–100. Rock crystal with traces of gold leaf, H: 90 mm; Diam: 144.5 mm

Plate 132
Amphoriskos (perfume vase), ca. 25 BC. Rock crystal, H: 57 mm; W: 36 mm

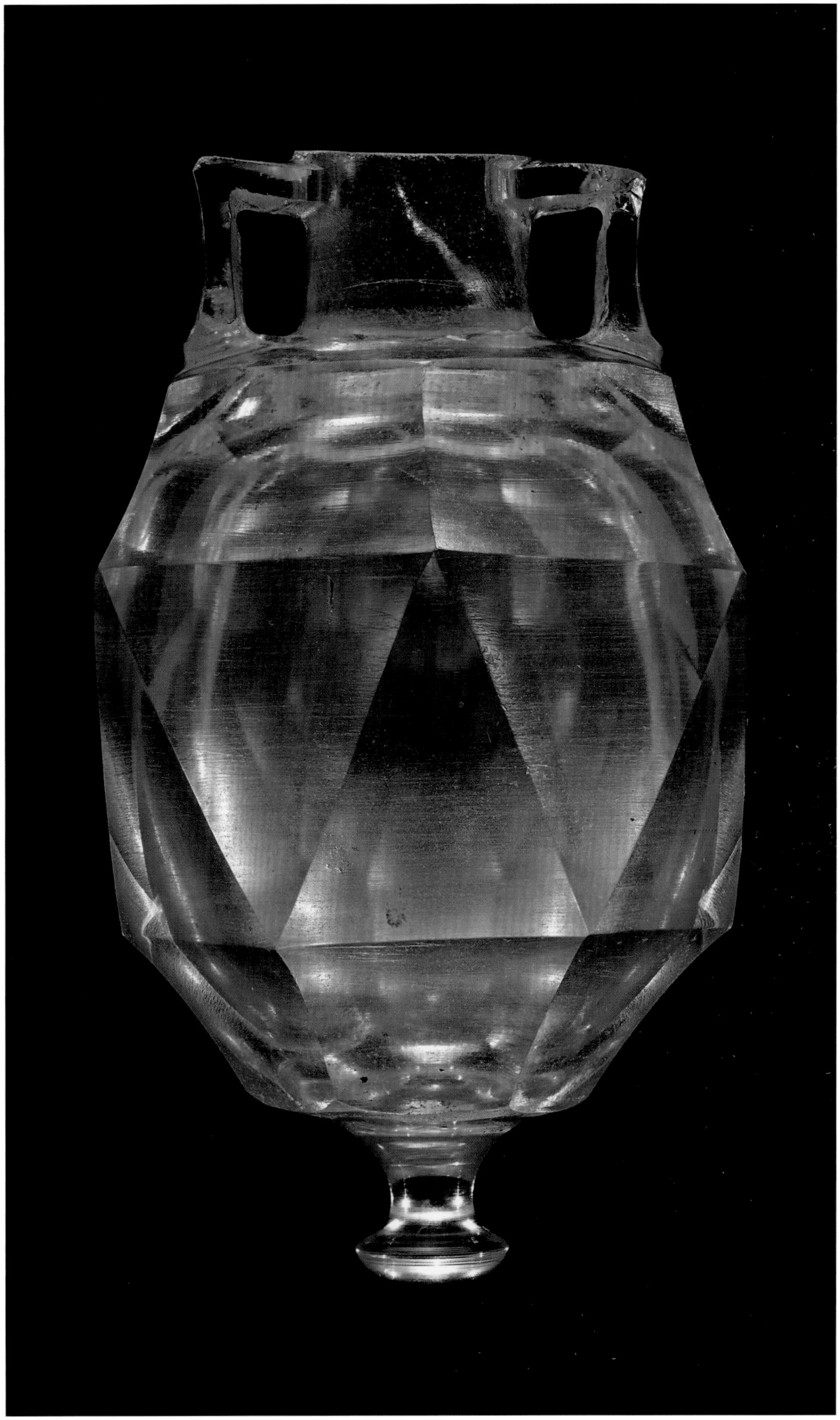

Plate 133
Kantharos (the Crawford Cup), ca. AD 1–100. Murrhine (fluorite), H: 97 mm; Diam: 107 mm; Wt: 867 grams

Plate 134 (opposite)
Cup with grapevines (the Barber Cup), ca. AD 1–100. Murrhine (fluorite), H: 135 mm; Diam: 95 mm; Wt: 1340 grams

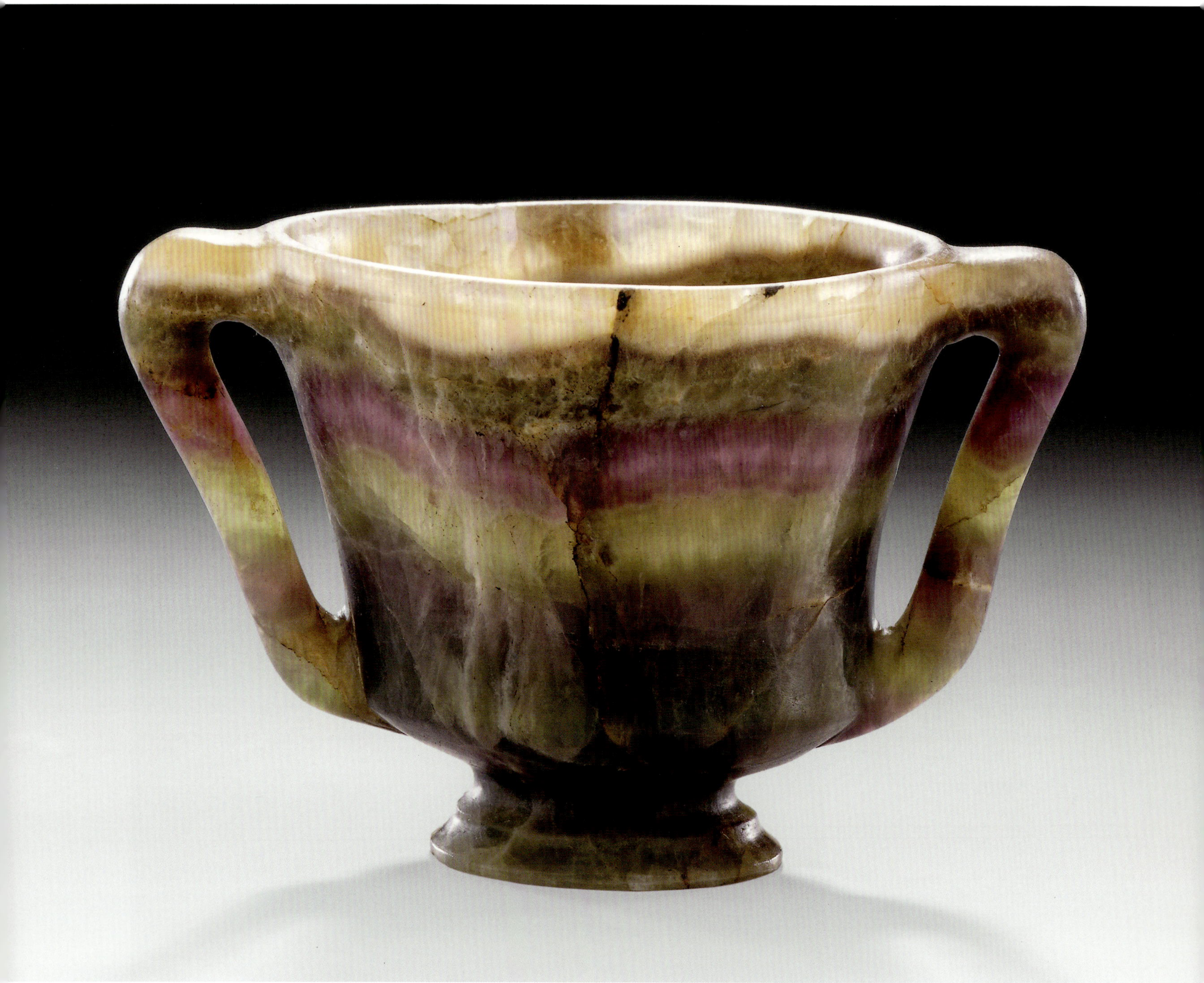

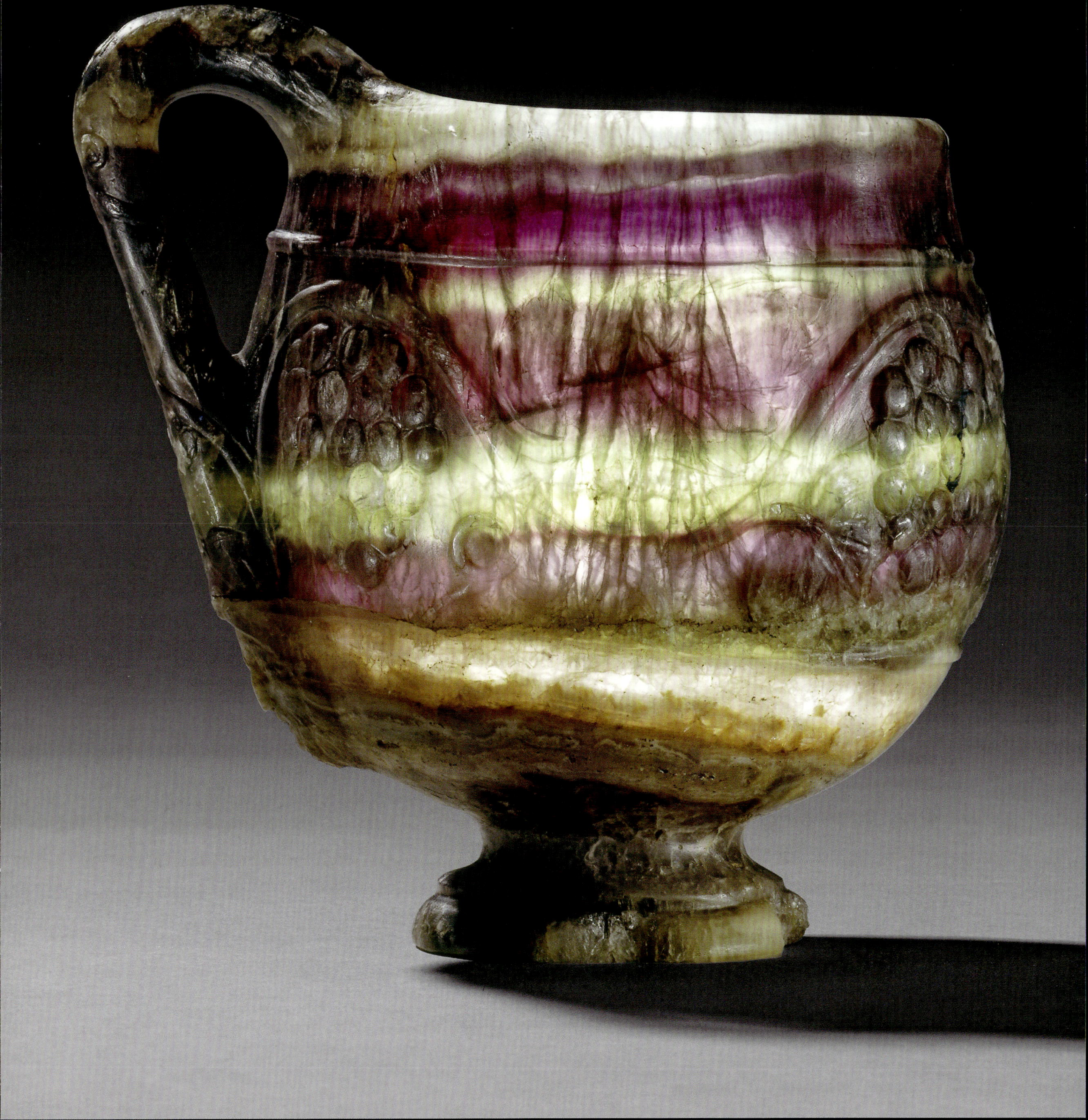

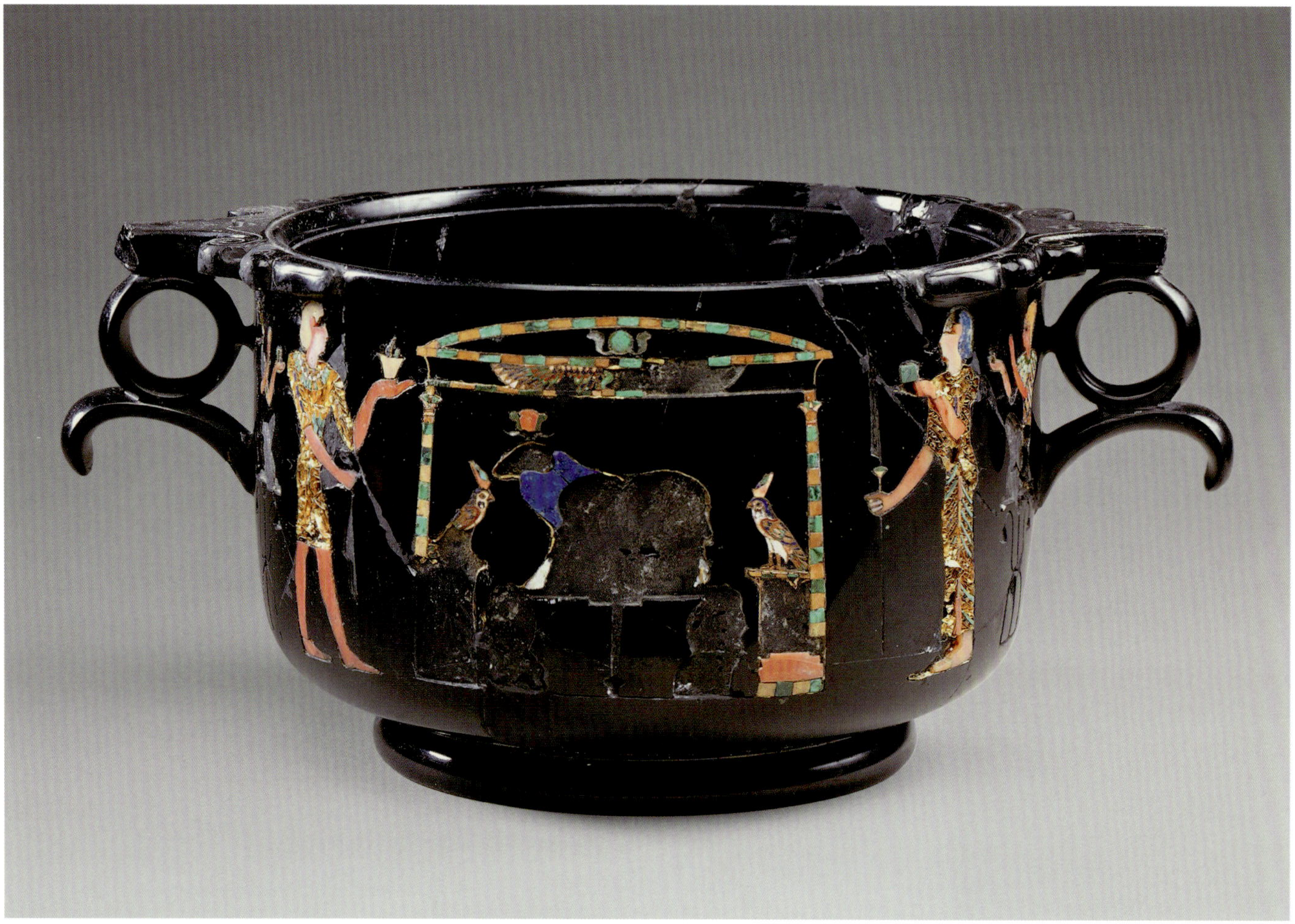

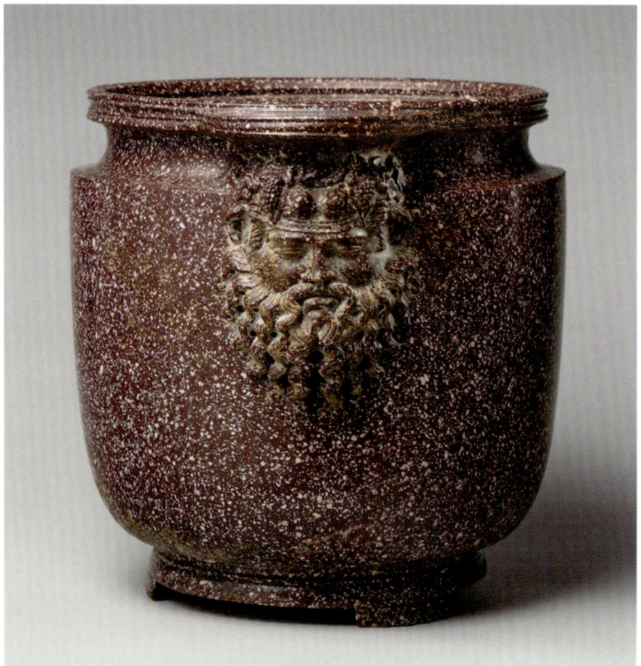

Plate 135
Skyphos with Egyptianizing scenes, first century BC–first century AD. Obsidian inlaid with pink and white coral, cornelian, yellow jasper, lapis lazuli, and malachite, set in gold, H: 125 mm; Diam: 182 mm

Plate 136
Situla (wine bucket) with masks of Silenoi, first to early second century AD. Porphyry, H: 25.5 cm; W: 30 cm; D: 24.8 cm; Diam (of rim): 22.5 cm

Plate 137 (opposite, top)
Bust of Berenike II, Queen of Egypt, ca. 225 BC. Garnet, H: 18 mm

Plate 138 (opposite, bottom)
Head of Herakles, second century BC(?). *Giallo antico*, H: 155 mm; W: 115 mm; D: 55 mm

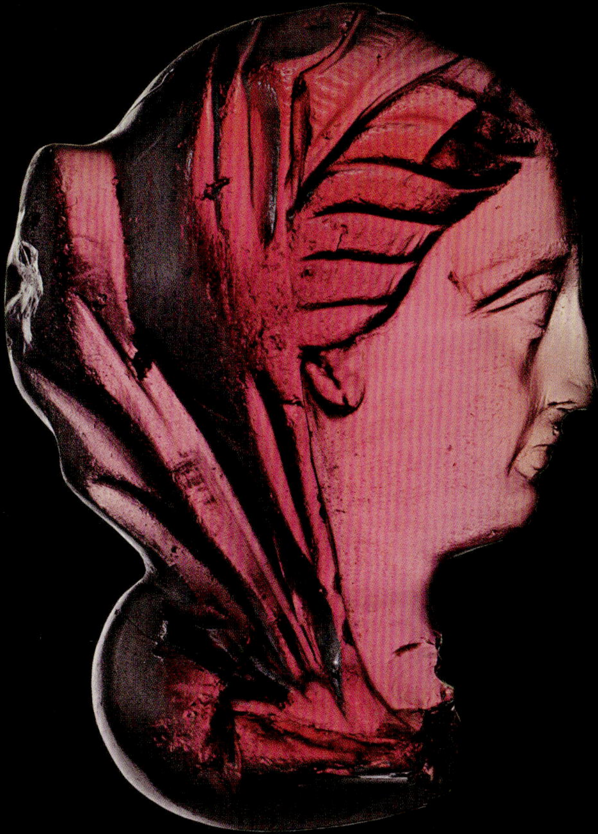

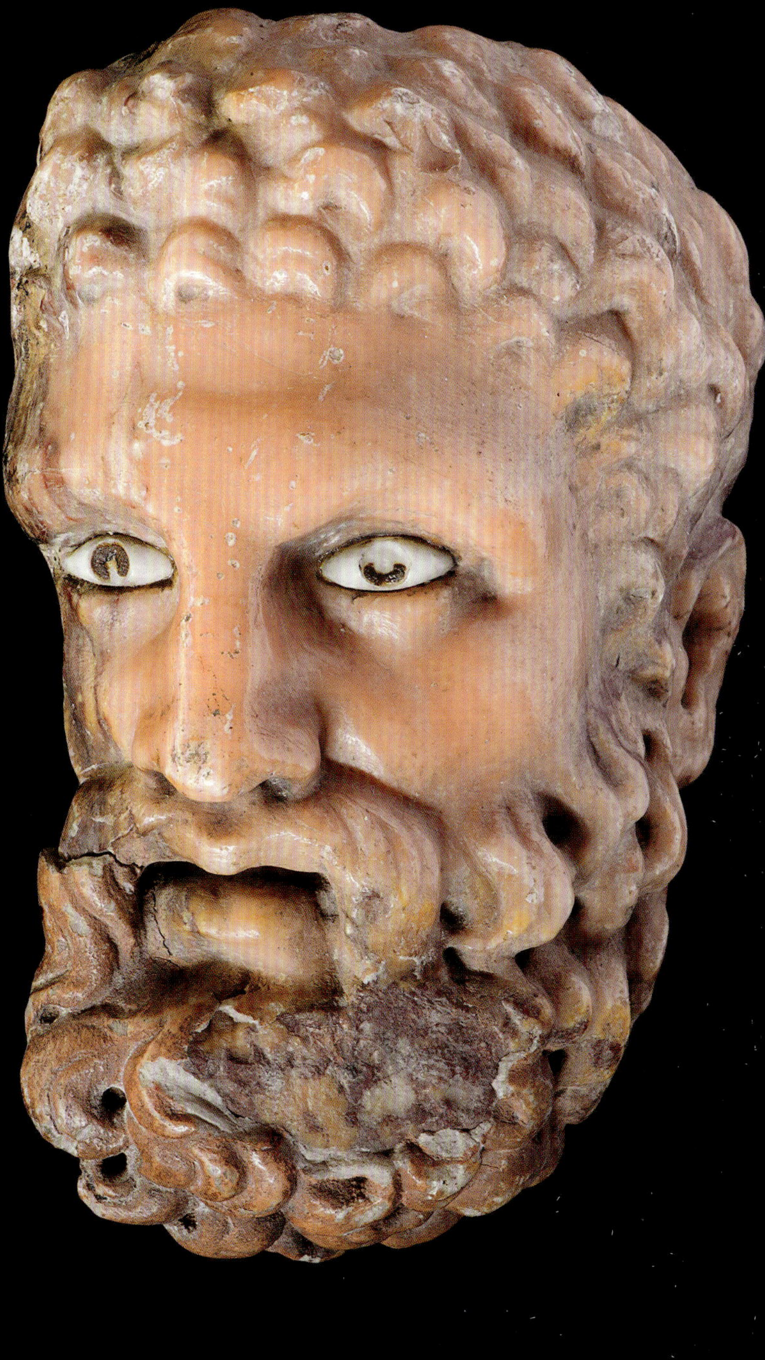

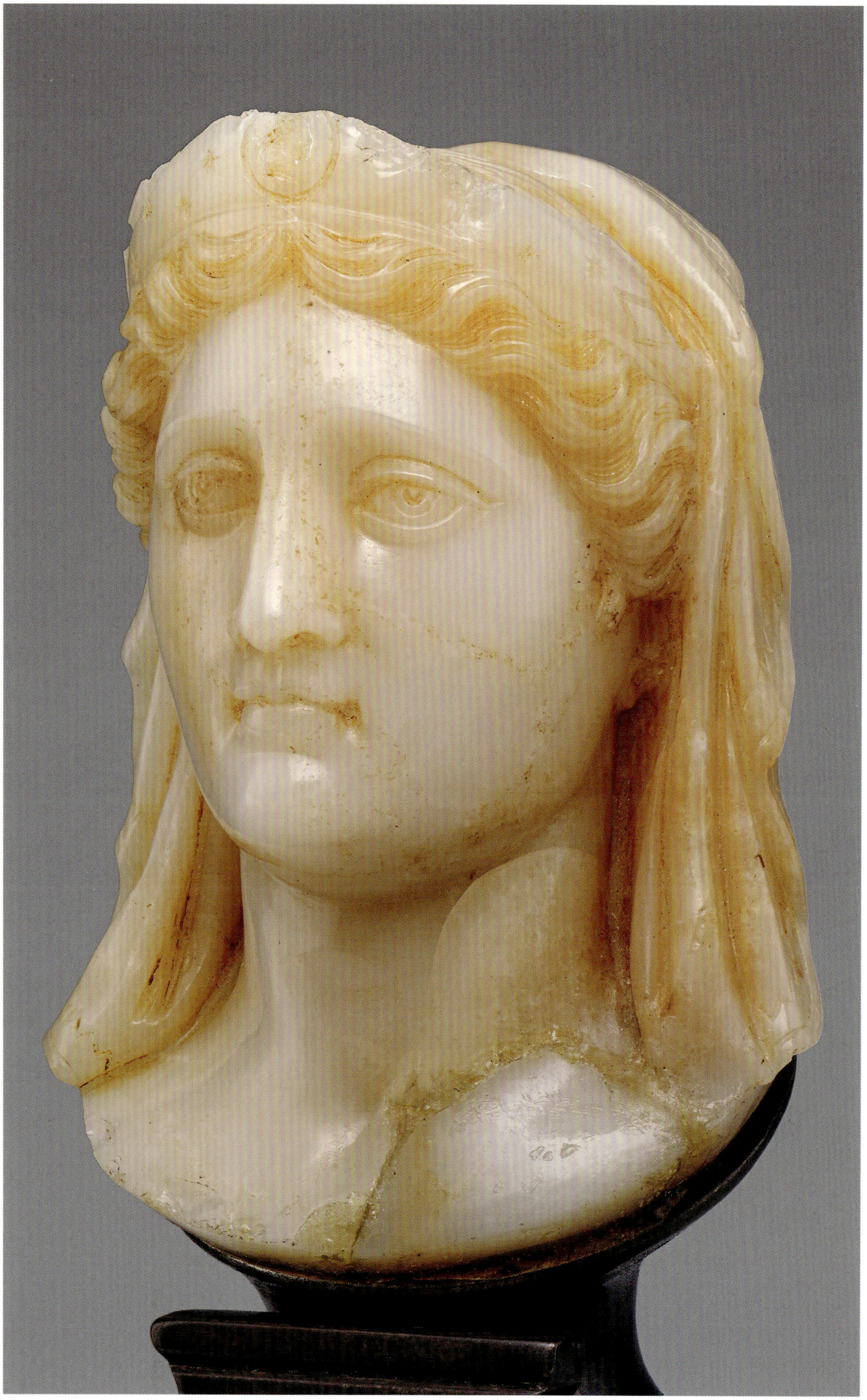

Plate 139

Head of Antonia Minor, ca. AD 37–54. Chalcedony, H: 50 mm

Plate 140 (opposite)

Head of a Julio-Claudian princess, ca. AD 40. Green chalcedony, H: 90 mm; W: 54.5 mm; D: 52 mm

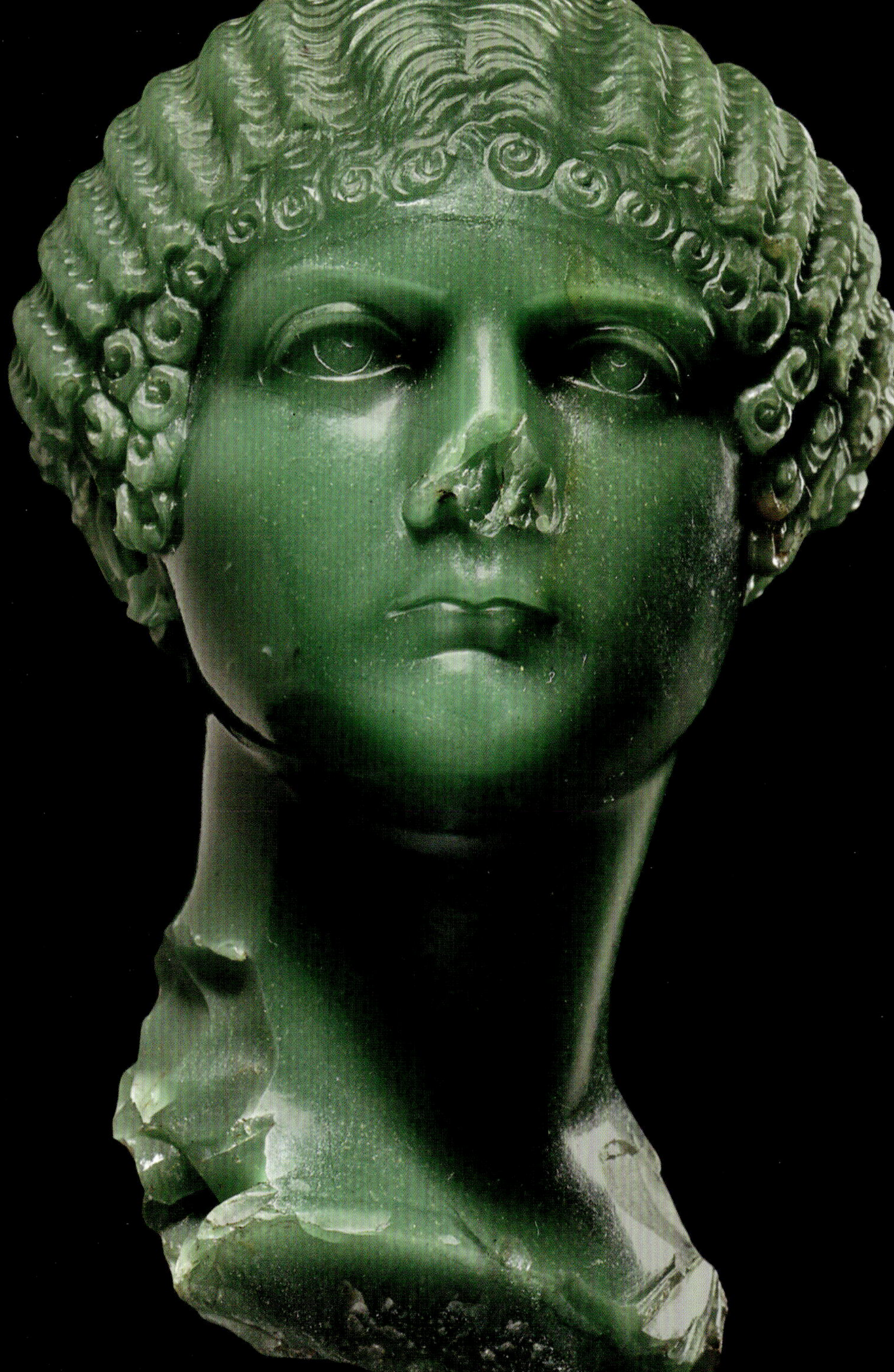

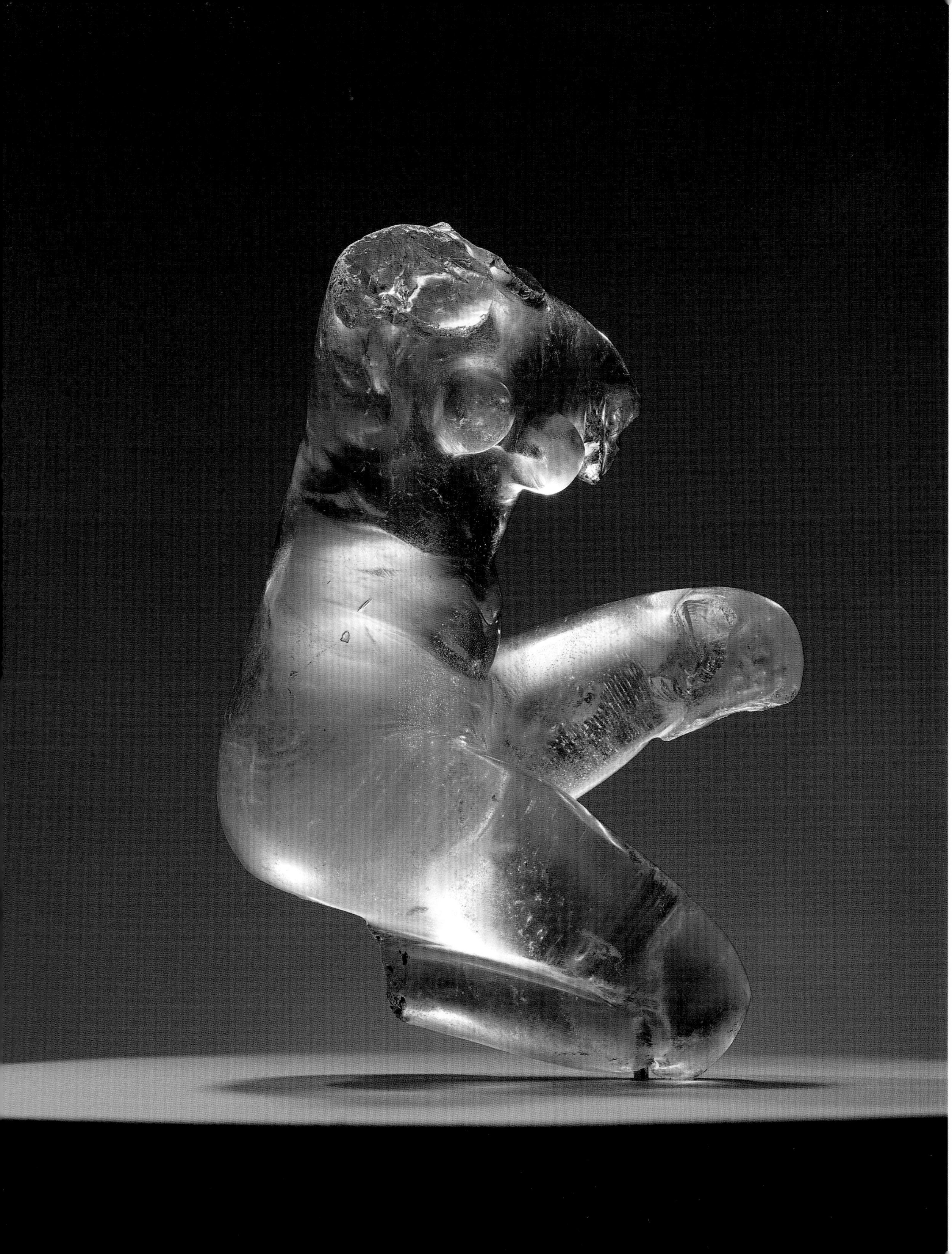

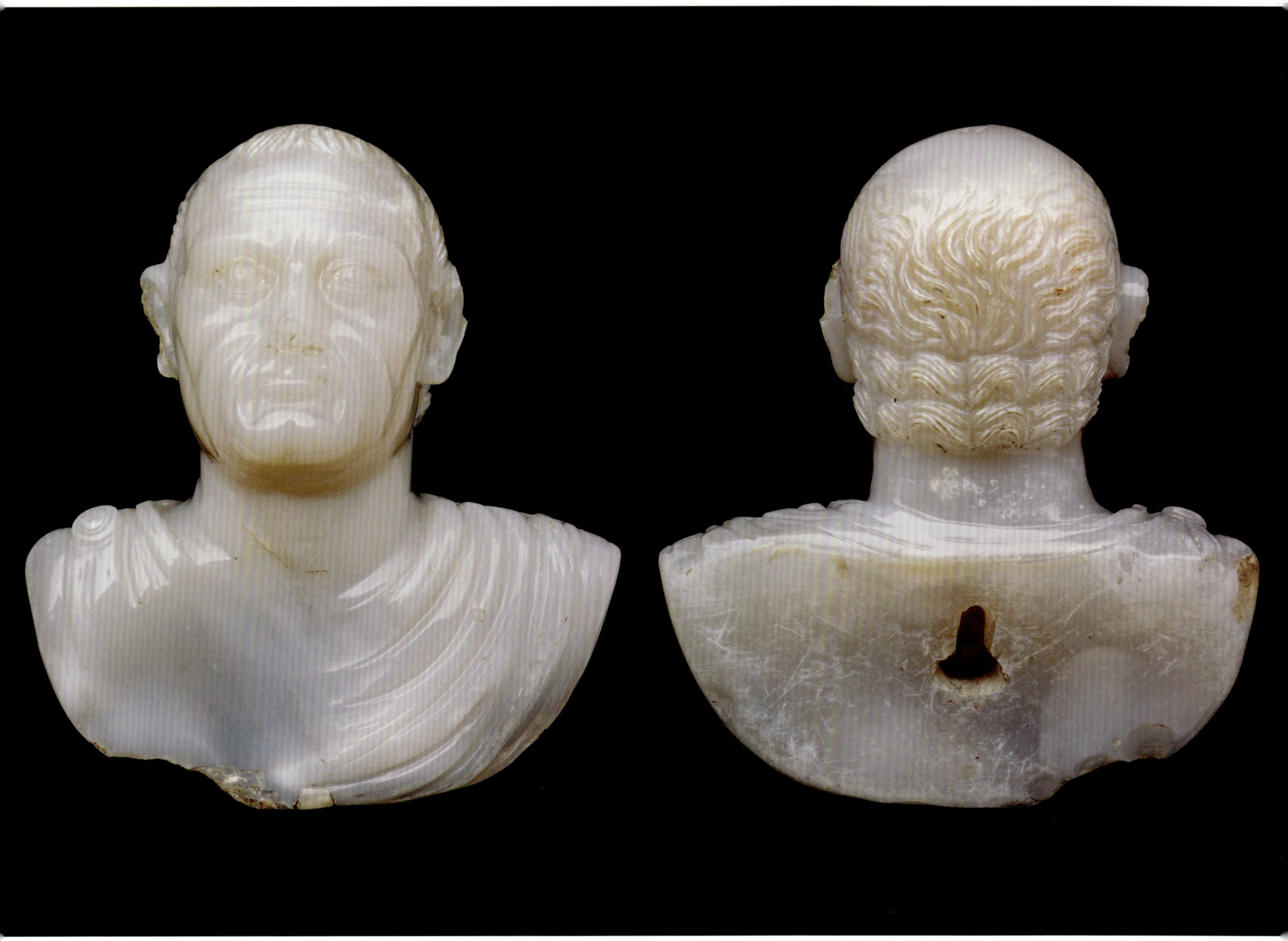

Plate 141 (opposite)
Statuette of the crouching Aphrodite, first century BC.
Rock crystal, H: 85 mm

Plate 142
Bust of a man, perhaps Vespasian (two views), ca. AD 70–96.
Chalcedony, H: 115 mm

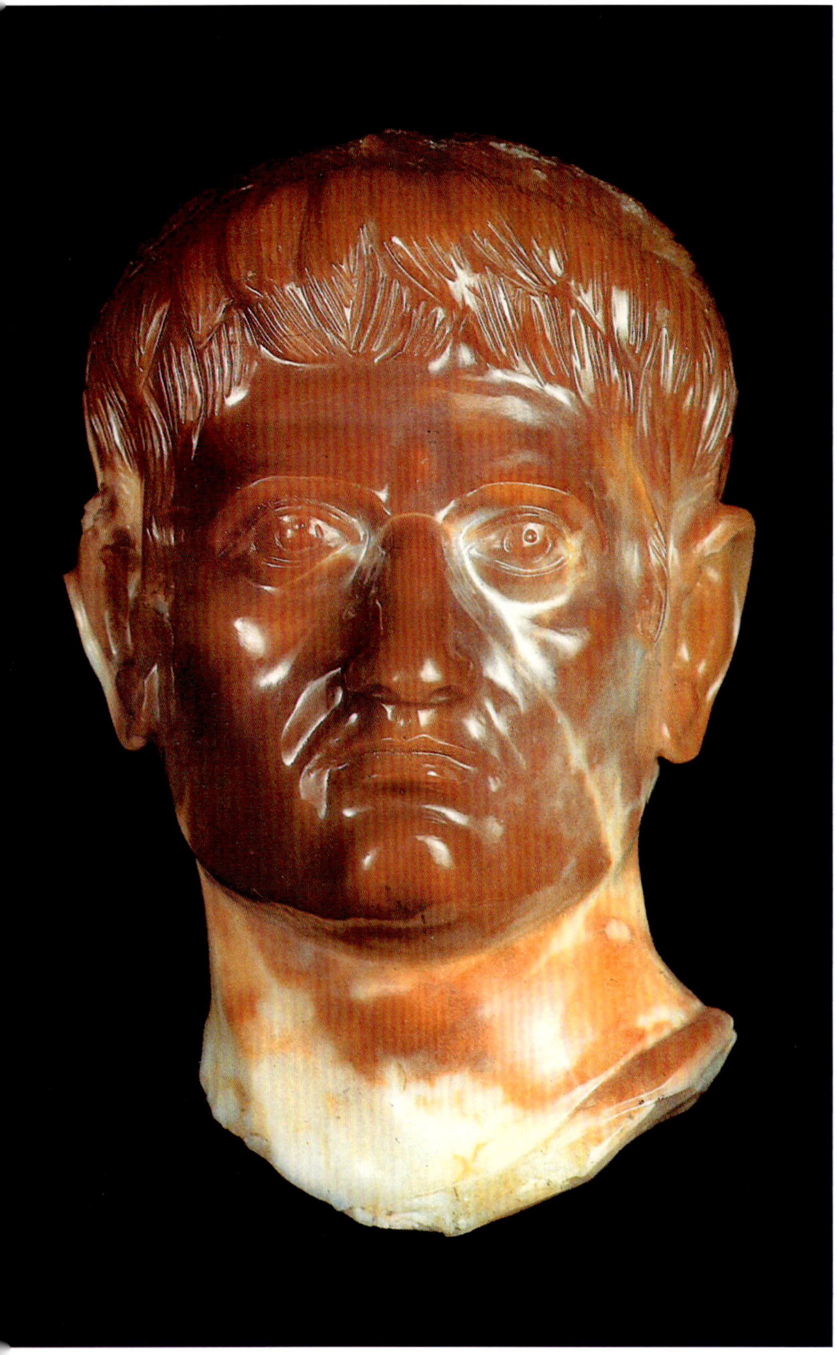

Plate 143
Head of Augustus, ca. AD 81, reworked after AD 96. Agate, H: 161 mm; W: 108 mm; Diam: 97 mm

Plate 144
Torso of a man wearing a toga, ca. AD 90. Jasper, H: 187 mm

Plate 145 (opposite)
Hand, ca. first–second century AD(?). Chalcedony with post-antique gilt-silver bracelet, L: 73 mm

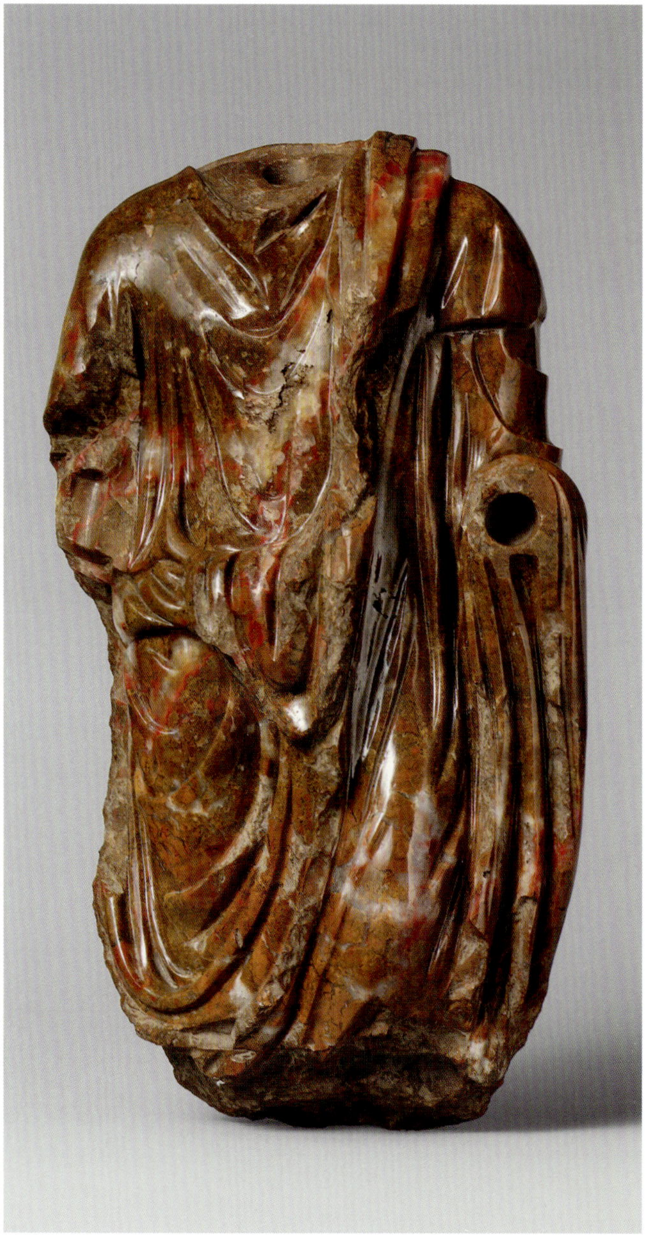

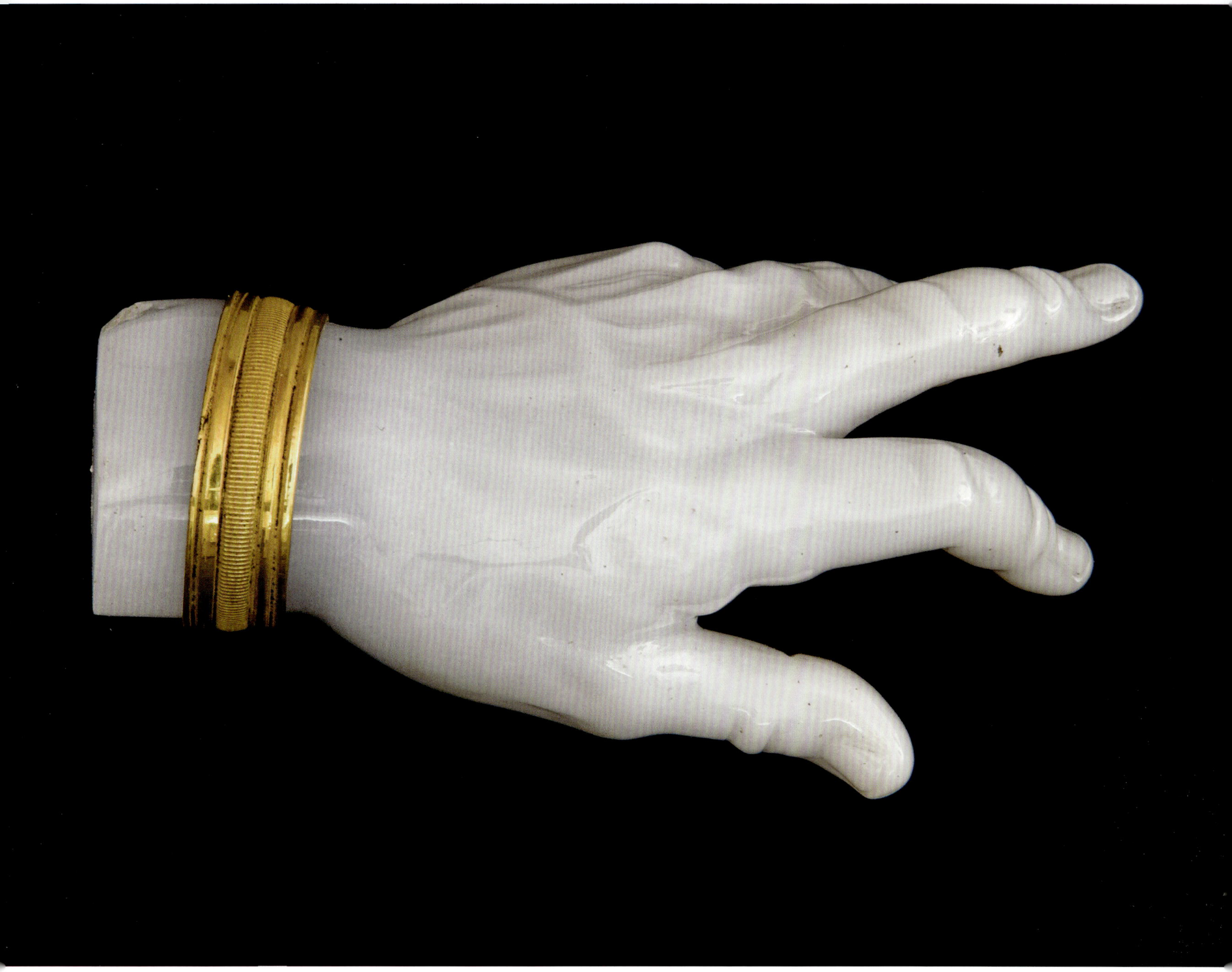

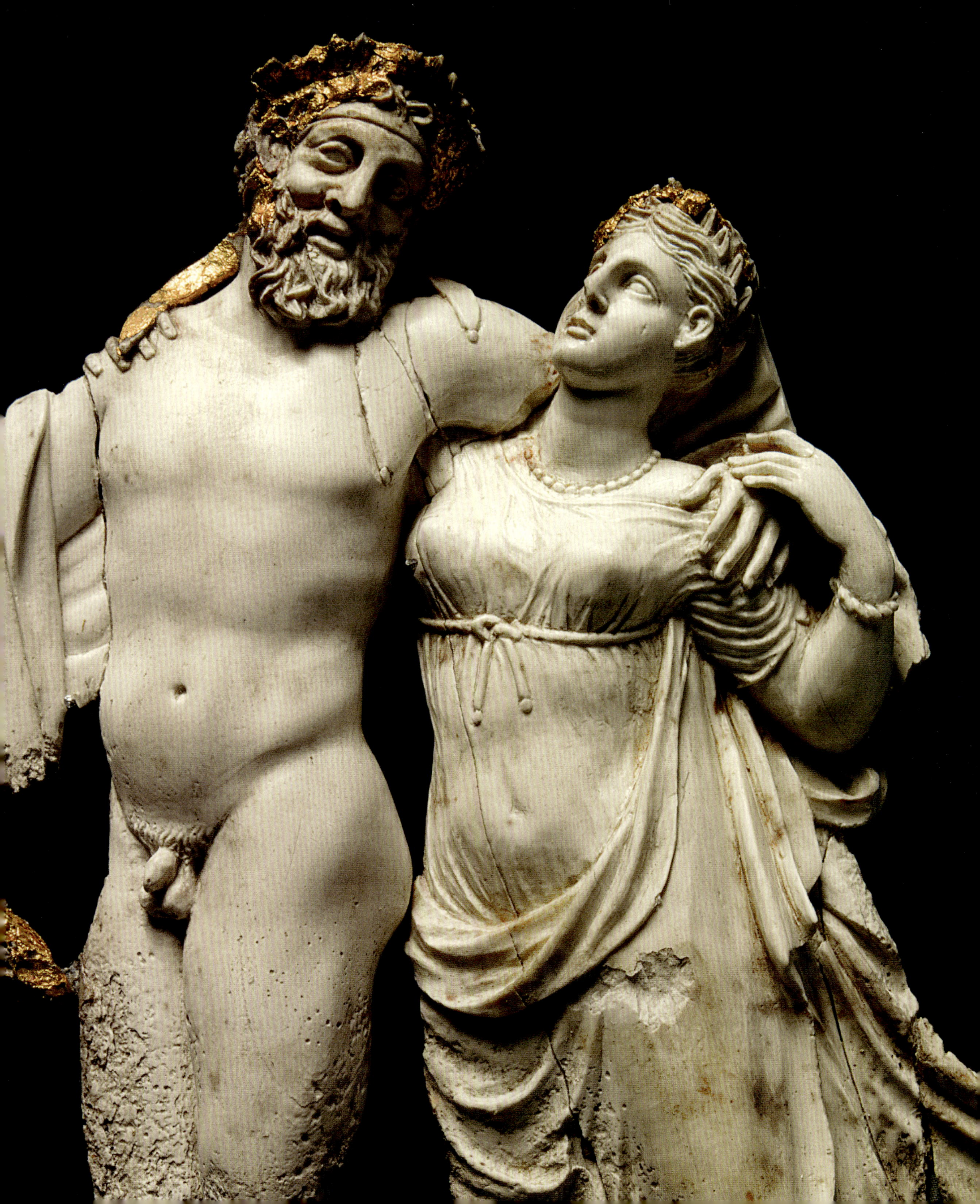

CHAPTER THREE

ORGANIC MATERIALS

The archaeological record can be misleading, for most artifacts are preserved by chance. The most numerous survivals from Greece and Rome were not necessarily the most plentiful in antiquity, nor the most important. Biodegradable objects fashioned from ivory, amber, pearl, and coral were always rare and treasured for their exotic origins, mythological associations, and particular characteristics. The same was true for some wooden items and textiles that stood out from the many everyday products of Greek and Roman society because of their materials and craftsmanship. These are seldom found among the myriad items that have come down to us, but nonetheless survive in greater numbers than we might imagine.

IVORY

White, gleaming, and lustrous, ivory has been prized since prehistory. Hard, yet elastic, it is both durable and flexible. Its fine grain allows it to hold detail, and it can be carved, incised, turned on a lathe, and molded, as well as painted and gilded. Imported to Greece and Italy from the Levant, North Africa, and, eventually, India, ivory was an exotic material. In the Aegean Bronze Age, it was combined with ebony, gold, rock crystal, and *kyanos* (apparently blue glass) on luxury furniture, as recorded on Linear B tablets. The fact that no ideogram exists for ivory in Mycenaean Greek would seem to be an indication of its rarity. Indeed, scribes emphasized the importance of the material by the large size of the word relative to others on the same tablets and by its prominent position when it is mentioned as a raw material.[1]

In the *Odyssey* Euryalos gives Odysseus an ivory-handled sword, which, he remarks, is very valuable. Other ivory objects described in the epics of Homer, such as the reins of Medon, the couch and key of Penelope, and the bed she shared with Odysseus, are symbols of royal affluence. Their son Telemachos was so awed by the palace of Menelaos, flashing with gold, silver, amber, and ivory, that he thought himself in Olympus.[2] In his list of the most valuable substances on earth, Pliny the Elder included ivory as the most costly product derived from a land animal. He also noted that elephant tusks "fetch a vast price, and supply a very elegant material for images of the gods." Pausanias concurred: "The Greeks [of earlier epochs] seem to me to have been especially lavish in honoring the gods, and not at all miserly of resources, in that they imported ivory from India and Ethiopia to make statues."[3]

Ivory's novelty and scarcity were certainly fundamental reasons for its value, but, even in Egypt and the Near East, where it was more readily available, the root of its desirability lay in the inherent beauty of its subtle, glowing color and smooth texture, qualities which could be highlighted and augmented by the skill of those who worked it as well as by the additional materials with which it was combined. Ivory's warmth and luminosity, so closely approximating human skin, made it appropriate for statuary. In the biblical Song of Solomon the poet likens his lover's neck to an ivory tower.[4] Homer recognized the resemblance of the material to flesh, not only in the *Iliad,* where Menelaos's wounded thigh, covered with blood, is likened to eastern ivory horse-trappings, stained with purple, "delight for a king," but also in the *Odyssey*, when Athena, desiring to give Penelope the surpassing beauty of Aphrodite, set her to sleep:

> Gave her immortal gifts, so that the Achaians might admire her.
> First she cleansed well her face with ambrosial beauty...
> And she made her taller and of goodlier build to behold,
> And then she made her whiter than sawn ivory.[5]

Greek and Latin poets followed Homer in comparing the most beautiful human skin to ivory, whose numinous quality they did not overlook. The topos was even applied by an infatuated patron to a Roman freedwoman.[6] The story of Pelops, whose shoulder, having been consumed by Demeter (or Thetis), was replaced by the gods in ivory, was told by Pindar and other ancient authors, and it has been suggested that this material was employed because it most closely approximated the divine substance of the gods' being. Yet, for some classical authors, as for some biblical prophets, ivory was also the embodiment of extravagance.[7]

Excavations of late Bronze Age and early Iron Age palaces in the Aegean and the Near East have recovered stores of ivory furnishings that represented real wealth for rulers.[8] Some early Greek ivories were deposited in tombs (plate 146), but most that have survived to this day derive from sanctuaries, where raw ivory as well as finished goods were offered to the gods. Ivory seals, pins, containers, and furniture with carved and appliqué figural decoration (plate 147), statues and statuettes, often part of larger ensembles (plates 148, 151), were dedicated as votives.[9] The finely carved figure of a kneeling or jumping youth, with inlaid eyes, brows, and earrings, and an amber-studded headband (plate 149) originally formed the arm of a lyre offered to Hera at Samos. In the temple of the same goddess at Olympia, Pausanias saw a centuries-old box of cedar wood and ivory carved with dozens of mythological scenes that had once belonged to the seventh-century BC tyrant Kypselos of Corinth. His detailed account of this box is the single longest description we have of any work of ancient art.[10] Gilt-ivory reliefs excavated at Delphi (plate 151) may have belonged to a similar item, or perhaps supported the arm of a throne, or functioned as components in some other piece of luxury furniture, as seen in representations of such objects in other media (figs. 29, 30).[11]

From the fifth century BC, Athenian inscriptions record ivory in temple inventories: not only complete objects, such as inlaid tables, thrones, statuettes, cups, lyres, and gilded flute cases, but also detached components, fragments, and

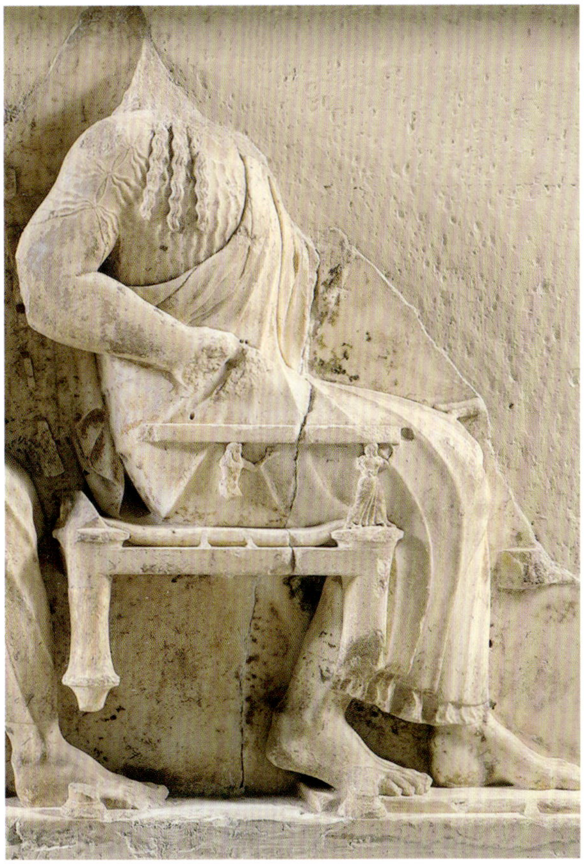

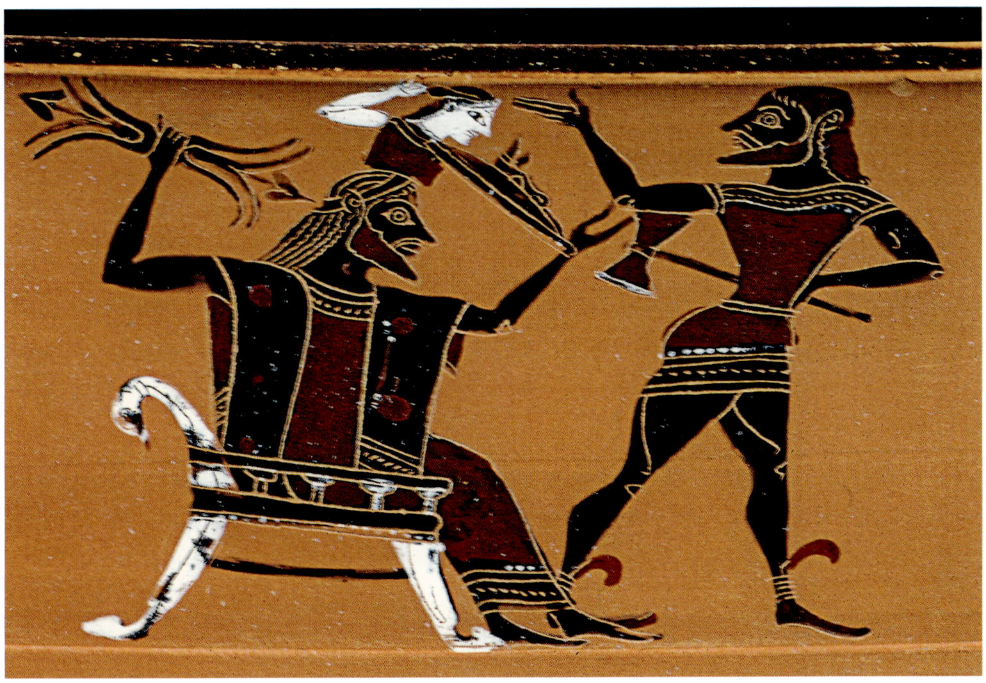

Figure 29
East frieze of the Treasury of the Siphnians at Delphi (detail), ca. 530 BC. Marble. Depictions of luxury furniture in Greek sculpture and vase painting indicate the use of wood and ivory for figural and other elements, which is also amply demonstrated by literary, epigraphical, and archaeological evidence. The armrest of the throne of Zeus is supported by a satyr pursuing a nymph or maenad.

Figure 30
Athenian black-figured "Little Master" cup (detail), signed by Phrynos as potter, ca. 550 BC. Terracotta, H: 20 cm, Diam: 28 cm. London, British Museum, 1867,0508.962 (B424). The white color of the swan back, legs, and other elements of Zeus's throne in this image of the Birth of Athena suggests that ivory is represented.

even containers full of ivory dust, which was considered to have medicinal and other values. (Scribonius Largus, court physician to Emperor Claudius, prescribed ivory dust mixed with honey as a cure for epilepsy.)[12] Ivory perfume containers, mirror handles, and fly whisks were dedicated at other sanctuaries, and elaborate panels of gilded ivory decorated the doors of temples. In fact, from the building accounts of the fourth-century BC Temple of Asklepios at Epidauros we know that "Sotairos took the contract to provide ivory for the door, for 3,150 drachmai" and that this sum constituted nearly 5 percent of the cost of the entire temple.[13]

From this same period, when Athens was enriched in the wake of the Persian Wars, comes the earliest surviving evidence for the precise value of ivory. Its actual cost, surprisingly, seems to have rarely equaled that of silver by weight, at least according to the few examples of prices that have been preserved.[14] Regardless of its monetary value, ivory was considered a luxury. It was not only dedicated to the gods, but rich Greeks and Romans, rulers and aristocrats alike, employed it to furnish their homes.[15] As an example of absurd extravagance, one of Aristophanes's characters mentions an ivory privy.[16] The wealthy inhabitants of Akragas in Sicily were said to have had couches of solid ivory,[17] rather than just furniture with veneers. Even the latter could be exquisite, as is clear from incised ivory sheets depicting the Judgment of Paris, dated ca. 400 BC, that once decorated a wooden sarcophagus recovered on the northern shore of the Black Sea (plate 152). Fourth-century BC Macedonian royal tombs, meanwhile, have yielded numerous stunning gilt-ivory appliqués that once adorned couches (plate 155), as well as a composite ivory, gilt-silver, and rock crystal inlaid parade shield, with images of Achilles and Penthesilea carved in ivory as its principal device (plate 154). The Athenian general Alkibiades is said to have had a golden shield, which may have been of a similar construction, with an ivory device of his own invention, Eros wielding a thunderbolt.[18] In the fourth century BC, the Athenian orator Demosthenes referred to his father's ownership of two workshops (*ergastria*), "neither one small," one of which produced swords, the other furniture. Each used approximately two minai's worth of ivory a month.[19]

In the wake of Alexander's conquests, ivory became more readily available and is markedly present in rich Macedonian tombs and Hellenistic sites farther east, such as Nysa and Aï Khanoum.[20] Among other luxuries displayed in the Grand Procession of Ptolemy II Philadelphos at Alexandria in the first half of the third century BC were six hundred tusks carried by Ethiopian tribute bearers. A century later, Antiochos IV Epiphanes displayed eight hundred tusks in a procession at Daphne, near Antioch.

Ptolemy IV Philopator lavishly decorated one of two huge ceremonial ships he built with gold and ivory, as well as exotic woods and jewels. Kallixeinos reports that the "twenty doors of the portico had been joined together from planks of citron-wood and decorated with ivory.... The column shafts were of cypress-wood, while the Corinthian capitals had been ornamented with ivory and gold. The entire architrave was made of gold, and a frieze that contained striking ivory figures more than a cubit high was attached to its top; the workmanship of the figures was indifferent, but the amount of money spent on them was astonishing."[21] The gold and ivory figures probably resembled in form, if not in quality, the splendid ivory reliefs on Macedonian couches mentioned above. Two centuries later, and from considerably farther east, is a splendid group of objects recovered from the storerooms of a royal palace excavated at the Parthian city of Nysa in modern Turkmenistan. This cache includes dozens of ivory rhyta and furniture legs that combine eastern and western forms and imagery (plates 156, 157).[22]

Although the Romans lauded simplicity and the peasant roots of their state, conquests across the Mediterranean brought luxuries to their city. From the Etruscans, they transformed the folding ivory campstool into the *sella curulis* (curule chair), the mark of magistrates holding the highest offices. As in Hellenistic Greece, ivory furniture and adornments were eagerly consumed by the powerful and prosperous. Lucius Cornelius Scipio Asiaticus displayed 1,231 tusks in the triumphal procession celebrating his victory over Antiochos III in 189 BC, and almost two centuries later the Augustan poet Horace referred to *captivum ebur* (captive ivory), ivory couches, and purple textiles as extravagances of city living.[23] Tripod tables with three tusks as legs and tops of exotic wood with complex grain patterns sold for vast sums (see below). As the empire expanded and trade flourished, ivory became still more plentiful and was employed for a wider variety of objects, such as hairpins, combs, knife handles, theater tokens, gaming pieces, and dice, all of which were also fashioned from cheaper and more readily available bone. A set of more than twenty exquisitely carved miniature ivory cosmetic and writing implements dating to the first century AD was nonetheless a luxury, designed to demonstrate the affluence, elegance, and intelligence of its owner (plate 163).[24]

Although some ancient authors thought that the tusks of elephants were horns, they are in fact, teeth—upper incisors to be precise—and like the tusks of other animals, they grow continuously throughout the life of the animal.[25] Because ancient Greeks knew the material, imported from Africa and the Levant, before they were introduced to the animal, the latter takes its name from the former, *elephas* in Greek. Hippopotamus tusks, too, provided ivory for ancient craftsmen, but predominantly in Egypt and during the Aegean Bronze Age, rather than the Classical period. Tusks of prehistoric mammoths, too, were occasionally found, and ancient authors referred to "buried" and "fossil" ivory. Cicero mentions two enormous tusks (*dentes eburneos incredibili magnitudine*) that Verres removed from the Temple of Juno near Melita on Malta.[26] These could have once belonged to either a large African elephant or an extinct species. If truly fossilized, such tusks would be difficult to carve, and on account of their size, they would, in any case, have better served as trophies, as did the alleged tusks of the Kalydonian Boar. These, Pausanias reports, were displayed in the Temple of Athena Alea at Tegea and transferred to Rome by Augustus, where, presumably, they were seen by Ovid, who compared them to the teeth of an Indian elephant. Pausanias mentions there being just one tusk in the sanctuary of Dionysos located in the gardens of Augustus; he was told that it was half a fathom (ca. one meter) long.[27] Four centuries later, Procopius reported seeing the tusks of the Kalydonian Boar in Beneventum and described what appear to have been mammoth tusks: "They are there even up to my time, a noteworthy sight and well worth seeing, measuring not less than three spans around and being in the form of a crescent."[28] Ancient sources record the exhibition of other tusks in temples, but there is no evidence that any of these once belonged to mammoths or other extinct species. Pausanias saw the "ivory horn" (*elephantos keras*) of Amaltheia dedicated by the men of Khersonnesos in the Treasury of the Sikyonians at Olympia and mentions an elephant skull in the sanctuary of Artemis in Campania.[29] The tusks in the shrine to Dionysos described by Lucian are said to be those that the god himself brought from Ethiopia (fig. 31).[30]

Although ancient writers—and nineteenth-century hunters and ivory dealers—were confident in their ability to distinguish among the "fresh" ivory of different elephant species and subspecies on the basis of color, density, and hardness, modern science has yet to definitively identify the source of ancient elephant ivories. The ultimate source of the material, of course, was the natural habitat of elephants, which ranged more extensively across Africa and Asia in antiquity than at present. Tusk size, however, varies not only among individuals but also between species; thus size can occasionally serve as a guide to an ivory's origin.[31]

Although the ancient ivory trade survived the fall of the great Bronze Age empires, it was disrupted by the extinction of the "Syrian" elephant in the eighth century BC. Early in the ninth century BC, King Hiram of Tyre and King Solomon of Judah sought to augment local supplies by sending a joint expedition to Ophir (India?) in order to obtain ivory and other exotic materials.[32] Phoenician colonists in North Africa tapped the local supply of elephants and exported ivory to Spain, Etruria, and, most likely, Sicily and Greece. It is uncertain whether they also sent ivory home, but Ezekiel reports that by the sixth century Phoenicians were importing

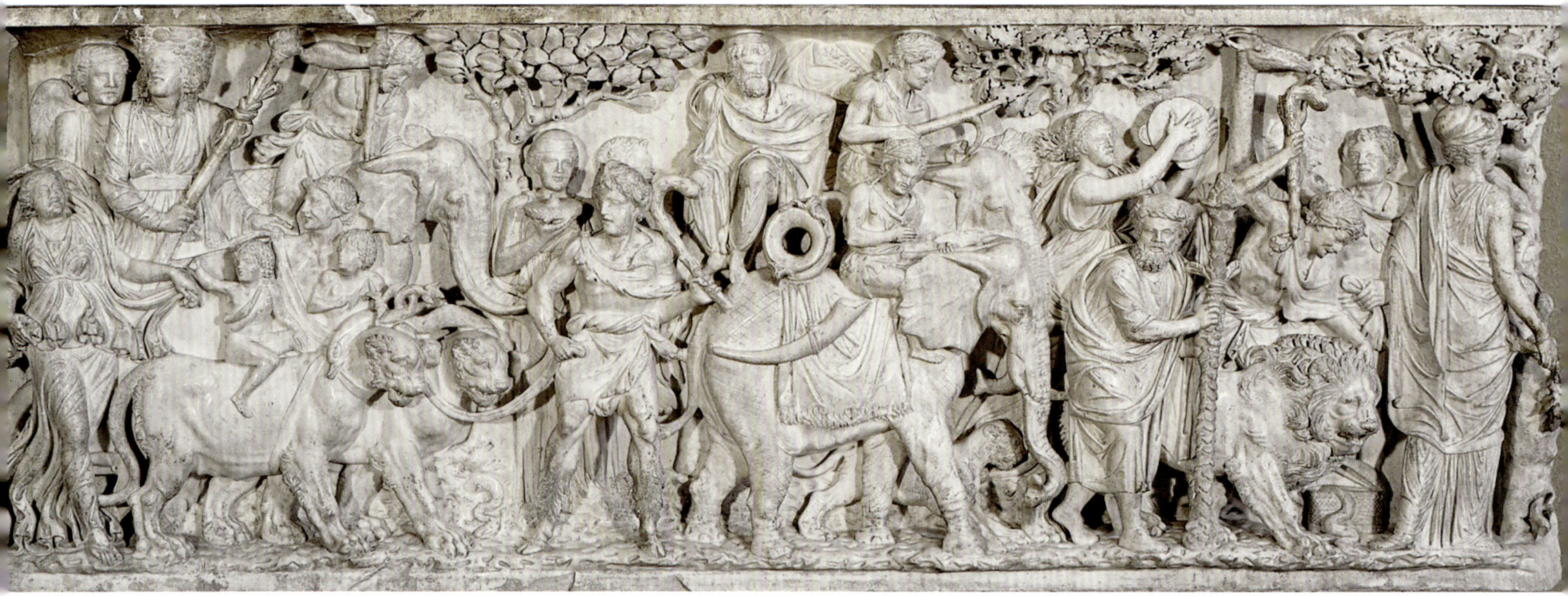

ivory from Dedan in western Arabia, whither it must have been brought from East Africa or India.[33] An inscription of the Persian king Darius relates that ivory from both Kush (Ethiopia) and India, as well as from Arachosia (Afghanistan), was employed in the decoration of his palace at Susa.[34] Herodotos records that every other year the Ethiopians delivered as tribute to the Persian king twenty great tusks, along with two *choinikes* of unrefined gold, two hundred blocks of ebony, and five Ethiopian boys.[35]

There is clear evidence that by the Classical period Africa, too, was supplying ivory to Greece. The comic poet Hermippos, writing in Athens circa 430–420 BC, reports that "Libya supplies ivory in plenty for trade."[36] The Carthaginian explorer Hanno saw elephants in northwest Africa, at the foot of the Atlas Mountains, after he sailed through the Strait of Gibraltar early in the fifth century BC. The author of *The Periplus* (Pseudo-Skylax) of circa 350 BC describes the island of Kerne on the west coast of Africa where Phoenicians traded Attic pottery, perfume, and "Egyptian stone" with Ethiopians (i.e., black Africans) for ivory tusks and animal skins.[37]

As Pausanias notes, few Greeks became familiar with elephants themselves prior to the eastern campaigns of Alexander, who first encountered them at the Battle of Gaugamela in 331

Figure 31
Sarcophagus, from the Via Salaria, Rome, ca. AD 190. Marble, H: 90 cm; W: 121 cm. Baltimore, Walters Art Museum, 23.31. The triumph of Dionysos returning from India is depicted here with exotic animals, including a giraffe, preceding the chariot of the god, which is drawn by panthers. In the center of the crowded composition is a pair of elephants, the one in the foreground carrying a tusk and a large vessel tied to its back as booty.

BC.[38] Alexander and his successors acquired Asian elephants both in battle and as diplomatic gifts.[39] By the second quarter of the third century BC, the Ptolemies were sponsoring expeditions along the coast of the Red Sea to capture and train African elephants as war machines. Such expeditions involved the foundation of cities and eventually extended beyond the straits of Bab-el-Mandeb, as far as Cape Guardafui in present-day Somalia. Here native *elephantomachoi* (elephant fighters) were skilled at killing elephants (which the Ptolemies, of course, wanted alive). In all likelihood they had long been engaged in the ivory trade. Evidence for trade between the Horn of Africa and India is considerable, and the author of the *Periplus Maris Erythraei* leaves no doubt that by the mid-first century AD, East Africa and India were still supplying a thriving trade in ivory.[40]

Roman exploitation of African and Asian elephants for both ivory and entertainment can be traced through literary evidence, but given the multiple sources of both animal and material, it is little wonder that Greek and Roman poets often appear to have employed the terms for both more out of a concern for meter than geography.[41] Elephants captured in battle were displayed in Roman triumphs and often in the amphitheater; others were imported specifically for the latter.[42] In either case, ivory from their tusks would not have been wasted. By the first century Pliny implied that exploitation was leading to a shortage of North African ivory and resulting in increased bone carving, for which there is considerable earlier evidence.[43] Indian ivories, in the meantime, were imported to Italy already carved (plate 159). Mosaics illustrating elephant hunts, such as those at Piazza Armerina in central Sicily and in Constantinople, are evidence of the continued trade in live African elephants for the games, while Roman expeditions as far as what is today known as the Ivory Coast in West Africa may have sought new sources of ivory.[44] In the fourth century AD, Themistius lamented the destruction of the elephants of North Africa, and by the seventh century they were gone, victims of both the ivory trade and the amphitheater.[45] India and East Africa, however, continued to supply ivory to the Mediterranean. Whether it traveled overland along the caravan routes, or via the Red Sea or Nile Valley, these sources of ivory were exploited throughout the imperial and early Byzantine periods.[46]

Techniques

Few ancient literary sources refer at any length to ancient methods of working ivory,[47] yet the processes by which tusks were prepared, and motifs were carved and subsequently decorated, can be reconstructed to some degree. Techniques can be inferred not only from numerous discrete passages of ancient authors but from the inherent qualities of the material, finds from a few excavated workshops, and, most importantly, from the surviving physical remains themselves. Although harder and finer than the hardest and finest of woods, ivory has long been worked in a similar manner. Once the tusks were removed from the animals (an arduous task that requires cutting through the animal's flesh as close as possible to the bone and which presumably was not undertaken by Mediterranean craftsmen), they might be transported whole or precut. Whether blocks or plaques were cut in advance for convenience in shipping, as a matter of economy, or gradually, as material was sold off at different ports of call, remains unknown.

Whether or not ivory, like fine woods, was "seasoned" to preclude later shrinkage remains uncertain. Modern ivory carvers have asserted that elephant ivory is best carved fresh, but the hoarding of tusks in antiquity indicates that fresh ivory was not necessarily held at a premium. Storage conditions affect the state of the material. Present-day anecdotal, rather than scientific, evidence appears to indicate that while a thinly cut section of elephant ivory is liable to warp and split and thus become unsuitable for carving, large pieces, including uncarved tusks, can remain relatively stable over many years, even in fluctuating conditions.

The outermost surfaces of tusks are mostly unusable and need to be removed. Cementum, a rough, hard, ridged material, covers the proximal end of the elephant tusk, binding it to the animal's gums. The older ivory that forms the natural outer surface of the tusk, frequently called the "bark" or "husk" (though often misidentified as enamel or cementum), was usually removed as well. Where it remains on carved ivories (necessarily at the edges) it often appears opaque and white.[48] Cementum at the proximal end of the tusk is likely to have been removed as part of the same process, as was the tip, as evidenced by the fine black cracks that frequently mar it. The cementum, enamel, and older, lower-quality ivory that form the outer surface of tusks might be cut away either before or after tusks were sawn into sections suitable for carving various objects. The hollow proximal portion of elephant tusks required little adaptation to furnish the body of *pyxides* and other containers. Flat panels, round or rectilinear in outline, might be cut horizontally or longitudinally from the remainder of the tusk, although longitudinal cuts appear to have been preferred.

The sculptor of statues and statuettes rather than plaques (although the same craftsman will often have produced both) could carve small- and medium-sized figures whole from elephant tusks of less than extraordinary size, as can be seen from numerous statuettes, such as the well-known females from the Kerameikos cemetery at Athens (plate 146). Larger one-piece carvings, up to about a meter in height, were certainly possible. No such monodontic ivory figure at this scale survives from antiquity, but it is tempting to think that the lost ivory statue of Athena Alea from Tegea "made of ivory throughout" that Pausanias attributes to the Archaic sculptor Endoios and that Augustus transferred to his forum in Rome may have been carved in one piece.[49]

Regardless of the scale and technique of Endoios's Athena Alea, other passages by Pausanias and numerous other ancient authors, as well as the physical remains of Greek and Roman ivories, indicate that statues usually comprised several individually carved components. The natural shape of elephant tusks requires little to be adapted to form forearms, several of which survive.[50] Faces, hands, and feet might have been carved whole or pieced, depending on scale. Two of the lesser-known companions of the famous Geometric statuette from the Kerameikos cemetery have separately carved ivory ears, and the arms of another are attached by iron pins.[51] Economy was practiced with clothed figures on a larger scale. Pausanias informs us that the sanctuary of Zeus at Megara housed a statue of Athena "gilt, except for the hands and feet; these and the face are of ivory"; and an image of the same goddess at Aigeira on the Gulf of Corinth had "the face and hands of ivory and also the feet; the rest is of wood, decorated throughout with gold and colors."[52] This appears to have been the technique of most composite ivory statues: precious imported ivory was reserved for exposed flesh; painted and gilded wood was employed for hair and drapery.

After a block suitable for the carving of the desired figure or component had been sawn from a tusk (if the entire tusk was not to be used), outlines might be drawn or incised with a point or awl; carving could then proceed with chisels or knives.[53] Drills, both solid and hollow, were employed for a variety of tasks: as a preliminary to chisel work and for undercutting, as in marble carving; for details such as eyes, ears, and nostrils; and, of course, for creating circular mortises into which dowels and pins for assembly were inserted.[54] Rectilinear and triangular mortises were also employed with tenons as well as dowels. Rasps and files of varying degrees of fineness brought the components/figures closer to their finished surfaces, and evidence of their use remains visible on the edges of some pieces. The marks of these tools, however, are often difficult to distinguish from those of the abrasives and polishes reserved for the final stages. Joins were secured with adhesives.[55] Cross-pins added extra security, and the pieces to be joined were often scored beforehand to provide a better grip.[56] Joins, moreover, were carefully placed so as to be unobtrusive and might be hidden further by jewelry (e.g., necklaces, bracelets) or drapery (e.g., sleeves, neck- and waist-lines).[57] Hence, the front part of feet (plate 165) and even individual toes were carved separately, as the heels would have been invisible underneath long, flowing robes.[58]

That ancient ivories were colored is most readily evident from literary sources. The physical remains tend to be poorly preserved: many ivories have been subjected to fire, and few have been examined microscopically for traces of pigment.[59] Egyptian, Near Eastern, Asian, and medieval Western European ivories, in contrast, occasionally retain much of their original polychromy, and it is to these we must turn to envision the original appearance of Mediterranean ivories, some of which, in the words of Pausanias, were "decorated throughout with gold and colors."[60] Just what these colors were, we cannot be certain, but traces of red pigment have been recognized on the lips of an Archaic Greek head from Crete and a Roman one from Italy, the last identified as cinnabar (mercuric sulfide, aka vermilion or minium).[61] This pigment is mentioned by Theophrastos, Vitruvius, the physician and author Dioscorides, and Pliny, and was also employed on Fayum portraits, Roman wall paintings, Byzantine frescoes, and Late Antique and Middle Byzantine ivories. These last, like Egyptian and ancient Near Eastern ivories, were further adorned with blues (ultramarine/lapis lazuli), greens (malachite or verdigris), and such colors are likely to have enhanced Greek works in ivory, just as they did those in stone.[62]

Although ivory was generally reserved for the flesh of anthropomorphic figures, it was nonetheless occasionally gilded, as in the case of a foot from Delphi whose finely carved ivory sandal straps retain traces of gold.[63] For the most part, however, wood appears to have served as the support for gold. Why waste precious imported ivory where it would not be seen? Some physical evidence for wooden cores for statues and statuettes has been recovered at Delphi in carbonized form, where gold-headed nails were found along with repoussé gold sheets.[64]

The means of attaching gold to chryselephantine statuary appears to have varied considerably. Heavier sheets of gold, gold-silver alloy, gilt-silver, or gilt-bronze, such as those from Delphi bearing repoussé decoration in the form of locks of hair, drapery folds, and embroidered figural scenes could be nailed to underlying wooden cores (plate 10a, b).[65] Lighter gold foils might have been attached by adhesive, so too thinner gold leaf.[66] The Egyptians employed egg white for this purpose, and this method, along with fish glue, is recommended by the twelfth-century Benedictine monk Theophilus.[67] Another technique for gilding wooden and composite statuary appears to have been water gilding. This method was employed in Egypt as well as in the Middle Ages and thereafter in Europe. Gold leaf was applied to a sticky wet bole (a fine, unctuous red clay) that had been laid over a preparation of chalk whiting or gesso.[68] In the case of wooden or composite figures, whiting might be applied directly to the core, but in both Egypt and Europe it frequently coated linen that had been glued to the surface of the wood. The gold was then burnished or might be punched or incised with patterns, as can today be observed on late medieval/early Renaissance European sculpture, as well as in the gold background of paintings of the same date.

The unfinished statue of *Zeus Olympios* at Megara, like Pheidias's *Athena* and *Zeus* and several other statues in their wake, was constructed on a colossal scale. Earlier techniques of carving individual components from sectioned tusks and assembling them on a wooden core would not suffice, for the exposed flesh of these statues far surpassed the size of any tusk. Greek and Latin authors suggest that by the mid-fifth century BC age-old techniques of furniture production had been developed to such a degree that tusks could be "unscrolled" into thin sheets of ivory with substantially larger dimensions than sectioned pieces; classical and medieval sources, moreover, preserve recipes for chemically softening ivory in order to mold it to a desired shape. These components were mounted to wooden cores, combined with gold sheets and other materials, including crystal, glass, amber, and obsidian, to create stunning representations of the gods and, from the late fourth century BC, a few mortals. Such chryselephantine statues were ranked among the highest artistic achievements of the classical world. Today their grandeur can only be imagined through the combination of descriptions of ancient authors, representations in other media, and a few surviving components of similar statues produced at a smaller scale.[69]

WOOD

In the classical world, as today, a great variety of woods was available for a wide range of purposes: the construction of buildings; of ships, chariots, carts, and other vehicles; of weapons, siege engines, and diverse machines; and for vessels, furniture, and statuary. Exotic woods, whether imported from distant lands or obtained nearer to home, were especially prized. Even the possession of certain types of trees in one's gardens could bring owners both pleasure and prestige, as is evident in ancient literature, Roman wall paintings, and at the few excavated sites where floral remains and ancient planting beds have been carefully studied.[70] Physical survivals of Greek and Roman woodwork, however, are few. Votive statuettes have been recovered from the waterlogged marshes of the Heraion of Samos, the sulfuric springs of Palma di Montechiaro in Sicily, and the source of the river Seine; the dry climate of Egypt has preserved examples of Graeco-Roman furniture, which have also been recovered from tombs on the shores of the Black Sea; Herculaneum, too, has yielded examples of intarsia tabletops, bedsteads, and ceiling coffers, as well as more mundane items.[71]

Ancient authors mention several important wooden statues, but these seem to have been venerated more for their age than for their materials.[72] Some early statues, however, were fashioned from woods that carried considerable meaning. The venerable "old statue" of Athena Polias on the Athenian Acropolis, for example, is variously said to have fallen from the heavens or to have been carved (or enhanced) by the sculptor Endoios. Whatever its origins, the fact that the figure was made of olive wood was certainly significant, for the olive was Athena's sacred tree, her gift to the people of Athens. This material was so holy that when the Epidaureans, suffering from drought, consulted the oracle at Delphi and were instructed to erect olive-wood statues of Damia and Auxesia, goddesses of fertility, they sought the raw material at Athens.[73] Statues of Dionysos on the Cycladic island of Naxos were carved of vine and of fig, the first closely linked to the god of wine and the second a tree the god is said to have discovered and whose fruit and leaves were thought to purge toxins.[74] Theokritos writes of a fig-wood statue surrounded by vines and grape clusters: a Priapus in the form of a phallus.[75] The specific materials of other wooden statues clearly mattered: Pausanias mentions an Asklepios at Sparta called *Agnitas* after its willow-like wood, *agnus castus*, whose medicinal powers were discussed by Aristotle and Dioscorides.[76] Myrtle-wood statues of Aphrodite were dedicated to the goddess in the distant past by Pelops at Temnos near Magnesia-on-Menander in Asia Minor, "when he was propitiating the goddess and asking for Hippodameia to be his bride,"[77] and by a certain Herostratos whom Athenaios reports the goddess rescued at sea.[78] Other ancient authors mention myrtle's associations with Aphrodite, sex, and marriage; the word was also a euphemism for the female pudenda and the upper part of the penis.[79]

Cedar, cypress, and boxwood, employed in ancient Egypt and the Near East for luxury furniture, were prized for their durability, pleasing fragrance, and imperviousness to insects. Ebony and citrus wood both became bywords for luxury.[80] Citrus, which the Greeks called *thyon*, was a desirable, aromatic North African hardwood, resistant to decay and rot, that was discussed at length by ancient writers. It was favored by ancient Greek aristocrats for furniture, doors, and statues.[81] It is mentioned in the epics of Homer and briefly by Theophrastos. Hieron II of Syracuse (r. 270–215 BC) used it on the doors of the shrine to Aphrodite installed on his massive ship, the *Syrakousia*. Ptolemy IV Philopator (r. 221–205 BC) commissioned a larger and still more luxurious vessel that likewise had doors of citrus and ivory. The earliest known reference to citrus wood by a Roman author is Cato's denunciation of its use as a monstrous extravagance. Generations later, Cicero, despite having accused Verres of confiscating a large and beautiful citrus-wood table from a Roman citizen in Sicily, and despite being constantly hard up for cash himself, bought one for half a million sesterces, the equivalent of half a senator's property qualification. Later, Seneca mentions citrus tables being worth a million sesterces, and the highest price mentioned by Pliny shortly thereafter is 1.3 million, enough to buy a large estate.

Pliny also reports that when Roman men mocked the extravagance of women when it came to jewelry, they countercharged with men's table-mania. Citrus-wood tables were valued in part by size, but also on account of their attractive grain patterns, which, according to Pliny, could be long and wavy, "which is called tiger wood, or have little spirals, which is called panther wood... yet another type is called parsley-wood because it has wavy lines that look like clusters of grains."[82] Expensive citrus-wood tabletops were often combined with legs fashioned from tusks of ivory, and workers in both materials belonged to the same guild, the *citrarii et eborarii*.[83] According to the historian Dio, Seneca had a collection of five hundred such tables, and in his philosophical treatise *On the Good Life* questioned his own conscience: "Why don't you live according to your principles? Why do you have such elegant furniture?"[84]

To make the most of such precious woods, the ancients developed and exploited techniques of veneering, which, as we have seen, were also applied to ivory (see plate 152). Athenian inscriptions recording the sale of property confiscated from Alkibiades and others accused of mutilating the Herms and profaning the Eleusinian mysteries in 415/14 BC list a low veneered couch (*chameuna parakollos*) that sold for seventeen drachmas. This may not seem like much, but the sale was a public auction, and the price is twice that of Milesian *klinai* (another type of couch).[85] Unfortunately the material of the veneer is unknown. Pliny places the advent of veneers at Rome much later, citing the Roman historian Fenestella, who said that furniture veneered with maple and citruswood began to be made in his boyhood, i.e., the mid-first century BC.[86] Techniques of veneering were applied also to other materials: cabinets and couches were plated with tortoiseshell, an innovation Pliny attributes to the first-century BC Roman equestrian Carvilius Pollio, "a man of prodigal habits and ingenious in inventing the refinements of luxury... the first to cut the shell of the tortoise into laminæ and to veneer beds and cabinets with it." Pliny also credits Pollio with being the first to adorn couches with silver "in the Carthaginian style."[87] Vergil and Ovid mention tortoiseshell doors and walls as marks of extravagance and royal riches, while Juvenal denounces tortoiseshell couches and cribs.[88] Pliny, however, notes that tortoiseshell was used to fake fine woods, suggesting a relative scale of value.[89]

AMBER

Amber is the hardened resin of prehistoric pines whose special properties made it highly valued in many ancient cultures.[90] Although amber has been found in Sicily, and ancient authors mention other sources in the east, most amber employed in the ancient Mediterranean world originated in the region of the Baltic Sea and was carried on the long "amber route" south to the shores of the Adriatic, whence it was distributed to peoples living in Italy, the Balkans, and beyond. Baltic amber was imported to Greece in the Bronze Age and deposited in the shaft graves at Mycenae. The material is mentioned in the Homeric poems, where it is called *elektron*, the same term used for gold-silver alloy, whose color it shares. Indeed, its name lies at the root of the modern word *electricity*, for it has electrostatic properties, which were noted by the early Greek natural philosopher Thales of Miletos (ca. 625–545 BC), who observed that, when rubbed, it gained the power to attract other objects, such as feathers and straw.[91]

The ancients told many tales about the origins of amber. Some thought it to be solidified urine of the lynx or some other animal, which hardened upon contact with the air, or the tears shed for Meleager by his sisters, who were transformed into birds called *meleagrides* (guinea fowl) that lived in the lands beyond India.[92] In the fifth century BC, Aischylos, Sophokles, and Herodotos all speculated as to its origins. Most common was the belief that amber was the solidified tears of the Heliades, the daughters of the sun god Helios, who wept inconsolably mourning the death of their brother Phaeton, for in color, gleam, and warmth the material seems to capture aspects of the sun.

Pliny recounts—and rejects—many of these theories, for he knew what amber was and described it as "the marrow that flows down from pine trees" (*defluens medulla pinei generis arboribus*), although his information about its geographical origins was somewhat less reliable. He differentiated between various types of amber on account of their color and transparency, noting particularly the high value of "Falernian" amber, which took its name from the similarity of its color to the prized wine. He notes that amber's "rating among luxuries is so high that a human figurine, however small, is more expensive than a number of human beings, alive and in good health." Indeed, he places it after rock crystal on his list of luxuries but notes that "it is fancied only by women" and that while crystal might be used for cold drinks, and murrhine for both hot and cold, "not even luxury has yet succeeded in inventing a justification for using amber."[93]

The historian Tacitus likewise takes a moralizing tone. In his *Germania* he notes that northern tribesmen, the Aestii, living on the shores of the sea that girdles the earth, "ransack the sea," collecting amber in the shallows and on the beaches. "Like true barbarians, they have never asked or discovered what it is or how it is made. For a long time, indeed, it lay unheeded like any other refuse of the sea, until Roman luxury made its reputation. They have no use for it themselves. They gather it crude, pass it on in unworked lumps, and are astounded at the price it fetches."[94] This account ignores the long history of amber being imported into pre-Roman Italy, where it was greatly prized by the Etruscans and other peoples, especially for its magical and medicinal properties, which the Romans also appreciated. Necklaces with amber beads and pendants of various shapes were worn as prophylactics against tonsillitis and afflictions of the throat, and the material was thought to cure fever and other ailments when mixed with honey, rose oil, and other substances.[95]

Amber survivals from Greece are rare, thus the small circular inlays in the headband of the ivory youth from Samos (plate 149) are exceptional. In the Roman world amber was employed for rings, beads, pendants, amulets, utensils, small vessels with Dionysiac subjects (plate 169), statuettes (plate 168), game pieces, dice, and other decorative objects. Although considerably softer than hard stones (about 2.5 on the Mohs scale), amber seems, on occasion, to have been worked by some of the same craftsman who carved gems.[96] Indeed, some Roman amber rings preserve inset cornelian intaglios.[97] The material survives today most often in tombs and may well have had some eschatological significance, but ancient literary sources report that it was employed also in the production of large-scale portraiture, such as the image of the emperor Augustus that Pausanias saw at Olympia.[98] Pliny reports that amber could be dyed and was sometimes used to make artificial amethysts.[99]

PEARLS

Pearls seem to have been rare in ancient Mesopotamia and early Egypt. In the Hellenistic period they were imported into the Mediterranean world from the Red Sea, the Persian Gulf, and India.[100] In fact, the Greek words *margarites* and *margaron* seem to be linked etymologically to the Old Indian word for pearl, *manjaram*. Pearls begin to appear in Greek jewelry in the third century BC (plate 170), but often they have not survived, leaving mere cavities where they once contributed to the polychromatic compositions that became popular in Hellenistic jewelry.

Pliny ranked pearls as the most expensive commodity to come from the sea. The ancients, he reports, valued them for their "brilliance, size, roundness, smoothness, and weight, qualities of such rarity that no two pearls are found that are exactly alike". He also explains how different terms evolved for differently shaped pearls, and how "women glory in hanging these on their fingers and using two or three for a single earring" (fig. 32).[101] Seneca, too, complained that one pearl was not enough for each ear. "The lobes of our ladies have attained a special capacity for supporting a great number.... The crazy fools seem to think that their husbands are not sufficiently tormented unless they wear the value of an inheritance in each ear."[102] Even more outrageous were the pearl-encrusted shoes worn by extravagant women and, apparently, Caligula, who also had pearls sewn to his clothes. Nero, too, seems to have decorated not only his shoes with pearls but also his

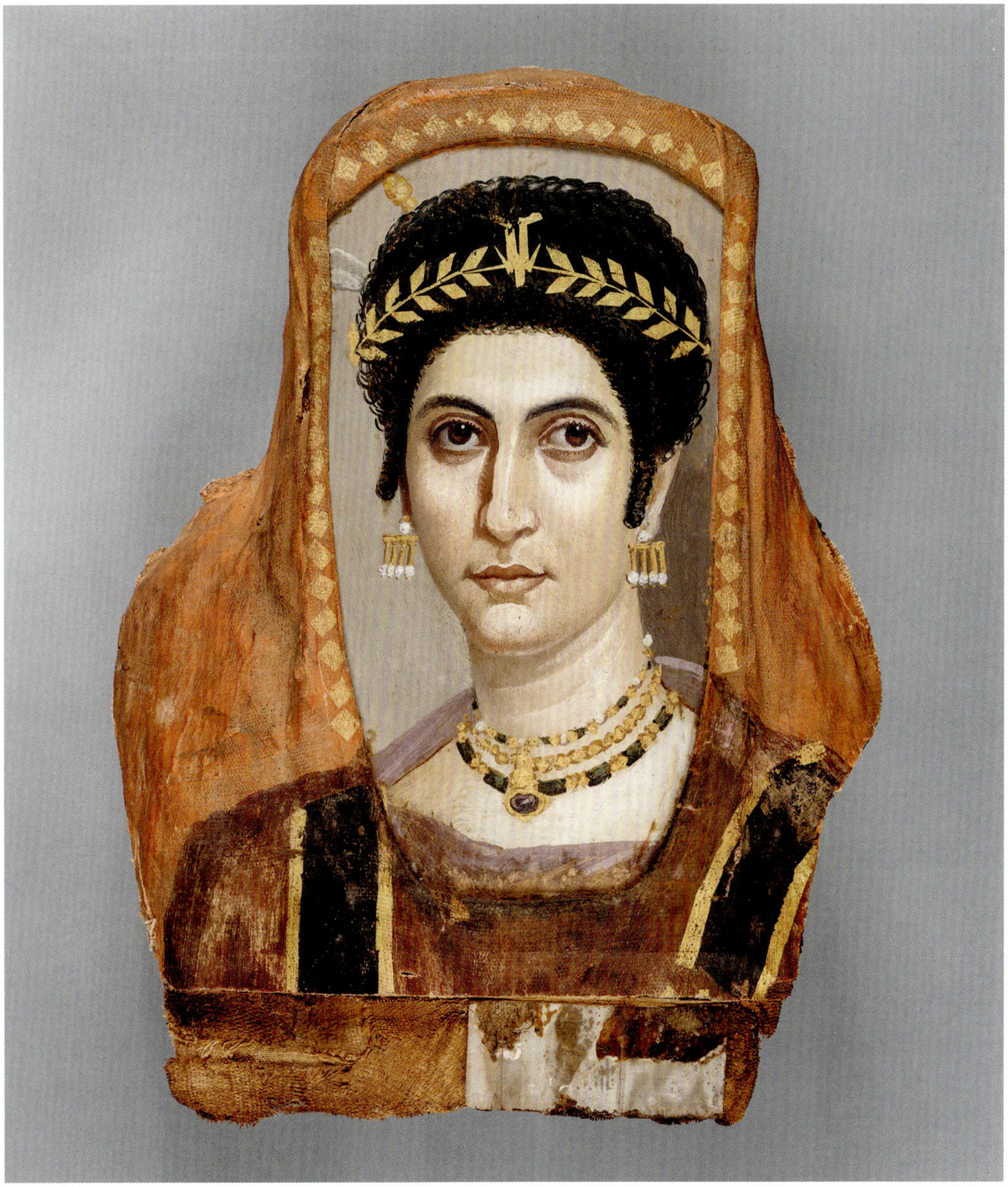

Figure 32
Mummy portrait of Isidora, ca. AD 100–110. Linen, wax, pigment, and gold on wood, H: 48 cm; W: 36 cm; D: 12.8 cm. Malibu, JPGM 81.AP.42. Isidora (her name is inscribed on the side of the portrait) wears earrings with multiple suspended pearls, perhaps the *crotalia* described by Pliny, as well as gold, pearl, emerald, and amethyst necklaces, a gold wreath, and hairpin.

traveling couches. He even provided actors in his theater with pearl masks.[103]

While the Greek taste for pearls seems to have originated with the eastern conquests of Alexander, Roman fashion for them apparently arose from Pompey the Great's conquests in the Mithradatic Wars of the late 60s BC. In his triumphal procession, thirty-three crowns of pearls, and numerous pearl ornaments, including a pearl portrait of the conqueror, were paraded through the streets of Rome.[104] Julius Caesar's invasion of Britain shortly thereafter provided a new source of pearls. Suetonius asserts that Caesar invaded the island in the hope of gaining pearls, some of which adorned sedan chairs and a breastplate he dedicated to Venus Genetrix, but they were small and of unpleasant color, lacking luster.[105] Pliny indignantly claims to have seen Lollia Paulina, the consort of Gaius Caligula, "at an ordinary betrothal banquet covered with emeralds and pearls interlaced alternately and shining all over her head, hair, ears, neck, and fingers, the sum total amounting to the value of 40 million sesterces" (see plate 171). But the cost of this ensemble pales before the value of the

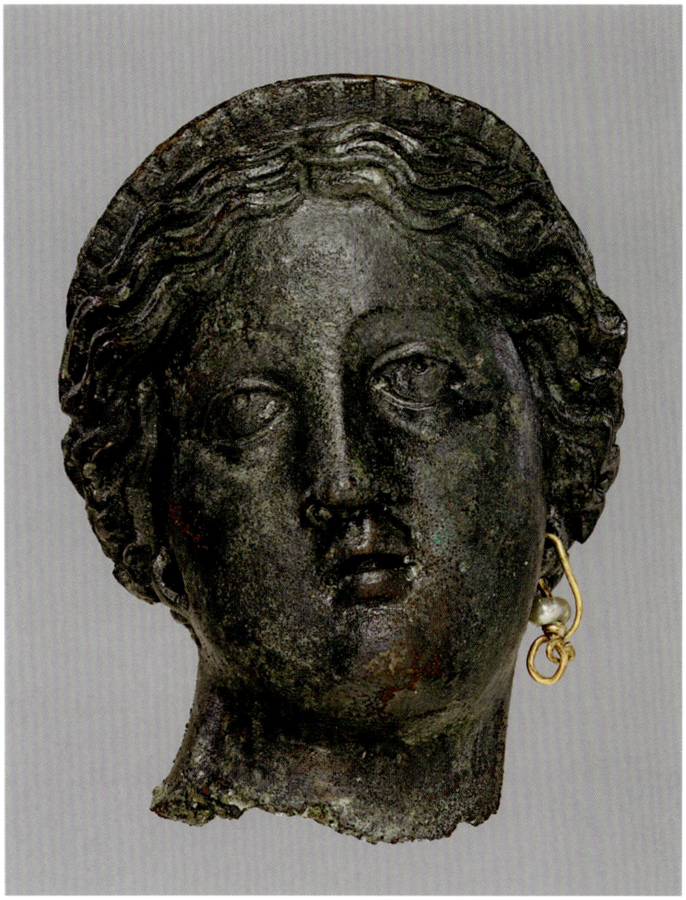

Figure 33
Head of a statuette of Venus, ca. AD 100. Bronze, H: 4.5 cm. Malibu, JPGM, 73.AB.24. One surviving gold-and-pearl earring illustrates that images, too, were adorned with jewelry.

single pearl that was consumed by Cleopatra, one of a pair of the largest ever seen, to win her famous wager with Mark Antony half a century earlier. Alone it was worth 10 million.[106] Emperor Vitellius, meanwhile, is said to have financed an entire military campaign by the sale of a single pearl from his mother's ear.[107] Various texts reveal that pearl earrings were also affixed to statues—the twin of Cleopatra's pearl was apparently later cut in half to adorn a statue of Venus at Rome,[108] and a small head of the same goddess detached from a bronze statuette preserves one of two minute gold and pearl earrings that originally hung from both pierced ears (fig. 33).

Merchants called *margaritarii* (singular *margaritarius*) traded in pearls; the names of more than twenty are known from ancient Latin funerary and votive inscriptions. These were carved between the first century BC and the third century AD and indicate that the *margaritarii* themselves were foreigners, freedmen, the freeborn sons of freedmen, and slaves. Most of the inscriptions are from early imperial Rome, but examples come also from Tusculum, Anzio, and Aquileia in Italy, and one from Spain. Not all of these *margaritarii* were necessarily merchants: some seem to be freedmen belonging to the imperial and other households who were entrusted with looking after pearls.

The work of setting pearls was undertaken by goldsmiths (*aurifices*). In Rome the goldsmiths worked alongside the *margaritarii* who had their shops on the Via Sacra that ran through the Forum. Whether this is also the location of the Porticus Margaritaria, recorded in the ancient catalogues of Rome's buildings, remains uncertain. The inscriptions indicate that some *margaritarii*, like goldsmiths, may have amassed considerable wealth.[109] Whether the same was true of those who forged pearls by coating a ball of wax with gum tragacanth, egg white, and ground mica, we do not know. Recipes for producing such fake pearls are preserved in ancient papyri, as are instructions for cleaning pearls by feeding them to chickens and roosters, whose digestive systems might render them as clean and shiny as when they were first extracted from their oysters, removing grime and stains without diminishing their luster. Modern experiments have demonstrated the validity of this technique.[110]

CORAL

Although some ancient writers understood that pearls were formed by alien particles that entered and irritated oysters, they were unaware that coral is the calcareous skeleton of a marine creature (anthozoan coelenterate), thinking it rather to be a petrified plant. In fact, Ovid, in the *Metamorphoses*, explains how it was formed when Perseus, having rescued Andromeda from the sea monster, exposed sea plants to the head of the Gorgon:

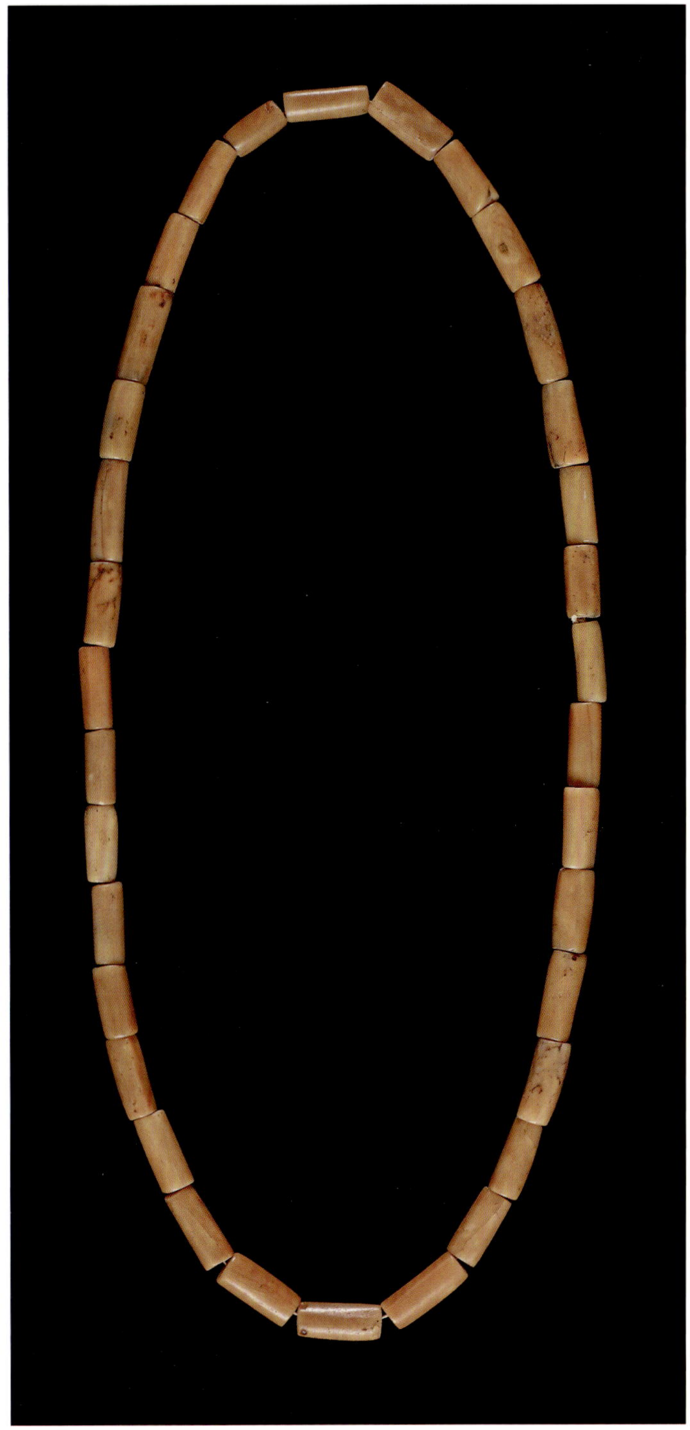

Figure 34
Necklace, from Naukratis, Egypt, ca. 500–400 BC. Coral, L: ca. 34 cm. London, British Museum, 1886,0401.1716 (Jewellery 2696).

> So that Medusa's head, covered with its snakes, is not bruised by the harsh sand, he makes the ground soft with leaves, and spreads out plants from below the waves, and places the head of that daughter of Phorcys on them. The fresh plants, still living inside, and absorbent, respond to the influence of the Gorgon's head, and harden at its touch, acquiring a new rigidity in branches and fronds. And the ocean nymphs try out this wonder on more plants, and are delighted that the same thing happens at its touch, and repeat it by scattering the seeds from the plants through the waves. Even now corals have the same nature, hardening at a touch of air, and what was alive, under the water, above water is turned to stone.[111]

Pliny notes that coral was also called *Gorgonia* (Gorgon stone)—or rather that the stone called Gorgonia was merely coral (*nihil aliud est quam coralium*), so named because it was "transformed into the hardness of stone after being softened in the sea."[112] Theophrastos and Dioscorides wrote of red corals found off the western coast of southern Italy, as did Pliny, who also was aware of coral from the Persian Gulf and Red Sea.[113] The author of the *Periplus of the Erythrean Sea* reports that coral was a valued export from the Mediterranean to India: it was shipped to Barbaricum at the mouth of the river Indus in present-day Pakistan, as well as to Barygaza farther south at the mouth of the Narmada in northwest India and to Muziris (perhaps modern Pattanam) on the southwest coast of the subcontinent, the last of which was a noted source for the export of spices, precious stones, pearls, and tortoiseshell.[114] Pliny, for his part, notes that coral was commonly used by the Gauls to adorn their swords, shields, and helmets before the Roman trade boom with India, where coral was held in as great demand as Indian pearls were in the Mediterranean: "At the present day, owing to the value set upon it as an article of exportation, it has become so extremely rare that it is seldom to be seen even in the regions that produce it."[115]

Pliny also mentions the various medicinal uses of coral: for example, depending on the preparation, it might bring relief for bowel pain, bladder afflictions, ulcers, and scars, among other conditions, and "branches of coral, hung at the necks of infants, are thought to act as a preservative against danger."[116] Whether such properties were imputed to a fifth-century BC coral necklace of thirty-four cylindrical coral beads excavated at the Greek settlement of Naukratis in the Nile Delta by Sir Flinders Petrie (fig. 34) we do not know.

The material was further thought to protect sailors from lightning and whirlwinds.[117] A Late Hellenistic Medusa head thought to be from Bactria (plate 172) may once have served such a purpose. Few other ancient coral artifacts survive, apart from beaded necklaces. A notable exception is a miniature bust of the god Serapis in the British Museum that is carved in a more recognizably Graeco-Roman style (plate 173).

TEXTILES

Physical survivals of ancient Greek and Roman textiles are rare. Scraps of woven wool and linen have been recovered from tombs on the Greek mainland and farther north, where they were exported to the shores of the Black Sea, as well as in southern Italy. Egypt has preserved considerably more examples because of its dry climate. Spindles, loom weights, and other implements used to spin thread and weave fabric excavated throughout the ancient Mediterranean world confirm literary and visual evidence for widespread textile production. Spinning and weaving were of considerable social and economic significance, both in individual households and in professional establishments.[118] Images on pots and statues provide some idea of the complex imagery woven into and painted and embroidered onto ancient luxury textiles, whose iconographical programs were often much more than merely decorative. Gods and goddesses on Athenian black- and red-figured ceramics as well as in statuary are sometimes represented wearing garments with complex geometric, floral, and figural decoration (figs. 35–37).[119] The name-vase of the Penelope Painter depicts the loyal wife of Odysseus weaving (or perhaps unraveling) such a cloth on an upright loom; Homer sang in the *Iliad* of Helen of Troy weaving during the course of the Trojan War; and ancient texts are replete with references to textiles of various kinds, from quotidian to luxurious.[120]

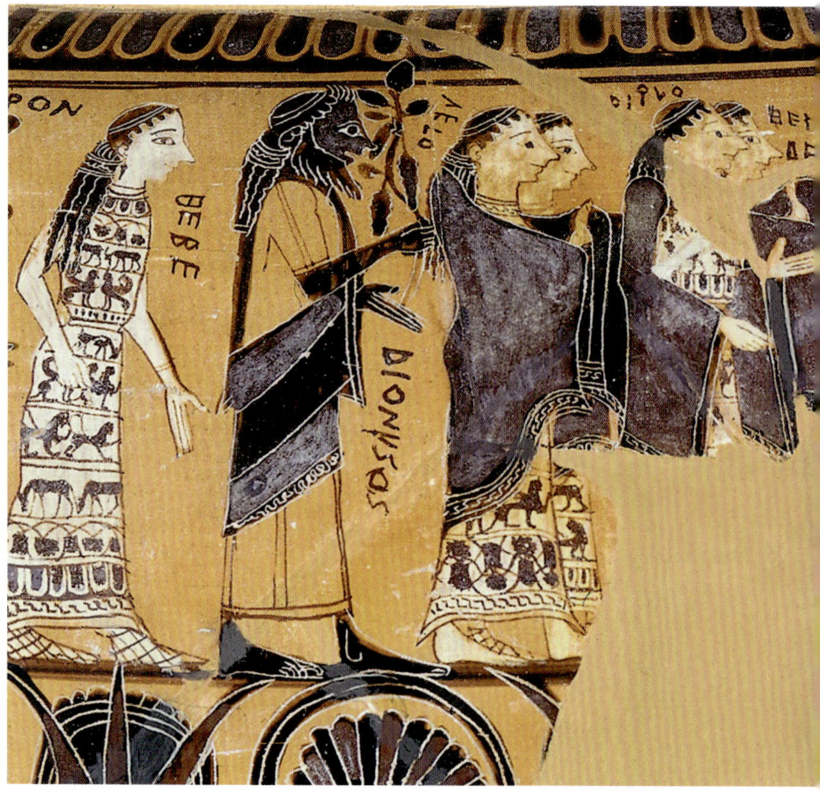

Figure 35
Athenian black-figured *dinos* (detail), signed by Sophilos as painter, ca. 580 BC. Terracotta, H (of detail): ca. 10 cm. London, British Museum 1971,1101.1. The procession of gods attending the wedding of Peleus and Thetis includes Hebe (left), Leto, Chariklo, and Hestia all wearing long white garments decorated with elaborate floral and animal friezes.

Figure 36 (opposite)
Athenian red-figured *skyphos* (detail), attributed to Makron as painter, ca. 500–480 BC. Terracotta, H (of vessel): 20 cm. London, British Museum, 1873,0820.375 (E140). The goddess Demeter holding grain and a torch wears a crown and earrings, as well as a fine sleeved *chiton* and a *himation* decorated with winged figures, racing chariots, runners, pegasoi, birds, panthers, dolphins, palmettes, spirals, stars, and zigzags.

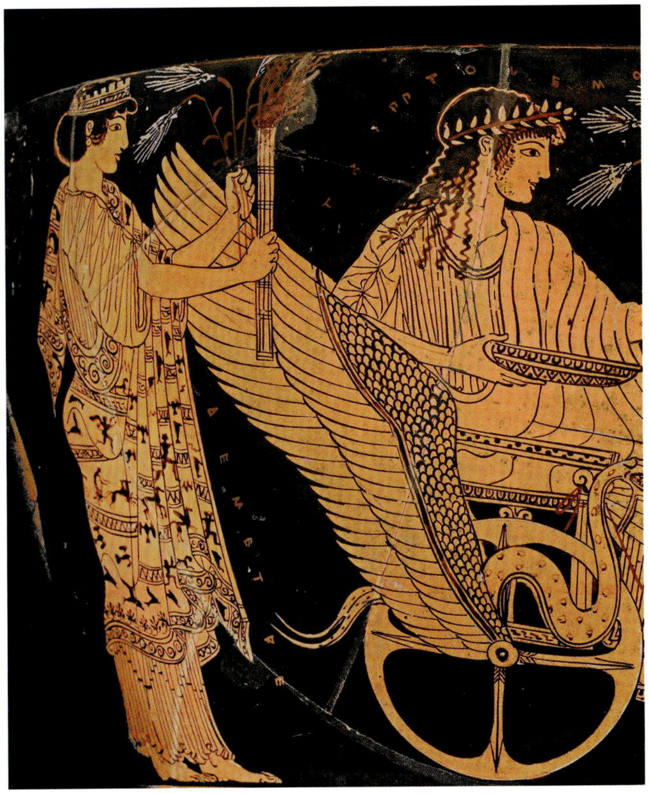

Sumptuous garments might be worn on special occasions by both men and women, offered to the gods, stored up for generations, or deposited in tombs. Wool and linen in several grades were the most common materials for fabrics. Scholars now debate whether silk was imported to Classical Greece, questioning the interpretation of earlier finds.[121] Certainly by the mid-fourth century BC Aristotle knew of wild silk moths associated with the island of Kos. Garments from that island became famous for their lightness, sheen, and transparency and became a byword for hedonism, especially in the Roman period. Latin writers referred to silk garments as *bombycinae, sericae*, and *metaxa*, emphasizing that they simultaneously covered but did not hide the physical charms of those who wore them. "So shines a woman's body through silk," wrote the poet Martial,[122] while Seneca remarked that "clad in silk no woman can honestly say she is not naked."[123] Caesar had curtains of silk, and Caligula was said to have worn silk garments, but Tacitus declared that "men should not disgrace themselves with silk clothing from the east."[124]

Purple textiles, produced using dyes from the transformed juices of marine gastropods of the genus *murex,* were especially valued because of their brightness and durability. There is physical evidence for the production of such dyes from virtually all shores of the Mediterranean, although they are most commonly associated with the Phoenicians, and particularly with the city of Tyre.[125] Tyrian purple, later known as imperial purple because it came to be reserved for Roman and Byzantine emperors, was known to the Minoans in the Bronze Age. In Greek myth, the dye was said to have been discovered by Herakles, or rather his dog, who stained his muzzle eating shellfish along the Phoenician coast. Purple cloths were the possession of gods and heroes. In the *Iliad*, Andromache, as yet unaware that her husband, Hektor, had fallen to Achilles, is weaving "a purple fabric that folds in two."[126] Euripides provides a lengthy description of luxury textiles in his play *Ion*, in which a messenger describes a banquet at Delphi, where guests are served from vessels of gold and silver beneath an amazing textile stretched to form the roof of a tent.

> Ion took from the temple's storehouse the sacred, beautiful tapestries, stretched them over the uprights and made a huge shady awning out of them for everyone to see and marvel at. Of these tapestries Ion placed first the garments which Herakles, son of Zeus, had dedicated to the temple. These were spoils that Herakles had gained from his war with the Amazons and on these garments were woven the following pictures: Heaven was gathering the stars into a circle in the sky and Helios was driving his horses towards the final blaze, dragging behind him the bright light of Esperos, the Evening star. Night in her black robe was racing a chariot with two horses at the yoke and alongside of her ran the stars. The Pleiads were flying through the center of Heaven and the swordsman, Orion, with the Bear above was turning her tail round the golden Pole. And the brilliant circle shone, cutting the month into two. The Hyades, a clear sign to the seafarers, and the light carrier Dawn were sending away the stars. Then Ion ordered more tapestries to be spread, this time work by

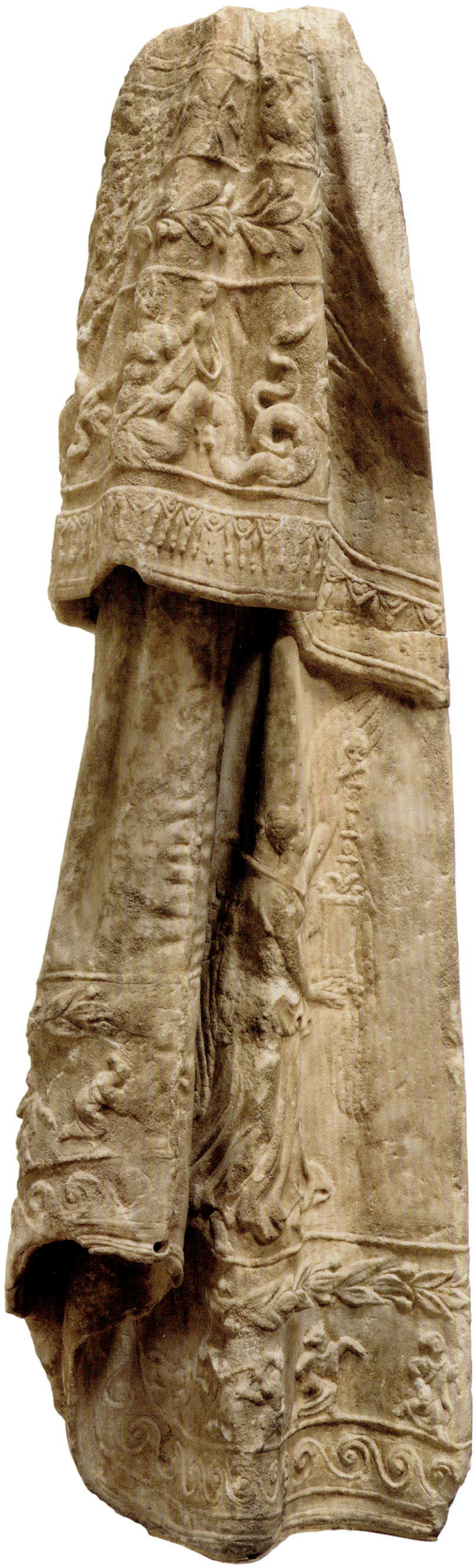

barbarians, upon which were agile, speedy ships, enemies to our own Greek ships and animals mixed of nature, half horse, half centaurs, horsemen chasing stags or hunting wild lions. Also, near the entrance of the tent was a picture of Kekrops, snakes twirled all round him and his daughters next to him. This was a picture that someone from Athens had dedicated to the temple of Apollo. Then Ion brought out great golden wine mixing bowls.[127]

According to Apollonios of Rhodes, writing centuries later, Athena gave to Jason a purple cloak whose brilliance outshone the rising sun: it was adorned with "ingenious designs" including, among many other scenes, the Cylopes making thunderbolts for Zeus, one of which "lay spurting flame as they beat it out with their hammers," and Aphrodite, her garment fallen from her shoulder exposing her breast, "all mirrored to perfection in the bronze shield she held in front of her."[128]

These may be fanciful descriptions of textiles, but that such items existed in reality as well as in myth is clear from references to the *peploi* woven for Athena at the Panathenaia. One was small, produced annually by a team of well-born

Figure 37
Part of the "Veil" of Despoina, carved by the workshop of Damophon of Messene, from Lykosoura, ca. 175–150 BC. Marble, H: 1.13 m. Athens, National Archaeological Museum, 1737. Profusely decorated, the veil incorporates many images significant to the cult of the goddess Despoina, an Arcadian variant of Persephone. Set between ornamental bands of tassels, olive sprays, running spirals, and eagles with winged thunderbolts, are figural friezes of Nereids and Tritons with hippocamps and dolphins, winged victories with incense burners, and animal-headed figures dancing and playing musical instruments.

girls, who also dedicated a gold *phiale* to the goddess. The other was larger, produced every four years by professional male weavers and served as the sail for the Panathenaic ship. Both were adorned with images of the Gigantomachy (battle of the gods and giants).[129] Other narrative weavings described by ancient authors depicted historical events, such as the Persian general "Datis dragging the island of Naxos from the sea, Artaphernes besieging Eretria, the victories claimed by Xerxes, the taking of Athens, the battle of Thermopylai, . . . and the drying up of the rivers, the bridging of the sea, the piercing of Mount Athos," which Philostratos reports Apollonios of Tyana saw in Babylon.[130]

Sumptuous purple garments were also owned by the well-to-do: the late fifth-century BC Athenian general Alkibiades profligately dragged a purple cloak on the ground as he swaggered through the Athenian Agora. Plutarch reports that such a garment might cost three minai (300 drachmai). [131] Around 400 BC the painter Zeuxis "became so wealthy that in order to make a show at Olympia, he displayed his name woven in golden letters in the figured parts of his garments."[132]

Mid-fourth-century BC inscriptions from the sanctuary of Artemis at Brauron, in eastern Attica, record, among many garments offered to the goddess, a *himation* dedicated by Luso "with letters of gold."[133] Inscribed woolen textiles showing evidence of ancient wear and repair have been recovered from fourth-century BC Skythian tombs on the northern shores of the Black Sea: Athena, Nike, Eris, Jokasta, Pheidra, Mopsos, Hippomedon, Iolaos, and Eulimene are all named amid the fragmentary figures and ornaments.[134] The motifs on this cloth are dyed, while those on others recovered nearby are embroidered (plate 175).

Golden garments, such as the *himation* of the orator Demosthenes, were surely more valuable; his was produced for him to wear in a Dionysiac procession.[135] Demetrios Poliorketes is said to have owned a robe with a lustrous dark background with gold stars and the twelve signs of the zodiac.[136] No such item with gold inscriptions survives from Greece, but a fifth-century tomb at Koropi in southeastern Attica has yielded scraps of linen embroidered with gold thread to create a series of lozenges, each with a striding lion within it (plate 174). Pliny credits Near Eastern kings with the invention of weaving with gold and notes its presence among the Etruscans.[137] Alexander the Great obtained golden garments when he captured Persepolis, and sumptuous eastern textiles are depicted in the Alexander Mosaic from the House of the Faun at Pompeii.[138] Ancient Roman authors report that members of the imperial family wore golden garments, in life and death, and these, not surprisingly, were not those noted for good rule: Agrippina, Nero, and Commodus.[139] Elagabalus occasionally wore "a tunic made wholly of cloth of gold, or one made of purple, or a Persian one studded with jewels, and at such times he would say that he felt oppressed by the weight of his pleasures."[140] Marcus Aurelius, in contrast, sold his wife's silk and golden garments to raise money to finance a military campaign, much as Vitellius had done by selling his mother's pearl earring a century earlier.[141]

Different kinds of gold thread are described by Pliny, who states that gold can be spun and woven just like wool.[142] Cloth of gold seems to have been a specialty of Pergamene workshops and was often referred to as "Attalid fabric" (*Attalica*).

Items woven from gold thread have been recovered not only from fifth-century BC Attica, as we have seen, but also from fourth-century BC Macedonia, which has yielded the most spectacular of all ancient textiles: two large panels of a gold and purple cloth wrapped around the cremated remains of a young woman placed in a golden chest in the antechamber of Tomb II at Vergina in Macedonia (plate 176). This textile was produced by weaving, rather than embroidering, gold strips just 0.25 mm thick into murex-dyed purple wool.[143] Late Classical, Hellenistic, and Roman gold-weave has been found in southern Italy, in the Vesuvian cities, and throughout the Roman Empire, including Britain, France, the Netherlands, Germany, Hungary, Ukraine, Spain, Turkey, Syria, Lebanon, Egypt, and Russia.[144] Roman funerary inscriptions commemorate specialist *aurinetices* and *aurivestrices* (weavers of golden garments); other inscriptions call similar workers *barbaricarii*.

By the fourth century the *barbaricarii* of Trier, Arles, Reims, Constantinople, and Antioch were all overseen by a state-run administration and supplied their wares to the imperial court. Diocletian's edict on prices set their pay at 1,000 denarii, more than any other textile makers.[145]

Most ancient textiles seem to have been produced as rectangles, and thus could serve flexibly as garments, hangings, or coverlets. "*Himatia* and precious linens" adorned Alexander the Great's wedding apartment, while Ptolemy II Philadelphos hung at a symposium "gold woven *chitones* and the most beautiful *ephaptides*, some of which were woven with portraits of the kings and other with mythical scenes."[146] It is only from later but better-preserved textiles from Roman Egypt that we can hope to recover a notion of the finest of these pictorial weavings, whose creators combined a variety of techniques to render in cloth highlights and shading to convincingly represent volume and depth. A number of splendid tapestries have been preserved in the dry climate of Antinoopolis, a city in Upper Egypt refounded by Emperor Hadrian to commemorate his young lover, Antinoos, who drowned in the Nile nearby in AD 132. Exceptional is a fragmentary woolen panel, parts of which are preserved in Paris and Lyon, that depicts different species of fish swimming in a blue-green sea (plate 179). The colors of the fish are vividly gradated and cast shadows, giving the impression that they exist in three dimensions, reflecting light as they swim in the sea. This tapestry was recovered from an ancient tomb in the early nineteenth century. We do not know whether, before it was employed as a funeral shroud, it functioned as decoration for a banqueting room, as did many Roman mosaics depicting marine life.

Another, slightly later, linen-and-wool tapestry now preserved in various museums depicts a Dionysiac *thiasos*, some of whose members are identified by name.[147] Its organization, with figures set in an arcade, has parallels in other textiles; such items must have served as impressive wall-hangings before their reuse in burial contexts. The figure of Dionysos himself (plate 177) is nude, but for a cloak behind him. He raises one hand to his head in a familiar gesture and holds a large golden cornucopia in the other. This is not the god's usual attribute, and it has been suggested that its presence here might be linked to its appearance in the Grand Procession of Ptolemy II Philadelphos at Alexandria.[148] The maenad playing a lyre (plate 178) who accompanies him wears a dotted crown, gold earrings, necklace, bracelets, and anklets, as well as a purple *peplos* with gold borders and an emerald cloak. The variable shading of the *peplos* not only gives added depth to the folds but also highlights the volume of the left leg pushing forward from underneath the drapery. Such splendid textiles provide only a glimpse of the fine work of weavers, dyers, and embroiderers that was so highly valued by the ancients.

NOTES

1 Lapatin 2001, 13. For much of what follows with regard to ivory, see Lapatin 2001, 8–21 (for greater detail and further references).

2 *Iliad* 5.582–83, 13.22; *Odyssey* 4.71–75, 8.403–5, 19.55–58, 21.5–7, 23.199–201.

3 *NH* 37.204, 8.31; Pausanias 5.12.3.

4 Song of Solomon 7:4.

5 *Iliad* 4.141–45; *Odyssey* 18.190–96.

6 *CIL* 6.37965 (the epitaph of Allia Potestas).

7 See LSJ, s.v.v. *elephantinos*, *elephas*; *Oxford Latin Dictionary*, s.v.v. *ebur*, *eburneus*, *eburnus*. See also Lapatin 2001, 15–16.

8 Barnett 1982, 25–28. That the hoarding of ivory continued into the Roman period is clear not only from the enormous number of tusks said to have been brought to Rome by *triumphatores*, presumably the stored wealth of Hellenistic kings (see Blümner 1905, esp. 2357), but also from a cache of tusks discovered in a magazine of the first-century AD palace at Wad ben Nagen, on the Nile south of Meroë in the Sudan (Vercoutter 1962, 280, pl. 20b).

9 The most notable collections of Greek votive ivories have been excavated in the sanctuaries of Artemis at Sparta and Ephesos, and of Hera at Argos, Perachora, and Samos; see Lapatin 2001 (with further references).

10 Pausanias 5.17–19.

11 See, e.g., Richter 1966; Andrianou 2006a, 2006b, 2009; Rhomiopoulou and Schmidt-Dounas 2010, esp. color pls. 2–3, pls. 14–33; Baughan 2013. See also plates 147, 148, 155, and 158 in this volume.

12 See previous note and Harris 1995. For ivory chips and dust, see Harris 1995, no. V.178; and *IDélos* 298A, 181. Scribonius Largus, *Compositiones*, ed. G. Helmreich (1877), xvi. 10(28)–11(15); cf. *NH* 29.113. Pliny (*NH* 35.42) also reports that Apelles discovered by burning ivory how to create the black pigment known even today as ivory black: *Apelles commentus est ex ebore combusto facere, quod elephantinum vocatur.*

13 Vickers 1987, 46; Oliver 1992; Pope and Schultz 2014.

14 See Gill 1992; Lapatin 2001, 14–15.

15 Blümner 1905, 2359–62.

16 Aristophanes, *Ploutos* 815.

17 Aelian, *Varia historia* 3.2 (citing Timaios).

18 Plutarch, *Alkibiades* 16.

19 Demosthenes, *Against Aphobos* 27.1.9–10. For an ivory-hilted sword, see, e.g., Andronicos 1984, 142–45; Kottaridi 2011, 70–71.

20 See Bernard 1970; Masson and Pugachenkova 1982; Andrianou 2006a; E. Pappalardo 2010, 2011; Rhomiopoulou and

Schmidt-Dounas 2010; Kottaridi 2011.
21 Kallixeinos *apud* Athenaios, *Deipnosophistai* 5.204–206c.
22 Barnett 1982, 66–67, pl. 67; Masson and Pugachenkova 1982; Vickers 1987, 49; E. Pappalardo 2010, 2011.
23 Horace, *Epistle* 2.1.193; *Satires* 2.6.103.
24 Cambridge, Fitzwilliam Museum, GR.2-27c.1980: Vassilika 1998, 118–19, no. 57. For a selection of ivories from the Roman settlement at Avenches in present-day Switzerland, see Bron 1985.
25 For the ancient debate as to whether tusks were horns rather than teeth, see, e.g., *NH* 8.7; Aelian, *Kynegetika* 4.31, 11.37; Philostratos 2.13; see also Scullard 1974.
26 Cicero, *In Verrem* 2.4.46, 103; for a large ivory ear of what may be a composite statue from the site, see Lapatin 2001, no. 34, fig. 145.
27 Pausanias 8.46.1, 5; Ovid, *Metamorphoses* 8.288.
28 Procopius, *De bello Gothico* 1.15.8.
29 Pausanias 6.19.6 and 5.12.3. Pliny (*NH* 8.3) mentions a "large quantity of tusks" (*magnitudo dentium*).
30 Lucian, *De dea Syria* 16.
31 Thus the so-called Mona Lisa from Nimrud, the diameter of which exceeds 13 cm, is believed to have been carved from the tusk of an African bush elephant (Barnett 1982, 51, pl. 46a–b). For the distribution of the elephant in antiquity and the sources of Mediterranean ivories, see Scullard 1974, 23–31, 61–63, 260–61; Barnett 1982, 3–8; Cutler 1985, 20–37; Krzyszkowska 1990, 12–19; Lapatin 2001, 10–13.
32 1 Kings 10:22; Barnett 1982, 9.
33 For the Phoenicians, see Ezekiel 27:15; Esse 1992. See also M. Polzer in Aroz, Graff, and Rakic 2014, 230, 232–34, for the cache of tusks from the seventh–sixth-century BC Bajo de la Campana shipwreck off the western coast of Spain.
34 For ivory in Arabia and farther east, see Scullard 1974, 260; Barnett 1982, 94n55.
35 Herodotos 3.97.
36 Hermippos *apud* Athenaios, *Deipnosopphistai* 1.27ff.
37 Pseudo Skylax 112. See Lapatin 2001, 11n53.
38 Pausanias 1.12.3–4. Herodotos (4.191) lists elephants among the animals of Libya, but apparently never encountered one himself. Ktesias of Knidos, who may have served as Persian court physician from 405 to ca. 387 BC, on the other hand, appears to have observed elephants closely. For his and other early accounts of elephants, prior to Aristotle, see Scullard 1974, 32–36.
39 Toynbee 1973, 32–38; Scullard 1974, 65–74 and passim.
40 Lapatin 2001, 12.
41 See, e.g., Blümner 1905; Toynbee 1973, 32–50; Scullard 1974, 260–61; Barnett 1982, 69–72; Buitron and Oliver 1985, 57–58; Cutler 1985, 20–26; Cutler 1987, 437–39; Belozerskaya 2006, 49–85.
42 Toynbee 1973, 46–49; Scullard 1974, 250–54; Belozerskaya 2006, 49–85.
43 *NH* 8.7: "*nuper ossa etiam in laminas secari coepere paenuria etinim rara amplitudo iam dentium praeterquam ex India reperitur, cetera in nostro orbe cessere luxuriate"* [Recently even bones have begun to be cut into veneers on account of the scarcity of ivory, inasmuch as an ample supply of tusks is now rarely obtained except from India, all the rest in our world having succumbed to luxury]; translation adapted from H. Rackham, 1940. For bone carving, which began at a much earlier date, see Lapatin 2001 (with references); St. Clair 2003; W. Stern and Thimme 2007. Bone and antler were also found among the ivory scraps excavated at Pheidias's workshop at Olympia; see Schiering 1991.
44 See Cutler 1985, 23.
45 Themistius 212.16–17 (ed. G. Downey, 1965). According to Isidore of Seville (quoted by Scullard 1974, 31), Mauretania Tingitana "was once full of elephants; now only India produces them."
46 Barnett 1982, 68–69; Cutler 1985, 22–24; St. Clair and McLachlan 1989, 2–3.
47 See, e.g., Lucian, *Quomodo historia conscribenda sit* 50; Philostratos, *Vita Apollonii* 5.20.9. Other comments of Lucian and Pausanias with regard to the production of monumental gold and ivory statues are discussed at length in Lapatin 1997, 2001.
48 Although cementum, like tree bark, was usually removed from elephant tusks prior to carving, it might, on occasion, have been left in place as its removal served to decrease the total size available to the craftsman. For the natural outer surface on the edges of some Byzantine ivories of the ninth to eleventh centuries AD, see Cutler 1985, 3–5.
49 Pausanias 8.46.1–5.
50 See Lapatin 2001, nos. 33.4, 44, 45.2, figs. 126–27, 227–30, 236–37.
51 Athens, National Museum, 777 and 779, with separately carved ears: Richter 1968a, figs. 20 and 22; Athens, National Museum, 778, with pinned arms (ibid., fig. 21). See also Carter 1985, 2, 40n5. The pieced ear of a face in Corfu (Lapatin 2001, no. 31) shows evidence of repair.
52 Pausanias 1.42.4; 7.26.4.
53 The position within a tusk whence a finished product has been extracted can sometimes be determined through careful study of ancient survivals, although the dearth of well-preserved figures makes generalizations concerning standard practices risky.
54 For the use of a drill for undercutting, see plate 165; for drilling as a preliminary to chisel work, see the eyebrows of the Delphi "Artemis" before its restoration: Lapatin 2001, no. 33.2, fig. 116; these holes may well be the remains of "honeycombing," a technique common in later stone sculpture, which is also present in the grooved brows of a small eighth-century chryselephantine head from the Northwest Palace at Kalhu.
55 Aelian, *De natura animalium* 17.32; *NH* 7.198.
56 Philostratos (*Imagines* 2.1) refers to an ivory statue of Aphrodite "constructed of closely joined ivory."
57 See, e.g., Lapatin 2001, nos. 4, 10, 33, 44, 45, figs. 6, 35–37, 114, 126–28, 227–30, 232–37. For such strategically located armbands and bracelets, see also Leipen 1971, 30.
58 See, e.g., Lapatin 2001, nos. 29, 33.10–11, figs. 107, 135–36. Compare no. 10, figs. 35–37, 39, where the front half of the feet were carved separately and attached to the legs, apparently for reasons of economy, like the forward-extended arms of Archaic marble *korai*.
59 See Connor 1998, though reviewers of this work have suggested, often vehemently, that some of the examples presented might have been re- or over-painted at a later date.
60 Pausanias 7.26.4.
61 See Plantzos 1996b; Lapatin 2001, nos. 22(E2) and 45.1.
62 For red, see Connor 1998, 28–29 (where the distinct processes of creating cinnabar and vermilion are outlined). Connor 1998, 23–65, also provides a detailed analysis of the pigments applied to Late Antique and Middle Byzantine ivories, and a survey "Ancient Tradition of Polychrome Ivories" employing ancient and medieval *testimonia*.
63 Lapatin 2001, no. 33.11, fig. 135.
64 Lapatin 2001, nos. 14, 33.6–7, figs. 47, 130–32.
65 Amandry 1939, 99–100, 115; Amandry 1991, 208–9.
66 According to Oddy 1985, 65n4, foil and leaf are both produced by hammering, but while foil can be handled with ease and can support its own weight, leaf is so thin that it folds over and clings to itself or whatever surface it comes into contact with. To prevent its sticking to the hammer or anvil, the medieval craftsman hammered gold leaf between sheets of parchment: Theophilus, *Schedula diversarum artium* 1.23; ancient craftsmen must have taken some similar precaution.
67 Dodwell 1961; Lucas and Harris 1962, 231–32. Connor 1998, 14, suggests that oil or resin might also have been used in Late Antiquity and the Middle Byzantine period. Vegetal gums may also have been used.
68 For gilt-gesso in Egypt, see Lucas and Harris 1962, 231–32; Penny 1993, 125, fig. 113.

69 See Lapatin 2001.
70 In general, see Jashemski 1979; Meiggs 1982; M. Carroll 2003; Bowe 2004.
71 Richter 1966; Vaulina and Wasowicz 1974; Hampe and Simon 1981; Kyrieleis 1981; Meiggs 1982, 323; Mols 1999; Lapatin 2001, 43; De Carolis 2007; Wallace-Hadrill 2011; Guidobaldi and Esposito 2012, esp. 163–69; Roberts 2013.
72 Romano 1980, 351–64; Meiggs 1982, 300–24; Donohue 1988.
73 Romano 1980, 42–57, 359–60; Meiggs 1982, 309; Donohue 1988; Ridgway 1992.
74 Athenaios, *Deipnosophistai* 3.78c; Romano 1980, 360.
75 Theokritos, *Epigram* 4 = *Anthologia Palatina* 9.437; see Donohue 1988, 44, 452–53, no. 364.
76 Pausanias 3.14.7; compare Aristotle, *Historia animalium* 627a7; Dioscorides, *Materia medica* 1.103.1–2.
77 Pausanias 5.13.7.
78 Athenaios, *Deipnosophistai* 15.675f–76c.
79 See also Pausanias 6.24.7; Artemidoros, *Oneirokritika*, 1.77; Vergil, *Eclogues* 8.61–63; Keuls 1993, 30, LSJ, 1155, s.v. *myrsinos*, no. 3.
80 Meiggs 1982, 279–94.
81 For much of what follows in still greater detail, see Meiggs 1982, 287–92; Lapatin 2001, 70–71; Barbera et al. 2010.
82 *NH* 13.96–97.
83 *CIL* 6.9528; Barnett 1982, 70–72.
84 Dio Cassius 61.10.3; Seneca, *De vita beata* 17.2.
85 Prichett 1953, 244 (I.231); Prichett 1956, 231–32.
86 *NH* 33.146.
87 *NH* 9.39; 33.144.
88 Vergil, *Georgics* 2.463; Ovid, *Metamorphoses* 2.737; *NH* 33.146; Juvenal 6.80, 11.94–95.
89 *NH* 16.233.
90 Mastrocinque 1991; Grimaldi 1996; Calvi 2005; Gagetti 2007, 2009; Nava and Salerno 2007; D'Ercole 2008; Sena Chiesa and Gagetti 2009; Causey 2011.
91 On Thales and the "magnetic" powers of amber, see Diogenes Laertius 1.24. See also Theophrastos, *History of Plants* 9.18.2; *NH* 37.48.
92 E.g., Ovid, *Metamorphoses* 15.413–15; Sophokles, frag. 830a. For these and other theories and their rejection, see *NH* 37.34–41.
93 *NH* 37.30–52.
94 Tacitus, *Germania* 45.
95 *NH* 37.44, 50–51.
96 Calvi 2005, 18–22.
97 See esp. Calvi 2005, 44–48; Gagetti 2007, 2009.
98 Pausanias 5.12.7.
99 *NH* 37.51.
100 Moorey 1994, 92–93; Athenaios, *Deipnosophistai* 3.93b; Ammianus Marcellinus 23.6.84; *NH* 9.106, 6.81, 6.110; Arrian, *Indika* 8.10–13; Theophrastos, *De lapidibus* 36; *Periplus maris Erythraei* 61. Pliny (*NH* 9.115) reports that the Thracian Bosphorus and Mauretania were additional sources.
101 *NH* 9.106–15.
102 Seneca, *De beneficiis* 7.9.
103 *NH* 37.17; Suetonius, *Gaius* 52.
104 *NH* 37.14–16.
105 *NH* 9.116; Suetonius, *Julius* 47; see also Tacitus, *Agrigola* 12; Aelian, *De natura animalium* 1.6; Ammianus Marcellinus 23.6.88; Tertulian, *De cultu feminarum* 1.6; Ausonius, *Mosella* 68.
106 *NH* 9.58.
107 Suetonius, *Vitellius* 7.
108 *NH* 9.119–21.
109 Calabi Limentani 1961; Granino Cecere 2012. For a marble portrait identified as the *margaritarius* Marcus Publius Ilarus, see Lipinsky 1975a, 314–15.
110 Caley 2008, 50–52, 53, 55, 62, 85–86; and especially Nassau and Hanson 1985. For the coating of small pearls with broken pearls to create larger pearls, see Tzetzes, *Chiliades* 11.493–95.
111 Ovid, *Metamorphoses* 4.740–52; translation by A. S. Kline, 2000. Compare *Metamophoses* 15.416–17: "coral, also, hardens the first time air touches it: it was a soft plant under the waves."
112 *NH* 37.164. See also Macrì 2009.
113 Theophrastos, *De lapidibus* 38; Dioscorides, *Materia medica* 5.139; *NH* 32.21–24 (compare Isidorus, *Origines* 16.8.1).
114 *Periplus of the Erythrean Sea* 28, 39, 49, 56.
115 *NH* 32.21–24. Several surviving Iron Age artifacts support this assertion; see, e.g., Stead and Rigby 1999, 58–59 (nos. 9–10), 94, 133.
116 *NH* 32.11.
117 *NH* 32.21–24, 37.164.
118 E.g., Pekridou-Gorecki 1989; Barber 1991, 1992; Vickers 1999a; Harlow and Nosch 2014.
119 See Dickens 1906–7, 392–95; Wace 1934; Richter 1965, 369–72; Stewart 1990, 94–96; Barber 1992; Vickers 1999a; Brøns 2014.
120 Vase: Chiusi, Museo Archeologico Nazionale, 1831; *Iliad* 3.125–27; see also previous notes.
121 Knigge 1991, 107–11; Margariti et al. 2013; Brøns 2014, 58–59.
122 Martial 8.68.7.
123 Seneca, *De beneficiis* 7.9.5.
124 Tacitus, *Annals* 2.33. See also Horace, *Satires* 1.2.101–5; *NH* 21.26; other sources collected by Richter 1929; Raschke 1978, esp. 622–37; Dalby 2000, 200.
125 See, e.g., Bruneau 1969; Reinhold 1970; Pekridou-Gorecki 1989; Vickers 1999a; Alfaro, Wild, and Costa 2004; Cardon 2007, 553–86; Margariti et al. 2013. Brøns 2014, 63–65, 167–170. See also *NH* 9.129–35.
126 *Iliad* 22.440–42.
127 Euripides, *Ion* 1141–66; slightly adapted from the translation by George Theodoridis, 2006. For literary and historical analyses, see, e.g., Goff 1988; Vickers 1999a, 15–19.
128 *Argonautika* 1722–67.
129 Mansfield 1985; Barber 1992; Vickers 1999a, 29–30.
130 Philostratos, *Vita Apollonii* 1.25; see Vickers 1999a, 19.
131 Plutarch, *Alkibiades* 16.1; *Moralia* 470f.
132 *NH* 35.62.
133 *IG* 2.754.8–9; *IG* 2^2.1529.14; Vickers 1999, 20; Cleland 2005, 40, 146, lines 318–19.
134 Minns 1913, 336, 212, fig. 113; Barber 1991, 206; Vickers 1999a, 20–21. See also Brøns 2014, 74–76.
135 Demosthenes 21.16, 22.
136 Plutarch, *Demetrios* 41.4; Douris *apud* Athenaios, *Deipnosophistai* 15.535ff.
137 *NH* 7.196, 19.57.
138 Diodoros 17.79.70.
139 For Agrippina: Tacitus, *Annales* 12.56; *NH* 33.63; for Nero: Suetonius, *Nero* 6.50; for Commodus: Scriptores Historiae Augustae, *Pertinax* 8.2–4.
140 Aelius Lampridicus, *Life of Antoninus Heliogabalus* (cited by Gleba 2008, 62).
141 Scriptores Historiae Augustae, *Marcus Aurelius* 17.4.
142 *NH* 33.62–63. See also Richter 1966, 118; Gleba 2008, 62.
143 Andronicos 1984, 191–95; Drogou 1987; Flury-Lemberg 1988, 234–37, 483, no. 51 ; Gleba 2008, 65; Kottaridi 2011, 96–97. For other examples of gold-threaded cloth, see, e.g., Vickers 1999a, 20–22; Gleba 2008.
144 Gleba 2008, 63–68, 70–73.
145 Gleba 2008, 63.
146 Chares and Kallixeinos *apud* Athenaios, *Deipnosophistai* 12.538d, 5.196e. For more examples, see Vickers 1999a, 28.
147 Arensberg 1977; Flury-Lemberg 1988, 384, 482, no. 47; Rutschowscaya 1990, 86–87. Compare Flury-Lemberg 1988, 364–83, nos. 93–94; Rutschowscaya 1990, 83–85.
148 Athenaios, *Deipnosophistai* 5.198c: D. Shepherd 1976, 8–9; see also Arensberg 1977, 8–10.

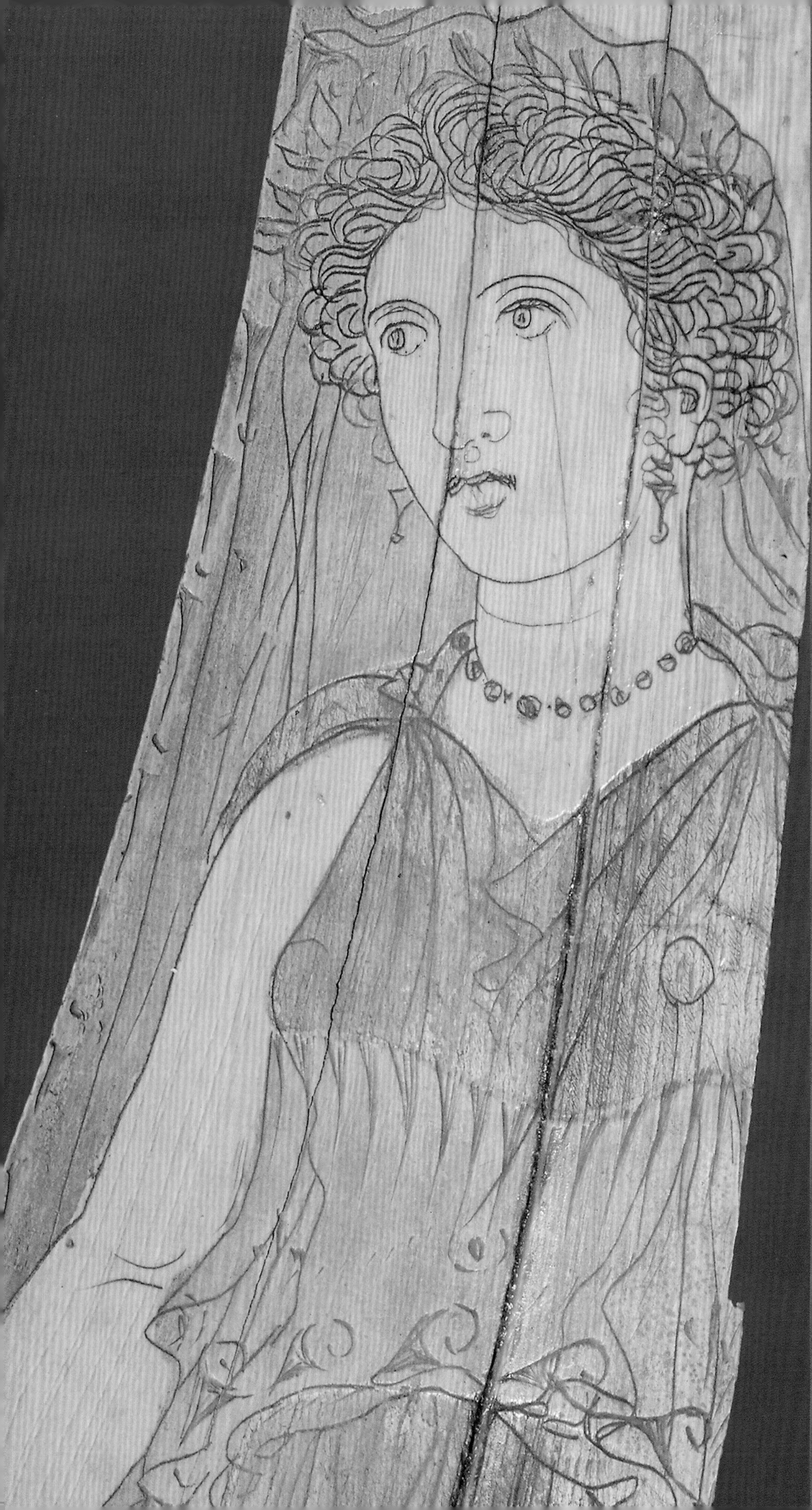

CHAPTER THREE

ORGANIC MATERIALS

PLATES 146–179

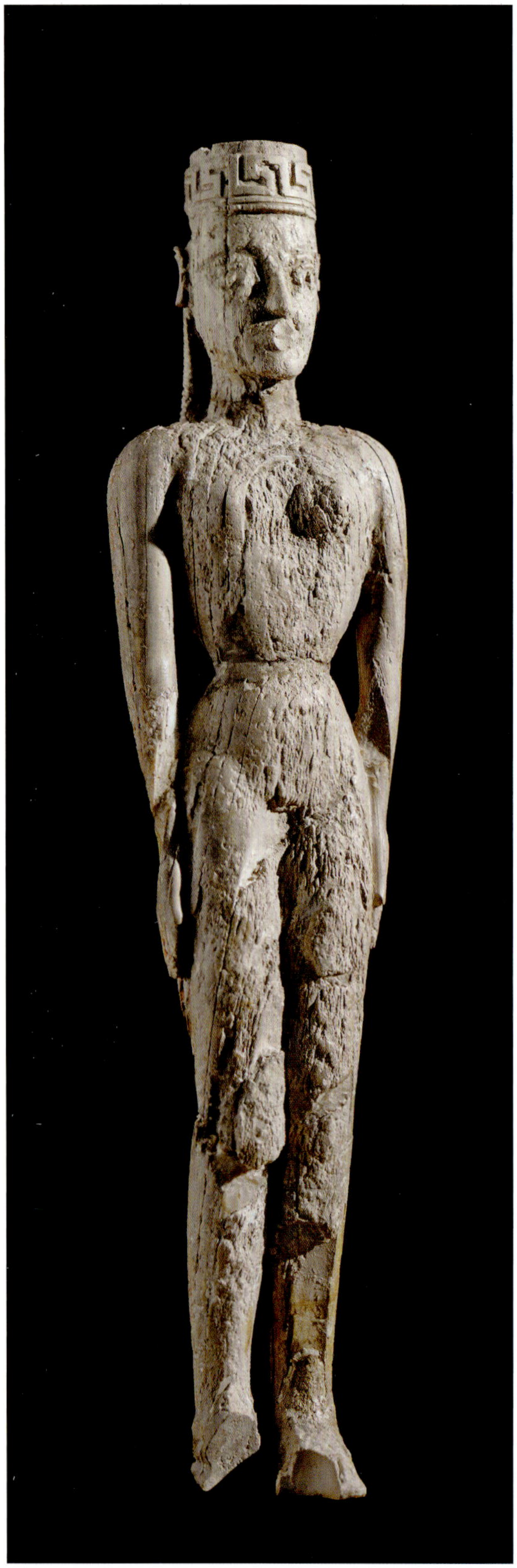

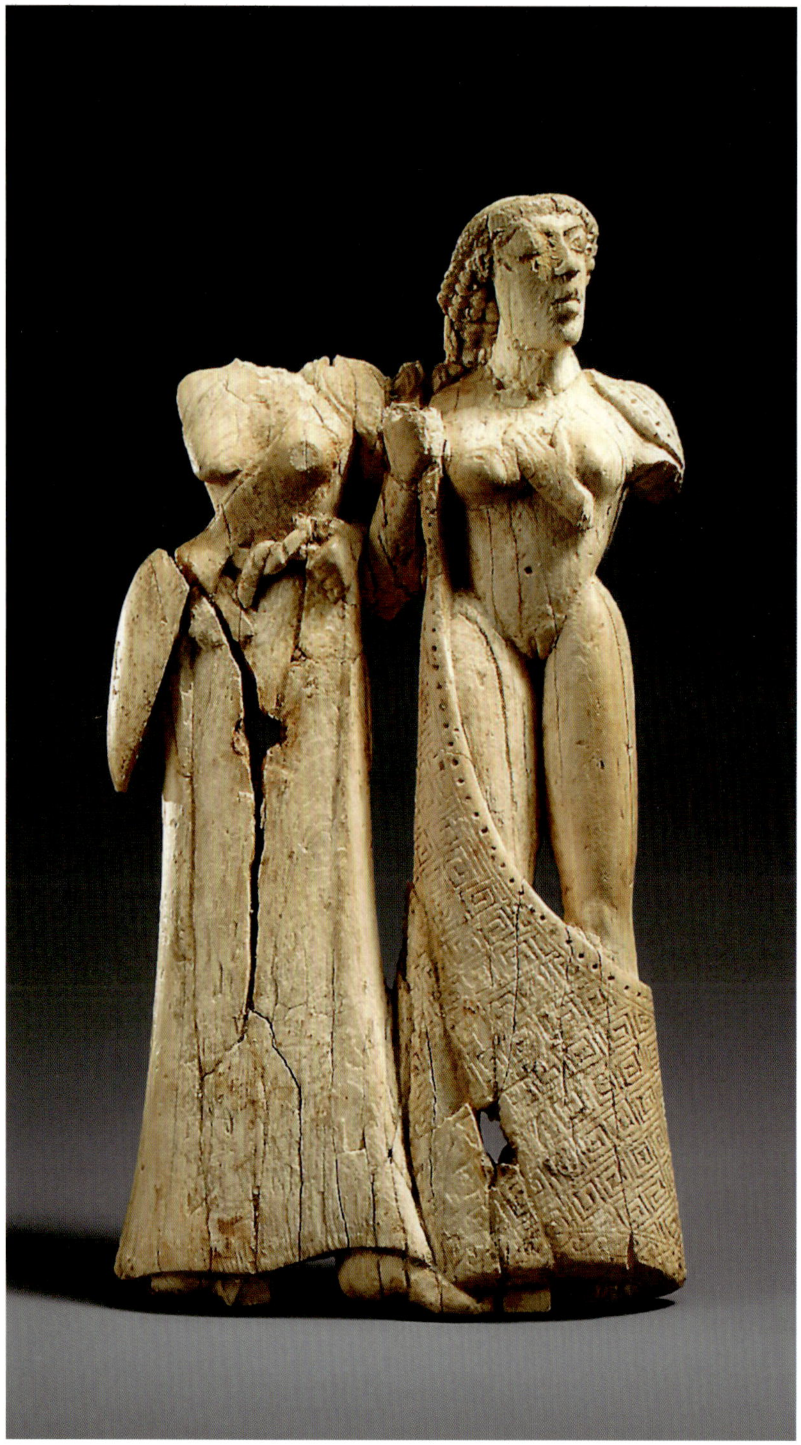

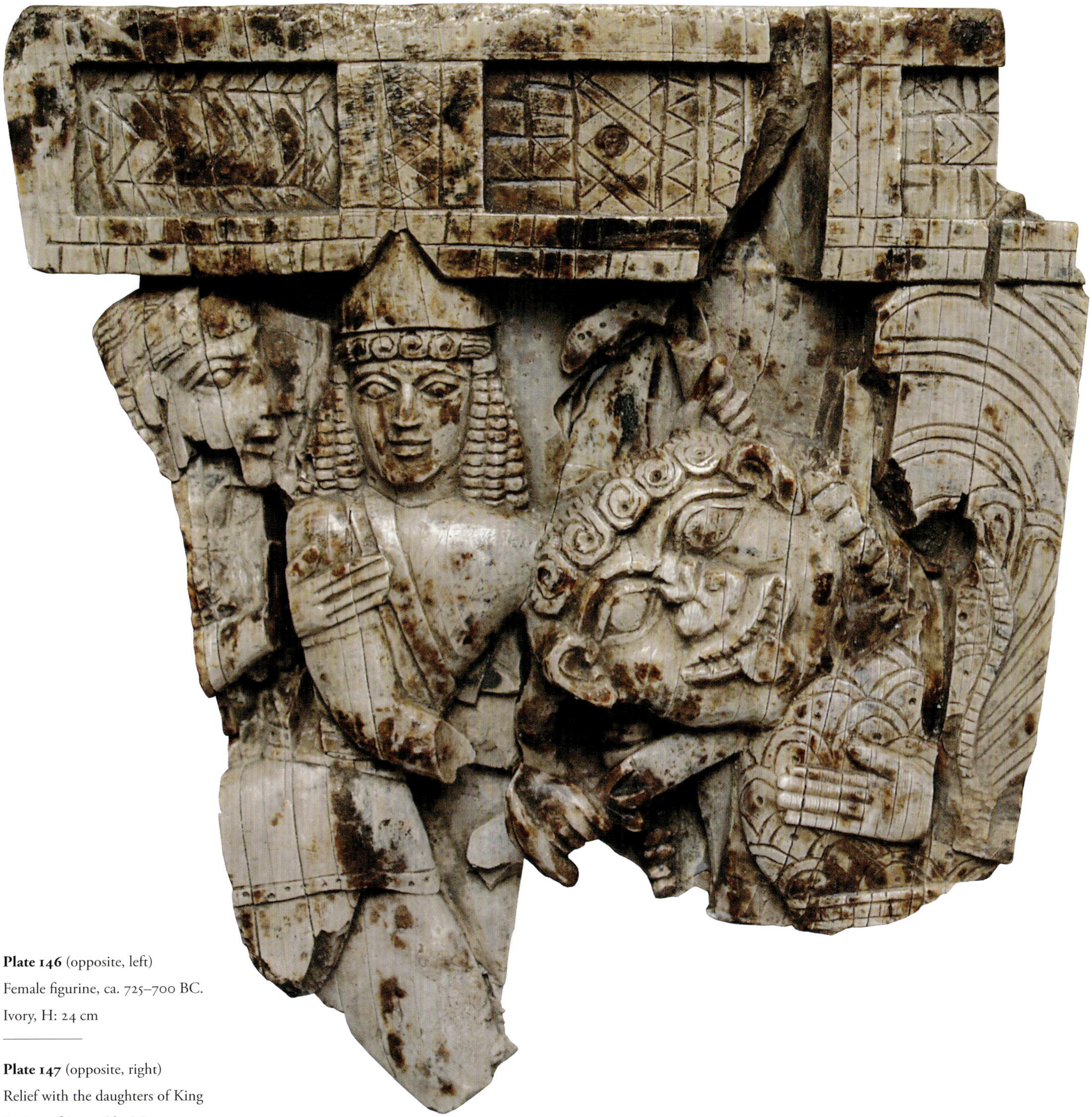

Plate 146 (opposite, left)
Female figurine, ca. 725–700 BC. Ivory, H: 24 cm

Plate 147 (opposite, right)
Relief with the daughters of King Proitos of Argos (the Morgan Ivory), ca. 650–625 BC. Ivory, H: 13.6 cm; W: 7 cm; D: 1.6 cm

Plate 148
Plaque with Perseus beheading the Gorgon, ca. 650–600 BC. Ivory, H: 10.6 cm; W: 10.2 cm; D: 1.1 cm

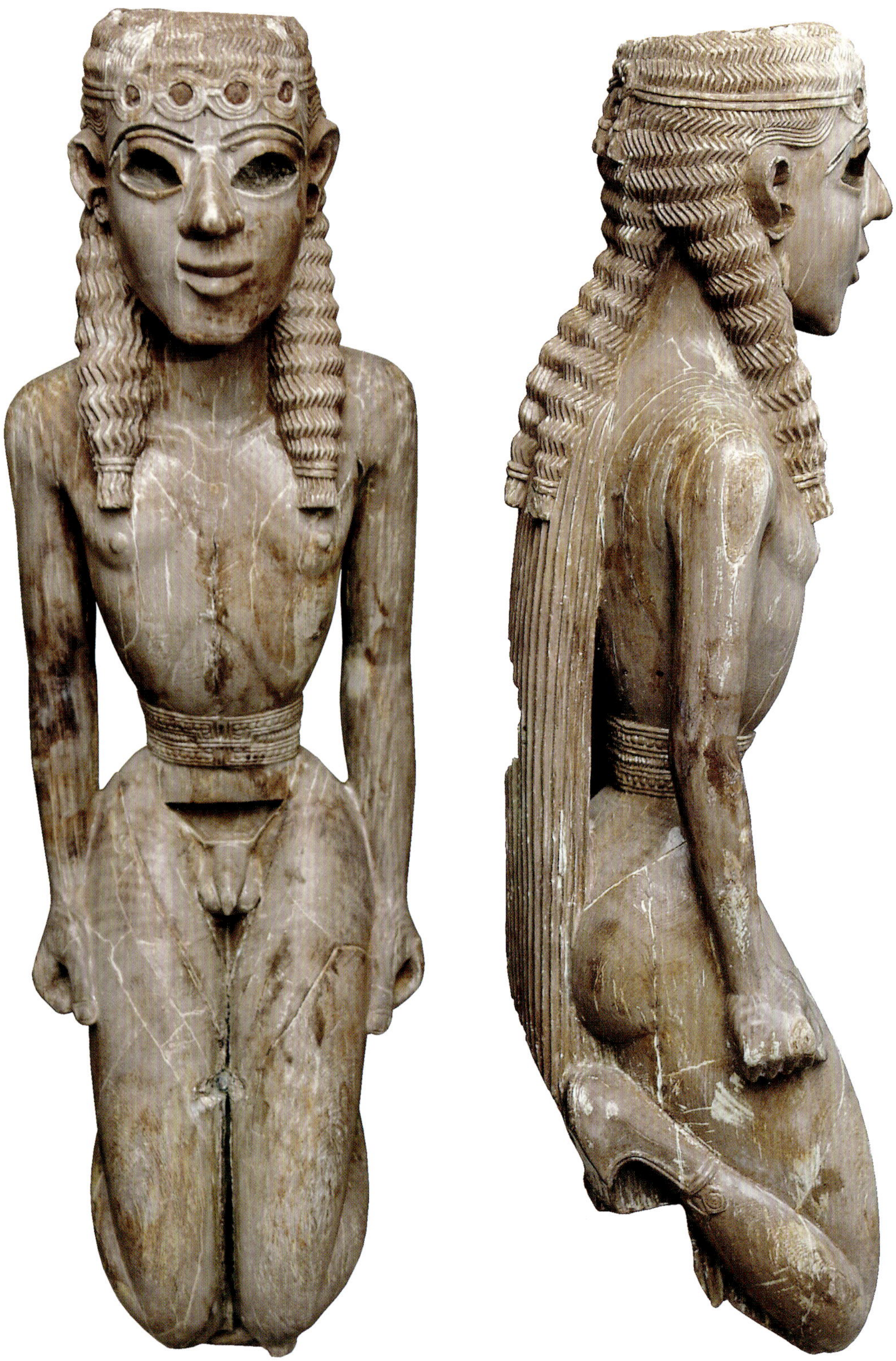

Plate 149

Lyre component in the form of a kneeling youth, ca. 650–625 BC. Ivory, H: 14.5 cm

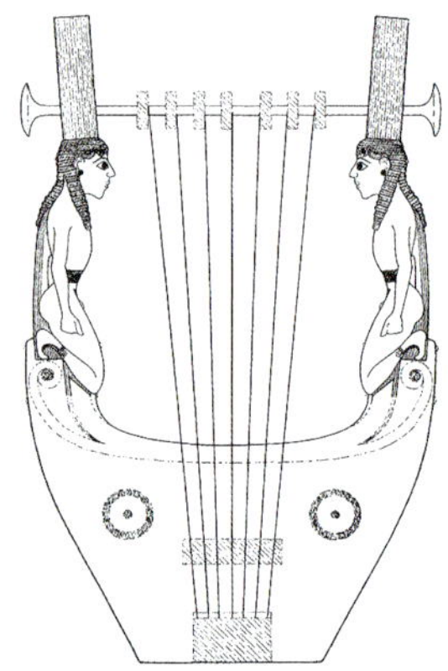

Plate 150
Head, ca. 600–550 BC. Ivory,
H: 1 cm; W: 1.6 cm; D: 1.3 cm

Plate 151
Plaque with the Boreids chasing the Harpies from the table of Phineus, ca. 570 BC. Ivory and gold, H: 7 cm

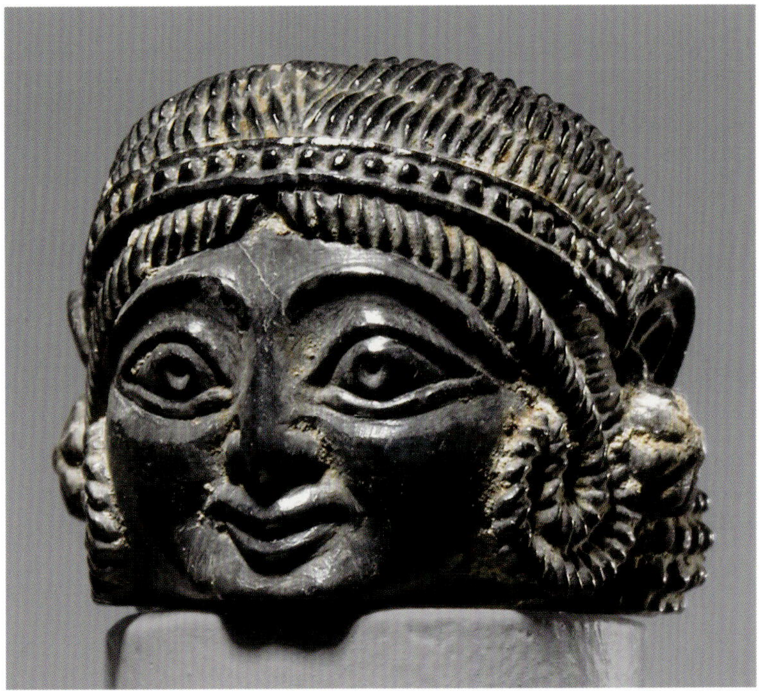

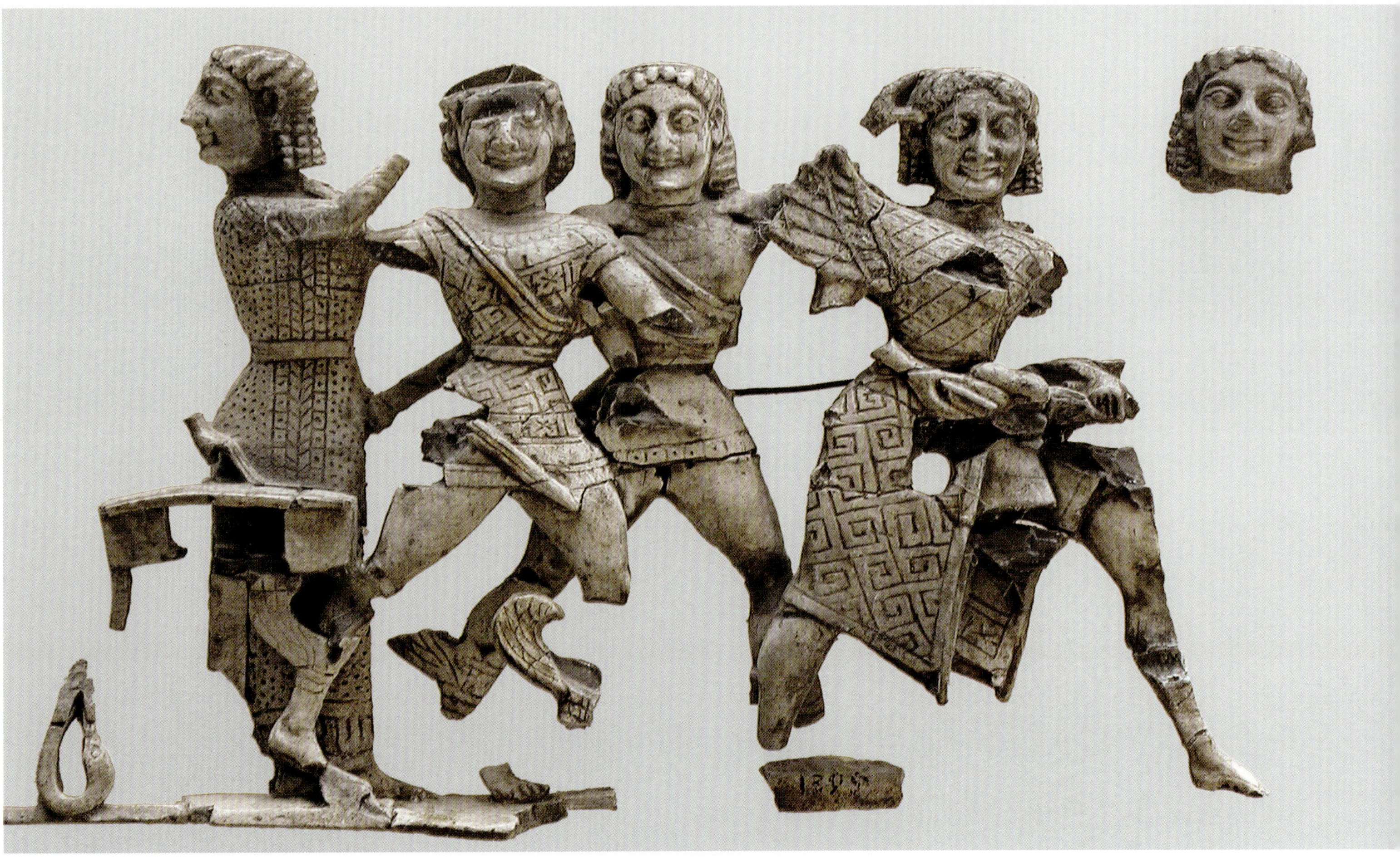

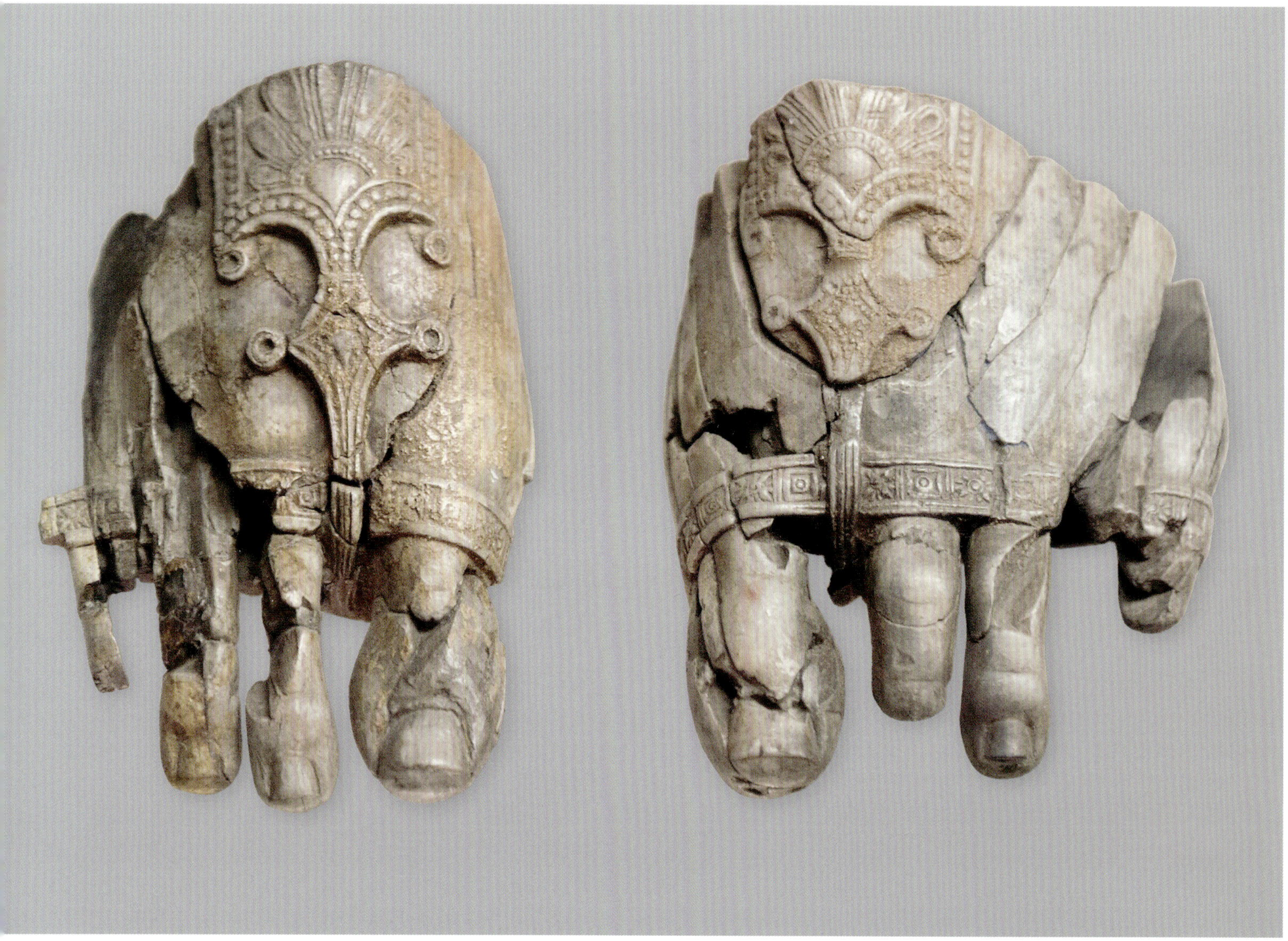

Plate 152

Feet of a composite statue, ca. 550 BC. Ivory and gold, L: ca. 8 cm. See also plate 10.

Plate 153 (opposite)

The Judgment of Paris, ca. 400 BC. Ivory, preserved H: 20.5 cm

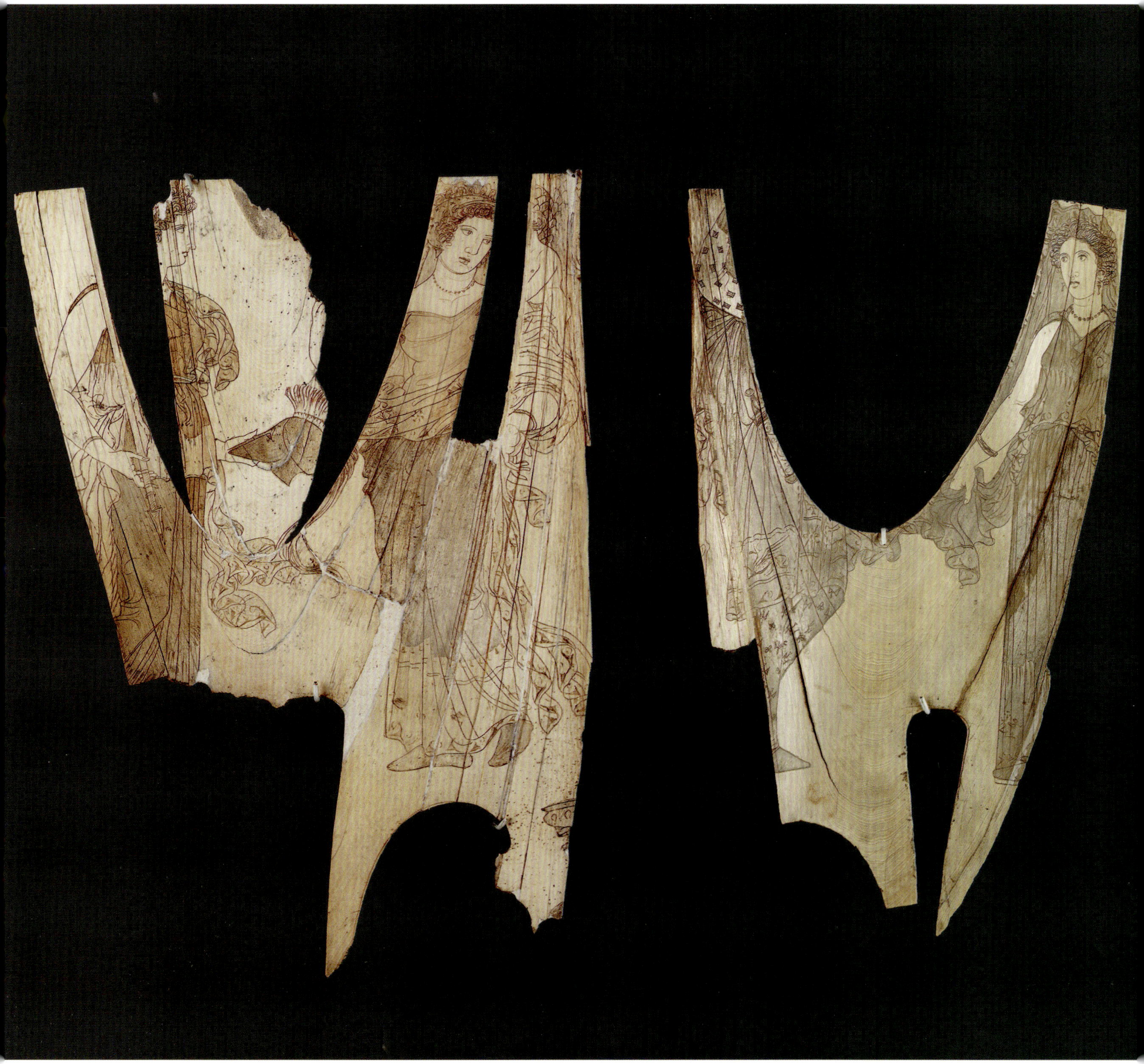

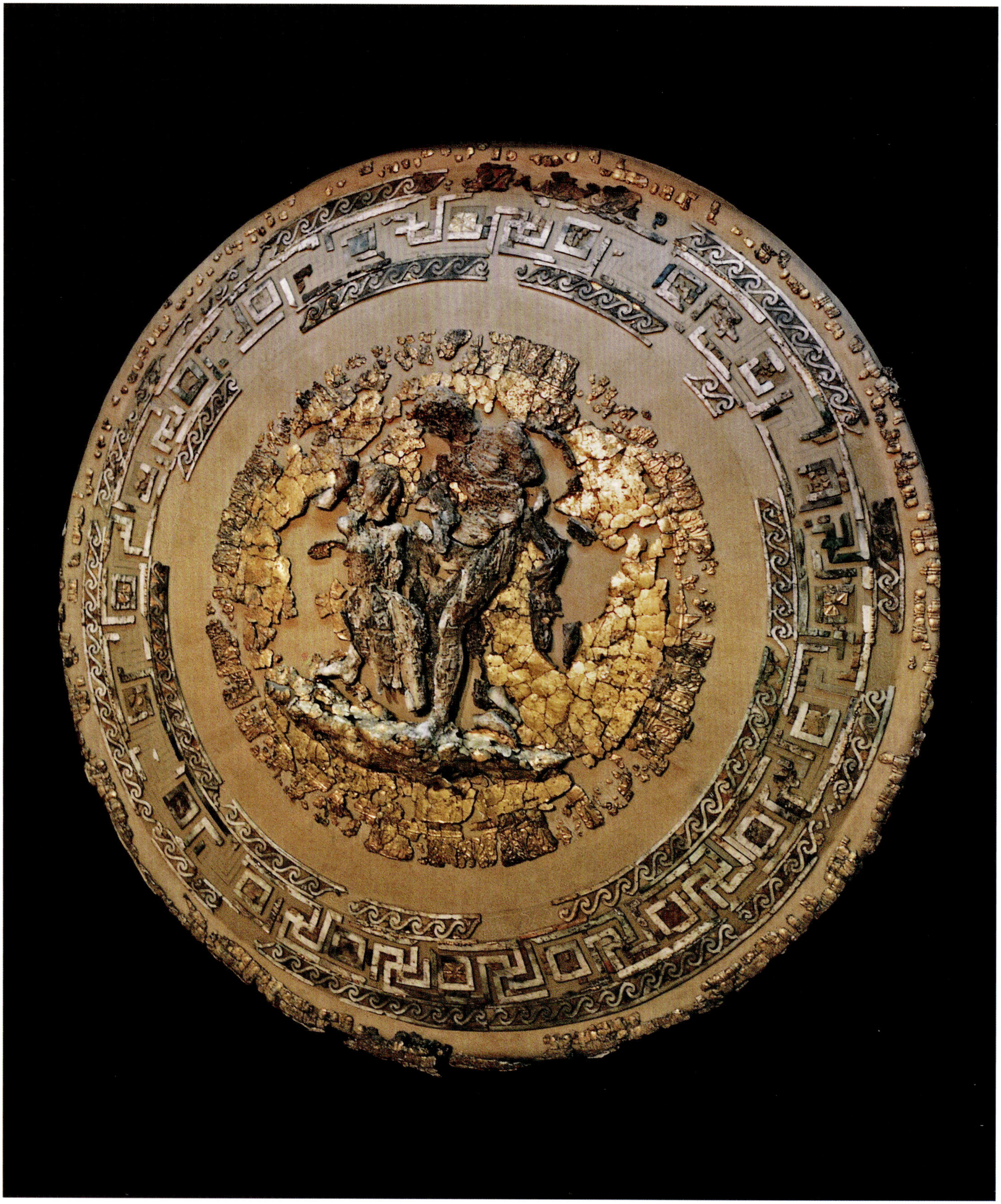

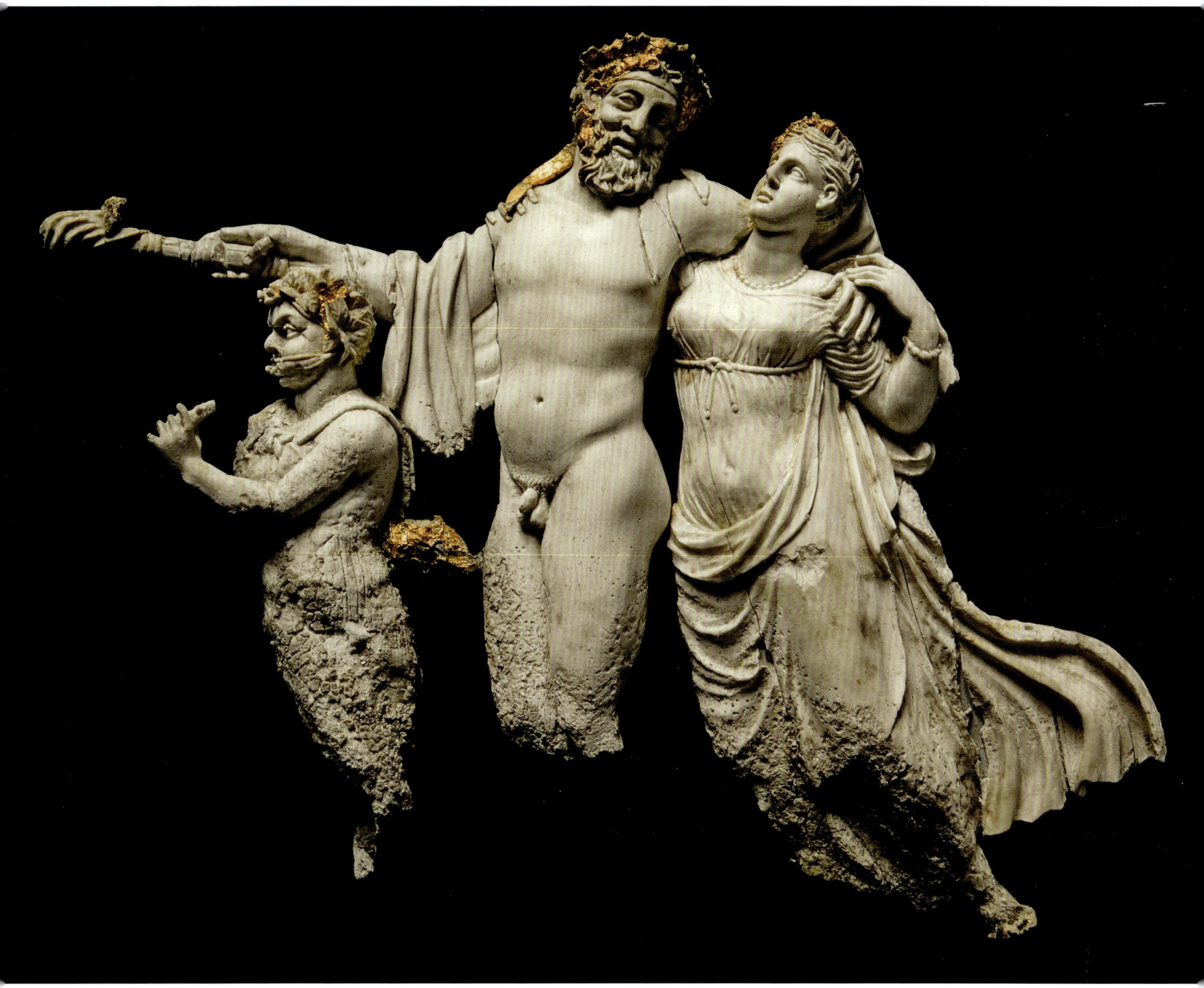

Plate 154 (opposite)
Parade shield with Achilles and Penthesilia, ca. 340–320 BC. Ivory, gold, silver, glass, leather, textile, stucco, and wood, H (of central figures): ca. 35 cm

Plate 155
Appliqué with Dionysos, Ariadne, and a Satyr, ca. 300 BC. Ivory and gold, H: ca. 10 cm

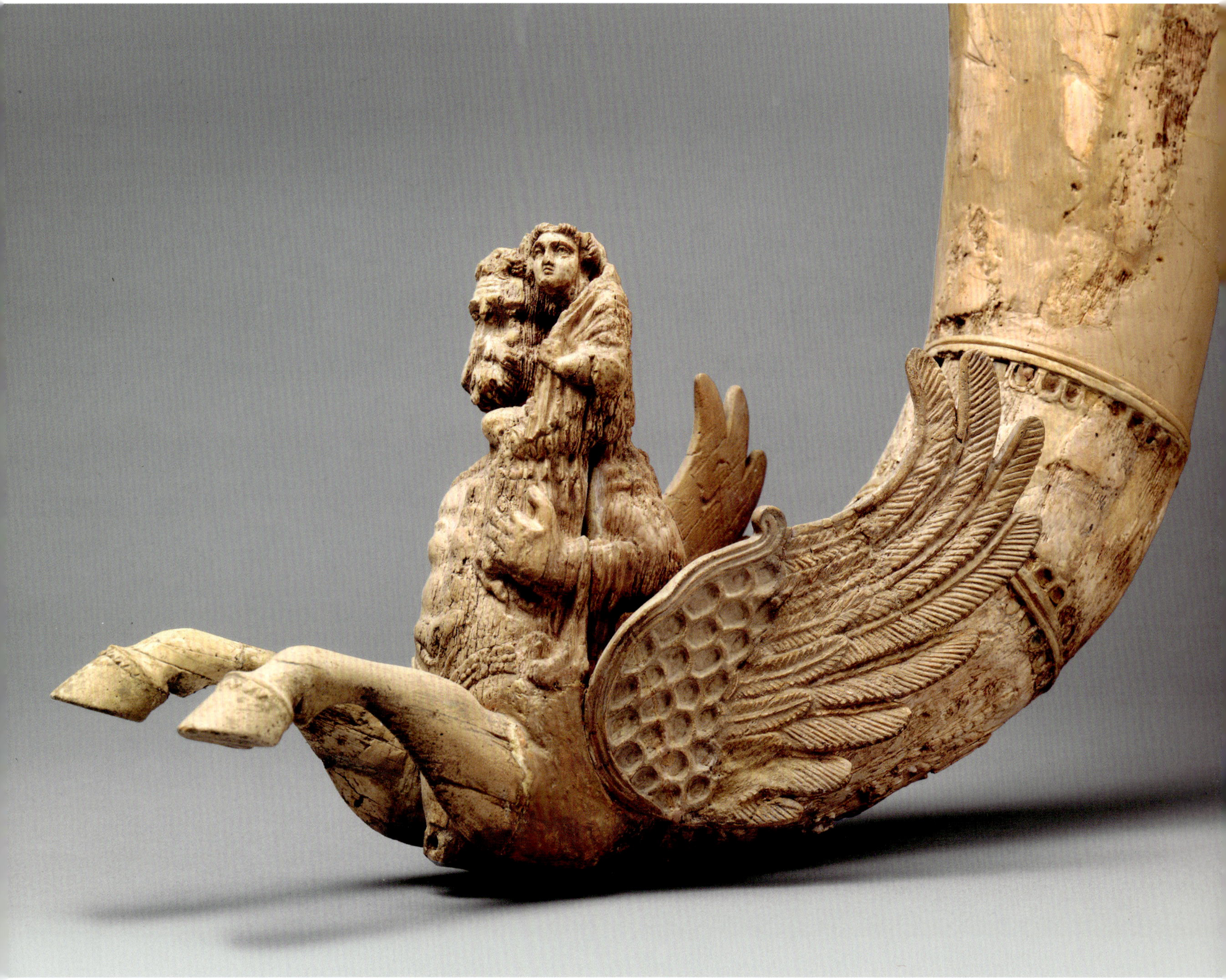

Plate 156
Rhyton with a winged centaur and nymph (detail), ca. 150–1 BC. Ivory, H: 63 cm; (figures) 17 cm

Plate 157 (opposite)
Rhyton with lion-griffin, ca. 150–1 BC. Ivory, H: 43.5 cm; (griffin) 13.5 cm

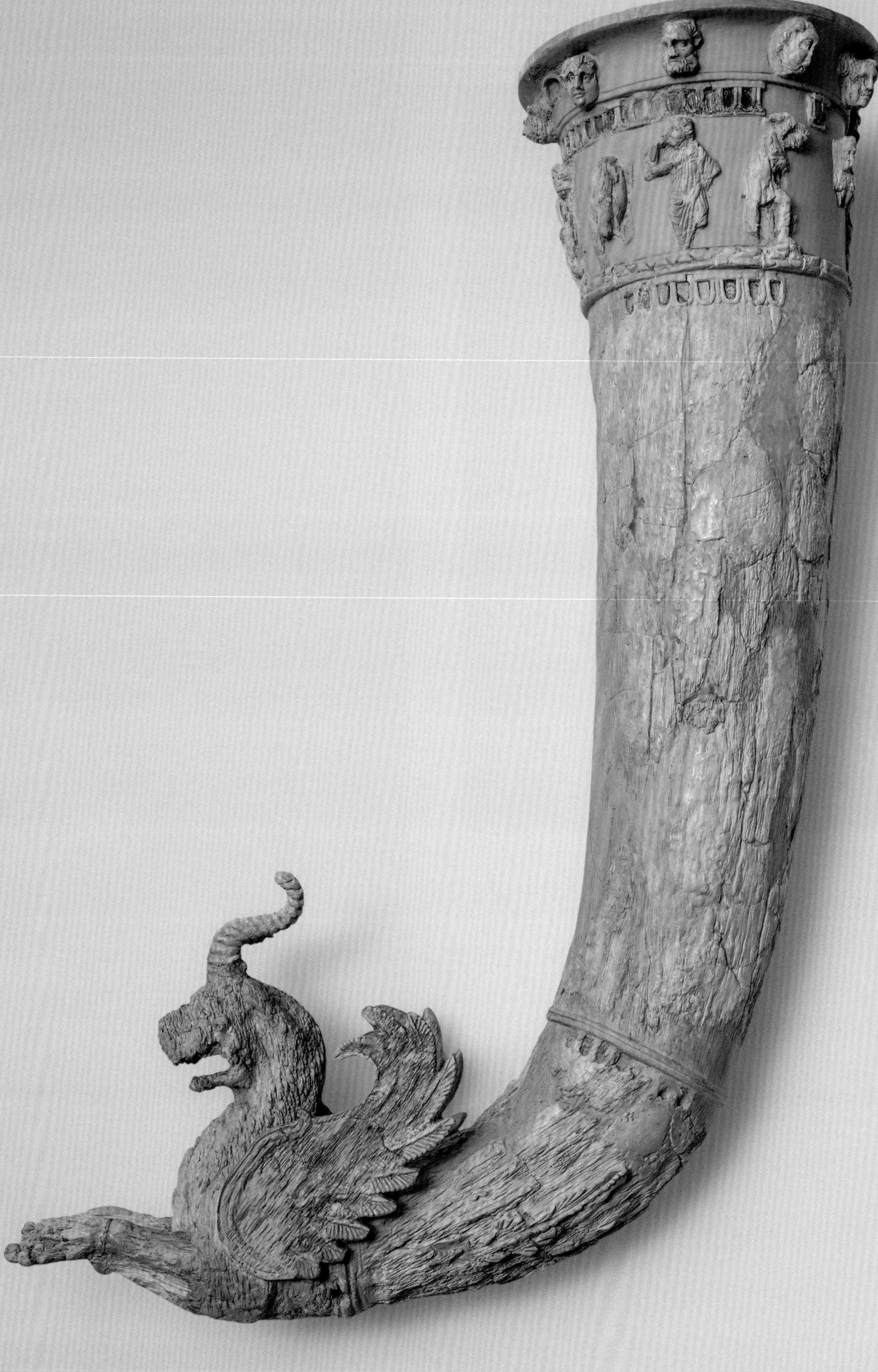

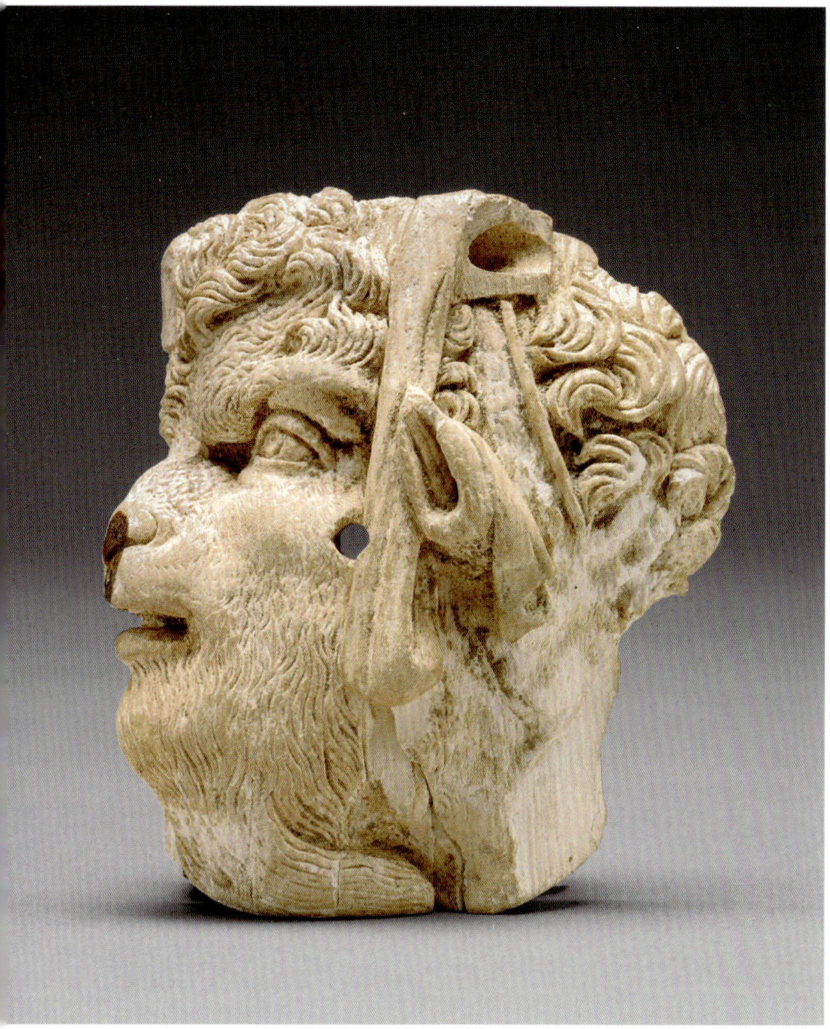

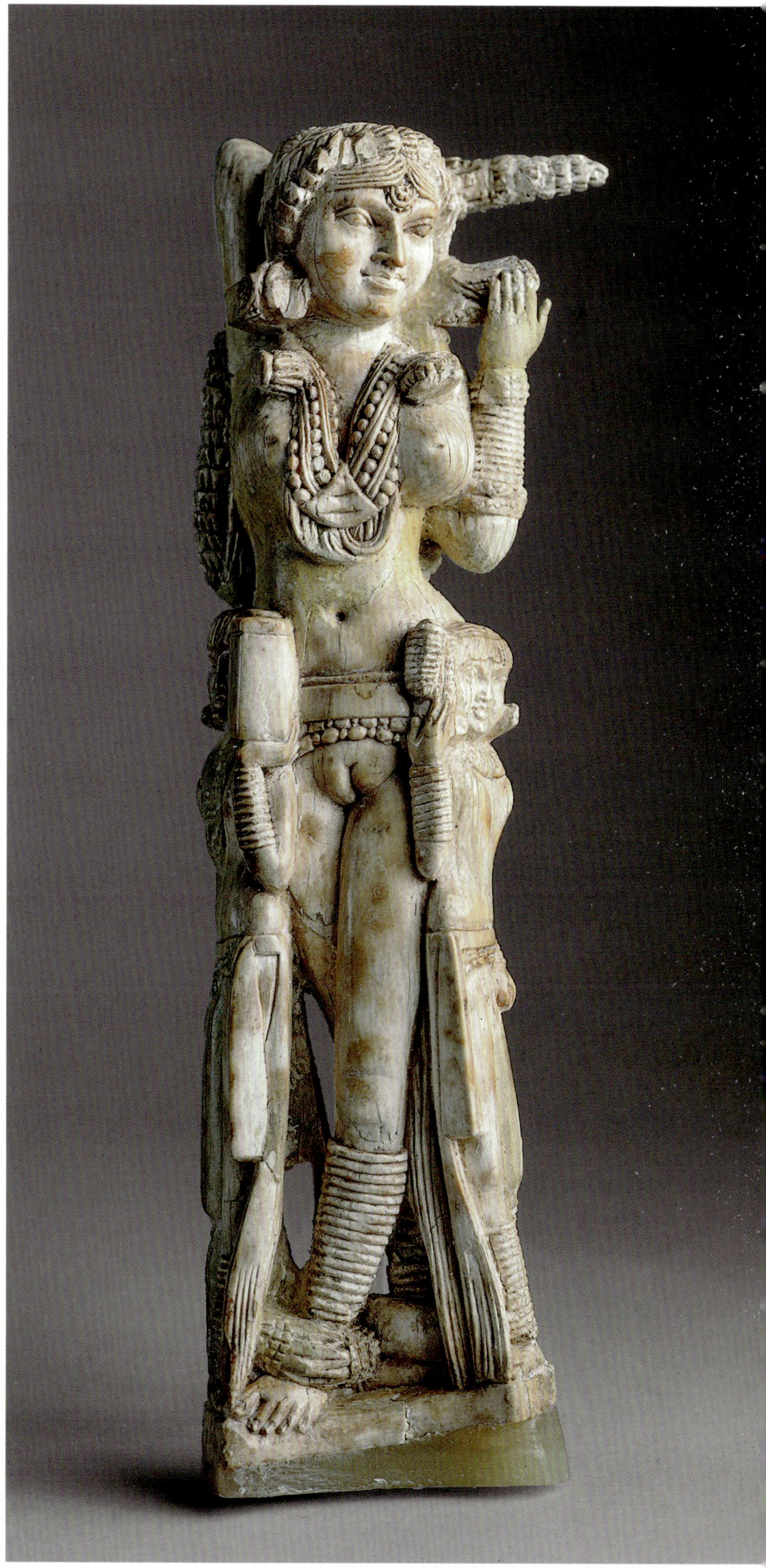

Plate 158
Appliqué with the head of Pan, ca. 100 BC. Ivory, H: 8.6 cm; W: 7.6 cm; D: 2.3 cm

Plate 159
Yakshi, ca. AD 1–79. Ivory, H: 24 cm; W: 5 cm; D: 6 cm

Plate 160 (opposite)
Statuette of Venus Anadyomene, ca. AD 1–79. Ivory, H: 10.5 cm

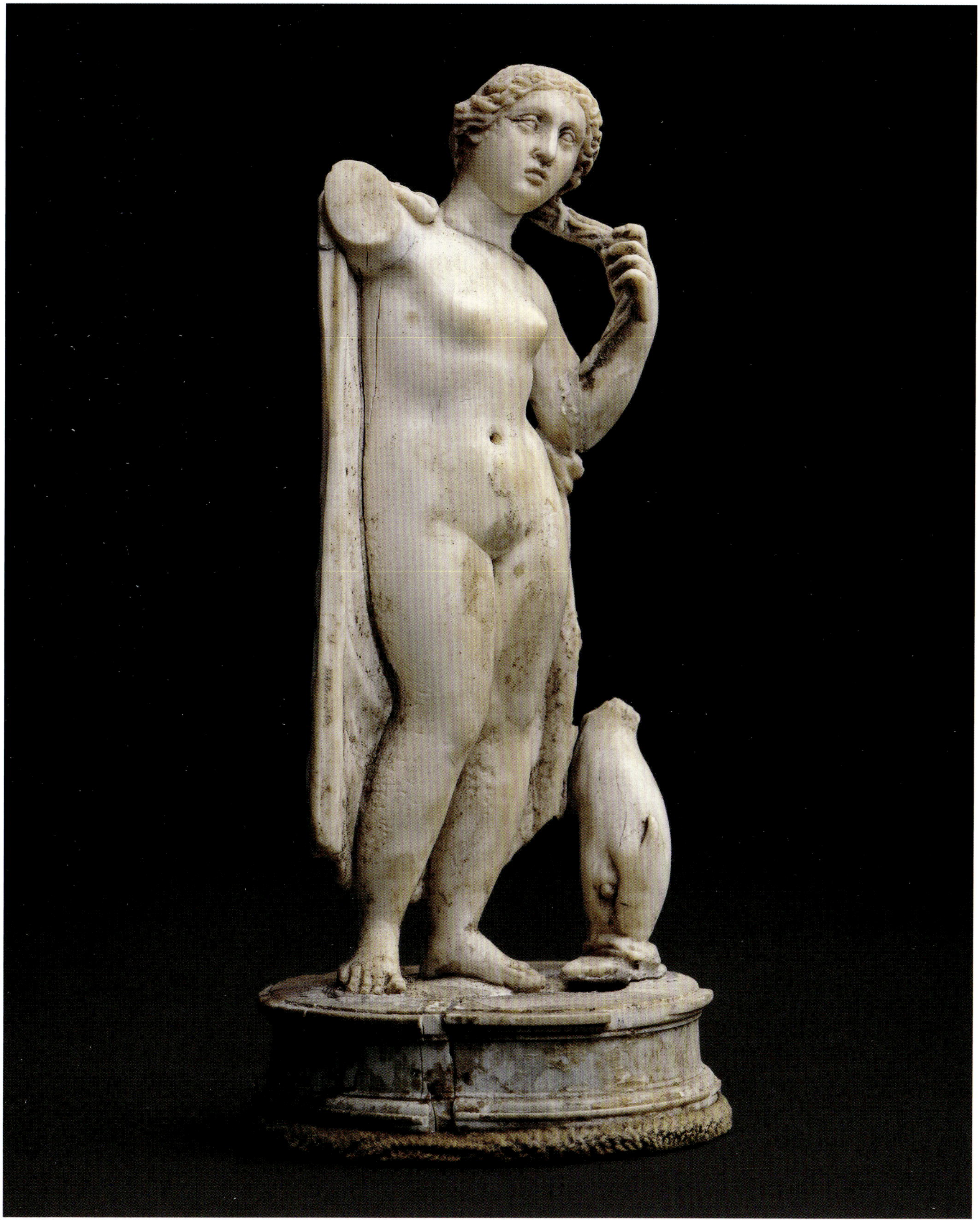

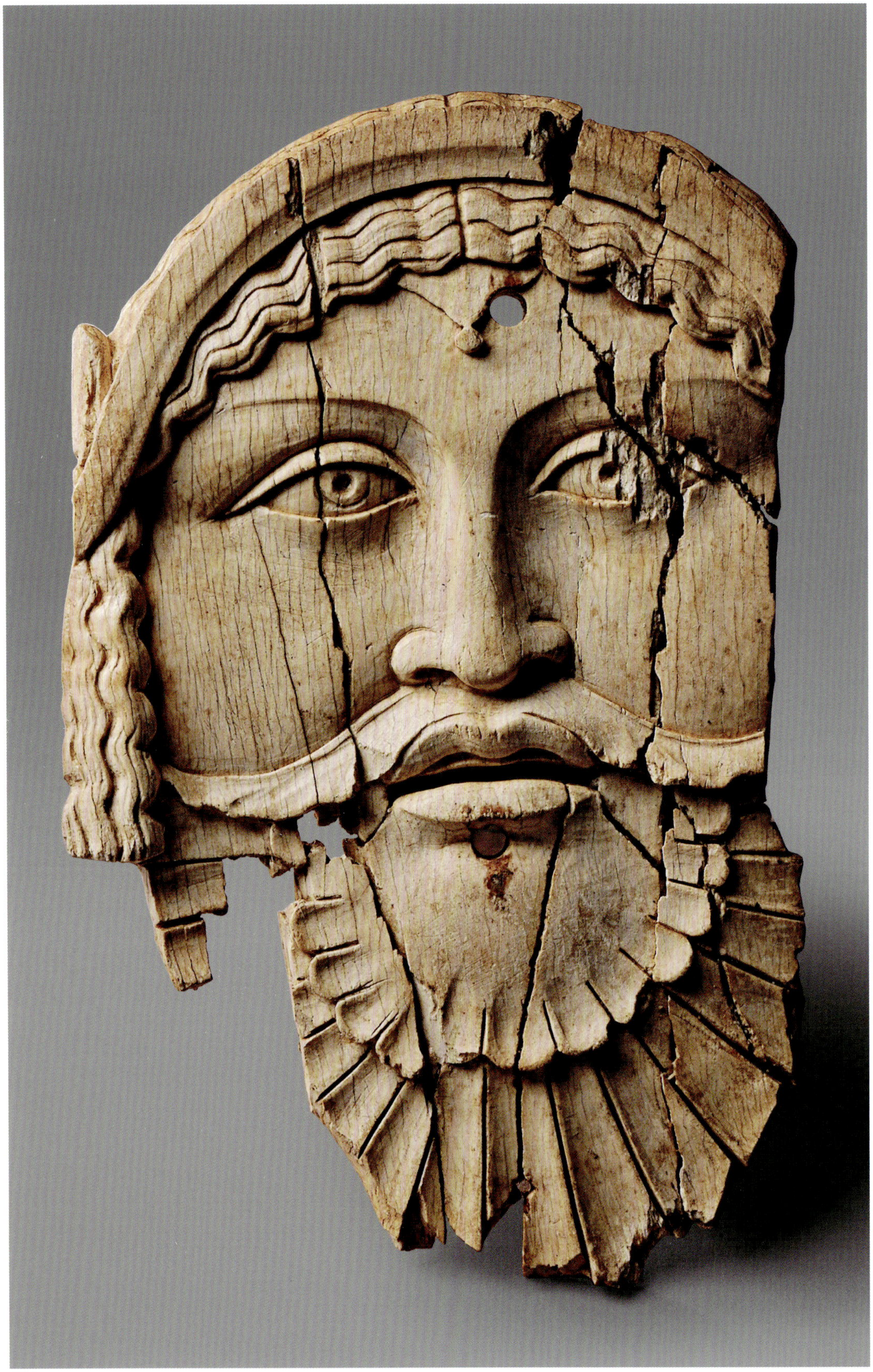

Plate 161
Appliqué of Dionysos,
ca. AD 1–100. Ivory, H: 17 cm

Plate 162 (opposite)
Face of a composite statue,
ca. 100 BC–AD 125. Ivory,
H: 20.2 cm; W: 14.5 cm

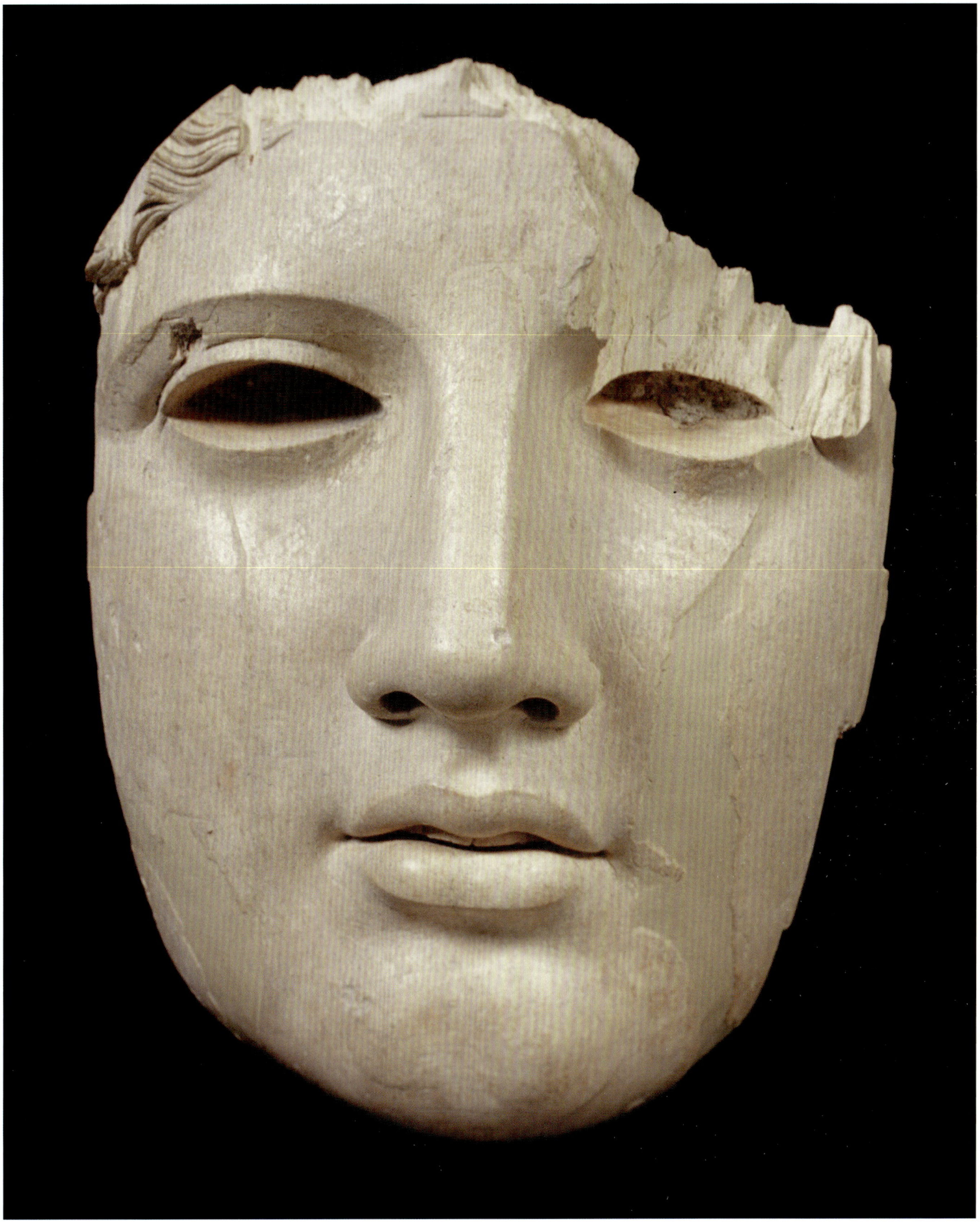

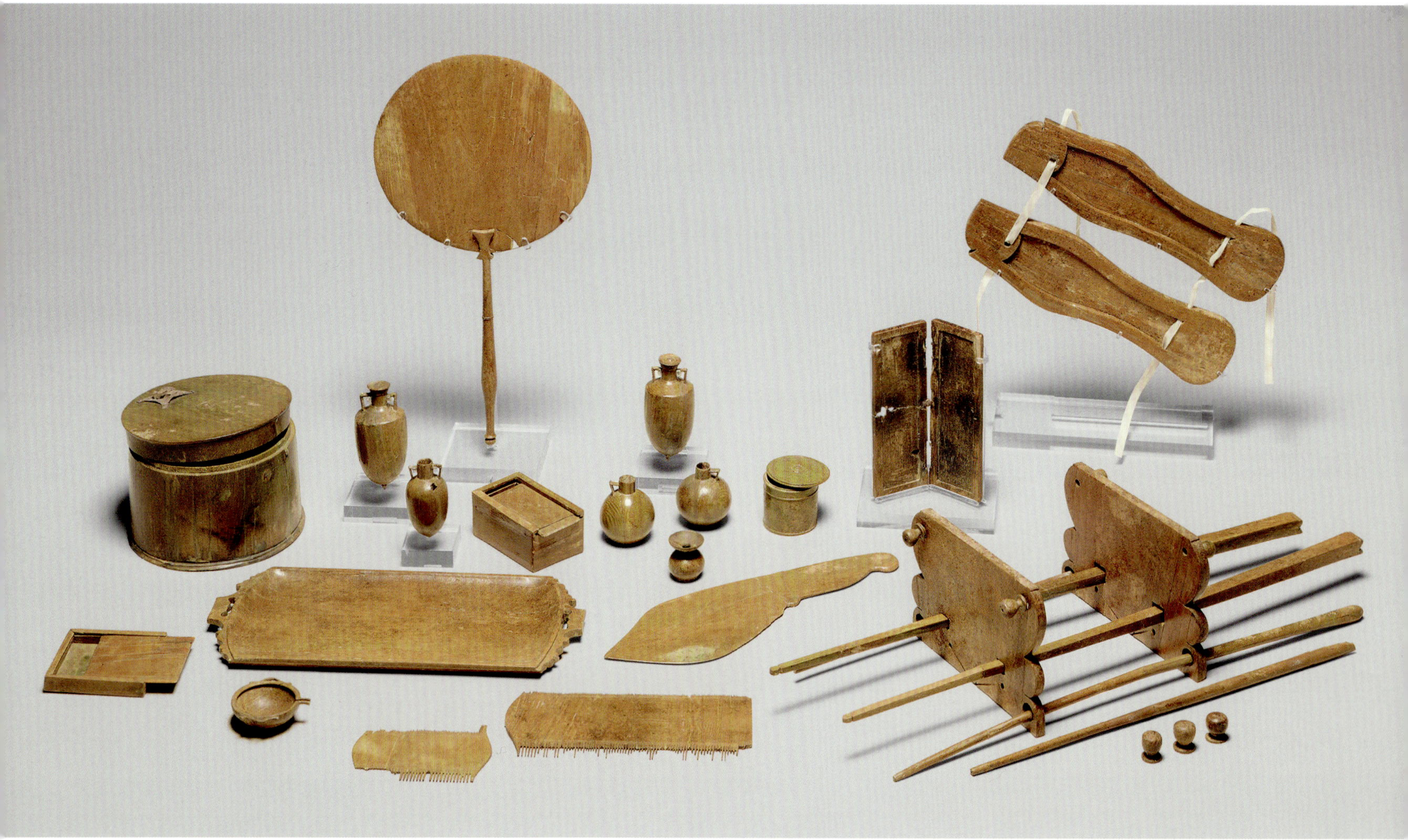

Plate 163

Set of cosmetic and writing implements, ca. AD 1–100(?). Ivory

Plate 164 (opposite)

Fragment of a tripod leg, ca. AD 1–79. Ivory

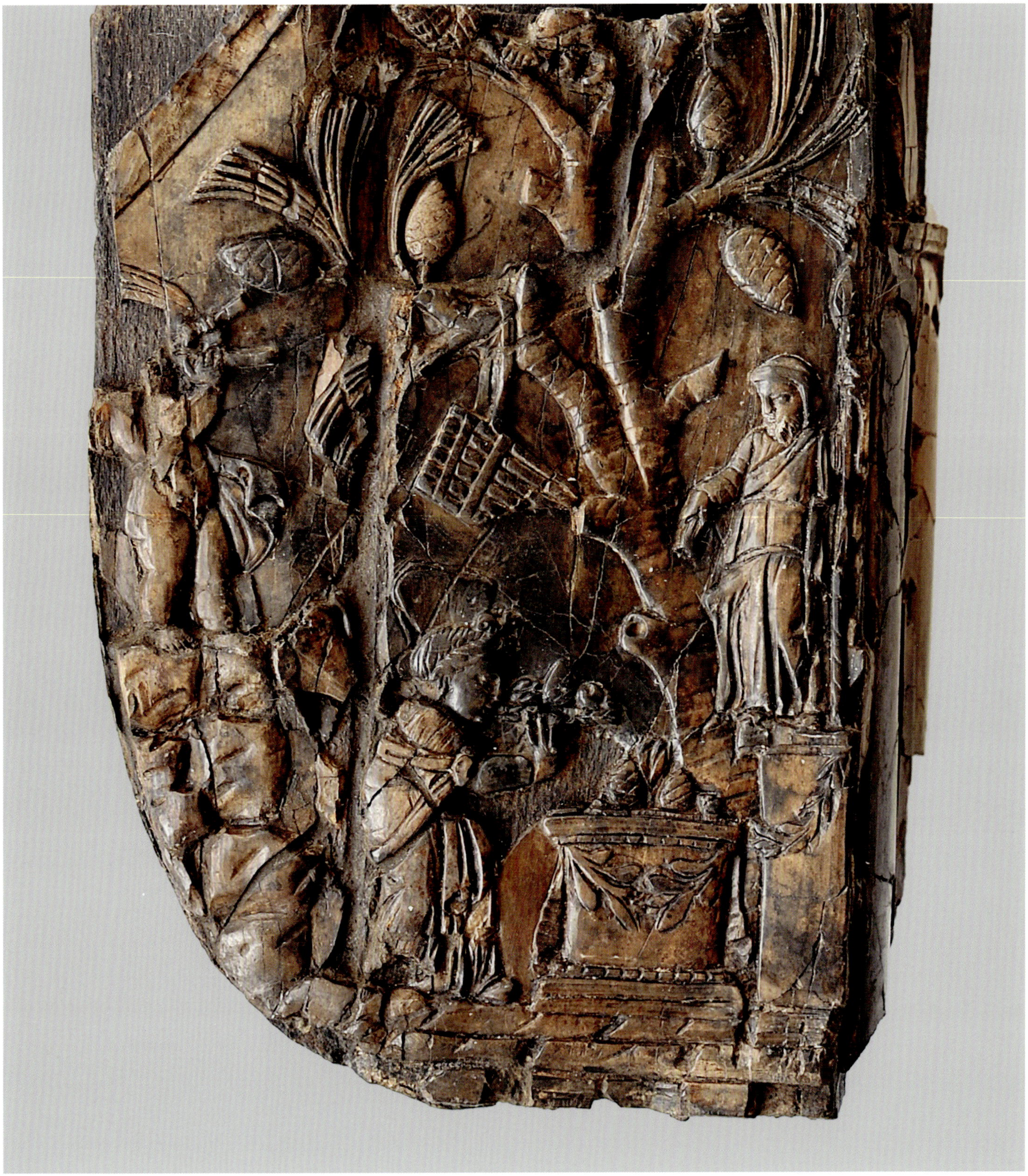

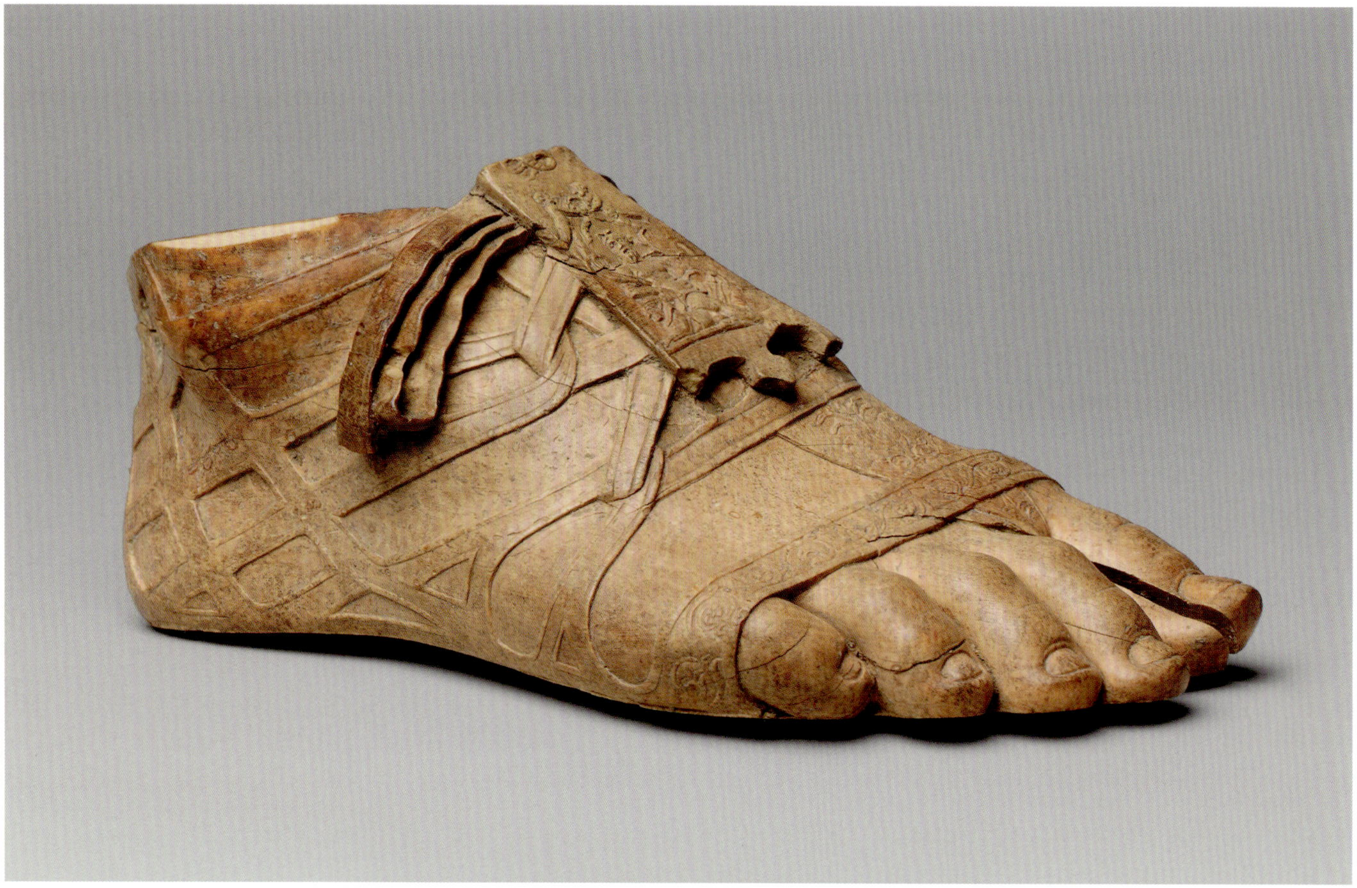

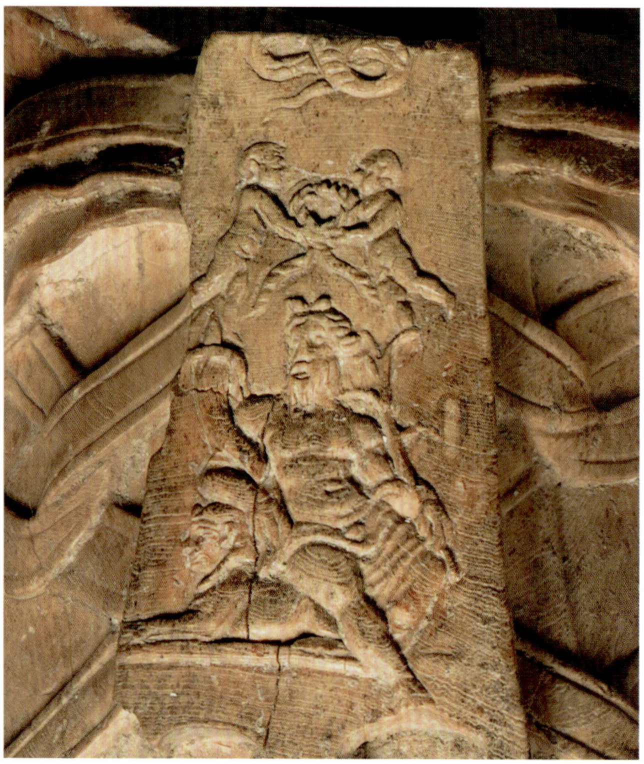

Plate 165 (above)
Sandaled foot of a composite statue, ca. AD 100–150. Ivory, H: 6 cm; L: 14.3 cm

Detail, plate 165, with the River Nile seated upon a sphinx

Plate 166 (opposite)
Portrait of Septimius Severus, ca. AD 193–211. Ivory, H: 24.8 cm; W: 17.5 cm; D: 10.5 cm

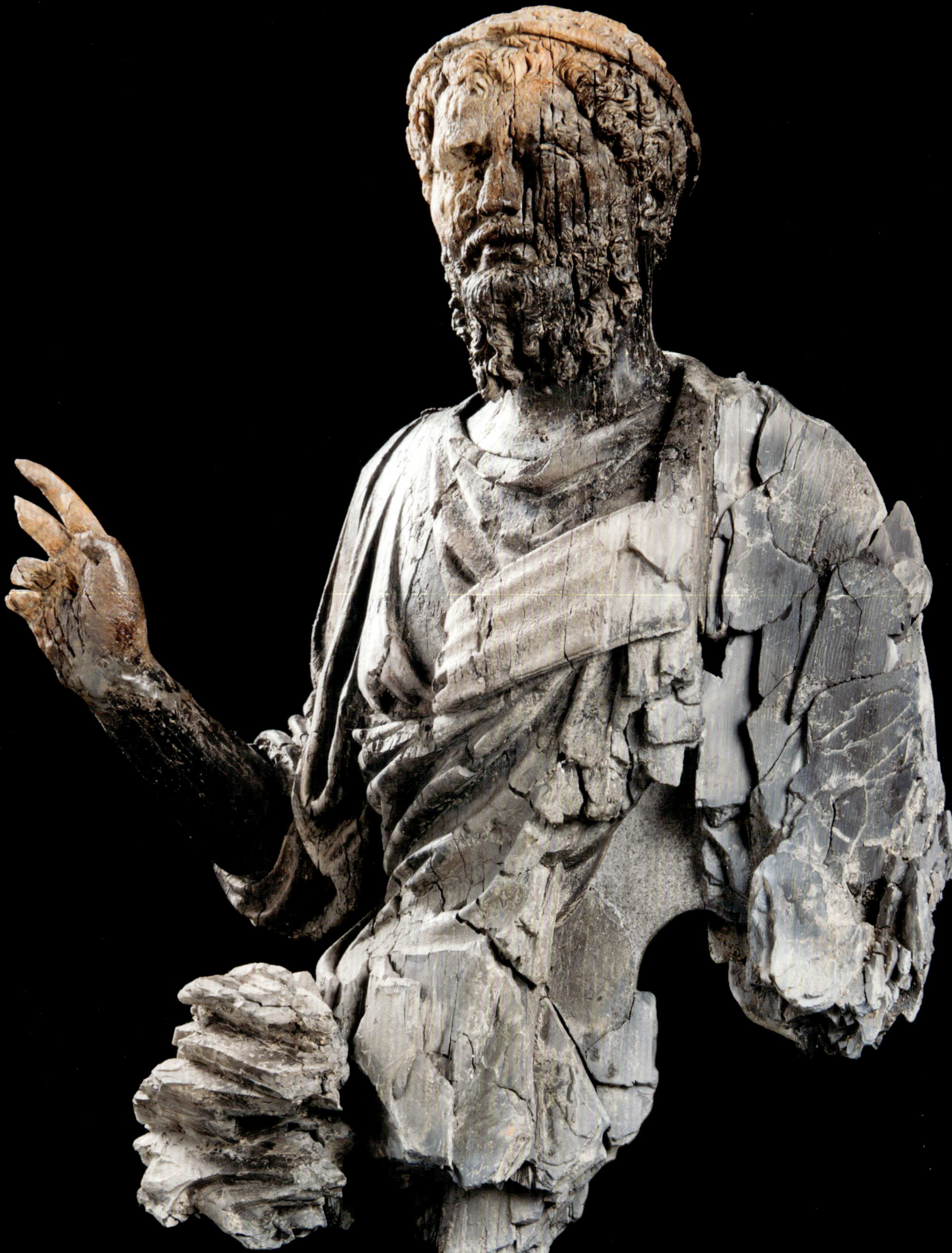

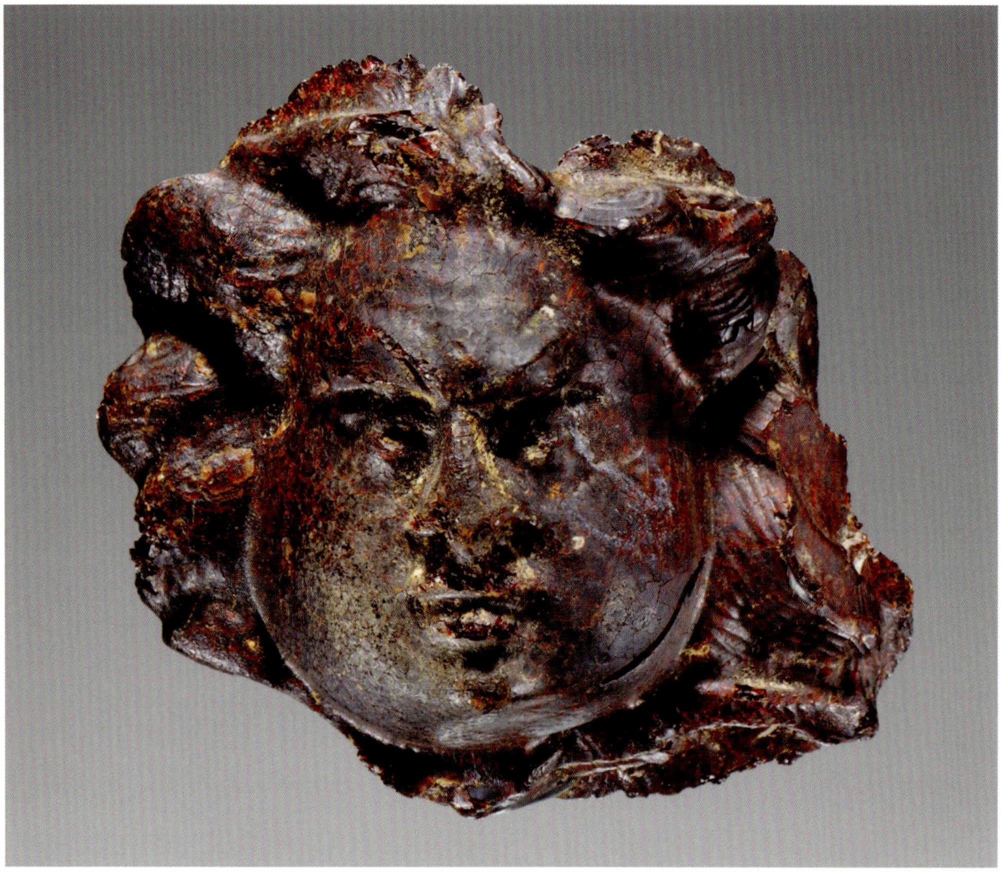

Plate 167
Medusa head, ca. AD 100. Amber, H: 5.8 cm; W: 5.8 cm; D: 3.2 cm

Plate 168
Cupids driving a cart, ca. AD 75–150. Amber, H: 6 cm; L: 11.4 cm; D: 2.3 cm

Plate 169 (opposite)
Perfume pot with vintaging cupids, ca. AD 100–120. Amber, H: 5.2 cm; W: 6.1 cm; Diam (at mouth): 2.5 cm

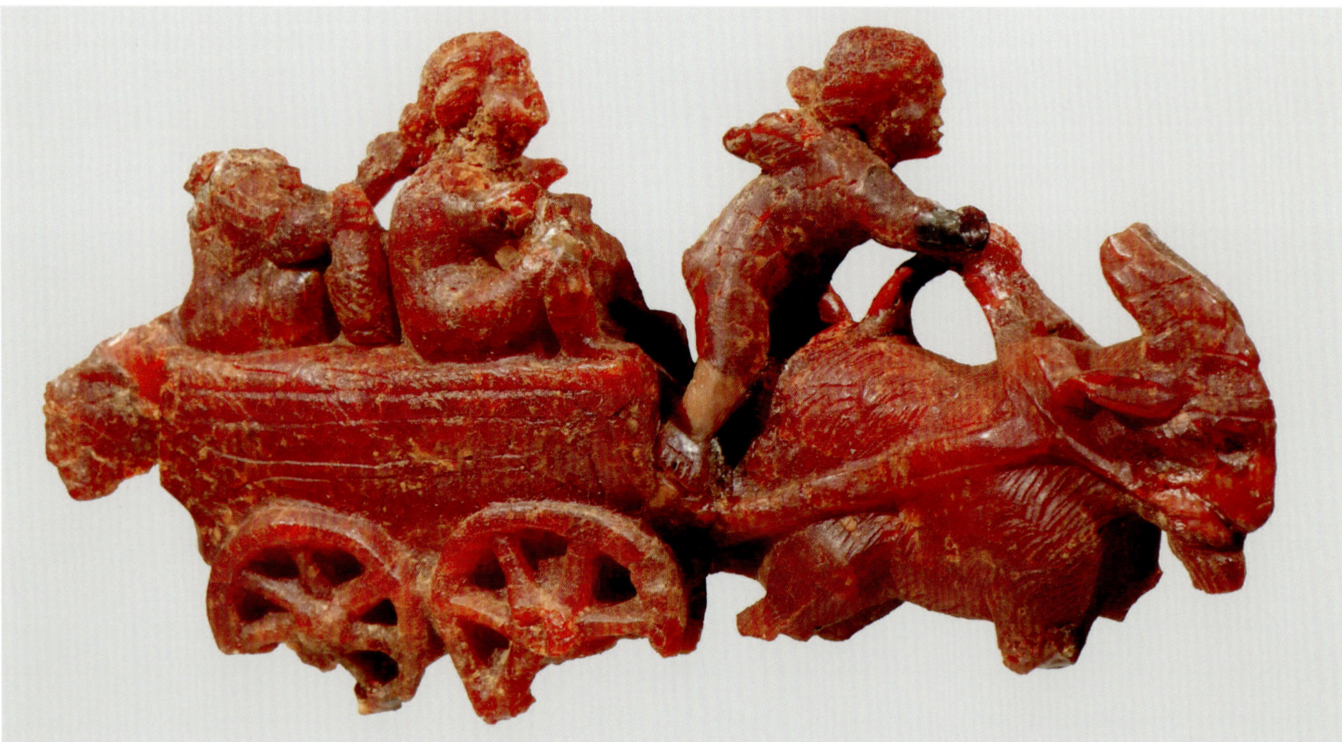

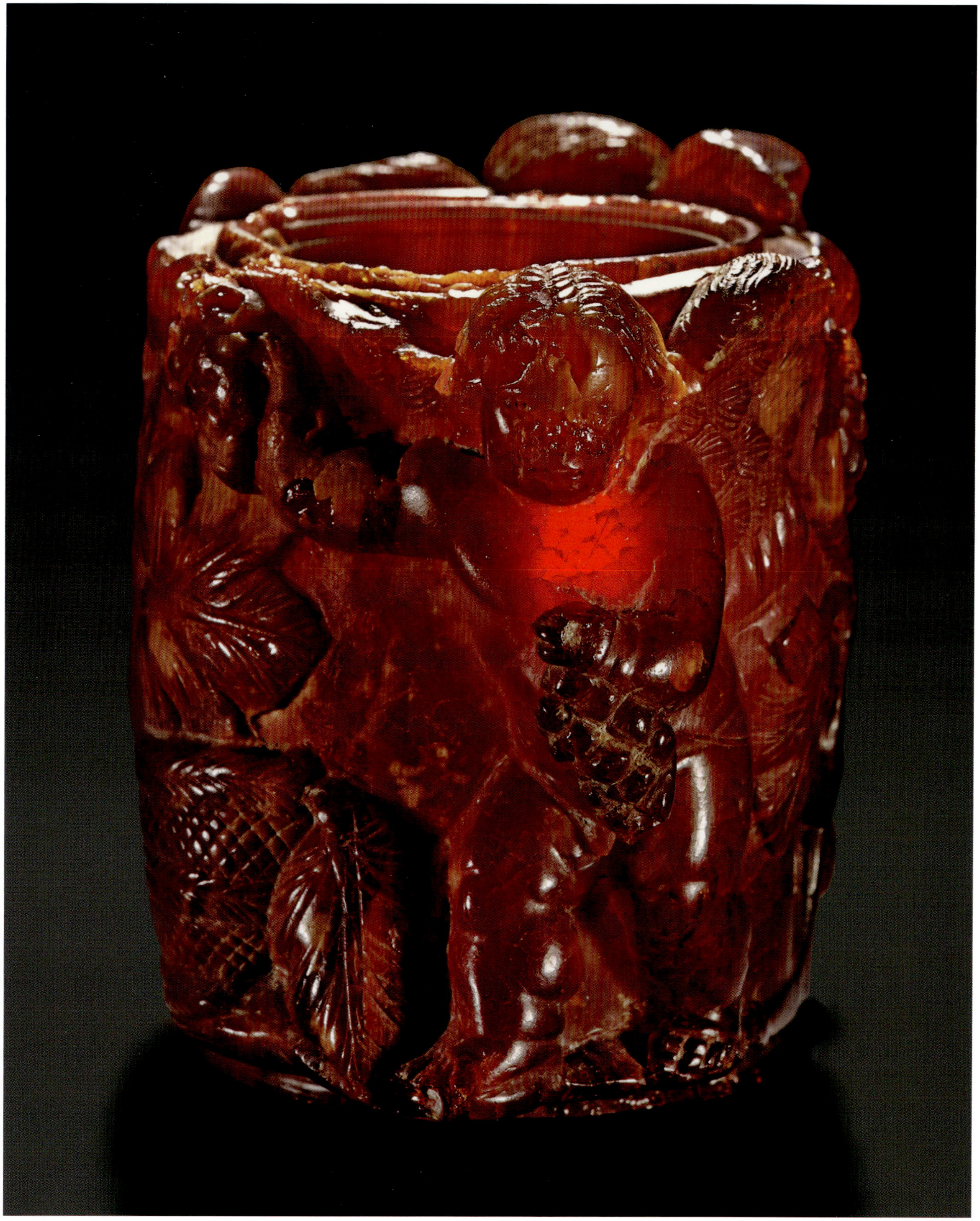

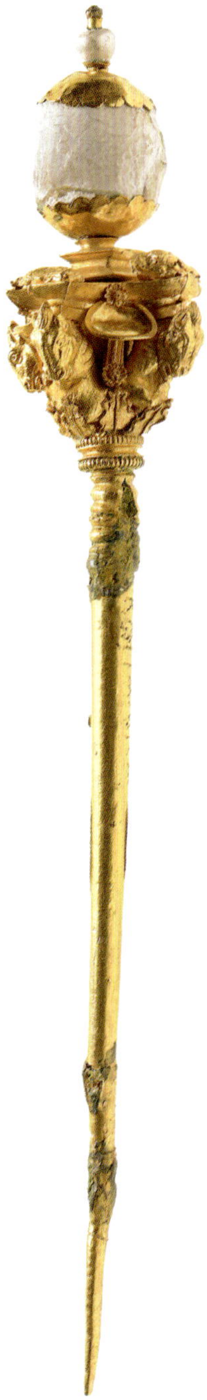

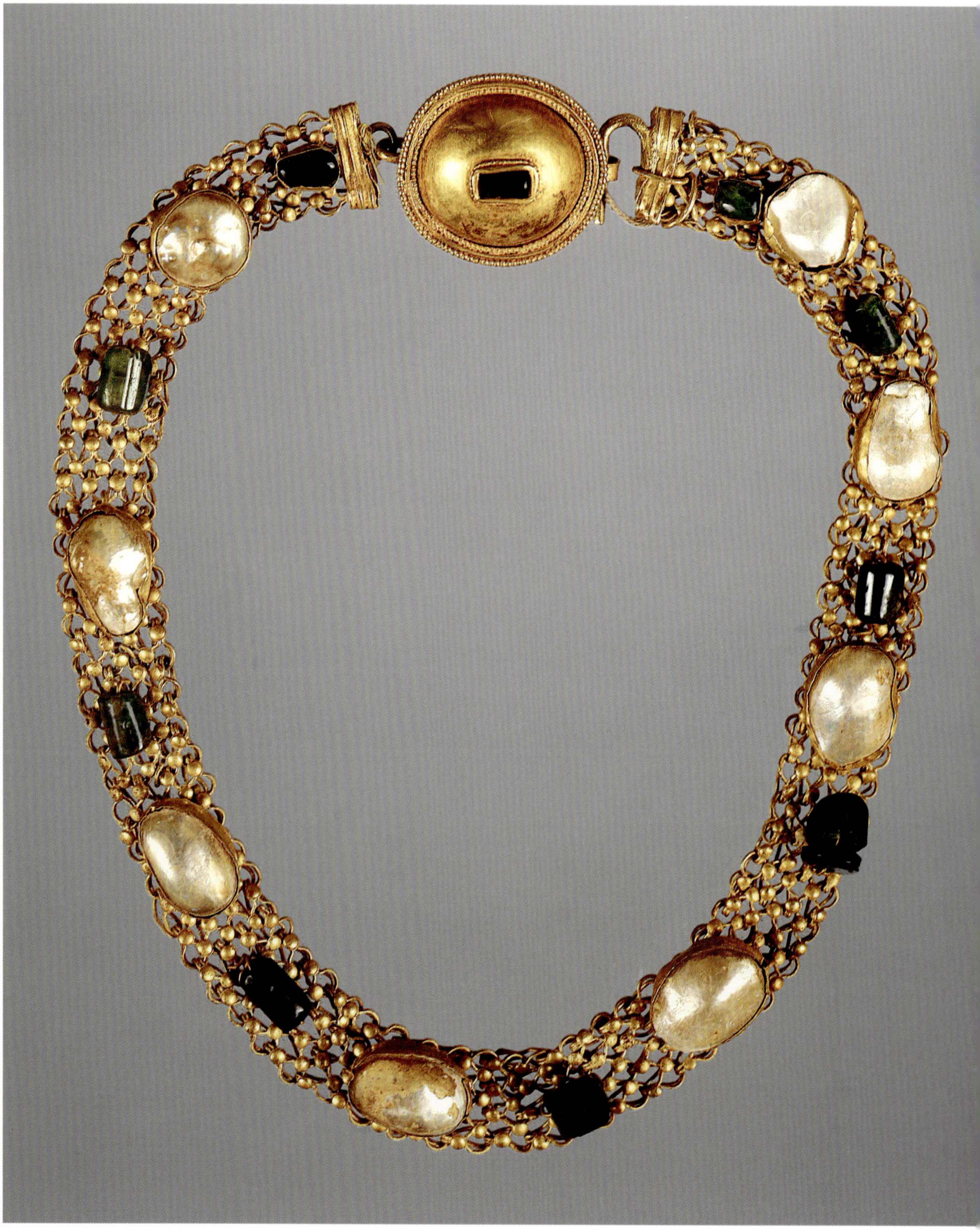

Plate 170 (opposite, left)
Pin, ca. 200–100 BC. Bronze, gold, pearls, H (overall): 17.8 cm; (of pearls): 1.4 and 0.4 cm

Plate 171 (opposite, right)
Necklace, ca. 100 BC–AD 79. Gold, mother-of-pearl, and emeralds, L: 34.5 cm

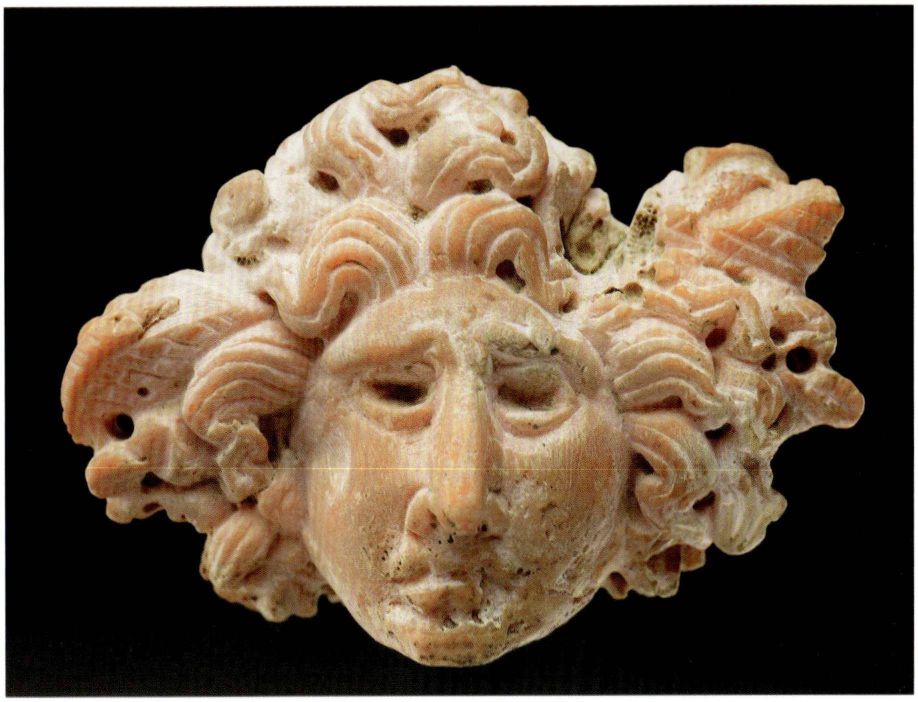

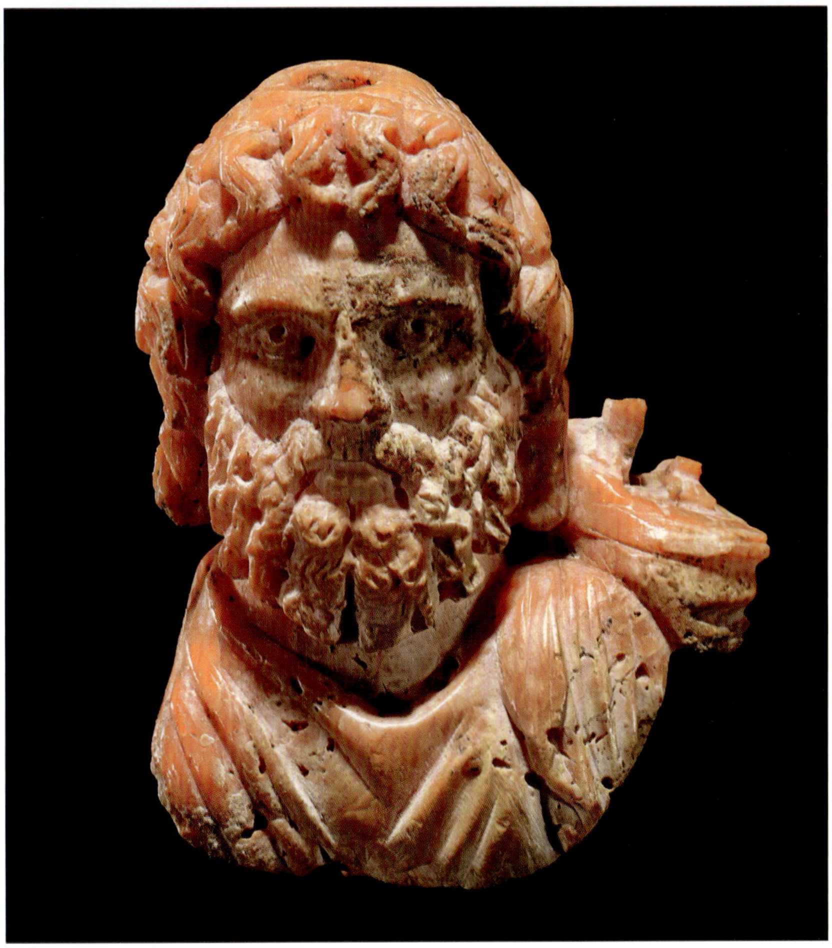

Plate 172
Head of Medusa, ca. 200–1 BC. Coral, H: 4.8 cm; W: 6.5 cm; D: 3.5 cm

Plate 173
Bust of Serapis, ca. AD 1–200. Coral, H: 6.2 cm; W: 4.8 cm; D: 3.2 cm

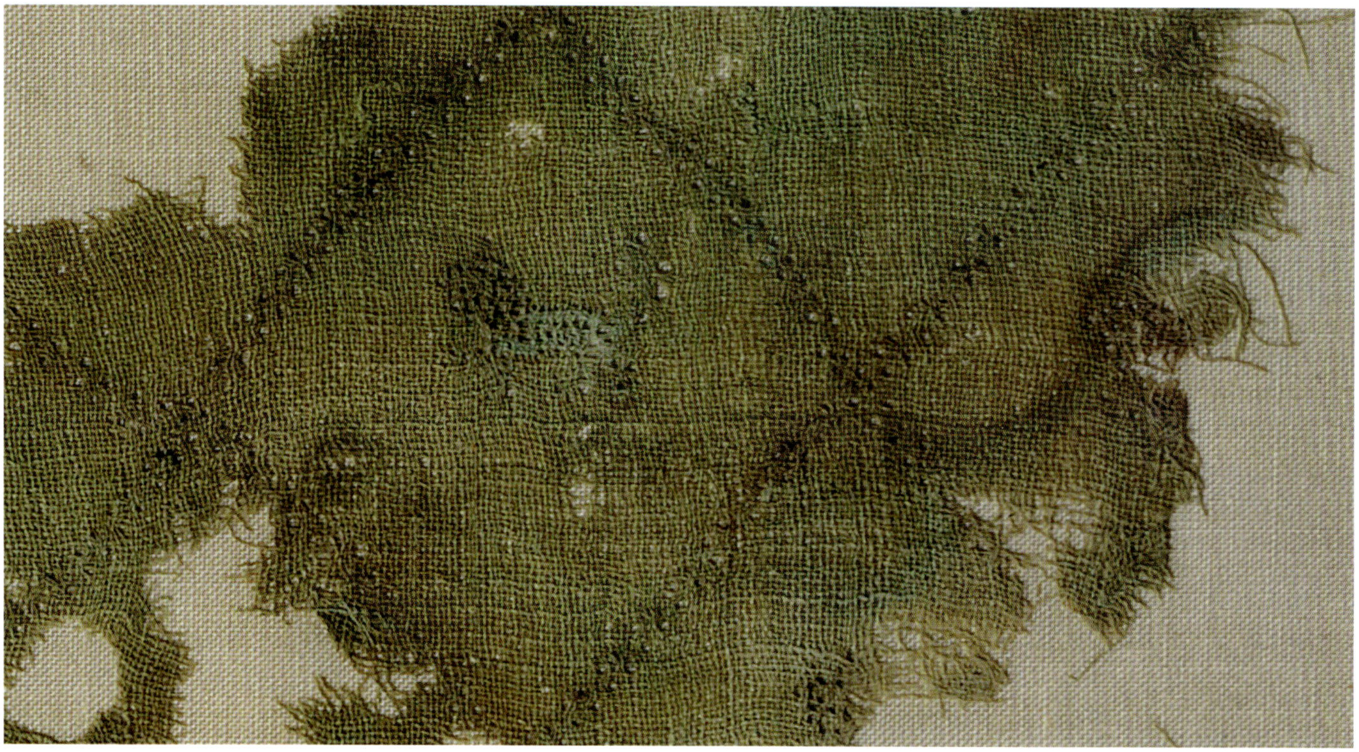

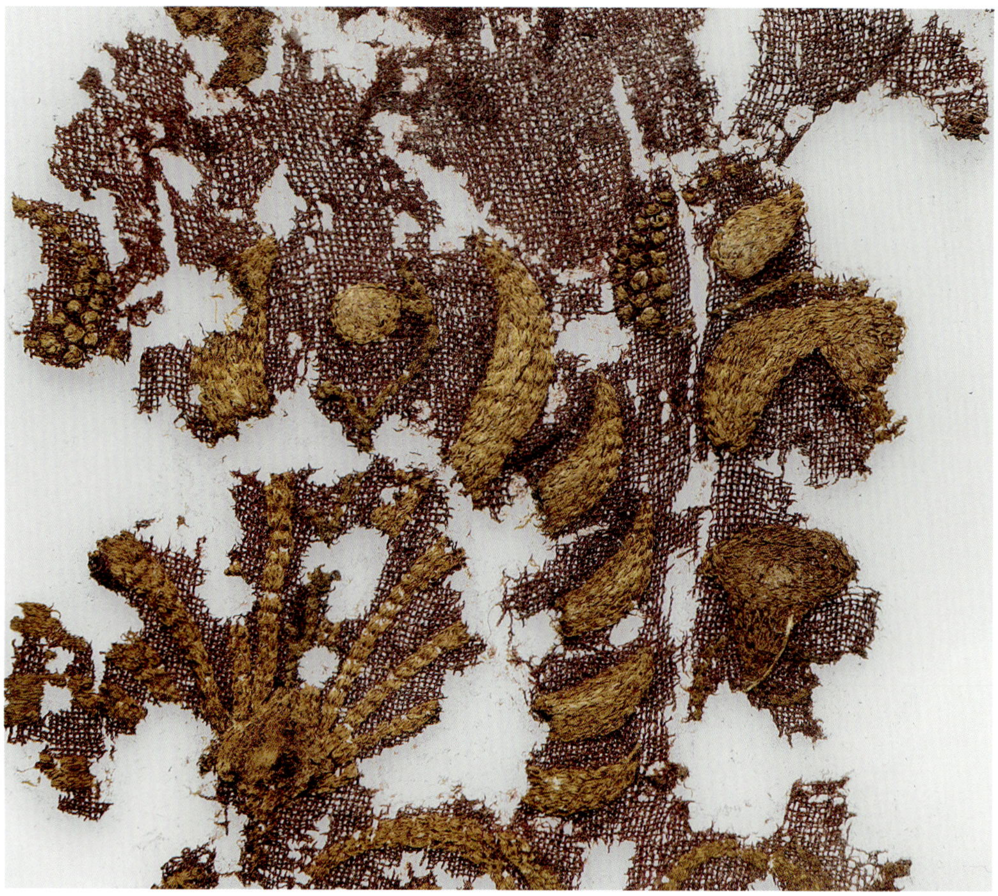

Plate 174
Textile fragments (detail), ca. 500–440 BC. Linen, silver, and gold, L (panel): 44.5 cm; W (panel): 27.3 cm

Plate 175
Textile fragment (detail), ca. 400–350 BC. Wool

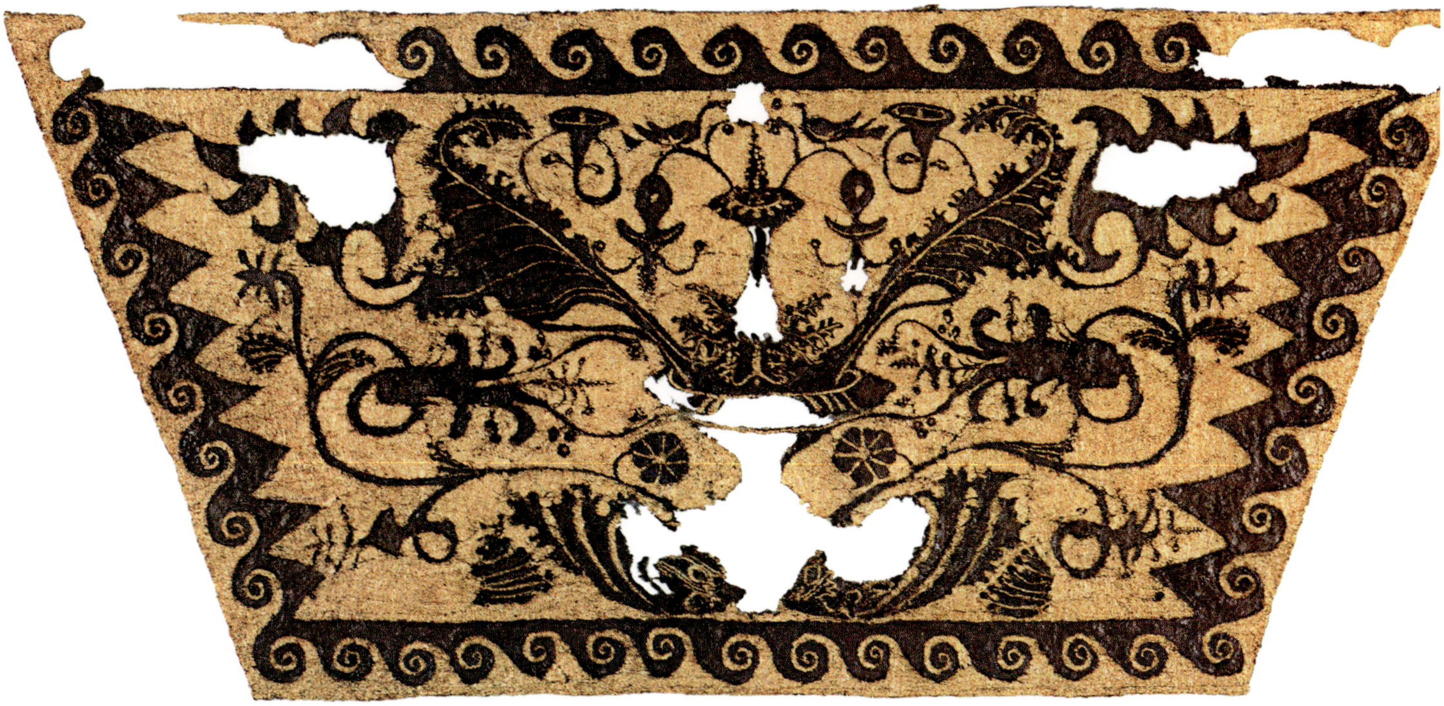

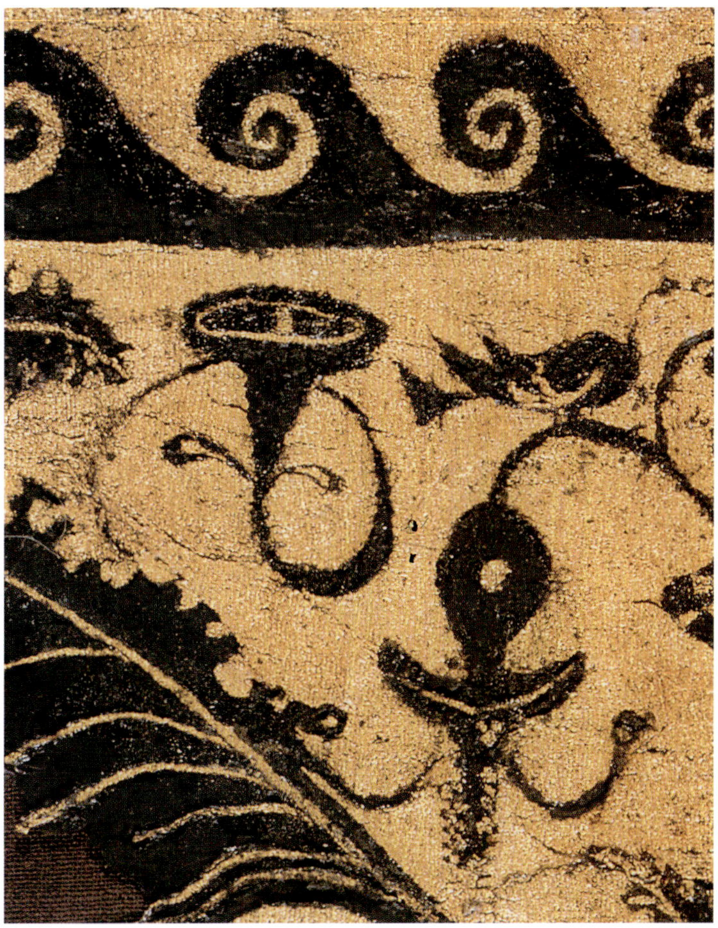

Plate 176

Gold and purple textile,
ca. 340–316 BC. Wool and gold,
H: 28.5 cm; W (max.): 61.5 cm

detail, plate 176

Plate 177
Tapestry fragments with Dionysos, ca. AD 300–500. Linen and wool, H: 139; W: 79 cm

Plate 178 (opposite)
Tapestry fragment with maenad, ca. AD 300–500. Linen and wool, H: 143 cm; W: 85.5 cm

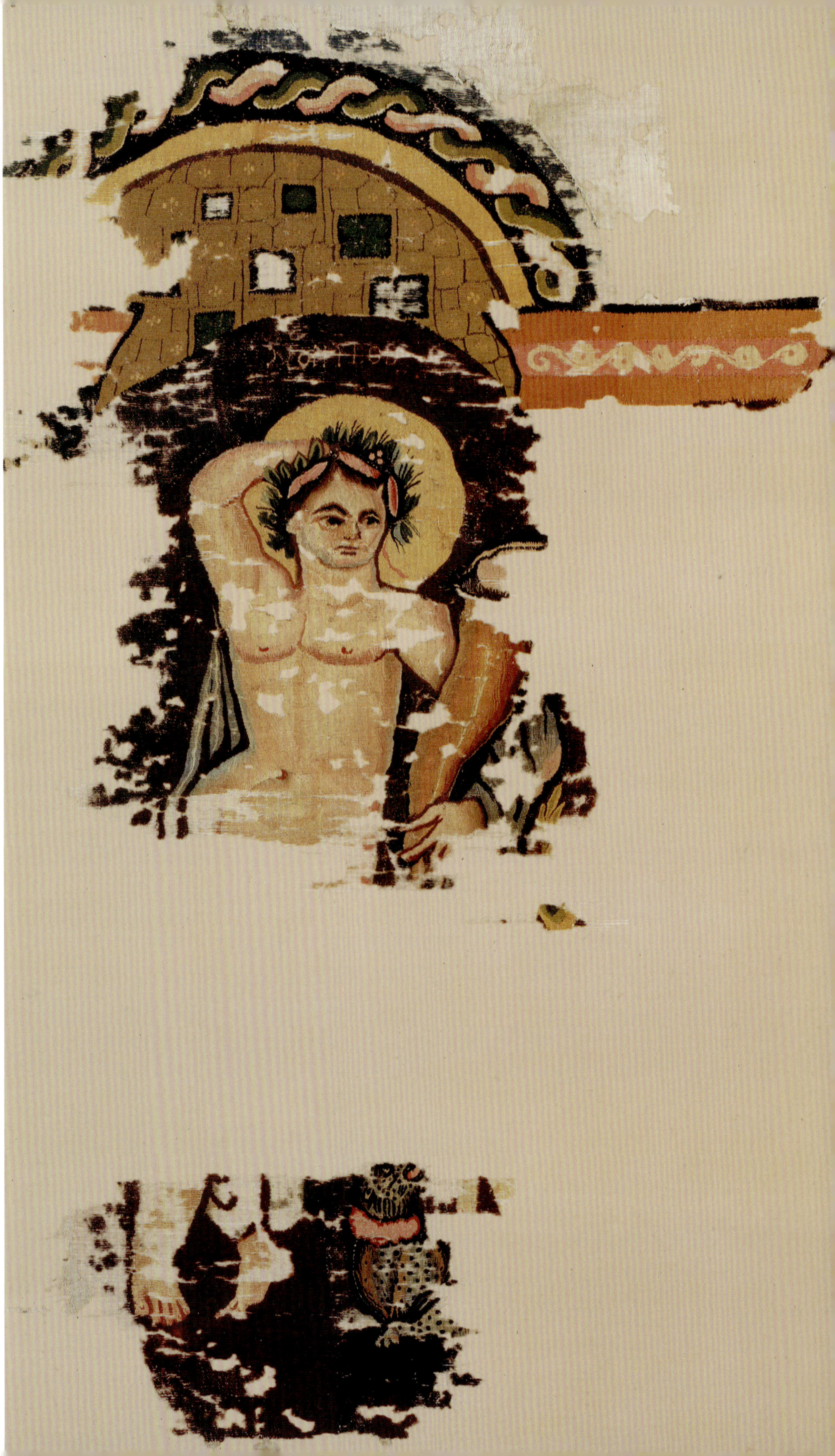

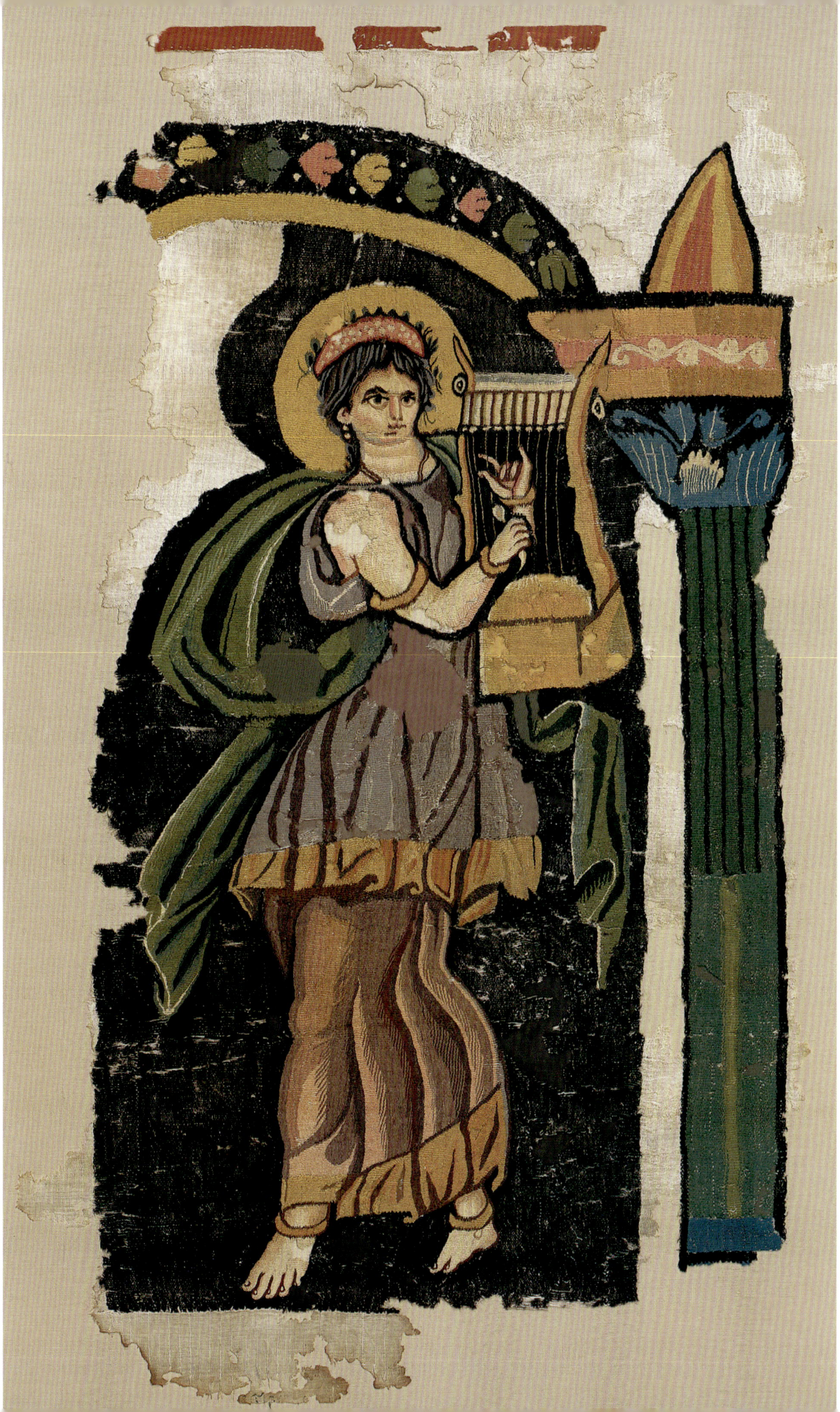

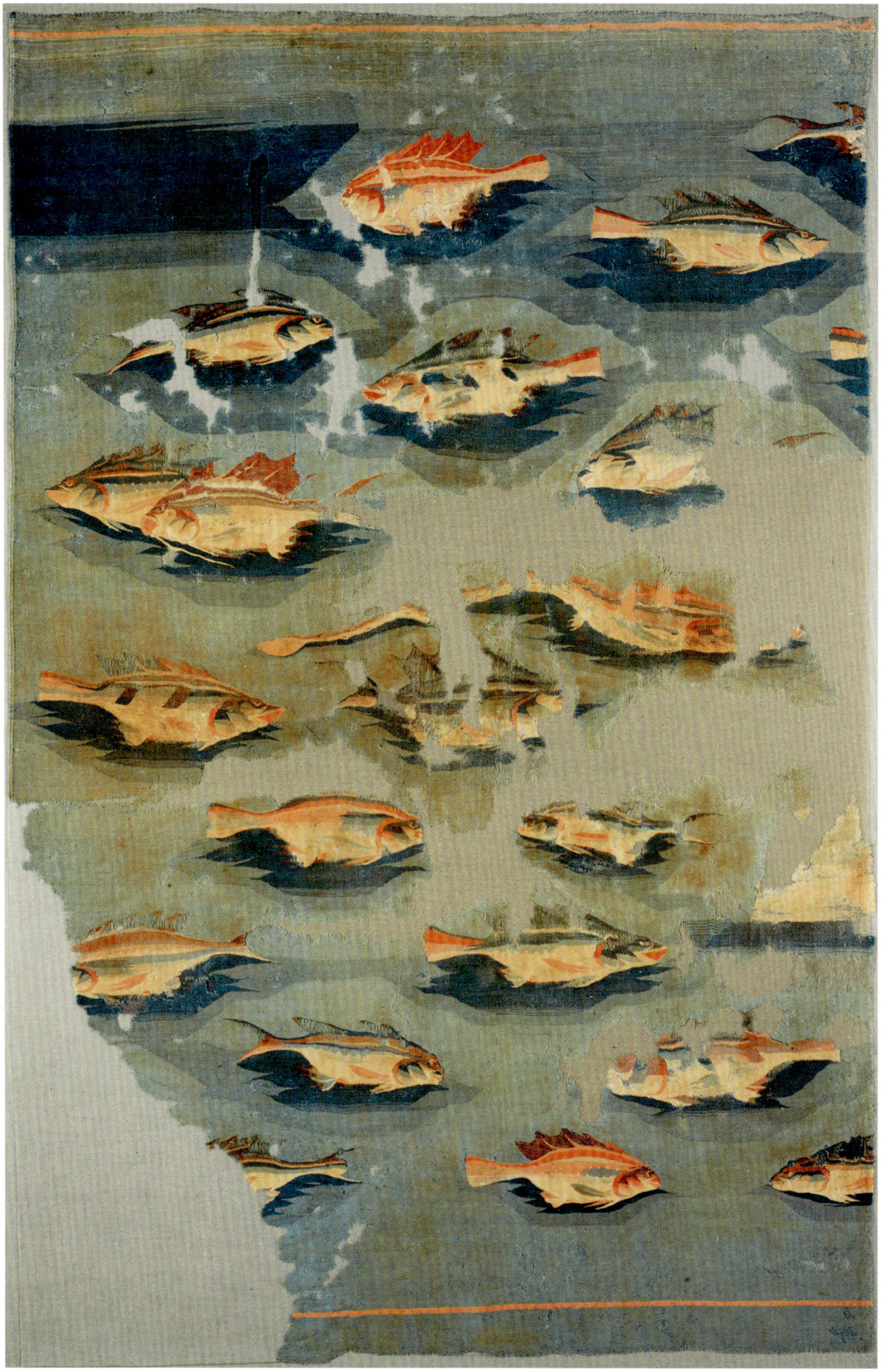

Plate 179

Tapestry with fish,
ca. AD 100–300. Wool,
H: 138 cm; W: 87 cm

EPILOGUE

Although presented in separate chapters in this book, luxury textiles, organic materials, hard stone objects, and items made of silver and gold did not operate in independent spheres in ancient Greece and Rome any more than in other places and periods. Whether paraded in funeral processions and deposited in tombs, exhibited during banquets and other ceremonial occasions, given as gifts, or offered to the gods, these items were commissioned, and acquired, to be seen and used together. They operated in a system, constituting what we might call the iconography of the precious, bestowing status, prestige, and cultural as well as economic capital on those who possessed and appreciated them. This is evident not only from caches of precious artifacts recovered archaeologically but also from the literary record, where fulsome descriptions of lavish displays move seamlessly from one material to another; for example, when diners wearing fine garments recline on sumptuous furniture decked with luxurious coverings, eating exotic foods and drinking rare wines from gold, silver, and hard stone vessels. Such accounts might be encomiastic or pejorative. On the one side we have glowing descriptions of Homeric hospitality, extensive inventories of Classical temple treasuries, and Kallixeinos's lengthy and admiring reports of the Grand Procession of Ptolemy II Philadelphos in Hellenistic Alexandria; on the other, there are the lampoons, such as Martial's of a certain Mamurra, who goes shopping among the riches of "golden Rome," where he carefully examines citrus-wood tables with ivory legs, tortoiseshell couches, antique silver, rock crystal, sardonyx, and murrhine vessels, pearl earrings and emeralds set in gold, but in the end buys only a pair of cheap cups (9.59).

More vehement is the presentation in the late first-century AD Book of Revelation of the imperial city as a woman "arrayed in purple and scarlet color, decked with gold and precious stones and pearls, having a golden cup in her hand full of abominations" (17:4); "And the merchants of the earth shall weep and mourn for her; for no man buyeth their merchandise any more: The merchandise of gold, and silver, and precious stones, and of pearls and fine linen, and purple, and silk, and scarlet, and all thyine wood, and all manner vessels of ivory, and all manner vessels of most precious wood" (18:4–5). So prevalent were such objects in the worldview of the ancients that they could function as a potent metaphor in the hands of dissidents desiring the collapse of the imperial power. The importance of the luxury arts is evident across the ages: prized by Homeric heroes, they were commissioned, collected, and exchanged by mortals who emulated them; they functioned as linchpins in the plots of Athenian tragedies; they were amassed and distributed by Hellenistic kings, and sought as trophies by Roman generals, who fought battles to gain them, displayed them prominently in their triumphs, and resold them to finance further campaigns.

Exquisitely fashioned by master craftsmen, the luxury arts of Greece and Rome often are decorated with scenes similar to those appearing in other media—images of divinities, heroic narratives, and personal portraits—but are rendered with consummate skill and detail. The outstanding qualities of the materials, which were entrusted to the most accomplished artisans, were exploited to their full potential. The results far surpass most works in better-surviving bronze, marble, and ceramic.

The decline of the classical world was not accompanied by the disappearance of the luxury arts. Far from it. In both the Latin west and the Byzantine east, precious objects crafted of gold, silver, hard stones, and exotic organic materials continued to be collected, commissioned, and displayed by patrons of the highest rank—and desired by those of lesser means. They were exhibited and admired at court ceremonials and served as dedications to a new Christian god and a bevy of his saints—despite the virtues of poverty and humility professed by the new religion. Such was their appeal. Ancient items carved from hard stone were occasionally repurposed: a Nike on an intaglio might be viewed as an angel and thus serve as a bishop's seal; a stone vessel could be remounted as a reliquary or reinterpreted as the Holy Grail. Most ancient luxury artifacts, however, were lost. Gold and silver tended to be melted down and refashioned, and organic materials disintegrated all too easily.

Those ancient luxury objects that did survive fascinated medieval, Renaissance, and Enlightenment viewers not only because of their materials and craftsmanship but also their rarity and association with a revered past. They were collected by princes of church and state, admired by artists such as Michelangelo and Rubens. More recently, however, they have fallen out of fashion both aesthetically and intellectually. I hope that the small selection of surviving artifacts presented in this volume—and the historical material gathered to contextualize them—will encourage renewed study, appreciation, and research, opening the door to a reevaluation of the artistic production of the classical world, a greater understanding of the many uses to which it was put, and a more holistic view of Greek and Roman art and society.

PLATE COMMENTARIES

CHAPTER ONE: METALS

Plate 1
Pair of earrings with geometric decoration, ca. 850 BC
From Athens
Gold, H: 6.4 and 6.5 cm; W: 2.5 and 2.1 cm; Wt: 5.9 and 6.2 grams
Athens, Agora Museum, J 148

These intricate gold earrings were excavated in the so-called Tomb of a Rich Lady on the northwest slope of the Areopagos in Athens. Recent research indicates that the deceased was pregnant, which may, in part, account for the extraordinary wealth of her grave goods, which included imported faience and glass beads, a rock crystal pendant, and two ivory seals, as well as six locally produced gold rings, impressive ceramics, and diverse other artifacts. The earrings are composed of double looped straps, a central trapezoid, and three hollow pomegranate pendants. Plain and twisted wire, filigree, and granulation enhance all three parts, accentuating the length of the straps, dividing the central element into multiple panels filled with abbreviated guilloche, and adorning the pomegranate finials with triangular leaves at the top and a corona at the bottom. These are the earliest known examples of granulation and filigree from Iron Age Greece, leading some scholars to suggest that they were imported or fashioned by an emigrant Phoenician craftsman for an Athenian client, rather than made locally. Yet domestic production seems just as likely given the geometric motifs of the decoration.
BIBLIOGRAPHY Smithson 1968, esp. 113–14, no. 77a–b, pls. 30, 32; Higgins 1969, 144–45, pl. 34j–k; Hampe and Simon 1981, 198–211, figs. 320–21; Higgins 1980, 97–98, pl. 13D, E; Deppert-Lippitz 1985, 58–59, fig. 24; Musti et al. 1992, no. 44; Despini 1996, 91, 222, fig. 59; Delivorrias in Georgoula 1999, 88, fig. 47; Liston and Papadopoulos 2004.

....

Plate 2
Pair of earrings with geometric decoration, ca. 750–700 BC
Gold, Diam (disks): 2.8 cm; Wt: 18.3 and 18.7 grams
Los Angeles County Museum of Art, M.47.6.1, .2, .8a–b

Each of these elaborate geometric gold earrings consists of a flat disk connected to a cone by a spiral rod. All the surfaces are adorned with complex patterns in granulation and filigree: crosses, triangles, chevrons, meanders, and tongues. The disks and the underside of the cones have circular and pendant-shaped cloisons (forming a rosette) that have lost their central inlays, perhaps rock crystal or some other stone, amber, or glass. The spiral rods, rectangular in section, are attached to the cones and fit into sockets at the back of the disks; perpendicular holes allow for a cross-pin or fine thread to hold the elements in place.
BIBLIOGRAPHY Higgins 1969, 148, pls. 39b–40; D. Carroll 1970; Higgins 1980, 98, no. 4, pl. 14C; Deppert-Lippitz 1985, 73–74, fig. 33; Musti et al. 1992, 245–56, no. 59; Despini 1996, 84, 219, fig. 45.

....

Plate 3
Diadem with animals, ca. 760–720 BC
From the Kerameikos cemetery, Athens
Gold, L: 38.5 cm; H: 3.4 cm; Wt: 20.7 grams
Paris, Musée du Louvre, MNC 1291 (BJ93)

Tombs often preserve objects not used in life. In the Geometric period, and later, thin gold diadems were sometimes placed on the head of the deceased. Here, the style and motifs of the stamped (repoussé) ornament are identical to that found in contemporary art in other media, such as painted pottery and bronze statuettes. Between two panels of stacked meanders, a central panel depicts a recumbent goat flanked by two deer, each attacked by lions. Holes at the edges were for the cord with which the band was tied around the head.
BIBLIOGRAPHY De Ridder 1924, 9; Ohly 1953, 31, 84ff., 97ff., no. 12, A13, pls. 4.1, 7.2; Coldstream 1977, 123–24, fig. 38c; Laffineur 1978, 82–84, fig. 15; Higgins 1980, 97–98, fig. 14; Musti et al. 1992, no. 49; Despini 1996, 28–29, 56, 211, figs. 9–10.

....

Plate 4
Diadem with dancing women, ca. 700 BC
From Corinth
Gold, L: 15.5 cm; H: 3.5 cm; Wt: 15 grams
Berlin, Staatliche Museen, Antikensammlung, 31093

Stamped (repoussé) decoration depicts seven dancing women wearing long skirts and holding branches in their joined hands. Concentric circles fill the spaces between them. Similar motifs appear on Geometric vases depicting funeral scenes.
BIBLIOGRAPHY Greifenhagen 1970–75, 24, pl. 6.1; Heilmeyer 1988, 303, no. 24; Despini 1996, 57, 212, no. 11; Delivorrias in Georgoula 1999, 91, fig. 49.

....

Plate 5
Necklace or pectoral with Artemis as Mistress of the Animals, ca. 660–620 BC
From Kamiros, Rhodes
Gold, H (plaques): 4.2 cm; L: 22.2 cm; Wt: 52.8 grams
London, British Museum, GR 1861,1111.1.3,.4 (Jewellery 1128–30)

This multipiece necklace or pectoral ornament consists of seven gold plaques depicting Artemis as the *Potnia Theron* (Mistress of the Animals), two large rosettes, and multiple pomegranate-shaped pendants. Three different punches were utilized to fashion the hammered (repoussé) reliefs representing the winged goddess and each of the two panthers she holds. These modeled sheets were then soldered to the underlying plaques as appliqués. While the relief decoration is identical, granulation was added in different patterns on the goddess's garments, as well as in the hair, diadem, necklace, bracelets, and stippled pelts of the panthers. Twisted wire filigree frames each plaque and three gold tubes at the top allowed them to be strung together. Five pomegranates originally hung from wire chains at the bottom of each plaque. Evidence of wear and ancient repair both indicate that this sumptuous object was worn in life and not just buried in the tomb as a grave offering. Kamiros has yielded several similar objects, some of which depict centaurs and Artemis as a bee goddess.

BIBLIOGRAPHY Marshall 1911, 90, nos. 1128–30, pl. 11; Coarelli 1970, no. 1; Laffineur 1978, 202n56, 203nn57–58, pls. 5.2, 7.4, 7.5, 8.1; Higgins 1980; Musti et al. 1992, 249, no. 76; Despini 1996, 146, 245, fig. 133.

....

Plate 6
Pair of earrings with rosettes, ca. 510 BC
From Tomb 67, Sindos, Macedonia
Gold, Diam: 5.5 and 5.7 cm
Thessaloniki, Archaeological Museum, 7975

Found on either side of the head of a female skeleton, each of these elaborate band earrings with floral terminals has a complex rosette with a central gold sphere mounted on a heavily granulated cone, from which spring two rows of petals with superimposed plain and beaded wire filigree edges. Two smaller flowers, similar, but lacking the lower row of petals, mark the join to a gradually thinning openwork band with plain, twisted, and beaded wire, in the widest part of which is a guilloche.

BIBLIOGRAPHY A. Despini in Votokopoulou et al. 1985, 194–95, no. 321; Musti et al. 1992, 180, 268, fig. 143.4; Despini 1996, 92–93, nos. 62–63; Ignatiadou 2012, 392, 402, no. 7.

....

Plate 7
Dress Pin with Animals, ca. 475–450 BC
Said to be from the Peloponnesos
Gold, L (pin): 11.8 cm; L (head): 4.2 cm; Wt: 14.2 grams
Boston, Museum of Fine Arts, 96.718

Three sphinxes, three lions, and three large bees perch upon the head of this elaborate dress pin, which takes the form of a rosebud, cylinder, and globe atop a tapering shaft. The sphinxes and lions are fashioned in two halves from sheet gold hammered into matrices, soldered together with median seams, and attached to the petals and leaves. Their tails are separately attached pieces of wire. The lions have chased leg muscles, ribs, manes, and facial features. The bees, which appear to suck nectar from the flower, are meticulously crafted from several elements, with separately fashioned wings and wire for legs and antennae. The leaves, like the column and top of the pin, are adorned with beaded wire filigree. While the upright leaves have a central filigree rib, the pendant leaves are further enhanced with filigree palmettes. The pin is said to have been found, connected by a gold chain to another gold pin, in a grave in the Peloponnesos at Aigion, or between Patras and Pyrgos, along with two Athenian red-figure *lekythoi*.

BIBLIOGRAPHY Segall 1941; Jacobsthal 1956, 65–82, figs. 274–76; Hoffmann and Davidson 1965, 181–83, no. 69. For dress pins in temple inventories see Brøns 2014, 40–45 and appendix 4.

....

Plate 8
Rosette with winged animals, ca. 650 BC
From Melos
Gold, Diam: 4.6 cm
Athens, National Archaeological Museum, Xr 1177-1181

This gold rosette with a central eagle and, alternating on six lower petals, bees and griffin heads was fashioned from sheet gold and extensively decorated with granulation and filigree, using both plain and twisted wire, and engraving for the bees' wings. It and other elaborate examples originally formed parts of diadems or, perhaps, arm bands.

BIBLIOGRAPHY Hampe and Simon 1981, 211–12, fig. 326; Deppert-Lippitz 1985, 106, pl. VI; Despini 1996, 59, 212, fig. 16; Delivorrias in Georgoula 1999, 92–93, figs. 51–52.

....

Plate 9
Phiale (libation bowl), dedicated by the sons of Kypselos, ca. 625 BC
Inscription: ϘΥΨΒΛΣΔΑΣΑΝΒΘΒΝ ΒΞΒΡΑΚΛΕΑΜ (Κυψελίδαι ἀνέθεν ἐξ Ἡρακλείας)
Said to be from Olympia
Gold, H: 15 cm; Diam: 16.8 cm; Wt: 835.5 grams
Boston, Museum of Fine Arts, 21.1843

The inscription on the rim of this solid-gold libation bowl (*phiale mesomphalos*) with nine lobes declares that "The sons of Kypselos [dedicated this] from [the spoils taken at] Herakleia." Kypselos ruled Corinth circa 657–627 BC. His successors constructed a treasury at Delphi that contained many rich offerings of the kings of Lydia. The exact identification of Herakleia remains uncertain, but among the several cities with that name the one on the Ambracian Gulf on the eastern coast of the Adriatic Sea, not far from the Corinthian colony at Korkyra, is a likely candidate. This vessel is said to have been discovered in the early years of the twentieth century at Olympia, east of the sacred precinct between the stadium and the river Alpheios. Its weight is the equivalent of 100 Corinthian staters, silver coins first minted by Kypselos or his son Periander that weighed 8.2–8.5 grams, approximating the Persian daric of 8.4 grams. Delicate stamped beaded decoration surrounds its central circular boss, although its shape is now slightly distorted. Similar fluted *phialai*, hammered from bronze sheet, have been recovered from excavations at Olympia and the Heraion at Samos, and ceramic examples are known from Corinth and Sparta.

BIBLIOGRAPHY Caskey 1922, 1926; Payne 1931, 161, 211–22; Luschey 1939, 87, 102, 133; Strong 1966, 57–58, pl. 8A; Vickers and Gill 1994, 46n113, 65, fig. 3.2; Hasserodt 2009, 296–67, 433, no. 177.

....

Plate 10

Fragmentary statue of Apollo, restored head and embossed sheets, ca. 550 BC
From the Halos deposit at Delphi
Gold, ivory, silver, and enamel, H (head): 24.5 cm (approx. life-size); and H (sheets): 35.5 and 35 cm; W: 13.5 and 14 cm
Delphi Archaeological Museum, 10413, 9796, 9797

Relatively little survives of ancient Greek and Roman chryselephantine (gold and ivory) statuary, but among the most impressive remains are components discovered, burned and badly damaged, in two pits underneath and alongside the Sacred Way in the area of the Halos at the Sanctuary of Apollo at Delphi in 1939. These were deliberately buried with other precious offerings to the god after a fire destroyed the building that housed them at the end of the fifth century BC, when they were already about a century and a half old. The components of at least seven chryselephantine statues were recovered: hammered gold and gilt-silver sheets for drapery and hair, as well as ivory faces, hands, arms, and feet. The statues can be divided into four groups according to their scale. The largest three, one male and two females, must represent Apollo and his sister and mother, Artemis and Leto. Fashioned from large hollow sections of elephant tusk, the heads were nonetheless pieced together: ears, for example, were carved separately and attached with dowels. The eyes were inlaid and set within golden lashes, using a technique analogous to that employed in bronze statuary. Eyebrows, too, were inlaid. Gold and gilt-silver sheet were embossed with wavy patterns to represent hair, and gold figural panels with orientalized animals were apparently meant to function as elaborately woven or embroidered drapery. Goats, Pegasoi, lions, panther, bulls, stags, and sphinxes are presented, mirroring one another. These panels, attached by gilt-silver nails with heads in the form of enamel rosettes, have been reconstructed as leggings, although it is far from certain that they served this purpose.

BIBLIOGRAPHY Amandry 1939, 1991; Lapatin 2001, 57–60; Aruz, Graff, and Rakic 2014, 309–10, no. 182a,b (A. Psalti).

....

Plate 11

Ring with bearded man and phallos, ca. 440–430 BC
Electrum, H (bezel): 1.7 cm; Wt: 5.9 grams
Berlin, Staaliche Museen, Antikensammlung, FG287

While most portraits from fifth-century BC Greece are highly idealized, this image of a bearded man in profile expertly engraved into the bezel of an electrum ring presents a balding individual, with furrowed brow, deep-set eyes, and large hooked nose. His thin, disheveled hair is drawn back with two distinctive curls on top. The male genitalia under his chin have been variously interpreted as having personal significance to the owner, perhaps punning on his name; serving an apotropaic function; or corresponding somehow to the penis on the shaft of ancient herms. In the eighteenth century J. J. Winckelmann wrongly associated the image with the fertility god Priapus. This ring has since been compared to gems engraved by Dexamenos of Chios (see plates 84, 85) on account of the quality of the carving.

BIBLIOGRAPHY Winckelmann 1760, 261, no. 1609; Furtwängler 1896, 28, no. 287; Furtwängler 1900, X.35; Becatti 1955, no. 322; Richter 1968b, 97, no. 324; Boardman 1970, 219, 284, fig. 220; Greifenhagen 1970–75, 72, pl. 54.11, 17; Higgins 1980, 131, pl. 31D; Despini 1996, 203, 264–65, no. 209: Platz-Horster 2002, 54–55, no. 32b.

....

Plate 12

Ring with Artemis pouring a libation, ca. 450–425 BC
Gold, H: 1.8 cm; Wt: 4 grams
London, British Museum, GR 1914,1017.2

Artemis, goddess of the hunt, holds two spears in one hand as she pours a libation over an altar from a foreshortened *phiale* in the other. She wears high boots, a short *chiton*, and a belted animal skin that leaves one breast bare, as well as a pendant necklace.

BIBLIOGRAPHY Boardman 1970, 216, pl. 662; Higgins 1980, pl. 24C; Williams and Ogden 1994, 52, no. 4.

....

Plate 13

Ring with head of a woman, ca. 400–350 BC
Gold, H (bezel): 1.9 cm; Wt: 8.9 grams
London, British Museum GR, 1884,0409.1 (Rings 53)

The fine, expressive engraving of this female portrait is exceptional. The unknown sitter wears a plain scarf wrapped around her wavy hair, a necklace with a single acorn pendant, and boat-shaped earring with two pendants—a type popular in the Greek cities of southern Italy and along the shores of the Black Sea (see plate 27).

BIBLIOGRAPHY Marshall 1907, 12, no. 53; Richter 1968b, 98, no. 320; Boardman 1970, 222, pl. 714; Williams and Ogden 1994, 220–21, no. 127.

....

Plate 14
Ring with a goddess, ca. 400–300 BC
Gold, H: 2.2 cm; Wt: 15 grams
London, Victoria and Albert Museum, 552-1910

A standing woman wears a *peplos*, *polos*, and a thin veil, as well as delicate sandals. She holds a scepter in her left hand and wears a bracelet on her right wrist. The revelatory gesture of pulling at the veil, as well as the other attributes, suggests that she is Hera.

BIBLIOGRAPHY Boardman 1970, 229, pl. 733; Boardman 1993, 130, no. 117D.

....

Plate 15
Ring with woman and eagle on altar, ca. 350 BC
Said to be from a tomb at Phokaia (western Turkey)
Gold, L (bezel): 2 cm; Wt: 11.3 grams
London, British Museum GR, 1917,0501.59 (Rings 59)

Engraved into the bezel of this gold ring is a woman dressed in a *chiton* and *himation* making an offering at an altar surmounted by an eagle. Poised with her weight on her left leg and the right bent, she delicately extends her right hand over the altar (depicted in three-quarter view) to offer incense or perhaps seed. Her hair is tied back in a bun, and she wears a simple drop earring, as well as bracelets and sandals. The folds of her drapery fall naturalistically and the details of her anatomy (breasts and navel) are visible through the thin fabric of her *chiton*. The eagle on the altar may indicate that she worships Zeus.

BIBLIOGRAPHY Marshall 1907, 13, no. 59; Richter 1968b, 82–83, no. 243; Boardman 1970, pl. 739; Williams and Ogden 1994, 105, no. 58.

....

Plate 16
Ring with nude woman, ca. 400–380 BC
Said to be from Macedonia
Gold, H (bezel): 2 cm; Wt: 15.8 grams
New York, Metropolitan Museum of Art, 06.1124

An early study of the female nude, this woman stands stretching, if not dancing, with her hands behind her sharply raised head. While most of her body is depicted in profile, her right foot and right breast are represented in three-quarter view. Her hair, tied in a topknot, is finely engraved, as are the folds of her disgarded garment, which is draped over an elegant *klismos* behind her.

BIBLIOGRAPHY Richter 1956, no. 77; Boardman 1970, 298, pl. 710; Williams and Ogden 1994, 64, no. 17.

....

Plate 17
Ring with the *Erotostasia*, ca. 350 BC
Gold, H (bezel): 2.2 cm; W (bezel): 1.7 cm; Wt: 12 grams
Malibu, JPGM, 85.AM.277

An elegantly dressed woman, wearing a sleeveless *chiton* belted at the waist and a heavier *himation* draped over her legs, sits on a stool holding a balance scale with two small winged Erotes. Her hair is rolled up on the sides and tied on top, and she appears to wear a wreath, as well as bracelets and sandals. Whether she is a mortal or the goddess Aphrodite is unclear, but similar scenes of the *Erotostasia* (weighing of loves) appear on Athenian and South Italian vases, as well as on other rings, and seem to reflect the Homeric tradition of the *Psychostasia* (weighing of souls).

BIBLIOGRAPHY Spier 1992, 34, no. 51; Lapatin and Wight 2010, 86.

....

Plate 18
Ring with Bellerophon, Pegasos, and the Chimaira, ca. 350–300 BC
Gold, H (bezel): 2 cm; W (bezel): 1.4 cm; D (box): 0.8 cm;
Wt: 8 grams
Malibu, JPGM, 88.AM.104

Bellerophon, mounted upon Pegasos, slays the Chimaira. The figural motif was embossed on a separate sheet of gold cut to fit the bezel of this hollow box ring, to which it was subsequently applied. The area around the mythical scene was then decorated with filigree floral decoration, as were the sides and bottom of the hollow box. Palmettes and tendrils adorn the top and sides and addorsed palmettes, a bellflower blossom, and tendrils, the bottom. The distinctive corkscrew coils of the bottom tendrils allow attribution of the ring to the anonymous goldsmith called the Santa Eufemia Master after similar works discovered at Santa Eufemia in Calabria, southern Italy. Heavier beaded wire surrounds the top and bottom of the box, and the hoop of the ring is composed of eight short strands of loop-in-loop chain, with terminals of plain and beaded wire surmounted by filigree palmettes.

BIBLIOGRAPHY Spier 1992, 41, no. 70; Hoffmann 1993; Lapatin and Wight 2010, 123. See also Williams 1988.

....

Plate 19
Pendant disk with head of *Athena Parthenos*, ca. 400–350 BC
From Kul Oba, Kerch, Crimea
Gold and enamel, H: 18.5 cm; Diam: 7.2 cm; Wt: 85.3 grams
St. Petersburg, State Hermitage Museum, KO 5

This elaborate object, one of a pair mirroring each other, is among the earliest surviving representations of the monumental gold and ivory statue that Pheidias fashioned for the interior of the Parthenon on the Athenian Acropolis. That work is lost, but ancient literary sources describe the goddess as wearing a helmet with three crests—a central sphinx flanked by Pegasoi—stag and griffin protomes on the visor, and griffins on the cheek pieces, all of which are visible here along with dotted spirals on the visor. Also rendered in repoussé are the goddess's disk-and-pyramid earrings, three-tier necklace, and the two snakes of her aegis. Her owl can be seen to her right. This embossed and chased disk is surrounded by a flat band of sheet gold with filigree ivy tendrils and leaf cloisons filled with blue and green enamel. This circular band is bordered by plain and beaded wire on the interior and exterior and is further decorated with ivy leaves (originally filled with enamel) and six-petaled rosettes of sheet gold and beaded wire filigree, five of which survive. From the disk hangs an elaborate network of fine double loop-in-loop chains, from which are suspended heavy wire spirals, rosettes, small gold disks with blue and green enamel, and embossed seed- or urn-like pendants decorated with filigree, granulation, and colored enamel.

BIBLIOGRAPHY Higgins 1980, 130, pl. 29; Boardman 1993, 131, no. 118A; Ogden and Williams 1994, 144–45, no. 87; Trofimova 2007, 243–44, no. 141.

....

Plate 20

Bracelet with sphinxes, ca. 400–350 BC
From Kul Oba, Kerch, Crimea
Gold and enamel, H: 11.5 cm; W: 10 cm; Wt: 176.2 grams
St. Petersburg, State Hermitage Museum, KO 19

The sphinxes at the terminals of this bracelet were assembled from numerous elements formed separately from gold sheet, with details added in wire (such as their diadems, each with a central rosette, earrings, and pendant necklaces) or rendered in repoussé (such as the veins on their bellies). Coiled wire with snake's heads links the sphinxes' front paws, and the fine lotus and palmette filigree decoration of the collars was originally bordered by colored enamel inlays, pale green and white or pale blue. Small beaded wires separate the floral friezes, while larger beaded wires frame the collars and run along the twisted hoop of the bracelet, which is filled with a brown resinous material. Damage to the bracelet, one of a pair, suggests that it was worn in life as well as death.

BIBLIOGRAPHY Higgins 1980, 131, pl. 30B; Deppert-Lippitz 1985, 189, fig. 138; Piotrovsky, Galanina, and Grach 1987, no. 182; Williams and Ogden 1994, 140–41, no. 83; Despini 1996, 198, 261, fig. 197; Kalashnik 2004, 28–29; Trofimova 2007, 242, no. 140.

....

Plate 21

Wreath with Nikai and Erotes, dedicated by Kreithonios,
ca. 350–300 BC
Inscribed: ΚΡΕΙΘΩΝΙΟΣΗΘΗΚΗΤΟΕΙΣΤΗΦΑΝΟΝ (Κρειθώνιος ἧθηκη τὸ εἰ[ς] στέφανον)
From a chamber tomb at Serra d'Oro, near Armento, southern Italy
Gold, H: 37 cm; Diam: 19 cm
Munich, Antikensammlungen, 2335 WAF

This extraordinary gold wreath, originally comprising over one thousand separate elements, consists of large and small sprigs of oak entwined with ivy, narcissus, myrtle, roses, and asters, in which sport bees and anthropomorphic figures. Embossed leaves, flowers, and rosettes, some with enameled decoration, as well as acorns and clusters of berries, all spring from wire tendrils. The bees, too, are fashioned by repoussé, as are six (of seven original) winged figures: three nude kneeling Erotes and two draped females. These flank a central female figure, wearing a *chiton* and granulation-decked *himation*, disk earrings, a necklace with cluster pendant, shoes, and a pointed crown topped by a rosette. In her left hand she holds a *phiale*; the pitcher originally in her right is lost. She stands on a pedestal adorned with acanthus, rosettes, bellflowers, and palmettes, which bears an inscription in filigree. The inscription has occasioned much discussion but seems to indicate that Kreithonios provided funds for the wreath. Excavated on August 2, 1814, and later acquired by Caroline Murat, the sister of Napoleon Bonaparte and sometime Queen of Naples, it was purchased by Ludwig I of Bavaria in 1826.

BIBLIOGRAPHY Becatti 1955, 192, no. 354; Lipinsky 1975a, 1975b; Higgins 1980, 124, pl. 23; De Juliis 1984, 100–1, no. 32; Lullies 1982; Deppert-Lippitz 1985, 196, fig. 145, pl. XXI; Musti et al. 1992, 150, 260, fig. 119; Guzzo 2001a, 283.

....

Plate 22

Pegasos protome, ca. 350 BC
From Vazovo, Bulgaria
Gold, H: 14.8 cm; Wt: 475.5 grams
Razgrad, Bulgaria, Regional History Museum, 1409

This representation of the mythical winged beast is a masterpiece of small-scale sculpture that must have appealed greatly to the horse-riding Thracians living to the north and east of the mainland Greeks. Originally part of a larger whole, the wings and legs of the beast were fashioned separately and joined to the body, but they share the realistic treatment of form and texture. The curved and straight feathers of the upturned wings are expertly embossed, as are the mane, neck muscles, forelocks, teeth, and fetlocks. Veins, muscles, and other features of the head are realistically rendered, but a curved horn has been added between the creature's ears. The harness and bridle are rendered by parallel rows of small dots. Recovered after illicit excavation.

BIBLIOGRAPHY Marazov et al. 1998, 136–37, no. 61; Nikolov 2007, 174–75, no. 123.

....

Plate 23
Phiale (libation bowl) with acorns, beechnuts, and bees, dedicated by Demarchos, son of Achyris, ca. 325–275 BC
Inscribed: ΔΑΜΑΡΧΟΥ ΑΧΥΡΙΟΣ ΧΡΥΣΟΙ ΠbÞ
From Monte Riperto, Caltavuturo, Sicily
Gold, H: 3.7 cm; Diam: 22.8 cm; Wt: 982.4 grams
Himera, Sicily, Antiquarium, 12184

This libation bowl (*phiale mesomphalos*) is decorated with three concentric rows of stamped acorns (thirty-six per row), each decreasing in size toward the center, and one row of beechnuts. These rows are interspersed with abbreviated florals and, in the outermost ring, bees. The area around the *omphalos* is separated from the beechnuts by beaded wire on the interior and decorated with repoussé lotuses and palmettes; the exterior is incised with fine ivy tendrils. A Greek inscription in carefully formed dotted letters on the exterior lip records that the vessel belonged to and/or was dedicated by Demarchos, son of Achyris (or the *demarch* [magistrate] Achyris), and that it weighs 115 gold pieces, meaning staters. Ancient Roman marble replicas of the badly damaged "caryatids" that supported the south porch of the Erechtheion on the Athenian Acropolis found at the villa of the Roman emperor Hadrian at Tivoli indicate that they originally carried *phialai* adorned with acorns, and *phialai akylotai* and *phialai balanotai* are mentioned in Greek temple inventories. Recovered after illicit excavation.
BIBLIOGRAPHY Spatafora and Vassallo 2005; Guzzo, Spatafora, and Vassallo 2010; Guzzo in Lyons et al. 2013, 44–47. Compare a similar vessel in New York (Metropolitan Museum of Art, 62.11.1); see von Bothmer 1962; Strong 1966, 97–98, pl. 23A; von Bothmer 1984, 10–11, 50, no. 86; Lewis 1985, 77–78; Mertens and Anderson 1987, 82, fig. 61; Vickers and Gill 1994, 43n80, fig. 2.4; Picón et al. 2007, 195, 450, no. 231.

....

Plate 24
Phiale (libation bowl) with Ethiopians and acorns, ca. 325–275 BC
From Panagyurishte in Thrace (southern Bulgaria)
Gold, H: 3.5 cm; Diam: 25 cm; Wt: 845.7 grams
Plovdiv, Bulgaria, Archaeological Museum, 3204

Ancient authors record that the late fifth-century BC statue of Nemesis, fashioned by the Athenian sculptor Agorakritos, in that goddess's temple at Rhamnous held a *phiale* adorned with the heads of Ethiopians, and Athenian temple inventories mention *phialai Aithiopides*. The appearance of these exotic humans on gold libation bowls may have been a reference to some distant source of the metal, as well as to the Africans' upright way of life. This *phiale mesomphalos* is decorated with five concentric rows of stamped ornament, each decreasing in size toward the center, with lotuses and palmettes interspersed. Three of the rows consist of the heads of Ethiopians (black Africans), and one each of acorns and rosettes. An inscription on the inside of the mouth consists of two linked letters, MY. Two inscriptions on the outside record the weight of the vessel: H = *hekato*, indicating 100 Persian darics or 100 staters of Lampsakos, a Greek city on the eastern side of the Hellespont; the other inscription, also in the akrophonetic system, records the equivalent in Athenian currency: 196 drachmai and 1/4 obol. This *phiale* was found with eight other gold vessels on December 8, 1949, in Panagyurishte in Thrace (southern Bulgaria) weighing a total of 6.16 kilograms. The other vessels (an amphora and seven rhytons) are decorated with scenes of Thracian myths in Hellenic style, apparently fashioned for local elites by Greek craftsmen.
BIBLIOGRAPHY Venedikov 1961, 17, figs. 35–38, no. 9; Kontoleon 1962; Strong 1966, 97; Venedikov and Gerassimov 1975, 359, figs. 131–32; Lewis 1985, 76–77; Musti et al. 1992, 203, 280, fig. 156.1; Marazov et al. 1998, 148, no. 76; Nikolov 2007, 202–3, no. 137b.

....

Plate 25
Kylix, ca. 350–300 BC
From the Goljama Kosmatka Tumulus, Bulgaria
Gold, H: 5.9 cm; Diam: 9.5 cm; Wt: 228 grams
Kazanlik, Bulgaria, Iskra Historical Museum, A1715

Excavated in the autumn of 2004 near Seuthopolis, the ancient capital of Thrace, the Goljama Kosmatka tumulus has been associated with the early third-century BC burial of King Seuthes II. Finds included fine armor and a helmet inscribed with the king's name, horse trappings, and drinking vessels, the shapes of which, like this *kylix* with elegant bent handles, appear elsewhere in silver as well as terracotta. Delicate incised palmettes decorate the interior.
BIBLIOGRAPHY Kitov 2005, 50, fig. 15; Nikolov 2007, 162, no. 118e.

....

Plate 26
Necklace, ca. 330–300 BC
From the Great Bliznitsa Kurgan, Crimea
Gold and enamel, L: 37.8 cm; H: 6 cm; Wt: 241.7 grams
St. Petersburg, State Hermitage Museum, BB34

This fine chain-strap necklace with three rows of pendants is one of the most impressive works of ancient Greek goldsmithing. Repoussé lion's head terminals with hoops in their mouths form the clasps. Flat collars with thin beaded wire filigree palmettes and tendrils, bordered by plain, twisted, and larger beaded wire borders, mask the join to a long, flat loop-in-loop chain. Additional ornaments are suspended in three rows from this chain, which is made up of alternating double rosettes and disks edged with beaded wire. Twenty-one beechnut pendants with filigree cloisons filled with green enamel hang from the disks, while three strands of single loop-in-loop chains are attached to the rosettes. The central chain supports twenty-two small vase-shaped pendants with embossed leaves and granulation, topped by a rosette. The outer chains support twenty-one larger vase-shaped pendants decorated with alternating patterns: embossed leaves with granulation and a central panel with beaded wire filigree spiral tendrils punctuated by enamel-filled petals.

BIBLIOGRAPHY Williams and Ogden 1994, 188–89, no. 121; Kalashnik 2004, 54–55, no. 28; Trofimova 2007, 273–74, no. 163.

....

Plate 27
Earring with Nikai, ca. 350 BC
From Kul Oba, Kerch, Crimea
Gold, cinnabar, and enamel, H: 9 cm; Diam (disk): 2.8 cm; Wt: 23.4 grams
St. Petersburg, State Hermitage Museum, KO7

Elaborate boat-shaped earrings were popular in the late Classical and Hellenistic periods, and this stunning example from Kul Oba in the Crimea combines a crescent-shaped boat with a large disk, repoussé Nikai, palmettes, rosettes, and tendrils, and beechnut-shaped pendants. The disk has a complex flower at the center, which was originally filled with cinnabar. Twisted wire filigree coils and tendrils attached to a flat background surround the flower and are surrounded in turn by a series of plain and twisted wire circles and, toward the edge, rows of superimposed granulated beads. The boat is suspended by two chains, and its ends are adorned with (now distorted) palmettes, the leaves of which have filigree edges, while their hearts were filled with cinnabar. Mirrored cut-out repoussé Nikai, nude but for drapery over one thigh, rest on each terminal adjusting a sandal. The body of the boat is decorated with granulation, its edges demarcated by beaded wire, and a central palmette with spiral tendrils rises from the center like an *akroterion* (the upper ornament of a Greek temple). Eight rosettes are attached to its bottom, and from these hang a series of loop-in-loop chains from which are suspended ribbed, plain, and granulated beechnut-shaped pendants, as well as further rosettes and small disks filled with blue and green enamel.

BIBLIOGRAPHY Williams and Ogden 1994, 149, no. 89.

....

Plate 28
Pair of earrings with Artemis, ca. 375–300 BC
From Nymphaion (Crimea)
Gold, H: 4.4 and 4.6 cm; W (each): 2.5 cm; Wt (each): 8.6 grams
St. Petersburg, State Hermitage Museum, GK/N.2

These earrings take the form of Artemis riding a stag. The goddess wears a sleeveless *peplos*, pinned at the shoulders and belted at the waist, over a *chiton*, vertical folds of which are visible at the ankles, as well as sandals, necklace, and earrings of her own. Holding a torch in one hand and an antler of her sacred stag in the other, she rides sidesaddle on the beast, whose pelt is rendered by fine wavy chased lines and whose muzzle is stippled. Both goddess and animal are constructed of several components of sheet metal, as are the torches, which consist of rods of wire bound with three bunches of three looped wires. The figural groups hang from a twelve-petaled rosette, bordered by beaded wire filigree, framing two rows of thinner petals formed by wire loops. Originally, the centers of both were filled with stamens with enamel anthers and a central bee of sheet gold, only one of which is preserved. The combination of motifs has been variously explained. Artemis is the patron of wild animals and was long linked with bees. Because of her association with purity and chastity, her image is appropriate for brides before marriage. She protected weddings, in which torches played a role, and aided in childbirth. Thus, it has been suggested that earrings such as these might have been an appropriate wedding or spousal gift. The goddess is also sometimes linked with the moon goddess Selene, and with Iphigenia, who had particular significance in the Crimea, where these were found. Alternately, an Orphic fragment preserves a tradition that Zeus sent Artemis to help look for Persephone. Thus, perhaps, the torch has funerary connotations.

BIBLIOGRAPHY Hoffmann and Davidson 1965, 80–82, fig. 12f; Williams and Ogden 1994, 173–74, no. 110; Kalashnik 2004, 40–41, fig. 15; Trofimova 2007, 232–33, no. 132.

....

Plate 29
Pair of earrings with Ganymede and the Eagle of Zeus, ca. 330–300 BC
Said to be from northern Greece
Gold, H (each): 6 cm; Wt: 15.1 and 16.5 grams
New York, Metropolitan Museum of Art, 37.11.9–.10

Winged figures were popular motifs for earrings, as when worn they seemed to fly or float in the air. This pair of mirrored figures represents the eagle of Zeus carrying the Trojan prince Ganymede off to Olympus. The bodies of boy and bird are cast, while the drapery and finely chased wings and tails are fashioned from sheet gold. Like the Nike in Boston (plate 30), these mythological figures hang from an elaborate flaming palmette, with a granulated center and leaves edged in beaded wire filigree. Some have seen in this group a reflection of the lost sculpture of the same subject by the fourth-century BC Athenian sculptor Leochares mentioned by Pliny (*NH* 34.79). Others see the subject, an ascent to Olympus, as appropriate for a funerary context. Allegedly found in northern Greece together with gold necklaces, pins, and a pair of rock-crystal bracelets.

BIBLIOGRAPHY Hoffmann and Davidson 1965, 80–82, fig. 12g; Higgins 1980, 129, 164, pl. 48A; Deppetz-Lippert 1985, 226–27, fig. 163; Williams and Ogden 1994, 76, no. 31; Despini 1996, 118, 234, no. 97; Picón et al. 2007, 170, 440, no. 197.

....

Plate 30
Earring with Nike driving a chariot, ca. 350–325 BC
Gold and enamel, H: 5 cm; Wt: 15.8 grams
Boston, Museum of Fine Arts, 98.788

An intricate miniature work of sculpture in the round, this gold earring depicts the goddess of victory leaning forward—balanced by her long, elegantly chased wings—holding the reins of her rearing horses in her left hand and a goad, only partially preserved, in her right. Wind sweeps through the skirt of her sleeveless *chiton*, which is belted at the waist and buttoned at both shoulders by granules of gold. She also wears bracelets and earrings. The horses (stallions) and their harness are rendered with no less detail: veins run along their bellies, and the hooves and leg and neck muscles are carefully rendered, as are the bits, headstalls, throat-lashes, breast-collars, and girths, the last two stamped, respectively, with circular punches and fashioned from twisted wire. The construction is complex: each horse was made in two halves, soldered together, with the legs added separately. Likewise, the goddess is hollow except for her arms. The chariot pole and axle are made of heavy wire; the wheels either cast or struck and attached so as to actually revolve. The elaborate palmette from which the whole is suspended by linking wire rings has been compared to an *akroterion*. Surrounding a central drop-shaped "fruit" filled with granulation and rimmed with filigree are sixteen sickle-shaped petals rimmed with beaded wire and fourteen circular stamens, rimmed with granulation, that were originally filled with polychrome enamel. Behind the palmette is a hook, terminating in a serpent's head. Not counting individual beads of granulation, the entire ensemble is composed of some 130 distinct pieces.

BIBLIOGRAPHY Segall 1942; Hoffmann and Davidson 1965, 76–82, no. 12; Deppert-Lippitz 1985, 226, fig. 164; Boardman 1993, 131, no. 118B.

....

Plate 31
Earring with Siren, ca. 330–300 BC
Gold, H: 4.4 cm; Wt: 7.3 grams
New York, Metropolitan Museum of Art, 08.258.49

Standing majestically on a double platform separated by gold spheres, this composite creature, half bird, half woman, was made in two halves (the seam of the gold sheets is visible on the right forearm), with the wings, tail, legs, diadem, earrings, *kithara*, and plectrum made separately. The three surviving strings of the instrument are made of thin gold wire, just 0.1 mm in diameter. The details of the siren's leg, tail, and wing feathers, as well as her hair, have been carefully chased. The figure is surmounted by a complex two-tiered palmette, consisting of two unequal rosettes with leaves and petals bordered by twisted wire. The end of the hook is in the form of a snake's head. Some have attributed this work to the same workshop that produced the Ganymede earrings (plate 29).

BIBLIOGRAPHY Hoffmann and Davidson 1965, 80–81, fig. 12e; Williams and Ogden 1994, 66, no. 19; Despini 1996, 120, 235, fig. 99.

....

Plate 32
Ear reel with Nereid and Eros, ca. 350–330 BC
From Kamiros, Rhodes
Gold, Diam: 2.3 cm; D: 1.1 cm; Wt: 4.1 grams
London, British Museum, GR1862,0530.8 (Jewellery 2067)

One of a pair now split between London and Paris, this repoussé ear reel is decorated on both sides with die-formed sheets attached to a spool-shaped side sheet. Both sides depict a mythological figure that slightly overlaps concentric circles. On one side, a Nereid rides a dolphin; her hair is tied up, and her sleeveless *chiton* is unbuttoned at the right shoulder exposing one breast. She carries a Corinthian helmet, one of the arms fashioned by Hephaistos for Achilles. On the other side, a nude winged Eros leans on a pillar, playing with a *iunx*, a kind of love charm in the form of a wheel on a string. Found within a marble *pyxis* along with an engraved gem. The same tomb contained a well-known *pelike* by the Marsyas Painter.

BIBLIOGRAPHY Marshall 1911, no. 2067; De Ridder 1924, no. 17; Williams and Ogden 1994, 90–91, no. 43; Treister 2001, 93n118.

....

Plate 33
Larnax, ca. 336–316 BC
From Tomb II at Vergina, Macedonia
Gold and enamel, H: 20.7 cm; W: 41 cm; D: 34 cm; Wt: 7.790 kg
Vergina Archaeological Museum, BM 2630

This sumptuous solid gold *larnax* (chest) was placed inside a marble box in the center of the western chamber of Tomb II in the large tumulus at Vergina in Macedonia. It contained a gold oak wreath and, wrapped with a gold and purple textile (plate 176), the cremated bones of a man, whom the excavator, Manolis Andronicos, believed to be Philip II, king of Macedon and father of Alexander the Great, but whom other scholars prefer to see as Philip III Arrhidaios, Alexander's half-brother. The four sides of the *larnax* are fashioned from two bent sheets of gold riveted together, with four longer pieces terminating in lion's paws at the corners. The lower edges of the sides are bent inward to support the bottom of the box, and the top of the back panel is connected to the lid with looped hinges held in place by a long pin. Graceful repoussé patterns and separately fashioned appliqués adorn the lid and sides of the *larnax*. The lid is edged with fine beading; within an embossed rectangle is a large embossed sixteen-point "Macedonian" star with eight shorter rays nestled within eight larger ones. A central embossed double circle surrounds a double ten-petaled rosette appliqué, the innermost petals of which are filled with blue glass paste that is attached by a gold rivet. Each of the sides is divided into three horizontal zones, apparently imitating similar items in wood: an embossed lotus and palmette chain above; a central recessed panel with ten-petaled gold and blue glass paste rosettes, five on the front and back, four on the two shorter sides; and a symmetrical embossed frieze of acanthus tendrils that sprout flowers and lilies. (The back has only the attached appliqués, not the embossed florals.) The longer corner pieces rest upon separately fashioned repoussé lion's paws, attached by rivets, and are decorated on both sides with a row of four double eight-petaled gold appliqué rosettes. Two large knobs near the corners of the lid and the front served as anchors for cord to tie the *larnax* closed.

BIBLIOGRAPHY N. Yalouris 1980, 186–87, fig. 36, no. 172; Andronicos 1984, 168–71; Tripodi 1985; Musti et al. 1992, 183, 270–71, fig. 147.1; Ginouvès 1994, 161–66, fig. 139; Borza and Palagia 2007; Kottaridi 2011, 74–77.

....

Plate 34
Gorgon appliqué, ca. 336–316 BC
From Tomb II at Vergina, Macedonia
Gold, H: 3.6 cm; W: 3.5 cm
Vergina Archaeological Museum, BM 2630

One of a pair thought to have originally been attached to a linen corselet that has largely disintegrated, this appliqué is of the earliest known depictions of the "beautiful" Gorgon type, in contrast to Archaic and early Classical Gorgons, which were represented with beards, wrinkled brows, lolling tongue, and fangs. Here the quality of the repoussé modeling and engraved details far surpasses the miniature scale of the object.

BIBLIOGRAPHY Andronicos 1984, 189–90, figs. 152–53; Musti et al. 1992, 189, fig. 147.13; Kottaridi 2011, 50–52, no. 175; Kottaridi et al. 2011, 91, 241, fig. 77, no. 91.

....

Plate 35
Diadem, ca. 200 BC
From the so-called Tomb of the Gold Ornaments, Canosa, southern Italy
Gold, enamel, cornelian, and garnet, L: 47.2 cm; Wt: 145 grams
Taranto, Museo Nazionale Archeologico, 22.437

This complex diadem consists of two flat semicircular gold sheets folded into tubes with beaded wire edges that are joined by a central hinge. Rings at the terminals, which are adorned with fine acanthus leaves, would have held the ribbon or cord with which the diadem was tied. The diadem presents vivid polychromatic contrasts. To its base are mounted spiral gold and enamel ribbons and some 150 small flowers, whose leaves, blossoms, and tendrils are edged with filigree and filled with white, blue, red, and dark and light green enamel. Colored glass beads and two small cornelians and two garnets attached by wires represent berries.

BIBLIOGRAPHY Becatti 1955, 191, no. 353; Coarelli 1970, no. 51; Higgins 1980, 157, pl. 45B; Deppert-Lippitz 1985, 244, fig. 179; De Juliis 1984, 110, 123–25, no. 54; De Juliis and Loiacono 1985, 314–35, fig. 370; Despini 1996, 78, 217, fig. 38; Guzzo 2001a, 118–20, 292 (B1), fig. 67.

....

Plate 36
Diadem in the form of a Herakles knot, ca. 200 BC
Said to be from Thessaly
Gold with garnet, agate, glass paste, and enamel, L: 52.5 cm; H: 4.5 cm
Athens, Benaki Museum, 1548

The central openwork motif of this diadem is connected by hinges to two trapezoidal plaques, the volutes of which recall Ionic capitals. Each plaque is connected to two flat-weave chains, with tassels hanging from the whole. The diadem is richly polychromatic, with profuse alternating green and blue enamel and cornelian cabochon inlays. Those in the Herakles knot are held in place by filigree bands of gold sheet and dentate triangles. At the center of the knot is rosette that has lost its inlay. It is flanked by opposing palmettes, and these elements are all edged with beaded wire filigree. Four smaller rosettes with granulated centers and edged with beaded wire filigree further adorn the knot. Four beaded wire volutes are partially tucked behind the sheet gold hinge plates, which are ornamented with filigree tongues and plain, double-twisted, and beaded wire filigree. Blue and green enamel decorate the central palmettes and the tongues on the bands in the knot and on the hinge plates. Colored enamel also decorates the borders of the central panels of both lateral plaques, the central panels of which are framed with plain, twisted, and beaded wire filigree. These panels are each filled with a single, teardrop cabochon at the center of a seven-leaved palmette, with two rosettes with beaded wire filigree edges above, and a double-twisted wire volute below. From each of these plaques extend two flat woven loop-in-loop chains with sheet gold terminals; these are ornamented with central palmettes edged and bordered by twisted wire filigree, some of which—again—are filled with alternating green and blue enamel. Each of the four terminals ends with a gold loop for a tie or clasp. Nine (of ten original) tassels of red, pink, and green glass beads hang from gold chains symmetrically positioned at each of the various elements. Said to have been found in Thessaly (at either Hamyros, near ancient Larissa Kremeste, or Karpenisi).

BIBLIOGRAPHY Segall 1938, 32–36, no. 28; Amandry 1953, 118; Hoffmann and Davidson 1965, 57, fig. 2c; Coarelli 1970, no. 45; N. Yalouris 1980, 143, no. 79A, color pl. 15; Higgins 1980, 158, pl. 46; Despini 1996, 74–75, 215, figs. 32–33; Delivorrias in Georgoula 1999, 202–3, no. 67, fig. 144.

....

Plate 37
Dress pin with crouching Aphrodite (detail), ca. 300–200 BC
Gold and garnet, H (figure): 1.8 cm
Athens, Benaki Museum, 2062

The goddess twists long locks of her hair with both hands, drying it after the bath, as seen in larger statues dependent on a prototype traditionally but erroneously attributed to Doidalsas of Bithynia based

on a corrupted passage from Pliny (*NH* 36.35). Wearing a diadem as well as a spiral necklace, she crouches on an elaborate triple openwork rosette of beaded wire set atop a Corinthian capital, the abacus of which is adorned on each side with garnet and emerald cabochons. Four winged Erotes sit or kneel at the corners of the abacus, each holding a different implement to assist the goddess: a mirror, a dress pin, an *alabastron* (perfume vase), and a fourth item that remains unidentified. Two long loop-in-loop chains hang from the bottom of the capital. They each have a hook at the end.
BIBLIOGRAPHY Despini 1996, 184–85, figs. 178–79; Oliver in Georgoula 1999, 200–1, no. 66, fig. 142. For dress pins in temple inventories see Brøns 2014, 40–45 and appendix 4.

....

Plate 38
Pair of earrings with doves, ca. 150–100 BC
From the Artjukhov Barrow, near Phanagoreia, Taman Peninsula, Russia
Gold, enamel, garnet, and cornelian, H: 6.5 cm
St. Petersburg, State Hermitage Museum, 40

Doves fashioned from white enamel with green wings and tail, inlaid gold eyes, gold beaks, and gold legs stand atop a gold platform. They are suspended between pendants of loop-in-loop chain and spiral twisted wire terminating in garnet beads with filigree caps. The elaborate disks have a garnet nucleus held in place by a granulated rosette-topped pin surrounded by a triple rosette of triangular cut-out leaves, originally enameled, with granulated clusters at the edge. Each disk is ringed by beaded and plain wire and filigree tongues. Above each disk is an "Isis crown," consisting of a pair of horns that frame a cornelian set within a circle of beaded wire, with two long feathers edged with beaded wire filigree, originally enameled. The dove is often associated with Aphrodite but also appears regularly in funerary contexts.
BIBLIOGRAPHY Higgins 1980, 164, pl. 48B; Despini 1996, 125, fig. 105.

....

Plate 39
Pair of armbands with Tritons and Erotes, ca. 200 BC
Gold, H: 25 and 26.5 cm; Wt (each): 186.5 grams
New York, Metropolitan Museum of Art, 56.11.5–.6

While snake bracelets are well known, this pair of armbands in the form of male and female Tritons (half-human, half sea-creature) is unique. The snake-bodied, fish-tailed creatures coil two-and-a-half times, and a third tight twist occurs just below their hips, where the transition between their impressive chased human musculature and scaly animal bodies is masked by acanthus leaves. Both the male and the female Triton hold an infant Eros in one arm, reaching upward and back with the other, perhaps to adjust the cloaks that billow behind their heads. Three rings behind each cloak may have been intended to link the armbands to a garment. While the exterior of both bands is finely chased, the interior has been lined with smooth sheet, on which is an inscription in dotted letters: ΖΩΙ. Similar inscriptions appear elsewhere and may be an abbreviation of the name of the goldsmith or, more likely, the owner.
BIBLIOGRAPHY Higgins 1980, 168, pl. 51B; Deppert-Lippitz 1985, 268, fig. 202; Mertens et al. 1987, 83, fig. 62; Williams and Ogden 1994, 82–83, no. 37; Despini 1996, 192–93, 260, figs. 192–93; Picón et al. 2007, 193, no. 229.

....

Plate 40
Assemblage of jewelry, ca. 220–100 BC
Said to be from Alexandria
Gold, garnet, cornelian, pearl, and glass
Malibu, JPGM, 92.AM.8.1–.11

This assemblage of eleven pieces of gold jewelry seems to have come from Hellenistic Alexandria. The diadem and hair-net are complex pieces, assembled from multiple components, with filigree, granulation, and added garnets, deep red stones imported from India that were extensively used in Hellenistic jewelry. The diadem has a central Herakles knot flanked by torch motives, profuse filigree, and hanging tassels. The hair-net has a central repoussé medallion of Aphrodite with a small winged Eros at her left shoulder. Two pairs of snake bracelets, two pairs of hoop earrings in the form of felines, a pair of pendant earrings depicting Eros, several gold cowry shells that would have formed a necklace, and two massive gold rings with cornelian intaglios depicting Artemis and Tyche complete the group.
BIBLIOGRAPHY Pfrommer 1999, 125–32; Pfrommer 2001; Lapatin and Wight 2010, 90–91.

....

Plate 41
Miniature shrine with Dionysos, ca. 200–100 BC
Said to be from Karpenisi, Thessaly
Gold, cornelian, and glass, H: 14.5 cm; W: 9 cm
Athens, National Archaeological Museum, 379 (232)

The god of wine, a satyr, and a panther in high relief are executed in repoussé applied to a stippled gold sheet and framed by separately worked Corinthian columns, socle, architrave, and pediment. Details have been added through chasing, filigree, appliqués, and cloisons with green and dark red glass and cornelian inserts. Dionysos stands frontally, off-center and off-balance, wearing a cloak pinned over his chest by a round medallion, which leaves his torso bare but sweeps across his thighs, covering his legs. He wears an ivy wreath with gold berries in his luxuriant hair and holds a *kantharos* in his right hand, while his left is thrown behind the shoulders of a muscular young satyr in a lively pose, whose rough skin contrasts with the smooth flesh of the god and the pelt of the frontal panther in the lower right-hand corner. A thyrsus with a spiral wand stands diagonally behind the god. Four gold "rings" with green and red glass cloisons hold the central sheet in position. The shrine itself consists of a base with alternating appliqués, glass cloisons, and rosettes with beaded wire petals, all framed by two strips of beaded wire filigree. The columns are set upon molded Ionic bases, with beaded wire filigree, and their lower sections have been left unfluted. The capitals rest atop two strands of beaded wire, with a smooth concave molding between them, and consist of vertical beaded wire and tightly wound wire volutes. Above double-twisted and plain wire filigree, the architrave resembles the base, except for a single central almond-shaped cloison filled with cornelian. Above that, between rows of filigree beaded wire, is a filigree frieze of eggs-and-darts and a row of embossed dentils. A separately fashioned pediment, framed by filigree eggs-and-darts, is filled by two large sheet gold rosettes with twisted wire filigree petals flanking a ten-pointed star, with five large closions filled with cornelian and five smaller ones filled with now-disintegrated glass paste, around a central round cornelian cloison. The central *akroterion* is largely lost, but the corner *akroteria* rise from a cornelian cloison with pointed and curved leaves, which were perhaps originally filled with some other material. While unique in gold, the form of this shrine has parallels in other materials.

BIBLIOGRAPHY Amandry 1946–48; Amandry 1953, 91–97, no. 445; Becatti 1955, 94–95, no. 445; Coarelli 1970, no. 42; S. Miller 1979, 10, pl. 19a; Musti et al. 1992, 197, fig. 150.3.

....

Plate 42
Head of a satyr, ca. 200–100 BC
Gold, H: 4.1 cm
Private collection

This highly expressive miniature sculpture representing one of the wild followers of the wine god Dionysos has a projecting perforated flange on the underside of its thick neck, perhaps indicating that it once served as the lid of a small vessel. The goldsmith has modulated the soft flesh of the satyr's heavily ridged brow, pug nose, thick lower lip, dimpled cheeks, and philtrum, in contrast to the apparent hardness of his widely spaced upper teeth and cleft chin. The bulging eyes are surrounded by heavy lids under turbulent, fleecy eyebrows that join at the bridge of the nose, communicating well the goaty character of this mythical creature. The thick spiked locks of hair—recalling those of the *Dying Gaul* and other Pergamene sculpture of the second century BC—curve back, diverging from the trajectory of the tall, pointed ears. The powerful vivacity of the figure, who turns his head to his left, stands out all the more in contrast to the delicate wreath of filigree ivy leaves and granulated berries at the back of the head, which has a double suspension loop and a pin threaded through it. Formerly in the Mathias Kormor collection.

BIBLIOGRAPHY Sotheby's, New York, November 21–22, 1985, lot 102; Christie's, New York, December 5, 2012 (sale 2770), lot 381.

....

Plate 43
Pair of earrings with Ethiopians, ca. 200 BC
From Tomb 3 at Vaccarella (Taranto)
Gold and garnet, H: 1.8 cm
Taranto, Museo Nazionale Archeologico, 22.634–5

This pair of earrings represents an Ethiopian (black African) couple, male and female. Their heads and necks, carved from garnets, have been inserted into sheet gold casings with collars at the bottom. From the collars twisted loop-in-loop chains emerge as the hoops of the earrings. They terminate in a smooth gold tail that hooks into a loop at the top of the head, which is composed of sheet gold covered with tight wire spiral curls that protrude from the surface, in the case of the man, and concentric waves, gathered at the neck in bun, for the woman. Similar earrings were produced in gold with amber inserts.

BIBLIOGRAPHY Becatti 1955, 199, no. 405; De Juliis 1984, 190–91, no. 130; Guzzo 2001a, 100, 259, fig. 53.

....

Plate 44a, b
Pair of engraved rings depicting a Ptolemy, ca. 186–145 BC
From Egypt
Gold, H: 3.4 and 2.6 cm; W: 2.5 and 1.9 cm
Paris, Musée du Louvre, Bj 1092, 1093

Both these rings bear engraved portraits of a Ptolemaic king (often identified as Ptolemy VI Philometer); one depicts him as a Hellenistic Greek monarch, the other in the guise of an Egyptian pharaoh. On the ring with a rectangular bezel, the ruler, with wide eyes, a large aquiline nose, small downturned mouth, and trim beard, wears a wide Egyptian collar with three tiers of ornament (dotted ovals, zigzags, and a simple battlement meander), as well as the double crown of upper and lower Egypt, which is tied with a ribbon knotted behind him. The tasseled ends of a wide cloth fillet, or diadem, emerge from beneath the crown and flutter behind him, while his unkempt hair emerges from the front. The ring with an oval bezel depicts the same man in Greek dress, a *chlamys* buttoned at the shoulder over a tunic, the double fold lines of which are also rendered. He, too, wears a diadem, the standard attribute of Hellenistic kings. Formerly in the collection of Napoleon III.

BIBLIOGRAPHY Furtwängler 1900, pl. xxxi.25–6; Richter 1968a, 158–59, nos. 625–26; Boardman 1970, 370–71, pl. 1010; Metzger in Rausch 1998, 203, nos. 147–48; Gerring 2000, 12, 174; Walker and Higgs 2001, 67, nos. 44–45; Stanwick 2003, 35, 53n42, 63n17, 73, figs. 224–25.

....

Plate 45
Ring with head of a woman, ca. 300–200 BC
From Mottola, southern Italy
Gold, H: 2.9 cm; W: 2.4 cm
Taranto, Museo Nazionale Archeologico, 54.117

This engraved ring, found with a gold necklace and two bracelets, depicts a fleshy-faced woman with a melon-style coiffure tied in a bun. She has been identified as the Ptolemaic queen Berenike II (died 211 BC), who sported a similar hairstyle. She wears an Eros-pendant earring as well as a linked necklace just above the wavy folds of her drapery.

BIBLIOGRAPHY Becatti 1955, 84, 188, no. 334 (compare pls. 96.373, 116.429); Richter 1968b, 161, no. 643; Boardman 1970, 371, pl. 1008; Coarelli 1970, no. 35; De Juliis 1984, 289–90, no. 210; De Juliis and Loiacono 1985, 309, fig. 358; Plantzos 1999a, pl. 89.1; Guzzo 2001a, 165, B3.

....

Plate 46

Ring inset with cast bust of Jupiter, ca. 50 BC–AD 20
From Petescia
Gold, H (bezel): 1.5 cm; W (bezel): 1.2 cm; Wt: 14 grams
Berlin, Staatliche Museen, Antikensammlung, Misc. 7051

The supreme god, his luxuriant hair falling over his draped shoulders, looks out from this ring in three-quarter view. His brow and cheeks are dramatically modeled, as are the corkscrew curls of his beard. His lips are parted, as if he is about to speak. The hoop and bust were each solid cast separately and subsequently joined. Whether this splendid ring belonged to a priest of Jupiter, a high-ranking soldier, or perhaps a goldsmith remains uncertain. It was found together with a hoard of other pieces of gold and silver jewelry, finely carved intaglios and cameos, and other luxury objects at Petescia in the Sabine Hills east of Rome in 1875.

BIBLIOGRAPHY Greifenhagen 1970–75, 80, pls. 58.9, 59.6; Heilmeyer 1988, 354–35, no. 16; Stefanelli 1992, 23, no. 10, figs. 12–13; Platz-Horster 2002, 84–87, no. 50.

....

Plate 47

Ring signed by Herakleidas, ca. 300–100 BC
Inscribed: ...ΑΚΛΕΙΔΑС ΕΠΟΕΙ
From Santa Maria Capua Vetere, Italy
Gold, H: 3.3 cm; W: 2.9 cm; Wt: 93.2 grams
Naples, Museo Archeologico Nazionale, 25085

Signed in Greek by the carver Herakleidas, this portrait of a beardless man was cut into a separate plate of gold and inserted into a larger ring mount. The serious expression of the face, with prominent cheekbones, deep-set eyes, and incised brows, has suggested to some scholars that the image is that of a Roman, perhaps Scipio Africanus, but others are less willing to be so precise.

BIBLIOGRAPHY Furtwängler 1900, pl. 33, no. 15; Becatti 1955, 214, no. 508; Vollenweider 1958; Stazio in *EAA* 3 (1960), 1149; Richter 1968b, no. 686; Boardman 1970, 361, 371, pl. 1005; Coarelli 1970, no. 56; Stefanelli 1992, 20, 229, figs. 2–3, no. 1; De Caro 1994, 57; Plantzos 1999a, 92, pl. 96.2: Guzzo 2001a, 165, no. 1.

....

Plate 48

Beaker, ca. 25 BC–AD 50
Found off the coast of Knidos (western Turkey)
Gold, H: 13.7 cm; Wt: 656.2 grams
Malibu, JPGM, 2001.6

This beaker is one of three vessels found by sponge divers in the early twentieth century. The elegant shape, raised by hammering and then turned on a lathe, is adorned only by a thin band slightly below its curved, offset lip. The weight of the vessel is recorded on the underside of its hollow flanged foot in dotted letters: *P II L I*, meaning two pounds, one sescuncia (1 1/2 ounces), which is the equivalent of 25 1/2 Roman ounces, that is to say 695.8 grams. Because the vessel weighs less, it is assumed to have lost its lid.

BIBLIOGRAPHY Lapatin 2008, 49, fig. 21; Lapatin and Wight 2010, 206; Lapatin 2014, 129–31.

....

Plate 49

Pitcher, ca. 25 BC–AD 50
Found off the coast of Knidos (western Turkey)
Gold, H: 19 cm; Wt: 673 grams
London, British Museum, GR 1894,0615.1 (Jewellery 3168)

Found with the beaker discussed above (plate 48), this vessel, too, has its weight inscribed on the base in dotted letters: *P II S L I = P(ondo) II, S(emissem), Semunciam (Scriptulum) I*, meaning 2 pounds, 6 and 13/24 ounces. Taking a Roman pound to be 327.5 grams, and the Roman ounce (1/12 of a pound) to be 27.3 grams, the recorded weight is 833.4 grams, which is 23 percent more than the present weight of the vessel. This shape, however, is widely attested in bronze as a pitcher, and it is likely that the handle originally attached to the body and neck was lost when the ancient join failed.

BIBLIOGRAPHY Marshall 1911, no. 3168; Lapatin 2014, 129–31.

....

Plate 50

Double-spouted lamp, ca. AD 50–79
From Pompeii
Gold, H: 15.1 cm; L: 32.2 cm; Wt: 801 grams
Naples, Museo Archeologico Nazionale, 25000

Found in 1863 in the area of the Temple of Venus at Pompeii, this double-spouted lamp is decorated with lotus leaves in repoussé on the body and a palmette on its large upright reflector. The handle, two spouts, and foot are undecorated, and the lid has been lost. Lamps, like jewelry and other precious items, were typical dedications in sanctuaries. Pausanias reports that one burned day and night in the so-called Erechtheion on the Athenian Acropolis. They are also closely associated with Venus/Aphrodite, and a pair of Latin graffiti in the House of Gaius Polybius at Pompeii suggests that Emperor Nero and his wife, Poppaea Sabina, may have dedicated this lamp and other gold vessels to the goddess when they visited the Bay of Naples in AD 64.

BIBLIOGRAPHY Carducci 1969, 46–47, pl. 47; Coarelli 1970, no. 64; Pozzi in Museo Archeologico Nazionale 1989, 80, 218, 219n80; De Caro 1994, 113.

....

Plate 51
Bust of an Emperor, ca. AD 180
From Aventicum (Switzerland)
Gold, H: 33.5 cm; Wt: 1.590 kg
Lausanne, Musée cantonal d'archéologie et d'histoire, 1939/134

This hollow gold image of a bearded emperor wearing a cuirass is generally thought to represent Marcus Aurelius (r. AD 161–180), but that identification is far from universally accepted because the portrait does not follow the standard iconography of that or, indeed, any other emperor. The short, wavy hair is drawn back from a furrowed brow; eyebrows are incised as are the irises and pupils of the wide, heavily lidded eyes, beneath which are fine lines and bags indicating the careworn life of the ruler. The nose is long and straight, while the mouth is small, with pursed lips. The beard and mustache are short, unlike those typical of late second-century emperors. The muscles of the neck are well defined, and the folds of a tunic are schematically rendered above the breastplate of the cuirass, which is adorned with a chubby-faced gorgoneion surrounded by feathers, rather than the more normal scales. This feather cuirass is the *lorica plumata*, known from ancient literature. The patterned texture of the feathers contrasts with the flat undecorated depiction of the leather straps and the *paludamentum* (cloak) over the emperor's right shoulder. Although gold portraits are frequently mentioned in ancient literature, survivals are rare. This example likely served as a portable *imago* of the emperor that would be carried by soldiers along with other legionary standards. Excavated in late Roman debris inside an aqueduct near a temple at Aventicum (Avenches, Switzerland).

BIBLIOGRAPHY Schazmann 1940; Riccardi 2002; Hochuli-Gysel 2008.

....

Plate 52
Bust of Septimius Severus, ca. AD 200
From Plotinoupolis (Didymoteichon, Thrace)
Gold, H: ca. 25 cm; Wt: 950 grams
Komotini, Greece, Archaeological Museum, 207

This gold bust of the emperor Septimius Severus (r. AD 193–211), like the previous bust, deviates from the emperor's official portrait types, in this case combining the small curls over his forehead that are present in his earliest marble portraits with the long split beard of later ones. Here the curly hair is more three-dimensional than that of the gold portrait from Aventicum, and the skin smoother and features more idealized. The emperor wears a *lorica plumata* (feather cuirass), which contrasts with the texture of the smooth leather straps and the twisted rope work at the cloth sleeves. Though smaller than the Aventicum portrait, this image also seems to have been intended to be carried on a pole as a military standard.

BIBLIOGRAPHY Vavritsas 1968, 1969; Riccardi 2002.

....

Plate 53
Patera from Rennes, ca. AD 210
From Rennes, Brittany
Diam: 25 cm; Wt: 1.35 kg
Paris, Bibliothèque nationale de France, Cabinet des médailles, 56.94

Discovered in 1774, during the demolition of a house in Rennes, Brittany, this solid gold bowl, known as the Rennes Patera, is richly decorated with Bacchic imagery surrounded by imperial gold coins. The central medallion (*emblema*) depicts the drinking contest between Bacchus and Hercules, which can be read as an allegory of the triumph of wine over physical strength. Beardless and crowned with ivy, the god of wine, surrounded by six of his followers—including a satyr playing the double pipes in the foreground and a horned Pan playing the panpipes—sits on an elaborate stool, holding a thyrsus and a poppy-shaped drinking horn. Beside him Hercules, identified by his lion skin and club, sits on a rock, holding a wine cup. Surrounding this scene is a frieze showing the triumph of Bacchus, who appears in a chariot drawn by two panthers. Hercules, drunk and supported by two companions, precedes the god, and these three are accompanied by the followers of Dionysos: satyrs, maenads, cupids, and Pans engaged in a variety of activities. Around the medallion is a laurel wreath and sixteen imperial gold coins set within crowns, alternately acanthus and laurel. These coins are the *aurei* of Antonine emperors and empresses from Hadrian (AD 76–138) to Geta (AD 189–211).

BIBLIOGRAPHY Avisseau-Broustet in Lapatin 2014, 160–64 (with further references).

....

Plate 54
Necklace, ca. AD 200–300
Said to be from Egypt
Gold, L (extended): 91.4 cm; Diam (medallions): 2.7 cm
Baltimore, Walters Art Museum, 57.1600

Eight gold medallions framed by two distinct types of pierced-work scroll decoration hang as pendants on this long necklace of four loop-in-loop chains. The length of the chains could be adjusted by moving the two large spherical beads, embossed with rosettes, palmettes, and shells. Because the end of each chain passes through one of the beads before being affixed to another, this adjustment could, depending on the length chosen, make it appear that part of the necklace consists of eight chains. Cylindrical spacers with chased decoration separate the medallions, seven of which hold *aurei* (gold coins) minted under

Vitellius, Vespasian, Domitian, Nerva, Faustina the Elder, and Marciana, that is, from AD 69 to 141. The eighth medallion has two thin plates embossed with images of the sun and moon. The insertion of gold coins into jewelry began in the second century and became popular in the third and fourth centuries. Several ornate examples similar to this one survive.

BIBLIOGRAPHY Stefanelli 1992, 208, figs. 260, 266, no. 227. Compare a similar necklace in New York (Metropolitan Museum of Art, 36.9.1; see Yeroulanou 1999, 38–39, 79–81, 109–11, 209, fig. 29, no. 2).

....

Plate 55
Bowl with floral decoration, ca. 250 BC
From a Hellenistic tomb at Canosa di Puglia, southern Italy
Gold glass, H: 11.4 cm; Diam: 20.3 cm
London, British Museum, 1871,0518.2

Gold glass is often associated with Byzantium and its mosaics, but the technique of backing glass—or rock crystal—with gold that has been cut, punched, or molded to shape is attested archaeologically as early as the fourth century BC, when hammered gold sheets were set under glass and crystal and used to decorate finger rings and pieces of luxury furniture. The technique appears to have been employed even earlier by Pheidias in the decoration of his monumental gold and ivory statue of Zeus at Olympia in the late fifth century BC. That sculpture subsequently came to be ranked among the Seven Wonders of the Ancient World. This bowl consists of two nesting white glass bowls with a thin layer of gold foil sandwiched between them. The gold has been meticulously cut to represent twinned running spirals at the rim and, on the body, large lotus and acanthus leaves and twisting tendrils, which arise from a double eight-petaled rosette on the bottom. Where the bowl was produced is not certain; Alexandria is often suggested.

BIBLIOGRAPHY Lapatin 2001, 82–83; Williams 2009, 190–91, no. 86.

....

Plate 56
Portrait of Gennadios, ca. AD 250–300
Inscribed: ΓΕΝΝΑΔΙ ΧΡΩΜΑΤΙ ΠΑΜΜΟΥϹΙ
Gold glass, Diam: 4.1 cm
New York, Metropolitan Museum of Art, 26.258

The most spectacular surviving gold glasses were produced at the height of the Roman Empire. Figural medallions were set into the bottoms of bowls that appear to have been given as gifts on special occasions. Some of these were subsequently cut from their bowls and set in the mortar of tombs in the Roman catacombs; others seem to have been made as disks to be mounted and worn as pendants. Few have primary archaeological contexts. Some of the most accomplished images were not just cut into the gold, but stippled so as to render complex patterns and chiaroscuro effects, sometimes with added color. The Greek inscription on this roundel of stippled gold and deep blue glass proclaims that its subject is "Gennadios most accomplished in the musical arts." As in the inscription on the medallion below (plate 58), the grammatical variants correspond to the Alexandrian dialect, suggesting the origins of this object. Wearing a mantle over his left shoulder, the beardless youth with thick, curly hair turns to his right, smiling slightly, his eyes alert under arched brows.

BIBLIOGRAPHY Morey 1959, 74, no. 454; Ostoia 1969, no. 2; Breckenridge in Weitzmann 1977, 287, no. 264.

....

Plate 57
Portrait of Eusebius, ca. AD 225–50
Inscribed: EVSEBI ANIMA DVLCIS
From Rome
Gold glass, silver, and pigment, Diam: 4.8 cm
Rome, Musei Vaticani (Museo Sacro della Biblioteca), 700 (469)

This gold glass roundel of a short-haired beardless man was found in the cemetery of St. Callistus, Rome. It is inscribed in Latin: "the sweet soul of Eusebius." Eusebius wears a cloak fastened on his right shoulder by a fibula, with a volute above and crosspiece below. Underneath his cloak he wears a tunic, the white sleeve of which is rendered in silver, while it appears to have an orange border visible at the neck. The pupil of his eye is reserved in blue glass and a highlight in the iris rendered by a gold dot. The shading, highlights, and illusionistic modeling of this roundel, apparently made in Italy and deposited in, if not intended for, a tomb, are no less accomplished than those thought to have been produced at Alexandria (see plates 56, 58).

BIBLIOGRAPHY Morey 1959, 3, no. 3; Zanchi Roppo 1969, 78–80, no. 84, fig. 26.

....

Plate 58
Portrait of two women and a youth, ca. AD 250
Inscribed: BOYNNEPI KEPAMI
Gold glass and silver, Diam: 6.1 cm
Brescia, Musei di Santa Giulia, Museo dell' Età Christiana

This gold glass medallion may never have gone underground, for in the eighth century it was set into the Cross of Desiderius. It depicts two women and a beardless youth. He has close-cropped hair and wears a white *pallium* over a white tunic, both garments rendered in silver and stippled to create folds and wrinkles, just as the stippled gold gives volume to his face and shadow to his neck and chin. His dark eyes, bushy brows, long nose, and small mouth are features he shares with the two women. The one in the center wears a mantle knotted over a tunic. Her hair is parted in the center, and she wears a dark necklace. The woman to the right has a more complex coiffure; she wears a pearl necklace and earrings and over her tunic an elaborately patterned mantle. The widely spaced Greek inscription has been variously interpreted; it may be written in Alexandrian Greek, suggesting the origin of the object. Whether the sitters are members of the imperial family, as was once thought, a mother with her children, or a couple about to be wed remains uncertain.

BIBLIOGRAPHY Morey 1959, 42, no. 237; Zanchi Roppo 1969, 22–25, no. 12; Hanfmann 1975, 318–19, no. 52; Boardman 1993, 338–40, no. 337; Sena Chiesa 2002, 159–60.

....

Plate 59

Portrait of a bearded man, ca. AD 200–250
Gold glass and pigment, Diam: 4.4 cm
Arezzo, Museo Archeologio Nazionale
"Gaio Cilnio Mecenate," 14973

This evocative image of a middle-aged man with thinning hair and sunken cheeks was rendered in gold glass with a thin coat of white paint for his tunic and diagonal *pallium* and reddish brown for the *clavus* (ceremonial stripe) on his right shoulder. The technique here is extraordinarily refined: stippling has rendered both shading and highlights that vividly present an individual who is far from idealized, although features such as the flamelike lock above the modulated brow and heavily lidded eyes appear in portraits in other media. The long, uneven nose, small mouth, wispy beard and, above all, the staring eyes convince us that we are face to face with a specific individual. Just who he is, however, remains a mystery.

BIBLIOGRAPHY Morey 1959, 41, no. 234; Pillinger 1984; E. Laurenzi in La Rocca 2009, 258, 309, no. VI.16.

....

Plate 60

Bull, ca. 600–550 BC
From the Halos deposit, Delphi
Silver, gold, and copper, original H: ca. 1.25 m; L: ca. 2.30 m
Delphi Archaeological Museum

Found in one of two pits dug underneath and alongside the Sacred Way at the Sanctuary of Apollo, along with other charred and damaged precious material (see plate 10), this life-size silver bull was a splendid votive offering dedicated to the god in his most important shrine. With gilt-silver horns, forehead, ears, dewlap, and hooves, the bull was composed of approximately sixteen repoussé silver plaques attached by silver nails to silvered copper bands set on a wooden core. The precise date and occasion of its dedication as well as the identity of its donor remain unknown, but other objects buried with it suggest that it may have been the offering of an East Greek or an eastern potentate. Certainly this gift in precious materials was more expensive and constituted a record of piety more permanent than the sacrifice of a live animal.

BIBLIOGRAPHY Amandry 1977; Amandry 1991, 202–5.

....

Plate 61

Fragmentary strip with mythological scenes, ca. 540–530 BC
Silver and gold, H: 9 cm; L: 27.5 cm
Malibu, JPGM, 83.AM.343

This fragmentary repoussé gilt-silver strip depicts several mythological scenes in discrete square panels. The original length and function of the strip remains unknown, but the surviving scenes all depict violent scenes with strong movement to the right. At far left a running figure, with winged boots, is a sister of the Gorgon Medusa, one of whose siblings is better preserved in the fourth panel. Like her better-preserved sister, she is in the so-called *Knielauf* position, a popular mode of depicting motion in Archaic Greek art. She wears a short skirt with ornamental borders; the body of a snake that was tied around her waist as a belt is visible below her right arm. In the next panel Zeus attacks the winged fish-tailed Typhon with a thunderbolt. The two figures look one another in the eye, as the god grasps the monster behind the neck before delivering the coup de grâce. In the third panel Orestes attacks his mother Klytemnestra over the fallen body of her lover Aigisthos. The hero's clothing and pose is similar to that of Zeus, but his right arm is lowered and holds a sword. He tramples the long-haired Aigisthos and grabs his mother's hair, as she extends a large nozzlelike breast toward him with her left hand and extends her open right, both useless gestures of supplication. The next panel is filled by another Gorgon, in the same pose as the first, but much better preserved. Her bearded face, framed by spiral locks, is frontal, with open mouth, fangs, and lolling tongue; her curved wings are extended, with open-mouthed snakes, tied around her waist, beneath them. In the next panel Athena, wearing a highly patterned cloak over a long *peplos*, urges Perseus to kill the Gorgon Medusa, who has not been preserved. He turns and looks back at the goddess, to avoid the fatal gaze of the Gorgon. The final panel (not shown), like the first, is highly fragmentary: Theseus grasps the horn of the frontal-faced bull-headed Minotaur, driving his sword into its neck. Similar mythological scenes, depicting the height of action, appear on sixth-century BC bronze shield bands, but this smaller object may have formed part of a ceremonial belt or, perhaps, have adorned a chest or some other piece of furniture. Its style suggests that it was made in one of the Greek colonies in South Italy.

BIBLIOGRAPHY Pfrommer 1983; Guzzo 1986; Musti et al. 1992, 144, 257, no. 107.

....

Plate 62

Two *kylikes*, ca. 625–575 BC
Silver, H: 10.2 and 7.4 cm; W: 22 and 14.7 cm;
Diam: 16.5 and 10.7 cm; Wt: 362.7 and 192.1 grams
Malibu, JPGM, 77.AM.68–.69

Terracotta cups of this so-called Ionian type were common in the seventh and early sixth centuries BC. Originally produced in Ionia

(East Greece and Asia Minor), the shape was widely exported to the west and also appears in depictions of mythological scenes, such as the blinding of Polyphemos by Odysseus, who first got the Cyclops drunk. Metal examples are much rarer: six are known in bronze and four in silver. The majority of these, when their findspots are known, come from tombs, but one in bronze was recovered from the Sanctuary of Hera at Perachora on the northern shore of the Gulf of Corinth. These two, whose different sizes and details suggest that they might not have been made or used as a pair, were each fashioned from four pieces of metal: a flaring ring foot and two horizontal handles, circular in section, were soldered to the deep bowl with a high offset lip. The joins where the handles of the larger cup are attached to the body are masked by thin plates adorned with tongues. The weight of the larger cup corresponds precisely to 65 Persian sigloi (5.6 grams). The smaller cup weighs just less than 44 Attic drachmai (4.4 grams) or 22 Euboian/Attic staters (8.7 grams). Whether this is a coincidence or somehow reflects the origins or use of either cup remains uncertain.

BIBLIOGRAPHY Guzzo 2001b.

....

Plate 63
Phiale (libation bowl) with *apobatai*, late fifth century BC
From the Basova Tumulus, near Duvanli, Bulgaria
Silver and gold, Diam: 20.5 cm; Wt: 428 grams
Plovdiv, Bulgaria, Archaeological Museum, 1515

Four gilt and incised four-horse chariots race around the raised central knob and palmette frieze in the interior of this libation bowl (*phiale mesomphalos*). This shape originated in the ancient Near East, but, by the late fifth century, when this example was fashioned, it was common in Greece (see plates 23, 24). A young charioteer with a long garment drives each of the chariots, while a warrior mounts, or dismounts, the car. These are *apobatai*, warriors who competed by running and jumping in and out of chariots at the Panathenaic games at Athens. The warriors are individualized not only in pose but also in equipment, each shield being held at a different angle (one in profile, another frontal, the third seen in three-quarter from the exterior, the last from the interior) and emblazoned with a different device (horse, lion, and centaur). The weight of the vessel is approximately 1 Attic mina (100 drachmai). This, along with the event depicted and the style of the imagery, which recalls contemporary red-figure vase painting, strongly suggests that this *phiale* was made in Athens and exported to the northern shores of the Black Sea, where it was given or traded to a local chieftain who provided grain to the Greek city. The tomb in which it was found also contained armor and other vessels in silver, bronze, and terracotta.

BIBLIOGRAPHY Strong 1966, 74–75; Venedikov and Gerassimov 1975, 362; Musti et al. 1992, 170, 266, no. 136; Vickers and Gill 1994, 40–41, 131–35; Marazov et al. 1998, 138–93, no. 64; Lapatin 2003, 76–77.

....

Plate 64
Kantharos with the death of Orpheus, late fifth century BC
Silver and gold, H: 16.4 cm; Diam: 11.8 cm; Wt: 408.9 grams
Vassil Bojkov collection

The shape of this *kantharos*, a drinking vessel with a high-pedestaled foot and flat looping handles rising far above the rim, was particularly associated with Dionysos, the god of wine, and he often appears holding such cups. Here expressive repoussé Silenos heads on the interior, at the terminations of the horizontal struts between the handles and the rim, and the gilt ivy wreath on the upper surface of the foot also recall the god. A second wreath of laurel leaves encircles the body of the vessel, just below the rim, and is largely overlapped by figures in the mythological scenes that make up the majority of the decoration. On one side, two Thracian women attack the poet Orpheus, whose name is inscribed beneath the lyre he holds before him in feeble defense. Beardless, with long, flowing hair, he wears sandals and a *himation* that leaves most of his chest bare and stands on a rocky outcrop before two ithyphallic herms. The Thracian women attack from the left: one, swathed in intricately patterned drapery, prepares to hurl a stone, her movement so violent that her *peplos* has come unpinned at the shoulder, leaving one breast bare; the other, brandishing a double axe, sports star-shaped tattoos on her upper arms, and zigzags on her calves and feet, as well as what seem to be bracelets at her wrists. These, and other details, such as eyebrows and eyelashes, are incised with masterful fluidity, recalling contemporary red-figure vase painting. The other side depicts in the same technique the Dioskouroi abducting one of the daughters of Leukippos in a two-horse chariot.

BIBLIOGRAPHY Votokopoulou 1997, no. 151; Marazov 2011, 79–81, no. 53.

....

Plate 65
Rhyton in the form of Pegasos, ca. 400 BC
From a tomb at Aul Uljap, Crimea
Silver and gold, H: 37.3 cm; Wt: ca. 1.43 kg
Moscow, State Museum of Oriental Art, 37 M-IV

Set on a modern stemmed foot, this spectacular rhyton with gilt-silver mane, wings, and decorative bands at various points on the horn originally also had inlaid eyes. The anatomy of the horse's muzzle has been sensitively worked in repoussé, while the hairs of the upright mane and feathers of the tripartite wings have been chased with exacting precision. Teardrop-shaped lozenges and a band of palmettes decorate the top of the horn. In the middle a complex lotus and palmette anthemion frieze is partially preserved above a series of square panels depicting the gods battling the giants. Dionysos and Hermes appear twice; Zeus and Hephaistos once, along with a goddess, perhaps Athena, wielding a temple key as a weapon. Given its weight (which is equal to 1/3 of 10 minai), style, and the presence of

Gigantomachy imagery (the battle of the gods and giants is represented as a series of duels on the east metopes of the Parthenon), this object has been plausibly attributed to an Athenian craftsman.

BIBLIOGRAPHY Leskow et al. 1989, 120–22, no. 101; Vickers and Gill 1994, 41–42, fig. 2.3; Vickers 1999b, 30.

....

Plate 66
Stag's head rhyton with warriors, ca. 400 BC
Silver and gold, L: 29 cm; Diam: 12.8 cm; Wt: 829.2 grams
George Ortiz collection

Rhyta, drinking horns in the shape of animal heads, were particularly popular among the Thracians and their neighbors, and immigrant Greek craftsmen seem to have journeyed to the shores of the Black Sea to satisfy the desire of wealthy clients for precious metal work. This magnificent stag's head rhyton was raised from silver sheet using the repoussé technique; handle, antlers, and ears were fashioned separately and attached. The forged handle was soldered, the cast antlers inserted and soldered into tubes driven through the head, and the hammered ears riveted in place. The eyes were inset in some other material, perhaps glass or enamel. Traces of niello have been recognized in the tear ducts, the nostrils, and the mouth. The surface of the skin was lightly stippled around the forehead, muzzle, and snout, adding greater naturalism to the animal form. Gilding enhanced the antlers, the inside of the ears, the beaded and ovolo moldings at the rim, and the weapons and pubic hair of the warriors on the neck. These six young men (all but one are beardless) carry large round shields and are nude except for their baldrics and headgear. Armed with swords and spears, four face each other over the stag's forehead, while the other two duel underneath the handle on the reverse. The craftsman clearly delighted in portraying overlapping figures in various foreshortened poses and with contrasting weaponry, especially the helmets of the figures, which include *pilos, petasos, kausia*, as well as Corinthian and Attic helmets.

BIBLIOGRAPHY N. Yalouris 1980, 128–29, no. 53; Ortiz 1996, no. 152.

....

Plate 67
Hydria and wreath, ca. 310 BC
Inscribed: MNAI E ΔPA ΞH
From Tomb III at Vergina, Macedonia
Silver and gold, H (hydria): 54 cm; Wt (hydria): 2.3 kg
Vergina Archaeological Museum, BE 96

This *hydria* (water jar) and gold oak wreath with acorns were discovered in the so-called Prince's Tomb at Vergina. The silver vessel, rising from a flaring foot with a concave profile, and with its ovoid body, flat shoulder, tall neck, and horizontal handles, has many parallels in terracotta and also a few in silver. This example, however, was not intended to hold liquid but was fashioned especially to serve as an ossuary. Made of separate pieces of hammered sheet joined by hinges just above the handles and provided with a false conical knobbed lid, it contained the bones of a young man about sixteen years old, wrapped in purple cloth. An inscription at the base of the neck records the weight of the vessel: 5 minai, 68 drachmai. Other silver vessels and the remains of sumptuous ivory furniture (see plate 155) were also deposited in this tomb, and many scholars believe the youth interred therein to have been Alexander IV of Macedon, the son of Alexander the Great, who was murdered by Kassander between 311 and 309 BC.

BIBLIOGRAPHY Andronicos 1984, 202, 212; Ginouvès 1994, 174; Gill 2008, 337; Zimi 2011, 179, no. 2; Kottaridi 2011, 116–17.

....

Plate 68
Emblema with Skylla, ca. 300–212 BC
From Morgantina, Sicily
Silver and gold, Diam: 10.5 cm; Thickness: 2 cm; Wt: 81 grams
Aidone, Italy, Museo Archeologico Regionale, 1981.11.22

The marine monster Skylla is first mentioned in Homer's *Odyssey*, where she is described as having twelve feet, six necks, and multiple heads, with triple rows of sharp teeth; her voice was compared to yelping dogs. In this *emblema* (relief medallion), as in later Greek literature, she is depicted as a beautiful woman—she even wears bracelets—with long, flowing hair, naked to below the waist. A thin, snakelike sea-dragon is wrapped around her torso, while a large, wide serrated leaf (or perhaps some kind of horizontal fin) separates her human from her animal form. From beneath the leaf emerge two large, powerful spiraling scaly fish tails, as well as the protomes of three dogs, two with webbed paws. The dog on the left holds an octopus in its jaws; the one in the center chews on a fish; and the one on the right eyes a dolphin that gambols in the waves. Skylla herself raises a boulder above her head. Legend had it that she would dash upon the rocks sailors attempting to pass through the straits that separated Sicily from the toe of Italy. This gilt *emblema* may once have originally decorated the lid of a *pyxis* or the interior of a drinking cup. It has been suggested that emerging from the swirling wine, which might have evoked thoughts of her companion, the whirlpool Charybdis, this Skylla might have playfully threatened a drinker with a potential headache. Whether cups with such splendid high relief *emblemata* were actually employed for drinking or were just made for display, however, remains a matter of debate. Certainly this *emblema* was carefully gilded for pictorial effect, for only Skylla's human flesh, the plain background, and some of the waves are silver. This object was deliberately buried beneath the floor of a house at the Greek city of Morgantina in central Sicily with fifteen other Hellenistic gilt-silver vessels prior to the sack of that city in 212 BC. Its owner never returned, and the hoard remained interred until it was illicitly removed from the site in the early 1980s. The treasure was subsequently acquired by the Metropolitan Museum of Art in New York, which returned it to Italy in 2010.

BIBLIOGRAPHY von Bothmer 1984, 55, no. 95; Guzzo 2003, 51–52, no. 4; Lyons et al. 2013, 71.

....

Plate 69
Hemispherical bowl with floral decoration and small animals, ca. 200–100 BC
Inscribed: MMASCAI PVIIↃ∴
From Novi Falerii (Civita Castellana, Latium, Italy)
Silver, gold, and garnet, Diam: 18.3 cm; Wt: 1.280 kg
Naples, Museo Archeologico Nazionale, 25285

One of a pair, this hemispherical gilt-silver bowl with garnet inlays consists of a smooth interior liner set inside a high relief gilt exterior that was initially cast, embossed, engraved, and joined to additional elements. From an eight-petaled rosette with a central garnet cabochon at the bottom springs a series of large acanthus leaves surrounded by smaller tendrils alternating with larger petals. The petals are filled with more vegetation, as well as a series of small animals consuming others (two swans have butterflies in their beaks, a snake eats a frog, and a lizard nibbles a leaf). Bands of guilloche, beads, and eggs-and-darts adorn the rim, and an inscription names one M. Mascai (?), presumably the owner of the set. It also gives a weight, perhaps for a larger group of objects, for along with this pair of bowls, a smaller hemispherical cup was found in the same spot, as was a centaur rhyton protome (plate 73) and other silver objects, now lost. On stylistic grounds the cups have been attributed to a Hellenistic workshop in East Greece, perhaps Pergamon or Syria, and they may have come to Italy either as booty from Rome's Asian wars in the second century BC or as part of the donation of the treasury of Attalos III to Rome in 133 BC. Formerly in the Borgia collection.

BIBLIOGRAPHY Visconti 1823; Strong 1966, 109–10; Stefanelli 1991, 6–7, 254, nos. 1–2; Lo Monaco in La Rocca, Parisi Presicce, and Lo Monaco 2010, 296, no. III.3 (with additional references).

....

Plate 70
Net-patterned bowl, ca. 100–1 BC
Silver, gold, and garnets, H: 5.1 cm; Diam: 20 cm; Wt: 433.8 grams
Malibu, JPGM, 86.AM.752.3

Hammered from a sheet of silver and decorated with elaborate patterns, gilding, and inset garnets, this bowl is a splendid example of the luxury plate produced in the eastern lands, which following the death of Alexander the Great were first ruled by the Seleucids and subsequently the Parthians. In the center, a garnet forms the heart of a floral calyx with silver and gold petals of various shapes. These overlap a net pattern of fourteen staggered pentagons; in the center of each is a different flower inset with a garnet. Garnets were rare in the west before the Hellenistic period, after which they remained precious but were more frequently obtainable. The ancients called them *carbunculi* on account of their fiery appearance, resembling burning charcoal, and Pliny mentions different kinds from a variety of sources, ranging from India and Ethiopia to Asia Minor (*NH* 37.92–98). The weight of this bowl corresponds to 1 Attic mina (100 drachmai).

BIBLIOGRAPHY Pfrommer 1993, 188–89, no. 72; Lapatin and Wight 2010, 93.

....

Plate 71
Handle in the form of a Triton, ca. 100–50 BC
Silver and gold, H: 27 cm; W: 9.5 cm; Wt: 455.3 grams
Malibu, JPGM, 85.AM.163

Fashioned to function as the handle of a pitcher, this well-modeled Triton, a mythical hybrid of man and sea serpent, once raised his extended right hand protectively over the liquid content of the vessel to which the handle was originally attached. The full beard, shaggy hair, and animal ears, as well as dynamic movement of the muscular torso, all give power to the figure, who may have held a trident, or perhaps a conch shell, in his left hand. A double calyx of large and small acanthus leaves at the creature's hips masks not only the transition between the anthropomorphic and animal elements of the creature but also the join of the handle to the rim of the now-lost vessel. The head, arms, and tail fins are solid cast, while the torso and serpent body are hollow. Traces of gilding survive on much of the handle's surface, indicating that hair, beard, acanthus leaves, and tail were golden, while face, torso, and arms of the Triton remained silver.

BIBLIOGRAPHY Barr-Sharrar 1993; Lapatin and Wight 2010, 94.

....

Plate 72
Centaur protome from a rhyton, ca. 160 BC
From Nova Falerii (Civiltà Castellana, Latium, Italy)
Silver and gold, H: 22 cm; Wt: 689 grams
Vienna, Kunsthistorisches Museum, ANSA VIIa 49.01

Found together at Nova Falerii with a bowl (plate 70) and other precious objects, this dynamic figure of a centaur once graced the end of a sumptuous rhyton (drinking horn) (see plates 65, 73, 156, 157). It is a masterpiece of the repoussé technique—the head and body were hammered from a single sheet of silver, while the arms and legs were cast separately and attached. The mythological figure, half-man, half-horse, originally held a stringed lyre in his left hand, and a plectrum (pick) remains in his right. This, and the wreath of vine leaves in his hair, are gilded. Although the bold musculature and wild beard and hair of this centaur recall the animalistic nature of the composite of beast and man, the fact that this creature plays the lyre indicates that he was one of the civilized centaurs, like Chiron, the teacher of Achilles and other heroes. The highly expressive face has been compared to those in the monumental marble frieze of the Altar of Zeus at Pergamon in western Asia Minor, carved in the first half of the second century BC. However, rhytons with centaur protomes are known only from areas under the control of the Seleucids, farther to the east.

BIBLIOGRAPHY Strong 1966, 109–10; Reinsberg 1980, 106ff, 111ff, 200; Valavanos and Lambrinoudakis 2010, 42–43; Hagg 2012, 122–23, no. 48.

....

Plate 73
Stag rhyton, ca. 50 BC–AD 50
Silver, gold, garnet, and glass, H: 27.4 cm; L: 46 cm;
Diam: 12.6 cm; Wt: 899.6 grams
Malibu, JPGM, 86.AM.753

Called *rhyta* (singular *rhyton*) from the Greek verb *rhuo* (to flow), drinking horns of this type were designed to aerate wine, which was poured through them, entering the wide mouth at the top and exiting from a small hole, in this case in the chest of the stag. The large horn of the vessel was produced by the repoussé technique. A delicate spiral adorns the rim, with a palmette frieze and larger olive wreath below. Most of the horn consists of elegant vegetal spirals, with overlapping leaves, tendrils, and flowers, which rise along with acanthus leaves from the ring that marks the transition to the body of the stag, which is rendered with taut muscles and protruding veins. Antlers, ears, and legs were separately cast and soldered to the body, and the eyes preserve their original inlays. Vessels of this shape were made in a variety of materials, ranging from relatively inexpensive terracotta and glass to precious ivory and hard stone (see plates 126, 156, 157). An inscription on the belly of the stag in Aramaic (?) script has yet to be convincingly deciphered. The forms of the floral motifs, however, are Hellenistic, suggesting that this object was made by a Greek craftsman for an eastern client.
BIBLIOGRAPHY Penny 1993, 223; Pfrommer 1993, 192–93, no. 74; Boardman 1996, fig. 284; Lapatin and Wight 2010, 99.

....

Plate 74
Statuette of a bull, ca. 100 BC–AD 79
Said to be from Pompeii
Silver and gold, H: 14 cm; Wt: 475 grams
Malibu, JPGM, 2001.7

Powerfully modeled, this statuette of a bull was hollow cast in silver and then entirely gilded. Standing erect with head raised, left foreleg bent, and tail (now partially broken) curled up into its flank, it likely stood with other statuettes of gods, goddesses, and divinities in a domestic shrine (*lararium*) in Pompeii, where it was said to have been found between 1780 and 1790. The beast probably represents Jupiter, the king of the gods who often assumed the guise of a bull, and served as an object of devotion and veneration. The sculptor has realistically rendered the loose skin under the animal's neck as a series of pliant folds and the thick, curly hair of the forehead. Soon after it was found, the statuette became part of the collection of Maria Christina of Savoy, queen of the Kingdom of the Two Sicilies.
BIBLIOGRAPHY Lapatin 2008, 126; Lapatin and Wight 2010, 207.

....

Plate 75
Cup in the form of a bull's head, ca. 100 BC–AD 100
Inscribed: ΔΡΑΧ ΞΖ
Silver and gold, H: 12.1 cm; Diam: 9.5 cm; Wt: 274 grams
Malibu, JPGM, 87.AM.58

This finely worked cup, with a separately made smooth inner liner, takes the form of a young bull, as evidenced by the small budding horns. These are gilded, as was often the practice with animals intended for sacrifice, and this cup may have been used on ritual occasions. The animal's mouth, the garland around the neck, and the tear ducts are also gilded, and the eyes were originally inlaid, perhaps with glass paste. Both cup and liner were hammered from silver sheet, while the protruding ears were fashioned separately. The highly naturalistic features of the hair on the forehead, sinews across the cheeks, and loose skin at the dewlap are enhanced by the fine chasing and stippling of the hide and snout, all adding vivacity to the beast. A Greek inscription on the rim records the weight and value of the object: 67 drachmai.
BIBLIOGRAPHY Pfrommer 1993, 220–21, no. 128; Lapatin and Wight 2010, 95.

....

Plate 76
Skyphos with Priam before Achilles, signed by Cheirisophos (Hoby Cup), ca. AD 1–25
Inscribed: ΧΕΙΡΙΣΟΦΟΣ ΕΠΟΙΕ
From a tomb on Lolland Island, Baltic Sea
Silver and gold, H: 10.9 cm; W (including handle): 21.7 cm;
Wt: 975.5 grams
Copenhagen, Nationalmuseet, 10/20

Discovered in a princely tomb at Hoby on Lolland Island, in the Baltic Sea, along with other precious Roman imports, this gilt-silver cup, one of a pair, seems to have been a gift to a native chieftain from a Roman general, Gaius Silius, who commanded Roman troops at Mainz between AD 14 and 21, for "Silius" is scratched on the bottom of both cups. Each cup, assembled from separately cast feet and handles, smooth inner liners, and repoussé figural shells, is signed with dotted inscriptions by the silversmith Cheirisophos ("skilled hand"), one in Greek and the other transliterated into Latin letters. On this cup the Trojan king Priam, bearded and wearing the sleeved tunic and trousers of "barbarians" living to the north of Rome, as well as a soft Phrygian cap and a belt with carefully incised flowers, kneels and kisses the hand of the Greek hero Achilles, as described in the twenty-fourth book of Homer's *Iliad*. For Homer, this scene of reconciliation constitutes the climax of his epic, but it is uncertain whether the reference would have been known to the cup's recipient. Silius may have intended that the chieftain see himself in the figure of Priam, subservient to the seated classical hero, who is short-haired and clean-shaven, with a naked muscular torso and bare feet, wearing a mantle; in short, the personification of Roman power. The other side of this cup presents more of the scene: Greek and Trojan

servants, Priam's chariot, the ransom for the body of Hector, and a sleeping guard of the Greek camp. The second cup depicts another episode from the Trojan War: Philoktetes's feet being washed after having been bitten by a snake and Odysseus's attempt, ten years later, to obtain from him the bow of Herakles. Thus the pair seems to encapsulate the beginning and the end of the war.
BIBLIOGRAPHY Vermeule 1963; Strong 1966, 136–37; Poulsen 1968; Jeppeson 1972; Künzl 1978; Künzl in Hofter et al. 1988, 569–71, nos. 396–97; Stefanelli 1991, 256–57; Müller 1994; Marvin 2008, 183–86; Squire 2011, 293–95; Grane 2012; F. Specque in La Rocca et al. 2013, 277–78, no. VII.8.

....

Plate 77
Pitcher with Achilles, AD 1–100
From Berthouville, France
Inscribed: MERCVRIO AVGVSTO Q. DOMITIVS TVTVS EX VOTO
Silver and gold, H: 31.5 cm; Wt: 1.159 kg
Paris, Bibliothèque national de France, Cabinet des médailles, 56.5

From the same deposit and dedicator as the centaur *scyphus* (plate 78) this pitcher, too, was one of a pair of vessels that spoke to one another. On the body Achilles holds a shield above his head, as if to protect himself from the agony of Hecuba and Priam, wailing from the walls of Troy in mourning for their son, Hector, whom the Greek hero drags from his chariot, as described by Homer in the *Iliad*. On the other side of the vessel, however, Achilles himself falls, fatally wounded by the arrow Paris shot into his heel. The companion pitcher represents Achilles mourning for the dead Patroclus and the weighing of the body of Hector against the ransom brought by Priam to Achilles. The neck of this pitcher depicts the Trojan spy Dolon about to be ambushed by Ulysses; that of the other pitcher shows Ulysses and Diomedes stealing the Palladion. Altars figure prominently in both scenes. Thus ancient viewers were encouraged to reflect upon and discuss what constituted heroism in battle, the proper response to the loss of a loved one, and piety to the gods.
BIBLIOGRAPHY Babelon 1916, 81–87, nos. 4–5; Lehmann-Hartleben 1938; Baratte 1984; Baratte and Painter 1989; Stefanelli 1991, 275, no. 102; Colonna in Lapatin 2014, 52–57.

....

Plate 78
Cup with Centaurs, ca. AD 1–100
From Berthouville, France
Inscribed: MERCVRIO AVGVSTO Q. DOMITIVS TVTVS EX VOTO
Silver and gold, H: 11.6 cm; W (including handles): 21.6 cm;
Diam: 15 cm; Wt: 1.653 kg
Paris, Bibliothèque nationale de France, Cabinet des médailles, 56.7

One of a pair, this *scyphus* (*skyphos* in Greek) was dedicated to Mercury by Quintus Domitius Tutus at a Gallo-Roman sanctuary near Berthouville in Normandy. Discovered by chance by a farmer in 1830, it is one of the outstanding surviving products of Roman silversmiths, with profuse decoration and relief at times so high that it constitutes sculpture in the round. The cup's tripartite handles, whose upper surface is decorated with floral motifs, bird's heads, and panthers, and the ring foot were cast separately and attached to a smooth inner liner, hammered from a sheet of silver, and to the elaborately decorated outer shell, fashioned through combined techniques of repoussé, embossing, engraving, and appliqué. The scenes on each side of this cup speak to each other and to those on both sides of its counterpart, inviting those who used them at banquets (*convivia*) in the years before they were dedicated to Mercury to reflect on and no doubt discuss the varying nature of Dionysos (Bacchus to the Romans), as the hybrid creatures who adorn them seem to be either tormented or experiencing ecstatic joy. Each scene features a male or female centaur surrounded by Erotes and Bacchic paraphernalia, including not only thyrsi, *tympana*, *cistae mysticae*, panpipes, incense burners, theatrical masks, and tables laden with elaborate silver vessels but also a young female satyr expressing milk from her breast, a baby sea serpent being force fed, a peacock, etc. Silver vessels appear throughout the composition, some decorated with mythological scenes, including, appropriately, Odysseus offering wine to Polyphemos. Ancient weight inscriptions in dotted letters on the bottom of the smooth inner liners of both cups, where they could only have been read before assembly of the components, were recently discovered through X-radiography. They record about 40 percent of the vessels' current weights, suggesting that the silver content of the liners, perhaps manufactured by an ancient subcontractor, was closely controlled in the workshop. The total preserved weight, including nineteenth-century restoration materials, is slightly over five Roman pounds.
BIBLIOGRAPHY Babelon 1916, 88–91, nos. 6–7; Strong 1966, 126; Künzl 1979, 216, no. 40; Baratte 1984; Van de Grift 1984; Baratte and Painter 1989, 82–84, no. 19; Stefanelli 1991, 276, no. 105; Colonna in Lapatin 2014, 46–51.

....

Plate 79
Cup with a medallion of Athena, ca. 75–50 BC
From Hildesheim, Germany
Silver and gold, Diam (cup): 32.5 cm; Diam (emblem): 16 cm;
Wt: 1.984 kg
Berlin, Staatliche Museen, Antikensammlung, 3779,1

Found in 1868 together with seventy other pieces of Roman silver that were buried in the second half of the first century at Hildesheim near Hannover in Germany, this "picture cup" with a high relief image of the goddess Athena was an object for display, rather than actual use as a drinking vessel. Inscriptions on stone indicate that such dishes were sometimes bequeathed to favorite relations. Here, set inside an elegant bowl with wide flat handles and a gilt frieze of palmettes and acanthus flowers, a separately fashioned *emblema* depicts Athena seated in three-quarter view on a rock. The goddess wears a triple-crested helmet, with a sphinx and Pegasoi, of the type invented in the late fifth century BC by Pheidias for his monumental gold and ivory statue erected within the Parthenon on the Athenian Acropolis (see plates 19, 92), as well as a scaly, snake-fringed aegis, a long sleeveless *peplos* belted just beneath her breasts, and a mantle draped over her left arm and legs. With her left hand she grasps the rim of her shield, and with her right a short staff, perhaps a rudder, which, unlike the other objects depicted here, is not a common attribute of the goddess. Opposite her, on a tall rocky outcrop tied with a fillet and an olive wreath—perhaps a reference to the Acropolis—perches a small owl. The technical skill of the silversmith who created this ensemble is unsurpassed, both for the complicated patterns of soft drapery folds rendered in hard metal and for the high relief of the extremities, including the goddess's helmet and right foot, which extend vivaciously beyond the borders of the tondo. Greek letters inscribed on the back of the *emblema* seem to be a weight inscription, but they correspond neither to the weight of the *emblema* nor the entire cup.

BIBLIOGRAPHY Küthmann 1959, 44–49; Strong 1966, 151; Gehrig 1980, 13, no. 1; Stefanelli 1991, 176, 271, fig. 167, no. 91. See also *CIL* 6.10029.

. . . .

Plate 80

Bust of Lucius Verus, AD 161–69
From Marengo, northern Italy
Silver, H: 55 cm; W: 51 cm; Wt: 2.850 kg
Turin, Museo di Antichità, 5456

This bust was found in 1928 outside Marengo, east of Turin in northern Italy, along with twenty-three pieces of silver, including elements of furniture and architectural decoration, rather than the abundance of drinking vessels more often found in ancient hoards. These objects range in date from the first to the third century and seem to have been gathered together for their monetary value before being deliberately buried. A third-century votive inscription to the goddess Fortuna on another object in the hoard suggests that some of the items might have been rescued or been the booty from an ancient sanctuary. This hollow bust of the emperor who ruled jointly with his brother Marcus Aurelius between AD 161 and 169 may have been an object of worship or it may have functioned as a military standard. The portrait conforms to the type used to depict the emperor early in his reign. His full hair has small curls and larger locks over the forehead, and the full beard has expressive corkscrew curls. The present asymmetry of the eyes may be due to the modern restoration of the bust, which was found smashed. The emperor wears a tunic and cuirass, the front of which takes the form of a scaly aegis with a central gorgoneion, a type first assumed by Hellenistic rulers who sought to associate themselves with Zeus and Athena and later adopted by Roman emperors in the first century.

BIBLIOGRAPHY Bendinelli 1937; Baratte 1998; Sena Chiesa 1998; Riccardi 2002; Brecciaroli Taborelli in Guzzo 2006b; Sena Chiesa 2008.

. . . .

CHAPTER TWO: HARD STONES

Plate 81

Scaraboid intaglio of a youth restraining a horse, ca. 500 BC
Inscribed: ΕΠΙΜΗΝΕΣ ΕΠΩΙΕ (Epimenes made this)
Said to be from the Nile Delta, perhaps Naukratis
Chalcedony, H: 17 mm; W: 19 mm; D: 9 mm
Boston, Museum of Fine Arts, 27.677

This splendid gem depicts a nude beardless youth restraining a restive horse. The carver, Epimenes, obviously delighted not only in rendering fine details, like the bridle, ornamental *peytrel*, and topknot of the horse, but also in representing the young man in a dynamic three-quarter rear view. Similar poses and renderings of musculature, as well as the facial profile and cross-hatched, pelleted hair, have allowed the attribution of other unsigned gems to the same carver (plates 82, 83). Why he signed only this gem, we cannot know, but it is certainly a miniature masterpiece, asserting command of the anatomical detail and overlapping and foreshortened limbs also found in Late Archaic painting and relief sculpture. The letter forms of the inscription suggest that Epimenes came from the Cyclades or the northern Greek islands. Formerly in the Tyszkiewicz and Lewes House collections.

BIBLIOGRAPHY Beasley 1920 (2002 ed.), no. 28; Boardman 1968a, no. 246; Boardman 1970, no. 355; Zwierlein-Diehl 2007, 41.

. . . .

Plate 82

Scaraboid intaglio of an archer testing his arrow, ca. 500 BC
Attributed to Epimenes
Said to be from Naukratis, Egypt
Chalcedony, H: 17 mm; W: 15 mm; D: 13 mm
New York, Metropolitan Museum of Art, 31.11.5.
Formerly in the Southesk collection

BIBLIOGRAPHY Boardman 1968a, no. 248; Boardman 1970, no. 357; Mertens and Anderson 1987, no. 38.

. . . .

Plate 83

Scaraboid intaglio of a youth scraping his leg with a strigil, ca. 500 BC
Attributed to Epimenes
Obsidian, H (gem): 16.2 mm; W: 12.9 mm; D: 6 mm
Set in a gold swivel ring
Malibu, JPGM, 85.AN.370.6
Formerly in the Mezzacappa and Kagan collection

BIBLIOGRAPHY Spier 1992, no. 17; Lapatin and Wight 2010, 83.

. . . .

Plate 84
Scaraboid intaglio of a heron, ca. 450–430 BC
Inscribed: ΔΕΧΑΜΕΝΟΣ ΕΠΟΙΕ ΧΙΟΣ (Dexamenos of Chios made [this])
From Burial Chamber 48, Kurgan 5, at Yuz Oba, Kerch, Crimea
Chalcedony, H: 17 mm; W: 22 mm
Set in a gold swivel ring
St. Petersburg, State Hermitage Museum, YU. O. 24

Excavated in a tomb also containing imported Athenian pottery dated circa 375–370 BC, this stunning intaglio seems to have been buried on the northern shore of the Black Sea as an heirloom. It depicts a heron in flight, the blue chalcedony illusionistically serving as the sky. The delicate engraving of the bird's crest, talon, and feathers—differently patterned on wings, body, and neck—is unsurpassed. Dexamenos's signature, in neatly aligned letters, like those on contemporary marble *stoichedon* inscriptions, was intended to be read on the stone itself, rather than in impression. Other gems signed by Dexamenos have been found in tombs along the northern shore of the Black Sea, suggesting that he may have worked there. The inclusion in this inscription of his home—the Aegean island of Chios—also supports the notion that he worked abroad. Some gems signed by the master, however, have been found on the Greek mainland (see plate 85).

BIBLIOGRAPHY Boardman 1969; Boardman 1970, no. 468; Neverov 1976, no. 20; Kalashnik 2004, 86–89; Neverov in Trofimova 2007, 62–63, 259, no. 154; Boardman and Wagner 2012, 212–13.

....

Plate 85
Scaraboid intaglio of a bearded man, ca. 450–430 BC
Inscribed: ΔΕΧΑΜΕΝΟΣ ΕΠΟΙΕ (Dexamenos made [this])
Said to be from Kara in Attica
Mottled jasper, H: 21 mm, W: 17 mm, D: 6 mm
Set in a gold swivel ring
Boston, Museum of Fine Arts, 23.580

Carved with great fluency, this intaglio depicts a middle-aged man with high forehead, straight nose, wavy hair, and trimmed beard and mustache. The fine engraving of the hair—thin on top, curling in front of the ears—is executed with long, fluid lines, which, at the back of the head, produce a sense of volume. The eyebrow and both upper and lower lashes are carved with extreme delicacy. Light incisions mark wrinkles in the forehead and the back of the neck, while the fleshy volumes of the nostrils and throat are more sculpturally modeled. The whole gives a strong impression of individuality. Arthur Evans, who once owned the gem, believed it represented the Athenian statesman Kimon, an early rival of Perikles. Scholars today are less confident as to the identity of the sitter. Formerly in the Soteriades, Rhousopoulos, Evans, and Lewes House collections.

BIBLIOGRAPHY Evans 1898; Beazley 1920 (2002 ed.), no. 50; Boardman 1969; Boardman 1970, no. 466; Boardman and Wagner 2012, 213.

....

Plate 86
Scaraboid intaglio of Nike, ca. 370–350 BC
Signed by Onatas(?)
From Kamiros, Rhodes
Chalcedony, H: 31 mm; W: 24 mm; D: 11 mm
London, British Museum, 1865,0712.86 (Gem 601)

Pierced lengthwise, this exceptionally large and exquisitely carved domed gem was originally mounted on a swivel. A Nike, in three-quarter view, her face in profile, hangs a sword on a trophy mounted on a tall tree stump. The composition recalls that of the parapet of the Temple of Athena Nike on the Athenian Acropolis. The trophy consists of a variety of arms: a helmet with a horizontal crest, lowered cheek pieces, and raised feathers; a round shield with a central boss; a linen corselet with rectangular *ptyrges* (flaps) and an under-tunic that blows as if in a light breeze. A folded piece of heavier cloth hangs from a lower branch, and a single greave appears to be nailed to the tree, while a second, larger shield with an offset rim leans against the trunk. A long double-headed spear stands opposite the Nike; from it a hangs a thin fluttering banner on which are inscribed letters that seem to read ONA..., perhaps the carver's signature. Onatas is otherwise unknown, but the engraver of this gem, whatever his name, was certainly a master. The wealth of fine detail, rendering of diverse textures, and the Nike's convincing anatomy and pose are unsurpassed. Her hair is finely engraved, coiled up around her head and tied in front. Her mantle, though still draped over her right arm, has slipped below her hips, exposing her breasts and stomach and fluttering around her legs in complex folds. Her right foot is in profile, while the left, with heel raised, is foreshortened. Even the feathers of the two large wings that rise above her head are individualized. The weapons on the trophy are of a type commonly used in South Italy, suggesting that this gem may have been carved there, despite the fact that it was found in Rhodes. Formerly in the Castellani collection.

BIBLIOGRAPHY Walters 1926, 601; Boardman 1970, no. 590; Zwierlein-Diehl 2007, 52, 363, fig. 170; Williams 2009, no. 64; Boardman and Wagner 2012, 214.

....

Plate 87
Intaglio of Philetairos of Pergamon, ca. 275–175 BC
Mottled chalcedony and jasper, H: 28 mm; W: 23 mm
London, British Museum, GR 1872,0604.1333 (Gem 1184)

Philetairos (343–263 BC), son of Attalos, founded the Attalid dynasty, which ruled Pergamon in western Turkey. After the death of

Alexander the Great in 323 BC, Philetairos served under his various successors, eventually being entrusted by Lysimachos to safeguard a treasure of 9,000 silver talents at Pergamon's mountaintop stronghold. Following the death of Seleukos in 281 BC, Philetairos essentially ruled independently, although he never declared himself king. He used the vast wealth at his disposal not only to improve the fortifications of Pergamon and construct temples and other buildings on its acropolis but also to benefit neighboring cities. He dedicated temples at Delos and Delphi, establishing a model for subsequent Pergamene cultural diplomacy. His nephew Eumenes, who succeeded him, placed his portrait on Pergamene coinage, as did subsequent rulers of the city. As in those numismatic portraits, Philetairos appears here clean-shaven, with short, curly hair, and a somewhat fleshy face (he was reportedly a eunuch). Whether this gem was carved during his lifetime or later is uncertain, for his image remained an emblem of the Attalid dynasty until his great-great-grandnephew Attalos III bequeathed the city to Rome in 133 BC. However, the fact that he appears here without the royal diadem suggests that this image may date to his lifetime. Formerly in the Castellani collection.

BIBLIOGRAPHY Walters 1926, 1184; Plantzos 1999a, no. 90; Williams 2009, no. 83.

....

Plate 88

Intaglio of a Ptolemaic king, second–first century BC
Cornelian, H: 20 mm; W: 17 mm; D: ca. 4 mm
Modern gold and enamel mount
Paris, Bibliothèque nationale de France, Cabinet des médailles, 2057

The subject of this bold portrait has been identified as either Ptolemy VI Philometor (r. 180–145 BC) or Ptolemy XII Neos Dionysos (r. 80–51 BC), who was also called *Auletes* (the flute player). Wearing a flat diadem whose ends flutter and twist behind him, the sharp-featured king wears a *chiton* pinned at the shoulders. The folds of drapery at his neck, like his finely incised locks of hair, overlap one another realistically. His face is marked by a wide bulging brow; long aquiline nose, fleshy nostrils and lips, and a pronounced chin, all rendered with great subtlety. Paradoxically, despite the masterful carving, it is difficult to determine whether the ruler represented here is Ptolemy VI, who appears bearded in Egyptian and Greek garb on a pair of gold rings (plate 44), or Ptolemy XII, some of whose coins the head resembles. Both were weak rulers protected by powerful Roman patrons. The intaglio, however, depicts a man of character and determination, in the mold of Alexander the Great, whose upward gaze and leonine coiffure he emulates.

BIBLIOGRAPHY Vollenweider and Avisseau-Broustet 1995, no. 102; Plantzos 1999a, no. 17.

....

Plate 89

Intaglio of the *Doryphoros* of Polykleitos, ca. 50–40 BC
Dark green chalcedony, H (gem): 22.4 mm; W: 17.3 mm
Malibu, JPGM, 75.AM.61

Romans demonstrated their status and taste by reference to famous works of Greek art and literature. The *Doryphoros* (Spearbearer) of the Argive sculptor Polykleitos, first cast in bronze ca. 440 BC, was highly renowned, in part because the sculptor wrote a treatise that explained the theory underlying its system of proportions. That work, called *The Kanon*, was read not only by other artists but also, to judge by the number of quotations and citations in surviving ancient literature, by poets, orators, and even physicians, who sought therein to understand better the principles of the ideal human body. This intaglio presents just the bust of the figure, which the Romans also excerpted in statuary, and may have been intended to signal not only the cultivation of its owner, but also his adherence to some kind of ideal.

BIBLIOGRAPHY Oliver 1980; Spier 1992, no. 221; Lapatin and Wight 2010, 200. See also Moon 1995.

....

Plate 90

Intaglio of a man, ca. 150 BC
Inscribed ΜΗΝΟΦΙΛΟΣ ΕΠΟΙΕ (Menophilos made [this])
Said to be from Syria
Garnet, H (gem): 23.5 mm; W: 18.5 mm; D: 7 mm;
H (ring): 34.4 mm; W: 29.1 mm
Set in a heavy gold ring with a stepped bezel
Chicago, Oriental Institute Museum, OIA29789,
purchased in Beirut in 1953 by Chester D. Tripp

This powerful portrait bears the only known signature of the engraver Menophilos. Nothing is known of him, but several contemporaries of the same name are attested, particularly in Asia Minor. None of these individuals can be linked to our engraver, however. The name was shared by several craftsmen working in other media, including at least two members of a family of sculptors from Ephesos who were active on the island of Delos in the second half of the second century BC. Although the subject of this portrait has been called Mark Antony, his identity remains uncertain, despite his individuality. He has a powerful neck and jaw, strong chin, thin lips, aquiline nose with fleshy nostril, sunken cheek, furrowed brow, and short hair arranged in unruly triangular locks. The convex form of the gem and the elaborate stepped bezel of its ring have parallels in the second century BC and may corroborate the story that this gem was found in Syria along with another engraved ring stone depicting the jugate heads Zeus-Serapis and Isis, two gold snake armbands, a gold bracelet, and coins of Asia Minor and the Seleucid mints of Syria, the latest belonging to the reign of Tryphon (142–138 BC).

BIBLIOGRAPHY Kraeling 1955; Vollenweider 1966, 38; Hoffmann and Davidson 1965, no. 56; Richter 1968b, no. 689; Grimm 1970, 166–67: Vollenweider 1972–74, no. 136.1; Higgins 1980, 170; Spier 1989, 30, H; Plantzos 1999a, no. 621; Zwierlein-Diehl 2005, 337; Platz-Horster 2012, 40, 43, no. B 10. See also R. Smith 1988, 127.

....

Plate 91
Intaglio of Sirius (the Dog Star), ca. 100 BC
Inscribed: ΓΑΙΟΣ ΕΠΟΙΕΙ (Gaius made [this])
Garnet, H: 21.5 mm; W: 15 mm; Thickness: 7 mm
Modern gold swivel ring
Boston, Museum of Fine Arts, 27.734

This exceptionally deeply cut intaglio, carved with great virtuosity, depicts the head of Sirius, the Dog Star, frontally, rather than in profile, as was far more common in ancient glyptic. The dog is of the Molossian type, with thick fur in striated tufts, pointed ears, particularly expressive brows, a long snout, open mouth, and teeth. Appropriately engraved in a fiery red garnet, the personification of the hottest days of summer is identifiable by the nine thin hooked rays he emits. The carver Gaius cleverly placed his signature in minute Greek on the dog's collar, integrating it into the composition. Other signed gems by Gaius do not survive, but his signature appears on clay sealings from an archive on Delos. This fine work has been admired since the eighteenth century, drawn and imitated by the master engraver Johann Lorenz Natter and many others. Formerly in the Chesterfield, Bessborough, Marlborough, and Lewes House collections.

BIBLIOGRAPHY Natter 1754; Beazley 1920 (2002 ed.), no. 114; Plantzos 1999a, no. 709; Zwierlein-Diehl 2007, 77-78; Boardman et al. 2009, 139, no. 293.

....

Plate 92
Intaglio of the *Athena Parthenos* of Pheidias, ca. 50–25 BC
Inscribed: ΑΣΠΑΣΙΟΥ (by Aspasios)
Red jasper, H: 35 mm; W: 28 mm
Rome, Museo Nazionale Romano,
Palazzo Massimo alle Terme, 52382

This large gem, one of five surviving works signed by Aspasios, is remarkable for its detailed rendition of the head and bust of the famous gold and ivory statue of Athena that Pheidias fashioned in the late fifth century BC for the interior of the Parthenon on the Athenian Acropolis. The statue, famous throughout antiquity, was some four hundred years old when Aspasios represented it here. Despite the many descriptions of Pheidias's work, this gem remains one of the most detailed documentations of its appearance. The patron goddess of Athens wears a helmet with three crests supported by a sphinx in the center flanked by two Pegasoi, a visor with Pegasoi and deer protomes, and rampant griffins on the raised cheek pieces (see also plate 19). Curls spiral out from the helmet over her shoulders and in front of her ears, which sport pendant earrings. She wears several necklaces and her trademark scaly aegis, with its central gorgoneion and snakes curling at the edges. Formerly in the Rondanini, and Ottoboni collections and that of the Kunsthistorisches Museum,Vienna.

BIBLIOGRAPHY Vollenweider 1966, 31; Richter 1971, no. 642; Lapatin 2001, 66, color pl. IX; Platt 2006, 234–35; Zwierlein-Diehl 2007, 111–12, no. 436.

....

Plate 93
Intaglio of Artemis, ca. 50–25 BC
Signed: ΑΠΟΛΛΩΝΙΟΥ (by Apollonios)
Amethyst, H: 25.7 mm; W: 13.8 mm
Naples, Museo Archeologico Nazionale, 26070

As if lost in thought, the virgin goddess of the hunt stands in a rustic sanctuary. Resting her crossed hands on a small pillar, she holds two burning torches downward over a rocky altar, while a higher outcrop rises behind her. Her pose is relaxed, with the weight on the left leg. She wears high, open-toed boots and a short *peplos,* pinned at the shoulder and belted at the waist, leaving her arms and legs bare. The garment's heavy over-fold falls to her hips; the end of her closed quiver and the tip of her bow are visible over her shoulder. First published in 1585, this gem has been misassociated with Apollonides, one of only four gem engravers mentioned by Pliny (*NH* 37.8), because the carver's minute signature ΑΠΟΛΛΩΝΙΟΥ, placed vertically alongside the pillar, was optimistically misread as ΑΠΟΛΛΩΝΙΔΟΥ. Formerly in the Tigrini, Orsini, and Farnese collections.

BIBLIOGRAPHY Zwierlein-Diehl 1986, no. 143 (compare 142); Pannuti 1994, no. 72; Gasparri 1994, no. 56; Zwierlein-Diehl 2007, 113, 279, no. 443.

....

Plate 94
Intaglio of Odysseus, Diomedes, and the Palladion (the Felix Gem), ca. 25 BC–AD 25
Inscribed: ΦΗΛΙΞ ΕΠΟΙΕΙ (Felix made [this]) and
ΚΑΛΠΟΥΡΝΙΟΥ ΣΕΟΥΗΡΟΥ (Belonging to Calpurnius Severus)
Agate, H: 26 mm; W: 35 mm; D: 3 mm
Oxford, Ashmolean Museum, AN1966.1808

The story of Diomedes's theft of the Trojan Palladion, a popular subject on gems (see plate 96), here receives its fullest narrative presentation in glyptic art. The hero sits on the altar holding the sacred image of Athena in one hand, a sword in the other, with a slain guard or priest at his feet and a statue of Poseidon on a tall pillar in the distance. The scene is set within the walls of Troy and includes Odysseus gesturing toward the dead man in protest of Diomedes's sacrilege. The inscription on the altar names the gem carver and the other its original owner, Calpurnius Severus, a member of the court of Emperor Tiberius (r. 14–37). The subsequent ancient history of the gem is unknown, but it has been well documented since the Renaissance. It was purchased by the Florentine humanist scholar Nicolò Niccoli and then passed into the hands of other aristocratic collectors, who showed it to artists in their circles. The carving inspired such Renaissance masters as Andrea Mantegna, Donatello, and Leonardo da Vinci. Felix, a common slave name, appears in a funerary inscription of the freedman Quintus Plotinus Felix among the names of a group of gem engravers who practiced their craft along the Sacred Way in Rome. Formerly in the Niccoli, Trevisan, Barbò, Gonzaga, Arundel, Marlborough, Bromilow, Evans, and Spencer-Churchill collections.

BIBLIOGRAPHY Boardman 1970, no. 1015; Henig and MacGregor 2004, no. 10.20; Marvin 2008, 187–89; Boardman et al. 2009, no. 165; *CIL* 6[2] 9535.

....

Plate 95
Intaglio of Apollo, Marsyas, and Olympos (the Seal of Nero), ca. 30 BC
Attributed to Dioskourides
Cornelian, H: 40.2 mm; W: 34 mm
Naples, Museo Archeologico Nazionale, 26051

Deeply carved with a complex composition and subtle modeling of anatomy, this gem is conventionally associated with Emperor Nero, who famously accompanied himself on a lyre like Apollo's as he sang while Rome burned. Some of Nero's coins also bear an image of the god playing the instrument. Apollo is depicted half nude, standing in a contrapposto pose with a lyre, having just defeated the satyr Marsyas in a musical contest. The satyr's son Olympos kneels at the feet of the god, begging for forgiveness. Marsyas himself sits with his hands bound to the leafless tree behind him, from which hangs the case for his double-pipes. The pipes themselves rise above his knee, near Lorenzo de' Medici's initials, which were cut into the gem in the late fifteenth century. The style and quality of the engraving suggest that this gem was carved by Dioskourides. Comparison of Marsyas's anatomy with that of Diomedes on another intaglio signed by the master (see plate 96); in particular the similar rendering of hip, buttocks, genitals, abdomen, and arm, supports this attribution. Augustus closely associated himself with Apollo, and this image of the god triumphing over the satyr, a follower of Dionysos, may reflect the victory over Mark Antony, who styled himself the "New Dionysos." As for Nero's actual seal, it was an image of Augustus passed down by his Julio-Claudian predecessors—carved by Dioskourides. Formerly in the Trevisan, Barbo, di Piero, Medici, and Farnese collections.

BIBLIOGRAPHY Pannuti 1994, no. 127; Gasparri 1994, no. 46; Gennaioli 2010, no. 35; Gennaioli 2012, no. 11.

....

Plate 96
Intaglio of Diomedes and the Palladion, ca. 40–30 BC
Inscribed: ΔΙΟCΚΟΥΡΙΔΟΥ (by Dioskourides)
Cornelian, H: 17.5 mm; W: 19 mm
Chatsworth, Devonshire Collection, Gem 13(1/5)

The ancients considered the fall of Troy necessary to the rise of Rome, for the Trojan Aeneas fled his shattered city and founded the new city on the Tiber. The theft of the Palladion, the talismanic Trojan statue of Athena by the Greek hero Diomedes, was a crucial element in the story, which was especially popular in Roman art of the late Republic and early Empire (see also plate 94). Here Dioskourides, one of the few gem engravers ancient writers mention by name, has not only depicted the Greek hero, holding the diminutive image of the goddess—recognizable by its crested helmet, shield, and spear—but he has also encapsulated the entire story in a small compass. Diomedes sits on an altar, sword in one hand, at his feet the body of the priest he has slain. Before him stands a statue of Poseidon on a pillar, its back to the hero, a signal of the god's disgust and the difficulties ahead. Not only is the inclusion of so many details exceptional in such a small space but so is the handling of the hero's anatomy. His dynamic pose is rendered sculpturally, with convincingly diverse textures of curly hair, smooth skin, firm muscle, and hard underlying bone. Formerly in the Seven collection and that of King Louis XIV.

BIBLIOGRAPHY Vollenweider 1966, 62, pl. 62; Richter 1971, no. 664; Scarisbrick 1986, 247, no. 13; Plantzos 1999b; Scarisbrick 2003.

....

Plate 97
Fragmentary intaglio of Apollo, ca. 30–20 BC
Attributed to Solon
Amethyst, H: 33 mm; W: 30 mm
Modern gold setting
Malibu, JPGM, 96.AN.290

Although not signed by the artist, this minutely detailed gem shares several features with the signed works of the engraver Solon (active 70–20 BC), including the intricately carved hair, hooked lock before the ear, large incised iris, and the curved line of the chin and jaw. Solon's signature is preserved on five ancient gems, and he seems eventually to have worked in Roman imperial circles, fashioning idealized portraits of the emperor Augustus and his sister, along with images of mythological figures. Apollo was a particular favorite of the emperor, who next to his home on Rome's Palatine Hill erected a temple to the god who had helped him defeat Antony and Cleopatra at Actium in 31 BC. The fact that this image of the god of moderation is engraved on an amethyst, which was often thought to protect against drunkenness, may also have political significance, for Mark Antony styled himself the "New Dionysos." Formerly in the de Béhague and Fleischman collections.

BIBLIOGRAPHY Spier 1991; see also Vollenweider 1966; Zwierlein-Diehl 2007, 114–15.

....

Plate 98
Intaglio of Zeus, late first century BC–early first century AD
Cornelian, H: 37 mm; W: 26 mm
St. Petersburg, State Heritage Museum, Ж 1216

The Classical style of fifth-century BC Greece was revived in Rome in engraved gems as well as in sculpture (see also plates 89, 92). Here the king of the Olympian gods stares coolly forward. The image seems to reference a famous passage from the first book of Homer's *Iliad* (528–30) that is said to have inspired Pheidias, the sculptor of the monumental gold and ivory statue of Zeus at Olympia, one of the Seven Wonders of the Ancient World: "'Nothing I do shall be vain nor revocable nor a thing unfulfilled when I bend my head in assent to it.' Thus spoke the son of Kronos, and nodded his dark brow, and the ambrosial locks waved from the king's immortal head and he made great Olympus quake." Here, the god's visage is stern. His beard is a mass of hooked curls and his coiffure complex: finely engraved parallel strands descend from the crown of his head, meeting a wreath of oak, recognizable by its serrated leaves and acorns. Behind the small, fleshy ear, a thick braided band wraps around the base of the head and two long corkscrew curls hang from it. In front of the ear shorter hooked curls are swept back from the bulging brow, while a blank eye stares forward, like that of a statue. Formerly in the collections of the duc d'Orleans and Catherine the Great.
BIBLIOGRAPHY Neverov 1976, no. 114; Kagan and Neverov 2001, 57, no. 29/1.

....

Plate 99
Intaglio of Demosthenes, ca. 25–1 BC
Inscribed: ΑΠΕΛΛΟΥ (by Apelles)
Cornelian, H (gem): 19 mm; W: 15 mm
Set in a gold ring
Malibu, JPGM, 90.AN.13

This deeply carved and well-modeled depiction of the famous fourth-century BC orator is based on the posthumous portrait commissioned by the Athenian state from the sculptor Polyeuktos in 280/79 BC. The gem-engraver Apelles is otherwise unknown but probably took his name from the famous Greek painter. Several other gem carvers share names with famous artists working in other media, such as Daidalos, Nikias, Polykleitos, Skopas, and Timanthes. We cannot know the motivation of the owner of this ring for choosing this device: he may have been named Demosthenes, desired oratorical success, admired the Athenian rhetorician, or shared his republican politics. The white bands that mar the image appear to be the result of alteration in the body of the stone (the carved features were originally transparent) caused by exposure to elevated temperatures and/or chemical exposure in an adverse environment.
BIBLIOGRAPHY Spier 1992, no. 220; Lapatin and Wight 2010, 201.

....

Plate 100
Intaglio of Octavian as Neptune, ca. 31–27 BC
Inscribed: ΠΟΠΙΛ ΑΛΒΑΝ (Popillius Albanus)
Said to be from Hadrumentum (in present-day Tunisia)
Cornelian, H: 17 mm; W: 21 mm
Modern gold setting
Boston, Museum of Fine Arts, 27.733

Although ancient literary sources make much of the modest public behavior of Octavian (who later assumed the name Augustus), he did not shun association with the gods in private luxury arts (see also plates 112, 113). Here he appears as Poseidon/Neptune, the ruler of the seas. Nude but for a cloak fluttering behind him, he holds a trident and the reins of a chariot drawn by four *hippocamps* (sea horses) as he drives them through a turbulent sea. His identity is certain, for he lacks the beard of the sea god, and his short hair and face are recognizable. Below the horses' hooves a Triton with a large pointed ear emerges from the water to swim alongside the emperor; a dolphin crests the waves in the middle of the gem. The carving is powerful, and although there is some repetition in the position of the horses' hooves, their spirited heads with distended nostrils and wild manes enliven the scene. The date is suggested by the coins of Octavian, minted in the years 31–27 BC, which display naval emblems celebrating his victory at Actium. Nothing is known of Popillius Albanus, whose name appears in the field above, but the Popillii were an important family during the Republic, its members holding consulships and achieving other honors in the second and early first centuries BC. The white clouding of the gem is likely the result of intense heat. Formerly in the Tyszkiewicz and Lewes House collections.
BIBLIOGRAPHY Beazley 1920 (2002 ed.), no. 105; Maderna-Lauter in Hofter et al. 1988, no. 247; Zanker 1988, 97–98; Plantzos 1999a, no. 633.

....

Plate 101
Intaglio of Julia, daughter of Titus, ca. AD 80–91
Inscribed: ΕΥΟΔΟC ΕΠΟΙΕΙ (Euodos made [this])
From the abbey of Saint-Denis, France
Beryl (aquamarine), H (gem): 50 mm; W: 37 mm
Carolingian gold, sapphire, and pearl setting
Paris, Bibliothèque nationale de France, Cabinet des médailles, 2089

Finely engraved with a wealth of detail, this large intaglio depicts the Flavian princess Julia (AD 61–89/90), daughter of the emperor Titus and rumored to be the lover of her uncle, the emperor Domitian. The folds of her tunic, braided *stola*, and soft mantle are all differentiated.

She wears a pearl pendant earring and thin strand of pearls around her fleshy neck. Above her wide eye and bushy brow, her elaborate coiffure is arranged in rows of curls stacked high above her forehead, and, separated by a diadem decorated with scrolls, thin braids are pulled back and tied in a swirling bun. This stunning image of the princess came to be associated with the Virgin Mary in the Middle Ages, and thus was placed at the apex of the so-called Escrain de Charlemagne that Charles the Bald donated to the French royal abbey of Saint-Denis about 870. In 1625 Jacques Doublet recognized the portrait as that of an ancient ruler, but he mistakenly believed the sitter to be Cleopatra. His friend the antiquarian Nicolas-Claude Fabri de Peiresc correctly identified Julia on the basis of her coin portraits. He also deciphered the carver's signature. No other gems by Euodos are known.

BIBLIOGRAPHY Zwierlein-Diehl 1986, no. 142; Vollenweider and Avisseau-Broustet 2003, no. 145; Zwierlein-Diehl 2007, no. 484.

....

Plate 102

Cameo of Alexander the Great with the horn of Zeus Ammon, ca. 320–200 BC(?)
Sardonyx, H (gem): 32 mm; W: 30 mm
Modern gold and enamel setting
Paris, Bibliothèque nationale de France, Cabinet des médailles, 222

According to Pliny, "Alexander the Great issued an edict forbidding his likeness to be engraved on stone by anyone except Pyrgoteles, who was undoubtedly the most brilliant in this field" (*NH* 37.8; see also *NH* 7.125). No gems bearing that carver's signature survive, but several have nonetheless been attributed to his hand, including this one. Alexander's image was widespread in antiquity, serving both as a talisman and as a symbol of political power. Here, in a three-layer sardonyx, he wears the royal diadem tied around his curly locks and, arcing over his ear, the horn of Zeus Ammon, an allusion to Zeus's utterance that Alexander was his son, would rule the world, and would be invincible until he rejoined the gods. Alexander appears in similar guise in the series of coins minted by his successor, Lysimachos, beginning in 297 BC. This cameo differs from the coins not only in the fineness of its detail but also in that Alexander has a double chin and the ram's horn here wraps around, rather than crosses over, his ear. Whenever it was carved and by whom, this outstanding work may capture something of the innovative style and superlative skill of Pyrgoteles, whom some modern scholars have credited with the invention of the cameo technique. Formerly in the collection of King Louis XIV.

BIBLIOGRAPHY Stewart 1993, passim, esp. 322n105; Vollenweider and Avisseau-Broustet 1995, no. 29. Compare Boardman and Vollenweider 1978, no. 280.

....

Plate 103

Double portrait of male and female rulers (the Gonzaga Cameo), third century BC or later(?)
Sardonyx, H: 157 mm; W: 118 mm
St. Petersburg, State Hermitage Museum, H 291

This magnificent, deeply carved cameo takes its name from the Gonzagas of Mantua, Italy; it is first recorded in a 1542 inventory of the antiquities collection of Isabella d'Este. The two figures depicted as *capita jugata* (yoked heads)—a composition first seen on the coinage of Ptolemy II Philadelphos and his sister/wife Arsinoe II—have been variously identified as that couple, as Alexander the Great and his mother Olympias, Augustus and Livia, Tiberius and Livia, Germanicus and Agrippina the Elder, Nero and Agrippina the Younger, Hadrian and Sabina, and others. Dates ascribed to the gem vary accordingly. Both figures wear laurel wreaths, the male over his helmet, which is decorated further by a winged snake, a star, a spiraling tendril, and a long white crest. He has leonine hair, reminiscent of Alexander the Great, long sideburns, and wears a wonderfully carved aegis, from whose scales emerge two white heads: the Gorgon Medusa's in front and a bearded male, plausibly identified as Phoibos, the personification of fear. In addition to the laurel wreath with berries, the woman wears a veil over her hair, which is arranged in tightly twisted curls. Her necklace, which also crosses the neck of her companion, is a modern repair. Formerly in the collections of the Gonzaga, Queen Christina of Sweden, Livio Odescalchi, Pope Pius VI, Napoleon Bonaparte and Josephine Beauharnais, and Czar Alexander I.

BIBLIOGRAPHY Kyrieleis 1971; Brown 1997, 85–107; Platz-Horster 1997; Zwierlein-Diehl 2007, 62–65; Casazza 2008, esp. 37–46, 304–5, no. 87.

....

Plate 104

Cameo of Zeus fighting the giants, ca. 150 BC
Inscribed: ΑΘΗΝΙΩΝ (by Athenion)
Sardonyx, H: 29 mm; W: 35 mm
Naples, Museo Archeologico Nazionale, 25848

This exuberant cameo, first published by J. J. Winckelmann in 1764, conveys the tumult of the Gigantomachy as the king of the gods, holding a scepter in his left hand and thunderbolt in his right, routs a pair of snake-legged giants. The god, chariot horses, and monsters all move dynamically in three dimensions, their muscles bulging in the expressive style of second-century BC Pergamene sculpture, which also provides the closest parallel for the giants as bifurcated anguipeds. The engraver Athenion is also known from two ancient glass cameos depicting a Hellnistic ruler in a chariot driven by Athena. Formerly in the Orsini and Farnese collections.

BIBLIOGRAPHY Gasparri 1994, no. 55; Pannuti 1994, no. 71; Zwierlein-Diehl 2007, 69.

....

Plate 105
Cameo of Hermaphroditus revealing him/herself, ca. 150–100 BC
Attributed to Protarchos
Sardonyx, H: 18 mm; W: 14 mm; D: 2 mm
Modern gold ring
Malibu, JPGM, 2001.28.9

The illusionistic possibilities of the cameo technique are pushed here to their limits, not only in the complex posture and vibrant, three-dimensional drapery folds but also in the subtle rendering of seemingly transparent cloth achieved by carefully exploiting the layered stone. The technical mastery and refined style of this small stone representing Hermaphroditus sitting on an altar recalls works signed by Protarchos, to whom have been attributed other cameos depicting the androgynous offspring of Hermes and Aphrodite. Formerly in the Arundel, Marlborough, and Ionides collections.
BIBLIOGRAPHY Boardman 1968b, no. 62; Boardman et al. 2009, no. 23; Lapatin and Wight 2010, 203. See also Vollenweider 1966, 23–25; Dacos, Giuliano, and Pannuti 1973, nos. 3–4; Gasparri 1994, no. 27; Zwierlein-Diehl 2007, 68–69.

....

Plate 106
Cameo of Dionysos and a satyr on a chariot drawn by Psychai and Erotes, ca. 50–30 BC
Sardonyx, H: 33.9 mm; W: 42.6 mm
Naples, Museo Archeologico Nazionale, 25840

One of the most famous ancient gems during the Renaissance, this cameo was inscribed in the late fifteenth century with the initials of Lorenzo de' Medici (LAV.R.MED.). The composition was popular in antiquity, but here it is engraved with exceptional skill and fluidity. Two Psychai with butterfly wings tug a chariot carrying an effeminate Dionysos, who reclines, legs crossed, supported by a young satyr, under billowing drapery. A knotty plane tree curves overhead. Standing on the chariot pole, a winged Eros holding the reins threatens the Psychai with a torch. A second, smaller Eros seems to be turning, or perhaps mischievously impeding, one of the chariot wheels. Details of fluttering drapery, complex poses, and varying textures are outstanding. On account of similarities to signed gems, this cameo has been attributed to Sosistratos and, because of its Dionysiac iconography, has been connected with the circle of Mark Antony, who styled himself the "New Dionysos." Formerly in the Barbo, Medici, and Farnese collections.
BIBLIOGRAPHY Vollenweider 1966, 32–33; Dacos, Giuliano, and Pannuti 1973, no. 8; Gasparri 1994, no. 30; Boardman 1997, 18–20; R. Gennaioli in Casazza 2008, no. 6; Gennaioli 2010, no. 12; Gennaioli 2012, no. 9.

....

Plate 107
Cameo of the Marriage of Cupid and Psyche(?)
(the Marlborough Cameo)
ca. 50–25 BC
Inscribed: ΤΡΥΦΩΝ ΕΠΟΙΕΙ (Tryphon made [this])
Sardonyx, H: 37 mm; W: 45 mm; D: 2.5 mm
Boston, Museum of Fine Arts, 99.101

One of the most famous and influential cameos in modern times, this stone is remarkable for its technique and detail. It bears the signature of the Greek carver Tryphon, who was praised in a poem preserved in the *Palatine Anthology* (9.544). Thus some scholars have questioned the authenticity of the inscription as too good to be true. Recent studies, however, have not only adduced ancient parallels for the elegant, if idiosyncratic letter forms but also demonstrated that the gem was rediscovered before 1572, when it was fully described by Costantino Felici. In the center a cupid with a long torch leads Psyche and a veiled cupid carrying a dove toward another cupid, who lifts a cloth covering objects on a stool. Another cupid holds a *liknon* (ritual basket) of pomegranates over the couple's heads. The cameo has inspired generations of artists and collectors, including Peter Paul Rubens, who once owned it. It has been depicted in numerous engravings, often with erroneous details, and was replicated by Josiah Wedgwood on plaques, vases, inkwells, and opera glasses. The imagery appears in eighteenth-century society portraits and interior furnishings, including a chimneypiece relief at Blenheim Palace, home of the dukes of Marlborough, who also owned the gem, and was so well known that it was adapted for late eighteenth-century caricatures. Formerly in the Ligorio(?), Rubens, Arundel, and Marlborough collections.
BIBLIOGRAPHY Vollenweider 1966, 36–37; Nonni 1995; Micheli 2008; Boardman et al. 2009, no. 1; Prioux 2012.

....

Plate 108
Cameo of the young Herakles, ca. 30–20 BC
Attributed to Gnaios
Sardonyx, H: 29.9 mm; W: 23 mm
Naples, Museo Archeologico Nazionale, 25851

Carved to exploit three layers of the stone, the contrasting colors of which appear to have been artificially enhanced, this depiction of the beardless young hero is marked by the extraordinarily fine engraving of the wavy mane of the lion skin, the hero's tight curls, and his smooth facial features. Herakles's lips are slightly parted, nostrils flared, and his eye is marked by fleshy lids, incised iris and pupil. Similar features appear on an aquamarine intaglio depicting the same hero, with a club rather than a lion skin as attribute, signed by the carver Gnaios (London, British Museum, 1867,0507.318 [Gem 1982]). Formerly in the Barbo, Medici, and Farnese collections.

BIBLIOGRAPHY Vollenweider 1966, 46; Dacos, Giuliano, and Pannuti 1973, no. 24; Pannuti 1994, no. 176; Gasparri 1994, no. 45; R. Gennaioli in Casazza 2008, no. 7.

....

Plate 109
Cameo of Herakles leashing Kerberos, ca. 40–30 BC
Inscribed: ΔΙΟCΚΟΥΡΙΔΟ[Υ] (by Dioskourides)
Sardonyx, H: 25.3 mm; W: 21.3 mm
Berlin, Staatliche Museen, Antikensammlung, FG 11062

Signed by the engraver who cut the seal of Emperor Augustus (see also plates 95, 96), this stone is remarkable both for its complex composition, based on earlier Hellenistic prototypes, and for the rounded modeling of its high-relief carving. Details such as the rocky ground line and oblique club behind the right rear leg of the hellhound add depth to the composition, as does the undercutting of the beast's left rear leg as it paws at the hero, whose bulging musculature is masterfully rendered. Although Kerberos has only two, rather than the canonical three, heads pinned between the hero's powerful thighs, the placement of Herakles's lion skin, depicted frontally, cleverly conflates the hero's first and last labors. Scholars debate whether this is the gem mentioned by Benvenuto Cellini in his *Autobiography* (1525), where he wrote that Michelangelo, too, admired its craftsmanship, saying that he had never seen anything so marvelous. Formerly in the collections of Friedrich III and the Electors of Brandenburg.
BIBLIOGRAPHY Zwierlein-Diehl 2007; Platz-Horster in Casazza 2008, no. 22; Platz-Horster 2012, no. 21.

....

Plate 110
Cameo of an eagle, ca. 27 BC(?)
Sardonyx, Diam: 220 mm
Vienna, Kunsthistorisches Museum, IXa 26

One of the largest surviving cameos from antiquity, this splendid carving encapsulates Roman power. Sculpted in high relief, the eagle of Jupiter perches majestically on a palm branch, the symbol of victory. The talons of the left foot grasp a wreath identifiable by its distinctive oak leaves and acorns as the *corona civica*, awarded to Emperor Augustus in January of 27 BC on account of his saving the lives of fellow citizens during the bloody civil wars that preceded his victory at Actium in 31 BC. The carver, working in the Hellenistic tradition, has subtly varied the pose of the eagle and especially the orientation and textures of its feathers. Those of the body seem to twist dynamically in response to the bird's movement and, along with those of the upper half of the wings, they are carved in relief, while those of the lower wings are incised, as is the skin of the bird's legs and feet.
BIBLIOGRAPHY Zwierlein-Diehl 2008, no. 4.

....

Plate 111
Cameo of Athena/Minerva, ca. 25–1 BC
Sardonyx, H: 68 mm; W: 60 mm; D: 11 mm
Late seventeenth-century gold and enamel setting
Paris, Bibliothèque nationale de France, Cabinet des médailles, 17

The goddess of war and wisdom wears an elaborate helmet decorated with a rampant griffin carved in relief, a visor with an incised scroll, and a long horsehair crest, fashioned from both mane and tail, that flows down to her shoulder, where it meets her own, more voluminous, wavy locks, tied near the end. The goddess's profile face is sympathetic, in contrast to the cold classicism of many contemporary gems; her body is presented in three-quarter view. The scaly aegis across her chest has a central gorgoneion (Medusa head) carved in relief and twisting snakes at the edges. Whether this and other cameos with similar profiles represent a Julio-Claudian princess in the guise of a goddess, as has been suggested, remains uncertain. The griffin, associated in ancient imagery with Nemesis, has been linked to the misbehavior and eventual banishment of Augustus's daughter Julia in 2 BC, but this event is unlikely to have been commemorated in so precious a medium. The griffin, moreover, had long been associated with Athena: as the guardian of gold, the beast appeared on the goddess's helmet in antiquity's most famous representation of her—Pheidias's monumental fifth-century BC gold and ivory statue in the Parthenon on the Athenian Acropolis (see plates 19, 92). Formerly in the collection of King Louis XIV.
BIBLIOGRAPHY Vollenweider and Avisseau-Broustet 2003, no. 67.

....

Plate 112
Cameo of Augustus, ca. 25–20 BC
From the reliquary of Saint Hilaire, abbey of Saint-Denis, France
Sardonyx, H: 49 mm; W: 40 mm
Late fourteenth-century gilt-silver, sapphire, ruby, and pearl setting
Paris, Bibliothèque nationale de France, Cabinet des médailles, 234

The first emperor of Rome is depicted facing right, wearing a double wreath of laurel intertwined with oak, tied with a ribbon fluttering in the rear. The laurel alludes to Augustus's close association with Apollo (see plate 95). The serrated leaves of oak together with the acorns are a reference to the *corona civica* that the emperor was awarded in 27 BC (see plate 110). The detailed engraving of the veins of the leaves and the coiffure contrasts with the soft, rounded modeling of the ear, nose, and neck. Despite such naturalistic details as the slightly furrowed brow and the finely rendered muscles of the neck, the image of the emperor is highly idealized; its closest parallels appear on his coins minted in the late 20s BC.
BIBLIOGRAPHY Vollenweider and Avisseau-Broustet 2003, no. 52; Roger in La Rocca et al. 2013, 218, no. IV.3.

....

Plate 113
The Gemma Augustea, ca. 12 BC–AD 14
Sardonyx, H: 187 mm; W: 223 mm; D: 3.5–14 mm
Seventeenth-century gold setting
Vienna, Kunsthistorisches Museum, IXa 30

One of the largest and most impressive ancient gems to survive, this cameo was cut from a large sardonyx that was artificially treated to achieve two uniform color layers: white above dark bluish brown. Now broken at the edges, it originally depicted more than twenty-five figures disposed in two tiers. Above, off center, Augustus sits, half-draped. Beneath his throne is the eagle of Jupiter, the supreme god whose guise the emperor assumes in this fusion of Rome and Olympus. Augustus is depicted as Pontifex Maximus, holding a scepter and a *lituus* (a ritual implement), the attribute of an augur. He is crowned with an oak wreath—the *corona civica*, an honor reserved for those who have saved the lives of Roman citizens (see plate 110)—by a veiled woman wearing a mural crown; she is *Oikomene*, the personification of the civilized world. In front of her are male and female personifications, variously identified as Ocean, Neptune, or Saturn, and Earth, or Italy, symbolizing sea and land or the Golden Age—or both. The woman wears a *bulla* and holds a cornucopia. Her two children, one holding ears of wheat, are the products of peace and fertility. The emperor shares his throne with an armed goddess, Roma, the personification of Rome. Her feet, like his, tread upon the arms of defeated enemies in this celebration of the extension of Roman rule. Between them a starred disk with the sign of Capricorn alludes to both the *sidus Julium* (the star whose appearance signaled the divinity of his adoptive father, Julius Caesar) and the month of Augustus's conception. Farther left stands a Roman soldier in battle armor. Next to him a four-horse chariot, driven by a winged Victory, brings another Roman, wearing a toga and laurel wreath. These are members of the Augustan dynasty, usually identified as Drusus (or Germanicus) and Tiberius.

While the precise dating and specific meaning of the cameo has been much debated by scholars, its overall significance is clear: the elevation of the emperor and his house as the bringers of peace and prosperity—the *Pax Augusta*—through continued military effort. The lower tier represents the triumph of Roman armies and the pacification of barbarian peoples, although individual figures are less readily identifiable. On the right, a standing man and a woman holding two spears, identified variously as Mercury and Diana or as the personifications of auxiliary troops, dominate vanquished Celts or Germans, a standing female and a kneeling male with shaggy hair and beard wearing a torque. While her hair is being pulled violently, he lowers his hands in a gesture of supplication. To the left, two armed soldiers and two unarmed assistants, perhaps Roman allies if not mythological heroes, raise a trophy above two captives, a bearded man with hands bound behind his back and a woman despondently resting her head on her hands.

Although carved in low relief, the cameo presents a wealth of detail: clothing, armor, weaponry, and other apparatus. Subtly overlapping and masterfully foreshortened figures stand in a variety of poses. Scholars have recognized portraits in many of the figures, and the clear association of the cameo with the court of Augustus has encouraged its attribution to Dioskourides or his workshop, perhaps his son, Hyllos (see plates 95, 96, 109, 114), but this is by no means certain. Nor is the ancient destination of the gem. Its visual language shares panegyrical themes, dynastic ambitions, and allusions to a golden age with much Augustan art and literature. If it was carved circa AD 12 to commemorate the victories of Livia's sons Tiberius and Drusus on the northern frontiers, their service to Augustus, and the establishment of the cult of Roma in the west, then it may have been a gift from Livia to the emperor. But several other interpretations are plausible: because Augustus resisted divine honors in the west, scholars have suggested that the gem may have been intended for a recipient in the provinces or an eastern client king; or that it was meant to be seen only by a select private audience as early as 12 BC; or that it was fashioned after Augustus's death in AD 14.

The cameo is first recorded in a mid-thirteenth-century inventory of the treasury of the church of Saint Sernin, in Toulouse, France, where, brought from Constantinople, it probably served as the centerpiece of an ecclesiastical breastplate. The raising of the trophy in its lower register was likely read in a Christian interpretation as preparation for the Crucifixion, while Augustus and Roma enthroned might have been taken to be Christ and the Virgin Mary in majesty. Some two hundred years later, the gem-collecting Renaissance pope Paul II so desired the cameo that he offered the people of Toulouse 10,000 gold pieces and construction of a bridge over the River Garonne in exchange for it, but the offer was refused. In 1533 King Francis I of France appropriated the gem, but it disappeared in 1590, when the Huguenots plundered Fontainebleau. It soon resurfaced in Venice, where it was purchased for 12,000 gold pieces by the Holy Roman emperor Rudolph II (r. 1576–1612). This rich history not only reflects the great value, prestige, and desirability of imperial cameos over the centuries but also demonstrates how this luxury art appealed to and was utilized for political declarations by lofty rulers across the ages on account of its costly materials and superb craftsmanship.

BIBLIOGRAPHY Doonan 1992; Pollini 1993; Lörz 2006; Zwierlein-Diehl 2008, no. 6 (with extensive bibliography).

....

Plate 114
Cameo of a laughing satyr, ca. AD 10
Inscribed: ΥΛΛΟΣ ΔΙΟΣΚΟΥΡΙΔΟΥ ΕΠΟΙΕΙ
(Hyllos, son of Dioskourides, made [this])
Sardonyx, H: 17.6 mm; W: 14.4 mm
Berlin, Staatliche Museen, Antikensammlung, FG 11063

This miniature cameo, barely larger than a thumbnail, is a tour de force of engraving. In less than two millimeters of relief, the carver has captured the ribald nature of a young satyr. A roughly textured *nebris* (fawn skin) delicately knotted at his shoulder (seen from behind in foreshortened three-quarter view) contrasts with the soft skin of his back and neck and the wild, fully dimensional hair. The satyr's pointed ear, alert eye, pug nose, full lips, and sharply delineated teeth are rendered flawlessly; the entire profile is undercut, adding depth to the composition. Like his brothers Eutyches and Herophilos, Hyllos followed his father in the craft of gem engraving. His minute, three-line signature here is another mark of his skill. Ten other cameos and intaglios signed by him survive, and several other unsigned works have been attributed to his hand. Some, like this gem, treat mythological subjects in an exuberant Late Hellenistic style; others adopt the cold neoclassicism of the early imperial age. Formerly in the collection of the Electors of Brandenburg.

BIBLIOGRAPHY Vollenweider 1966, 69–72; Zwierlein-Diehl 2007, 119–21; Platz-Horster 2012, no. 28.

....

Plate 115

Cameo of a centaur, ca. AD 50–150
Sardonyx, H: 51 mm; W: 42.5 mm
Naples, Museo Archeologico Nazionale, 25889

Carved so as to feature a dark figure on a light ground, this stone depicts a centaur carrying implements for a Dionysiac celebration. His left hand holds a candelabrum, while the right grasps the rim of a *krater* (large mixing bowl) balanced on his back. A lion skin flutters behind him, which like his proper left limbs, is rendered in a translucent honey-colored layer of the stone, giving the cameo both a sense of depth and a multicolored effect. The detail and quality of the carving is virtuosic: not only are the body and limbs of the centaur fully modeled but his front right equine leg is undercut. The centaur's head is bent forward, and his facial features express the burden of the weight he carries. The *krater* itself is adorned with an incised ivy wreath. Inscribed LAV·R·MED in the late fifteenth century, it was formerly in the Medici and Farnese collections.

BIBLIOGRAPHY Dacos, Giuliano, and Pannuti 1973, no. 35; Pannuti 1994, 167; Gasparri 1994, no. 52.

....

Plate 116

Cameo of Jupiter, ca. AD 14–37
Sardonyx, H: 94 mm; W: 63.5 mm; Thickness: ca. 8 mm
Fourteenth-century gold, silver, and enamel setting
Paris, Bibliothèque nationale de France, Cabinet des médailles, 1

On this large cameo, expressively carved through three layers (brown, white, and black) in very shallow relief (ca. 1.5 mm), the king of the gods stands holding a thunderbolt in his right hand and a scepter in his left. Alongside his sandaled feet, the left foreshortened and overlapping the exergue, his eagle turns to look back up toward him. Jupiter wears an oak wreath with acorns and a mantle draped over his left shoulder, leaving his muscular chest and abdomen bare. The carver has not only exploited the regular layers of the stone to contrast the god's brown hair, mantle, and thunderbolt with his white flesh (and the eagle's body and wings), but he has also cut more thinly the brown layer between the god's lower legs to give the cloth a sense of transparency and, most impressively, to create a highlight along the outer edge of the left leg, giving volume to the figure. Scholars have seen in the face of the god the features of Emperor Tiberius and have attributed the carving of the cameo to Hyllos (see plate 114); it also exhibits similarities to cameos depicting the emperor Claudius. In the Middle Ages the god was identified as Saint John the Evangelist because of the eagle, prompting King Charles V to donate the cameo to the cathedral of Chartres.

BIBLIOGRAPHY Megow 1987, 208, no. A87; Vollenweider and Avisseau-Broustet 2003, no. 83; Avisseau-Broustet in Lapatin 2014, 134–37.

....

Plate 117

Cameo with double portrait of Trajan and Plotina, ca. AD 105–115
Sardonyx, H: 50 mm; W: 43 mm; D: 12 mm
London, British Museum, GR 1824,0301.97 (Gem 3610)

Following the tradition of Hellenistic double portraits (see plate 103), the carver of this multilayered cameo depicted the imperial couple with a combination of natural and idealized features. Like other cameos representing the emperor and his family, this one was probably a gift to a member of the Roman court intended to manifest a close connection to the ruler. Various textures of soft skin, wavy and tightly curled hair, and veined laurel leaves are skillfully differentiated in the hard stone. Trajan (r. 98–117) and Plotina married in the early 90s, before he became emperor, but they are represented here in middle age, suggesting a date in the early second century. The modeling of soft flesh at the neck and the crows' feet at the eyes is especially fine. Formerly in the Payne Knight collection.

BIBLIOGRAPHY Walters 1926, no. 3610.

....

Plate 118

Cameo with double portrait of Septimius Severus and Julia Domna, ca. 207–211
Sardonyx, H (gem): 50 mm; W: 42 mm; H (with setting): 75 mm; W: 60 mm
Ancient gold setting
Kansas City, The Ferrell Collection

This deeply cut cameo depicts the emperor and his wife not in profile, as was customary in cameos, but in three-quarter view. The emperor wears a laurel wreath with three inset jewels and, over a scallop-necked tunic, a *paludamentum* (military cloak) pinned at his right shoulder.

At his chest is a winged gorgoneion. Behind the emperor is his wife, with her typical long wavy locks, adorned only by a beaded (pearl?) necklace. The facial features of both are sensitively rendered, with incised eyebrows, fleshy eyelids, and large irises with hollow pupils. The emperor's long, curly beard, divided in the middle, and the four corkscrew locks on his brow are typical of his later portraits in which he assumes characteristics of his patron god, Serapis.

BIBLIOGRAPHY Spier 2010, no. 50.

....

Plate 119

Askos, ca. 200–100 BC
From Amisos (Samsun), Turkey
Banded agate, with gold lid and foot, H: 65 mm; W: 84 mm
Cleveland Museum of Art, 1964.92

This charming container, intended to hold perfumed oil, mimics the form of larger vessels in the shape of wine skins. Dated to the middle Hellenistic period by parallels in other media, this example not only has a gold lid, with an adjustable disk to regulate the flow of precious liquid, but also a gold foot. A crab has been cut into the body behind the rectilinear handle. While this might have had some now-lost meaning for the unknown owner, or implications for the intended contents of the vessel, it may just as likely have been cut to remove and mask the presence of a natural flaw in the stone (compare plate 124).

BIBLIOGRAPHY Cooney 1965; Bühler 1973, no. 22; Oliver 1975, 167.

....

Plate 120

Rhyton in the form of a gazelle, ca. 300–100 BC(?)
From Hejiacun, Xi'an, China
Banded agate, with gold muzzle, H: 65 mm; L: 156 mm;
Diam: 59 mm; Thickness: 2 mm
Shaanxi, China, History Museum

Discovered in 1970 in a large cache of precious objects of diverse dates and origins belonging to a member of the T'ang elite and deliberately buried in the mid-eighth century, this gold-muzzled animal-head rhyton has been variously attributed to Chinese, Central Asian, Sogdian, Sassanian, Parthian, Ghandaran, Persian, and Ptolemaic manufacture. Although general parallels are found in various materials and multiple cultures—the hoard includes objects ranging from fifth-century BC Chinese bronzes to early Byzantine gold coins—the closest comparandum is an agate calf's-head rhyton found in the Egyptian desert, along with seven other agate vessels (see plate 121). The Hejiacun rhyton is larger and more finely carved, and the lively, naturalistic depiction of the beast finds its nearest analogues in Hellenistic works. The pierced mouth, surrounded by granulated gold beads, makes this object a true rhyton. The sensitively carved eyes, pointed ears, and ridged recurving horns allow the animal to be identified as a Persian or north African gazelle (*Gazella subgutturosa subgutturosa* or *Gazella dorcas*). Wherever this remarkable object was carved, it evidently played a part in the extensive cosmopolitan luxury culture that followed the conquests of Alexander, for it eventually made its way east via the Silk Road and, to protect it from invading armies, was buried almost a thousand years after its creation.

BIBLIOGRAPHY Oliver 1975, 167; Parlasca 1975; Gasparri 1979, 5; Grimm 1981, 19; Parlasca 1985; Grimm 1998, 118–21; Dongfang 2003; Hansen 2003; Slavazzi 2003, 439; Louis 2007.

....

Plate 121

Bowl, ca. 300–100 BC
From Egypt
Banded agate, H: 42 mm; Diam: 98 mm; Wt: 508 grams
Malibu, JPGM, 72.AI.38

Found in a tomb in the Egyptian desert between Qift and Qusseir in 1930, along with seven other agate vessels, this splendid bowl, with a slightly raised base and three delicate horizontal flutes beneath a subtly recurved lip, has been dated as early as the eighth century BC and as late as the fourth century AD. It has also been attributed to both Persian and Egyptian craftsmen, but its closest parallel was found in the cemetery of Priscilla in Rome in 1731. Neither burial, however, is closely dated, and both may well have contained earlier heirlooms and exotic imports. Similar shapes in glass, along with the find context, suggest a Hellenistic date. Formerly in the collection of King Farouk I.

BIBLIOGRAPHY Engelbach 1931; Habachi and Biers 1969, 32; Bühler 1973, no. 10; Parlasca 1985; Slavazzi 2003, 438–39.

....

Plate 122

Cup fragment with Eros, ca. 100 BC–AD 100
Banded agate, H: 47.9 mm; W: 47.2 mm; Thickness: 4.2 mm
Phoenix Ancient Art

This charming fragment of a cameo-cut cup, originally approximately 65 mm high and 100 mm in diameter, preserves an Eros riding a panther. The winged god of love, with a quiver full of arrows hanging behind him from a baldric slung over his left shoulder, holds a spear aloft in his right hand. His fleshy chest, stomach, and limbs are softly rendered, in contrast to his alert face. His sharply carved hair is tied in the back, and he is crowned with a wreath. The beast he rides without reins is powerfully modeled, with bulging brow, wide eyes, and slightly opened mouth. It finds its closest parallels in a series of elaborate table legs in colored marbles from the first century AD. Eros is usually seen riding lions, dolphins, birds, and other animals, but he appears on a panther—the Dionysiac animal par excellence—on a marble relief of the first century BC; on a silver drinking vessel, terracotta revetments, and bronze appliqués of the first century AD; and on mosaics and marble sarcophagi of the second. In the later representations, Erotes atop panthers and other animals are

often associated with the seasons, but in earlier works they appear in more strictly Dionysiac contexts—appropriate on a luxurious drinking vessel such as this—with satyrs, maenads, and Dionysiac paraphernalia. Formerly in the collection of Derek Content.
UNPUBLISHED: compare *LIMC* 3: 996, 1001 (Eros/Amor, Cupido), nos. 338–40, 344, 389 (see also no. 410).

....

Plate 123
Ribbed cup (Chalice of Abbot Suger), ca. 200–1 BC
From the abbey of Saint-Denis, France
Banded agate, H (including postantique mounts): 184 mm
Twelfth-century gem-, glass-, and pearl-studded gilt-silver mount
Washington, DC, National Gallery of Art, 1942.9.277

This steep-walled, ribbed vessel is a masterpiece of stone carving. The deep vertical flutes cut into the body increase the exterior surface area of the vessel and enhance the play of color in the stone, which ranges from creamy white to honey yellow to dark brown, changing under different lighting conditions. Indeed, in 1148 Abbot Suger of Saint-Denis described in the report on his administration his purchase of this "precious chalice made of a block of sardonyx, a gem partly sard and partly onyx, in which the red sard's hue, vying with the blackness of the onyx, is variegated in such a manner that the properties of both seem to compete in trespassing on each other." The interior of the cup is smooth. The small, elegant pedestal foot, visible in a 1633 watercolor, can no longer be seen, as it is hidden by the pearl-studded circlet above the knob. Although ancient sources record the combination of stone vessels with gold accoutrements, and a few examples survive (see plates 119, 120), the elaborate carving of this cup was a tour de force. A similarly ribbed breccia cup, now in Lisbon, and several glass vessels help to date this example and attribute it to an Alexandrian workshop. Formerly in the Townley and Widener collections.
BIBLIOGRAPHY Verdier 1990, 1993.

....

Plate 124
Phiale (libation bowl) with an allegorical scene and the head of Medusa
(the Tazza Farnese), ca. 100 BC(?)
Double-sided, cameo-cut, banded agate, H: 40 mm; Diam: 217 mm; Wt (including modern silver mount): 1.420 kg
Naples, Museo Archeologico Nazionale, 27611

Exceptional for its size and quality, this shallow circular bowl was cut from a single piece of banded agate, whose multiple colors range through various shades of dark and light brown, rust, orange, golden and honeyed yellow, light grayish blue, ivory, and white. Carving the vessel on both sides was technically daring, risking damaging one side while working the other. Modern carvers estimate that such a project would have taken several years. (The hole drilled through the center, defacing the composition on the exterior, appears to be postantique; it was probably used for the addition of some kind of foot; compare plate 123.)

The exterior, carved in low relief, depicts the head of Medusa. The Gorgon is framed by wild, wavy, finely cut locks of hair radiating in all directions. Her incised brows are long and mobile; her chin dimpled. Above her temples emerge two small wings and snakes, whose tails are tied under her chin, while numerous others are coiled and knotted at the folded edge of the scaly aegis behind her. A deep irregular cutting below her chin must have been made to remove a flaw in the stone.

The interior, carved in considerably higher relief, is a tour de force of cameo cutting. The variegated bands of color that made up the stone are evident in the vessel's lip. The carver, although to some degree limited by the nature of the stone, has exploited the white layer for most of the seven full-bodied figures, as well as for the head of the Sphinx crouching at the bottom of the composition. This beast faces right, wearing a typical pharaonic headdress with the uraeus of Osiris at the forehead. The female figure reclining on its back seems to symbolize the fertility of Egypt, for both her breasts are bare, and she holds two ears of grain in her raised right hand. She wears a flat headband over her centrally parted hair, which falls to her shoulders in corkscrew curls typical of Africans in Hellenistic art. A twisted bracelet adorns each of her wrists; her visible foot is bare; and her legs are modeled by the vertical folds of her thick drapery, which becomes transparent over her belly, revealing her navel. The folds of her drapery as well as her anatomy and jewelry are rendered in considerable detail, including the joints of her fingers and toes, as well as their nails and cuticles.

Above her a bearded male sits on a knotted tree stump, his lower body draped, but his fleshy torso bare, conveying his age, power, and prosperity. His extended left arm holds the top of a large horn in his lap. His face, like his body, shows signs of age. Before him stands a youth wearing only an *exomis* (tunic with one sleeve). His right hand, partially obscured by the bearded figure's cornucopia, holds what appears to be a plow; in his left is a blade (perhaps a pruning hook or plowshare), while a seed bag hangs from his left wrist. Unlike the older, bearded male, this figure's muscles are well defined and tense, imparting a dynamism that is enhanced by his striding gait. This and his coiffure recall depictions of satyrs and Gauls in ancient sculpture.

These three principal figures and the Sphinx are accompanied by two smaller pairs. At the right sit two sensuous, half-draped females facing the center of the tondo. One, with her curving spine to the viewer, holds a *phiale*. Her finely carved hair is tied in a topknot. Her companion, whose belly and breasts are exposed, holds a cornucopia while adjusting her shoulder-length hair with her other hand. Behind her rise ears of grain. Above, two smaller, muscular, beardless youths fly through the sky. With his right arm extended before him, one tightly grasps a piece of drapery that arcs back over his head and wraps around his left wrist. He looks back to his companion, who blows into the shell in his right hand.

While the exact meaning of the interior scene continues to elude scholars, its Egyptian associations have long been recognized. The value of the material, quality of the workmanship, and highly rhetorical visual language leave little doubt that the *phiale* is the sophisticated product of "court art." The earliest interpreters identified the central, striding youth as Alexander the Great and the bearded male and reclining female as Ptolemy I Soter and his queen, Berenike I. Later interpretations have proposed that the Tazza Farnese presents an allegory of the Nile. The heavy, bearded male is taken to be the personification of the river; the female reclining on the Sphinx—the symbol of Egypt—is Isis; Horus, her son by Osiris, occupies the middle ground; the two females to the right have been read as Memphis and Anchirroe, the daughters and principal branches of the Nile; and the two males above as the Etesian winds, which blow during the flood season. A Greek reading of the imagery conflates the figures with Hellenic divinities: Isis becomes Isis/Euthenia, the personification of abundance and prosperity; Horus is syncretized with the Eleusinian hero Triptolemos, who first brought the arts of agriculture to mankind; the daughters of the Nile become two of the Horai (seasons), who, as they are associated with the grain and a wine bowl, might personify summer and autumn; and the winds above have also been read specifically as those that blow in the winter (Boreas) and spring (Zephyros). More complex astronomical, astrological, and cosmological readings based on ancient texts have also been proposed. Another line of investigation into the meaning—and date—of the *phiale* has been to recognize the features of specific historical individuals in the figures, and thus to add to the allegory of fertility and regeneration a more specific political layer of interpretation. The "portraits" on the *phiale* are far from specific, however, and the Ptolemaic associations of the Tazza have also been called into question. The authors of the *interpretationes Romanae* take the Tazza to be a Roman commission produced to commemorate the victory of Augustus over Antony and Cleopatra at Actium in 31 BC, or to herald the inception of the Golden Age at the *Ludi Saeculares* celebrated in Rome in 17 BC.

Whatever its precise ancient context, the Tazza Farnese presents a complex allegory of abundance, plenty, and regeneration related to Egypt in general and to the inundation of the Nile specifically. With its precious material, fine carving, and recondite iconography, it is likely to have belonged to a royal patron and to have been used sparingly. Being carved on both sides, it was not suited to rest on a table. Rather, like all *phialai,* it might have been employed to make libations. It is perhaps significant that when the *phiale* is used as an offering bowl, its inner scene, with light figures on the dark background, would be revealed when liquid was poured out as a libation to the gods. Indeed, there can be little doubt that the scenes on both sides of the object are highly charged. Held in the hands of a ruler making a libation, the Medusa on the outside would have served its apotropaic function, dispelling evil spirits from the site of sacrifice. The interior, when emptied of its liquid contents, would have revealed a cosmic allegory of inundation and regeneration, the achievement of which was dependent on the ruler who held it. Formerly in the collections of Frederick II of Sicily (?), Timur the Great, Alfonso of Aragon, Ludovico Trevisan, Pietro Barbo (Pope Paul II), Lorenzo de' Medici, and the Farnese.

BIBLIOGRAPHY Heikamp and Grote 1974, no. 43; La Rocca 1984; Gasparri 1994, esp. 74–83; Pannuti 1994, no. 68; Slavazzi 2003, 439–41; Zwierlein-Diehl 2007, 67–68; Belozerskaya 2012.

....

Plate 125

Kantharos with Bacchic paraphernalia (the Cup of the Ptolemies), ca. 50 BC–AD 50
From the abbey of Saint-Denis, France
Banded gate, H: 84 mm; W: 184 mm; Diam: 125 mm
Paris, Bibliothèque nationale de France, Cabinet des médailles, 368

This splendid cup was first associated with the Hellenistic rulers of Egypt by Tristan de Saint-Amant, who in 1644 identified it with the "onyx *kantharoi*" described as having been displayed at Alexandria in the early third century BC during the grand Dionysiac procession of Ptolemy II Philadelphos. Its shape and decoration, however, find their closest parallels in Roman silver vessels (see plates 76, 78). Rising from a small pedestal foot, the almost cylindrical vessel is profusely decorated with two similar scenes, separated by undulating double handles carved free of the vessel, incised with grapevines, and terminating in poppy buds. The body of the cup is a riot of deeply carved Dionysiac paraphernalia, arranged in picturesque disorder as if in preparation for a Bacchic festival. Two trees enveloped by grapevines spring from the bases of the handles and spread their branches, tied with veils, across the body of the cup. Tables supported by sphinxes on one side and by legs terminating in lion's paws on the other carry luxurious vessels, including a rhyton, *krater*, pitcher, and incense burner, as well as cups and baskets, a Priapic herm, and a statuette of a woman (Ceres?) holding two torches. Wreaths, garlands, baskets, panpipes, and a tympanum further populate the scenes, along with a panther, goats, birds, and a snake emerging from a *cista mystica,* as well as a dozen tragic and comic masks carved in exceptionally high relief. Traditionally thought to have been dedicated to Saint Denis by the French king Charles the Bald (r. 840–877), the cup has been stripped of its elaborate medieval mount, which drawings suggest was similar to that of the Chalice of Abbot Suger (see plate 123).

BIBLIOGRAPHY Bühler 1973, 18; Alcouffe et al. 1991, no. 11; Avisseau-Broustet 1996; Plantzos 1999a, 102; Slavazzi 2003, 440–42; Zwierlein-Diehl 2007, 67–68.

....

Plate 126
Alabastron (perfume vase), ca. 40–10 BC
From Nottuln Abbey, near Münster, northwest Germany
Banded agate, H: 88.3 mm; Diam (max): 33.2 mm
Berlin, Staatliche Museen, Antikensammlung, FG 11362

Cut from a four-layered stone, this finely carved vessel, which has lost both lip and foot, is divided into two scenes, one with three women holding an infant male (a), the other depicting the Venus Victrix (b). The first is a ritual scene, in which the woman on the right presents the nude child to her companion, who raises one hand in toward the boy while resting the other on a short pillar. A third woman stands between and behind them, facing frontally, holding an amphora on her left shoulder. The goddess on the other side of the vessel (b–c) turns sharply to observe this scene. She sits between a small temple on a rocky outcrop and a trophy erected over a tall tree stump. Her long hair is tied atop her head, and most of her backside is exposed, her drapery covering only her legs. In her left hand she holds a round shield with a scaly aegis and central gorgoneion. Beneath the goddess a barbarian captive wearing trousers and long sleeves sits at the base of the trophy with hands bound. A Corinthian helmet, bow, and small round shield rest on the ground.

Venus was the divine ancestor of the *gens Julia*, and the precious material and fine workmanship of this vessel, too, link it with the imperial house. The precise identity of the young male, whose birth this object seems to celebrate, however, remains uncertain. Scholars have suggested that he is Marcus Claudius Marcellus, born in 42 BC, the son of Octavia and nephew and heir of the future emperor Augustus, which would make this vessel the earliest preserved Roman political/allegorical cameo. Other candidates have been proposed for the newborn, and the women have been variously identified as historical members of the Julio-Claudian house (e.g., Octavia, Livia, Julia) or mythological figures (e.g., the Roman birth goddesses Carmenta, Porrima, and Posverta, or the three Fates). Precisely when and how this vessel entered the medieval abbey at Nottuln, where it served as a reliquary, is unknown.

BIBLIOGRAPHY Bühler 1973, 59–63, no. 68; Zwierlein-Diehl 1999; Zwierlein-Diehl 2007, 169–70; Platz-Horster 2012, 93–94, no. 86 (with full bibliography).

....

Plate 127
Simpulum (ladle), ca. AD 1–200
Banded agate, H: 127 mm; Diam: 50 mm; Thickness: 2 mm
Florence, Museo degli Argenti, 532

Cut from a single block, this elegant vessel consists of a circular cup with ring base and molded lip, from which rises a vertical tapering handle that curls out at the top, terminating in a tab adorned with a leaf carved in relief. The inner surface of the handle is flat, while the exterior is decorated with a stylized (olive?) vine. At either side of the transition to the bowl, the handle widens in the form of stylized duck's heads, typical of the handle attachments of contemporary metal vessels. While possibly once used in a domestic context, the *simpulum* was also a ritual implement, and as such it often appears on Roman coins and sacral friezes. Recent research suggests that this object, first recorded in Florentine archives in 1566, is one of the thirty-nine vessels of rock crystal and eight of agate discovered in Rome on February 4, 1544, in the tomb of Empress Maria, wife of Honorius and daughter of Stilicho, in the course of the construction of St. Peter's Basilica. Maria died in AD 423, but it is likely that this and several other of the implements interred with her, most of which are lost, were, in fact, heirlooms. Formerly in the Medici collection.

BIBLIOGRAPHY Bühler 1973, no. 64; Heikamp and Grote 1974, no. 3; Gasparri 1975, 362; A. Paolucci in Acidini Luchinat et al. 1997, no. 117; Slavazzi 2003, 446; Venturelli 2009, no. 19.

....

Plate 128
Cup, first century BC–fourth century AD
Banded agate, H: 311 mm; Diam: 117 mm; Thickness: 3.0–3.5 mm
Fifteenth-century gilt-silver mount
Florence, Museo degli Argenti, 503

This tall, slightly tapering, straight-walled beaker with elegant triple-scroll handles, curved base, and stepped foot is the most elaborately carved and best preserved of a series of ancient agate vessels of similar shape that made their way into European ecclesiastical and princely collections in the Middle Ages and Renaissance. Most have lost their handles and/or been cut down. This example, inscribed LAV.R.MED. in the late fifteenth century, was at some point in antiquity engraved on both sides with a fillet tied around a double-headed thyrsus. This Dionysiac motif is rare, but crossed double-headed thyrsi appear on the bronze coinage of Chios and marble sarcophagi in the second century. Tall, straight-walled beakers of similar shape (without the fine handles) are attested in glass from the first century onward. The thin wall and the delicacy of the carving of this cup also suggest it was carved at an early date. Much later, it held the relics of Saints Gregory Nazianzus, Nicolas of Myrna, and Leonard the Confessor. Formerly in the Medici collection.

BIBLIOGRAPHY Bühler 1973, no. 86; Heikamp and Grote 1974, no. 6; Gasparri 1979, 12; Venturelli 2009, no. 2. Compare Alcouffe 1984, no. 24; Alcouffe 2001, no. 1; Slavazzi 2003, 446, 450; M. Sframeli in Casazza 2008, no. 19.

....

Plate 129
The Rubens Vase, ca. AD 400
Cameo-cut agate with modern gold lip, H: 186 mm; W: 185 mm; D: 120 mm
Baltimore, Walters Art Museum, 42.562

Named after one of its many illustrious owners, the Flemish painter Peter Paul Rubens, who acquired it in 1619 and subsequently drew and molded it, this thinly carved oval vessel is almost transparent. It is entwined by high-relief twisting vines, leaves, and grape clusters that sprout from large acanthus leaves below two heads of Pan which serve as handles on opposite sides. Virtuoso carving is evident in the curling edges and veins of the leaves and especially in the vigorous, expressive mustachioed Pans, with their wide eyes, bushy brows, wrinkled faces, and toothy grins. Both wear acorn wreaths, and their thin, tall recurved horns are dramatically undercut. An elaborate rosette is carved on the underside of the slightly flaring foot. Formerly in the collections of the dukes of Anjou, King Charles V of France, Peter Paul Rubens, Emperor Jahangir of India, and the dukes of Hamilton.

BIBLIOGRAPHY Ross 1943; Bühler 1973, no. 109; Gasparri 1979, 5–6, 8; Weitzmann 1979, no. 313; Slavazzi 2003, 446–47.

....

Plate 130
Skyphos, ca. 25 BC–AD 15
From S. Maria Capua Vetere, Italy
Rock crystal, H: 120 mm, W: 150 mm
Naples, Museo Archeologico Nazionale, 124701

Rising from a low ring base, the nearly cylindrical body of this deep cup has an offset lip from which extend the flat thumb-plates of two long, vertical ribbon handles. A gracefully undulating vine carved in relief adorns the body; the veins of its lanceolate leaves are engraved. Found in a tomb in the necropolis of Ponte San Prisco with an alabaster *calyx-krater*, this vessel has been dated to the Augustan period.

BIBLIOGRAPHY Spinazzola 1928, pl. 222; Gasparri 1979, 4–5; Museo Archeologico Nazionale 1986, 228–29, no. 7; De Caro 1994, 234; V. Arveiller in La Rocca et al. 2013, 280, no. VII.10.2. Compare Hahnloser 1971, no. 5.

....

Plate 131
Skyphos/Kantharos, ca. AD 1–100
From Field II, Room 13, Begram, Afghanistan
Rock crystal with traces of gold leaf, H: 90 mm; Diam: 144.5 mm
Kabul, National Museum of Afghanistan, MK 04.136

Although similar in shape to the crystal *skyphos* from Capua (plate 130), this vessel has a more elegant outwardly tapering shape, with *kantharos*-like handles that rise above its lip, which is engraved with an ovolo pattern. Twisted vine shoots and grape leaves have been cut into the body. Traces of gold leaf are preserved in some of the carved decoration.

BIBLIOGRAPHY Menninger 1996, 46–49, no. 121; Hiebert and Cambon 2008, 200–1, no. 214. Compare Hahnloser 1971, no. 5.

....

Plate 132
Amphoriskos (perfume vase), ca. 25 BC
Rock crystal, H: 57 mm; W: 36 mm
Malibu, JPGM, 83.AN.331

Miniature vessels of diverse shapes were cut from rock crystal. Their forms vary considerably, just like their counterparts in terracotta, glass, and other materials. Some, with wide feet, are able to stand on their own, while others, like this example, with only a delicate knob at the bottom, were originally suspended from cords or chains attached to their necks or handles. Some are narrow and rounded, with curvilinear handles, while others are faceted. Faceting seems to play on the fact that rock crystals are naturally hexagonal, but here the geological form has been transformed by the craftsman. The original mouth is lost. Two flat angular handles flank the thin-walled (1.7 mm thick) cylindrical neck. At the shoulder the circular form becomes hexagonal, with a series of six wheel-cut trapezoidal facets, below which twelve isosceles triangles, alternatingly upright and pendant, decorate the body. The vessel narrows to another six trapezoids, the midpoint of each being centered on the "joins" of the trapezoids above. Thus, the vessel negates entirely the natural form of the crystal from which it was formed, not only through the combination of round and angled forms but also in the manipulation of the crystalline structure.

BIBLIOGRAPHY *JPGMJ* 12 (1984): 259, no. 148. For a similar vessel, see Bühler 1973, no. 56; *Allen Memorial Art Museum Bulletin* 18 (1961): 260, no. 166. For a variety of other examples, see Bühler 1973, passim; Oliver 1975; Gasparri 1975; Vickers 1996; E. Stern 1997.

....

Plates 133, 134
Kantharos (the Crawford Cup), ca. AD 1–100
From Cilicia
Murrhine (fluorite), H: 97 mm; Diam: 107 mm; Wt: 867 grams
London, British Museum, GR 1971,0419.1

Cup with grapevines (the Barber Cup), ca. AD 1–100
From Cilicia
Murrhine (fluorite), H: 135 mm; Diam: 95 mm; Wt: 1340 grams
London, British Museum, 2003,1202.1

Found together, containing ashes, in an ancient tomb in Cilicia, on the border of modern Turkey and Syria, during World War I, these two cups are the best-preserved examples of the *vasae murrinae* that were greatly prized by the Romans. Pliny and other Latin authors leave no doubt as to the high value of such vessels of rare colorfully banded fluorite, imported to the Mediterranean from Parthia (modern Iran). The stone is rather friable and considerably softer than other precious stones (4 on the Mohs scale). Thus, before carving it was apparently dipped in resin, perhaps myrrh, giving it its name and its attractive fragrance. Indeed, Pliny reports that one wealthy Roman so enjoyed the flavor that he gnawed on the edge of his cup. The pedestaled two-handled *kantharos* is a rather heavy version of a shape that also survives in agate (see plate 125), silver, and glass. The one-handled Barber Cup is unparalleled. Its shape was likely adapted by a craftsman who originally intended to fashion a round, high-walled, two-handled *kantharos*. It has low-relief decoration: vine leaves and grape clusters symmetrically disposed around the body and tendrils rising up the handle from a bearded head of Bacchus at the base. Formerly in the Stóclet collection.

BIBLIOGRAPHY Lowenthal and Harden 1949; Harden 1954; Vickers 1997b; Slavazzi 2003, 445; Williams 2004; Tressaud and Vickers 2007; Williams 2009, no. 137.

....

Plate 135

Skyphos with Egyptianizing scenes, first century BC–first century AD
From the so-called Villa di San Marco at Stabiae, Italy
Obsidian inlaid with pink and white coral, cornelian, yellow jasper, lapis lazuli, and malachite, set in gold, H: 125 mm; Diam: 182 mm
Naples, Museo Archeologico Nazionale, 294473

This is one of a pair of large *skyphoi* buried in a luxury villa south of Pompeii by the eruption of Mount Vesuvius in AD 79. Carved from a large block of obsidian, the *skyphos* closely imitates contemporary silver vessels in shape (see plates 76, 78). Both sides are decorated with almost identical scenes rendered in precious inlays held in place by thin gold bands. Within a stylized building supported by colorful lotus columns, an Apis bull stands on a sacrificial table flanked by Horus falcons wearing the double crown of Upper and Lower Egypt. The curved pediment of the building contains a solar disk flanked by two snake uraei above a winged sun disk. From either side sumptuously dressed male and female attendants approach, bearing garlands, flowers, and other offerings, while a servant with perfume vases kneels behind each of them on a platform supported by thin lotus stalks. Although often ascribed to Alexandrian craftsmen, these scenes are nonsensical, combining Egyptian funerary iconography with a Roman sympotic shape. Pliny reports that Ethiopia was the source of obsidian, but recent analysis suggests that the obsidian of these cups originated there. Other objects of Roman obsidian inlaid with classical rather than Egyptianizing motifs, combined with the lack of similar objects from Egypt, suggest Italian manufacture.

BIBLIOGRAPHY Elia 1957; De Caro 1994, 234; Leospo 1999; M. Borriello in Ciarallo and De Carolis 1999, 162; M. Cima in De Caro 2006, 212–14; Lapatin 2008, 46–47; Mattusch 2008, no. 31. See also Dohrn 1965.

....

Plate 136

Situla (wine bucket) with masks of Silenoi, first to early second century AD
Porphyry, H: 25.5 cm; W: 30 cm; D: 24.8 cm; Diam (of rim): 22.5 cm
New York, Metropolitan Museum of Art, 2014.215

Situlae were employed in wine making. Examples of the shape in metal and other materials had long flexible handles attached to the rim or shoulder. Although this example was not functional, its deep red color and decoration, as well as its shape, appropriately reference the wine-god Dionysos. Below the flat handles on each side are the heads of bearded Silenoi wearing fillets and finely carved wreaths with berries. Like satyrs, these followers of the god have pointed ears. This vessel was probably intended to hold cremated remains. Because the gifts of Dionysos freed mortals from the cares of life, Dionysiac motifs were popular in funerary contexts. Formerly in the López-Willshaw collection.

BIBLIOGRAPHY Del Bufalo 2012, 25, 138, no. V7.

....

Plate 137

Bust of Berenike II, Queen of Egypt, ca. 225 BC
Garnet, H: 18 mm
Malibu, JPGM, 81.AN.76.59

This miniature hard stone relief is technically a cameo. Carved of garnet, rather than sardonyx, it was probably intended to be mounted into a ring. Examples of similar small busts cut from other stones survive from the fourth century BC in Greece, and from much earlier in Egypt and the Levant. Here a woman who appears to be the wife of Ptolemy III Euergetes wears a fillet and a veil over her melon-style coiffure, which is tied in a bun in the back. Following the death of her husband, Berenike ruled Egypt jointly with her eldest son, Ptolemy IV, but was murdered by him soon after his accession in 221 BC. Formerly in the Pappalardo collection.

BIBLIOGRAPHY Boardman 1975, no. 59; Spier 1989; Plantzos 1996a, 1996b; Lapatin and Wight 2010, 84.

....

Plate 138

Head of Herakles, second-first century BC(?)
Giallo antico, H: 155 mm; W: 115 mm; D: 55 mm
Florence, Museo degli Argenti, Gem 825

This head was first noted in Medici inventories of 1736 as being located in a cupboard in the Tribuna degli Uffizi and erroneously characterized as being made of coral. It was later described as *giallo antico carnicino* and reported to be a relief, although its rough and uneven back surface indicates that it is actually a fragment of a well-modeled carving in the round. The lower part of the beard has been restored in painted plaster, and the inset white eyes, which have lost their irises and pupils, may not be original. The short curly locks of hair and beard, the cauliflower ear, modulated brow, and small mouth, however, all place this head firmly in the Hellenistic tradition, if not in the Hellenistic period. The carving of the soft flesh of the cheeks and lower eyelids is especially sensitive. The statue to which this head presumably once belonged was about one-third life-size. Called *marmor numidicum* by the Romans, *giallo antico* was quarried since at least the second century BC at Smitthus, modern Chemtou, in Tunisia and exported to Italy soon after the Roman conquest of Carthage in 146 BC. It was eventually rated as one of the most expensive colored marbles in the price edit of Diocletian (AD 301).

BIBLIOGRAPHY Rusconi 1935, 8, fig. 45; Morassi 1963, 10, pl. 2.

....

Plate 139
Head of Antonia Minor, ca. AD 37–54
Chalcedony, H: 50 mm
Malibu, JPGM, 81.AN.101

Cut for insertion into a statuette or a bust fashioned from some other material, this exquisitely carved head—formerly identified as Livia, the wife of Augustus—represents Antonia Minor (36 BC–AD 37), Augustus's favorite niece, grandmother of Emperor Caligula, and mother of Emperor Claudius. Wearing a diadem and veil with edges incised with zigzags over her wavy locks, the imperial princess is presented in the guise of the goddess Juno. In AD 37, a few months before her death, the Roman senate, at the urging of Caligula, voted her the title Augusta. Earlier, following the death of Empress Livia in AD 29, she had served as priestess of the cult of Divine Augustus, a fact evidently alluded to here in her diadem, which is adorned by a central engraving of the laureate profile head of the first emperor, as well as stars and lozenges, the first and last apparently representing inset gems. Formerly in the Smith, Mayer, and Hertz collections.

BIBLIOGRAPHY Simon 1982, 342; Megow 1987, no. D5; Spier 1992, no. 432; Borromeo 1993, no. 22; Dahmen 2001, no. 78; Gagetti 2006, no. B7.

....

Plate 140
Head of a Julio-Claudian princess, ca. AD 40
Green chalcedony, H: 90 mm; W: 54.5 mm; D: 52 mm
London, British Museum, 1907,0415.1 (Gem 3946)

Scholars do not agree as to whether this exquisitely carved head represents Agrippina the Younger (d. AD 51), sister of Caligula, fourth wife of the emperor Claudius, and mother of Nero; one of her two sisters, Julia Drusilla (d. AD 38) or Julia Livilla (d. AD 41 or 42); or the third wife of Claudius, Valeria Messalina (d. AD 48). All were represented with similar coiffures: face framed by tight snail curls, above which wavy locks flow from a central part. Here, the details of the hair are carved with impressive depth and vitality, their matte finish contrasting with the smooth, polished skin. Holes drilled in (but not through) the ears may indicate the original presence of earrings, presumably in gold, perhaps adorned with small pearls, as attested in other statues (see fig. 33). Beneath a low brow, the wide-set eyes, with pupils and irises finely delineated, are surrounded by fleshy lids. The mouth is small, the lips thin, yet fleshy. A bit of drapery at the lower break suggests that this object may have originally formed part of a bust, rather than a complete statue. Similar portraits in amethyst and green jasper may represent the same imperial princess. Of the candidates for identification, Drusilla was Caligula's favorite sister (and alleged to be his lover); after her death in AD 41 he had her consecrated as Diva Drusilla Panthea. Formerly in the Pierpont Morgan collection.

BIBLIOGRAPHY Walters 1926, no. 3946; Megow 1987, no. D33; Dahmen 2001, no. 81; Gagetti 2006, no. B10; Williams 2009, no. 138.

....

Plate 141
Statuette of the crouching Aphrodite, first century BC
Rock crystal, H: 85 mm
Malibu, JPGM, 78.AN.248

In a garbled passage (*NH* 36.25), Pliny mentions a statue of Aphrodite, the goddess of love, cleansing herself (*Venerem lavantem se*). Many examples of a statue type depicting Aphrodite nude and crouching, as if in a bath, survive in diverse materials. Scholars today debate the degree to which any of these figures can be associated with Pliny's text, but this statuette in rock crystal represents a variant of the main type, perhaps developed on the island of Rhodes, in which the goddess turns to face the viewer while her lower body remains in profile. Although the head and arms are lost, it seems from examples in other materials that this statuette conflates the image of the kneeling goddess with the so-called *anadyomene* type, in which the she is depicted wringing her hair, having just emerged from the sea. Because the ancients considered rock crystal to be super-frozen ice, the aquatic associations of this material might seem appropriate to Aphrodite (whose name means "born from the foam"). However, the representation of the soft body of the goddess of love here might also appear paradoxical. Her fleshy thighs, buttocks, and abdomen are sensuously rendered in this hard mineral; the breasts less successfully so, although their awkwardness is partially explained by the material and would have been less noticeable before the arms and head were lost. Held in the hand, the transparent material would have taken on the color of human flesh.

BIBLIOGRAPHY Krug 1982; *LIMC* 2: 106 (Aphrodite), no. 1039; Padgett 1995, no. 22; Gagetti 2006, no. G31.

....

Plate 142
Bust of a man, perhaps Vespasian, ca. AD 70–96
Chalcedony, H: 115 mm
Boston, Museum of Fine Arts, 98.768

This expressively rendered balding man with a deeply lined face wears a *paludamentum* (military cloak) fastened on his right shoulder. He has been alternately identified as Emperor Vespasian (r. AD 69–79), recut from a portrait of Nero, or an otherwise unknown private individual. Although the arrangement of the hair at the nape of the neck recalls the long hair sometimes worn by Nero, these horizontal waves do appear, arranged somewhat differently, in portraits of Vespasian and his son Domitian (r. AD 81–96). Moreover, despite damage to the nose, ears, and chest there is no compelling evidence of this figure having actually been recut (compare plate 143). A keyhole-shaped notch at the back of the bust, however, indicates that it may have served as an *imago clipeata*, a portrait projecting from a circular frame (like a shield). This, the precious material, and the *paludamentum* all suggest that this portrait may well be an idiosyncratic representation of Vespasian. Formerly in the Tyszkiewicz collection.

BIBLIOGRAPHY Megow 1987, no. E1; J. J. Hermann in Hermann et al. 1999, no. 212; Dahmen 2001, no. 193; Varner 2004, 55, no. 2.16; Gagetti 2006, no. D3.

....

Plate 143
Head of Augustus, ca. AD 81, reworked after AD 96
From Municipium Turiaso, Saragossa (Zaragoza), Spain
Agate, H: 161 mm; W: 108 mm; Diam: 97 mm
Spain, Museo de Zaragoza, 80.5.1

Cut slightly below the neck for insertion into a body fashioned from a different material, this large agate head was found, after what seems to have been a long and eventful life, in the reservoir of a fountain destroyed in the third century AD. The coiffure over the ears, at the top, and the back of this large head conforms to the arrangement seen on portraits of Emperor Domitian (r. 81–96) made at the time of and after his accession. Although Domitian's rule was in many ways successful, his increasingly autocratic tendencies alienated the upper classes, and he was eventually assassinated. The senate voted to erase his memory (one of the few true instances of *damnatio memoriae* in Roman history), and many of his portraits were destroyed or reworked. This head, which retains traces of a *paludamentum* at the lower left, was refashioned into an image of Augustus (r. 27 BC–AD 14) of the Prima Porta type, as evidenced by the distinctive arrangement of locks over the forehead. Perhaps this occurred early in the reign of Trajan, the first Spanish-born emperor of Rome, in honor of Augustus, the first emperor and founder of the colony in which the head was discovered.

BIBLIOGRAPHY Beltrán Lloris 1984; Borromeo 1993, no. 8; Dahmen 2001, no. 76; Varner 2004, no. 5.47; Gagetti 2006, no. A22.

....

Plate 144
Torso of a man wearing a toga, ca. AD 90
Jasper, H: 187 mm
New York, Metropolitan Museum of Art, 17.230.54

Relatively large cuttings for dowels indicate that the head, arms, and legs of this statuette were carved separately in another material, probably another stone, such as chalcedony (see plate 145), rather than considerably lighter ivory. The right to wear the toga was reserved for Roman citizens, and different colorations of the garment distinguished degrees of status. Most exclusive was the *toga picta*, dyed purple and embroidered with gold. It was worn by generals in triumphal processions, magistrates of the highest rank, and emperors. While the white-and red-veined jasper used here might not represent the *toga picta* as naturalistically as, say, porphyry, the rarity and expense of the material would have expressed the high status of the figure represented, perhaps a divinity if not the emperor himself. The arrangement of the folds suggests a late Flavian date, and the reversal of the standard pose, with the weight of the figure on the right leg, rather than the left, might indicate that the figure was fashioned as a pendant to another, or that the workshop that carved it was particularly creative.

BIBLIOGRAPHY Gagetti 2006, D20; Picón et al. 2007, no. 386.

....

Plate 145
Hand, ca. first–second century AD(?)
Chalcedony, silver, and gold, L: 73 mm
Florence, Museo degli Argenti, Gem 826

Exquisitely carved of hard stone, this left hand, missing most of its smallest finger, was acquired in 1672 for Cardinal Leopoldo de' Medici from the Florentine jeweler Marco Gamberucci. Its origins are unknown. Details of veins, sinews, joints, and cuticles are rendered with extraordinary precision, and the varied positions of the fingers and thumb enliven the object. The gilt-silver bracelet appears to be modern, but a similar band may originally have masked a join at the wrist, if the object were not slotted directly into a garment. There is no evidence of a cutting for attachment, and it remains possible that the object was originally longer and was broken and cut down at a later date.

BIBLIOGRAPHY M. Casarosa in Gennaioli 2010, no. 118; Gennaioli 2012, no. 45.

....

CHAPTER THREE: ORGANIC MATERIALS

Plate 146
Female figurine, ca. 725–700 BC
From the Kerameikos cemetery, Athens
Ivory, H: 24 cm
Athens, National Archaeological Museum, 776

Five nude female ivory figurines of diminishing size were among the rich contents of a late Geometric grave excavated in a tomb near the Dipylon gate in the Kerameikos cemetery at Athens. Whether or not all five of the statuettes were carved from a single imported tusk, as has been suggested, they all show the Greek adoption of foreign materials and types and their adaptation to serve local needs in a local style. Both the material and the pose of the figures were imported. Female nudity is typical of ancient Near Eastern handles for fans, mirrors, and fly whisks depicting the goddess Astarte. Yet the proportions of this figure and her "sisters," the clear articulation of the body, and the meander that adorns the low cylindrical headpiece all find direct parallels in locally produced figures in other materials. Unfortunately, we do not know precisely what function these ivories served before they were interred, nor how they might have been displayed during the laying out of the body of the deceased and the procession to the tomb, but they must have been important elements of self-fashioning by the deceased and/or identity construction by the living. These ivories seem to have been commissioned in emulation of foreign models, and thus provide evidence of not only the desire of early Greek elites to possess and display imported luxury goods but also the willingness and ability of local artisans to learn, master, and even invent the techniques necessary to produce them.
BIBLIOGRAPHY Richter 1968a, figs. 16–19; Weber 1974; Boardman 1978, fig 19; Barnett 1982, 56, pl. 56d–e; Carter 1985, 1–7; Stewart 1990, 105, pl. 18; Lapatin 2001, 44–45.
....

Plate 147
Relief with the daughters of King Proitos of Argos (the Morgan Ivory), ca. 650–625 BC
Ivory, H: 13.6 cm; W: 7 cm; D: 1.6 cm
New York, Metropolitan Museum of Art, 17.190.73

Holes for attachment indicate that this thick plaque, flat at the back and partially cut as openwork, was created as an appliqué intended for adornment of a chest, such as that of the Corinthian ruler Kypselos, described at length by the later Greek traveler Pausanias, or for some other piece of furniture. Some scholars have suggested that the two female figures might represent Peitho, the personification of persuasion, and Aphrodite, the goddess of love, but most consider them to be the daughters of King Proitos of Argos, who were driven mad by Dionysos because they refused to recognize his divinity. Thus they committed a series of improper acts, including stripping off their clothes, as seen here. While the woman on the left adjusts her belt, the intricate, meander-patterned garment of her companion has fallen to her knees. Although no traces of pigment remain, ivories were usually painted and/or gilded, and color would have further enlivened this scene. Placed on some object intended for use by the women of a well-to-do household, this relief, like those depicting other mythological narratives, would have provided an example of proper—or improper—behavior.
BIBLIOGRAPHY Richter 1945; Robertson 1975, 141; Barnett 1982, 60, pl. 60a; Picón et al. 2007, 57, 416, no. 43; Annie Caubet in Aruz, Graff, and Rakic 2014, 293, no. 161.
....

Plate 148
Plaque with Perseus beheading the Gorgon, ca. 650–600 BC
From the Heraion at Samos
Ivory, H: 10.6 cm; W: 10.2 cm; D: 1.1 cm
Athens, National Archaeological Museum, 201/726

Originally attached to some object dedicated to the goddess Hera, this fragmentary plaque depicts Perseus slaying the Gorgon Medusa. Assisted by Athena, who stands at the broken left edge of the relief, her right hand touching his right arm in a traditional gesture of support, the young beardless hero grabs with his left hand a snake protruding from the monster's head as he drives his sword into her neck from below. Perseus, like the Gorgon, is depicted with a frontal face, for he dares not look in her direction, lest he be turned to stone. He wears a conical cap, whose point intrudes into the geometric frieze that borders the scene, perhaps the cap that some ancient authors said made him invisible. His low forehead, the row of curls across his brow, and the triangular bands of beaded hair framing his face are typical of the "Daidalic" style of Greek art of the seventh century BC. The oversized head of Medusa, who is already collapsing, closely resembles contemporary representations of her in other media: she has large eyes, a wrinkled nose, fleshy cheeks, and a toothy grimace with a protruding tongue. The feathers of her wings and her scaly chest are neatly incised. Paint and perhaps gilding would have further enlivened the composition. Whether this plaque was made in Samos, where it was found under the steps of the so-called Polykrates Temple, or imported from Sparta, whence there are parallels, remains uncertain.
BIBLIOGRAPHY Freyer-Schauenburg 1966, 4, 30–39, no. 5 (E1); Marangou 1969, 72–76; Hampe and Simon 1981, 230, fig. 348; Kyrieleis 1981, 39, fig. 27.
....

Plate 149
Lyre component in the form of a kneeling youth, ca. 650–625 BC
From the Heraion at Samos
Ivory, H: 14.5 cm
Athens, National Archaeological Museum, E88

Cuttings for attachment in the head, back, and bottom of this exquisitely carved figure of a kneeling youth, certainly one of the finest of all ivories to survive from antiquity, indicate that it originally formed one arm of a complex lyre that was dedicated to Hera in her sanctuary on Samos. The circles of the headband are inlaid with amber, and additional inlays, now lost, originally adorned the eyes, eyebrows, earlobes, and pubic hair. Nude, but for an intricately patterned belt, the youth's body is taut. Although the kneeling pose might have been copied from eastern art, the vigor and elasticity of the figure, as well as the male nudity, place it firmly in the Greek sphere, as does the stylized rendering of the high arched rib cage, and the finely patterned hair. Later dedications of gilt ivory lyres (now lost) are recorded in the inventories of the treasures stored in the temples on the Athenian Acropolis.

BIBLIOGRAPHY Ohly 1959; Freyer-Schauenburg 1966, 3, 19–26, no. 3 (E88); Boardman 1978, fig. 54; Kyrieleis 1981, 29–31, fig. 18; Barnett 1982, 59, pl. 62a–c; Vickers 1987, 42–43; Stewart 1990, pls. 24–25; Boardman 1993, 34, no. 15. See also Harris 1995.

....

Plate 150
Head, ca. 600–550 BC
Ivory, H: 1 cm; W: 1.6 cm; D: 1.3 cm
Atlanta, Michael C. Carlos Museum, 2007.8.1

Although blackened by fire, this deftly carved head is well preserved, but for slight damage at the rear. Cut flat at the bottom and drilled for attachment, it may originally have been part of a composite statue or perhaps a finial of some sort. The face is framed by neat short linear strands of hair, which, beneath a dotted diadem or fillet, flow from a small central part into two large curls before the ears, which are adorned with large rosette earrings. Below the low brow, strongly arching eyebrows accentuate the wide almond-shaped eyes, with raised irises and drilled pupils. The nose is long, lips smiling, chin sharp, and cheeks fleshy. The style of the features and liveliness of the figure recall other East Greek and Lydian ivories and figures in other media.

UNPUBLISHED. Compare plate 149 above; Barnett 1982, pls. 56–58; Fitton 1992; Lapatin 2001, pls. 83–87, 108.

....

Plate 151
Plaque with the Boreids chasing the Harpies from the table of Phineus, ca. 570 BC
From the Halos deposit at Delphi
Ivory and gold, H: 7 cm
Delphi Archaeological Museum, 9944

This ivory plaque was found in the same deposit of burnt and broken precious offerings buried under and alongside the Sacred Way in the sanctuary of Apollo at Delphi as other gold and ivory objects (see plates 10, 152). Carved for the most part as openwork and preserving visible traces of gilding, the relief depicts two of the Argonauts, Zetes and Kalaïs, sons of Boreas, coming to the aid of Phineus, the blind king of Thrace, whose food was forever being stolen or despoiled by the Harpies. Only Phineus's hand, pressed onto the table at the far left, remains. A woman standing nearby looks back while gesturing in alarm. She wears a tight-fitting tunic and a skirt with incised linear patterns. The first two of the other four figures—all facing forward but moving decisively to the right—wear short tunics and baldrics for their swords. As befitting the sons of Boreas, the god of the north wind, they have wings at their ankles. The one at the middle of the composition reaches out and grabs the hair of the first of the Harpies, whose large wing sprouts from her shoulder. She wears an even more elaborate garment, incised with diagonally running meanders, and holds some of the stolen food in her hand. A drill hole between her legs indicates how the appliqué was attached to some larger object. Little remains of the second Harpy, and it is unclear how much farther to the right the composition may have originally extended. Also uncertain is the precise number and identity of these Harpies, two of whom ancient literary sources named Okypete (swift-flying) and Podarge (fleet-of-foot). Regardless, such decoration was certainly appropriate for a luxurious dining couch or banqueting table, if not a chest or some other piece of furniture. Similar reliefs, analogous in size, technique, and style, were also found at Delphi. They depict a battle scene and a warrior mounting a chariot as other men look on.

BIBLIOGRAPHY Amandry 1939; Petrakos 1977, figs. 24–25, 33; Barnett 1982, 60, pl. 63d; Amandry 1991.

....

Plate 152
Feet of a composite statue, ca. 550 BC
From the Halos deposit at Delphi
Ivory and gold, L: ca. 8 cm
Delphi Archaeological Museum, 9946, 9947

Much of the ivory recovered from the impressive cache of chryselephantine (gold-and-ivory) statuary that was recovered burned and badly damaged in the sanctuary of Apollo at Delphi has been heavily restored (see plate 10), but this well-carved pair of sandaled feet, though blackened by fire, is relatively well preserved. They belong to one of the intermediary figures, about two-thirds life-size, and the high quality of their craftsmanship is clear. Painstakingly carved low relief floral and geometric decoration adorns the intricately shaped thongs and horizontal straps of the sandals, which were likely to have been further adorned with paint and gilding (which survives on other feet from the cache). The soft flesh and other anatomical details—including the joints and contours of the toes, nails, and even the cuticles—have received no less attention. The identity of the figure represented remains unknown, but the statue must have been a stunning dedication to the god.

BIBLIOGRAPHY Amandry 1939, 1991; Lapatin 2001, 57–60, no. 33.10.

....

Plate 153
The Judgment of Paris, ca. 400 BC
From Kul Oba, Kerch, Crimea
Ivory, preserved H: 20.5 cm
St. Petersburg, Hermitage State Museum, KO 116

These magnificent incised ivory veneers originally adorned a sumptuous cedar-wood sarcophagus recovered from a rich Skythian tomb at Kul Oba on the Kerch peninsula on the northern shore of the Black Sea in 1830. They depict one of the key episodes of Greek mythology, the contest of three goddesses, Hera, Athena, and Aphrodite, for the golden apple inscribed "To the fairest." This competition ultimately precipitated the Trojan War, when Aphrodite bribed the judge, the Trojan prince Paris, with Helen, wife of the Greek king Menelaus. The thinly cut ivory has split along naturally curving lines, but enough survives to allow us to recognize the figures in the scene and to admire the extraordinary quality of the craftsmanship, which parallels in style and surpasses in quality the finest Athenian red-figure vase painting of the period. At the far left, Athena, holding a spear and a crested Corinthian-type helmet, faces Aphrodite, who turns toward the young Eros perched on her shoulder. Paris is only partially preserved in his barbarian finery. He looks right toward Hera, who is veiled and crowned with a floral wreath. All three goddesses wear necklaces and bracelets, as well as garments whose lively folds flutter in complex patterns. Pigments applied to the ivory add variety to the composition and, where absent, the illusion of transparency to the drapery. Other incised ivory veneers from the same tomb depict the Dioskouroi abducting the daughters of Leukippos. Some scholars have attributed the engraving of these veneers to an Athenian craftsman; amidst the many local and imported gold objects deposited within the tomb was a gold and enamel pendant depicting the Athena Parthenos (see plate 19).

BIBLIOGRAPHY Minns 1913, 204–5, figs. 100–1; Artamonov 1969, pls. 257–62; Vaulina and Wasowicz 1974, 45–51, no. 1, pl. VIII; Boardman 1993, 144, no. 138; Williams and Ogden 1994, 136, fig. 48.

....

Plate 154
Parade shield with Achilles and Penthesilia, ca. 340–320 BC
From Vergina, Macedonia
Ivory, gold, silver, glass, leather, textile, stucco, and wood,
H (of central figures): ca. 35 cm
Vergina Archaeological Museum

Found in fragments in Tomb II at Vergina, this splendid composite gold and ivory parade shield, like the gold *larnax* (plate 33) from the same tomb, has been associated alternately with the Macedonian king Philip II, the father of Alexander the Great, who was assassinated in 336 BC, and with his son Philip III Arrhidaios, who was executed by order of his stepmother in 317/16. It was constructed on a wooden core with a leather and cloth interior, where embossed gilt-silver strips depicting Nikai, antithetical lions, the club of Herakles, and floral ornament anchored its handle and suspension straps. The sumptuous exterior was composed of gilt stucco into which were set circles of cutout running spirals and meanders in ivory, the latter containing silver-backed inset glass plaques. The central device, carved in high relief, is an ivory group of Achilles slaying the Amazon queen Penthesilia. The two are interlocked, as the Greek hero stands over the fallen woman, pulling back her head, about to apply the coup de grâce—the moment at which, according to some authors, he fell in love with her. A similar composition appeared on one of the west metopes of the Parthenon and the frieze of the Maussolleion at Halikarnassos; it may have also featured in the Amazonomachy on the exterior of the shield held by Pheidias's gold and ivory Athena inside the Parthenon. Significantly, it appears later on gold and brass medallions as the device on shields held by Alexander the Great, who claimed descent from Achilles. Here most of the surface of the ivory relief is badly deteriorated, but the virtuosity of the carving remains evident not only in the meanders and spirals but especially in the feet of both heroic figures, which are relatively undamaged. His right foot is delicately arched, poised on the rocky outcrop that serves as a ground for both figures, its ankle bone subtly modeled; hers are both extended, dragging limp behind her.

BIBLIOGRAPHY Andronicos 1984, 134–40; Borza and Palagia 2007, 113–17; Kottaridi 2011, 71–74.

....

Plate 155
Appliqué with Dionysos, Ariadne, and a Satyr, ca. 300 BC
From Vergina, Macedonia
Ivory and gold, H: ca. 10 cm
Vergina Archaeological Museum

Found in the so-called Prince's Tomb in the Macedonian royal cemetery at Vergina, this delicately carved gilt-ivory relief was once attached to a sumptuous *kline* (couch), along with a series of ivories depicting a bearded figure wearing oriental dress and a Phrygian cap, which seems to represent Sabazios, a Thracian variant of Dionysos;

cavorting satyrs, maenads, and griffins; and tripods (prizes given to dramatic victors). Here, in the center, stands Dionysos himself, bearded, but still youthful of body, supported by his consort, probably Ariadne, and a young satyr, who plays the double pipes. Gold survives on Dionysos's hair, fillet, and part of his beard, the hair and tail of the satyr, and Ariadne's crown, as well as on other fragments. The preservation and sensitivity of the carving is extraordinary, particularly the fleshiness of the god's cheeks, which, along with his need for support, suggest slight inebriation. The fine detail of the figures' hair, the delicacy of their hands, and the varied folds of the woman's drapery, whether crimped under the cord tied beneath her breasts, bunched on her upper arm, or fluttering behind her, are all expertly rendered. The torch held laterally by the god is appropriate symbolically for a funerary couch, but Dionysos and his companions would, of course, be suitable for the decoration of an object to be used at a drinking party, and it seems likely that the sumptuous couch to which the relief was originally attached was enjoyed by its owner and demonstrated his high status in life before being deposited in his tomb. There, it seems, a warrior's panoply (including swords, greaves, a cuirass, and a helmet) was placed upon it, while the cremated remains of the deceased, perhaps Alexander IV, the son of Alexander the Great, were deposited inside a silver hydria festooned with a gold wreath (plate 67).

BIBLIOGRAPHY Andronicos 1984, 207–8; Kottaridi 2011, esp. 112–16; Baughan 2013, 268–69. See also Rhomiopoulou and Schmidt-Dounas 2010, 87–99.

....

Plates 156, 157

Rhyton with winged centaur and nymph, ca. 150–1 BC
From Old Nysa, Turkmenistan
Ivory, H: 63 cm; (figures) 17 cm
Ashkabat, National Museum of Turkmenistan

Rhyton with lion-griffin, ca. 150–1 BC
From Old Nysa, Turkmenistan
Ivory, H: 43.5 cm; (griffin) 13.5 cm
Moscow, State Museum of Oriental Art, 3949111

The Parthian capital of Old Nysa, located east of the Caspian Sea in modern Turkmenistan, was founded by Mithradates I (r. 171–138 BC) and called Mitradatkart in Parthian. Soviet excavations in 1948 uncovered a treasury of thirty-three ivory furniture components, as well as a group of almost fifty splendid ivory rhyta (drinking horns), a shape better attested in metal and other materials (see plates 65, 73, 120). Composed of up to four different components, these vessels range in size from 30–60 cm in height. Although much degraded they have been skillfully restored, each from hundreds of fragments. Their decoration combines eastern and western forms and iconographies, as one might expect, given their findspot; some terminate with the foreparts of centaurs, others with winged and horned lion-griffins. At the top they have Greek moldings and relief friezes of classical figures: Olympian gods, female figures, including the Muses and followers of Dionysos, and sacrificial scenes. One even preserves part of an inscription in Greek.

BIBLIOGRAPHY Masson and Pugachenkova 1982; Barnett 1982, 66–67, pl. 67; Vickers 1987, 49; E. Pappalardo 2010, 2011.

....

Plate 158

Appliqué with the head of Pan, ca. 100 BC
Ivory, H: 8.6 cm; W: 7.6 cm; D: 2.3 cm
Malibu, JPGM, 87.AI.18

Expressively carved in high relief to depict Pan, the goatish follower of Dionysos, this roundel was cut flat at the back and drilled through the cheek for attachment, probably to form part of the *fulcrum* (back support) of a luxurious *kline* (couch). Images of Dionysos himself, and especially satyrs, maenads, and other followers of the gods, were popular decorations for furniture (see also figure 19, plates 151, 155), which were produced in a variety of materials. Ancient literary sources often mention ivory couches as being particularly luxurious, and the detailed representation of Pan here is among the finest surviving ivory carvings of the Hellenistic age. More goat than human, Pan is depicted with wild deeply carved hair, pointed ear, and abundant finely carved facial hair, which extends into a goatee tucked back under his chin. The demigod's mouth is open, revealing his teeth, and his eye is wide and alert between fleshy lids. A horn, now lost, was separately carved and attached by means of the hole above the ear. A flat cloth ribbon, or fillet, another attribute of Dionysos, is wrapped around the base of the horn and hangs down over the cheek, adding yet another contrasting texture represented here by the anonymous master carver.

BIBLIOGRAPHY Doumeyrou 1989; Lapatin and Wight 2010, 101.

....

Plate 159

Yakshi, ca. AD 1–79
From Pompeii
Ivory, H: 24 cm; W: 5 cm; D: 6 cm
Naples, Museo Archeologico Nazionale, 149425

Discovered in Pompeii in the remains of a wooden chest located in a garden in the so-called House of the Four Styles (I.8.5; now also known as the House of the Indian Statuette), this intricately carved figurine of a female figure and two smaller companions is striking testimony to contacts between ancient Rome and India. Like the two handmaidens at her sides bearing toiletries, the principal figure is nude but for a diadem, necklace on her chest, and numerous bracelets and anklets. Carved fully in the round and with a deep hole cut into the top of the head, this object was originally intended to serve either as a handle or, more likely, as the leg of a chair, table, or some other luxury furnishing. The principal figure has often been identified as Lakshmi, the wife of Vishnu, the Hindu goddess of wealth, prosperity, and generosity and the embodiment of beauty, grace, and charm. That goddess, however, is usually depicted with four arms, dressed in fine garments, standing on a lotus flower, flanked by elephants. The woman depicted here, with sexual attributes emphasized, may rather be a *yakshi*, an earth spirit of great fertility, though it is likely that her Pompeian owners would have thought of her as a kind of Indian Venus (see plate 160). A single letter inscribed on the base in Kharoshthi script suggests that the object was created in the northwest region of the subcontinent. It may have been brought to Campania by Nabatean merchants, who are known to have lived in the port of Puteoli, north of Pompeii, and traded in pearls, gemstones, and other precious materials that had been transported from the shores of the Indian Ocean and along the coast of the Red Sea.

BIBLIOGRAPHY Barnett 1982, 69, pl. 75b–e; De Caro 1994, 274; Asaka and Iorio 2005; Basu 2010.

....

Plate 160
Statuette of Venus Anadyomene, ca. AD 1–79
From Pompeii
Ivory, H: 10.5 cm
Naples, Museo Archeologico Nazionale, 110924

Well preserved apart from the loss of the right arm, hand, strand of hair, and dolphin's tail, this figurine reproduces a Hellenistic statue of the goddess of love wringing her hair upon emerging from the sea (or her bath), which was perhaps derived from a famous painting by Apelles. Here the craftsman deviates from the standard depiction of the goddess as completely nude by adding a long cloak, presumably originally colored, which frames and highlights the display of her sensuous body. The warmth, gleam, and apparent softness of the ivory aptly capture and convey the flesh of the goddess. The type was extremely popular and was widely produced in diverse materials for a variety of settings. Examples have been found in sanctuaries, graves, baths, and fountain houses, as well as homes, where they were sometimes placed in *lararia* (small shrines) with other household gods. This example was found alongside a bronze statuette of Jupiter holding a silver scepter in the tablinum of the so-called House of the Greek Epigrams (V.1.18) at Pompeii, where it would have been displayed prominently. Bronze and silver vessels and other implements were also found in this prosperous Pompeian house, which was first built in the third or second century BC and enlarged at the end of the Republican period, when dining rooms as well as a large peristyle garden were added following the owner's acquisition of adjacent property. While much of the decoration of the tablinum does not survive, a fresco of Venus and Adonis is preserved, as are several other frescoes elsewhere in the house depicting the goddess, including Venus and Mars, the Judgment of Paris, and Cupid Wrestling Pan, perhaps further indications of the owner's devotion to the goddess.

BIBLIOGRAPHY Museo Archeologico Nazionale 1986, 110, 230–31, no. 1; De Caro 1994, 275; Lapatin 2008, 37. See also Wardle 2010, esp. 201–26.

....

Plate 161
Appliqué of Dionysos, ca. AD 1–100
From Saepinum
Ivory, H: 17 cm
Campobasso, Italy, Museo Provinciale Sannitico, 1.311

Two holes drilled through the forehead and beneath the lower lip in this large, flat relief of the wine god Dionysos indicate that it was intended to serve as an appliqué attached to some larger object, perhaps a couch, chest, or some other piece of furniture. As often in Greek and Roman art, the god confronts the viewer directly. His wide, almond-shaped eyes, with drilled pupils and incised irises, are surrounded by sensitively rendered lids, and his fleshy lips, parted to reveal his upper teeth, are framed by a long mustache and beard, which falls in two tiers of scalloped locks. The god wears a cloth fillet above wavy locks of hair, which flow from a central part and arc over his low forehead; an odd triangular ornament with a round terminal seems to fall out from under his hair over his forehead. Long, wavy locks of hair once framed the sides of his face—only those on the proper right survive. Saepinum was a Samnite hill town that became prosperous following the Social Wars of the early first century BC, particularly during the rule of the emperor Augustus and his successors. This splendid object, appropriate in both a banqueting and a funeral context, would have demonstrated the wealth and refinement of its owner as well as his devotion to the god.

BIBLIOGRAPHY Adam-Veleni 2011, 9, 177, fig. 2, no. 1.

....

Plate 162
Face of a composite statue, ca. 100 BC–AD 125
Said to be from north of Rome
Ivory, H: 20.2 cm; W: 14.5 cm
Rome, Museo Nazionale Romano,
Palazzo Massimo alle Terme, 508646

This magnificent face, slightly over life-size, along with nine other ivory components of at least three composite statues, was recovered in 2003 by Italian authorities, having been illicitly excavated a decade earlier apparently near Vitellara, Cesano, some thirty kilometers north of Rome, perhaps from a ancient villa. Exquisitely carved from a single large tusk, the face is difficult to date precisely, although its style is decidedly Classical. The crispness of the eyebrows and especially the eyelid, perhaps overemphasized by the loss of the original inlaid eyes, suggests a date in the early second century AD, during the classicizing revival of Hadrian, who himself commissioned the largest known composite gold and ivory statue, the colossal *Zeus Olympios* at Athens. However, Roman generals removed smaller chryselephantine statues from Greece in the first century BC, and ancient literary sources record the production of several new statues in the technique at Rome in the first centuries BC and AD. This example is one of the finest known survivals: the rendering of the nostrils is particularly sensitive, and the teeth are visible through the expressive slightly parted lips. Traces of wavy hair are visible above the brow, and the statue may have worn a crown or diadem. The ears were carved separately and attached; the left survives. The preserved left hand may have grasped a scepter, while the right, palm open, may have been intended to hold an offering bowl. The identity of the figure remains uncertain. While some scholars have suggested the face might be a portrait of a member of the imperial family, assimilated to divinity, it seems too idealized to be anything but a god. Even its gender cannot be determined with certainty.

BIBLIOGRAPHY Giuliano et al. 2003; Talamo 2013.

....

Plate 163

Set of cosmetic and writing implements, ca. AD 1–100(?)
Ivory
Cambridge, Fitzwilliam Museum, GR.2-27c.1980

Both the size and material of most of these two dozen objects, ranging from a tray measuring 21.5 by 9.8 cm to miniature vessels, suggest that they were not designed for actual use but rather intended to convey the wealth, refinement, and literary pretension of their owner, presumably a woman. Several objects seem to have to do with writing: sandal-shaped and rectangular writing tablets, the interiors of which would have originally been lined with wax, what appears to be a mechanism for unrolling and reading a papyrus scroll, and a sword-shaped spatula. A variety of containers, boxes with sliding lids, two combs with broken tines, and round fan or imitation mirror on a long handle, in turn, attest to the values of beauty and elegance. While the larger objects could have been fashioned from blocks of ivory, and the *pyxides* (circular boxes) cut from sections of tusks, the elegant small vessels were turned on a lathe with special care.

BIBLIOGRAPHY Vassilika 1998, 118–19, no. 57.

....

Plate 164

Fragment of a tripod leg, ca. AD 1–79
From Herculaneum
Ivory
Pompei, Soprintendenza Archeologica di Pompei e Ercolano, Herc R4

Excavations in 2007 along the ancient shoreline of Herculaneum, which was buried by the same eruption of Mount Vesuvius that destroyed Pompeii in AD 79, uncovered a luxury seaside pavilion that was part of the so-called Villa dei Papiri, which seems to have been owned in the first century BC by Lucius Calpurneus Piso Caesoninus, the father-in-law of Julius Caesar. Among the finds were fragments of carbonized wooden furniture and ivory veneers exquisitely carved in low relief. The surviving pieces apparently belonged to two tables and four ornamental tripods of the kind that appear in ancient Roman wall paintings. Although discolored, the ivories are relatively well preserved and most depict scenes from the life of Bacchus and his companions. One shows the god nude, except for an ivy wreath and cloak pulled up over his head and shoulders, holding a thyrsus in his left hand. Another depicts satyrs and cupids engaged in wine making and other activities. Here, beneath a pruned pine tree, a winged Psyche places fruits on a garlanded altar before a statue of Dionysos, draped and holding a thyrsos. Behind her a cupid stands on a rocky outcrop playing the double pipes. Above her, panpipes hang from the tree.

BIBLIOGRAPHY Guidobaldi 2010; Guidobaldi and Esposito 2010, 51–55; Wallace-Hadrill 2011, 118; Guidobaldi and Esposito 2012, 163–64; Roberts 2013, 199.

....

Plate 165

Sandaled foot of a composite statue, ca. AD 100–150
Said to be from Rome
Ivory, H: 6 cm; L: 14.3 cm
New York, Metropolitan Museum of Art, 25.78.43

Like the pair of feet from Delphi (plate 152), but considerably later, this delicately carved foot was part of a composite statue whose flesh parts were rendered in ivory and draped elements in other materials, probably wood covered with gold and paint. The sensitive carving of the toes, which not only presents such details as cuticles and wrinkles at the joints but also provides a sense of the bones underneath the flesh, is matched by the detailed rendering of the sandal, whose leather straps are pulled tight around the foot but flutter where loose. The band above the toes is carved in such low relief that it appears as if it were stamped with a decorative pattern of acanthus tendrils and flowers, and an acanthus palmette adorns the thong rising from between toes. The most detail, however, is on the tongue (see detail), where the personification of the river Nile sits cross-legged on a sphinx, holding a cornucopia in his right hand and a reed in the left. Two young boys crown him with a wreath and above them are the lower coils of a serpent, the *Agathodaimon* (personification of good fortune), which continued on another separately carved component. Because of the high quality of the craftsmanship and the connection of the imagery with Egypt, this object has been dated in the Hellenistic period and to the reign of Emperor Augustus, who defeated Antony and Cleopatra at the Battle of Actium in 31 BC and subsequently annexed Egypt. But the closest parallels for the depiction of the Nile and other imagery on the sandal itself are found on Alexandrian coins minted during the reigns of Emperors Trajan (AD 98–117), Hadrian (AD 117–138), Antoninus Pius (AD 138–161), and their successors, suggesting that the foot, too, was carved in the second century.

BIBLIOGRAPHY Lapatin 2001, 130–32; Picón et al. 2007, 362, 487, no. 420.

....

Plate 166
Portrait of Septimius Severus, ca. AD 193–211
From the Temple of Peace, Rome
Ivory, H: 24.8 cm; W: 17.5 cm; D: 10.5 cm
Rome, Museo Nazionale Romano, Palazzo Massimo alle Terme

This exceptional portrait of Septemius Severus was discovered during excavations in the area of the Templum Pacis (Temple of Peace) in the Roman Forum. The temple was built by the emperor Vespasian and inaugurated in AD 75, but it was badly damaged by a fire in AD 192 and rebuilt by Septemius Severus, which may have been the reason for the placement within of this image, which, in turn, was destroyed by another fire in late antiquity. The emperor can be recognized by comparison of his physiognomy, especially his long beard, to portraits on coins and in marble. Raising his right hand in a gesture of address (*ad locutio*), he is depicted seated (as indicated by slight remains of his left leg), wearing a sleeved tunic and a *toga contabulata* with a diagonal *umbo* across his chest. Although presented in the guise of a philosopher, he is crowned by a *taenia*, or fillet, with small drill holes, perhaps for insertion of some other material (compare plates 118, 139). Another, later ivory portrait of a beardless youth, perhaps the emperor Julian, was found nearby.
BIBLIOGRAPHY Spinola 2014, 165–74, figs. 7a–c.

....

Plate 167
Medusa head, ca. AD 100
Amber, H: 5.8 cm; W: 5.8 cm; D: 3.2 cm
Malibu, JPGM, 71.AO.355

This thick piece of amber, now broken at the edges, has been skillfully fashioned into head of the Gorgon Medusa. The monster has wild, deeply carved hair with wide incised locks, a furrowed brow, arched eyebrows above narrow staring eyes with drilled pupils, a prominent nose, fleshy mouth, and extremely puffy cheeks. Only one of the pair of snakes tied underneath the chin in a Herakles knot is well preserved, its head marked by drilled eyes. A larger boring drilled through the hair at the top, now partially broken, held a pin to affix this appliqué to some larger object.
BIBLIOGRAPHY Causey 2011, 71, fig. 31.

....

Plate 168
Cupids driving a cart, ca. AD 75–150
From Azay-le-Rideau, France
Amber, H: 6 cm; L: 11.4 cm; D: 2.3 cm
Paris, Bibliothèque nationale de France, Cabinet des médailles, Froehner 1135

This large sculptural group was discovered around 1800 in the richly appointed tomb of a young girl, along with gold jewelry, a gold ring set with a jasper, two rings of rock crystal, statuettes of ivory, additional ambers, and other objects, which have since been dispersed. Carved on both sides to be viewed entirely in the round, it presents a winged cupid holding the reigns of a goat that draws a four-wheeled cart carrying two additional figures, both of which are damaged and whose identities are uncertain. Details such as the hair, wings, and even the toes of the cupid and the beard and hair of the goat are finely incised. It has been suggested that the figures on the cart might be Dionysos and Ariadne, but the resemblance of the forwardmost figure's chubby body and hair to those of the cupid suggest that a child is represented here. The group recalls not only similar scenes on Roman sarcophagi, where deceased children are associated with Erotes, but also the presence of children and cupids together on other carved ambers.
BIBLIOGRAPHY D'Ercole 2008, 94–106, no. 17.

....

Plate 169
Perfume pot with vintaging cupids, ca. AD 100–120
Said to be from Aquileia
Amber, H: 5.2 cm; W: 6.1 cm; Diam (at mouth): 2.5 cm
London, British Museum, 1866,0412.3 (Amber 114)

Two winged cupids, carved in high relief, cut and gather clusters of grapes from a sturdy vine with large leaves. One cupid stands, holding two clusters, apparently about to place them in a basket. His companion seems to sit on the vine, holding a drinking horn in one hand and in the other a bunch of grapes, which has attracted the notice of a crouching panther below. A large two-handled wine vessel with a ribbed body and neck stands before the panther. The concentric circles at the bottom of this pot were turned on a lathe.
BIBLIOGRAPHY Strong 1966, 92–93, no. 114; Nava and Salerno 2007, 284, no. IV.45; Williams 2009, 310–11, no. 143.

....

Plate 170
Pin, ca. 200–100 BC
From the sanctuary of Aphrodite at Paphos, Cyprus
Bronze, gold, and pearls, L (overall): 17.8 cm; L (of pearls): 1.4 and 0.4 cm
London, British Museum, 1888,1115.2 (Jewellery 1999)

The inscription on the shaft of this pin indicates that it was dedicated to Aphrodite in fulfillment of a vow by Tamisa and Eubola, the wife of Aratas, a member of the Ptolemaic court. (During much of the Hellenistic period Cyprus was under Egyptian control.) The two pearls at the top of the pin have both disintegrated slightly and lost much of their original luster, but the lower one is the largest to have survived from classical antiquity. Given Aphrodite's association with the sea, pearls constituted a highly appropriate dedication to the goddess. Beneath the pearls the head of the pin is decorated with four goat's heads separated by lotus flowers, acanthus foliage, and four drinking doves.

BIBLIOGRAPHY Landman et al. 2001, 64; Williams 2009, 224–25, no. 102. For dress pins dedicated at sanctuaries see Brøns 2014, 40–45, and appendix 4.

....

Plate 171
Necklace, ca. 100 BC–AD 79
From Pompeii
Gold, mother-of-pearl, and emeralds, L: 34.5 cm
Naples, Museo Archeologico Nazionale, 113576

Found in the so-called *contrada Bottaro* southwest of Pompeii in 1881, this stunning necklace is composed of a mesh of gold loops set with eight large oblong iridescent pieces of mother-of-pearl and nine smaller emeralds, two, at the ends, encased in gold, like the mother-of-pearl, the others "sewn" in place by gold wires. The clasp consists of a circular domed boss with triple wire filigree at the edge and a rectangular stone; a loop on the underside received a simple hook. The overall effect of extreme liveliness in this necklace and others, less complex, results from the pleasing color contrast of gold, white pearl, and bright green emerald.

BIBLIOGRAPHY Breglia 1941, 62, no. 473; Coarelli 1970, no. 60; Museo Archeologico Nazionale 1989, 216–17, no. 70; Stefanelli 1992, 113, no. 40, fig. 78; De Caro 1994, 280; Lapatin 2008, 43.

....

Plate 172
Head of Medusa, ca. 200–1 BC
Coral, H: 4.8 cm; W: 6.5 cm; D: 3.5 cm
Oxford, Ashmolean Museum, EA1993.19

Carved from a large piece of pink coral, this round face can be identified as the Gorgon Medusa by not only the wild hair but especially by the wing protruding from the proper right side of the head and the remains of a snake on the left. The strongly arched eyebrows, hollow eyes with fleshy lids, and wide cheeks are typical of Graeco-Roman images of Gorgons, but the long, wide nose is not, and stylistically this carving seems to fall outside the tradition of classical sculpture. Its provenance and style suggest, rather, that it is a Gandharan or Bactrian work, for ancient sources write of coral being prized in and around India and of its having been imported from the Mediterranean in exchange for pearls and other commodities. Here, the carver seems to have exploited the naturally porous quality of the material and cut the monster's thick, curving, incised locks of hair around preexisting holes, drilling additional ones to enhance the effect. Whether the story of coral's origins as sea plants petrified by contact with the severed head of Medusa, which could turn those who looked upon it to stone, was known to the carver of this object or his patrons we do not know.

UNPUBLISHED.

....

Plate 173
Bust of Serapis, ca. AD 1–200
Coral, H: 6.2 cm; W: 4.8 cm; D: 3.2 cm
London, British Museum, 1814,0704.1123 (Gem 3940)

This miniature bust, with a flat, subtriangular back and vertical rectilinear support post, depicts the god Serapis, who is recognizable by the characteristics of his symmetrically arranged curly hair and beard with corkscrew locks, which are further articulated by incision. Intense eyes with drilled pupils and tear ducts stare out from pronounced eyelids. A hole in the top of the head was likely intended for the attachment of a separately fashioned *modius*, a grain measure that was a typical attribute of the deity, a Hellenistic assimilation of the Greek Hades and the Egyptian Osiris, who was the god of fertility as well as the Underworld. Also typical of Serapis iconography are the tunic with V-shaped folds over the chest and the wider fold of a mantle falling forward over the proper left shoulder. This imagery likely derives from a famous statue that ancient authors attributed to the sculptor Bryaxis, who seems to have sought to rival the majesty of Pheidias's *Zeus Olympios*. According to Clement of Alexandria, writing in the late second century, Bryaxis's *Serapis* was fashioned from a mixture of precious materials: "There were filings of gold and silver on its surface, and also of bronze, iron, and lead, and in addition to these tin. Nor did it lack any of the Egyptian gems—fragments of sapphire, hematite, and emerald, and still others of topaz. After grinding all these to a powder he colored the mixture to a dark blue tone" (*Protreptikos* 4.48.3). Although different in color, this miniature coral bust, too, was precious and presents an element not apparent in other representations of the god. On his proper left shoulder are the remains of the feet of a small figure standing on a molded base. These may have belonged to Harpokrates, the son of Osiris/Serapis and the goddess Isis. Formerly in the collection of Charles Townley.

BIBLIOGRAPHY Walters 1926, no. 3940. See also Pollitt 1986, 279–80.

....

Plate 174
Textile fragments, ca. 500–440 BC
From Koropi, Attica
Linen, silver, and gold, H (panel): 44.5 cm; W (panel): 27.3 cm
London, Victoria and Albert Museum, T.220 to B-1953

Found at Koropi in southeast Attica in a bronze *kalpis* (water jar) with bones and the powdered remains of other even more degraded textiles, these linen fragments are embroidered with silver-gilt thread in a diaper pattern with small striding lions, forepaws and tails raised, in the center of each lozenge. Gold-threaded textiles are not only mentioned in ancient literature as the garments of heroes and divinities but also appear in historical accounts as being worn by the rich and in temple inventories as dedications to the gods.

BIBLIOGRAPHY Beckwith 1954; Richter 1965, 371, fig. 495; Richter 1966, 118, fig. 589; Barber 1991, 206; Gleba 2008, 65. See also Cleland 2005; Y. Spantidaki and Mulhérat 2012; Brøns 2014.

....

Plate 175
Textile fragment, ca. 400–350 BC
From the Pavlovskij Barrow, Kerch, Crimea
Wool
St. Petersburg, State Hermitage Museum

A frieze of elaborate palmettes with spiraling tendrils was embroidered with yellow, green, and black thread on a red/purple wool background on this fragment of a garment found buried with a woman on Kerch peninsula, on the northern shore of the Black Sea. Another fragment of the same garment preserves an Amazon mounted on horseback, brandishing a spear.
BIBLIOGRAPHY Minns 1913, 336–37, fig. 244; Richter 1965, 370, fig. 491; Richter 1966, 118, fig. 590; Pekridou-Gorecki 1989, 44–48; Barber 1991, 207–9; Brøns 2014, 70; Spantidaki 2014.
....

Plate 176
Gold and purple textile, ca. 340–316 BC
From Tomb II at Vergina, Macedonia
Wool and gold, H: 28.5 cm; W (max.): 61.5 cm
Vergina Archaeological Museum

Found wrapped around the cremated bones of a young woman placed in a gold *larnax* in the antechamber of Tomb II at Vergina, this badly damaged and restored cloth, woven with gold strips and threads of purple-dyed wool, is without doubt the finest surviving weaving from Classical Greece. Recent research suggests that the two surviving trapezoidal panels were originally rectangular—their present shape the result of distortion—and that the cloth itself originally consisted of four such panels, folded over one another. Each panel has a border of running spirals surrounding a riotous, yet symmetrical acanthus that rises from a central stem flanked by a pair of large leaves. Twisting and spiraling tendrils, leaves, buds, blossoms, calyxes, and flowers fill the space. At center top two small birds perched on delicate stems face one another. There is no indication that these gold threads were wrapped around a fabric core, as were later gold threads. They measure just 0.25 mm wide and were woven at a density of approximately seventy per centimeter. Analysis of the purple dye indicates that it was derived from murex.
BIBLIOGRAPHY Andronicos 1984, 191–95; Drogou 1987; Flury-Lemberg 1988, 234–37, 483, no. 51; Gleba 2008, 65; Kottaridi 2011, 96–97.
....

Plates 177, 178
Tapestry fragment with Dionysos, ca. AD 300–500
Linen and wool, H: 139 cm; W: 79 cm
Boston, Museum of Fine Arts, 1973.290

Tapestry fragment with maenad, ca. AD 300–500.
Linen and wool, H: 143 cm; W: 85.5 cm
Riggisberg, Switzerland, Abegg Stiftung, 1637

Both these fragments depict the world of Dionysos. In the Boston fragment the god is largely nude, wearing an ivy wreath in his hair and a cloak that falls behind his back and wraps around his left arm, which cradles a large golden cornucopia. He raises his right arm to his head in a familiar gesture; his lower body is largely lost, but he was originally depicted seated with his legs crossed and a small panther at his feet. Shading and highlights have been employed to render more effectively the god's body, his drapery, and the cornucopia. Dark brown outlines separate his raised arm and neck from the halo behind him, but darker lines at his shoulders and beneath his pectorals give volume to his muscles, while still more subtle shading and highlights animate his face, the drapery folds, and even the edges of the red ribbon of his wreath. The cornucopia has been rendered in seven different colors, ranging from deep browns and oranges to bright yellow to suggest the shine of light on metal. A wide orange horizontal band with a white and yellow floral scroll on a pink band within forms part of an arcade of yellow arches, each surmounted by a different ornamental band: here a braid of white, pink, dark, and olive green. Below is a golden apse decorated with gold polygons and green squares, perhaps suggesting emeralds set in a gold ground if not a coffered ceiling. Before being reemployed as a funerary shroud this weaving may well have adorned a dining room. Its imagery was equally appropriate for both functions. The dark purple background and complex architectural structure link this panel to the Riggisberg panel, which depicts a maenad playing a lyre. She wears a red crown with yellow dots topped by green leaves; and drop earrings, a gold necklace, armlet, bracelets, and anklets. Her purple peplos has gold trim, and she also wears a green mantle. Behind her head is a gold halo, and the architecture that surrounds her is also polychromatic. Another related panel (Cleveland Museum of Art, 1975.6) depicts a satyr and maenad.
BIBLIOGRAPHY D. Shepherd 1976; Arensberg 1977; Flury-Lemberg 1988, 384, 482, cat. no. 47; Rutschowscaya 1990, 86–87.
....

Plate 179
Tapestry with fish, ca. AD 100–300
From Antinoopoulos (Antinoë), Egypt
Wool, H: 138 cm; W: 87 cm
Lyon, Musée des Tissus, 28927

Presented in profile and swimming in different directions, a variety of fish are presented on this large fragment of a splendid wool textile from Upper Egypt. Gradations of color and cast shadows illusionistically convey light reflecting off the scales of the fish underwater and add to the sense of their three-dimensionality. Paintings and mosaics of marine life decorated Roman baths and dining rooms. A sumptuous tapestry such as this would likely have been hung in the latter before it was reused as a funeral shroud at Antinoopoulos, the city renamed for Hadrian's lover, Antinoos, who drowned nearby in the river Nile.
BIBLIOGRAPHY Martiniani-Reber 1986; Rutschowscaya 1990, 62, 68; Stauffer et al. 1995, 9; Stauffer 2006.
....

REFERENCES

ABBREVIATIONS

AJA	*American Journal of Archaeology*
BCH	*Bulletin de correspondance hellénique*
BSA	*Annual of the British School at Athens*
CIL	*Corpus Inscriptionum Latinarum* (Berlin, 1893–)
EAA	*Enciclopedia dell'arte antica, classica e orientale* (Rome, 1958–97)
IDélos	*Inscriptions de Délos* (Paris, 1926–72)
IG	*Inscriptiones graecae*
JdI	*Jahrbuch des Deutschen Archäologischen Instituts*
JPGM	The J. Paul Getty Museum
JPGMJ	*The J. Paul Getty Museum Journal*
JRA	*Journal of Roman Archaeology*
JRS	*Journal of Roman Studies*
LIMC	*Lexicon Iconographicum Mythologiae Classicae* (Zürich, 1981–2009)
LSJ	H. G. Liddell, R. Scott, and H. Stuart Jones, *Greek-English Lexicon*
MÉFRA	*Mélanges de l'École française de Rome, Antiquité*
NH	Pliny the Elder, *Natural History*
OLD	*Oxford Latin Dictionary*
RE	*Paulys Real-Encyclopädie der classischen Altertumswissenschaft.* Georg Wissowa, ed. (Stuttgart, 1893–)
REA	*Revue des études anciennes*
RM	*Mitteilungen des Deutschen Archäologischen Instituts, Römische Abteilung*
ZPE	*Zeitschrift für Papyrologie und Epigraphik*

Acidini Luchinat et al. 1997
Acidini Luchinat, Cristina, et al. 1997. *Magnificenza alla corte dei Medici: Arte a Firenze alla fine del Cinquecento.* 1997. Exh. cat., Florence, Museo degli Argenti, Palazzo Pitti. Milan: Electa.

Acosta-Hughes and Kosmetatou 2002
Acosta-Hughes, Benjamin, and Elizabeth Kosmetatou 2002. *New Poems Attributed to Posidippus: A Text in-Progress.* Milan: Center for Hellenic Studies.

Acosta-Hughes, Kosmetatou, and Baumbach 2004
Acosta-Hughes, Benjamin, Elizabeth Kosmetatou, and Manuel Baumbach, eds. 2004. *Labored in Papyrus Leaves: Perspectives on an Epigram Collection Attributed to Posidippus (P.Mil. Vogl. VIII 309).* Washington, DC: Center for Hellenic Studies.

Adam-Veleni 2011
Adam-Veleni, Polyxeni, ed. 2011. *Il dono di Dioniso: Mitologia del vino nell'Italia centrale (Molise) e nella Grecia del Nord (Macedonia)* / Το δωρο του Διονυσου: μυθολογια του κρασιου στην κεντρικη Ιταλια *(Molise)* και τη βορεια Ελλαδα *(*Μακεδονια*)* / *The Gift of Dionysos: Mythology of Wine in Central Italy (Molise) and Northern Greece (Macedonia).* Exh. cat. Thessalonike: Archaiologiko Mousseio Thessalonikes.

Adams 2011
Adams, Noël. 2011. "The Garnet Millennium: The Role of Seal Stones in Garnet Studies." In Entwistle and Adams 2011, 10–24.

Ager 2006
Ager, Sheila L. 2006. "The Power of Excess: Royal Incest and the Ptolemaic Dynasty." *Anthropologica* 48, no. 2: 165–86.

Aillagon 2008
Aillagon, Jean-Jacques, ed. 2008. *Rome and the Barbarians: The Birth of a New World.* Exh. cat., Venice, Palazzo Grassi. Milan: Skira.

Alcouffe 1984
Alcouffe, Daniel. 1984. "Classical, Byzantine and Western Hardstone-Carving." In *The Treasury of San Marco, Venice*, edited by David Buckton, 73–108. Exh. cat., New York, Metropolitan Museum of Art. Milan: Olivetti.

Alcouffe 2001
Alcouffe, Daniel. 2001. *Les gemmes de la Couronne.* Exh. cat. Paris, Musée du Louvre. Paris: Réunion des Musées Nationaux.

Alcouffe 2003
Alcouffe, Daniel, ed. 2003. *Les vases en pierres dures: Actes du colloque organisé au Musée du Louvre par le Service culturel le 9 juin 2001.* Paris: Documentation française.

Alcouffe et al. 1991
Alcouffe, Daniel, et al. 1991. *Le trésor de Saint-Denis.* Exh. cat., Paris, Musée du Louvre. Paris: Réunion des Musées Nationaux.

Aleshire 1989
Aleshire, Sara B. 1989. *The Athenian Asklepieion: The People, Their Dedications, and the Inventories.* Amsterdam: J. C. Gieben.

Alfaro and Karali 2008
Alfaro, Carmen, and L. Karali, eds. 2008. *Purpureae Vestes II: Vestidos, textiles y tintes; estudios sobre la producción de bienes de consumo en la Antigüedad; actas del II Symposium Internacional sobre textiles y tintes del Mediterráneo en el mundo antiguo.* Valencia: Universitat de València.

Alfaro, Wild, and Costa 2004
Alfaro Giner, Carmen, John Peter Wild, and Benjami Costa, eds. 2004. *Purpureae vestes: Actas del I Symposium Internacional sobre Textiles y Tintes del Mediterráneo en Época Romana.* Valencia: Universitat de València.

Amandry 1939
Amandry, Pierre. 1939. "Rapport préliminaire sur les statues chryséléphantines de Delphes." *BCH* 63: 86–119.

Amandry 1946–48
Amandry, Pierre. 1946–48. "Naiskos de la collection H. Stathatos." *Annuario della Scuola archeologica di Atene e missioni italiane in Oriente* 24–26: 181–98.

Amandry 1953
Amandry, Pierre. 1953. *Collection Hélène Stathatos: Les bijoux antiques.* Strasbourg: Institut d'Archéologie de l'Université.

Amandry 1977
Amandry, Pierre. 1977. "Statue de taureau en argent." *Études delphiques* (*BCH* Suppl. 4): 273–93.

Amandry 1991
Amandry, Pierre. 1991. "Les fosses de l'Aire." In *Guide de Delphes: Le musée*, 191–226. Paris: École Française d'Athènes.

Ampolo 1984
Ampolo, Carmine. 1984. "Il lusso funerario e la città archaica." *Annali dell'Istituo universitario orientali di Napoli (AION)* 6: 71–102.

André-Salvini 1999
André-Salvini, Béatrice. 1999. "L'idéologie des pierres en Mésopotamie." In Caubet 1999, 273–93.

Andrianou 2006a
Andrianou, Dimitra. 2006. "Chairs, Beds, and Tables: Evidence for Furnished Interiors in Hellenistic Greece." *Hesperia* 75: 219–66.

Andrianou 2006b
Andrianou, Dimitra. 2006. "Late Classical and Hellenistic Furniture and Furnishings in the Epigraphical Record." *Hesperia* 75: 561–84.

Andrianou 2009
Andrianou, Dimitra. 2009. *The Furniture and Furnishings of Ancient Greek Houses and Tombs.* New York: Cambridge University Press.

Andronicos 1984
Andronicos, Manolis. 1984. *Vergina: The Royal Tombs and the Ancient City.* Athens: Ekdotike Athenon.

Appadurai 1986
Appadurai, Arjun. 1986. *The Social Life of Things: Commodities in Cultural Perspective.* Cambridge: Cambridge University Press.

Arensberg 1977
Arensberg, Susan Macmillan. 1977. "Dionysos: A Late Antique Tapestry." *Boston Museum Bulletin* 75: 4–25.

Artamonov 1969
Artamonov, Mikhail Illarionovich. 1969. *Treasures from Scythian Tombs in the Hermitage Museum, Leningrad.* London: Thames & Hudson.

Aruz, Graff, and Rakic 2014
Aruz, Joan, Sarah B. Graff, and Yelena Rakic, eds. 2014. *Assyria to Iberia at the Dawn of the Classical Age.* Exh. cat. New York: Metropolitan Museum of Art.

Asaka and Iorio 2005
Asaka, T., and V. Iorio. 2005. "'. . . lucroque India admota est': Contatti tra l'India e l'area vesuviana." In *Omni pede stare: Saggi architettonici e circumvesuviani in memoriam Jos de Waele*, edited by Stephan T. A. M. Mols and Eric M. Moormann, 325–30. Naples: Electa Napoli.

Aßkamp 2007
Aßkamp, Rudolf, ed. 2007. *Luxus und Dekadenz: Römisches Leben am Golf von Neapel.* Exh. cat., multiple venues. Mainz: Philipp von Zabern.

Austin and Bastianini 2002
Austin, Colin, and Guido Bastianini, eds. 2002. *Posidippi Pellaei Quae Supersunt Omnia.* 2nd ed. Milan: LED (Edizioni Universitarie di Lettere Economia Diritto for the University of Milan).

Avisseau-Broustet 1996
Avisseau-Broustet, M. 1996. "Coupe des Ptolémées." In *Trésors de la Bibliothéque nationale de France*, vol. 1, edited by M.-H. Tesnière, 55. Paris: Bibliothèque nationale de France.

Babelon 1916
Babelon, Ernest. 1916. *Le trésor d'argenterie de Berthouville, près Bernay (Eure) conservé au Département des médailles et antiques de la Bibliothèque nationale.* Paris: Librairie Centrale des Beaux-Arts.

Baldini and Guaitoli 2009
Baldini Lippolis, Isabella, and Maria Teresa Guaitoli, eds. 2009. *Oreficeria antica e medievale: Tecniche, produzione, società.* Ornamenta 1. Bologna: Ante quem.

Baldini and Morelli 2011
Baldini Lippolis, Isabella, and Anna Lina Morelli, eds. 2011. *Oggetti-Simbolo: Produzione, uso e significato nel mondo antico.* Ornamenta 3. Bologna: Ante quem.

Baldini and Morelli 2012
Baldini, Isabella, and Anna Lina Morelli, eds. 2012. *Luoghi, artigiani e modi di produzione nell'oreficeria antica.* Ornamenta 4. Bologna: Ante quem.

Ball 1950
Ball, Sydney H. 1950. *A Roman Book on Precious Stones Including an English Modernization of the 37th Booke of the Historie of the World by C. Plinius Secundus.* Los Angeles: Gemological Institute of America.

Balty 1977
Balty, Jean-Charles. 1977. "Tryphe." In *LIMC* 8: 96–97.

Baratte 1978
Baratte, François. 1978. "L'ingots d'or et d'argent en rapport avec l'atelier de Sirmium." *Sirmium* 8: 99–111.

Baratte 1984
Baratte, François. 1984. *Römisches Silbergeschirr in den gallischen und germanischen Provinzen.* Stuttgart: Gesellschaft für Vor- und Frühgeschichte in Württemberg und Hohenzollern.

Baratte 1985
Baratte, François. 1985. "À propos de la vaisselle d'argent romain: Valeur métallique, valeur artistique." *Bulletin de la Societé française de Numismatique* 50: 625–29.

Baratte 1986
Baratte, François. 1986. *Le trésor d'orfèvrerie romaine de Boscoreale.* Paris: Réunion des Musées Nationaux.

Baratte 1988
Baratte, François. 1988. "The Treasure of Boscoreale." In *Il Tesoro di Boscoreale: Una collezione di argenti da mensa tra cultura ellenistica e mondo romano,* 27–32. Exh. cat., Casina dell'Aquila, Pompeii. Milan: Franco Maria Ricci.

Baratte 1991
Baratte, François. 1991. "Arts précieux et propagande impériale au début de l'Empire romain: L'example des deux coupes de Boscoreale." *Revue du Louvre* 1: 24–40.

Baratte 1992
Baratte, François. 1992. "Les trésors de temples dans le monde romain: Une expression particulière de la piété." In *Ecclesiastical Silver Plate in Sixth-Century Byzantium: Papers of the Symposium Held May 16–18, 1986 at The Walters Art Gallery, Baltimore, and Dumbarton Oaks, Washington, D.C.,* edited by Susan A. Boyd and Marlia Mundell Mango, 111–21. Washington, DC: Dumbarton Oaks Research Library and Collection.

Baratte 1998a
Baratte, François. 1998. *Silbergeschirr, Kultur und Luxus in der römischen Gesellschaft.* 15. Trierer Winckelmannsprogramm. Mainz: Philipp von Zabern.

Baratte 1998b
Baratte, François. 1998. "Il tesoro di Marengo." In Mercando 1998, 369–80.

Baratte and Painter 1989
Baratte, François, and Kenneth Painter, eds. 1989. *Trésors d'orfèvrerie gallo-romains.* Exh. cat. Paris, Musée du Luxembourg; Lyon, Musée de la Civilasation Galloe Romaine. Paris: Éditions de la Réunion des Musées Nationaux.

Barber 1991
Barber, E. J. W. 1991. *Prehistoric Textiles.* Princeton: Princeton University Press.

Barber 1992
Barber, E. J. W. 1992. "The Peplos of Athena." In *Goddess and Polis: The Panathenaic Festival in Ancient Athens,* edited by Jenifer Neils, 103–17. Exh. cat. Hanover, NH: Hood Museum of Art, Dartmouth College; Princeton: Princeton University Press.

Barbera et al. 2010
Barbera, Mariarosaria, Salvo Barrano, Giacomo De Cola, Silvia Festuccia, Luca Giovannetti, Oberdan Menghi, and Manola Pales. 2010. "La villa di Caligola: Un nuovo settore degli *Horti Lamiani* scoperto sotto la sede dell'ENPAM a Roma." *Fasti Online Documents & Research.* www.fastionline.org/docs/FOLDER-it-2010-194.pdf.

Barnett 1982
Barnett, Richard D. 1982. *Ancient Ivories in the Middle East and Adjacent Countries. Qedem* 14. Jerusalem: Institute of Archaeology, Hebrew University of Jerusalem.

Barr-Sharrar 1993
Barr-Sharrar, Beryl. 1993. "A Silver Triton Handle in the Getty Museum." *Studia Varia from the J. Paul Getty Museum* 1 (*Occasional Papers on Antiquities* 8): 99–106.

Basu 2010
Basu, Chandreyi. 2010. "The Heavily Ornamented Female Figure from Pompeii." In *Il fascino dell'Oriente nelle collezioni e nei musei d'Italia,* edited by Beatrice Palma Venetucci, 59–63. Rome: Artemide.

Baughan 2013
Baughan, Elizabeth P. 2013. *Couched in Death: Klinai and Identity in Anatolia and Beyond.* Madison: University of Wisconsin Press.

Beard 2003
Beard, Mary. 2003. "Mrs. Arthur Strong, Morelli, and the Troopers of Cortés." In *Ancient Art and Its Historiography*, edited by Alice A. Donohue and Mark D. Fullerton, 148–70. Cambridge: Cambridge University Press.

Beard 2007
Beard, Mary. 2007. *The Roman Triumph.* Cambridge, MA: Belknap Press of Harvard University Press.

Beazley 1920 (2002 ed.)
Beazley, John Davidson. 2002. *The Lewes House Collection of Ancient Gems* [Now at the Museum of Fine Arts, Boston]. Edited by John Boardman. Revised reprint of 1920 ed. BAR International Series 1074. Oxford: Archaeopress.

Becatti 1955
Becatti, Giovanni. 1955. *Oreficerie antiche dalle minoiche alle barbariche.* Rome: Instituto Poligrafico dello Stato.

Beckwith 1954
Beckwith, John. 1954. "Textile Fragments from Classical Antiquity: An Important Find at Koropi, near Athens." *Illustrated London News* 224 (January 23): 114–15.

Belozerskaya 2005
Belozerskaya, Marina. 2005. *Luxury Arts of the Renaissance.* Los Angeles: JPGM.

Belozerskaya 2006
Belozerskaya, Marina. 2006. *The Medici Giraffe and Other Tales of Exotic Animals and Power.* New York: Little, Brown.

Belozerskaya 2012
Belozerskaya, Marina. 2012. *Medusa's Gaze: The Extraordinary Journey of the Tazza Farnese.* Oxford: Oxford University Press.

Beltrán Lloris 1984
Beltrán Lloris, Miguel. 1984. "El retrato de 'Divus Augustus' del Municipium Turiaso (Tarazona, Zaragosa): Un palimpsesto de época Trajanea." *Madrider Mitteilungen* 25: 103–34.

Bendinelli 1937
Bendinelli, Goffredo. 1937. *Il tesoro di argenteria di Marengo.* Turin: Vincenzo Bona.

Benson 1991
Benson, Carol A. 1991. "Ancient Ornaments of Beaten Gold." *Ornament* 15, no. 1 (September): 56–59.

Bent 1885
Bent, J. Theodore. 1885. "On the Gold and Silver Mines of Siphnos." *Journal of Hellenic Studies* 6: 195–98.

Bernard 1970
Bernard, Paul. 1970. "Sièges et lits en ivoire d'époque hellenistique en Asie centrale." *Syria* 47: 327–43.

Bernhardt 2003
Bernhardt, Rainer. 2003. *Luxuskritik und Aufwandsbeschränkungen in der griechischen Welt.* Historia Einzelschrift 168. Stuttgart: Steiner.

Berry 1994
Berry, Christopher J. 1994. *The Idea of Luxury: A Conceptual and Historical Investigation.* Cambridge: Cambridge University Press.

Bing 2005
Bing, Peter. 2005. "The Politics and Poetics of Geography in the Milan Posidippus, Section One: On Stones (AB 1–20)." In *The New Posidippus: A Hellenistic Poetry Book*, edited by Kathryn Guzwiller, 119–40. Oxford: Oxford University Press.

Bispham, Harrison, and Sparkes 2006
Bispham, Edward, Thomas Harrison, and Brian A. Sparkes. 2006. *The Edinburgh Companion to Ancient Greece and Rome*. Edinburgh: Edinburgh University Press.

Bluhm et al. 1996
Bluhm, Andreas, et al. 1996. *The Colour of Sculpture, 1840–1910*. Exh. cat., Amsterdam, Van Gogh Museum; Leeds, Henry Moore Institute. Zwolle: Waanders.

Blümner 1905
Blümner, H. 1905. "Elfenbein." In *RE*, vol. 5, part 2: 2356–66.

Boardman 1968a
Boardman, John. 1968. *Archaic Greek Gems: Schools and Artists in the Sixth and Early Fifth Centuries B.C.* Evanston, IL: Northwestern University Press.

Boardman 1968b
Boardman, John. 1968. *Engraved Gems: The Ionides Collection*. London: Thames and Hudson.

Boardman 1969
Boardman, John. 1969. "Three Greek Gem Masters." *Burlington Magazine* 111, no. 799 (October): 587–96.

Boardman 1970
Boardman, John. 1970. *Greek Gems and Finger Rings*. London: Thames and Hudson. 2nd ed., 2001.

Boardman 1975
Boardman, John. 1975. *Intaglios and Rings: Greek, Etruscan, and Eastern from a Private Collection.* London: Thames and Hudson.

Boardman 1978
Boardman, John. 1978. *Greek Sculpture: The Archaic Period*. London: Thames and Hudson.

Boardman 1993
Boardman, John, ed. 1993. *The Oxford History of Classical Art*. Oxford: Oxford University Press.

Boardman 1996
Boardman, John. 1996. *Greek Art*. 4th ed. London: Thames and Hudson.

Boardman 1997
Boardman, John. 1997. "Classical Gems and Media Interaction." In Brown 1997, 13–21.

Boardman et al. 2009
Boardman, John, et al. 2009. *The Marlborough Gems Formerly at Blenheim Palace, Oxfordshire.* Oxford: Oxford University Press.

Boardman and Vollenweider 1978
Boardman, John, and Marie-Louise Vollenweider. 1978. *Catalogue of the Engraved Gems and Finger Rings in the Ashmolean Museum.* Vol. 1, *Greek and Etruscan*. Oxford: Clarendon Press.

Boardman and Wagner 2012
Boardman, John, and Claudia Wagner. 2012. "Luxury Arts." In T. Smith and Plantzos 2012, vol. 1: 200–220.

Boetzkes and Stein 1997
Boetzkes, Manfred, and Helga Stein, eds. 1997. *Der Hildesheimer Silberfund: Original und Nachbildung; vom Römerschatz zum Bürgerstolz.* Hildesheim: Gerstenberg.

Borromeo 1993
Borromeo, Georgina E. 1993. "Roman Small-Scale Portrait Busts." PhD diss., Brown University, Providence, RI.

Borza and Palagia 2007
Borza, Eugene N., and Olga Palagia. 2007. "The Chronology of the Royal Macedonian Tombs at Vergina." *JdI* 122: 81–125.

von Bothmer 1962
von Bothmer, Dietrich. 1962. "A Gold Libation Bowl." *Bulletin of the Metropolitan Museum of Art*, n.s., 21: 154–66.

von Bothmer 1984
von Bothmer, Dietrich. 1984. "A Greek and Roman Treasury." *Bulletin of the Metropolitan Museum of Art*, n.s., 42.

Boussac 1988
Boussac, Marie-Françoise. 1988. "Sceaux déliens." *Revue archéologique* 1, no. 2: 307–40.

Boussac 1992
Boussac, Marie-Françoise. 1992. *Les sceaux de Délos / Τα Σφραγισματα της Δηλου*. Vol. 1. Paris: Boccard.

Bowe 2004
Bowe, Patrick. 2004. *Gardens of the Roman World.* Los Angeles: JPGM.

Breck 1927
Breck, Joseph. 1927. "The Ficoroni Medallion and Some Other Gilded Glasses in the Metropolitan Museum of Art." *Art Bulletin* 9, no. 4 (June): 353–56.

Breglia 1941
Breglia, Laura. 1941. *Catalogo delle oreficerie del Museo Nazionale di Napoli.* Rome: Libreria dello Stato.

Briant 2002
Briant, Pierre. 2002. "History and Ideology: The Greeks and 'Persian Decadence.'" In *Greeks and Barbarians,* edited by Thomas Harrison, 193–210. New York: Routledge.

Brinkmann, Primavesi, and Hollein 2010
Brinkmann, Vinzenz, Oliver Primavesi, and Max Hollein, eds. 2010. *Circumlitio: The Polychromy of Antique and Mediaeval Sculpture.* Frankfurt: Schriftenreihe der Liebieghaus Skulpturensammlung.

Bromehead 1952
Bromehead, C. E. N. 1952. "What Was Murrhine?" *Antiquity* 26, no. 102: 65–70.

Bron 1985
Bron, Ch. 1985. "Les ivoires sculptées d'Avenches." *Bulletin de l'Association pro Aventico* 29: 27–47.

Brøns 2014
Brøns, Cecilie. 2014. "Gods and Garments: Textiles in Greek Sanctuaries in the 7th–1st Centuries B.C." PhD diss., University of Copenhagen.

Brown 1997
Brown, Clifford M., ed. 1997. *Engraved Gems: Survivals and Revivals.* Studies in the History of Art 54. Washington, DC: National Gallery of Art.

Bruce 2014
Bruce, Will. 2014. "Gold Refining and Religious Cult in Lydian and Achaemenid Sardis." In *Archaeological Institute of America. 115th Annual Meeting Abstracts. January 2–5, 2014, Chicago, Illinois,* 20. Boston.

Bruneau 1969
Bruneau, Philippe. 1969. "Documents sur l'industrie Délienne de la Pourpre." *BCH* 93: 759–91.

Bühler 1973
Bühler, Hans-Peter. 1973. *Antike Gefäße aus Edelsteinen.* Mainz: Philipp von Zabern.

Buitron and Oliver 1985
Buitron, Diana, and Andrew Oliver. 1985. "Greek, Etruscan, and Roman Ivories." In Richard H. Randall et al., *Masterpieces of Ivory from the Walters Art Gallery,* 54–79. New York: Hudson Hills Press.

Buttrey 2007
Buttrey, T. V. 2007. "Domitian, the Rhinoceros, and the Date of Martial's *Liber De Spectaculis*." *JRS* 97: 101–12.

Cahn 1960
Cahn, Herbert A. 1960. "Die Gewichte der Goldgefässe." *Antike Kunst* 3: 26.

Cahn and Kaufmann-Heinimann 1984
Cahn, Herbert A., and Annemarie Kaufmann-Heinimann, eds. 1984. *Der spätrömische Silberschatz von Kaiseraugst.* Derendigen: Habegger.

Calabi Limentani 1958a
Calabi Limentani, I. 1958. "*Argentarius.*" In *EAA*, vol. 1: 619–21.

Calabi Limentani 1958b
Calabi Limentani, I. 1958. "*Aurifex.*" In *EAA*, vol. 1: 930–32.

Calabi Limentani 1959
Calabi Limentani, I. 1959. "*Caelator.*" In *EAA,* vol. 2: 250–52.

Calabi Limentani 1960
Calabi Limentani, I. 1960. "*Gemmarius.*" In *EAA*, vol. 3: 808–9.

Calabi Limentani 1961
Calabi Limentani, I. 1961. "*Margaritarius.*" In *EAA*, vol. 4: 832–33.

Calandra 2011
Calandra, Elena. 2011. *The Ephemeral and the Eternal: The Pavilion of Ptolemy Philadelphos in the Court of Alexandria.* Athens: Scuola Archeologica Italiana di Atene.

Caley 2008
Caley, Earle Radcliffe. 2008. *The Leyden and Stockholm Papyri: Greco-Egyptian Chemical Documents from the Early 4th Century AD.* Edited by William B. Jensen. Cincinnati: Oesper Collections in the History of Chemistry.

Caley and Richards 1956
Caley, Earle Radcliffe, and John F. C. Richards, trans. and eds. 1956. *Theophrastus On Stones.* Columbus: Ohio State University.

Callataÿ 1989
Callataÿ, François de. 1989. "Les trésors achéménides et les monnayages d'Alexandre: Espèces immobilisées et espèces circulantes?" *REA* 91: 259–74.

Calvi 2005
Calvi, Maria Carina. 2005. *Le ambre romane di Aquileia.* Aquileia: Associazione Nazionale per Aquileia.

Cardon 2007
Cardon, Dominique. 2007. *Natural Dyes: Sources, Tradition, Technology and Science.* Translated by Caroline Higgitt. London: Archetype.

Carducci 1969
Carducci, Carlo. 1969. *Gold and Silver Treasures of Ancient Italy.* London: Abbey Library.

Carey 2000
Carey, Sorcha. 2000. "The Problem of Totality: Collecting Greek Art, Wonders and Luxury in Pliny the Elder's *Natural History.*" *Journal of the History of Collections* 12, no. 1: 1–13.

D. Carroll 1970
Carroll, Diane Lee. 1970. "A Group of Asymmetrical Spiral-Form Earrings." *AJA* 74: 37–42.

M. Carroll 2003
Carroll, Maureen. 2003. *Earthly Paradises: Ancient Gardens in History and Archaeology.* Los Angeles: JPGM.

Carter 1985
Carter, Jane Burr. 1985. *Greek Ivory-Carving in the Orientalizing and Archaic Periods.* New York: Garland.

Casazza 2008
Casazza, Ornella, ed. 2008. *Il cammeo Gonzaga: Arti preziose alla corte di Mantova.* Exh. cat., Mantua, Fruttiere di Palazzo Te. Milan: Skira.

Caskey 1922
C[askey], L[acey] D[avis]. 1922. "A Votive Offering of the Kypselids." *Museum of Fine Arts Bulletin* (Boston) 20, no. 122: 65–68.

Caskey 1926
C[askey], L[acey] D[avis]. 1926. "Note on the Kypselid Bowl." *Bulletin of the Museum of Fine Arts* (Boston) 24, no. 143: 50–51.

Casson 1926
Casson, Stanley. 1926. *Macedonia, Thrace and Illyria: Their Relations to Greece from the Earliest Times to the Time of Philip, Son of Amyntas.* Oxford: Oxford University Press.

Castiglione 2006
Castiglione, Marianna. 2006. "*In argento plane studiosus sum:* Un'esibizione di privata *luxuria.*" In Guzzo 2006a, 45–59.

Caubet 1989
Caubet, Annie. 1989. "Pygmalion et la statue d'ivoire." In *Architecture et poésie dans le monde grec: Hommage à George Roux,* edited by Roland Étienne et al., 247–54. Lyon: Maison de l'Orient.

Caubet 1999
Caubet, Annie, ed. 1999. *Cornaline et pierres précieuses: La Méditerranée, de l'Antiquité á l'Islam; Actes du colloque organisé au Musée du Louvre par le Service culturel les 24 et 25 novembre 1995.* Paris: Documentation française.

Causey 2011
Causey, Faya. 2011. *Amber and the Ancient World.* Los Angeles: JPGM.

Cauuet 1999
Cauuet, Béatrice, ed. 1999. *L'or dans l'antiquité: De la mine à l'objet.* Aquitania suppl. 9. France: Ministère de la Culture et de la Communication.

Chankowski 2011
Chankowski, Véronique. 2011. "Divine Financiers: Cults as Consumers and Generators of Value." In *The Economies of Hellenistic Societies, Third to First Centuries BC,* edited by Zosia H. Archibald, John K. Davies, and Vincent Gabrielsen, 142–65. Oxford: Oxford University Press.

Chkonia and Lordkipanidze 2007
Chkonia, Ana, and Nino Lordkipanidze. 2007. *Medeas Gold: Neue Funde aus Georgien.* Exh. cat., Tiflis, Georgisches Nationalmuseum; Antikensammlung, Staatlichen Museen zu Berlin. Tiflis: Georgisches Nationalmuseum.

Ciarallo and De Carolis 1999
Ciarallo, Annamaria, and Ernesto De Carolis, eds. 1999. *Pompeii: Life in a Roman Town.* Exh. cat., Los Angeles County Mseum of Art. Milan: Electa.

Cicirelli 1993
Cicirelli, Caterina. 1993. *Mulierum ornamenta: Ori e gemme dalle ceneri del Vesuvio.* Exh. cat., Torre del Greco, Palazzo Vallelonga. Torre del Greco: Banca di Credito Popolare.

Cima and La Rocca 1986
Cima, Maddalena, and Eugenio La Rocca, eds. 1986. *Le tranquille dimore degli dei: La residenza imperiale degli horti Lamiani.* Exh. cat., Rome, Campidoglio, Palazzo dei Conservatori. Venice: Cataloghi Marsilio.

Cima and Talamo 2008
Cima, Maddalena, and Emilia Talamo. 2008. *Gli horti di Roma antica.* Milan: Electa.

Cimok 2000
Cimok, Fatih, ed. 2000. *Antioch Mosaics: A Corpus.* Istanbul: A Turızm Yayınlari.

Clark 1986
Clark, Grahame. 1986. *Symbols of Excellence: Precious Materials as Expressions of Status.* Cambridge: Cambridge University Press.

Cleland 2005
Cleland, Liza. 2005. *The Brauron Clothing Catalogues: Text, Analysis, Glossary and Translation.* BAR International Series 1428. Oxford: John and Erica Hedges.

Coarelli 1970
Coarelli, Filippo. 1970. *Greek and Roman Jewellery.* London: Hamlyn.

Coldstream 1977
Coldstream, J. N. 1977. *Geometric Greece.* London: E. Benn.

Collareta 1995
Collareta, Marco. 1995. "L'historien et la technique: Sur le rôle de l'orfèvrerie dans les *Vite* de Vasari." In *Histoire de l'histoire de l'art: Cycles de conférences organisés au Musée du Louvre par le Service culturel,* edited by Edouard Pommier, vol. 1: *De l'antiquité au XVIIIe siècle,* 165–76. Paris: Musée du Louvre.

Collon 1997
Collon, Dominique, ed. 1997. *7000 Years of Seals.* London: British Museum.

Connor 1998
Connor, Carolyn L. 1998. *The Color of Ivory: Polychromy on Byzantine Ivories.* Princeton: Princeton University Press.

Conophagos 1980
Conophagos, Constantin Elia. 1980. *Le Laurium antique et la technique grecque de la production de l'argent.* Athens: Ekdotike Hellados.

Cook 1997
Cook, Robert Manuel. 1997. *Greek Painted Pottery.* 3rd ed. London: Routledge.

A. Cooley and M. Cooley 2004
Cooley, Alison, and M. G. L. Cooley. 2004. *Pompeii: A Sourcebook.* London: Routledge.

Cooney 1965
Cooney, J. D. 1965. "A Perfume Flask from Antiquity." *Bulletin of the Cleveland Museum of Art* 52: 45–46.

Cormack 2007
Cormack, Sarah. 2007. "The Tombs at Pompeii." In *The World of Pompeii,* edited by John Joseph Dobbins and Pedar William Foss, 585–606. London: Routledge.

Cozzoli 1980
Cozzoli, Umberto. 1980. "La τρυφή nella interpretazione delle crisi politiche." In *Tra Grecia e Roma: Temi antichi e metodologie moderne,* edited by Massimiliano Pavan, 133–45. Rome: Istituto della Enciclopedia italiana.

Cutler 1985
Cutler, Anthony. 1985. *The Craft of Ivory. Sources Techniques, and Uses in the Mediterraean World: A.D. 200–1400.* Washington, DC: Dumbarton Oaks, Research Library and Collection.

Cutler 1987
Cutler, Anthony. 1987. "Prolegomena to the Craft of Ivory Carving in Late Antiquity and the Early Middle Ages." In *Artistes, artisans et production artistique au Moyen Age,* edited by Xavier Barral i Altet, vol. 2, 431–75. Paris: Picard.

Cutler 1994
Cutler, Anthony. 1994. "Uses of Luxury: On the Function of Consumption and Symbolic Value in Byzantine Culture." In *Byzance et les images: Cycle de conferences organisé au Musée du Louvre par le Service culturel du 5 octobre à 7 décembre 1992,* edited by André Guillou and Jannic Durand, 287–327. Paris: Documentation française.

Dacos, Giuliano, and Pannuti 1973
Dacos, Nicole, Antonio Giuliano, and Ulrico Pannuti. 1973. *Il tesoro di Lorenzo il Magnifico.* Vol. 1, *Le gemme.* Exh. cat., Florence, Palazzo Medici Riccardi. Florence: Sansoni.

Dahmen 2001
Dahmen, Karsten. 2001. *Untersuchungen zu Form und Funktion kleinformatiger Porträts der römischen Kaiserzeit.* Münster: Scriptorium.

Dalby 2000
Dalby, Andrew. 2000. *Empire of Pleasures: Luxury and Indulgence in the Roman World.* London: Routledge.

D'Ambrosio and De Carolis 1997
D'Ambrosio, Antonio, and Ernesto De Carolis. 1997. *I monili dall'area vesuviana.* Ministero per i Beni culturali ed ambientali, Soprintendenza Archeologica di Pompei, cataloghi 6. Rome: "L'Erma" di Bretschneider.

Dari-Mattiacci and Plisecka (2010) 2012
Dari-Mattiacci, Giuseppe, and Anna E. Plisecka. 2012. "Luxury in Ancient Rome: Scope, Timing

and Enforcement of Sumptuary Laws" (November 22, 2010). *Legal Roots*, vol. 1 (2012). Amsterdam Center for Law & Economics Working Paper No. 2010-03. Available at SSRN: http://ssrn.com/abstract=1616712.

Dasen 2011
Dasen, Véronique. 2011. "Magic and Medicine: Gems and the Power of Seals." In Entwistle and Adams 2011, 69–74.

Daumas 1956
Daumas, François. 1956. "La valeur de l'or dans la pensée égyyptienne." *Revue de l'histoire des religions* 149: 1–17.

Davidson 1998
Davidson, James N. 1998. *Courtesans and Fishcakes: The Consuming Passions of Classical Athens.* Hammersmith, London: Fontana Press.

J. Davies 2007
Davies, John K. 2007. "The Phokian Hierosylia at Delphi: Quantities and Consequences." In *Corolla Cosmo Rodewald* (*Akanthina* 2), edited by Nick Sekunda, 75–96. Gdansk: Foundation for the Development of Gdansk University.

O. Davies 1935
Davies, Oliver. 1935. *Roman Mines in Europe.* Oxford: Clarendon Press.

De Angeli 1992
De Angeli, Stefano. 1992. *Templum divi Vespasiani.* Rome: De Luca.

De Caro 1994
De Caro, Stefano. 1994. *Il Museo Archeologico Nazionale di Napoli.* Naples: Electa Napoli.

De Caro 2006
De Caro, Stefano, ed. 2006. *Egittomania: Iside e il mistero.* Exh. cat., Museo Archeologico Nazionale di Napoli. Milan: Electa.

De Carolis 2007
De Carolis, Ernesto. 2007. *Il mobile a Pompei ed Ercolano: Letti, tavoli, sedie e armadi.* Rome: "L'Erma" di Bretschneider.

De Juliis 1984
De Juliis, Ettore M. 1984. *Gli ori di Taranto in età ellenistica.* Exh. cat., Milan, Brera 2. Milan: A. Mondadori.

De Juliis and Loiacono 1985
De Juliis, Ettore M., and E. Loiacono. 1985. *Taranto: Il Museo Archeologico.* Taranto: Mandese.

Del Bufalo 2012
Del Bufalo, Dario. 2012. *Porphyry. Red Imperial Porphyry: Power and Religion.* Turin: Umberto Allemandi.

Dentzer 1962
Dentzer, J.-M. 1962. "La tombe de C. Vestorius Priscus dans la tradition de la peinture italique." *MÉFRA* 74: 533–94.

Deppert-Lippitz 1985
Deppert-Lippitz, Barbara. 1985. *Griechischer Goldschmuck.* Mainz: Philipp von Zabern.

Deppert-Lippitz 1992
Deppert-Lippitz, Barbara. 1992. "Three Early Byzantine Ornaments." *Muse: Annual of the Museum of Art and Archaeology, University of Missouri-Columbia* 26: 46–52.

Deppert-Lippitz 1993a
Deppert-Lippitz, Barbara. 1993. "A Group of Late Antique Jewelry in the Getty Museum." *Studia Varia from the J. Paul Getty Museum* 1 (*Occasional Papers on Antiquities* 8): 107–40.

Deppert-Lippitz 1993b
Deppert-Lippitz, Barbara. 1993. "L'opus interrasile des orfevres romains." In *Outils et ateliers d'orfèvres des temps anciens*, edited by Christiane Eluère, 69–72. Antiquités nationales, Mémoire 2. Saint-Germain-en-Laye: Société des Amis du Musée des Antiquités nationales.

D'Ercole 2008
D'Ercole, Maria Cecilia. 2008. *Ambres gravés du département des monnaies, médailles et antiques.* Paris: Bibliothèque nationale de France.

De Ridder 1924
De Ridder, André. 1924. *Musée national du Louvre: Catalogue sommaire des bijoux antiques.* Paris: Musées nationaux.

Despini 1996
Despini, Aikaterini. 1996. *Greek Art: Ancient Gold Jewellery.* Athens: Ekdotike Athenon.

Devoto 2003
Devoto, Guido. 2003. "Tecniche di lavorazione glittica nell'antichità e diagnosi micromorfoscopica (exoscopia) delle gemme incise." In Zanettin 2003, 343–86.

Dickens 1906–7
Dickens, Guy. 1906–7. "Damophon of Messene, II." *BSA* 13: 357–404.

Dignas 2002
Dignas, Beate. 2002. "'Inventories' or 'Offering Lists'? Assessing the Wealth of Apollo Didymaeus." *ZPE* 138: 235–44.

Dittenberger 1920
Dittenberger, Wilhelm. 1920. *Sylloge inscriptionum Graecarum.* Vol. 3. 3rd ed. Leipzig: Hirzel.

Dodds 1951
Dodds, Eric Robertson. 1951. *The Greeks and the Irrational.* Berkeley: University of California Press.

Dodwell 1961
Dodwell, Charles Reginald, ed. 1961. *Theophilus: The Various Arts.* London: T. Nelson.

Dohrn 1965
Dohrn, Thomas. 1965. "Crustae." *RM* 72: 127–41.

Dolcini and Zanettin 1999
Dolcini, Loretta, and Bruno Zanettin, eds. 1999. *Cristalli e gemme: Realtà fisica e immaginario, simbologia, technique e arte.* Exh. cat., Venice, Palazzo Loredan. Venice: Istituto Veneto di Scienze, Lettere et Arti.

Domergue 2008
Domergue, Claude. 2008. *Les mines antiques: La production des métaux aux époques grecque et romaine.* Paris: Picard.

Donohue 1988
Donohue, Alice A. 1988. *Xoana and the Origins of Greek Sculpture.* Atlanta: Scholars Press.

Donohue 1995
Donohue, Alice A. 1995. "Winckelmann's History of Art and Polyclitus." In *Polykleitos, the Doryphoros, and Tradition*, edited by Warren G. Moon, 327–53. Madison: University of Wisconsin Press.

Doonan 1992
Doonan, Owen. 1992. "Gemma Augustea: A New Interpretation." *Revue des archéologues et historiens d'art de Louvain* 25: 25–30.

Doumeyrou 1989
Doumeyrou, Elisabeth. 1989. "An Ivory Fulcrum." *JPGMJ* 17: 5–14.

Drayman-Weisser 2000
Drayman-Weisser, Terry, ed. 2000. *Gilded Metals: History, Technology and Conservation.* London: Archetype.

Drogou 1987
Drogou, S. 1987. "To hyphasma tis Verginas: Protes paratiriseis." In *Ametos: Timetikos tomos gia ton kathegete Manole Androniko*, vol. 1, 303–22. Thessalonike: Aristoteleion Panepistemion Thessalonikes.

Dross-Krüpe and Paetz gen. Schieck 2014
Dross-Krüpe, Kerstin, and Paetz gen. Schieck, Annette. 2014. "Unravelling the Tangled Threads of Ancient Embroidery: A Compilation of Written Sources and Archaeologically Preserved Textiles." In *Greek and Roman Textiles and Dress: An Interdisciplinary Anthology*, edited by Mary Harlow and Marie-Louise Nosch. Oxford: Oxbow.

Dubois-Pelerin 2008
Dubois-Pelerin, Éva. 2008. *Le luxe privé à Rome et en Italie au Ier siècle après J.-C.* Naples: Centre Jean Bérard.

Eichholtz 1962
Eichholtz, D. E., trans. 1962. *Pliny, Natural History.* Vol. 10, *Libri XXXVI–XXXVII.* Cambridge, MA: Harvard University Press.

Eichholtz 1965
Eichholtz, D. E., trans. and ed. 1965. *Theophrastus: De lapidibus.* Oxford: Clarendon.

Elia 1957
Elia, Olga. 1957. "Le coppe ialine di Stabiae." *Bolletino d'arte* 42: 97–103.

Engelbach 1931
Engelbach, Reginald. 1931. "Recent Acquisitions in the Cairo Mueum, I, Set of Agate Vessels." *Annales du Service des Antiquités de l'Égypte* 31: 126–27.

Entwistle and Adams 2011
Entwistle, Christopher, and Noël Adams, eds. 2011. *"Gems of Heaven": Recent Research on Engraved Gemstones in Late Antiquity, c. AD 200–600.* British Museum Research Publications 177. London: British Museum.

Erskine 2013
Erskine, Andrew. 2013. "Hellenistic Parades and Roman Triumphs." In *Rituals of Triumph in the Mediterranean World*, edited by Anthony Spalinger and Jeremy Armstrong, 37–55. Leiden: Brill.

Esse 1992
Esse, Douglas L. 1992. "Phoenician and Greek Ivories in the Late Eighth Century B.C.: Some Common Ground." *AJA* 96: 339.

Evans 1898
Evans, Arthur J. 1898. "The Athenian Portrait-head by Dexamenos of Chios." *Revue archéologique* 32: 337–55.

Faraone 2001
Faraone, Christopher A. 2001. *Ancient Greek Love Magic.* Cambridge, MA: Harvard University Press.

Faraone 2011
Faraone, Christopher A. 2011. "Text, Image and Medium: The Evolution of Graeco-Roman Magical Gemstones." In Entwistle and Adams 2011, 50–61.

Faraone 2015
Faraone, Christopher A. 2015. "A Case of Cultural (Mis)translation? Egyptian Eyes on Two Greek Amulets for Opthalmia." In *Festschrift for Heinrich von Staden*, edited by B. Holmes et al. Forthcoming.

Fitton 1992
Fitton, J. Lesley, ed. 1992. *Ivory in Greece and the Eastern Mediterranean from the Bronze Age to the Hellenistic Period.* British Museum Occasional Paper 85. London: British Museum.

Flury-Lemberg 1988
Flury-Lemberg, Mechthild. 1988. *Textile Conservation and Research.* Bern: Abegg-Stiftung Bern.

Fontanella 2009
Fontanella, Elena, ed. 2009. *Luxus: Il piacere della vita nella Roma imperiale.* Exh. cat., Turin, Museo di Antichità. Rome: Istituto Poligrafico e Zecca dello Stato.

Frazer 1913
Frazer, J[ames] G[eorge], trans. 1913. *Pausanias's Description of Greece.* London: Macmillan.

Freyer-Schauenburg 1966
Freyer-Schauenburg, Brigitte. 1966. *Elfenbeine aus dem samischen Heraion.* 2nd ed. 6 vols. Hamburg: Cram, De Gruyter.

Frielinghaus 2011
Frielinghaus, Heide. 2011. *Die Helme von Olympia.* Olympische Forschungen 33. Berlin: De Gruyter.

Fuqua 2007
Fuqua, Charles. 2007. "Two Aspects of the *Lithika.*" *Classical Philology* 102: 281–91.

Fuqua 2008
Fuqua, Charles. 2008. "An Internal Ring Composition in Posidippus' *Lithika.*" *Classical World* 102: 3–12.

Furtwängler 1896
Furtwängler, Adolf. 1896. *Beschreibung der geschnittenen Steine im Antiquarium: Königliche Museen in Berlin.* Berlin: W. Spemann.

Furtwängler 1900
Furtwängler, Adolf. 1900. *Die Antiken Gemmen: Geschichte der Steinschneidekunst im klassischen Altertum.* 3 vols. Leipzig and Berlin: Giesecke & Devrient.

Gagetti 2004–5
Gagetti, Elisabetta. 2004–5. "'*. . . galeae gemmis radientur et auro*': Roman Visor Helmets with Gems." *Anodos: Studies of the Ancient World* 4–5: 79–92.

Gagetti 2006
Gagetti, Elisabetta. 2006. *Preziose sculture di età ellenistica e romana.* Milan: LED.

Gagetti 2007
Gagetti, Elisabetta. 2007. "*locum in deliciis . . . sucina optinent:* Le ambre di Aquileia e di Spalato." In *Le regioni di Aquileia e Spalato in epoca romana: Proceedings of the International Conference (Udine, 2006)*, edited by Maurizio Buora, 135–61. Udine: Castello.

Gagetti 2009
Gagetti, Elisabetta. 2009. "Ambra: Il puro gusto del lusso." In Fontanella 2009, 178–89.

Gagetti 2014
Gagetti, Elisabetta. 2014. "Transparente bellezza, oscure identità: Un ritratto rilavorato di dama in cristallo di rocca." In *Costantino il Grande a 1700 anni dall' "Editto di Milano": Atti della XLIV settimana di studi Aquileiesi 30 maggio–1 giugno 2013*, edited by Giuseppe Cuscito, 367–86. Antichità Altoadriatiche LXXVIII. Trieste: Editreg.

Gantz 1993
Gantz, Timothy. 1993. *Early Greek Myth.* Baltimore: Johns Hopkins University Press.

Garland 1989
Garland, Robert. 1989. "The Well-Ordered Corpse: An Investigation into the Motives behind Greek Funerary Legislation." *Bulletin of the Institute of Classical Studies* 36: 1–15.

Garrett and Kurke 1994
Garrett, Andrew, and Leslie Kurke. 1994. "Pudenda Asiae Minoris." *Harvard Studies in Classical Philology* 96: 75–83.

Gasparri 1975
Gasparri, Carlo. 1975. "A proposito di un recente studio sui vasi antichi in pietra dura." *Archeologia classica* 27: 350–77.

Gasparri 1979
Gasparri, Carlo. 1979. "Vasi antichi in pietra dura a Firenze e Roma." *Prospettiva* 19: 4–13.

Gasparri 1994
Gasparri, Carlo, ed. 1994. *Le gemme Farnese.* Naples: Electa Napoli.

Gasparri 2003
Gasparri, Carlo. 2003. "Vases antiques inédits en pierres dures." In Alcouffe 2003, 11–29.

Gehrig 1980
Gehrig, Ulrich. 1980. *Hildesheimer Silberschatz im Antikenmuseum.* Berlin: Staatliche Museen Preussicher Kulturbesitz.

Gennaioli 2010
Gennaioli, Riccardo, ed. 2010. *Pregio e bellezza: Cammei e intagli dei Medici.* Exh. cat., Florence, Museo degli Argenti, Palazzo Pitti. Livorno: Sillabe.

Gennaioli 2012
Gennaioli, Riccardo, ed. 2012. *Gems of the Medici.* Exh. cat., Houston Museum of Natural Science; Bowers Museum, Santa Ana, CA. Florence: Contemporanea Progetti.

Georgoula 1999
Georgoula, Electra, ed. 1999. *Greek Jewellery from the Benaki Museum Collections.* Athens: Adam Editions.

Gerring 2000
Gerring, Britta. 2000. *Sphragides: Die gravierten Fingerringe des Hellenismus.* Oxford: Archaeopress.

Gill 1992
Gill, David W. J. 1992. "The Ivory Trade." In Fitton 1992, 233–37.

Gill 2008
Gill, David W. J. 2008. "Inscribed Silver Plate from Tomb II at Vergina: Chronological Implications." *Hesperia* 77: 335–58.

Ginouvès 1994
Ginouvès, René. 1994. *Macedonia from Philip II to the Roman Conquest.* Princeton: Princeton University Press.

Giuliani and Schmidt 2010
Giuliani, Luca, and Gerhard Schmidt. 2010. *Ein Geschenk für den Kaiser: Das Geheimnis des grossen Kameo.* Munich: Beck.

Giuliano et al. 2003
Giuliano, Antonio, et al. 2003. *Il volto d'avorio: L'eccezionale recupero di un'opera trafugata.* Exh. cat., Parco della Musica, Auditorium Arte, Rome. Rome: "L'Erma" di Bretschneider.

Gleba 2008
Gleba, Margarita. 2008. "*Auratae Vestes*: Gold Textiles in the Ancient Mediterranean." In Alfaro and Karali 2008, 61–77.

Goff 1988
Goff, Barbara. 1988. "Euripides' *Ion* 1132–1165: The Tent." *Proceedings of the Cambridge Philological Society* 34 (January): 42–54.

Gordon 2011
Gordon, Richard. 2011. "Archaeologies of Magical Gems." In Entwistle and Adams 2011, 39–49.

R. Gorman and V. Gorman 2007
Gorman, Robert J., and Vanessa Gorman. 2007. "The *Tryphê* of the Sybarites: A Historiographical Problem in Athenaeus." *Journal of Hellenic Studies* 127: 38–60.

Graham 1957
Graham, J. W. 1957. "Auri Sacra Fames." *Phoenix* 11 (Autumn): 112–20.

Grand-Clément 2011
Grand-Clément, Adeline. 2011. *La fabrique des couleurs: Histoire du paysage sensible des Grecs anciens (VIIIe–début du Ve siècle av. n. è.).* Paris: Boccard.

Grane 2012
Grane, Thomas. 2012. "Pliny and the Wandering Mountain." *Analecta Romana Instituti Danici* 37: 7–28.

Granino Cecere 2012
Granino Cecere, Maria Grazia. 2012. "Margaritarii tra committenza privata e mercato urbano." In Baldini and Morelli 2012, 25–36.

Greifenhagen 1970–75
Greifenhagen, Adolf. 1970–75. *Schmuckarbeiten in Edelmetall. Staatliche Museen Berlin. Stiftung Preußischer Kulturbesitz. Antikenabteilung.* Vol. 1: *Fundgruppen;* vol. 2: *Einzelstücke.* Berlin: Mann.

Griffiths 1943
Griffiths, Anna Henwood. 1943. *Temple Treasures: A Study Based on the Works of Cicero and the* Fasti *of Ovid.* Philadelphia: N.p.

Grimaldi 1996
Grimaldi, David A. 1996. *Amber: Window to the Past.* Exh. cat., New York, American Museum of Natural History. New York: Abrams.

Grimm 1970
Grimm, Günter. 1970. "Zu Marcus Antonius und C. Cornelius Gallus." *JdI* 85: 158–70.

Grimm 1981
Grimm, Günter. 1981. "Orient und Okzident in der Kunst Alexandriens." In *Alexandrien: Kulturbegegnungen dreier Jahrtausende im Schmelztiegel einer mediterranen Großstadt*, edited by Norbert Hinske, 13–25. *Aegyptiaca Treverensia* 1. Mainz: Philipp von Zabern.

Grimm 1998
Grimm, Günter. 1998. *Alexandria: Die erste Königsstadt der hellenistischen Welt.* Mainz: Philipp von Zabern.

Grubessi, Aurisicchio, and Castiglioni 1990
Grubessi, O., C. Aurisicchio, and A. Castiglioni. 1990. "The Pharaohs' Forgotten Emerald Mines." *Journal of Gemmology* 22, no. 3: 164–77.

Gruen 1992
Gruen, Erich S. 1992. *Culture and National Identity in Republican Rome.* Ithaca, NY: Cornell University Press.

Gruen 2011
Gruen, Erich S., ed. 2011. *Cultural Identity in the Ancient Mediterranean.* Los Angeles: Getty Research Institute.

Guidobaldi 2010
Guidobaldi, Maria Paola. 2010. "Arredi di lusso in legno e avorio da Ercolano." *LANX* 6: 63–99.

Guidobaldi and Esposito 2010
Guidobaldi, Maria Paola, and Domenico Esposito. 2010. "New Archaeological Research at the Villa of the Papyri in Herculaneum." In *The Villa of the Papyri at Herculaneum: Archaeology, Reception, and Digital Reconstruction,* edited by Mantha Zarmakoupi, 21–62. Berlin: De Gruyter.

Guidobaldi and Esposito 2012
Guidobaldi, Maria Paola, and Domenico Esposito. 2012. *Ercolano: Colori da una città sepolta.* San Giovanni Lupatoto (Verona): Arsenale.

Gutzwiller 1995
Gutzwiller, Kathryn J. 1995. "Cleopatra's Ring." *Greek, Roman and Byzantine Studies* 36: 383–98.

Gutzwiller 2005
Gutzwiller, Kathryn J., ed. 2005. *The New Posidippus: A Hellenistic Poetry Book.* New York: Oxford University Press.

Guzzo 1986
Guzzo, Pier Giovanni. 1986. "Una lamina d'oro arcaica d'incerta provenienza." *Studi urbinati* 59, no. 3: 35–43.

Guzzo 2001a
Guzzo, Pier Giovanni. 2001. *Oreficerie dalla Magna Grecia.* Taranto: La Colomba.

Guzzo 2001b
Guzzo, Pier Giovanni. 2001. "Coppe ioniche in argento." *Studia Varia from the J. Paul Getty Museum* 2 (*Occasional Papers on Antiquities* 10): 1–6.

Guzzo 2003
Guzzo, Pietro Giovanni. 2003. "A Group of Hellenistic Silver Objects in the Metropolitan Museum." *Metropolitan Museum Journal* 38: 45–94.

Guzzo 2006a
Guzzo, Pietro Giovanni, ed. 2006. *Argenti a Pompei.* Exh. cat., Museo Archeologico Nazionale di Napoli. Milan: Electa.

Guzzo 2006b
Guzzo, Pietro Giovanni, ed. 2006. *Argenti: Pompei, Napoli, Torino.* Exh. cat., Turin, Museo di Antichità. Milan: Electa.

Guzzo 2007
Guzzo, Pier Giovanni, ed. 2007. *Pompeii: Tales from an Eruption.* New ed. Exh. cat., Birmingham, AL, Birmingham Museum of Art; Houston, Museum of Fine Arts. Milan: Mondadori Electa.

Guzzo, Spatafora, and Vassallo 2010
Guzzo, Pier Giovanni, Francesca Spatafora, and Stefano Vassallo. 2010. "Una phiale d'oro iscritta dall'entroterra di Himera: Dalla Sicilia a New York e ritorno." *MÉFRA* 122: 451–77.

Habachi and Biers 1969
Habachi, Labib, and Jane C. Biers. 1969. "An Agate Bowl from Egypt." *Muse: Annual of the Museum of Art and Archaeology, University of Missouri-Columbia* 3: 29–34.

Hackens and Moucharte 1989
Hackens, Tony, and Ghislaine Moucharte, eds. 1989. *Technology and Analysis of Ancient Gemstones: Proceedings of the European Workshop Held at Ravello, European University Centre for Cultural Heritage, November 13–16 / Technologie et analyse des gemmes anciennes; actes de l'Atelier européen tenu à Ravello, Centre universitaire européen pour les Biens Culturels, 13–16 novembre 1987.* PACT 32. Strasbourg: Council of Europe.

Hackens and Winkes 1983
Hackens, Tony, and Rolf Winkes, eds. 1983. *Gold Jewelry: Craft, Style and Meaning from Mycenae to Constantinopolis.* Exh. cat., Providence, Museum of Art, Rhode Island School of Design. Aurifex 5. Louvain-La-Neuve: Institut Supérieur d'Archéologie et d'Histoire de l'Art, Collège Erasme.

Haevernick 1963
Haevernick, Thea Elizabeth. 1963. "Beiträge zur Geschichte des antiken Glases: XI. Obsidianarbeiten." *Jahrbuch des Römisch-Germanischen Zentralmuseums Mainz* 10: 118–38.

Hagg 2012
Hagg, Sabine, ed. 2012. *Masterpieces in the Collection of Greek and Roman Antiquities: A Brief Guide to the Kunsthistorisches Museum.* 2nd ed. Vienna: Kunsthistorisches Museum.

Hahnloser 1971
Hahnloser, Hans R., ed. 1971. *Il tesoro di San Marco.* Vol. 2, *Il tesoro e il museo.* Florence: Sansoni.

Halleux and Schamp 1985
Halleux, Robert, and Jacques Schamp 1985. *Les lapidaires grecs.* Paris: Les Belles Lettres.

Hamilton 2000
Hamilton, Richard. 2000. *Treasure Map: A Guide to the Delian Inventories.* Ann Arbor: University of Michigan Press.

Hampe and Simon 1981
Hampe, Roland, and Erika Simon. 1981. *The Birth of Greek Art, from the Mycenaean to the Archaic Period.* New York: Oxford University Press.

d'Hancarville 1766–67
d'Hancarville, Pierre François Hugues. 1766–67. *Antiquités étrusques, grecques et romaines, Tirées du cabinet de M. William Hamilton, Envoyé extraordinaire de S. M. Britannique en Cour de Naples.* 4 vols. Naples: F. Morelli.

Hanfmann 1975
Hanfmann, George M. A. 1975. *Roman Art: A Modern Survey of the Art of Imperial Rome.* New York: Norton.

Hansen 2003
Hansen, Valerie. 2003. "The Hejia Village Hoard: A Snapshot of China's Silk Road Trade." *Orientations* 34, no. 2 (February): 14–19.

Harden 1954
Harden, Donald B. 1954. "*Vasa Murrina* Again." *JRS* 44, no. 1–2: 53.

Hardiman 2012
Hardiman, Craig. 2012. "'Popular' Aesthetics and Personal Art Appreciation in the Hellenistic Age." In *Aesthetic Value in Classical Antiquity,* edited by Ineke Suiter and Ralph M. Rosen, 265–83. Leiden: Brill.

Harlow and Nosch 2014
Harlow, Mary, and Marie-Louise Nosch, eds. 2014. *Greek and Roman Textiles and Dress: An Interdisciplinary Anthology.* Oxford: Oxbow.

Harris 1988
Harris, Diane. 1988. "Nikokrates of Kolonos, Metal Worker to the Parthenon Treasures." *Hesperia* 57: 329–37.

Harris 1995
Harris, Diane. 1995. *Treasures of the Parthenon and Erechtheion.* Oxford: Clarendon Press.

Harward 1982
Harward, Vernon J. 1982. "Greek Domestic Sculpture and the Origins of Private Art Patronage." PhD diss., Harvard University, Cambridge, MA.

Haskell 1984
Haskell, Francis. 1984. "The Baron d'Hancarville: An Adventurer and Art Historian in Eighteenth-Century Europe." In *Oxford, China and Italy: Writings in Honour of Sir Harold Acton,* edited by Edward Chaney and Neil Ritchie, 177–91. London: Thames and Hudson. Reprinted in Francis Haskell, *Past and Present in Art and Taste: Selected Essays* (1987).

Hasserodt 2009
Hasserodt, Monika. 2009. *Griechische und orientalische Metallphialen des frühen ersten Jahrtausends v. Chr. in Griechenland.* Bonn: Habelt.

Heikamp and Grote 1974
Heikamp, Detlef, and Andreas Grote. 1974. *Il tesoro di Lorenzo il Magnifico.* Vol. 2, *I vasi.* Exh. cat., Florence, Palazzo Medici Riccardi. Florence: Sansoni.

Heilmeyer 1988
Heilmeyer, Wolf-Dieter. 1988. *Antikenmuseum Berlin: Die ausgestellten Werke.* Berlin: Staatliche Museen Preussischer Kulturbesitz.

Heinen 1983
Heinen, H. 1983. "Die Tryphè des Ptolemaios VIII. Euergetes II." In *Althistorische Studien: Hermann Bengtson zum 70. Geburtstag dargebracht von Kollegen und Schülern,* 116–28. Wiesbaden: Steiner.

Henig 1983
Henig, Martin. 1983. "The Luxury Arts: Decorative Metalwork, Engraved Gems and Jewellery." In *A Handbook of Roman Art: A Survey of the Visual Arts of the Roman World,* edited by Martin Henig, 139–65. Oxford: Phaidon.

Henig 1990
Henig, Martin. 1990. *The Content Family Collection of Ancient Cameos.* Oxford: Ashmolean Museum.

Henig 2006
Henig, Martin. 2006. "Gems, Jewellery and Glass." In Bispham, Harrison, and Sparkes 2006, 217–30.

Henig and MacGregor 2004
Henig, Martin, and Arthur MacGregor. 2004. *Catalogue of the Engraved Gems and Finger-Rings in the Ashmolean Museum.* Vol. 2, *Roman.* Oxford: Archaeopress.

Henig and Plantzos 1999
Henig, Martin, and Dimitris Plantzos, eds.. 1999. *Classicism to Neo-classicism: Essays Dedicated to Gertrud Seidmann.* Oxford: Archaeopress.

Hermann et al. 1999
Hermann, John, et al. 1999. *Art of the Ancient Mediterranean World*. 1999. Exh. cat. Nagoya: Nagoya/Boston Museum of Fine Arts.

Hiebert and Cambon 2008
Hiebert, Fredrik, and Pierre Cambon, eds. 2008. *Afghanistan: Hidden Treasures from the National Museum, Kabul*. Exh. cat., Washington, D.C., National Gallery of Art, and other venues. Washington, DC: National Geographic Society.

Higbie 2003
Higbie, Carolyn. 2003. *The Lindian Chronicle and the Greek Creation of Their Past*. Oxford: Oxford University Press.

Higgins 1969
Higgins, Reynold Alleyne. 1969. "Early Greek Jewellery." *BSA* 64: 143–53.

Higgins 1980
Higgins, Reynold Alleyne. 1980. *Greek and Roman Jewellery*. 2nd ed. London: Methuen.

Hochuli-Gysel 2008
Hochuli-Gysel, Anne. 2008. "The Bust of Marcus Aurelius." In Aillagon 2008, 82–83, no. I.20.

Hoffmann 1993
Hoffmann, Herbert. 1993. "Bellerophon and the Chimaira in Malibu: A Greek Myth and an Archaeological Context." In *Studia Varia from the J. Paul Getty Museum* 1 *(Occasional Papers on Antiquities* 8): 63–70.

Hoffmann and Davidson 1965
Hoffmann, Herbert, and Patricia F. Davidson. 1965. *Greek Gold: Jewelry from the Age of Alexander*. Exh. cat., Boston, Museum of Fine Arts; Brooklyn Museum; Richmond, Virginia Museum of Fine Arts. Boston: Museum of Fine Arts.

Homolle 1882
Homolle, Théophile. 1882. "Comptes des hiéropes du Temple d'Apollon Délien." *BCH* 6: 1–167.

Hunt 1996
Hunt, Alan. 1996. *The Governance of Consuming Passions: A History of Sumptuary Law*. New York: St. Martin's Press.

Hunter 2004
Hunter, Richard. 2004. "Notes on the *Lithika* of Posidippus." In Acosta-Hughes, Kosmetatou, and Baumbach 2004, 94–104.

Hutchinson 2002
Hutchinson, G. O. 2002. "The New Posidippus and Latin Poetry." *ZPE* 138: 1–10.

Ignatiadou 2012
Ignatiadou, Despoina. 2012. "The Sindos Priestess." In *"Princesses" of the Mediterranean in the Dawn of History*, edited by Nikolaos Chr. Stampolidis with Mimika Giannopoulou, 338–411. Exh. cat. Athens: Museum of Cycladic Art.

Invernizzi et al. 2004
Invernizzi, Antonino, et al. 2004. *Seleucia al Tigri: Le impronte di sigillo dagli archivi*. Alessandria: Edizioni dell'Orso.

Isager 1991
Isager, Jacob. 1991. *Pliny on Art and Society*. Odense: Odense University Press.

Jacobsthal 1956
Jacobsthal, Paul. 1956. *Greek Pins and Their Connexions with Europe and Asia*. Oxford: Clarendon Press.

Jashemski 1979
Jashemski, Wilhelmina. 1979. *The Gardens of Pompeii: Herculaneum and the Villas Destroyed by Vesuvius*. New Rochelle, NY: Caratzas Bros.

Jenkins and Sloan 1996
Jenkins, Ian, and Kim Sloan, eds. 1996. *Vases and Volcanoes: Sir William Hamilton and His Collections*. Exh. cat. London: British Museum.

Jenkyns 1980
Jenkyns, Richard. 1980. *The Victorians and Ancient Greece*. Cambridge, MA: Harvard University Press.

Jeppeson 1972
Jeppeson, Kristian. 1972. "An Inside View of the Hoby Cups." *Acta Archaeologica* 43: 1–18.

Jex-Blake and Sellers 1896
Jex-Blake, K., trans. and E. Sellers, ed. 1896. *The Elder Pliny's Chapters on the History of Art*. London: Macmillan. Reprinted Chicago, 1967.

Johns 1990
Johns, Catherine. 1990. "Research on Roman Silver Plate." *JRA* 3: 28–43.

Johns 1996
Johns, Catherine. 1996. *The Jewellery of Roman Britain: Celtic and Classical Traditions*. London: Routledge.

Johns 1997
Johns, Catherine. 1997. *The Snettisham Roman Jeweller's Hoard*. London: British Museum.

Johns 2010
Johns, Catherine. 2010. *The Hoxne Late Roman Treasure: Gold Jewellery and Silver Plate*. London: British Museum.

Johns and Potter 1983
Johns, Catherine, and Timothy W. Potter. 1983. *The Thetford Treasure: Roman Jewellery and Silver*. London: British Museum.

Junius 1694 (1991 ed.)
Junius, Franciscus. 1694. *Catalogus Architectorum, Mechanicorum sed praecipue Pictorum, Statuariorum, Caelatorum, Tornatorum, aliorumque Artificum*. Rotterdam: Leers. Translation: *Franciscus Junius, The Literature of Classical Art*. Vol. 2, *A Lexicon of Artists & Their Works*. Edited and translated by Keith Aldrich, Philipp P. Fehl, and Raina Fehl. Berkeley: University of California Press, 1991.

Kacharava et al. 2008
Kacharava, Darejan D., et al. 2008. *Wine, Worship, and Sacrifice: The Golden Graves of Ancient Vani*. Exh. cat., Arthur M. Sackler Gallery, Smithsonian Institution, Washington, DC; Institute for the Study of the Ancient World, NYU. New York: Institute for the Study of the Ancient World; Princeton: Princeton University Press.

Kagan and Neverov 2000
Kagan, Julia, and Oleg Neverov. 2000. *Splendeurs des collections de Catherine II de Russie*. Exh. cat. Paris: Centre Culturel du Panthéon.

Kagan and Neverov 2001
Kagan, Julia, and Oleg Neverov, eds. 2001. *Sud'ba odnoj kollekcii: 500 reznyh kamnej iz kabineta gercoga Orleanskogo/Le destin d'une collection: 500 pierres gravées du cabinet du Duc d'Orléans*. Exh. cat., St. Petersburg, State Hermitage Museum. St. Petersburg: Slavija.

Hofter et al. 1988
Hofter, Mathias, et al. 1988. *Kaiser Augustus und die verlorene Republik*. 1988. Exh. cat., Berlin, Martin-Gropius-Bau. Mainz: Philipp von Zabern.

Kalashnik 2004
Kalashnik, Yuri. 2004. *Greek Gold: From the Treasure Rooms of the Hermitage*. Exh. cat. Amsterdam: Hermitage Amsterdam.

Kalavrezou 2012
Kalavrezou, Ioli. 2012. "Light and the Precious Object, or Value in the Eyes of the Byzantines." In *The Construction of Value in the Ancient World*, edited by John K. Papadopoulos and Gary Urton, 354–69. Los Angeles: Cotsen Institute of Archaeology Press.

Keesling 2006
Keesling, C. 2006. "Heavenly Bodies: Monuments to Prostitutes in Greek Sanctuaries." In *Prostitutes and Courtesans in the Ancient World*, edited by Christopher A. Faraone and Laura K. McClure, 59–76. Madison: University of Wisconsin Press.

Kent and Painter 1977
Kent, J[ohn] P. C., and K[enneth] S. Painter, eds. 1977. *Wealth of the Roman World: AD 300–700*. Exh. cat. London: British Museum.

Keuls 1993
Keuls, Eva C. 1993. *The Reign of the Phallus: Sexual Politics in Ancient Athens*. Reprint of 1985 ed. Berkeley: University of California Press.

Kitov 2005
Kitov, Georgi. 2005. "The Newly Discovered Tomb of the Thracian Ruler Seuthes III." *Archaeologia Bulgarica* 9, no. 2: 39–54.

R. Klemm and D. Klemm 2013
Klemm, Rosemarie, and Dietrich Klemm. 2013. *Gold and Gold Mining in Ancient Egypt and Nubia: Geoarchaeology of the Ancient Gold Mining Sites in the Egyptian and Sudanese Eastern Deserts*. Berlin: Springer.

Kloft 1996
Kloft, Hans. 1996. "Überlegungen zum Luxus in der frühen römischen Kaiserzeit." In *Energeia: Studies on Ancient History and Epigraphy Presented to H. W. Pleket*, edited by J. H. M. Strubbe, R. A. Tybout, and H. S. Versnel, 113–34. Amsterdam: J. C. Gieben.

Knigge 1991
Knigge, Ursula. 1991. *The Athenian Kerameikos: History—Monuments—Excavations*. Translated by Judith Binder. Athens: Krene.

Kondoleon 2000
Kondoleon, Christine, ed. 2000. *Antioch: The Lost Ancient City*. Exh. cat., Worcester Art Museum and other venues. Princeton: Princeton University Press.

Kontoleon 1962
Kontoleon, Nikolaos. 1962. "The Gold Treasure of Panagurischte." *Balkan Studies* 3: 185–200.

Kosmetatou 2003
Kosmetatou, Elizabeth. 2003. "Poseidippos Epigr. 8 and Early Ptolemaic Cameos." *ZPE* 142: 35–42.

Kosmetatou 2004a
Kosmetatou, Elizabeth. 2004. "On Large Gemstones." *ZPE* 146: 81–84.

Kosmetatou 2004b
Kosmetatou, Elizabeth. 2004. "Rhoxane's Dedications to Athena Polias." *ZPE* 146: 75–80.
Kottaridi 2011
Kottaridi, Angeliki. 2011. *Macedonian Treasures: A Tour through the Museum of the Royal Tombs of Aigai*. Translated by Alexandra Doumas. Athens: Kapon.
Kottaridi et al. 2011
Kottaridi, Angeliki, et al. 2011. *Heracles to Alexander the Great: Treasures from the Royal Capital of Macedon, a Hellenic Kingdom in the Age of Democracy*. Exh. cat. Oxford: Ashmolean Museum.
Kraeling 1955
Kraeling, Carl H. 1955. "Hellenistic Gold Jewelry in Chicago." *Archaeology* 8: 252–95.
Krug 1982
Krug, Antje. 1982. "Die 'Kauernde Aphrodite' in Kristall." *JPGMJ* 10: 145–52.
Krumeich 2007
Krumeich, Ralf. 2007. "Human Achievement and Divine Favor: The Religious Context of Early Hellenistic Portraiture." In *Early Hellenistic Portraiture: Image, Style, Context*, edited by Peter Schultz and Ralf von den Hoff, 161–80. Cambridge: Cambridge University Press.
Krzyszkowska 1990
Krzyszkowska, Olga. 1990. *Ivory and Related Materials: An Illustrated Guide. Bulletin of the Institute of Classical Studies* suppl. 59. London: Institute of Classical Studies.
Krzyszkowska 2005
Krzyszkowska, Olga. 2005. *Aegean Seals: An Introduction*. Bulletin of the Institute of Classical Studies suppl. 85. London: Institute of Classical Studies.
Krzyszkowska and Morkot 2000
Krzyszkowska, Olga, and Robert Morkot. 2000. "Ivory and Related Materials." In *Ancient Egyptian Materials and Technology*, edited by Paul T. Nicholson and Ian Shaw, 320–31. Cambridge: Cambridge University Press.
Kunsthistorisches Museum Wien 1991
Kunsthistorisches Museum Wien. 1991. *The Secular and Ecclesiastical Treasuries: Illustrated Guide*. Contributions by Rotraud Bauer et al.; translated by Sophie Kidd and Peter Waugh. Salzburg: Residenz.
Künzl 1978
Künzl, Ernst. 1978. "Quod sine te factum est hoc magis archetypum est? (Martialis 8.34)." *Archäologisches Korrespondenzblatt* 8: 311–17.
Künzl 1979
Künzl, Ernst. 1979. "Le argenterie." In *Pompei 79: Raccolta di studi per il decimonono centenario dell'eruzione vesuviana*, edited by Fausto Zevi, 211–28. Naples: G. Macchiaroli.
Kurke 1992
Kurke, Leslie. 1992. "The Politics of ἁβροσύνη in Archaic Greece." *Classical Antiquity* 11: 91–120.
Kurke 1995
Kurke, Leslie. 1995. "Herodotus and the Language of Metals." *Helios* 22: 36–64.
Kurke 1999
Kurke, Leslie. 1999. *Coins, Bodies, Games, and Gold: The Politics of Meaning in Archaic Greece*. Princeton: Princeton University Press.
Kurtz 1985
Kurtz, Donna C., ed. 1985. *Beazley and Oxford*. Oxford: Oxford University Committee for Archaeology.
Küthmann 1959
Küthmann, Harald. 1959. *Untersuchungen zur Toreutik des zweiten und ersten Jahrhunderts vor Christus*. Kallmünz: Lassleben.
Kuttner 1995
Kuttner, Ann L. 1995. *Dynasty and Empire in the Age of Augustus: The Case of the Boscoreale Cups*. Berkeley: University of California Press.
Kuttner 2005
Kuttner, Ann L. 2005. "Cabinet Fit for a Queen: The Λιθικά as Posidippus' Gem Museum." In Gutzwiller 2005: 141–63.
Kyrieleis 1971
Kyrieleis, Helmut. 1971. "Der Kameo Gonzaga." *Bonner Jahrbücher des Rheinischen Landesmuseum in Bonn* 171: 162–93.
Kyrieleis 1981
Kyrieleis, Helmut. 1981. *Führer durch das Heraion von Samos*. Athens: Krene.
La Chau and Le Blond 1780
La Chau, Géraud de, and Gaspar M. Le Blond. 1780. *Description des principales pierres gravées du cabinet de S. A. S. Monseigneur le duc d'Orleans. . . .* Vol. 1. Paris: La Chau.
Laffineur 1978
Laffineur, Robert. 1978. *L'orfèvrerie rhodienne orientalisante*. Paris: Boccard.
Lahusen 1978
Lahusen, Götz. 1978. "Goldene und vergoldete römischen Ehrenstatuen und Bildnisse." *RM* 85: 385–95.
Landman et al. 2001
Landman, Neil H., et al. 2001. *Pearls: A Natural History*. Exh. cat., New York, American Museum of Natural History. New York: Abrams.
Lang 2012
Lang, Jörn. 2012. *Mit Wissen geschmückt? Zur bildlichen Rezeption griechischer Dichter und Denker in der römischen Lebenswelt*. Monumenta Artis Romanae 39. Wiesbaden: Reichert.
Lapatin 1997
Lapatin, Kenneth. 1997. "Pheidias ἐλεφαντουργός." *AJA* 101: 663–82.
Lapatin 2001
Lapatin, Kenneth. 2001. *Chryselephantine Statuary in the Ancient Mediterranean World*. Oxford: Oxford University Press.
Lapatin 2003
Lapatin, Kenneth. 2003. "The Fate of Plate and Other Precious Materials: Towards a Historiography of Ancient Greek Minor(?) Arts." In *Ancient Art and Its Historiography*, edited by A. A. Donohue and Mark D. Fullerton, 69–91. Cambridge: Cambridge University Press.
Lapatin 2005
Lapatin, Kenneth. 2005. "The Statue of Athena and Other Treasures in the Parthenon." In *The Parthenon from Antiquity to the Present*, edited by Jenifer Neils, 261–91. Cambridge: Cambridge University Press.
Lapatin 2008
Lapatin, Kenneth. 2008. "Luxus." In Mattusch 2008, 31–51.
Lapatin 2012
Lapatin, Kenneth. 2012. "Ancient Writers on Art." In T. Smith and Plantzos 2012, vol. 1: 273–89.
Lapatin 2014
Lapatin, Kenneth, ed. 2014. *The Berthouville Silver Treasure and Roman Luxury*. Los Angeles: JPGM.
Lapatin 2015
Lapatin, Kenneth. 2015. "Luxury Arts." In *A Companion to Roman Art*, edited by Barbara E. Borg. Malden, MA, and Oxford: Wiley-Blackwell.
Lapatin and Wight 2010
Lapatin, Kenneth, and Karol Wight, eds. 2010. *The J. Paul Getty Museum: Handbook of the Antiquities Collection*. 2nd ed. Los Angeles: JPGM.
La Rocca 1984
La Rocca, Eugenio. 1984. *L'età d'oro di Cleopatra: Indagine sulla Tazza Farnese*. Rome: "L'Erma" di Bretschneider.
La Rocca 1986
La Rocca, Eugenio. 1986. "Il lusso come espressione di potere." In Cima and La Rocca 1986, 3–35.
La Rocca 2009
La Rocca, Eugenio, ed. 2009. *Roma, la pittura di un impero*. Exh. cat., Rome, Scuderie del Quirinale. Milan: Skira.
La Rocca, Parisi Presicce, and Lo Monaco 2010
La Rocca, Eugenio, Claudio Parisi Presicce, and Annalisa Lo Monaco, eds. 2010. *I giorni di Roma: L'età della conquista*. Exh. cat., Rome, Musei Capitolini. Milan: Skira.
La Rocca et al. 2013
La Rocca, Eugenio, Claudio Parisi Presicce, Annalisa Lo Monaco, Cécile Giroire, and Daniel Roger, eds. 2013. *Augusto*. Exh. cat., Rome, Scuderie del Quirinale. Milan: Electa.
Laum 1924
Laum, Bernhard. 1924. *Heiliges Geld: Eine historische Untersuchung über den sakralen Ursprung des Geldes*. Tübingen: Mohr.
Lawton 1995
Lawton, Carol L. 1995. *Attic Document Reliefs: Art and Politics in Ancient Athens*. Oxford: Clarendon Press.
Lehmann-Hartleben 1938
Lehmann-Hartleben, Karl. 1938. "Two Roman Silver Jugs." *AJA* 42: 82–105.
Leipen 1971
Leipen, Neda. 1971. *Athena Parthenos: A Reconstruction*. Toronto: Royal Ontario Museum.
Leospo 1999
Leospo, Enrichetta. 1999. "Le coppe di ossidiana." In *La Villa di San Marco a Stabia*, edited by Alix Barbet and Paola Miniero Forte, 333–41. Naples: Centre Jean Bérard; Rome: École française de Rome; Pompeii: Soprintendenza Archeologica di Pompei.
Leppmann 1970
Leppmann, Wolfgang. 1970. *Winckelmann*. New York: Knopf.
Leskow et al. 1989
Leskow, A[leksandr] M[ikhailovich], et al. 1989. *Gold- und Kunsthandwerk vom antiken Kuban: Neue archäologische Entdeckungen aus der Sowje-*

tunion. Translated by I. Weigold-Hess. Exh. cat., Städtisches Reiss-Museum Mannheim, Archäologische Sammlungen. Stuttgart: Theiss.

Lewis 1955
Lewis, David M. 1955. "The Public Seal of Athens." *Phoenix* 9: 32–34.

Lewis 1985
Lewis, D[avid] M. 1985. "Temple Inventories in Ancient Greece." In *Pots & Pans: A Colloquium on Precious Metals and Ceramics in the Muslim, Chinese and Graeco-Roman Worlds*, edited by Michael Vickers, 71–81. Oxford: Oxford University Press.

Linders 1972
Linders, Tullia. 1972. *Studies in the Treasure Records of Artemis Brauronia Found in Athens*. Stockholm: Svenska Institutet i Athen.

Linders 1975
Linders, Tullia. 1975. *The Treasures of the Other Gods in Athens and Their Functions*. Meisenheim am Glan: Anton Hain.

Linders 1987
Linders, Tullia. 1987. "Gods, Gifts, Society." In *Gifts to the Gods: Proceedings of the Uppsala Symposium 1985*, edited by Tullia Linders and Gullög Nordquist, 115–22. Boreas 15. Uppsala: Uppsala Universitet.

Linders 1997
Linders, Tullia. 1997. "Gaben an die Götter oder Goldreserve?" In *Kult und Kultbauten auf der Akropolis*, edited by Wolfram Hoepfner, 31–36. Berlin: Archäologisches Seminar der Freien Universität Berlin.

Lipinsky 1975a
Lipinsky, Angelo. 1975. *Oro, argento, gemme e smalti: Tecnologia delle arti dalle origini alla fine del Medioevo, 3000 a.C.–1500 d.C.* Florence: Olschki.

Lipinsky 1975b
Lipinsky, Angelo. 1975. "La corona votiva aurea da Armento." In *Antiche civiltà lucane*, edited by Pietro Borraro, 59–98. Galatina: Congedo.

Liston and Papadopoulos 2004
Liston, Maria A., and John K. Papadopoulos. 2004. "The 'Rich Athenian Lady' Was Pregnant: The Anthropology of a Geometric Tomb Reconsidered." *Hesperia* 73: 7–38.

Loewental and Harden 1949
Loewental, A. I., and D. B. Harden. 1949. "Vasa Murrina." *JRS* 39: 31–37.

Longus 1709
Longus, Georgius, 1709. *De anulis signatoriis antiquorum*. Frankfurt and Leipzig: Bachmann.

Lorber 2008
Lorber, Catharine. 2008. "Weight Standards of Thracian Toreutics and Thraco-Macedonian Coinages." *Revue belge de numismatique et de sigillographie* 154: 1–29.

Lorimer 1936
Lorimer, H. L. 1936. "Gold and Ivory in Greek Mythology." In *Greek Poetry and Life: Essays Presented to Gilbert Murray on His 70th Birthday*, 14–33. Oxford: Clarendon Press.

Lörz 2006
Lörz, Markus. 2006. "Die mittelalterliche Geschichte der Gemma Augustea." *Concilium Medii Aevi* 9: 159–73.

Louis 2007
Louis, François. 2007. "The Hejiacun Rhyton and the Chinese Wine Horn (*Gong*): Intoxicating Rarities and Their Antiquarian History." *Artibus Asiae* 67: 201–42.

Lucas and Harris 1962
Lucas, A[lfred], and J. R. Harris. 1962. *Ancient Egyptian Materials and Industries*. 4th ed. London: E. Arnold.

Lullies 1982
Lullies, Reinhard. 1982. "Abermals: Zur Bedeutung des Kranzes von Armento." *JdI* 97: 91–117.

Luschey 1939
Luschey, Heinz. 1939. *Die Phiale*. Bleicherode am Harz: C. Nieft.

Lyons et al. 2013
Lyons, Claire L., Michael Bennett, Clemente Marconi, with Alexandra Sofroniew, eds. 2013. *Sicily: Art and Invention between Greece and Rome*. Exh. cat., Malibu, Getty Villa; Cleveland Museum of Art; Los Angeles: JPGM.

Macrì 2009
Macrì, Sonia. 2009. *Pietre viventi: I minerali nell'immaginario del mondo antico*. Turin: UTET libreria.

Maiuri 1933
Maiuri, Amedeo. 1933. *La casa del Menandro e il suo tesoro di argenteria*. 2 vols. Rome: La Libreria dello Stato.

Mallwitz and Herrmann 1980
Mallwitz, Alfred, and Hans-Volkmar Herrmann, eds. 1980. *Die Funde aus Olympia: Ergebnisse hundertjähriger Ausgrabungstätigkeit*. Athens: S. Kasas.

Manojlović-Marijanski 1973
Manojlović-Marijanski, Mirjana. 1973. "Der Fund von Berkasovo, Jugoslawien." In *Spätrömische Gardehelme*, edited by Hans Klumbach, 15–38. Munich: Beck.

Mansfield 1985
Mansfield, John Magruder. 1985. "The Robe of Athena and the Panathenaic Peplos." PhD diss., University of California, Berkeley.

Manzelli 1994
Manzelli, Valentina. 1994. *La policromia nella statuaria greca arcaica*. Rome: "L'Erma" di Bretschneider.

Marangou 1969
Marangou, Lila I. 1969. *Lakonische Elfenbein- und Beinschnitzereien*. Tübingen: Wasmuth.

Marazov 2011
Marazov, Ivan. 2011. *Thrace and the Ancient World: Vassil Bojkov Collection*. Exh. cat., Sofia, National Museum of History, Sofia, Bulgaria: Thrace Foundation.

Marazov et al. 1998
Marazov, Ivan, Margarita Tacheva, Ivan Venedikov, and Alexander Fol. 1998. *Ancient Gold: The Wealth of the Thracians; Treasures from the Republic of Bulgaria*. Exh. cat., Saint Louis Art Museum and other venues. New York: Abrams.

Margariti et al. 2013
Margariti, Christina, Stavros Protopapas, Norman Allen, and Vladimir Vishnyakov. 2013. "Identification of Purple Dye from Molluscs on an Excavated Textile by Non-destructive Analytical Techniques." *Dyes and Pigments* 96: 774–80.

Mariette 1750
Mariette, P.-J. 1750. *Traité des pierres gravées*. 2 vols. Paris: De l'imprimerie de l'auteur.

Marshall 1907
Marshall, F. H. 1907. *Catalogue of the Finger Rings, Greek, Etruscan and Roman, in the Departments of Antiquities, British Museum*. London: Printed by order of the Trustees.

Marshall 1911
Marshall, F. H. 1911. *Catalogue of the Jewellery, Greek, Etruscan, and Roman, in the Departments of Antiquities, British Museum*. London: Printed by order of the Trustees.

Martiniani-Reber 1986
Martiniani-Reber, Marielle. 1986. *Lyon, Musée historique des tissus: Soieries sassanides, coptes et byzantines, Ve–XIe siècles*. Paris: Réunion des Musées Nationaux.

Marvin 2008
Marvin, Miranda. 2008. *The Language of the Muses: The Dialogue between Roman and Greek Sculpture*. Los Angeles: JPGM.

Masson and Pugachenkova 1982
Masson, M. E., and G. A. Pugachenkova. 1982. *The Parthian Rhytons of Nisa*. Translated by Caroline M. Breton Bruce. Florence: Le Lettere Licosa.

Mastrocinque 1991
Mastrocinque, Attilio. 1991. *L'ambra e l'Eridano: Studi sulla letteratura e sul commercio dell'ambra in età preromana*. Este: Zielo.

Mastrocinque 2011
Mastrocinque, Attilio. 2011. "The Colours of Magical Gems." In Entwistle and Adams 2011, 62–68.

Mattusch 2008
Mattusch, Carol C., ed. 2008. *Pompeii and the Roman Villa: Art and Culture around the Bay of Naples*. Exh. cat., Washington, DC, National Gallery of Art; Los Angeles County Museum of Art. Washington, DC: National Gallery of Art; London: Thames & Hudson.

Mayor 2000
Mayor, Adrienne. 2000. *The First Fossil Hunters: Paleontology in Greek and Roman Times*. Princeton: Princeton University Press.

Mayor 2010
Mayor, Adrienne. 2010. *The Poison King: The Life and Legend of Mithradates, Rome's Deadliest Enemy*. Princeton: Princeton University Press.

Megow 1987
Megow, Wolf-Rüdiger. 1987. *Kameen von Augustus bis Alexander Severus*. Berlin: De Gruyter.

Meiggs 1982
Meiggs, Russell. 1982. *Trees and Timber in the Ancient Mediterranean World*. Oxford: Clarendon Press.

Menninger 1996
Menninger, Michael. 1996. *Untersuchungen zu den Gläsern und Gipsabgüssen aus dem Fund von Begram (Afghanistan)*. Würzburger Forschungen zur Altertumskunde 1. Würzburg: Ergon.

Mercando 1998
Mercando, Liliana, ed. 1998. *Archeologia in Piemonte*. Vol. 2, *L'età romana*. Turin: Umberto Allemandi.

Mertens and Anderson 1987
Mertens, Joan, and Maxwell L. Anderson. 1987. *The Metropolitan Museum of Art: Greece and Rome.* New York: Metropolitan Museum of Art.

Michel 2004
Michel, Simone. 2004. *Die Magischen Gemmen: Zu Bildern und Zauberformeln auf geschnittenen Steinen der Antike und Neuzeit.* Studien aus dem Warburg-Haus 7. Berlin: Akademie.

Micheli 2008
Micheli, Maria Elisa. 2008. "Tryphon a *Sentinum*?" In *Sentinum 295 a.C., Sassoferrato 2006: 2300 anni dopo la battaglia; una città romana tra storia e archeologia; convegno internazionale, Sassoferrato, 21–23 settembre 2006*, edited by Maura Medri, 127–39. Rome: "L'Erma" di Bretschneider.

Miles 2008
Miles, Margaret M. 2008. *Art as Plunder: The Ancient Origins of Debate about Cultural Property.* Cambridge: Cambridge University Press.

Miles 2015
Miles, Margaret M. 2015. "Collecting the Past, Creating the Future: Art Displays in the Hellenistic Mediterranean." In *Museum Archetypes and Collecting in the Ancient World*, edited by Maria W. Gahtan and Donatella Pegazzano, 33–44. Leiden: Brill.

M. Miller 1990
Miller, Margaret C. 1990. "Peacocks and *Tryphe* in Classical Athens." *Archaeological News* 15: 1–10.

M. Miller 1997
Miller, Margaret C. 1997. *Athens and Persia in the Fifth Century BC: A Study in Cultural Receptivity.* Cambridge: Cambridge University Press.

S. Miller 1979
Miller, Stella G. 1979. *Two Groups of Thessalian Gold.* Berkeley: University of California Press.

Minns 1913
Minns, Ellis H. 1913. *Scythians and Greeks: A Survey of Ancient History and Archaeology on the North Coast of the Euxine from the Danube to the Caucasus.* Cambridge: University Press.

Mols 1999
Mols, Stephan T. A. M. 1999. *Wooden Furniture in Herculaneum: Form, Technique and Function.* Translated by Rob Bland. Amsterdam: Gieben.

Moon 1995
Moon, Warren G., ed. 1995. *Polykleitos, the Doryphoros, and Tradition.* Madison: University of Wisconsin Press.

Moorey 1994
Moorey, P. R. S. 1994. *Ancient Mesopotamian Materials and Industries: The Archaeological Evidence.* Oxford: Clarendon. Reprinted Winona Lake, IN: Eisenbrauns, 1999.

Morassi 1963
Morassi, Antonio. 1963. *Il tesoro dei Medici: Oreficerie, argenterie, pietre dure.* Milan: Silvana Editoriale d'Arte.

Morey 1959
Morey, Charles Rufus. 1959. *The Gold-Glass Collection of the Vatican Library; with Additional Catalogues of Other Gold-Glass Collections.* Edited by Guy Ferrari. Vatican City: Biblioteca Apostolica Vaticana.

Morris 1992–93
Morris, Ian. 1992–93. "Law, Culture and Funerary Art in Athens, 600–300 B.C." *Hephaistos* 11/12: 35–50.

Müller 1994
Müller, Carl Werner. 1994. "Das Bildprogramm der Silberbecher von Hoby: Zur Rezeption frühgriechischer Literatur in der römischen Bildkunst der augusteischen Zeit." *JdI* 109: 321–52.

Mura Sommella 1983
Mura Sommella, Anna, ed. 1983*Crepereia Tryphaena: Le scoperte archeologiche nell'area del Palazzo di Giustizia.* Exh. cat., Rome, Palazza dei Conservatorio. Venice: Marsilio.

Museo Archeologico Nationale 1986
Museo Archeologico Nationale di Napoli. 1986. *Le Collezioni del Museo Nazionale di Napoli.* Vol. 1, *I mosaici, le pitture, gli oggetti di uso quotidiano, gli argenti, le terrecotte invetriate, i vetri, i cristalli, gli avori.* Rome: De Luca.

Museo Archeologico Nationale 1989
Museo Archeologico Nationale di Napoli. 1989. *Le Collezioni del Museo Nazionale di Napoli.* Vol. 2, *La scultura greco-romana, le sculture antiche della collezione Farnese, le collezioni monetali, le oreficerie, la collezione glittica.* Rome: De Luca.

Musti et al. 1992
Musti, Domenico, Mario Benzi, Luigi Rocchetti, Pier Giovanni Guzzo, Giuliana Calcani, and Fiorenzo Catalli. 1992. *L'oro dei Greci.* Novara: Istituto Geografico De Agostini.

Mylonas 1983
Mylonas, George E. 1983. *Mycenae, Rich in Gold.* Athens: Ekdotike Athenon.

Nagy 2011
Nagy, Árpád M. 2011. "Magical Gems and Classical Archaeology." In Entwistle and Adams 2011, 75–81.

Nassau 1994
Nassau, Kurt. 1994. *Gemstone Enhancement: History, Science, and State of the Art.* 2nd ed. London: Butterworth Heinemann.

Nassau and Hanson 1985
Nassau, Kurt, and A. E. Hanson. 1985. "The Pearl in the Chicken: Pearl Recipes in Papyrus Holmiensis." *Gems & Gemology* 21: 223–321.

Natter 1754
Natter, Lorenz. 1754. *Traité de la méthode antique de graver en pierres fines, comparée avec la méthode moderne, et expliquée en diverses planches.* London: Printed by J. Haberkorn.

Naumann-Steckner 2007
Naumann-Steckner, Friederike. 2007. "*Foedula vivas* – Pummelchen lebe hoch! Inschriften auf römischem Tafelsilber." In *Kosmos der Zeichen: Schriftbild und Bildformel in Antike und Mittelalter*, edited by Dietrich Boschung and Hansgerd Hellenkemper, 295–317. Exh. cat., Römisch-Germanisches Museum der Stadt Köln. Wiesbaden: Reichert.

Nava and Salerno 2007
Nava, Maria Luisa, and Antonio Salerno, eds. 2007. *Ambre: Trasparenze dall'antico.* Exh. cat., Museo Archeologico Nazionale di Napoli. Milan: Electa.

Nenna 1998
Nenna, M. D. 1998. "Gemmes et pierres dans le mobilier alexandrin." In Rausch 1998, 156–61.

Neverov 1976
Neverov, Oleg. 1976. *Antique Intaglios in the Hermitage Collection.* Leningrad: Aurora.

Nicholson and Shaw 2000
Nicholson, Paul T., and Ian Shaw, eds. 2000. *Ancient Egyptian Materials and Technology.* Cambridge: Cambridge University Press.

Nicolini 1990
Nicolini, Gérard. 1990. *Techniques des ors antiques: La bijouterie ibérique du VIIᵉ au IVᵉ siècle.* Paris: Picard.

Nikolov 2007
Nikolov, Vassil. 2007. *Kultur und Kunst des vorgeschichtlichen Thrakiens.* Translated by Zlatka Parpulova. Plovdiv, Bulgaria: Lettera.

Nonni 1995
Nonni, Giorgio. 1995. "Le nozze mistiche di Amore e Psiche: Storia di una gemma ellenistica ritrovata a Sentinum nel XVI secolo." *Studi umanistici piceni* 15: 169–78.

Oddy 1981
Oddy, Andrew. 1981. "Gilding through the Ages." *Gold Bulletin* 14: 75–79.

Oddy 1985
Oddy, W. A. 1985. "Vergoldungen auf prähistorisch und und klassischen Bronzen." In *Archäologische Bronzen, antike Kunst, moderne Technik*, edited by Hermann Born, 64–71. Berlin: Dietrich Reimer.

Oddy, Bimson, and La Niece 1983
Oddy, W. A., M. Bimson, and S[usan] La Niece. 1983. "The Composition of Niello Decoration on Gold, Silver, and Bronze in the Antique and Mediaeval Periods." *Studies in Conservation* 28: 29–35.

Ogden 1982
Ogden, Jack. 1982. *Jewellery of the Ancient World.* London: Trefoil.

Ogden 1991
Ogden, Jack. 1991. "Classical Gold Wire: Some Aspects of Its Manufacture and Use." *Jewellery Studies* 5: 95–105.

Ogden 1992a
Ogden, Jack. 1992. *Ancient Jewellery.* London: British Museum.

Ogden 1992b
Ogden, Jack. 1992. "Gold in Antiquity." *Interdisciplinary Science Reviews* 17, no. 3: 261–70.

Ogden 1993a
Ogden, Jack. 1993. "Aesthetic and Technical Considerations Regarding the Colour and Texture of Ancient Goldwork." In *Metal Plating and Patination: Cultural, Technical and Historical Developments*, edited by Susan La Niece and Paul Craddock, 39–49. Oxford: Butterworth-Heinemann.

Ogden 1993b
Ogden, Jack. 1993. "Granulation and a Greek Astronaut." *Jewellery Studies* 6: 73–74.

Ohly 1953
Ohly, Dieter. 1953. *Griechische Goldbleche des 8. Jahrhunderts v. Chr.* Berlin: Mann.

Ohly 1959
Ohly, Dieter. 1959. "Zur Rekonstruktion des samischen Geräts mit dem Elfenbeinjüngling." *Athenische Mitteilungen* 74: 48–56.

Oliver 1975
Oliver, Andrew, Jr. 1975. Review of Bühler 1973. *AJA* 79: 165–67.

Oliver 1977
Oliver, Andrew, Jr. 1977. *Silver for the Gods: 800 Years of Greek and Roman Silver*. Exh. cat. Toledo, OH: Toledo Museum of Art.

Oliver 1980
Oliver, Andrew, Jr. 1980. "A Set of Ancient Silverware in the Getty Museum." *JPGMJ* 8: 155–66.

Oliver 1992
Oliver, Andrew, Jr. 1992. "Ivory Temple Doors." In Fitton 1992, 227–32.

Oliver 2004
Oliver, Andrew, Jr. 2004. "The Changing Fashions of Roman Silver." *Record of the Art Museum, Princeton University* 63: 2–27.

Oliver and Shelton 1979
Oliver, Andrew, Jr., and John Shelton. 1979. "Silver on Papyrus: A Translation of a Roman Silver Tableware Inventory." *Archaeology* 32, no. 1: 21–28.

Orejas and Sánchez-Palencia 2002
Orejas, Almudena, and F. Javier Sánchez-Palencia. 2002. "Mines, Territorial Organization, and Social Structure in Roman Iberia: Carthago Noua and the Peninsular Northwest." *AJA* 106: 581–99.

Ortiz 1996
Ortiz, George. 1996. *In Pursuit of the Absolute: Art of the Ancient World; the George Ortiz Collection*. Rev. ed. Exh. cat., Berlin, Altes Museum. Bern: Benteli.

Ostoia 1969
Ostoia, Vera K. 1969. *The Middle Ages: Treasures from the Cloisters and the Metropolitan Museum of Art*. Exh. cat., New York, Metropolitan Museum of Art; Los Angeles County Museum of Art; Art Institute of Chicago. Los Angeles: Los Angeles County Museum of Art.

Overbeck 1868
Overbeck, Johannes. 1868. *Die antiken Schriftquellen zur Geschichte der bildenden Künste bei den Griechen*. Leipzig: W. Engelmann. Reprinted Hildesheim: Olms, 1959.

Padgett 1995
Padgett, J. Michael. 1995. "A Chalcedony Statuette of Herakles." *Record of the Art Museum, Princeton University* 54, no. 1: 2–22.

Padgett 2003
Padgett, J. Michael, ed. 2003. *The Centaur's Smile: The Human Animal in Early Greek Art*. Exh. cat., Princeton University Art Museum; Houston, Museum of Fine Arts. Princeton: Princeton University Art Museum.

Painter 2001
Painter, Kenneth S. 2001. *The Insula of the Menander at Pompeii*. Vol. 4, *The Silver Treasure*. Oxford: Clarendon.

Panagopoulou 2007
Panagopoulou, Katerina. 2007. "Between Necessity and Extravagance: Silver as a Commodity in the Hellenistic Period." *BSA* 102: 315–43.

Pannuti 1983
Pannuti, Ulrico. 1983. *Museo Archeologico Nazionale di Napoli: Catalogo della collezione glittica*. Vol. 1. Rome: Istituto Poligrafico e Zecca dello Stato.

Pannuti 1994
Pannuti, Ulrico. 1994. *Museo Archeologico Nazionale di Napoli: Catalogo della collezione glittica*. Vol. 2. Rome: Istituto Poligrafico e Zecca dello Stato.

Panzanelli, Schmidt, and Lapatin 2008
Panzanelli, Roberta, with Eike D. Schmidt and Kenneth Lapatin, eds. 2008. *The Color of Life: Polychromy in Sculpture from Antiquity to the Present*. Exh. cat., Malibu, Getty Villa. Los Angeles: JPGM.

Papadopoulos and Urton 2012
Papadopoulos, John K., and Gary Urton, eds. 2012. *The Construction of Value in the Ancient World*. Los Angeles: Cotsen Institute of Archaeology Press.

E. Pappalardo 2010
Pappalardo, Eleonora. 2010. *Nisa Partica: I rhyta ellenistici*. Florence: Le Lettere.

E. Pappalardo 2011
Pappalardo, Eleonora. 2011. "I rhyta in avorio." In *Gli splendori di Nisa Partica: Scavi italiani in Turkmenistan,* edited by Carlo Lippolis and Niccolò Manassero, 36–40. Exh. cat., Turin, Istituto San Giuseppe. Turin: Centro Ricerche Archeologiche e Scavi di Torino per il Medio Oriente e l'Asia.

U. Pappalardo 1986
Pappalardo, Umberto. 1986. "Gli argenti." In Museo Archeologico Nazionale 1986, 91–101, 206–17.

U. Pappalardo 2003
Pappalardo, Umberto. 2003. "Le argenterie." In *Menander: La Casa del Menandro di Pompei*, edited by Grete Stefani, 90–107. Exh. cat., Boscoreale, Antiquarium. Milan: Electa.

U. Pappalardo 2008
Pappalardo, Umberto. 2008. *The Splendor of Roman Wall Painting*. Los Angeles: JPGM.

Parlasca 1975
Parlasca, Klaus. 1975. "Ein hellenistisches Achat-Rhyton in China." *Artibus Asiae* 37: 280–90.

Parlasca 1985
Parlasca, Klaus. 1985. "Neue Beobachtungen zu den hellenistichen Achatgefäßen aus Ägypten." *JPGMJ* 13: 19–22.

Passerini 1934
Passerini, A[lfredo]. 1934. "La τρυφή nella storiografia ellenistica." *Studi italiani di filologia classica* 11: 35–56.

Paton 1916–18.
Paton, W. R. 1916–18. *The Greek Anthology*. 5 vols. London: Heinemann.

Pavesi and Gagetti 2001
Pavesi, Giuseppina, and Elisabetta Gagetti. 2001. *Arte e materia: Studi su oggetti di ornamento di età romana*. Edited by Gemma Sena Chiesa. Bologna: Cisalpino.

Payne 1931
Payne, Humfry. 1931. *Necrocorinthia: A Study of Corinthian Art in the Archaic Period*. Oxford: Clarendon Press.

Pekàry 1968
Pekàry, T. 1968. "Goldene Statuen der Kaiserzeit." *RM* 75: 144–48.

Pekridou-Gorecki 1989
Pekridou-Gorecki, Anastasia. 1989. *Mode im antiken Griechenland*. Munich: Beck.

Penny 1993
Penny, Nicholas. 1993. *The Materials of Sculpture*. New Haven: Yale University Press.

Petrain 2005
Petrain, David. 2005. "Gems, Metapoetics, and Value: Greek and Roman Responses to a Third-Century Discourse on Precious Stones." *Transactions of the American Philological Association* 135: 329–57.

Petrakos 1977
Petrakos, Basil. 1977. *Delphi*. Athens: Clio.

Pfeiler 1970
Pfeiler, Bärbel. 1970. *Römischer Goldschmuck des ersten und zweiten Jahrhunderts n. Chr. nach datierten Funden*. Mainz: Philipp von Zabern.

Pfrommer 1983
Pfrommer, Michael. 1983. "Griechische Originale und Kopien unter römischem Tafelsilber." *JPGMJ* 11: 135–46.

Pfrommer 1993
Pfrommer, Michael. 1993. *Metalwork from the Hellenized East: Catalogue of the Collections*. Malibu: JPGM.

Pfrommer 1999
Pfrommer, Michael. 1999. *Alexandria: Im Schatten der Pyramiden*. Mainz: Philipp von Zabern.

Pfrommer 2001
Pfrommer, Michael; with Elana Towne Markus. 2001. *Greek Gold from Hellenistic Egypt*. Los Angeles: J Paul Getty Trust.

Picón et al. 2007
Picón, Carlos A., Joan R. Mertens, Elizabeth J. Milleker, Christopher S. Lightfoot, and Seán Hemingway. 2007. *Art of the Classical World in the Metropolitan Museum of Art: Greece, Cyprus, Etruria, Rome*. New York: Metropolitan Museum of Art.

Pillinger 1984
Pillinger, Renate. 1984. *Studien zu römischen Zwischengoldgläsern*. Vol. 1, *Geschichte der Technik und das Problem der Authentizität*. Vienna: Verlag der Österreichischen Akademie der Wissenschaften.

Piotrovsky, Galanina, and Grach 1987
Piotrovsky, Boris, Liudmila Galanina, and Nonna Grach. 1987. *Scythian Art*. Translated by Viacheslav Sobolev. Oxford: Phaidon; Leningrad: Aurora.

Plantzos 1996a
Plantzos, Dimitris. 1996. "Hellenistic Cameos: Problems of Classification and Chronology." *Bulletin of the Institute of Classical Studies* 41: 115–31.

Plantzos 1996b
Plantzos, Dimitris. 1996. "Ptolemaic Cameos of the Second and First Centuries BC." *Oxford Journal of Archaeology* 15: 39–61.

Plantzos 1997
Plantzos, Dimitris. 1997. "Crystals and Lenses in the Graeco-Roman World." *AJA* 101: 451–64.

Plantzos 1999a
Plantzos, Dimitris. 1999. *Hellenistic Engraved Gems*. Oxford: Clarendon Press.

Plantzos 1999b
Plantzos, Dimitris. 1999. "The Price of Sacrilege: Diomedes, the Palladion and Roman Taste." In Henig and Plantzos 1999, 39–47.

Platt 2006
Platt, Verity. 2006. "Making an Impression: Replication and the Ontology of the Graeco-Roman Seal Stone." *Art History* 29: 233–57.

Platz-Horster 1987–94
Platz-Horster, Gertrud. 1987–94. *Die antiken Gemmen aus Xanten.* 2 vols. Cologne: Rheinland-Verlag; Bonn: Habelt.

Platz-Horster 1997
Platz-Horster, Gertrud. 1997. "Der Capita-iugata-Kameo in Berlin." In *La glyptique des mondes classiques: Mélanges en hommage à Marie-Louise Vollenweider*, edited by Mathilde Avisseau Broustet, 55–70. Paris: Bibliothèque nationale de France.

Platz-Horster 2002
Platz-Horster, Gertrud. 2002. *Ancient Gold Jewellery. Altes Museum: A Selection from the Permanent Collection.* Translated by Michael Vickers and Mira Hofmann. Mainz: Philipp von Zabern.

Platz-Horster 2008
Platz-Horster, Gertrud, ed. 2008. *Mythos und Macht: Erhabene Bilder in Edelstein.* Berlin: Staatliche Museen zu Berlin, Antikensammlung.

Platz-Horster 2012
Platz-Horster, Gertrud. 2012. *Erhabene Bilder: Die Kameen in der Antikensammlung Berlin.* Wiesbaden: Reichert.

Pollini 1993
Pollini, John. 1993. "The Gemma Augustea: Ideology, Rhetorical Imagery, and the Creation of a Dynastic Narrative." In *Narrative and Event in Ancient Art*, edited by Peter J. Holliday, 258–98. Cambridge: Cambridge University Press.

Pollitt 1974
Pollitt, J. J. 1974. *The Ancient View of Greek Art: Criticism, History, and Terminology.* New Haven: Yale University Press.

Pollitt 1986
Pollitt, J. J. 1986. *Art in the Hellenistic Age.* Cambridge: Cambridge University Press.

Pollitt 1990
Pollitt, J. J. 1990. *The Art of Ancient Greece: Sources and Documents.* 2nd ed. Cambridge: Cambridge University Press.

Pope and Schultz 2014
Pope, Spencer, and Peter Schultz. 2014. "The Chryselephantine Doors of the Parthenon." *AJA* 118: 19–31.

Porter 2011
Porter, James I. 2011. "Against *leptotes*: Rethinking Hellenistic Aesthetics." In *Creating a Hellenistic World*, edited by Andrew Erskine and Lloyd Llewellyn Jones, 271–312. Swansea: Classical Press of Wales.

Porter 2012
Porter, James I. 2012. "Is the Sublime an Aesthetic Value?" In *Aesthetic Value in Classical Antiquity*, edited by Ineke Sluiter and Ralph M. Rosen, 47–70. Leiden: Brill.

Poulsen 1968
Poulsen, Vagn H. 1968. "Die Silberbecher von Hoby." *Antike Plastik* 8: 69–74.

Powers 2011
Powers, Jessica. 2011. "Beyond Painting in Pompeii's Houses: Wall Ornaments and Their Patrons." In *Pompeii: Art, Industry, and Infrastructure*, edited by Eric Poehler, Miko Flohr, and Kevin Cole, 10–32. Oxford: Oxbow Books.

Prioux 2008
Prioux, Évelyne. 2008. *Petits musées en vers: Épigramme et discours sur les collections antiques.* Paris: INHA.

Prioux 2010
Prioux, Évelyne. 2010. "Visite au cabinet des gemmes: Images et idéologie lagides dans un cycle d'épigrammes hellénistiques." In *Métamorphoses du regard ancien*, edited by Évelyne Prioux and Agnès Rouveret, 29–66. Nanterre: Presses Universitaires de Paris-Ouest.

Prioux 2012
Prioux, Évelyne. 2012. "Addaios, Épigrammes, 9 Gow-Page," texte n° 252231. In *CALLYTHEA*, www.cn-telma.fr/callythea/extrait252231. First posted May 6, 2012; modified March 14, 2013.

Pritchett 1953
Pritchett, W. Kendrick. 1953. "The Attic Stelai: Part I." *Hesperia* 22: 225–99.

Pritchett 1956
Pritchett, W. Kendrick. 1956. "The Attic Stelai: Part II," with a contribution by Anne Pippin. *Hesperia* 25: 178–317.

Prückner 1968
Pruckner, Helmut. 1968. *Die lokrischen Tonreliefs: Beitrag zur Kultgeschichte von Lokroi Epizephyrioi.* Mainz: Philipp von Zabern.

Qi 2003
Qi, Dongfang. 2003. "The Burial Location and Dating of the Hejia Village Treasures." *Orientations* 34, no. 2: 20–24.

Quagliati 1908
Quagliati, Q[uintino]. 1908. "Rilievi votivi arcaici in terracotta di Lokroi Epizephyrioi." *Ausonia: Rivista della Società italiana di archeologia e storia dell'arte* 3: 136–234.

Ramage and Craddock 2000
Ramage, Andrew, and Paul Craddock. 2000. *King Croesus' Gold: Excavations at Sardis and the History of Gold Refining.* London: British Museum.

Rapin 1987
Rapin, Claude. 1987. "La trésorerie hellénistique d'Aï Khanoum." *Revue archéologique*, n.s., fasc. 1: 41–70.

Rapin 1992
Rapin, Claude. 1992. *La trésorerie du palais hellénistique d'Aï Khanoum: L'apogée et la chute du royaume grec de Bactriane.* Fouilles d'Aï Khanoum 8; Mémoires de la Délégation archéologique française en Afghanistan 33. Paris: Boccard.

Raschke 1978
Raschke, Manfred G. 1978 "New Studies in Roman Commerce with the East." In *Aufstieg und Niedergang der römischen Welt*, part 2, vol. 9, no. 2, edited by Hildegard Temporini and Wolfgang Haase, 604–1378. Berlin: De Gruyter.

Rausch 1998
Rausch, A., ed. 1998. *La Gloire d'Alexandrie.* Exh. cat., Paris, Musée du Petit Palais. Paris: Paris-musées.

Reeder 1976
Reeder Williams, Ellen. 1976. "Ancient Clay Impressions from Greek Metalwork." *Hesperia* 45: 41–66.

Reeder 1988
Reeder, Ellen D. 1988. "The Hellenistic Minor Arts." In *Hellenistic Art in the Walters Art Gallery*, edited by Ellen D. Reeder, 45–51. Exh. cat. Baltimore: Walters Art Gallery.

Reeder 1999
Reeder, Ellen D., ed. 1999. *Scythian Gold: Treasures from Ancient Ukraine.* Exh. cat., San Antonio Museum of Art and other venues. New York: Harry Abrams in association with the Walters Art Gallery, Baltimore.

Reinhold 1970
Reinhold, Meyer. 1970. *History of Purple as a Status Symbol in Antiquity.* Brussels: Latomus.

Reinsberg 1980
Reinsberg, Carola. 1980. *Studien zur hellenistischen Toreutik: Die antiken Gipsabgüsse aus Memphis.* Hildesheim: Gerstenberg.

Reuterswärd 1960
Reuterswärd, Patrik. 1960. *Studien zur Polychromie der Plastik.* Vol. 2, *Griechenland und Rom.* Stockholm: Almqvist & Wiksell.

Reynolds, Roueché, and Bodard 2007
Reynolds, Joyce, Charlotte Roueché, and Gabriel Bodard. 2007. *Inscriptions of Aphrodisias.* London: King's College. http://insaph.kcl.ac.uk/iaph2007/index.html.

Rhomiopoulou and Schmidt-Dounas 2010
Rhomiopoulou, Katerina, and Barbara Schmidt-Dounas. 2010. *Das Palmettengrab in Lefkadia. Mitteilungen des Deutschen Archäologischen Instituts, Athenische Abteilung*, Beiheft 21. Mainz: Philipp von Zabern.

Riccardi 2002
Riccardi, Lee Ann. 2002. "Military Standards, *Imagines* and the Gold and Silver Imperial Portraits from Aventicum, Plotinoupolis, and the Marengo Treasure." *Antike Kunst* 45: 86–100.

Rice 1983
Rice, E. E. 1983. *The Grand Procession of Ptolemy Philadelphus.* Oxford: Oxford University Press.

L. Richardson 1988
Richardson, Lawrence. 1988. *Pompeii: An Architectural History.* Baltimore: Johns Hopkins University Press.

R. Richardson 1911
Richardson, Rufus B. 1911. *A History of Greek Sculpture.* New York: American Book Company.

Richter 1929
Richter, Gisela M. A. 1929. "Silk in Greece." *AJA* 33: 27–33.

Richter 1945
Richter, Gisela M. A. 1945. "An Ivory Relief in the Metropolitan Museum of Art." *AJA* 49: 261–69.

Richter 1956
Richter, Gisela M. A. 1956. *Catalogue of Engraved Gems: Greek, Etruscan and Roman. The Metropolitan Museum of Art, New York.* Rome: "L'Erma" di Bretschneider.

Richter 1965
Richter, Gisela M. A. 1965. *A Handbook of Greek Art.* 4th ed. London: Phaidon.

Richter 1966
Richter, Gisela M. A. 1966. *The Furniture of the Greeks, Etruscans and Romans.* London: Phaidon.

Richter 1968a
Richter, Gisela M. A. 1968. *Korai: Archaic Greek Maidens*. London: Phaidon.

Richter 1968b
Richter, Gisela M. A. 1968. *Engraved Gems of the Greeks, Etruscans, and Romans*. Part 1, *Engraved Gems of the Greeks and the Etruscans: A History of Greek Art in Miniature*. London: Phaidon.

Richter 1971
Richter, Gisela M. A. 1971. *Engraved Gems of the Greeks, Etruscans, and Romans*. Part 2, *Engraved Gems of the Romans*. London: Phaidon.

Ridgway 1992
Ridgway, Brunilde S. 1992. "Images of Athena on the Acropolis." In *Goddess and Polis: The Panathenaic Festival in Ancient Athens,* edited by Jenifer Neils, 119–42. Exh. cat. Hanover, NH: Hood Museum of Art, Dartmouth College; Princeton: Princeton University Press.

Ridgway 1994
Ridgway, Brunilde S., ed. 1994. *Greek Sculpture in the Art Museum, Princeton University: Greek Originals, Roman Copies and Variants*. Princeton: The Museum.

Rigato 2011
Rigato, Daniela. 2011. "Tra *pietas* e magia: Gemme e preziosi offerti alle divinità." In Baldini and Morelli 2011, 41–55.

Roberts 2013
Roberts, Paul. 2013. *Life and Death in Pompeii and Herculaneum*. Exh. cat. London: British Museum.

Robertson 1975
Robertson, Martin. 1975. *A History of Greek Art*. 2 vols. Cambridge: Cambridge University Press.

Robertson 1991
Robertson, Martin. 1991. "Adopting an Approach, I." In *Looking at Greek Vases,* edited by Tom Rasmussen and Nigel Spivey, 1–12. Cambridge: Cambridge University Press.

Rodríguez-Almeida 1994
Rodríguez-Almeida, Emilio. 1994. "Marziale in Marmo." *MÉFRA* 106: 197–217.

Rogers 1991
Rogers, Guy MacLean. 1991. *The Sacred Identity of Ephesos: Foundation Myths of a Roman City*. London: Routledge.

Romano 1980
Romano, Irene B. 1980. "Early Greek Cult Images." PhD diss., University of Pennsylvania, Philadelphia.

Rosenfeld, Dvoracheck, and Amorai-Stark 2003
Rosenfeld, Amnon, Michael Dvoracheck, and Shua Amorai-Stark. 2003. "Roman Wheel-cut Engraving, Dyeing and Painting Microquartz Gemstones." *Journal of Archaeological Science* 30: 227–38.

Ross 1943
Ross, Marvin Chauncey. 1943. "The Rubens Vase: Its History and Date." *Journal of the Walters Art Gallery* 6: 9–39.

Rouse 1902
Rouse, William Henry Denham. 1902. *Greek Votive Offerings: An Essay in the History of Greek Religion*. Cambridge: Cambridge University Press.

Roux 1995
Roux, Valentine. 1995. "Le travail des lapidaires." In Tallon 1995, 39–44.

Rubel 2014
Rubel, Alexander. 2014. *Fear and Loathing in Ancient Athens: Religion and Politics during the Peloponnesian War*. Edited and translated by Michael Vickers. Abingdon, Oxon, and New York: Routledge.

Rubin 1995
Rubin, Patricia Lee. 1995. *Giorgio Vasari: Art and History*. New Haven: Yale University Press.

Rusconi 1935
Rusconi, Arturo Iahn. 1935. *Il Museo degli Argenti in Firenze*. Rome: La Libreria dello Stato.

Russo 1999
Russo, Simona. 1999. *Gioielli nei papiri di età greco-romana*. Florence: Istituto Papirologico "G. Vitelli."

Rutschowscaya 1990
Rutschowscaya, Marie-Hélène. 1990. *Coptic Fabrics*. Paris: Adam Biro.

Sas and Thoen 2002
Sas, Kathy, and Hugo Thoen, eds. 2002. *Schone Schijn: Romeinse juweelkunst in West-Europa / Brillance et prestige: La joaillerie romaine en Europe occidentale*. Exh. cat., Provinciaal Gallo-Tomeins Museum te Tongeren. Leuven: Uitgeverij Peeters.

Scarisbrick 1986
Scarisbrick, Diana. 1986. "The Devonshire Parure." *Archaeologia* 108: 239–54.

Scarisbrick 2003
Scarisbrick, Diana. 2003. "The Devonshire Gems and Parure." In *The Devonshire Inheritance: Five Centuries of Collecting at Chatsworth,* edited by Nicolas Barker, 64–74. Exh. cat. Alexandria, VA: Art Services International.

Scatozza Höricht 1989
Scatozza Höricht, Lucia Amalia. 1989. *I monili di Ercolano*. Rome: "L'Erma" di Bretschneider.

Schazmann 1940
Schazmann, Paul. 1940. "Buste en or représentant l'empereur Marc-Aurèle trouvé à Avenches en 1939." *Zeitschrift für schweizerische Archaeologie und Kunstgeschichte* 2: 69–93.

Schiering 1991
Schiering, Wolfgang. 1991. *Die Werkstatt des Pheidias in Olympia*. Vol. 2, *Werkstattfunde*. Olympische Forschungen 18. Berlin: De Gruyter.

E. Schmidt 1957
Schmidt, Erich F. 1957. *Persepolis*. Vol. 2, *Contents of the Treasury and Other Discoveries*. Chicago: University of Chicago Press.

G. Schmidt 2008
Schmidt, Gerhard. 2008. "Erfahrungen und Fragen beim Nachschneiden der drei größten Sardonyx-Kameen der Antike: Tazza Farnese, Gemma Augustea, und Grand Camée de France." In Platz-Horster 2008, 6–12.

Schur 2004
Schur, David. 2004. "A Garland of Stones: Hellenistic *Lithika* as Reflections on Poetic Transformations." In Acosta-Hughes, Kosmetatou, and Baumbach 2004, 118–22.

Scott 1931
Scott, Kenneth. 1931. "The Significance of Statues in Precious Metals in Emperor Worship." *Transactions and Proceedings of the American Philological Association* 62: 101–23.

Scullard 1974
Scullard, H. H. 1974. *The Elephant in the Greek and Roman World*. London: Thames & Hudson.

Seaford 1994
Seaford, Richard. 1994. *Reciprocity and Ritual: Homer and Tragedy in the Developing City-State*. Oxford: Clarendon Press.

Segall 1938
Segall, Berta. 1938. *Museum Benaki Athen: Katalog der Goldschmiede-Arbeiten*. Athens: Pyrsos.

Segall 1941
Segall, Berta. 1941. "Two Gold Pins in the Classical Collection." *Bulletin of the Museum of Fine Arts* (Boston) 39, no. 234: 54–58.

Segall 1942
Segall, Berta. 1942. "The Earring with Winged Charioteer in the Classical Department: An Interpretation." *Bulletin of the Museum of Fine Arts* (Boston) 40, no. 239: 50–54.

Sekora 1977
Sekora, John. 1977. *Luxury: The Concept in Western Thought, Eden to Smollett*. Baltimore: Johns Hopkins University Press.

Sena Chiesa 1966
Sena Chiesa, Gemma. 1966. *Gemme del Museo Nazionale di Aquileia*. Aquileia: Museo Nazionale di Aquileia.

Sena Chiesa 1998
Sena Chiesa, Gemma. 1998. "Un pezzo eccezionale del Tesoro di Marengo: Il ritratto di Lucio Vero." In Mercando 1998, 359–68.

Sena Chiesa 2002
Sena Chiesa, Gemma, ed. 2002. *Gemme dalla corte imperiale alla corte celeste*. Milan: Università degli Studi di Milano.

Sena Chiesa 2003
Sena Chiesa, Gemma. 2003. "Arte e prestigio nella glittica di età romana," with contributions by Elisabetta Gagetti and A. Magni. In Zanettin 2003, 387–436.

Sena Chiesa 2008
Sena Chiesa, Gemma. 2008. "*Imago Caesaris argentea:* Il busto di Lucio Vero del Tesoro di Marengo." *LANX* 1: 1–25. Electronic ed.: http://riviste.unimi.it/index.php/lanx/article/view/123/274.

Sena Chiesa 2012
Sena Chiesa, Gemma, ed. 2012. *Constantino 313 d.C.* Exh. cat., Milan, Palazzo Reale. Milan: Electa.

Sena Chiesa and Gagetti 2009
Sena Chiesa, Gemma, and Elisabetta Gagetti. 2009. "I manufatti di lusso." In *Moenibus et portu celeberrima. Aquileia: Storia di una città,* edited by Francesca Ghedini, Michele Bueno, and Marta Novello, 253–72. Rome: Libreria dello Stato.

Shaw, Bunbury, and Jameson 1999
Shaw, Ian, Judith Bunbury, and Robert Jameson. 1999. "Emerald Mining in Roman and Byzantine Egypt." *JRA* 12: 203–15.

D. Shepherd 1976
Shepherd, Dorothy G. 1976. "A Late Classical Tapestry." *Bulletin of the Cleveland Museum of Art* 63: 307–13.

R. Shepherd 1993
Shepherd, Robert. 1993. *Ancient Mining*. London: Elsevier Applied Science.

Sherlock 1996
Sherlock, David. 1996. "Silver and Silversmithing." In Strong and Brown 1976, 11–23.
Simon 1966
Simon, Erika. 1966. "Toreutica." In *EAA* vol. 7: 919–48.
Simon 1982
Simon, Erika. 1982. "Vier iulisch-claudische Büsten: Augustus und Antonia Minor in Kurashiki/Japan." *Archäologischer Anzeiger* 1981: 332–43.
Slavazzi 2003
Slavazzi, Fabrizio. 2003. "Vasi in pietra dura nell'età ellenistico-romana." In Zanettin 2003: 437–58.
M. Smith 2004
Smith, Martyn. 2004. "Elusive Stones: Reading Posidippus' *Lithika* through Technical Writing on Stones." In Acosta-Hughes, Kosmetatou, and Baumbach 2004, 105–17.
R. Smith 1988
Smith, R. R. R. 1988. *Hellenistic Royal Portraits*. Oxford: Clarendon Press.
T. Smith and Plantzos 2012
Smith, Tyler Jo, and Dimitris Plantzos, eds. *A Companion to Greek Art*. 2 vols. Malden, MA, and Oxford: Wiley-Blackwell.
Smithson 1968
Smithson, Evelyn Lord. 1968. "The Tomb of a Rich Athenian Lady, ca. 850 B.C." *Hesperia* 37: 77–116.
S. Spantidaki 2014
Spantidaki, Stella. 2014. "Embellishment Techniques of Classical Greek Textiles." In *Greek and Roman Textiles and Dress: An Interdisciplinary Anthology*, edited by Mary Harlow and Marie-Louise Nosch. Oxford: Oxbow.
Y. Spantidaki and Moulhérat 2012
Spantidaki, Youlie, and Moulhérat, Christophe. 2012. "Greece." In *Textiles and Textile Production in Europe from Prehistory to AD 400*, edited by Margarita Gleba and Ulla Mannering, 185–200. Oxford: Oxbow.
Spano 1943
Spano, Giuseppe. 1943. "La tomba dell'edile C. Vestorio Prisco in Pompei." *Atti della Accademia nazionale dei Lincei: Memorie della Classe di scienze morali, storiche e filologiche*, ser. 7, 3, fasc. 6: 237–315.
Sparkes 2006
Sparkes, Brian A. 2006. "Pottery and Metalwork." In Bispham, Harrison, and Sparkes 2006, 206–16.
Spatafora and Vassallo 2005
Spatafora, Francesca, and Stefano Vassallo. 2005. *La phiale aurea di Caltavuturo*. Palermo: Soprintendenza ai Beni Culturali Ambientali, Servizio Beni Archeologici.
Spier 1989
Spier, Jeffrey. 1989. "A Group of Ptolemaic Engraved Garnets." *Journal of the Walters Art Gallery* 47: 21–38.
Spier 1991
Spier, Jeffrey. 1991. "Two Hellenistic Gems Rediscovered." *Antike Kunst* 34: 91–96.
Spier 1992
Spier, Jeffrey. 1992. *Ancient Gems and Finger Rings: Catalogue of the Collection. The J. Paul Getty Museum*. Malibu: JPGM.
Spier 2010
Spier, Jeffrey. 2010. *Treasures of the Ferrell Collection*. Wiesbaden: Reichert.
Spinazzola 1928
Spinazzola, Vittorio. 1928. *Le arti decorative in Pompei e nel Museo nazionale di Napoli*. Milan: Bestetti e Tumminelli.
Spinola 2014
Spinola, Giandomenico. 2014. "I ritratti dei poeti, filosofi, letterati e uomini illustri nelle biblioteche romane." In *La biblioteca infinita: I luoghi del sapere nel mondo antico*, edited by Roberto Meneghini and Rossella Rea, 155–75. Exh. cat., Rome, Colosseum. Milan: Electa.
Springer 1949
Springer, Lawrence A. 1949. "Temple Treasures: A Study Based on Livy." PhD diss., University of Pennsylvania, Philadelphia.
Squire 2011
Squire, Michael. 2011. *The Iliad in a Nutshell: Visualizing Epic on the Tabulae Iliacae*. Oxford: Oxford University Press.
Stampolides 1992
Stampolides, Nikolaos Chr. 1992. *Les sceaux de Délos / Τα Σφραγισματα της Δηλου*. Vol. 2. Paris: Boccard.
Stanwick 2003
Stanwick, Paul Edmund. 2003. *Portraits of the Ptolemies: Greek Kings as Egyptian Pharaohs*. Austin: University of Texas Press.
Stauffer 2006
Stauffer, Annemarie. 2006. "Zum Nachleben babylonischer Wirktradition im Nahen Osten." *Damaszener Mitteilungen* 15: 303–20.
Stauffer et al. 1995
Stauffer, Annemarie, Marsha Hill, Helen Evans, and Daniel Walker. 1995. *Textiles of Late Antiquity*. Exh. cat. New York: Metropolitan Museum of Art.
St. Clair 2003
St. Clair, Archer. 2003. *Carving as Craft: Palatine East Discoveries and the Greco-Roman Bone and Ivory Carving Tradition*. Baltimore: Johns Hopkins University Press.
St. Clair and McLachlan 1989
St. Clair, Archer, and Elizabeth Parker McLachlan, eds. 1989. *The Carver's Art: Medieval Sculpture in Ivory, Bone, and Horn*. Exh. cat. New Brunswick, NJ: Jane Voorhees Zimmerli Art Museum, Rutgers.
Stead and Rigby 1999
Stead, I. M., and V. Rigby. 1999. *The Morel Collection: Iron Age Antiquities from Champagne in the British Museum*. London: British Museum.
Stefanelli 1991
Stefanelli, Lucia Pirzio Biroli. 1991. *L'argento dei Romani: Vasellame da tavola e d'apparato*. Rome: "L'Erma" di Bretschneider.
Stefanelli 1992
Stefanelli, Lucia Pirzio Biroli. 1992. *L'oro dei Romani: Gioielli di età imperiale*. Rome: "L'Erma" di Bretschneider.
E. Stern 1997
Stern, E. Marianne. 1997. "Glass and Rock Crystal: A Multifaceted Relationship." *JRA* 10: 192–206.
W. Stern and Thimme 2007
Stern, Wilma Olch, and Danae Hadjilazaro Thimme. 2007. *Kenchreai: Eastern Port of Corinth*. Vol. 6, *Ivory, Bone, and Related Wood Finds*. Leiden: Brill.
Stewart 1990
Stewart, Andrew. 1990. *Greek Sculpture: An Exploration*. New Haven: Yale University Press.
Stewart 1993
Stewart, Andrew. 1993. *Faces of Power: Alexander's Image and Hellenistic Politics*. Berkeley: University of California Press.
Strong 1966
Strong, D[onald] E. 1966. *Catalogue of the Carved Amber in the Department of Greek and Roman Antiquities*. London: British Museum.
Strong and Brown 1976
Strong, Donald E., and David Brown, eds. 1976. *Roman Crafts*. London: Duckworth.
Talamo 2013
Talamo, Emilia. 2013. "Statue in avori da Cesano." In *Palazzo Massimo alle Terme: Le collezioni*, edited by Carlo Gasparri and Rita Paris, 302–8. Milan: Electa.
Tallon 1995
Tallon, Françoise, ed. 1995. *Les pierres précieuses de l'orient ancien des Sumériens aux Sassanides*. Exh. cat., Paris, Musée du Louvre. Exposition-dossier du Département des antiquités orientales 49. Paris: Réunion des Musées Nationaux.
Tamm 2004
Tamm, John. 2004. "Roman Drinking Silver: Terms, Forms, and Functions; Some Notes." In *Daimonopylai: Essays in Classics and the Classical Tradition Presented to Edmund G. Berry*, edited by Rory B. Egan and Mark A. Joyal, 453–67. Winnepeg: University of Manitoba Centre for Hellenic Civilization.
Tamm 2005
Tamm, John. 2005. "Argentum Potorium and the Campanian Wall-Painter: The Priscus Service Revisted." *Bulletin antieke beschaving: Annual Papers on Classical Archaeology* 80: 73–90.
Themelis 1983
Themelis, Petros G. 1983. "An 8th Century Goldsmith's Workshop at Eretria." In *The Greek Renaissance of the Eighth Century B.C: Tradition and Innovation*, edited by Robin Hägg, 157–65. Stockholm: Svenska Institutet i Athen.
Thoresen and Schmetzer 2013
Thoresen, Lisbet, and Karl Schmetzer. 2013. "Greek, Etruscan and Roman Garnets in the Antiquities Collection of the J. Paul Getty Museum." *Journal of Gemmology* 33, nos. 7–8: 201–22.
Toher 1991
Toher, Mark. 1991. "Greek Funerary Legislation and the Two Spartan Funerals." In *Georgica: Studies in Honour of George Cawkwell*, edited by Michael A. Flower and Mark Toher, 159–75. London: University of London, Institute of Classical Studies.
Tolstikov and Treister 1996
Tolstikov, Vladimir, and Michail Treister. 1996. *The Gold of Troy: Searching for Homer's Fabled City*. Exh. cat., Moscow, Pushkin State Museum of Fine Arts. New York: Ministry of Culture of the Russian Federation in association with Abrams.

Tondo and Vanni 1990
Tondo, Luigi, and Franca Maria Vanni. 1990. *Le gemme dei Medici e dei Lorena nel Museo Archeologico di Firenze.* Florence: Centro Di.

Tondriau 1948
Tondriau, Julien. 1948. "La *tryphè*, philosophie royale ptolémaïque." *REA* 50: 49–54.

Toynbee 1973
Toynbee, J. M. C. 1973. *Animals in Roman Life and Art.* London: Thames and Hudson.

Treister 1996
Treister, Michail Y. 1996. *The Role of Metals in Ancient Greek History.* Leiden: Brill.

Treister 2001
Treister, Michail Y. 2001. *Hammering Techniques in Greek and Roman Jewellery and Toreutics.* Leiden: Brill.

Tressaud and Vickers 2007
Tressaud, Alain, and Michael Vickers. 2007. "Ancient Murrhine Ware and Its Glass Evocations." *Journal of Glass Studies* 49: 143–52.

Tripodi 1985
Tripodi, Bruno. 1985. "Le larnakes di Vergina: Considerazioni sui cinerari macedoni del IV sec. a.C." *Rivista storica dell'antichità* 15: 53–65.

Trofimova 2007
Trofimova, Anna A., ed. 2007. *Greeks on the Black Sea: Ancient Art from the Hermitage.* Exh. cat., Malibu, The Getty Villa. Los Angeles: JPGM.

Tsimbidou-Avloniti 2005
Tsimbidou-Avloniti, Maria. 2005. Μακεδονικοί τάφοι στο Φοίνικα και στον Άγιο Αθανάσιο Θεσσαλονίκης, Συμβολή στη μελέτη της εικονογραφίας των ταφικών μνημείων της Μακεδονίας / *The Macedonian Tombs at Phinikas and Ayios Athanasios in the Area of Thessaloniki: Contribution to the Iconography of the Funerary Monuments of Macedonia.* Athens: Ekdose tou Tameiou Archaiologikon Poron kai Apallotrioseon.

Valavanos and Lambrinoudakis 2010
Valavanos, Panos, and Vasileios K. Lambrinoudakis. 2010. *Mousei Historias tes Technes: Vienna.* He Hellenike techne sta mouseia tou kosmou 5. [Athens]: Viliotheke Technes he Kathemerine.

Van de Grift 1984
Van de Grift, Jon. 1984. "Tears and Revel: The Allegory of the Berthouville Centaur Scyphi." *AJA* 88: 377–88.

Van Zanten 1977
Van Zanten, David. 1977. *The Architectural Polychromy of the 1830's.* New York: Garland.

Varner 2004
Varner, Eric R. 2004. *Mutilation and Transformation: Damnatio Memoriae and Roman Imperial Portraiture.* Leiden: Brill.

Vassilika 1998
Vassilika, Eleni. 1998. *Greek and Roman Art.* Fitzwilliam Museum Handbooks. Cambridge: Cambridge University Press.

Vaulina and Wasowicz 1974
Vaulina, Maria, and Aleksandra Wasowicz. 1974. *Bois grecs et romains de l'Ermitage.* Translated by Maria Drojecka. Warsaw: Zaklad Narodowy im. Ossolinskich.

Vavritsas 1968
Vavritsas, Andreas. 1968. "Χρυσῆ Προτομὴ ἐκ Διδυμοτείχου"[Gold bust from Didymoteichon]. *Athens Annals of Archaeology* 1: 194–97.

Vavritsas 1969
Vavritsas, Andreas. 1969. "Eine Goldbüste aus Didymoteichon." In *Actes du Ier Congrès international des études balkaniques et sud-est européennes*, vol. 2: 419–22. Sofia: Académie Bulgare des Sciences.

Venedikov 1961
Venedikov, Ivan. 1961. *The Panagyurishte Gold Treasure.* Translated by Alexander Risov. Sofia: Bulgarski Houdozhnik.

Venedikov and Gerassimov 1975
Venedikov, Ivan, and Todor Gerassimov. 1975. *Thracian Art Treasures.* Translated by Marguerite Alexieva and Petco Drenkov. London: Caxton.

Venturelli 2009
Venturelli, Paola. 2009. *Il tesoro dei Medici al Museo degli argenti: Oggetti preziosi in cristallo e pietre dure nelle collezioni di Palazzo Pitti.* Florence: Giunti.

Vercoutter 1962
Vercoutter, Jean. 1962. "Un palais des 'Candaces', contemporain d'Auguste (Fouilles à Wad-ban-Naga 1958–1960)." *Syria* 39: 263–99.

Verdier 1990
Verdier, Philippe. 1990. "Chalice of the Abbot Suger of Saint-Denis." *Studies in the History of Art* 24: 9–29.

Verdier 1993
Verdier, Philippe. 1993. "Chalice of the Abbot Suger of Saint-Denis." In Rudolf Distelberger, Alison Luchs, Philippe Verdier, and Timothy H. Wilson, *Western Decorative Arts, Part I: Medieval, Renaissance, and Historicizing Styles Including Metalwork, Enamels, and Ceramics*, 4–12. The Collections of the National Gallery of Art Systematic Catalogue. Washington, DC: National Gallery of Art.

Vermeule 1963
Vermeule, Cornelius C. 1963. "Augustan and Julio-Claudian Court Silver." *Antike Kunst* 6: 33–40.

Vermeule 1974
Vermeule, Cornelius C. 1974. *Greek and Roman Sculpture in Gold and Silver.* Boston: Museum of Fine Arts.

Vickers 1984
Vickers, Michael. 1984. "Demus' Gold Phiale." *American Journal of Ancient History* 9: 48–53.

Vickers 1985
Vickers, Michael. 1985. "Early Greek Coinage, a Reassessment." *Numismatic Chronicle* 145: 1–44.

Vickers 1987
Vickers, Michael. 1987. "Early Civilizations" and "Rome and the Eastern Empire." In *Ivory, a History and Collector's Guide*, edited by Fiona St Aubyn, 32–67. London: Thames and Hudson.

Vickers 1989a
Vickers, Michael. 1989. "Panagyurishte, Dalboki, Loukovit and Rogozen: Questions of Metrology and Status." In *The Rogozen Treasure: Papers of the Anglo-Bulgarian Conference, 12 March 1987*, edited by B. F. Cook, 101–11. London: British Museum.

Vickers 1989b
Vickers, Michael. 1989. "Persian Gold in Parthenon Inventories." *REA* 91: 249–57.

Vickers 1990a
Vickers, Michael. 1990. "Golden Greece: Relative Values, Minae, and Temple Inventories." *AJA* 94: 613–25.

Vickers 1990b
Vickers, Michael. 1990. "The Impoverishment of the Past: The Case of Classical Greece." *Antiquity* 64: 455–63.

Vickers 1994
Vickers, Michael. 1994. "Nabataea, India, Gaul, and Carthage: Reflections on Hellenistic and Roman Gold Vessels and Red-Gloss Pottery." *AJA* 98: 231–48.

Vickers 1996
Vickers, Michael. 1996. "Rock Crystal: The Key to Cut Glass and *Diatreta* in Persia and Rome." *JRA* 9: 48–65.

Vickers 1997a
Vickers, Michael. 1997. "Glassware and the Changing Arbiters of Taste." *Expedition* 39, no. 2: 4–14.

Vickers 1997b
Vickers, Michael. 1997. "Hamilton, Geology, Stone Vases and Taste." *Journal of the History of Collections* 9: 263–73.

Vickers 1999a
Vickers, Michael. 1999. *Images on Textiles: The Weave of Fifth-Century Athenian Art and Society. Xenia: Konstanzer Althistorische Vorträge und Forschungen* 42. Konstanz, Germany: Universitätsverlag Konstanz.

Vickers 1999b
Vickers, Michael. 1999. *Skeuomorphismus oder die Kunst, aus wenig viel zu machen.* Trierer Winckelmannsprogramm 16. Mainz: Philipp von Zabern.

Vickers and Gill 1994
Vickers, Michael, and David Gill. 1994. *Artful Crafts: Ancient Greek Silverware and Pottery.* Oxford: Clarendon Press.

Visconti 1823
Visconti, Alessandro. 1823. "Dissertazione su di una nuova argenteria." *Dissertazioni dell'Accademia Romana di Archeologia* 1, part 2: 301–17.

Vollenweider 1958
Vollenweider, Marie-Louise. 1958. "Das Bildnis des Scipio Africanus." *Museum Helveticum* 15: 27–45.

Vollenweider 1966
Vollenweider, Marie-Louise. 1966. *Die Steinschneidekunst und ihre Künstler in spätrepublikanischer und augusteischer Zeit.* Baden-Baden: Grimm.

Vollenweider 1972–74
Vollenweider, Marie-Louise. 1972–74. *Die Porträtgemmen der römischen Republik.* 2 vols. Mainz: Philipp von Zabern.

Vollenweider and Avisseau-Broustet 1995
Vollenweider, Marie-Louise, and Mathilde Avisseau-Broustet. 1995. *Camées et intailles: Catalogue raisonné.* Vol. 1, *Les portraits grecs du Cabinet des médailles.* Paris: Bibliothèque nationale de France.

Vollenweider and Avisseau-Broustet 2003
Vollenweider, Marie-Louise, and Mathilde Avisseau-Broustet. 2003. *Camées et intailles: Catalogue raisonné.* Vol. 2, *Les portraits romains du Cabinet des médailles.* Paris: Bibliothèque nationale de France.

Votokopoulou et al. 1985
Votokopoulou, Ioulia, ed. 1985. *ΣΙΝΔΟΣ. Κατάλογος της Εκθεσης*. Exh. cat. Thessalonike: Archaiologiko Mouseio Thessalonikes.

Votokopoulou 1997
Votokopoulou, Ioulia. 1997. *Argyra kai chalkina erga technes sten archaioteta*. Athens: Ekdotike Athenon.

Wace 1934
Wace, Alan J. B. 1934. "The Veil of Despoina." *AJA* 38: 107–11.

Wagner and Weisgerber 1988
Wagner, Günther A., and Gerd Weisgerber, eds. 1988. *Antike Edel- und Buntmetallgewinnung auf Thasos*. Bochum: Deutsches Bergbau-Museum.

Wagner, Weisgerber, and Kroker 1985
Wagner, Günther A., Gerd Weisgerber, and Werner Kroker. 1985. *Silber, Blei und Gold auf Sifnos: Prähistorische und antike Metallproduktion*. Bochum: Vereinigung der Freunde von Kunst und Kultur im Bergbau.

Walker and Higgs 2001
Walker, Susan, and Peter Higgs, eds. 2001. *Cleopatra of Egypt: From History to Myth*. Exh. cat., Rome, Palazzo Ruspoli, and other venues. London: British Museum.

Wallace-Hadrill 1990
Wallace-Hadrill, Andrew. 1990. "Pliny the Elder and Man's Unnatural History." *Greece & Rome*, ser. 2, 37: 80–96.

Wallace-Hadrill 2008
Wallace-Hadrill, Andrew. 2008. *Rome's Cultural Revolution*. Cambridge: Cambridge University Press.

Wallace-Hadrill 2011
Wallace-Hadrill, Andrew. 2011. *Herculaneum: Past and Future*. London: Frances Lincoln.

Walters 1921
Walters, H[enry] B. 1921. *Catalogue of Silver Plate (Greek, Etruscan, and Roman) in the British Museum*. London: Trustees of the British Museum.

Walters 1926
Walters, H[enry] B. 1926. *Catalogue of the Engraved Gems and Cameos, Greek, Etruscan and Roman in the British Museum*. Rev. ed. London: Trustees of the British Museum.

Wardle 2010
Wardle, Marianne E. 2010. "Naked and Unashamed: A Study of the Aphrodite Anadyomene in the Greco-Roman World." PhD diss., Duke University, Durham, NC.

Weber 1974
Weber, Martha. 1974. "Zu frühen attischen Gerätfiguren." *Athenische Mitteilungen* 89: 27–46.

Weitzmann 1979
Weitzmann, Kurt, ed. 1979. *Age of Spirituality: Late Antique and Early Christian Art, Third to Seventh Century*. Exh. cat., New York, Metropolitan Museum of Art, 1977–78. New York: Metropolitan Museum of Art.

Weeber 2003
Weeber, Karl-Wilhelm. 2003. *Luxus im alten Rom: Die Schwelgerei, das süsse Gift*. Darmstadt: Wissenschaftliche Buchgesellschaft.

Weeber 2006
Weeber, Karl-Wilhelm. 2006. *Luxus im alten Rom: Die öffentliche Pracht*. Darmstadt: Primus.

Whitehouse 2001
Whitehouse, David. 2001. *Roman Glass in the Corning Museum of Glass*. Vol. 2. Corning: Corning Museum of Glass.

Whitley 1997
Whitley, James. 1997. "Beazley as Theorist." *Antiquity* 71, no. 271: 40–47.

Williams 1988
Williams, Dyfri. 1988. "Three Groups of Fourth Century South Italian Jewellery in the British Museum." *RM* 95: 75–95.

Williams 1996
Williams, Dyfri. 1996. "Refiguring Attic Red-figure." *Revue archéologique* 1996, no. 2: 227–52.

Williams 1998
Williams, Dyfri, ed. 1998. *The Art of the Greek Goldsmith*. London: British Museum.

Williams 2003
Williams, Dyfri. 2003. "Gilded Pottery and Golden Jewellery." In *The Macedonians in Athens, 322–229 B.C.*, edited by Olga Palagia and Stephen V. Tracy, 226–35. Oxford: Oxbow.

Williams 2004
Williams, Dyfri. 2004. "Crystalline Matter." *British Museum Magazine*, no. 48 (Spring): 47.

Williams 2009
Williams, Dyfri. 2009. *Masterpieces of Classical Art*. London: British Museum.

Williams and Ogden 1994
Williams, Dyfri, and Jack Ogden. 1994. *Greek Gold: Jewellery of the Classical World*. Exh. cat. London: British Museum.

Wilton and Bignamini 1996
Wilton, Andrew, and Ilaria Bignamini, eds. 1996. *Grand Tour: The Lure of Italy in the Eighteenth Century*. Exh. cat., London, Tate Gallery; Rome, Palazzo delle Esposizioni. London: Tate Gallery.

Winckelmann 1755 (1987 ed.)
Winckelmann, Johann Joachim. 1755. *Gedanken ueber die Nachahmung der griechischen Werke in der Malerei und Bildhauerkunst*. Dresden. Facsimile ed. with English translation by Elfriede Heyer and Roger C. Norton, *Reflections on the Imitation of Greek Works in Painting and Sculpture*. La Salle, IL: Open Court, 1987.

Winckelmann 1760
Winckelmann, Johann Joachim. 1760. *Description des pierres gravées du feu Baron de Stosch dediée à son Eminence Monseigneur le Cardinal Aléxandre Albani par M. l'Abbé Winckelmann, Bibliothecaire de son Eminence*. Florence: Chez André Bonducci.

Winckelmann 1764
Winckelmann, Johann Joachim. 1764. *Geschichte der Kunst des Alterthums*. 2 parts. Dresden: In der Waltherischen Hof-Buchhandlung.

Winter 1994
Winter, Irene J. 1994 "Radiance as an Aesthetic Value in the Art of Mesopotamia." In *Art, the Integral Vision: A Volume of Essays in Felicitation of Kapila Vatsyayan*, edited by B. N. Saraswati, S. C. Malik, and Madhu Khanna, 123–32. New Delhi: D. K. Printworld.

Wyetzner 2002
Wyetzner, Peter. 2002. "Sulla's Law on Prices and the Roman Definition of Luxury." In *Speculum Iuris: Roman Law as a Reflection of Social and Economic Life in Antiquity*, edited by Jean-Jacques Aubert and Boudewijn Sirks, 15–33. Ann Arbor: University of Michigan Press.

A. Yalouris and N. Yalouris 1987
Yalouris, Athanasia, and Nicholas Yalouris. 1987. *Olympia: The Museum and the Sanctuary*. Translated by Louise Turner. Athens: Ekdotike Athenon.

N. Yalouris 1980
Yalouris, Nicholas. 1980. *The Search for Alexander*. Exh. cat., National Gallery of Art, Washington, DC, and other venues. Boston: New York Graphic Society.

Yeroulanou 1999
Yeroulanou, Aimilia. 1999. *Diatrita: Gold Pierced-Work Jewellery from the 3rd to the 7th Century*. Athens: Benaki Museum.

Zanchi Roppo 1969
Zanchi Roppo, Franca. 1969. *Vetri paleocristiani a figure d'oro conservati in Italia*. Bologna: R. Pàtron.

Zanda 2011
Zanda, Emanuela. 2011. *Fighting Hydra-Like Luxury: Sumptuary Regulation in the Roman Republic*. London: Bristol Classical Press.

Zanettin 2003
Zanettin, Bruno, ed. 2003. *Cristalli e gemme: Realtà fisica e immaginario, simbologia, techniche e arte*. Venice: Istituto Veneto di Scienze, Lettere ed Arti.

Zanker 1988
Zanker, Paul. 1988. *The Power of Images in the Age of Augustus*. Translated by Alan Shapiro. Ann Arbor: University of Michigan Press.

P. Zazoff and H. Zazoff 1983
Zazoff, Peter, and Hilde Zazoff. 1983. *Gemmensammler und Gemmenforscher: Von einer noblen Passion zur Wissenschaft*. Munich: Beck.

Zimi 2011
Zimi, Eleni. 2011. *Late Classical and Hellenistic Silver Plate from Macedonia*. Oxford: Oxford University Press.

Zwierlein-Diehl 1986
Zwierlein-Diehl, Erika. 1986. *Glaspasten im Martin-von-Wagner-Museum der Universität Würzburg*. Munich: Prestel.

Zwierlein-Diehl 1990
Zwierlein-Diehl, Erika. 1990. "Griechische Gemmenschneider und augusteische Glyptik." *Archäologischer Anzeiger* 1990, no. 4: 539–57.

Zwierlein-Diehl 1999
Zwierlein-Diehl, Erika. 1999. *Das Onyx-Alabastron aus Stift Nottuln in Berlin*. Winckelmannsprogramm der Archäologischen Gesellschaft zu Berlin, 138. Berlin: De Gruyter.

Zwierlein-Diehl 2005
Zwierlein-Diehl, Erika. 2005. "Gemmen mit Künstlerinscriften." In *Meisterwerke: Internationales Symposion anläßlich des 150. Geburtstages von Adolf Furtwängler, Freiburg im Breisgau 30. Juni–3. Juli 2003*, edited by Volker M. Strocka, 321–43. Munich: Hirmer.

Zwierlein-Diehl 2007
Zwierlein-Diehl, Erika. 2007. *Antike Gemmen und ihr Nachleben*. Berlin: De Gruyter.

Zwierlein-Diehl 2008
Zwierlein-Diehl, Erika. 2008. *Magie der Steine: Die antiken Prunkkameen im Kunsthistorischen Museum*. Vienna: Christian Brandstätter; Kunsthistorisches Museum Wien.

ACKNOWLEDGMENTS

This book has had a lengthy gestation, and I am grateful to the many colleagues and friends who have generously provided information, encouragement, and insight over the years. A grant from the Bogliasco Foundation supported initial research under optimal conditions. Some of the material presented in the introduction first appeared in slightly different form in my essay "The Fate of Plate and Other Precious Materials: Towards a Historiography of Ancient Greek Minor (?) Arts," in *Ancient Art and Its Historiography* (Cambridge University Press, 2003), 69–91. That volume's editors, A. A. Donohue and M. D. Fullerton, as well as Beatrice Rehl and Asya Graf of Cambridge University Press, kindly provided permission to include a revised version of it here. Part of chapter 3, on ivory, first appeared in my monograph *Chryselephantine Statuary in the Ancient Mediterranean World* (Oxford University Press, 2001).

Luxus would not have come into being without the enthusiasm of Marion True, Chris Hudson, Mark Greenberg, and Benedicte Gilman, all formerly of the J. Paul Getty Trust. To them I extend my warmest thanks. My current coworkers have taught me much and aided me immensely. I am extremely grateful to Marcus Adams, Al Aguilar, Peter Bonfitto, Shelby Brown, Jens Daehner, Claire Lyons, Susan Lansing Maish, Jeffrey Maish, Jerry Podany, Erik Risser, Eduardo Sanchez, David Saunders, Michael Smith, Jeffrey Spier, Marie Svoboda, Sahar Tchaitchian, and to the librarians at the Getty Research Institute, who greatly facilitated this project.

It is also a pleasure to acknowledge the kind assistance of Benjamin Acosta-Hughes, Polyxeni Adam-Veleni, Gianfranco Adornato, Fred Albertson, Pierre Amandry, Joan Aruz, Matilde Avisseau-Broustet, Alexandre Baralis, Beryl Barr-Sharrar, Mary Beard, Michael Bennett, Max Bernheimer, Sandra Blakely, John Boardman, Barbara Borg, Clare Browne, Lucilla Burn, Rika Burnham, Shane Butler, Elena Calandra, Faya Causey, Jennifer Chi, Gemma Sena Chiesa, Louise Chu, Chavdar Chushev, Maria Teresa Cinquantaquatro, Diane Harris Cline, Robert Cohon, Kathleen Coleman, Cécile Colonna, Derek Content, Kara Cooney, Robin Cormack, Antony Cutler, Andrew Dalby, Veronique Dasen, Francesco de Angelis, Maria Cecilia D'Ercole, Ariane Marie Sophie de Saxcé, Sophie Descamps-Lequime, Renee Dreyfus, Stella Drougou, Susanna Ebbinghaus, Chris Entwistle, Lucia Faedo, Christopher Faraone, James Ferrell, J. Lesley Fitton, Hallie Franks, Elisabetta Gagetti, Jasper Gaunt, Gaëlle Gautier, Riccardo Gennaioli, David Gill, Vaidehi Glibert, Hans Rupprecht Goette, Richard Gordon, Jack D. M. Green, Erich S. Gruen, Maria Paola Guidobaldi, Chris Hallett, Yannis Hamilakis, Sean Hemingway, Martin Henig, Despoina Ignatiadou, Thomas R. James, Christine Kondoleon, Angeliki Kottaridi, Antje Krug, Alexander Kruglov, Olga Krzyszkowska, Ann Kuttner, Lorenzo Lazzarini, Ann-Sophie Lehmann, Sarah Lepinski, Alexander Leskov, Emma Libonati, Christopher Lightfoot, Pascale Linnant de Bellefonds, Carlo Lipollis, François Lissarrague, Karen Manchester, Clemente Marconi, Elizabeth Marlow, Miranda Marvin, Richard Mason, Attilio Mastrocinque, Luigia Melillo, Joan Mertens, Margaret M. Miles, Margaret Miller, Sarah Morris, Árpád M. Nagy, Ruth Newby, Marden Nichols, Barbara Niemeyer, Marie-Louise Nosch, Jack Ogden, J. Michael Padget, Olga Palagia, Valerio Papaccio, John Papadopoulos, Eleonora Pappalardo, Rachel Patt, David Petrain, Carlos Picón, Joanne Pillsbury, Dimitris Plantzos, Verity Platt, Georg Plattner, Gertrud Platz-Horster, Jim Porter, Évelyn Prioux, Aurora Raimondi-Comenesi, Andrew Ramage, Nancy Ramage, Hadrien Rambach, Bodil Bundgaard Rasmussen, Lee Ann Riccardi, Brunhilde Sismondo Ridgway, Corinna Riva, Paul Roberts, Rea Rossella, Agnès Rouveret, Caroline Sauvage, Andreas Scholl, Phoebe Segal, Piper Severance, Maria Sframeli, Erika Simon, Fabrizio Slavazzi, R. R. R. Smith, Alexandra Sofroniew, Ambra Spinelli, Jennifer Stager, Lucia Pirzio Biroli Stefanelli, Niki Stellings-Hertzberg, Andrew Stewart, Marianne Stern, Molly Swetnam-Burland, Nancy Thomas, Lisbet Thoresen, Andrew Topsfield, Anna Trofimova, Francesca Tronchin, Marjorie Trusted, Claudia Wagner, Susan Walker, Andrew Wallace-Hadrill, Dyfri Williams, Roger Wilson, Irene Winter, Ruth Wolff, Ann Marie Yasin, Konstantinos Zachos, Paul Zanker, Mantha Zarmakoupi, Eleni Zimi, and Erika Zweirlein-Diehl.

Special thanks are due to Marina Belozerskaya, Laure Marest-Caffey, Carol C. Mattusch, and Michael Vickers, each of whom read the manuscript as it neared completion and provided valuable comments, suggestions, and corrections. If I failed to accept all of them, it is due to my own stubbornness, and I alone am responsible for remaining errors. Hans Rupprecht Goette and Tahneee Cracchiola provided stunning photographs, with customary speed and generosity. I am also indebted to IKONA/Rome and to all others who supplied images.

At Getty Publications, Publisher Kara Kirk strove to make this book appropriately splendid; Dinah Berland coordinated the project; Cindy Edwards copyedited the manuscript; Jean Wagner edited the bibliography; Elizabeth Kahn oversaw production; Kurt Hauser is responsible for the sumptuous design; Pam Moffatt acquired most of the photographs; Paul S. Tyler proofread the book; and Harvey L. Gable Jr. wrote the index. I am grateful to all of them for working so hard to create a volume that, I hope, does justice to its subject.

I dedicate this book to the memory of Audrey, *animae incomparabili et bene merenti.*

ILLUSTRATION CREDITS

Fig. 1: Princeton University Art Museum / Art Resource, NY

Fig. 2: Courtesy A Turizm Yayinlari, Istanbul. Photo: Suat Eman

Figs. 3, 11, 13, 22, 30, 34–36; plates 5, 12, 13,15, 32, 49, 55, 87, 117, 133, 134, 140, 169, 170, 173: © The Trustees of the British Museum / Art Resource, NY

Fig. 4: Courtesy of Soprintendenza Speciale per i Beni Archeologici di Napoli e Pompei and Museo Archeologico Nazionale di Napoli, Laboratorio di Conservazione e Restauro

Fig. 5; plates 7, 9, 30, 81, 85, 91, 100, 107, 142, 177: © 2015 Museum of Fine Arts, Boston

Fig. 6: Getty Research Institute (85-B16748)

Fig. 7: © Marie Mauzy / Art Resource, NY

Fig. 8a; plate 135: © DeA Picture Library / Art Resource, NY

Fig. 8b; plates 63, 171: Alfredo Dagli Orti / The Art Archive at Art Resource, NY

Fig. 9; plates 53, 88, 168: © Bibliothèque national de France

Fig. 10: Lessingimages.com

Fig. 14: Ashmolean Museum, University of Oxford

Fig. 15; plates 37, 47, 59, 69, 159: Scala / Art Resource, NY

Fig. 17: © Greg Balfour Evans / Alamy

Fig. 18: © Roemer-und-Pelizaeus Museum Hildesheim

Figs. 19, 23, 32, 33; plates 17, 18, 40, 48, 61, 62, 70, 71, 73–75, 77, 78, 83, 89, 97, 99, 105, 121, 132, 137, 139, 141, 149, 158, 167: The J. Paul Getty Museum, Los Angeles

Fig. 20; plate 119: Bridgeman Images

Figs. 21, 27: Archivio fotografico dei Musei Capitolini

Fig. 25; plates 29, 31, 39, 56, 136, 144, 147, 165: www.lacma.org

Fig. 26: © akg-images / The Image Works

Fig. 28: Scala / Ministero per i Beni e le Attività culturali / Art Resource, NY

Fig. 29: De Agostini Picture Library / G. Nimatallah / Bridgeman Images

Fig. 31; plates 54, 129: Walters Art Museum, Baltimore

Fig. 37: Photo: Hans R. Goette

Plate 1: Gianni Dagli Orti / The Art Archive at Art Resource, NY

Plate 2: Photo © Museum Associates / LACMA

Plates 3, 44: © RMN–Grand Palais / Art Resource, NY

Plates 4, 11, 46, 109, 126: bpk, Berlin / Antikensammlung, Staatliche Museen / Johannes Laurentius / Art Resource, NY

Plates 6, 154: De Agostini Picture Library / Bridgeman Images

Plate 8: Athens, National Archaeological Musem. Photo by Giannis Patrikianos © Hellenic Ministry of Culture / Archaeological Receipts Fund

Plates 10, 33: De Agostini Picture Library / G. Dagli Orti / Bridgeman Images

Plates 14, 174: V&A Images, London / Art Resource, NY

Plates 16, 82, 165: Image copyright © The Metropolitan Museum of Art. Image source: Art Resource, NY

Plates 19, 103: HIP / Art Resource, NY

Plates 20, 26–28, 38, 84, 98, 153: © The State Hermitage Museum

Plates 21, 124, 152: © Vanni Archive / Art Resource, NY

Plate 22: © Georgios Kefalas/epa/Corbis

Plate 23: Photo © Ira Block. Su concessione della Regione Siciliana, Assessorato dei Beni Culturali e dell'Identità Siciliana. Dipartimento dei Beni Culturali e dell'Identità Siciliana. Unauthorized reproduction prohibited

Plates 24, 60, 72, 113, 125: Erich Lessing / Art Resource, NY

Plate 25: © Iskra Historical Museum, Kazanlak, Bulgaria

Plate 34: Mondadori Portfolio / Bridgeman Images

Plate 35: Araldo De Luca / The Art Archive at Art Resource, NY

Plate 36: © 2015 Benaki Museum, Athens

Plate 41: Bridgeman-Giraudon / Art Resource, NY

Plate 42: © Christie's Inc.

Plate 43: Scala / White Images / Art Resource, NY

Plate 45: Su concessione del Ministero del Benii Culturali–Soprintendenza Archeologica della Puglia

Plates 50, 93, 95, 106, 130, 160: www.lucianopedicini.com

Plate 51: © Site et Musée romains d'Avenches, Photography, Jürg Zbinden, Berne

Plate 52: © Hercules Milas / Alamy

Plate 57: Archivio Fotografico Musei Vaticani, Rome

Plate 58: Album / Art Resource, NY

Plate 64: Thrace Foundation

Plates 65, 157: © The State Museum of Oriental Art (Moscow), 2014

Plates 67, 155: Mondadori Portfolio / akg-images

Plate 68: Su autorizzazione del Museo Regionale di Aidone (Prot 2138)

Plate 76: Nationalmuseet, Copenhagen, Denmark / Bridgeman Images

Plate 79: bpk, Berlin / Antikensammlung, Staatliche Museen / Art Resource, NY

Plate 80: De Agostini Picture Library / M. Carrieri / Bridgeman Images

Plate 90: Photography © The Art Institute of Chicago

Plate 92: Museo delle Terme, Archivio Fotografico

Plates 94, 172: Ashmolean Museum, University of Oxford, UK / Bridgeman Images

Plate 96: © Devonshire Collection, Chatsworth. Reproduced by permission of Chatsworth Settlement Trustees

Plates 101, 102, 111, 112, 116: © Bibliothèque national de France, Dist. RMN-Grand Palais / Art Resource, NY

Plates 104, 108: © Archivio dell'Arte / Luciano Pedicini

Plates 110, 146: Nimatallah / Art Resource, NY

Plate 114: bpk, Berlin / Antikensammlung, Staatliche Museen / Ingrid Geske/ Art Resource, NY

Plate 115: Alinari / Art Resource, NY

Plate 118: Photograph © Bruce M. White 2010

Plate 120: Henry Westheim Photography / Alamy

Plate 122: Stefan Hagen

Plate 123: Courtesy National Gallery of Art, Washington, DC

Plates 127, 138, 145: Gabinetto Fotografico del Polo Museale Fiorentino, Firenze

Plate 128: Finsiel / Alinari / Art Resource, NY

Plate 131: © Thierry Ollivier

Plate 143: Museo de Zaragoza (P. J. Fatás)

Plates 148, 149, 151: Photo: Hans R. Goette

Plate 150: © Michael C. Carlos Museum, Emory University. Photo by Bruce M. White, 2009

Plate 156: Photo by R. Gonella, archive of the Centro Ricerche Archeologiche e Scavi di Torino

Plate 161: Per concessione del Ministero dei Beni e delle Attività Culturali e del Turismo. Direzione Regionale per i Beni Culturali del Molise

Plates 162, 166: Per concessione del Ministero dei Beni e delle Attività Culturali e del Turismo. Sovrintendenza Archeologica di Roma

Plate 163: Fitzwilliam Museum, University of Cambridge, UK / Bridgeman Images

Plate 164: Per concessione del Ministero dei Beni e delle Attività Culturali e del Turismo, Soprintendenza PES

Plate 175: © The State Hermitage Museum / photo by Daria Bobrova

Plate 178: © Abegg-Stiftung, CH-3132 Riggisberg, 2003; (photo: Christoph von Viràg)

Plate 179: © Lyon, MTMAD–Pierre Verrier

INDEX OF WORKS

NOTE: Page numbers in *italic* refer to illustrations.

Published by the J. Paul Getty Museum, Los Angeles
Getty Publications
1200 Getty Center Drive, Suite 500
Los Angeles, California 90049-1682
www.getty.edu/publications

Dinah Berland, *Project Editor*
Cynthia Edwards, *Manuscript Editor*
Kurt Hauser, *Designer*
Elizabeth Chapin Kahn, *Production*
Diane Franco, *Typesetting*

Color separations by Prographics
Printed in Hong Kong

Library of Congress Cataloging-in-Publication Data

Lapatin, Kenneth D. S., author.
Luxus : the sumptuous arts of Greece and Rome / Kenneth Lapatin.
pages cm
Includes bibliographical references and index.
ISBN 978-1-60606-422-1 (hardcover)
1. Luxuries—Greece. 2. Luxuries—Rome. 3. Art objects, Greek. 4. Art objects, Roman. 5. Jewelry, Classical. 6. Goldwork, Ancient. 7. Silverwork, Ancient. 8. Greece—Antiquities. 9. Rome—Antiquities. I. J. Paul Getty Museum, issuing body. II. Title.
NK665.L37 2015
745.0938—dc23

2014041391

FRONT JACKET, *top row*: Earring with Nike driving a chariot (gold), ca. 350–325 BC (plate 30); Face of a composite statue (ivory), ca. 100 BC–AD 125 (plate 162); Cup fragment with Eros (banded agate), ca. 100 BC–AD 125 (plate 122); *bottom row*: Cameo of a laughing satyr (sardonyx), ca. AD 10 (plate 114); Centaur protome from a rhyton (silver and gold), ca. 160 BC (detail, plate 72); Portrait of a bearded man (gold glass and pigment), ca. AD 200–250 (plate 59)

BACK JACKET: Ring with head of a woman (gold), ca. 300–200 BC (plate 45); Head of a Julio-Claudian princess (green calcedony), ca. AD 40 (detail, plate 140); Scaraboid intaglio of a bearded man (mottled jasper), ca. 450–430 BC (plate 85)

HALF-TITLE PAGE: *Amphoriskos* (perfume vase) (rock crystal), ca. 25 BC (detail, plate 132); PAGE ii: Double portrait of male and female rulers (the Gonzaga Cameo; sardonyx), third century BC or later(?) (detail, plate 103); PAGE iii: *Patera* from Rennes (gold), ca. AD 210 (detail, plate 53); PAGE iv: Cup with centaurs (gilt silver), ca. AD 1–100; PAGE v: Intaglio of the *Athena Parthenos* of Pheidias (red jasper), ca. 50–25 BC (detail, plate 92); PAGE vi: Pegasos protome (gold), ca. 350 BC (detail, plate 22); PAGE viii: Tapestry with fish (wool), ca. AD 100–300 (detail, plate 179); PAGE ix (*top to bottom*): Portrait of Gennadios (gold glass), ca. AD 250–300 (detail, plate 56); Fragmentary intaglio of Apollo (amethyst), ca. 30–20 BC (detail, plate 97); Bust of Serapis (coral), ca. AD 1–200 (detail, plate 173); PAGE x: The Rubens Vase (cameo-cut agate with modern gold lip), ca. AD 400 (detail, plate 129); PAGE xii: Portrait of two women and a youth (gold glass and silver), ca. AD 250 (detail, plate 58); PAGE 45: *Phiale* (libation bowl) with Ethiopians and acorns (gold), 325–275 BC (detail, plate 24); PAGE 106: *Skyphos* with Egyptianizing scenes (obsidian), first century BC–first century AD (detail, plate 135); PAGE 129: Cameo of Jupiter (sardonyx in a medieval gold and enamel mount), ca. AD 14–37 (detail, plate 116); PAGE 170: Appliqué with Dionysos, Ariadne, and a satyr (ivory and gold), ca. 300 BC (detail, plate 155); PAGE 193: The Judgment of Paris (ivory), ca. 400 BC (detail, plate 153)

Illustration Credits

Every effort has been made to contact the owners and photographers of objects reproduced in this book whose names do not appear in the captions or illustration credits listed on the previous page. Anyone having further information concerning copyright holders is asked to contact Getty Publications so this information can be included in future printings.

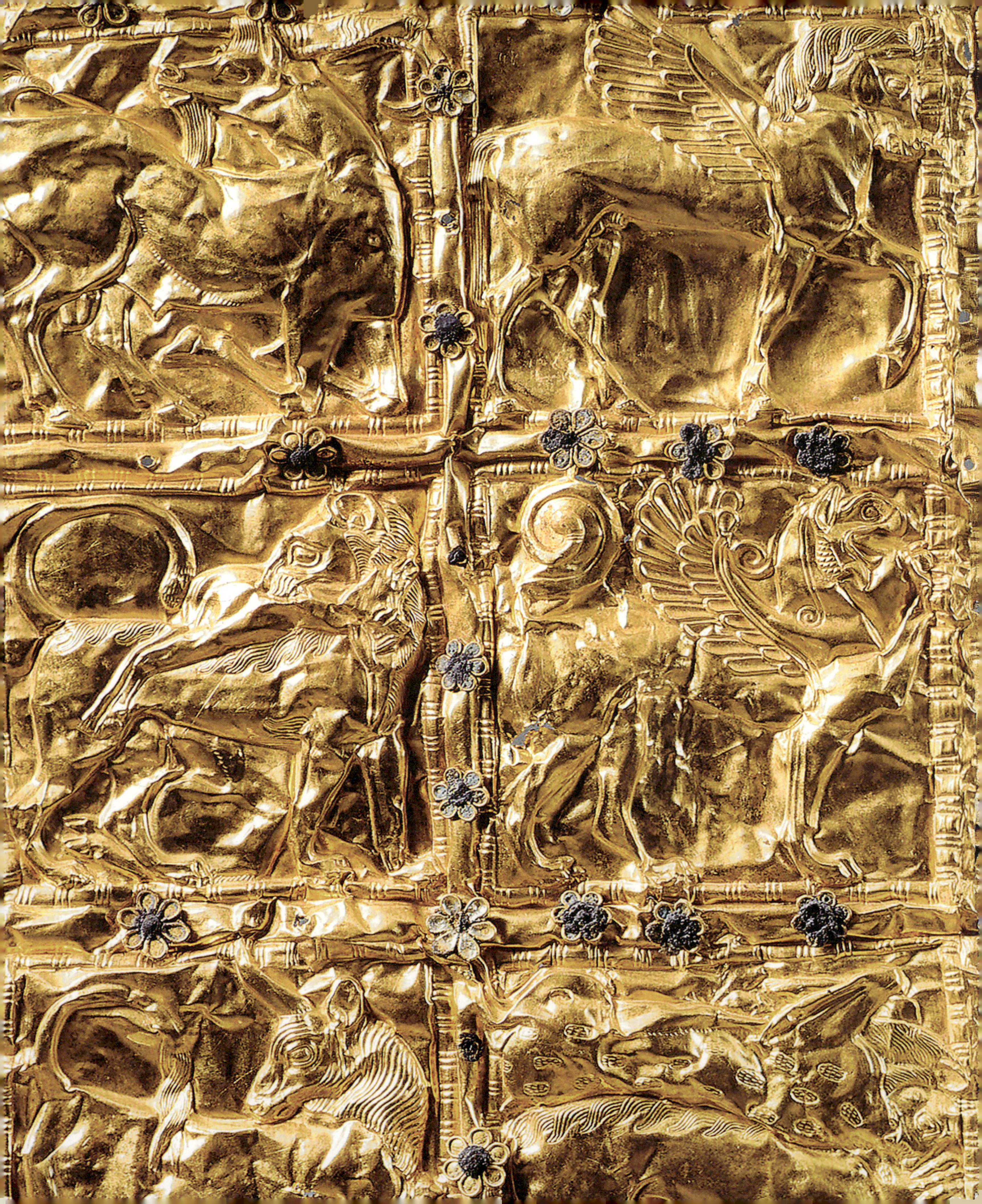